Fourth Edition

THE GLOBAL EXPERIENCE
Readings in World History Since 1500
Volume II

Philip F. Riley
Frank A. Gerome
Henry A. Myers
Chong-Kun Yoon

James Madison University

Prentice
Hall

Upper Saddle River, New Jersey 07458

Library of Congress Cataloging-in-Publication Data

The global experience / [edited by] Philip F. Riley . . . [et al.]—4th ed.
p. cm.
Contents: v. 2. Readings in world history since 1550.
ISBN 0-13-019569-3 (v. 2)
1. World history. I. Riley, Philip F.

D23.G57 2002
909—dc21

00-140088

VP Editorial Director: Charlyce Jones Owen
Senior Acquisitions Editor: Charles Cavaliere
VP, Director of Manufacturing
   and Production: Barbara Kittle
Senior Managing Editor: Jan Stephan
Production Liaison: Fran Russello
Project Manager: Linda B. Pawelchak
Manufacturing Manager: Nick Sklitsis
Prepress and Manufacturing Buyer: Tricia Kenny
Art Director: Jayne Conte
Cover Art: New York Convention & Visitors Bureau
AVP Director of Marketing: Beth Gillett Mejia

This book was set in 10/11 Janson Text
by Carlisle Communications Ltd.
and was printed and bound by RR Donnelley & Sons Company.
The cover was printed by Phoenix Color Corp.

Printed in the United States of America
10 9 8 7 6 5 4 3 2 1

ISBN 0-13-019569-3

Prentice-Hall International (UK) Limited, *London*
Prentice-Hall of Australia Pty. Limited, *Sydney*
Prentice-Hall Canada Inc., *Toronto*
Prentice-Hall Hispanoamericana, S.A., *Mexico*
Prentice-Hall of India Private Limited, *New Delhi*
Prentice-Hall of Japan, Inc., *Tokyo*
Pearson Education Asia Pte. Ltd., *Singapore*
Editora Prentice-Hall do Brasil, Ltda., *Rio de Janeiro*

For
Raymond C. Dingledine Jr.
1919–1990
Teacher, Scholar, Friend

confused

Contents

PART II
Global Patterns of Politics and Culture

PART III
Revolutions and Rebellions

PART IV

Empires and Upheavals

England's Imperial March   179

Japan: Tradition and Transformation 189

U.S. Expansion: Two Perspectives   201

PART V

An Era of Global Violence

World War I   209

PART VI
The Later Twentieth Century

PART VII
The Twenty-first Century

Human Rights and International Relations 351

Enduring Problems 62

Preface

This anthology is a brief, balanced collection of primary materials organized chronologically and focused on global themes.

In preparing this collection, we had three concerns in mind. First, any informed understanding of the world at the opening of the third millennium when the world is rapidly becoming one must begin with history. We believe the most useful mode of historical study—particularly for college students—is world history. Because men and women make history, the documents we have depict the variety of their experiences over time on a global scale. To help students study and appreciate these experiences, we have included excerpts both from classic texts and from less familiar but equally illustrative material. The resulting selection of readings illustrates patterns of global change and exchange, as well as the distinct features of the major civilizations.

Second, to encourage the comparative study of world history and to reinforce the underlying links between civilizations, we have organized the readings into chronological sections. By doing so, we hope to underscore global patterns of development and, at the same time, give our readers access to documents of special interest.

Third, to help with the understanding and retention of our reading selections, particularly those likely to be unfamiliar to students, we have included introductory comments as well as questions to consider. We hope this material will help students gain a better understanding of the text and connect their historical study to contemporary problems and issues.

Our students, particularly in their questions and criticisms, have shaped our work from the outset more than they know. Many of our colleagues at James Madison University have also helped immeasurably. They provided insights and suggestions to make this a better book. Michael J. Galgano, Head, Department of History, has assisted us at every turn: He enthusiastically found for us the means and time to complete this project. Mary Louise Loe not only contributed the selections on Russia and Soviet history but helped us throughout our work. Nicholas Miller of Boise State University; John A. Murphy of University College, Cork, Republic of Ireland; and John O. Hunwick of Northwestern University kindly advised us on Serbian, Irish, and African selections.

The fourth edition of *The Global Experience: Readings in World History* contains new sections, new selections, and new translations, as well as some changes in the selections published in our third edition. In Volume I, approximately twenty-five percent of the selections are new. Among the new selections in Volume I are The Egyptian Creation Story: "The Creation According to Ra"; The Babylonian Code of Hammurabi; Homer, *The Iliad;* Pure Land Scripture, *Sukhavativyuha;* Thucydides on the Plague and *Peloponnesian War;* Plutarch, "Lycurgus," on the Spartan Way of Life; St. Augustine of Hippo, The Just War; Paulus Orosius, *History Against the Pagans;* Procopius, *History of the Wars* and *The Secret History;* Law Codes of the Salian Franks; Ibn Fadlan, Impressions of Vikings in Early Russia; Michael Psellus, *Chronographia,* "Empress Zoe"; Murasaki Shikibu, *The Tale of Genji; Charles Borromeo, Instructions to Confessors;* Bernardino de Sahagún, Aztec Festival and the Conquest; An Aztec Account of the Conquest of Mexico: *The Broken Spears;* Pope Paul III, "Indians are Men," 1537; Sepúlveda, Just War Against Barbarians, 1550.

Among the new additions to Volume II are An Aztec Account of the Conquest of Mexico: *The Broken Spears;* James Harrington, "The Commonwealth of Oceana"; Sir William Petty, *Political Arithmetic; Enfumades* in French Algeria: Three Reports; Arthur de Gobineau, *The Inequality of Human Races;* U.S. Congress, The Chinese Exclusion Acts, 1882, 1892; Russo-Japanese War, 1904–1905, *Imperial Rescript;* John Rabe, The Diaries of the Nanking Massacre; Roupen of Sassoun, Eyewitness to Armenia's Genocide; Marie Claude Valliant-Couturier, Testimony on the Gassing at Auschwitz; Chong K. Yoon, The Korean War: A Personal Account; Henry A. Myers, "East Berliners Rise Up Against Soviet Oppression"; Gen. Douglas MacArthur, Report to Congress, April 19, 1951, "Old Soldiers Never Die"; Fidel Castro, Second Declaration of Havana; Teeda Butt Mam, Worms from Our Skin; Theresa Andrews, *Letters from a 1990s Bush Doctor* (revised and updated with the coup in Sierra Leone); Keith B. Richburg, A Black Man Confronts Africa; Dalai Lama (Tenzin Gyatso), Nobel Peace Prize Lecture; Japan: The Post-Postwar Generation; and Henry A. Myers, Now, in the Twenty-first Century. In this volume, we have expanded sections on Early Modern Political Economy; Nationalism and Romanticism; Racism; World War I; World War II: Asia and Europe; Patterns of Genocide; The Cold War; Decolonization: Africa, Latin America, and India; America and the Second Indo-china War; Human Rights and International Relations; and Enduring Problems. Under the section The Cold War, we have added two personal accounts, one on Berlin and the other on Korea.

In making these revisions, we were guided by the advice and criticism of our colleagues, Chris Arndt, Jack Butt, Steven W. Guerrier, Raymond M. Hyser, Michael Galgano. Sheila Riley helped with the final editing of the first three editions; Bradley Arnold and Beth Poplin worked on copyright permission requests; and Jae Kim and Jae Yang provided efficient clerical assistance. Gordon Miller, reference librarian, and the James Madison University's Inter-library Loan staff tirelessly and skillfully assisted us in obtaining materials.

We continue to welcome comments and criticism, which we appreciate in connection with our ongoing project of updating and improving this work. Please send your comments and suggestions to Philip F. Riley or Chong K. Yoon or any of the coeditors, Department of History, James Madison University, Harrisonburg, VA 22807.

Philip F. Riley
Chong K. Yoon

Part I
Global Contacts

Early Modern Exploration and Expansion

Almost a century before Portuguese captain Vasco da Gama successfully rounded the Cape of Good Hope and reached the Malabar coast of India in 1498, in 1405, Emperor Yung-lo (1403–1424) of the Ming dynasty (1368–1644) had launched the first of a series of grand-scale maritime expeditions. Over the next twenty-eight years, the Chinese court dispatched six more large-scale naval expeditions to Southeast Asia, India, Persia, and the east coast of Africa. These gigantic expeditions involved more than 70,000 men, engaged hundreds of vessels, and covered thousands of nautical miles. In contrast with the goals of the European adventurers who came to Asia several decades later, the main purpose of these grand undertakings was neither conquest nor trade. The Ming government was mainly interested in spreading and enhancing its dynastic prestige and power as well as winning for China the nominal control of those distant regions. By 1415, nineteen kingdoms had sent tributes to the Ming court; however, after nearly three decades of naval expeditions, not a single permanent overseas Ming colony was established.

Then, in 1433, the great Ming naval expeditions suddenly ceased, never to resume. Although scholars do not know the precise reasons why China refused to embark on her own Age of Exploration, possible explanations might include the high cost of the naval expeditions; China's long-held tradition of anti-commercialism; and the ruling Confucian scholars' and officials' prejudice toward the seafaring people, who neglected to observe two important Confucian virtues—namely, filial piety and ancestor worship. Had those Chinese seafarers sustained support from a leader such as Portugal's Prince Henry, the course of world history might have been quite different; certainly China would have "discovered" such distant lands as Spain, England, and France. A little more than six decades after the last Ming naval expedition of 1433, Vasco da Gama opened an era of European domination of the Asian waters. The compass and gunpowder, two important gifts of China to the West, permitted the Europeans to develop empires in Asia.

As the demand for Oriental products increased in Western Europe in the fifteenth century, merchants and monarchs, hoping to break the Italian monopoly of that trade, began their search for an all-water route to the East. Another powerful impetus was a strong sense of Christian duty to convert pagans and infidels. For centuries, Portuguese and Spaniards had struggled to expel the Muslims who occupied their land. That effort generated a religious fervor and missionary zeal and also helped establish a sense of national identity. By the early fifteenth century, Portugal had become a unified state, separate from the expanding Spanish kingdoms of Leon and Castile. The Iberians, with their strategic location facing the Atlantic and with new knowledge of navigation and shipbuilding gained from Italian seafarers on the Mediterranean, initiated the age of European exploration and expansion.

After establishing a colonial base in the Caribbean following the four voyages of Columbus, the governor of Cuba sent Hernán Cortés in 1519 to the mainland of North America and began the conquest of the indigenous population, which he completed two years later with the conquest of the Aztecs. Later in the sixteenth century, Spanish missionaries who had learned Indian languages provided another version of the conquest.

1 Cheng Ho [Zheng He],¹ Ming Maritime Expeditions

Most of the large naval expeditions of the Ming dynasty were led by a Muslim court eunuch named Cheng Ho (1371–1433). The following selection describes China's Columbus and the maritime explorations he led.

QUESTIONS TO CONSIDER

1. What does the size, organization, and nature of the Ming maritime fleet indicate about China's capabilities in the early fifteenth century?
2. What do the Ming emperor's bans on imperial naval explorations suggest about Chinese views of the world?
3. Compare and contrast the Ming maritime expeditions with the Age of Discovery in Western history. What motives inspired Cheng Ho and Columbus?

Cheng Ho (1371–1433), eunuch and commander-in-chief of the Ming expeditionary fleets in the early years of the 15th century, was born into a family named Ma at K'un-yang in central Yunnan [Kunyang]. His great-grandfather was named Bayan, and his grandfather and father were both named Ḥājjī, which suggests that the two probably visited Mecca and that the family had a long tradition of Islamic faith and may have been of Mongol-Arab origin. At the beginning of the Ming dynasty, a number of generals who fought on the frontier were in charge of recruiting eunuchs for the court. In 1381, when Yunnan was pacified by an army under Fu Yu-de, Cheng Ho, at that time about ten years old, was one of the children selected to be castrated. As a trainee for eunuch service, he was assigned to the retinue of Chu Ti [Zhu Di] [Emperor Yung-lo]. In his early twenties, he accompanied Chu Ti on a series of military campaigns and in the course of them took up a career in the army. As his family records relate, "when he entered adulthood, he reportedly became seven feet tall and had a waist about five feet in circumference. His cheeks and forehead were high but his nose was small. He had glaring eyes and a voice as loud as a huge bell. He knew a great deal about warfare and was well accustomed to battle.". . .

Cheng Ho first achieved official prominence early in 1404 when he was promoted to the position of director of eunuch affairs and granted the surname of Cheng

¹There are at least two ways to transcribe Chinese in the English-speaking world: the Wade-Giles system and the Pinyin system. The Wade-Giles system was first developed by an English sinologist, Thomas F. Wade, in 1867 and was later modified by Herbert Giles in 1912. It became the standard way of transcribing Chinese. But this system has now either been replaced or is in the process of being replaced by Pinyin, the official transcription system of the People's Republic of China. Hereafter, the Pinyin transcriptions will be provided in brackets on the first occurrence of Chinese terms in each reading where they occur. If no transcription appears, the term is the same in both systems.

[Zheng]. Shortly afterward he received the appointment of commander-in-chief of the first expedition. Meanwhile local officials of the eastern coastal regions were ordered to build ocean-going vessels. By July, 1405, some 1,180 ships of various sizes and types had been constructed. The large or treasure ships were, according to measures of that time, as much as 440 feet long and 186.2 wide, and those of medium size, or horse ships, 370 feet long and 150 wide. There were supply ships which measured 280 feet in length and 120 in breadth, and billet ships measuring 240 feet by 94. The battle-ships equipped with cannon were much smaller, measuring only 180 feet by 68. Most of the treasure ships were the product of the Lung-chiang [Long Jiang] shipyard near Nanking [Nanjing]. None of these has survived, but near the site of the shipyard was recently discovered (1957) a large wooden rudder (length 11 meters) thought to have been fashioned for one of the bigger vessels. It is now preserved in the Kiangsu [Jiangsu] provincial museum.

The first voyage began in the summer of 1405 with a 27,800 man crew and 62 (or 63) large and 255 smaller vessels. . . . [In the second voyage, which was launched in late autumn of 1407, the expedition sailed into the Indian Ocean.]

In the summer of 1409 Cheng Ho returned to Nanking to report on his mission to the emperor. Here he built a temple in honor of T'ien-fei [Tianfei], the goddess of the sea, to whose virtue and power he attributed the safe voyages of his fleets. The in-scription on the stele erected later (May 3, 1416) has been partly translated into French by Claudine Lombard-Salmon; the complete Chinese text may be found in the book by Louis Gaillard.

After a brief stay in the capital, Cheng Ho was again sent overseas, accompanied by Wang Chiang-hung [Wang Jinghong] and Hou Hsien [Hou Xian]. His third voy-age was comparable to the first and second in the number of men but with only 48 ves-sels; it lasted from September, 1409, to June, 1411. This expedition reached the same destination on the Malabar coast of India, but along the way several excursions were made, including brief visits to Siam, Malacca, Sumatra, and Ceylon. It also undertook lumbering operations and gathered fragrant herbs in the Sembilan Islands. . . .

It was the fourth voyage, which began in 1413 and ended in August, 1415, that took the expedition far beyond its earlier destinations. Under the same command but with a crew of 27,670 men and some 63 large vessels, the expedition touched at a num-ber of new places, including the Maldives, Hormuz, the Hadramaut coast, and Aden. In Sumatra the expedition became involved in a local power struggle at Ch'iao-shan [Qiaoshan] (Samudra-Pasai). A usurper by the name of Su-wa-la, after murdering the king, directed his forces against the expedition, but was subsequently defeated and pursued as far as Lambri, where he and his family were captured. The prisoners were taken to Nanking on the return of the fleet. As a result of this voyage, nineteen coun-tries sent envoys and tribute to the Ming court. Chu Ti was so pleased with the results that he rewarded all participants in the expedition according to their ranks.

In December, 1416, Cheng Ho was commissioned to escort home the envoys of the nineteen states, and embarked, possibly in the autumn of 1417, on his fifth voyage, which lasted up to August, 1419. The returning envoys, who had witnessed the delight of the Ming emperor at his first sight of a giraffe, spread the news to other countries. Hence an impressive collection of strange animals, among them lions, leopards, single-humped camels, ostriches, zebras, rhinoceroses, antelopes, and giraffes offered by rulers of several states highlighted this journey.

The spring of 1421 saw the launching of the sixth voyage, but Cheng may not have joined the fleet until later. It returned on September 3, 1422, accompanied by a large number of envoys from such states as Hormuz, Aden, Djofar, La-sa (Al-shsā?), Brawa, Mogadishu, Calicut, Cochin, Cail, Ceylon, the Maldive Islands, Lambri, Sumatra, Aru, Malacca, Kan-pa-li (Coyampadi?), Sulu, Bengal, Borneo, Ku-ma-la (-lang, Cabarruyan Islands?), and Ts'eng-pa (Zanzibar). The number of countries visited on this trip has not been listed, but the expedition reached at least as far as Aden, near the mouth of the Red Sea, and Mogadishu and Brawa on the coast of east Africa. . . .

In the meanwhile Chu Ti had died (August 12, 1424), and almost at once the idea of another maritime expedition came under attack. The emperor designate, Chu Kao-chih [Zhu Gaozhi], promptly (August 28) released from prison Hsia Yüan-chi [Xia Yuanji], perhaps the most outspoken critic of the treasure fleets, and on September 7, the very day of Chu's accession to the throne as the fourth Ming emperor, other voices joined Hsia's in recommending their abolition. This protest seems to have settled the matter, for in the following February Cheng Ho received an appointment as garrison commander of the Nanking district, and was told to maintain order in his own expeditionary forces, and consult with Wang Ching-hung and two other eunuchs. . . .

Only a few months later the fourth emperor died and for several years the plan to launch another expedition lay dormant. Finally in June, 1430, his successor, the fifth emperor, Chu Chan-chi [Zhu Zhanji], issued an order for the seventh (and what proved to be the last) voyage, but it was not to leave the Fukien [Fujian] coast until a year and a half later. It returned in July, 1433. The mission was intended to regenerate the tributary relationships once maintained under Chu Ti, which had significantly weakened since his death. A score of states were revisited, including those along the coasts of the Arabian peninsula and eastern Africa. In this instance two ambassadors returned with the fleet, bringing such gifts as giraffes, elephants, and horses. Cheng Ho, who was already in his sixties, did not perhaps visit all of them in person, and some of the side missions were conducted by his aides. . . .

What happened to Cheng Ho from this point is not clear. It has customarily been said that he died in 1435 or 1436 at the age of sixty-five, no specific date or site of burial being indicated in contemporary sources. A later source, the *T'ung-chih Shang Chiang liang-hsien chih* [*Tongzhi Shang Jiang liangxian Zhi*] (preface of 1874), 3/39a, however, maintains that Cheng Ho died at Calicut and was buried at Niushou-shan outside Nanking. If this be true, he must have passed away early in 1433.

2 Vasco da Gama, *Journey to India*

Vasco da Gama (1460?–1524) was one of the great mariners who helped Portugal take the lead in the era of explorations. In 1497, with four ships and 168 men, da Gama sailed down the west coast of Africa, rounded the Cape of Good Hope, fought Muslims along the way, and reached India. He did not return to Lisbon until 1499, after a voyage of two years and two months, but he brought back pepper, cloves, nutmeg, cinnamon, and precious stones. Shortly after da Gama's return, another explorer, Pedro Cabral, assembled a fleet and set out for India. According to the official account, his ships were blown far off their course and on April 22, 1500, they sighted the coast of Brazil. Although with this discovery the

Portuguese Crown could then boast of an empire and stake out its claim in America, Portugal devoted far more interest and attention to its growing empire in the East. The following reading is an excerpt from da Gama's journal of his voyage to India in 1497–1499.

QUESTIONS TO CONSIDER

1. Describe the Portuguese impressions of the inhabitants of Calicut.
2. Compare and contrast da Gama's historic voyage with that of the other explorers in this section.
3. Do you sense some deception or self-deception in the reporting of strong Christian influences in Calicut (modern Kozhihode)?
4. What were the consequences of the discovery of an ocean route to India at the close of the fifteenth century?

The city of Calicut is inhabited by Christians. They are of tawny complexion. Some of them have big beards and long hair, whilst others clip their hair short or shave the head, merely allowing a tuft to remain on the crown as a sign that they are Christians. They also wear moustaches. They pierce the ears and wear much gold in them. They go naked down to the waist, covering their lower extremities with very fine cotton stuffs. But it is only the most respectable who do this, for the others manage as best they are able.[1]

The women of this country, as a rule, are ugly and of small stature. They wear many jewels of gold around the neck, numerous bracelets on their arms, and rings set with precious stones on their toes. All these people are well disposed and apparently of mild temper. At first sight they seem covetous and ignorant.

When we arrived at Calicut, the captain-major sent two men to the King with a message, informing him that an ambassador had arrived from the King of Portugal with letters.

The king presented the bearers of this message with much fine cloth. He sent word to the captain bidding him welcome.

A pilot accompanied our two men, with orders to take us to a place called Pandarani, below the place [Capua] where we anchored at first. At this time we were actually in front of the city of Calicut. We were told that the anchorage at the place to which we were to go was good, whilst at the place we were then it was bad, with a stony bottom, which was quite true; and, moreover, that it was customary for the ships which came to this country to anchor there for the sake of safety. We ourselves did not feel

---

[1]The visitors thus became at once acquainted with the various castes constituting the population of Calicut, including the Nairs, or fighting caste of Malabar, who eat meat (which shows a servile origin), but wear the thread of the Dwija (twice-born), rank next to the Brahmans, and practice polyandry; and the turbulent Moplah, who are descendants of Arab fathers and native women. These latter are the "native" Moors.

From *Portuguese Voyages, 1498–1663*, ed. Charles David Ley (London: J. M. Dent & Sons Ltd; New York: E. P. Dutton & Co., 1947), pp. 27–38, *passim*. Reprinted by permission.

comfortable, and the captain-major had no sooner received this royal message than he ordered the sails to be set, and we departed. We did not, however, anchor as near the shore as the king's pilot desired.

When we were at anchor, a message arrived informing the captain-major that the king was already in the city. At the same time the king sent a *bale* [governor], with other men of distinction, to Pandarani, to conduct the captain-major to where the king awaited him. This *bale* is always attended by two hundred men armed with swords and bucklers. As it was late when this message arrived, the captain-major deferred going.

On the following morning, they took us to a large church, and this is what we saw:

The body of the church is as large as the monastery, all built of hewn stone and covered with tiles. At the main entrance rises a pillar of bronze as high as a mast, on the top of which was perched a bird, apparently a cock. In addition to this, there was another pillar as high as a man, and very stout. In the center of the body of the church rose a chapel, all built of hewn stone, with a bronze door sufficiently wide for a man to pass, and stone steps leading up to it. Within this sanctuary stood a small image which they said represented *Our Lady*. Along the walls, by the main entrance, hung seven small bells. In this church the captain-major said his prayers, and we with him.

We did not go within the chapel, for it is custom that only certain servants of the church should enter. These men wore some threads passing over the left shoulder and under the right arm, in the same manner as our deacons wear the stole. They threw holy water over us, and gave us some white earth, which the Christians of this country are in the habit of putting on their foreheads, breasts, around the neck, and on the forearms. They threw holy water upon the captain-major and gave him some of the earth, which he gave in charge of someone, giving them to understand that he would put it on later.

Many other saints were painted on the walls of the church, wearing crowns. They were painted variously, with teeth protruding an inch from the mouth, and four or five arms.

The captain, on entering, saluted in the manner of the country: by putting the hands together, then raising them towards Heaven, as is done by Christians when addressing God, and immediately afterwards opening them and shutting the fists quickly.

And the captain told the king that he was the ambassador of a king of Portugal, who was lord of many countries and the possessor of great wealth of every description, exceeding that of any king of these parts; that for a period of sixty years his ancestors had annually sent out vessels to make discoveries in the direction of India, as they knew that there were Christians kings there like themselves. This, he said, was the reason which induced them to order this country to be discovered, not because they sought for gold or silver, for of this they had such abundance that they needed not what was to be found in this country. He further stated that the captains sent out traveled for a year or two, until their provisions were exhausted, and then returned to Portugal, without having succeeded in making the desired discovery. There reigned a king now whose name was Dom Manuel, who ordered him not to return to Portugal until he should have discovered the king of the Christians, on pain of having his head cut off. That a letter had been entrusted to him to be presented in case he succeeded in discovering him, and, finally, he had been instructed to say by word of mouth that he [the king of Portugal] desired to be his friend and brother.

In reply to this the king said that he was welcome; that, on his part, he held him as a friend and brother, and would send ambassadors with him to Portugal. This latter had been asked as a favor, the captain pretending that he would not dare to present himself before his king and master unless he was able to present, at the same time, some men of this country.

On Tuesday the captain got ready the following things to be sent to the king: twelve pieces of *lambel*, four scarlet hoods, six hats, four strings of coral, a case containing six washstand basins, a case of sugar, two casks of oil, and two of honey. And as it is the custom not to send anything to the king without the knowledge of the Moor [who advised him on commercial matters], and of the *bale*, the captain informed them of his intention. They came, and when they saw the present they laughed at it, saying that it was not a thing to offer to a king, that the poorest merchant from Mecca, or any other part of India, gave more, and that if he wanted to make a present it should be in gold, as the king would not accept such things. When the captain heard this he grew sad, and said he had brought no gold, that, moreover, he was no merchant, but an ambassador; that he gave of that which he had, which was his own [private gift] and not the king's; that if the King of Portugal ordered him to return he would entrust him with far richer presents; and that if King Samolin would not accept these things he would send them back to the ships. Upon this they declared that they would not forward his presents, nor consent to his forwarding them himself. When they had gone there came certain Moorish merchants, and they all depreciated the present which the captain desired to be sent to the king.

When the captain saw that they were determined not to forward his present, he said that he would go to speak to the king, and would then return to the ships. They approved of this, and told him that if he would wait a short time they would return and accompany him to the palace. And the captain waited all day, but they never came back. The captain was very wroth at being among so phlegmatic and unreliable a people, and intended, at first, to go to the palace without them. On further consideration, however, he thought it best to wait until the following day. As to us others, we diverted ourselves, singing and dancing to the sound of trumpets, and enjoyed ourselves much.

On Wednesday morning the Moors returned, and took the captain to the palace. The palace was crowded with armed men. Our captain was kept waiting for fully four long hours, outside a door, which was only opened when the king sent word to admit him, attended by two men only, whom he might select. It seemed to him, as it did to us, that this separation portended no good.

When he had entered, the king said that he had expected him on Tuesday. The captain said that the long road had tired him, and that for this reason he had not come to see him. The king then said that he had told him that he came from a very rich kingdom, and yet had brought him nothing; that he had also told him that he was the bearer of a letter, which had not yet been delivered. To this the captain rejoined that he had brought nothing, because the object of his voyage was merely to make discoveries, but that when other ships came he would then see what they brought him; as to the latter, it was true that he had brought one, and would deliver it immediately.

The king then asked what kind of merchandise was to be found in his country. The captain said that there was much corn, cloth, iron, bronze, and many other things. The king asked whether he had any merchandise with him. The captain replied that he had a little of each sort, as samples, and that if permitted to return to the ships he would order it to be landed, and that meantime four or five men would remain at the lodgings assigned them. The king said no. He might take all his people with him, securely moor his ships, land his merchandise, and sell it to the best advantage. Having taken leave of the king the captain returned to his lodgings, and we with him. As it was already late no attempt was made to depart that night.

The next morning the captain asked for boats to take him to his ships. They began to whisper among themselves, and said that we should have them if we would order our vessels to come nearer to the shore. The captain said that if he ordered his vessels to approach his brother would think that he was being held a prisoner, and that he gave this order on compulsion, and would hoist the sails to return to Portugal. They said that if we refused to order the ships to come nearer we should not be permitted to embark. The captain said that King Samolin had sent him back to his ships, and that as they would not let him go, as ordered by the king, he should return to the king, who was a Christian like himself. If the king would not let him go, and wanted him to remain in his country, he would do so with much pleasure. They agreed that he should be permitted to go, but afforded him no opportunity for doing so, for they immediately closed all the doors, and many armed men entered to guard us, none of us being allowed to go outside without being accompanied by several of these guards.

On the following day, these gentlemen [i.e., the *bale* and others] came back, and this time they "wore better faces." They told the captain that as he had informed the king that he intended to land his merchandise, he should now give orders to have this done. The captain consented, and said that he would write to his brother to see it being done. They said this was well, and that immediately after the arrival of the merchandise he would be permitted to return to his ship. The captain at once wrote to his brother to send certain things, and he did so at once. On their receipt the captain was allowed to go on board, two men remaining behind with the things that had been landed.

At this we rejoiced greatly, and rendered thanks to God for having extricated us from the hands of the people who had no more sense than beasts, for we knew well that once the captain was on board those who had been landed would have nothing to fear. When the captain reached his ship he ordered that no more merchandise should be sent.

3 An Aztec Account of the Conquest of Mexico

A number of Spaniards wrote accounts of the conquest of Mexico in 1521. The following reading, however, is an account translated from the Aztec Nahuatl language by Spanish missionaries after the conquest.

QUESTIONS TO CONSIDER

1. What was the "great plague" that spread throughout the Aztec capital of Tenochtitlán? How important was disease as a factor in the Spanish victory over the Aztecs?
2. Consider how this account of the conquest reveals other factors which indicate how relatively few Spaniards were able to conquer so many? Can you think of other instances in which disease played a decisive role in determining the outcome of such an encounter? Explain.

THE PLAGUE RAVAGES THE CITY

While the Spaniards were in Tlaxcala, a great plague broke out here in Tenochtitlán. It began to spread during the thirteenth month and lasted for seventy days, striking everywhere in the city and killing a vast number of our people. Sores erupted on our faces, our breasts, our bellies; we were covered with agonizing sores from head to foot.

The illness was so dreadful that no one could walk or move. The sick were so utterly helpless that they could only lie on their beds like corpses, unable to move their limbs or even their heads. They could not lie face down or roll from one side to the other. If they did move their bodies, they screamed with pain.

A great many died from this plague, and many others died of hunger. They could not get up to search for food, and everyone else was too sick to care for them, so they starved to death in their beds.

Some people came down with a milder form of the disease; they suffered less than the others and made a good recovery. But they could not escape entirely. Their looks were ravaged, for wherever a sore broke out, it gouged an ugly pockmark in the skin. And a few of the survivors were left completely blind.

The first cases were reported in Cuatlán. By the time the danger was recognized, the plague was so well established that nothing could halt it, and eventually it spread all the way to Chalco. Then its virulence diminished considerably, though there were isolated cases for many months after. The first victims were stricken during the fiesta of Teotleco, and the faces of our warriors were not clean and free of sores until the fiesta of Panquetzaliztli.

DEFENSIVE TACTICS OF THE AZTECS

When the Aztecs discovered that the shots from the arquebuses and cannons always flew in a straight line, they no longer ran away in the line of fire. They ran to the right or left or in zigzags, not in front of the guns. If they saw that a cannon was about to be fired and they could not escape by running, they threw themselves to the ground and lay flat until the shot passed over them. The warriors also took cover among the houses, through a desert.

Then the Spaniards arrived in Huitzillán, where they found another wall blocking the road. A great crowd of our warriors was hiding behind it to escape gunfire.

THE SPANIARDS DEBARK

The brigantines came up and anchored nearby. They had been pursuing our war canoes in the open lake, but when they had almost run them down, they suddenly turned and sailed toward the causeway. Now they anchored a short distance from the houses. As soon as the cannons in their bows were loaded again, the soldiers aimed and fired them at the new wall.

From Miguel Leon-Portilla, *The Broken Spears: The Aztec Account of the Conquest of Mexico*, pp. 92–93, 96–101. © 1962, 1990 by Miguel Leon-Portilla. Expanded and Updated Edition © 1992 by Miguel Leon-Portilla. Reprinted by permission of Beacon Press, Boston.

The first shot cracked it in a dozen places, but it remained standing. They fired again: this time it cracked from one end to the other and crumpled to the ground. A moment later the road was completely empty. The warriors had all fled when they saw the wall collapsing; they ran blindly, this way and that, howling with fear.

Then the Spaniards debarked and filled the canal. Working hurriedly, they threw in the stones from the shattered wall, the roof beams and adobe bricks from the nearest houses, anything they could find, until the surface of the fill was level with the causeway. Then a squad of about ten horsemen crossed over it. They galloped to and fro, scouting both sides of the road; they raced and wheeled and clattered back and forth. Soon they were joined by another squad that rode up to support them.

A number of Tlatelolcas had rushed into the place where Motecuhzoma lived before he was slain. When they came out again, they unexpectedly met the Spanish Cavalry. The lead horseman stabbed one of the Tlatelolcas, but the wounded man was able to clutch the lance and cling to it. His friends ran to his aid and twisted it from the Spaniards hands. They knocked the horseman from his saddle, beat and kicked him as he lay on his back on the ground, and then cut off his head.

The Spaniards now joined all their forces into one unit and marched together as far as the Eagle Gate, where they set up the cannons they had brought with them. It was called the Eagle Gate because it was decorated with an enormous eagle carved of stone. The eagle was flanked on one side by a stone jaguar; on the other side there was a large honey bear, also of carved stone.

Two rows of tall columns led into the city from this gate. Some of the Aztecs hid behind the columns when they saw the Spaniards and their guns; others climbed onto the roofs of the communal houses. None of the warriors dared to show his face openly.

The Spaniards wasted no time as they loaded and fired the cannons. The smoke belched out in black clouds that darkened the sky, as if night were falling. The warriors hidden behind the columns broke from cover and fled; those on the rooftops climbed down and ran after them. When the smoke cleared away, the Spaniards could not see a single Aztec.

THE SPANIARDS ADVANCE TO THE HEART OF THE CITY

Then the Spaniards brought forward the largest cannon and set it up on the sacrificial stone. The priests of Huitzilopochtili immediately began to beat their great ritual drums from the top of the pyramid. The deep throbbing of the drums resounded over the city, calling the warriors to defend the stairway to the temple platform, cut the priests down with their great swords, and pitch them headlong over the brink.

The great captains and warriors who had been fighting from their canoes now returned and landed. The canoes were paddled by the younger warriors and the recruits. As soon as the warriors landed, they ran throughout the streets, hunting the enemy and shouting: "Mexicanos, come find them!"

The Spaniards, seeing that an attack was imminent, tightened their ranks and clenched the hilts of their swords. The next moment, all was noise and confusion. The Aztecs charged into the plaza from every direction, and the air was black with arrows and gunsmoke.

The battle was so furious that both sides had to pull back. The Aztecs withdrew to Xoloco to catch their breath and dress their wounds, while the Spaniards retreated to their camp in Acachinanco, abandoning the cannon they had set up on the sacrificial stone. Later the warriors dragged this cannon to the edge of the canal and toppled it in. It sank at a place called the Stone Toad.

THE AZTECS TAKE REFUGE

During this time the Aztecs took refuge in the Tlatelolco quarter. They deserted the Tenochtitlán quarters all in one day, weeping and lamenting like women. Husbands searched for their wives, and fathers carried their small children on their shoulders. Tears of grief and despair streamed down their cheeks.

The Tlatelolcas, however, refused to give up. They raced into Tenochtitlán to continue the fight and the Spaniards soon learned how brave they were. Pedro de Alvarado launched an attack against the Point of the Alders, in the direction of Nonhualco, but his troops were shattered as if he had sent them against a stone cliff. The battle was fought both on dry land and on the water, where the Indians had to draw back to Tlacopán.

On the following day, two brigantines came, up loaded with troops, and the Spaniards united all their forces on the outskirts of Nonhualco. The soldiers in the brigantines came ashore and the whole army marched into the very heart of Tenochtitlán. Wherever they went, the found the streets empty, with no Indians anywhere in sight.

THE LAST STAND

Then the great captain Tzilcatzin arrived, bringing with him three large, round stones of the kind used for building walls. He carried one of them in his hand; the other two hung from his shield. When he hurled these stones at the Spaniards, they turned and fled the city.

Tzilactzin's military rank was that of Otomi, and he clipped his hair in the style of the Otomies. He scorned his enemies, Spaniards as well as Indians; they all shook with terror at the mere sight of him.

When the Spaniards found out how dangerous he was, they tried desperately to kill him. They attacked him with their swords and spears, fired at him with their cross bows and arquebuses, and tried every other means they could think of to kill or cripple him. Therefore he wore various disguises to prevent them from recognizing him.

Sometimes he wore his lip plug, his gold earrings and all the rest of his full regalia, but left his head uncovered to show that he was an Otomi. At still other times, he wore only his cotton armor, with a thin kerchief wrapped around his head. At still other times, he put on the finery of the priests who cast the victims into the fire: a plumed headdress with the eagle symbol on its crest, and gleaming gold bracelets on both arms, and circular bands of gleaming gold on both ankles.

The Spaniards came back again the next day. They brought their ships to a point just off Nonhualco, close to the place called the House of Mist. Their other troops arrived on foot, along with the Tlaxcaltecas. As soon as they had formed ranks, they charged the Aztec warriors.

The heaviest fighting began when they entered Nonhualco. None of our enemies and none of our warriors escaped harm. Everyone was wounded, and the toll of the dead was grievous on both sides. The struggle continued all day and all night.

Only three captains never retreated. They were contemptuous of their enemies and gave no thought whatever to their own safety. The first of these heroes was Tzoyectzin; the second, Temoctzin; and the third, the great Tzilcatzin.

At last the Spaniards were too exhausted to keep on fighting. After one final attempt to break the Aztec ranks, they withdrew to their camp to rest and recover, with their allies trailing behind.

West Comes East: China and Japan

Driven by the love for gold, God, and glory, hardy and adventurous European traders, dedicated missionaries, and daring explorers took to the open seas and reached the shores of Asia in the last decade of the fifteenth and early decades of the sixteenth centuries. But while these Europeans were looking beyond the European horizon and venturing out on the stormy seas, Asian empires were generally turning inward, overwhelmed by internal decay, civil war, and dynastic transition. When Portuguese captain Vasco da Gama successfully led three small ships around the Cape of Good Hope and reached the western shores of the Indian subcontinent in 1498, the last ruling dynasty of the Delhi sultanate (1206–1526) was in its final stages of disintegration. In 1549, Japan was at the tail end of a century-long series of civil wars when a founding member of the Society of Jesus, St. Francis Xavier, arrived in western Japan and introduced Christianity to that country. In China, by the time Portuguese explorers reached an off-shore island near Canton in 1514, the once powerful Ming dynasty had begun to enter a long, drawn-out period of dynastic decline. Such fluid circumstances created favorable opportunities for European adventurers to establish their footholds on Asian shores.

The most dedicated and successful pioneers were the Jesuit missionaries. During the span of about two centuries—from St. Francis Xavier's first unsuccessful attempt to enter China in 1547 to the dissolution of the Jesuit order in 1773—several hundred "soldiers of the cross" were dispatched to China. Among the early Jesuit pioneers, the single most successful and important figure was Matteo Ricci, an Italian Jesuit (1551–1610). Besides his skillful approach to proselytism, Ricci's contributions to the bridging of East and West were invaluable and enduring.

Early Europeans in Asian ports brought not only Bibles but also firearms. Among the items that Portuguese traders first brought to Japan in 1543 was the arquebus, an early portable gun, which greatly fascinated the Japanese, who had long held a tradition of glorifying warriors and were in the midst of feudal wars. The "barbarian" firearms became avidly sought by Japanese feudal lords, and Japanese blacksmiths reproduced them in large quantities. Cannons appeared in Japan about 1558. In 1575, by employing 3,000 musketeers, Oda Nobunaga (1534–1582), a powerful warlord during the warring state period, won a decisive victory at the Battle of Nagashino over his enemies, who were armed with swords, bows, arrows, and pikes (long spears). After a century of disruption and disunity in the land, this victory paved the way for the unification of Japan. Thus, Japanese feudal lords with greater resources were now able to arm their soldiers with modern firearms and build larger, improved castles that could withstand musket and cannon attacks.

In addition, the European missionaries had phenomenal success in converting the Japanese to Christianity. Within a half century after St. Francis Xavier had first begun preaching in Japan in 1549, seventy-five Jesuit missionaries had won some 300,000 converts and established more than two hundred churches. This was the Jesuit missionaries' greatest success story in Asia. But a reversal of fortunes soon followed. In 1587, the new military master of Japan, Toyotomi Hideyoshi, became suspicious of the loyalty of the Japanese converts, and although the order was not rigorously enforced, he ordered all missionaries deported from Japan. The persecution of Christians was intensified when a new military government under Tokugawa Ieyasu was established in 1603. The early rulers of Tokugawa Japan regarded Christianity as subversive and ideologically incompatible with Tokugawa feudal principles. The Tokugawa paranoia about a secret collusion between the restless Japanese dissidents and the European powers resulted in a ban on travel by Japanese nationals to and from foreign lands. The Spanish and Portuguese missionaries were suspected to be the vanguard of aggression. For these reasons, the Tokugawa government closed the country to the outside world. This self-imposed isolation of Japan was to last more than two centuries until 1854, when American Commodore Matthew C. Perry signed the Treaty of Kanagawa.

4 Fernão Mendes Pinto, *The Travels of Mendes Pinto*

Fernão Mendes Pinto (1510?–1583) was born in Portugal and was in his late twenties when he sailed for India in 1537. He became wealthy as a merchant adventurer and spent many years in China and Japan. His account of his travels became important in Portuguese literature. The following selections describe his adventures on the China coast, where the Portuguese had established Ning-po as an enclave near Canton.

QUESTIONS TO CONSIDER

1. What was the Portuguese motive in attacking Nouday?
2. What practices of warfare on both sides could be seen as making Chinese-Portuguese relations difficult, in spite of the fact that China and Portugal were officially at peace?
3. How does religion enter into Pinto's narrative?
4. What are some ways in which Pinto's approach to exploration and contact with natives differs from that of the earlier Chinese explorer Cheng Ho (see Reading 1)?

THE SACK OF NOUDAY

The following morning, shortly before daybreak, Antonio de Faria sailed up the river with the three junks, the *lorcha*,[1] and the four fishing barges he had seized, and dropped anchor in six and a half fathoms of water right up against the walls of the city. Dispensing with the noisy salvo of artillery, he lowered the sails and hoisted the flag of commerce in keeping with the Chinese custom, intent upon observing all the outward signs of peace and leaving nothing undone by way of complying with the formalities, though he knew full well, from the way matters stood with the mandarin, that it would do him no good.

From here he sent him another letter which was extremely polite and friendly in tone, offering to raise the ransom for the captives; but it made that dog of a mandarin so angry, that he had the poor Chinese messenger crucified on an X-shaped cross and exhibited from the top of the wall in full view of the fleet. The sight was enough to make Antonio de Faria abandon the last shred of hope to which some of the men still made him cling, and at the same time, it made the soldiers so furious that they told him that, as long as he had decided to go ashore, there was no point in his waiting any longer because he would just be giving the enemies time to increase their strength.

---

[1]A junk is a Chinese sailing vessel distinguished by a high poop, overhanging stem, little or no keel, high pole masts and a deep rudder. A lorcha is a three-masted sailing vessel combining features of Chinese and European ship-building.

From Fernão Mendes Pinto, *The Travels of Mendes Pinto*, ed. and trans. Rebecca D. Catz (Chicago: University of Chicago Press, 1989), pp. 123–27. Reprinted with permission of The University of Chicago Press.

Since this seemed like good advice to him, he embarked immediately with all the men who were determined to go ashore, leaving orders behind for the junks to direct a steady barrage of fire against the enemies and the city, wherever major gatherings were to be seen, provided he was not engaged in a battle with them. And after disembarking at a spot about a culverin[2]-shot's distance below the roadstead, without encountering the slightest opposition, he marched along the shore in the direction of the city where, by this time, many people were stationed on top of the walls, waving an enormous number of silk banners, trying to put on a brave show by shouting and playing their martial music and generally carrying on like people who put more stock in words and outward appearances than in actual deeds.

As our men came within a musket-shot's distance of the moat surrounding the wall, about 1,000 to 1,200 soldiers—a guess hazarded by some—sallied forth from two gates; and of this number, about 100 to 120 were mounted on horseback, or to put it in a better way, they were mounted on some rather sorry looking nags. They began by putting on a fine show of skirmishing, running back and forth just as free and easy as you please, getting in each other's way most of the time, and often colliding and falling down in heaps of three and four, from which it was obvious that they were country bumpkins who were there not so much out of a desire to fight, but because they had been forced to come.

Antonio de Faria gently spurred his men on, and after signalling to the junks, he waited for the enemy out in the field, for he thought that they would want to engage him there, judging by the brave show they were putting on. But instead, they went right on with their skirmishing, running around in circles for a while, as though they were threshing wheat, thinking that this alone would be enough to scare us off. However, when they saw that we would not turn tail and run as they thought or probably hoped we would, they got together in a huddle and remained that way for a while, in a single body, in great disorder, without coming any closer.

Seeing them in that way, our captain ordered all the muskets, which had been silent until then, to fire at once; and, as God willed, they hit the mark so well that more than half of the cavalrymen, who were in the vanguard, were knocked to the ground. Off to a good start, we rushed them all together, calling on the name of Jesus as we went; and he, in his mercy, caused the enemy to abandon the field to us and sent them fleeing so wildly that they were falling on top of each other; and when they reached the bridge spanning the moat, they got themselves jammed in there so tightly that they were unable to move either backward or forward.

At this juncture, the main body of our men caught up to them and handled them so efficiently that, before long, more than three hundred of them were lying on top of each other—a pitiful sight indeed—for not a single one of them ever drew a sword.

Exhilarated by this victory, we made a dash for the gate, and there in the entrance we found the mandarin, surrounded by nearly six hundred men, mounted astride a fine horse, wearing an old-fashioned gilt-studded breastplate of purple velvet, which we found out later had belonged to a certain Tome Pires, whom King Manuel, of glorious memory, had sent as an ambassador to China. . . . The mandarin and his men tried to stop us at the entrance, where a cruel battle ensued, during which, little by little, in the time it would take to recite four or five Credos, they began to drive us back with a lot less fear than the ones on the bridge had shown, and they would have given us a

[2]A long cannon.

little difficult time had it not been for one of our slave boys who knocked the mandarin off his horse with a musket ball that struck him right in the chest. At that, the Chinese became so frightened that they all spun around immediately and began retreating through the gates in complete disorder, and we along with them, knocking them down with our lances, while not a single one of them had enough presence of mind to shut the gates. And off we went, chasing them before us like cattle, down a very long road, until at last they swept through another gate that led to the forest where every last one of them disappeared from sight.

Next, to prevent disorder, Antonio de Faria gathered his soldiers together and, in a single corps, marched with them straight to the prison where they were holding our men, who at the sight of us let out such a loud and terrifying cry of "Lord God, have mercy on us!" that it was enough to send the shivers down one's spine. He immediately had the prison doors and bars broken with axes, a task that our men threw themselves into with such great enthusiasm that it took but a moment to smash everything to bits and remove the prisoners' shackles, so that in a very short time all our companions were unfettered and free.

The order was given to our soldiers and the others in our company that each man was to lay hold of as much as he could for himself, because there would be no sharing of the spoils, and everyone was to keep whatever he could carry; but he asked them to be quick about it, for he would allow them no more than the brief space of half an hour in which to do it. And they all answered that they would be perfectly satisfied with that.

And then they all disappeared into the houses, while Antonio de Faria headed straight for the mandarin's, which he had staked out for himself, and there he found eight thousand taels in silver alone, as well as five huge jars of musk, all of which he had gathered up. The rest, which he left for the slaves accompanying him, consisted of large quantities of silk, yarn, satin, damask, and fine-quality porcelain packed in straw, which they carried until they were ready to collapse.

As a result, the four barges and three sampans that had been used as landing craft had to make four trips to transfer the loot to the junks, and there was not a slave or sailor among them who did not speak of his booty in terms of whole cases and bales of piece goods, to say nothing of the secrets each one kept locked in his heart.

When he saw that more than an hour and a half had gone by, Antonio de Faria quickly ordered the men to return to the ships, but there was absolutely no way of getting them to stop their looting, and this was especially true of the men of most account. But with night coming on, he was afraid some disaster might befall them, and he had the torch put to the city in ten or twelve different places; and since most of the buildings were constructed of pine and other woods, the fire spread so fiercely that in less than a quarter of an hour it looked like a blazing inferno.

Withdrawing to the beach with all the men, he embarked, with not a murmur of protest from any of them, for they were all leaving very rich and happy; and they had many pretty girls in tow, which was really pathetic to see, for they were tied up with musket wicks by fours and fives, and they were all crying while our men were laughing and singing.

PIRATES AT THE GATES OF NING-PO

Since it was already late when Antonio de Faria and all his men got back to the ship, there was no time left for anything but to attend to the wounded, who numbered fifty—eight of them Portuguese and the rest slaves and sailors—and to bury the dead, who numbered nine, counting one Portuguese.

And after spending the night with a careful lookout on account of the junks up the river, at daybreak he departed for a small town located at water's edge on the opposite bank, and discovered that it was completely deserted, all the inhabitants having fled. But he found the houses filled to overflowing with their goods and enormous quantities of food which Antonio de Faria had loaded on board the junks out of fear that in the ports along the way people would refuse to sell him anything because of what he had done.

After that was decided, since everyone thought it best and advised him to do so, that the three winter months he still had to wait before he could set out on his voyage should be spent on a deserted island called Pulo Hinhor, located out to sea fifteen leagues from Ning-po, where there was fresh water and good anchorage, because he thought that his presence in Ning-po would be detrimental to the commerce of the Portuguese merchants who spent their winters there peacefully carrying on their trade. And everyone praised him highly for this decision and his good intentions.

We departed from the port of Nouday, and after five days of sailing between the mainland and the islands of Comolem, at midday on a Saturday we were attacked by a robber named Premata Gundel, a bitter enemy of the Portuguese people, who had already done them a great deal of harm several times before, not only in Patani but in Sunda and Siam and other places as well, wherever he chanced to meet them in a way that suited his purposes. Mistaking us for Chinese, he attacked us with two huge junks carrying two hundred fighting men, not counting the crew that worked the sails. One of them, after sinking its grappling hooks into Mem Taborda's junk, nearly finished him off. However, when Quiay Panjao, who was a little way out to sea, saw what was happening, he turned back and rammed the enemy junk, going after it under full sail and smashing into its starboard quarter with such force that both of them promptly sank to the bottom, leaving Mem Taborda free of the danger threatening him. Then three of our *lorchas*, which Antonio de Faria had brought from the port of Nouday, came running to the rescue at top speed and—thanks be to God—they saved most of our people while those on the enemy side all drowned.

About this time, Premata Gundel had reached the big junk that Antonio de Faria was on and tackled it with a pair of grappling hooks attached to very long iron chains, immobilizing him fore and aft, and engaging him in a battle that was truly remarkable to see. For more than half an hour the enemy fought so bravely that most of Antonio de Faria's men were wounded, leaving him, on two occasions, in danger of being taken. However, at that point the three *lorchas* and a small junk commanded by Pero da Silva came to his aid, and—as God willed—with their help our men soon regained the ground they had lost. They pressed the enemy so hard that in no time at all the whole business was over, ending with the death of the eighty-six Moors who had boarded Antonio de Faria's junk and given him such a bad time that the only part of the ship still held by our men was the poop deck. And from here, they boarded the pirate's junk and put everyone they found on it to the sword, sparing none, though the crew had already dived into the sea.

However, the price of this victory was not cheap by any means, for it cost us the lives of seventeen men, five of them Portuguese—the best and bravest soldiers in the whole company—and left forty-three badly wounded, one of them Antonio de Faria, who came out of it with a spear injury and two sword cuts.

The battle over, an inventory was taken of what was found on the enemy junk and the booty was appraised at eighty thousand *taels*, the bulk of it in Japanese silver that the pirate had stolen from three merchant junks. That meant that, on this ship alone, the pirate was carrying 120,000 *cruzados*; and they said that he had been carrying almost as much on the junk that went down, which aggrieved many of our men.

With this prize, Antonio de Faria withdrew to a little island called Buncalou, located three or four leagues to the west where there was fresh water and good anchorage. He went ashore and remained there for eighteen days, sleeping in huts that were improvised for the large numbers of wounded men where—as it pleased the Lord—all of them regained their health.

And from there, we proceeded on our determined course with Antonio de Faria on his big junk, Mem Taborda and Antonio Henriques on theirs, Pero da Silva on the small one that had been captured in Nouday, and Quiay Panjao and all his people on the one just taken from the robber, which was given to him to compensate him for the one he had lost, in addition to twenty thousand *taels* from the common funds, with which he felt completely satisfied and well paid for his trouble; and all our men were also pleased with this arrangement because Antonio de Faria had been most adamant about it and had promised to make up for it handsomely in the future.

We went sailing along in this manner, and within six days we reached the Gates of Ning-po, which are actually two islands located three leagues from where the Portuguese traded in those days. It was a town they had built ashore with over a thousand houses that was governed by a city council, a high court magistrate, constables, six or seven judges, and administrative officers of state, where the notaries would sign the legal documents they drew up in the following manner: "I, So-and-So, Notary Public of the Archives and Judiciary of the city of Ning-po, in the name of His Majesty, the King . . .," as though it were situated between Santarem and Lisbon. And they felt so sure of themselves and were so complacent about it that they had gone so far as to build homes costing between three and four thousand *cruzados*, all of which, from large to small, were later destroyed and completely leveled by the Chinese—for our sins—with not a trace of them left to show for it, as I will explain more fully at the proper time when I come to it. And then it will be plain to see how uncertain things are in China, about which there is such great interest in Portugal and for which some people mistakenly have such high regard, for at every hour of the day they are exposed to all kinds of disasters and misfortunes.

5 Matteo Ricci, *Journals*

Matteo Ricci reached Macao in 1582. He had to overcome seemingly insuperable difficulties before gaining a foothold in China, which was rigidly Confucian and xenophobic. Ricci was quick to realize that the Jesuits could not hope to succeed in China if they adopted the same proselytizing approach that other missionaries had used. Immediately he set out to work from the top down: He began to penetrate the Chinese ruling class, not so much as a Christian missionary but rather as a learned friend and scientist. To dispel suspicion on the part of Chinese scholars and officials, he at first wore the robes of the Buddhist monk and then changed to those of the Confucian scholar-official class. Besides his mastery of the Chinese language and the classics, he made an intense study of Chinese history, customs, geography, philosophy, and government. He also knew how to arouse the curiosity and fancy of Chinese officials and scholars by presenting them with gifts previously unknown to them, such as clocks, sundials, clavichords, and astrolabes. As a result, Ricci won the respect, admiration, and friendship of the Chinese scholar-officials. At last, in 1601, after eighteen strenuous years, Ricci was allowed by the Chinese emperor to establish his residence at the imperial capital, where he stayed until his death in 1610. Ricci was buried in a plot donated by the emperor.

For a period of twenty-eight years, with patience, keen intellect, tact, and dedication, Ricci laid a permanent foundation for Christianity in China. Hundreds of fellow Jesuits followed in his footsteps to China and won thousands of Chinese converts. At the same time, Ricci and many of the Jesuits who later came to China developed a respect and fascination for Chinese civilization. Because of this scholarly interest, many of these Jesuits, starting with Ricci, emerged as pioneers in sinology in the West. They built a bridge between the two worlds. They introduced Confucius to Europe, and the Bible, Copernicus, and Euclid to China. Their letters and writings on Chinese history, government, society, philosophy, geography, and customs became the chief reference sources on China for the Europeans.

In particular, Ricci's diary, *De Propagatione Christiana apud Sinas* (On the Propagation of Christianity Among the Chinese), contributed greatly to Europe's understanding of China. The diary was posthumously published in 1615 by Ricci's co-worker, the Belgian Jesuit Nicholas Trigault, who edited and translated the original Italian into Latin. This diary was widely read in seventeenth-century Europe and appeared in several European languages. Ricci described various aspects of Chinese life and institutions such as Confucian philosophy, the imperial examination system, the bureaucracy, the arts and sciences, customs, and religions. Thus, Ricci's journal reopened China to Europe three centuries after Marco Polo had first bridged the gap through his famous travelogue. The following selection is Ricci's description, as presented by Father Trigault, of China's pacifistic tradition and the triennial rotation system of the imperial government.

QUESTIONS TO CONSIDER

1. How do you compare the people and society of China described by Ricci with those of Europe in the sixteenth century?
2. How did Ricci describe China's pacifistic tradition? Do you agree or disagree with Ricci's assessment? Why?

Before closing this chapter on Chinese public administration, it would seem to be quite worthwhile recording a few more things in which this people differ from Europeans. To begin with, it seems to be quite remarkable when we stop to consider it, that in a kingdom of almost limitless expanse and innumerable population, and abounding in copious supplies of every description, though they have a well-equipped army and navy that could easily conquer the neighboring nations, neither the King nor his people ever think of waging a war of aggression. They are quite content with what they have and are not ambitious of conquest. In this respect they are much different from the people of Europe, who are frequently discontent with their own governments and covetous of what others enjoy. While the nations of the West seem to be entirely consumed with the idea of supreme domination, they cannot even preserve what their ancestors have bequeathed them, as the Chinese have done through a period of some thousands of years. This assertion seems to have some bearing upon what many of our writers maintain relative to the initial founding of the empire, when they assert that the Chinese not only subjugated the neighboring nations but extended their sway even as far as India. After diligent study of the history of China, covering a period of more than four thousand years, I must admit that I have never seen any mention of such conquest, nor have I ever heard of them extending the boundaries of their empire. On the contrary, in frequent inquiry among learned Chinese historians, relative to this assertion, their answer has always been the same; that it was not so and could not possibly be so. Not to question the reputation of the writers who have recorded the error, the mistake may have arisen from the fact that certain evidences of the presence of the Chinese have been discovered beyond the confines of the kingdom. For example, one might cite the Philippine Islands, to which they found their way in private enterprise rather than on any official commission by their government.

Another remarkable fact and quite worthy of note as marking a difference from the West, is that the entire kingdom is administered by the Order of the Learned, commonly known as the Philosophers. The responsibility for orderly management of the entire realm is wholly and completely committed to their charge and care. The army, both officers and soldiers, hold them in high respect and show them the promptest obedience and deference, and not infrequently the military are disciplined by them as a schoolboy might be punished by his master. Policies of war are formulated and military questions are decided by the Philosophers only, and their advice and counsel has more weight with the King than that of the military leaders. In fact very few of these, and only on rare occasions, are admitted to war consultations. Hence it follows that those who aspire to be cultured frown upon war and would prefer the lowest rank in the philosophical order to the highest in the military, realizing that the Philosophers far excel military leaders in the good will and the respect of the people and in opportunities of acquiring wealth. What is still more surprising to strangers is that these same Philosophers, as they are called, with respect to nobility of sentiment and in contempt of danger and death, where fidelity to King and country is concerned, surpass even those whose particular profession is the defense of the fatherland. Perhaps this sentiment has its origin in the fact that the mind of man is ennobled by the study of letters. Or again, it may have developed from the fact that from the beginning and foundation of this empire the study of letters was always more acceptable to the

From *China in the Sixteenth Century: The Journals of Matthew Ricci, 1583–1610*, by Matthew Ricci, translated by Louis J. Gallagher, S. J. (New York: Random House, 1953), pp. 54–56, 58–59. Copyright 1942 and renewed 1970 by Louis J. Gallagher, S. J. Reprinted by permission of Random House, Inc.

people than the profession of arms, as being more suitable to a people who had little or no interest in the extension of the empire.

The order and harmony that prevails among magistrates, both high and low, in the provinces and in the regal Curia is also worthy of admiration. Their attitude toward the King, in exact obedience and in external ceremony, is a cause of wonderment to a foreigner. The literati would never think of omitting certain customary formal visits to one another or the regular practice of freely offering gifts. In the courts and elsewhere, inferiors always bend the knee when speaking to a superior, and address him in the most dignified language. The same is true of the people toward their prefects and toward the mayor of the city, even though these officers may have arisen from the lowest state in life before attaining their literary degrees and admittance to the magistracy. The term of office of all the dignitaries we have been discussing is three years, unless one be confirmed in his position or promoted by order of the crown. Usually they are promoted but not for the same locality, lest they should develop friendships and become lenient in the administration of justice, or develop a following in the province in which they are so influential. The experience of past ages has taught them that a magistrate burdened with favors is likely to incline toward the introduction of novelties and away from the rigor of the law.

No one is permitted to carry arms within city limits, not even soldiers or officers, military prefects or magistrates, unless one be en route to war or on the way to drill or to a military school. Certain of the higher magistrates, however, may be accompanied by an armed guard. Such is their dislike for arms that no one is allowed to have them in his home, except perhaps a metal dagger which might be needed on a journey as protection against robbers. Fighting and violence among the people are practically unheard of, save what might be concluded by hair pulling and scratching, and there is no requiting of injuries by wounds and death. On the contrary, one who will not fight and restrains himself from returning a blow is praised for his prudence and bravery.

6 Seclusion Edict of 1636

Of the five seclusion edicts issued by the Tokugawa government over a period of twenty-seven years, from 1612 to 1639, the edict reproduced here, issued on May 19, 1636, contained all essential aspects of the national seclusion.

QUESTIONS TO CONSIDER

1. What were the reasons for the self-imposed isolation of Japan under Tokugawa rule?
2. What were some of the short- and long-term effects of the Tokugawa seclusion policy?

1. Japanese ships shall by no means be sent abroad.
2. No Japanese shall be sent abroad. Anyone violating this prohibition shall suffer the penalty of death, and the shipowner and crew shall be held up together with the ship.
3. All Japanese residing abroad shall be put to death when they return home.
4. All Christians shall be examined by official examiners.
5. Informers against Christians shall be rewarded.
6. The arrival of foreign ships must be reported to Edo, and watch kept over them.
7. The Namban people (Spaniards or Portuguese) and any other people with evil titles propagating Christianity shall be incarcerated in the Omura prison as before.
8. Even ships shall not be left untouched in the matter of exterminating Christians.
9. Everything shall be done in order to see that no Christian is survived by descendants, and anyone disregarding this injunction shall be put to death, while proper punishment shall be meted out to the other members of his family according to their deeds.
10. Children born of the Namban people (Spaniards or Portuguese) in Nagasaki and people adopting these Namban children into their family shall be put to death; capital punishment shall also be meted out to those Namban descendants if they return to Japan, and their relatives in Japan, who may communicate with them, shall receive suitable punishment.
11. The samurai shall not purchase goods on board foreign ships directly from foreigners.
12. The white yarns (raw silk) sent on foreign ships shall be allotted to the five privileged cities and other quarters as stipulated after establishing their prices.
13. After the settling of the price of raw silk, the sale of any goods other than raw silk may be freely carried on between the dealers concerned. It is to be added that, as Chinese ships are small and cannot, therefore, bring large consignments, the authorities may issue orders for sale at their discretion. The delivery of goods other than raw silk shall be effected within twenty days after the settling of their prices.
14. The date of departure homeward of foreign ships shall not be later than September 20th. Any ships arriving in Japan later than usual shall sail for home within fifty days after their arrival. No date is fixed for departure of Chinese ships. They shall be caused to set sail a little later than Portuguese or Spanish ships at the discretion of the authorities concerned.
15. Foreign ships shall take back with them all they are unable to sell of their cargo.
16. The arrival in Nagasaki of representatives of the five cities (representatives of the privileged silk merchants of Kyoto, Sakai, Edo, Nagasaki, and Osaka) shall not be later than July 5th. Any of them arriving at the destination later than this date shall lose the privilege of the sale of raw silk.
17. Ships arriving at Hirado shall not transact business pending the establishment of prices at Nagasaki.

From Yosoburo Takekoshi, *The Economic Aspects of the History of the Civilization of Japan*, Vol. 2 (New York: Macmillan, 1930), pp. 128–29.

The African Slave Trade

Certainly one of the most lucrative items in the mercantile world of the Atlantic trader was African slaves. From the end of the fifteenth to the end of the nineteenth centuries, slavers pillaged Africa for cheap labor to work the plantations, and in Iberian America also the mines, of the New World. Twelve to 15 million Africans were sold into slavery and crossed the Atlantic, but it is estimated that perhaps 20 to 25 million died in the turmoil and warfare that accompanied this passage to the New World.

Although Europeans purchased captive Africans, they seldom undertook raids to capture slaves by themselves, much preferring to buy them from the various African slave dealers. This was one reason that Europeans showed no more humanitarian concern for slaves from Africa than the dealers did. The Europeans rationalized their part in the slave trade by telling themselves that slavery was a common institution among Africans themselves, that "normally" at least the men who were members of a group that had lost a tribal conflict would be killed by the victors. Being sold to Europeans, therefore, spared their lives. Another rationalization shored up this thinking: Converting captured Africans to Christianity saved their souls, which otherwise would have been lost.

The fact is that in the earliest stage of the Atlantic slave trade Europeans had some grounds for believing that they were buying Africans previously captured in tribal conflicts; however, the sheer numbers who were soon involved refuted any perception that anything other than slave raids or kidnapping (not tribal warfare) was the major source of African slaves. By the turn of the nineteenth century, European indignation over the inhuman practices of the slave traders grew to the point that most European countries made slavery illegal. Centuries before the Atlantic slave trade began, however, Arab slave traders bought and sold Africans; and, particularly at points on the East African coast, slavery directed at markets in the Middle East continued. In fact, it was one of the ironies of later history that Europeans used the rationalization of halting the African–Middle Eastern slave trade to justify their takeover of territories in East Africa toward the end of the nineteenth century.

7 Olaudah Equiano, *The Life of Olaudah Equiano, or Gustavus Vassa, The African*

One African who survived the journey was Olaudah Equiano (ca. 1745–1797), an Ibo born in eastern Nigeria near Benin. When Equiano was ten years old, he and his sister were captured from their home by local robbers who quickly sold the children to slavers. Equiano served a series of masters, first in Barbados and later in Virginia; he was finally bought by a British naval officer who took him to Canada, England, and then back to the West Indies. This owner gave Equiano the new name of Gustavus Vassa. In 1766, by luck and frugal trading, Equiano had saved the hefty sum of forty pounds sterling, which was enough money to buy his freedom. As a free man, he returned to England, where he worked as a barber, a domestic servant, and a sailor.

In 1789, he published a two-volume set of memoirs in English, describing his life in Africa and his experiences as a slave. His account, excerpted in the following reading, became a best-seller in England and soon enabled Equiano; to become active in the English antislavery movement.

QUESTIONS TO CONSIDER

1. What does this memoir tell us about the organization and extent of slavery in the eighteenth-century Atlantic world?
2. What does this selection indicate about Equiano's African home and African culture?
3. What does the memoir, particularly its title, *The Life of Olaudah Equiano, or Gustavus Vassa, The African,* tell us about the cultural effects of slavery upon Africans in the eighteenth century?

One day, when all our people were gone out to their works as usual and only I and my dear sister were left to mind the house, two men and a woman got over our walls, and in a moment seized us both, and without giving us time to cry out or make resistance they stopped our mouths and ran off with us into the nearest wood. Here they tied our hands and continued to carry us as far as they could till night came on, when we reached a small house where the robbers halted for refreshment and spent the night. . . .

The first object which saluted my eyes when I arrived on the coast was the sea, and a slave ship which was then riding at anchor and waiting for its cargo. These filled me with astonishment, which was soon converted into terror when I was carried on

From Olaudah Equiano, *The Life of Olaudah Equiano, or Gustavus Vassa, The African, Written by Himself* (Boston: I. Knapp, 1837), 31–32, 43–44, 47–48, 50–52.

board. I was immediately handled and tossed up to see if I were sound by some of the crew, and I was now persuaded that I had gotten into a world of bad spirits and that they were going to kill me. Their complexions too differing so much from ours, their long hair and the language they spoke (which was very different from any I had ever heard) united to confirm me in this belief. Indeed such were the horrors of my views and fears at the moment that, if ten thousand worlds had been my own, I would have freely parted with them all to have exchanged my condition with that of the meanest slave in my own country. When I looked round the ship too and saw a large furnace or copper boiling and a multitude of black people of every description chained together, every one of their countenances expressing dejection and sorrow, I no longer doubted of my fate; and quite overpowered with horror and anguish, I fell motionless on the deck and fainted. When I recovered a little I found some black people about me, who I believed were some of those who had brought me on board and had been receiving their pay; they talked to me in order to cheer me, but all in vain. I asked them if we were not to be eaten by those white men with horrible looks, red faces, and loose hair. They told me I was not, and one of the crew brought me a small portion of spirituous liquor in a wine glass, but being afraid of him I would not take it out of his hand. One of the blacks there took it from him and gave it to me, and I took a little down my palate, which instead of reviving me, as they thought it would, threw me into the greatest consternation at the strange feeling it produced, having never tasted any such liquor before. Soon after this the blacks who brought me on board went off, and left me abandoned to despair. . . .

The stench of the hold while we were on the coast was so intolerably loathsome that it was dangerous to remain there for any time, and some of us had been permitted to stay on the deck for the fresh air; but now that the whole ship's cargo were confined together it became absolutely pestilential. The closeness of the place and the heat of the climate, added to the number in the ship, which was so crowded that each had scarcely room to run himself, almost suffocated us. This produced copious perspirations, so that the air soon became unfit for respiration from a variety of loathsome smells, and brought on a sickness among the slaves, of which many died, thus falling victims to the improvident avarice, as I may call it, of their purchasers. This wretched situation was again aggravated by the galling of the chains, now become insupportable, and the filth of the necessary tubs, into which the children often fell and were almost suffocated. The shrieks of the women and the groans of the dying rendered the whole a scene of horror almost inconceivable. Happily perhaps for myself I was soon reduced so low here that it was thought necessary to keep me almost always on deck, and from my extreme youth I was not put in fetters. . . .

At last we came in sight of the island of Barbados, at which the whites on board gave a great shout and made many signs of joy to us. We did not know what to think of this, but as the vessel drew nearer we plainly saw the harbour and other ships of different kinds and sizes, and we soon anchored amongst them off Bridgetown. Many merchants and planters now came on board, though it was in the evening. They put us in separate parcels and examined us attentively. They also made us jump, and pointed to the land, signifying we were to go there. We thought by this we should be eaten by these ugly men, as they appeared to us; and when soon after we were all put down under the deck again, there was much dread and trembling among us, and nothing but bitter cries to be heard all the night from these apprehensions, insomuch that at last the white people got some old slaves from the land to pacify us. They told us we were not to be eaten but to work, and were soon to go on land where we should see many of our country people. This report eased us much; and sure enough soon after we were landed there came to us Africans of all languages. We were conducted immediately to the merchant's yard, where we were all pent up together like so many sheep in a fold without regard to sex or age. As every object was new to me everything I saw filled me with surprise. What struck me first was that the houses were built with storeys, and in every other respect different from those in Africa: but I was still more astonished on seeing people on horseback. I did not know what this could mean, and indeed I thought these people were full of nothing but magical arts. While I was in this astonishment one of my fellow prisoners spoke to a countryman of his about the horses, who said they were the same kind they had in their country. I understood them though they were from a distant part of Africa, and I thought it odd I had not seen any horses there; but afterwards when I came to converse with different Africans I found they had many horses amongst them, and much larger than those I then saw. We were not many days in the merchant's custody before we were sold after their usual manner, which is this: On a signal given, (as the beat of a drum) the buyers rush at once into the yard where the slaves are confined, and make choice of that parcel they like best. The noise and clamour with which this is attended and the eagerness visible in the countenances of the buyers serve not a little to increase the apprehensions of the terrified Africans, who may well be supposed to consider them as the ministers of that destruction to which they think themselves devoted. In this matter, without scruple, are relations and friends separated, most of them never to see each other again. I remember in the vessel in which I was brought over, in the men's apartment there were several brothers who, in the sale, were sold in different lots; and it was very moving on this occasion to see and hear their cries at parting. O, ye nominal Christians! might not an African ask you, Do unto all men as you would men should do unto you? Is it not enough that we are torn from our country and friends to toil for your luxury and lust of gain? Must every tender feeling be likewise sacrificed to your avarice? Are the dearest friends and relations, now rendered more dear by their separation from their kindred, still to be parted from each other and thus prevented from cheering the gloom of slavery with the small comfort of being together and mingling their sufferings and sorrows? Why are parents to lose their children, brothers their sisters, or husbands their wives? Surely this is a new refinement in cruelty which, while it has no advantage to atone for it, thus aggravates distress and adds fresh horrors even to the wretchedness of slavery.

8 Commerce, Slavery, and Religion in North Africa

The purchase of slaves by North African merchants through the agency of rulers on the southern Saharan fringes began as early as the ninth century A.D. and was brought to an end only at the beginning of the twentieth century. West African Muslim rulers played an important controlling role in all external trade, and North African merchants could operate only with their consent. From the nineteenth-century evidence we have from the northern regions of what is now Nigeria, it is clear that rulers had first choice of merchandise from the large caravans and paid for it in slaves—a commodity that could be obtained at will by raiding the large non-Muslim populations surrounding these Muslim states. The enslavement of non-Muslims was permitted by Islamic law as a by-product of *jihād*—"war for the expansion of the domain of Islam," but the random rounding up of non-Muslim populations to pay off a debt, such as is illustrated in the following piece, hardly comes under this rubric. Nevertheless, the narrator seeks some religious justification for carrying off black Africans into slavery inasmuch as their routinized mass "conversion" to Islam en route ensures their salvation. As he acknowledges, piety and commerce may be mutually reinforcing.

The following account was given to General E. Daumas, a French officer serving in Algeria in the 1830s, by a member of a caravan headed by a Tuareg guide (*khabīr*) called Cheggueun, which set out from Metlily in the Algerian Sahara to do business in Katsina in the far north of present-day Nigeria. Katsina was one of the emirates that formed part of a large Islamic empire founded in the early years of the nineteenth century with its capital at Sokoto.

QUESTIONS TO CONSIDER

1. How did the Muslim Holy men (Marabouts) influence the commerce in African slavery?
2. How does the organization of the slave trade in North Africa in the nineteenth century compare with the organization of the slave trade in West Africa in the eighteenth century (see Reading 7)?

THE SLAVE TRADE

We had been at Katsina for ten days and when the story had got around in the surrounding villages that a rich caravan had arrived, all the petty merchants hastened to the town. Moreover, since those of Katsina were pressing us it was decided to put our merchandise on sale and Cheggueun went to tell Omar[1] what we intended to do. The response of the serki (ruler) was that we could do as we liked, but that he would reserve the sale of all our broadcloths, in the name of the sultan. His oukil (agent) made a list the same day and took us to the palace to discuss the price with the serki himself.

"Khabir (caravan leader)," said Omar to our chief, "according to what my agent has told me, the broadcloths of your merchants are of inferior quality and are worth no more than a single slave, negro or negress, per cubit." "Sir, it shall be done ac-

---

[1]'Umar Dallāji, emir of Katsina, 1806–1835.

Abridged and trans. John O. Hunwick from Gen. E. Daumas, *Le Grand Désert. Itinéraire d'une caravane du Sahara au pays des nègres, royaume de Haoussa,* 4th ed., (Paris, 1860), pp. 199–247.

cording to your justice. We are your servants," replied Cheggueun, and we all put our fist on our chest as a sign of consent, for in fact we were getting a good deal. "Go in peace, then," replied the serki, "I do not have enough slaves to pay you today. But, by the grace of God, Mohammed Omar shall not fail in his word."

As we went out of the palace a regular low pitched sound caught our attention. It came from the center of the town and we made for it. It led us to the Makhzen (army) square where, from every street, a crowd came running like us. At the center of the square was placed a huge drum which a strapping Negro beat with a knobbed stick with all his might. This is the sultan's drum. It is never beaten for anything but assembling the army.

We had discovered the secret of the strange noise that had moved us and this proclamation of the chief of the Mekhazenia informed us for what purpose they were gathered: "This is the will of the serki. In the name of sultan Bello the Victorious,[2] may God bless him, all of you, are summoned to present yourselves here at daybreak, armed and mounted, with sufficient provisions to go, some to Zenfra [Zamfara] and others to Zendeur [Zinder] to hunt the idolatrous Koholanes[3]—enemies of the glorious sultan our master—may God curse them." "All that the sultan orders is good," responded the soldiers. "Let it be done according to the will of our lord and master."

The following day, in fact, the Mekhazenia (soldiery), prompt to the appointed meeting, divided themselves into two goums (companies), one taking the east and the other the south-west with orders to attack places without defences and to carry off the inhabitants as well as seizing all peasants busy cultivating their fields. At the same time orders were given to track down the idolatrous Koholanes in the interior.

Whilst waiting for the return of the goums that Omar had despatched to hunt Negroes, we went every day to the slave market where we bought at the following prices:

A Negro with beard	10 or 15,000 cowries

They are not considered as merchandise since one has little chance of preventing them from escaping.

An adult Negress, same price for the same reasons	10 or 15,000 cowries
An adolescent Negro	30,000 cowries
A young Negress	50–60,000 cowries
(The price varies according to whether she is more or less beautiful.)	
A male Negro child	45,000 cowries
A female Negro child	35–40,000 cowries

The seller gives the buyer the greatest possible chance to examine the slaves and one has three days to give notice of concealed faults.

---

[2]Muhammad Bellow (d. 1837) was the ruler of the Sokoto empire of which the emirate of Katsina formed a constituent part.

[3]In Saharan Arabic *kuḥlān* (sing. *akḥal)* is the equivalent of *sūdān*—"blacks" with a pejorative connotation.

THE RETURN OF OMAR'S GOUM

The goum of serki Omar had been on campaign for about a month when we learnt from a messenger that the double raid launched against Zinder and Zamfara had been completely successful and that the makhzen, bringing back two thousand slaves would return to Katsina the next day. In a few hours this good news had spread throughout the town and at daybreak the next day the entire population crowded the gardens on the east side where the two armies that had the previous day joined up ought to arrive.

A cloud of dust soon announced it and as they crossed the outer wall where the route was better marked and the terrain more solid, their confused mass began to make itself out from the veil of sand that they had raised on the plain. The prisoners walked at the head, men, women, children, the elderly, almost all naked or half covered in rags of blue cloth. The women and the elderly were unbound but tightly packed together; the children were piled onto camels with some sitting on their mothers' backs in a piece of cloth doing duty as a bag. The men had been chained, five or six to the same chain, their necks fixed in a strong iron ring closed by a padlock and their hands bound with palm ropes. The strongest and most resistant were tied down to the tails of horses. Women moaned and children cried. Men, in general, seemed more resigned, but the bloody cuts that the whip had made on their shoulders bore witness to their tough struggle with the horsemen of the serki.

The convoy steered itself towards the palace and its arrival was announced to Mohammed Omar by musicians. At the first sound of the music the serki came out of his palace followed by his agent and some dignitaries. On seeing him all the slaves threw themselves on their knees and the musicians attacked their instruments with a passion that bordered on fury. The serki, approaching the goum, complimented its leaders, examined the slaves and gave the order for them to be taken to the market. There they were placed in two rows in sheds, women on one side and men on the other, and on the next day we were invited to go and choose those which suited us. Cheggueun and the palace agent went with us and after very careful examination each of us obtained as many Negroes and Negresses as he had handed over cubits of broadcloth to the serki. Nevertheless, we only accepted those whose sound constitutions were a surety against the hazards of the long journey we had to make. The elderly, small children and pregnant women were sold to the people of Katsina or given by Omar as gifts to the leaders of his mekhazenias.

DEPARTURE OF THE CARAVAN

We were now in the month of April and the season was favorable for leaving. We hastened to gather provisions of maize, millet, dried meat, butter and honey sufficient for each person for three months and we bought baggage camels in sufficient number to insure against accidents en route and some oxhide tents. Finally, our caravan which had set out from Metlily (in Algeria) with sixty-four camels and only sixteen persons, was now augmented by four hundred slaves, of whom three hundred were women, and had a total of almost six hundred camels.

The people of Touat [Tuwāt][4] who joined with us, had increased in number similarly. They had purchased fifteen hundred slaves and their camels had risen in num-

---

[4]Tuwāt is a large oasis in the central Algerian Sahara.

ber to two thousand. Altogether we formed a company of about two thousand one hundred men and two thousand six hundred camels. Katsina had no square big enough to contain us and so, under the name of the Touat caravan, we went to establish ourselves in one of the great empty spaces set up in the middle of the gardens.

Finally we saw successively arriving the three caravans of Ghadames, Ghat and the Fezzan.[5] The first had penetrated as far as Nupe on the banks of the Bahar-el-Nil [river Niger] to the south of Sokoto. It brought back three thousand slaves and three thousand five hundred camels. The second had pushed down to Kano to the south-east of Katsina. It only numbered seven or eight hundred camels and four or five hundred slaves. The third came back from Sokoto and was no larger than the preceding one.

At daybreak our camels were loaded, the Negro children perched atop the baggage, the male Negroes secured by their chains in the center of the convoy and the Negro females grouped in eights or tens under the watch of men carrying whips. The departure signal was given and the first caravan moved. It was at this point that suddenly a confused noise of cries and sobs passed from one group of slaves to another and reached our own. All, together, wept and moaned, called out and uttered farewells. They were terrified of being eaten during the journey. Some rolled on the ground, clung to bushes and absolutely refused to walk. Nothing had any effect on them, neither kind words nor threats. They could only be got up with mighty lashes of the whip and by rendering them completely bloody. Despite their obstinacy, no one of them resisted this extreme measure. Moreover, joined together as they were, the less fearful or more courageous, struggling with the weaker ones, forced them to walk.

The first day we halted at only three leagues[6] from Katsina on a huge plain where we found pools and plenty of grass and wood. Each caravan established its camp separately. As soon as our camels had crouched down and after having, first and foremost, chained up our Negresses by the foot in groups of eight or ten, we forced our Negroes to help us, using their left hand which we had left free, in unloading our animals, marking out a circle with our loads and putting up the ox-hide tents we had brought from Katsina within this perimeter. Two or three of the older Negresses whom we had not chained together, but who nevertheless had their feet shackled, were set to preparing something for us to dine on.

The next day we loaded up early and this time the Ghat caravan took the lead. Although calmer than they were the evening before, our slaves were still very irritable. To tire them out and weaken them we made the slaves carry their irons, their dishes and the mortars for pounding maize and millet. And so that our entire attention could be concentrated on them, each of us tied his camels together in a single file. Watching over them thus became easier and if one of them fell down or a load fell off, we could in this way halt them all at once and we avoided the whole group bolting as we got one on its feet or reloaded another.

ESCAPE, RECAPTURE, PUNISHMENT

[The narrator's personal slave, Mebrouk, could not reconcile himself to his condition, despite his owner's blandishments, and led a party of six slaves—all chained together

---

[5]Ghadames and Ghat are Libyan oases close to the Algerian border. Fezzan is a large oasis region in southern Libya.
[6]The conventional distance of a league is three miles.

for the night—in an escape. Two were recaptured; two others chained together were attacked by a lion and one was mauled to death while the other eventually died of fright. Mebrouk and one other slave were never found.]

When news of this event was noised abroad our khebirs, each followed by fifteen horsemen, set off at a gallop and explored the countryside far and wide. But it is full of scrub and so dotted with hillocks that they could only find two of the fugitives. As a lesson for the future, it remained for us to learn from the two recaptured fugitives by what clever means they and their companions had slipped their chains. But neither kindness nor patience on the part of Cheggueun who was interrogating them, could make their tongues wag and, seized by anger, he ordered that they should be flogged in front of the other slaves. In no time all these pagans were lined up on the side of a hillock. Two powerful men seized one of the two Negroes, threw him to the ground and sat astride his heels and neck. At the same time two chaouchs (assistants) had taken up their stations, canes in hand, one on the right and the other on the left of the guilty one.

"Go to it," said Cheggueun. At the first blow the canes were white. At the fiftieth they were red and blood ran on the thighs and sides of the victim. But the obstinate fellow had still said nothing. Only his fitful breathing and some movement of his loins bore witness to the fact that they were not beating a corpse. Finally he cried out, "Abi (father)! Serki (chief)! I will tell all. Stop the beating." A gesture from Cheggueun brought the chaouchs to a halt.

"Speak," he said to the Negro. "What did you do to break your chains and what happened to them?"

"O Serki! I touched them with my kerikeri (amulet) and made them melt."

"Chaouchs!" responded Cheggueun, "Beat him harder. He lies."

The canes descended on the liar so hard that they removed a strip of his skin.

"Abi! Serki! I will talk. I will talk," he cried.

"Dog of a pagan," said Cheggueun, "I will have you killed if you lie to me again."

"By my father's neck," replied the slave, "here is the truth. During the night, by slithering on the sand, Mebrouk came over to us. He had some hot water in a calabash and he poured some of this in the lock of our chains. Thus wetted, when we tapped it on its side we made the bolt slide and we opened it. Out of the five, however, two had to escape attached to one another, carrying the chain with them."

"O my children," Cheggueun said to us, "you hear him. Above all, those of you whose Negroes are chained up with old chains, never go to sleep without seeing with your eye and touching with your hand the padlocks which protect your fortune. Let this be a good lesson to you all!"

The slave was seated and the chaouchs helped him to stand up. Limping and groaning he dragged himself to the feet of his master, prostrated with his face on the ground and poured sand over himself as a sign of his repentance and submission. It had taken no less than one hundred and twenty strokes of the cane to drag out his secret from him and good justice would have required that his accomplice receive the same. But his owner objected that two such wounded men would be an embarrassment for everyone, that they might die of exhaustion and that his loss was already great. Cheggueun, who had a heart of gold, was easily convinced by these good reasons and he gave orders that on departure the next morning the sick man should be put on a camel.

WITH THE MARABOUTS

[The caravan halted at a place called Aghezeur, probably near Agades in present-day Niger, to take on provisions and to reclaim some items they had deposited there on the southbound journey in the keeping of a community of "marabouts" (Muslim holymen).]

With our preparations for departure complete we were of a mind to set out on the third day after our arrival, but the marabouts of the zaouïa (lodge) of Sidi Ahmed who had come to our camp and called us together for prayer held us back with these words: "O Muslims! These negroes you are bringing are idolators. We must make them know the One God; we must teach them to pray and how to perform ablutions; we must circumcise them today. God will reward you for it. Make your slaves assemble. By God's grace we know their language; we will put ourselves in the middle of them and teach them what it is good for them to know."

We understood well, for the Lord loves him who causes the number of His servants to be increased; moreover, there is, from the point of view of sales, a great advantage in turning an idolator into a Muslim. Almost all of our slaves already knew the *shahāda* (declaration of faith) and the name of the Prophet and God. Frequently, during leisure time at camp we would teach them the basic tenets of the religion, speaking broken gnāwiyya[7] to them while they spoke broken Arabic to us. To the best behaved we offered some concessions; to the obdurate some harsh discipline; thus self-interest, if not conviction, had readied them for the solemn ceremony which would today make them into Muslims.

In front of the *zāwiya* of Sidi Ahmed is a huge open space. Each one of us led his Negroes there and made them sit on the ground and soon their number sketched out a gigantic thick semi-circle facing the zaouïa. Like a muezzin calling to prayer, the imam climbed up on the mosque and uttered these words:

"God is One; He has no associates. He is unique of His kind and none is comparable to Him. He is the Sovereign and Incomparable Lord. He is from all time and shall endure for all time. Eternity shall not destroy Him and time and the centuries do not change Him. He is the First, the Last, the Manifest and the Hidden. He knows what is in the inside of bodies. Nothing is similar to Him; He is superior to all things. His superiority and His exhaltation, instead of distancing Him from His worshippers, brings Him closer to His creatures. He is All-Seeing, All-Knowing, He is Omnipresent. He is Holy and no place can encompass Him. Only the saints can look upon Him in the places where His dwelling is sempiternal, as has been established by the verses of the Qur'ān and the accounts of the ancients. He is Living, He is Powerful, He is Almighty, He is Superb, He is Severe; idleness and weakness are remote from Him."

"He forgets not, He sleeps not. His is the command and to Him belongs the vastness of the universe. To Him belong honor and omnipotence. He created creatures and their acts. When He wishes a thing, it is. When He does not wish it, it is not. He is the Beginning and the End, the Doer of His will. Everything that is in the world— movement, rest, good, evil, profit, loss, faith, infidelity, obedience and disobedience— all come from God. There is no bird that flies with its wings, no beast that walks on

---

[7]"Blacks" language, i.e., Hausa.

its feet, no serpent that glides on its stomach, no leaf that grows or falls and no light or darkness without the almighty will of God. Everything that exists is created; God exists from eternity and all that has been created demonstrates His unity. Man's petition to God is prayer and prayer itself only exists by the will of God. If you put your confidence in God, He will care for you as He cares for the birds of the heavens who set out hungry and return full. He does not bring food to their nests, but he puts in them the instinct to search for it."

I would not dare to say that this speech made a lively impression on the Negroes, but the solemnity of the new spectacle for them, the receptivity with which we, their masters and the holy marabout, listened certainly made them ready for the carrying out of the religious act that would make them Muslims. When time for the operation came, though all or almost all showed themselves surprised, not one refused to undergo it, for they take pride in having no fear of pain. As soon as they had been marked with the symbol of the Muslims, they had their wounds staunched by us with an astringent powder made of dried ground leaves of arrar [juniper] and el-aazir, blended with butter.[8]

The marabouts then prayed over them in gnāwiyya, saying: "O you Negroes, give thanks to God! Yesterday you were idolators and today you are Muslims. Depart with your masters who will clothe you, feed you and love you like their brothers and children. Serve them well and they will give you your liberty in a while. If you are comfortable with them you shall stay there. If not you shall return to your land."

That day and the next we took particular care of our slaves. We fed them good meat and let them sleep in tents to keep them from the cold and dew of the nights. Thanks to such attentions our caravan did not lose a single one. In the other caravans, however, some of the older ones died.

9 Thomas Nelson, Slavery and the Slave Trade of Brazil

Under pressure from Britain, Brazil agreed to abolish its slave trade in 1826, but contraband traffic in slaves continued unabated in subsequent decades. Meanwhile, Britain claimed the right to search and arrest suspected slave ships. During the 1840s, Thomas Nelson served as a surgeon aboard a British frigate, the H.M.S. *Crescent,* and his duties included the inspection and treatment of contraband slaves intercepted en route to Brazil. The following reading is an excerpt from his book describing the conditions of the Africans he encountered.

QUESTIONS TO CONSIDER

1. What diseases did Nelson describe as being most prevalent among the Africans who survived the Atlantic crossing? Roughly what proportion of slaves arrived in Brazil compared to those who left American ports?

---

[8]El-Aazir has not been identified. The "butter" referred to was no doubt *samm*—"clarified butter" or "ghee," not the type one is accustomed to spread on bread.

2.   Compare Nelson's account of conditions aboard slave ships with Equiano's personal memoir (see Reading 7).

A few minutes after the vessel dropped her anchor, I went on board of her, and although somewhat prepared by the previous inspection of two full slavers to encounter a scene of disease and wretchedness, still my experience, aided by my imagination, fell short of the loathsome spectacle which met my eyes on stepping over the side. Huddled closely together on deck, and blocking up the gangways on either side, cowered, or rather squatted, three hundred and sixty-two negroes, with disease, want, and misery stamped upon them with such painful intensity as utterly beggars all powers of description. In one corner, apart from the rest, a group of wretched beings lay stretched, many in the last stage of exhaustion, and all covered with the pustules of smallpox. Several of these I noticed had crawled to the spot where the water had been served out, in the hope of procuring a mouthful more of the precious liquid; but unable to return to their proper places, lay prostrate around the empty tub. Here and there, amid the throng, were isolated cases of the same loathsome disease in its confluent or worst form, and cases of extreme emaciation and exhaustion, some in a state of perfect stupor, others looking piteously around, and pointing with their fingers to their parched mouths whenever they caught an eye who they thought would relieve them. On every side, squalid and sunken visages were rendered still more hideous by the swollen eyelids and the puriform discharge of a virulent ophthalmia, with which the majority appeared to be afflicted; added to this were figures shriveled to absolute skin and bone, and doubled up in a posture which originally want of space had compelled them to adopt, and which debility and stiffness of the joints compelled them to retain.

On looking more leisurely around, after the first paroxysm of horror and disgust had subsided, I remarked on the poop another wretched group, composed entirely of females. Some were mothers with infants who were vainly endeavoring to suck a few drops of moisture from the lank, withered, and skinny breasts of their wretched mothers; others were of every intermediate age. The most of them destitute even of the decency of a rag, and all presenting as woeful a spectacle of misery as it is possible to conceive.

While employed in examining the negroes individually, and separating and classifying the sick, who constituted by far the majority, I obtained a closer insight into their actual condition. Many I found afflicted with a confluent smallpox, still more with purulent ophthalmia, and the majority of what remained, with dysentery, ulcers, emaciation, and exhaustion. In several, two or three of these were met. Not the least distressing sight on that pest-laden deck was the negroes whom the ophthalmia had struck blind, and who cowered in seeming apathy to all that was going on around. This was indeed the ultimatum of wretchedness, the last drops of the cup of bitterness. Deprived of liberty, and torn from their native country, there was nothing more of human misery but to make them the victims of a physical darkness as deep as they had already been made of a moral one.

The stench on board was nearly overwhelming. The odor of the negroes themselves, rendered still stronger by their filthy and crowded condition, the sickening

From Thomas Nelson, *Remarks on the Slavery and Slave Trade of the Brazils* (London: J. Halchard and Son, 1846), pp. 43–56 *passim*.

smell of the suppurative stage of smallpox, and the far more disgusting effluvium of dysenteric discharge, combined with bilge water, putrid jerked beef, and numerous other matters to form a stench, it required no little exertion of fortitude to withstand. To all this, hunger and thirst lent their aid to finish the scene; and so poignant were they, that the struggles to obtain the means of satisfying them were occasionally so great as to require the interference of the prize crew. The moment it could be done, water in abundance and a meal was provided them; and none but an eyewitness could form an idea of the eagerness with which the former luxury was coveted and enjoyed. For many days, it seems, the water had not only been reduced in quantity, but so filled with impurities, and so putrid, that nothing but the most stringent necessity could have induced the use of it. . . .

Early yesterday morning (11th of September, 1843) the decks of the *Crescent* were again thronged by a miserable crowd of liberated Africans. The vessel in which they had been conveyed from the "coast" was captured a few days ago by one of the boats belonging to H.M.S. *Frolic,* a little to the northward of Rio.

Previously to the removal of the negroes, Dr. Gunn (the surgeon of the *Crescent*) and myself went on board the slaver, and stepping over the side, were astonished at the smallness of the vessel, and the number of wretched negroes who had been thrust on board of her. Below, the hold was crowded to excess; and above, the deck was so closely packed with the poor creatures, that we had to walk along the top of the low bulwarks in order to get aft. Of the appearance of the negroes, no pen can give an adequate idea. In numbers, the different protuberances and anatomical peculiarities of the bones can be distinctly traced by the eye, and appear, on every motion, ready to break through the skin, which is, in fact, all that covers them. Nor has this been confined to appearance; in many, at the bend of the elbows and knee-joints, over the hip-joints and lower part of the spine, the integuments have given way, and caused the most distressing and ill-conditioned sores. A great number of the Africans, especially the younger, cannot stand upright even when assisted, and the moment they are left to themselves, they double up their knees under their chins, and draw their legs so closely to their bodies, that they scarcely retain the form of humanity. So weak and so cramped are the most of them that they had to be carried in the arms of the seamen, one by one, up the *Crescent*'s ladder. All those not affected with contagious diseases are now on board the *Crescent,* and the most of them look like animated skeletons. From one of the Portuguese crew, who is at present under treatment for smallpox, I learn that the name of the vessel is the *Vencedora,* and that she left Benguela on the coast of Africa with four hundred and sixty slaves on board. But of this number only three hundred and thirty-eight have been counted over the side, a circumstance which will appear the less surprising when the space in which they were stowed comes to be considered. . . .

Just as the negroes who remained of the *Vencedora* had entirely recovered their wonted health and vigor, and were fit to be sent to one of our colonies, H.M.S. *Dolphin,* on the 15th of November, 1843, brought into harbor a full slaver, which she had captured a day or two before, a little to the northward of Rio. The crew of the slaver had actually run her ashore, and had begun to throw the negroes overboard into the sea, in order that they might be induced to swim for the land, when the boats of the *Dolphin* came up and obliged them to stop and effect their own escape.

This vessel is the largest I have yet seen employed in this traffic, and is better fitted and found than the common run of slavers; she is American built, and several of her fittings bear the name of American tradesmen. But, as usual, the Africans benefit nothing from the greater size of the vessel. The additional room has not been devoted to give increased accommodation, but to carry a greater number from the coast. The hold, instead of being fitted with one slave deck, has two; so that, in fact, the negroes have been as badly off, if not worse, than they would have been in a smaller vessel.

On attempting to go down into the hold, and satisfy myself with an examination before the Africans were removed, I was forced, after one or two unsuccessful attempts, to give it up;—the effluvium was perfectly overwhelming, and the heat so great, that the moment I left the square of the hatchway, the sensation approached suffocation. The decks furnished a melancholy spectacle of disease and wretchedness; but the most prominent and widely spread scourge is purulent ophthalmia. Numbers of the poor creatures are squatting down in corners or groping about the deck deprived of all sight. Their immensely swollen eyelids, contrasting with their haggard and wasted features, and the discharge which keeps constantly trickling down their cheeks, and which they have not even a rag to wipe away, gives them an appearance of ghastly, murky misery which it is impossible for me to describe.

Many eyes, I am afraid, are irretrievably lost, and several poor wretches must remain forever totally blind. Dysentery, too, that fellest of all diseases in the negro race, is at work amongst them, and will undoubtedly commit fearful ravages. Five hundred and seventy-two Africans were found on board. What the number was at starting there is no means of ascertaining. One of the crew, a slave, who acted on board in the capacity of a cook, and who preferred being captured by Englishmen to escaping with his master, told me that many had died and were thrown overboard during the passage. The exact number taken on board, however, he could not tell. In all probability, it was not under seven hundred; but of course this is only mere conjecture.

Part II

Global Patterns of Politics and Culture

Degrees of Religious Toleration

From the fourth century, when Christianity was established as the Roman state religion, well into the seventeenth century, religious toleration made no sense to the great majority of Europeans. For them, believing the right things would gain them salvation; believing the wrong things would send them to hell. Heresy, the crime of harboring and spreading false doctrine, was often compared with counterfeiting coins or with spreading a disease worse than leprosy.

The kingdom of Poland experimented briefly and unsuccessfully with religious toleration in the sixteenth century, but it was only in the English North American colonies, Prussia, and the Netherlands that religious toleration made headway in the seventeenth century. Then, with the Enlightenment of the eighteenth century, religious toleration gained widespread acceptance in many parts of Europe.

The following three selections illustrate this change. In his Act Concerning Religion (1649), now usually called the Maryland Toleration Act, Lord Baltimore—himself a member of the Catholic minority in England—granted toleration to what we now call "mainline" Christian denominations. At the same time, he established ferocious punishments for what he construed as blasphemy. Even though these punishments were seldom implemented, they reveal how even a farsighted and relatively tolerant seventeenth-century statesman was unwilling to risk the stability of his government by granting too much religious freedom. On the other hand,

Gotthold Ephraim Lessing, a leading German poet and playwright, and Thomas Paine, an influential figure in both the American and French Revolutions, spoke for the eighteenth-century Enlightenment. For them, complete religious toleration was the only rational approach for policy makers to adopt. Paine's statement appears in *The Rights of Man* (1792), a defense of the French Revolution. Lessing's statement is made by the Jewish title character in his play *Nathan the Wise Man* (1779), as he defends the right of Jews to remain faithful to their religion.

10 The Maryland Toleration Act

In 1632, Charles I issued a charter to Cecilius Calvert, second Baron of Baltimore, as lord proprietor of the territory that is now Maryland. The Calverts were among the few active and politically prominent Catholic families of the time, and Maryland became the only seventeenth-century British colony in North America where Catholics were particularly welcome. The following selection reveals Lord Baltimore's attitude toward religious toleration.

QUESTIONS TO CONSIDER

1. What sort of dissent was Lord Baltimore willing to tolerate? What limits did he put on religious dissent?
2. What punishments did Lord Baltimore establish for those who exceeded the limits of religious toleration? Why were the punishments so severe?
3. Compare this view of religious freedom with that of the English experience in India (see Reading 45).

An Act concerning Religion: Forasmuch as in a well-governed and Christian commonwealth matters concerning religion and the honor of God ought in the first place to be taken into serious consideration and endeavored to be settled, be it therefore ordered and enacted by the Right Honorable Cecilius Lord Baron of Baltimore, absolute Lord and Proprietary of this province, with the advice and consent of this General Assembly that:

Whatsoever person or persons within this province and the islands thereunto belonging shall from henceforth blaspheme God, that is, curse Him, or deny our Sav-

From Assembly Proceedings, April 2–21, 1649, in *The Archives of Maryland*, Vol. 1, ed. W.H. Browne (Baltimore: Maryland Historical Society, 1883), pp. 244–47. Reprinted by permission of the Maryland Historical Society.

iour, Jesus Christ, to be the Son of God, or shall deny the Holy Trinity—the Father, Son, and Holy Ghost—or the godhead of any of the said three persons of the Trinity, or the unity of the Godhead, or shall use or utter any reproachful speeches, words or language concerning the said Holy Trinity, or any of the said three persons thereof, shall be punished with death and confiscation or forfeiture of all his or her lands to the Lord Proprietary and his heirs. . . .

Whatsoever person or persons shall from henceforth use or utter any reproachful words or speeches concerning the blessed Virgin Mary, the Mother of our Saviour, or the Holy Apostles or Evangelists, or any of them, shall in such case for the first offense forfeit to the Lord Proprietary. . . the sum of five pounds sterling or the value thereof. . . . But, in case such offender or offenders shall not then have goods and chattels sufficient for the satisfying of such forfeiture, or that the same be not otherwise speedily satisfied, . . . then such offender shall be publicly whipped and be imprisoned during the pleasure of the Lord Proprietary or the . . . chief Governor of this province for the time being. . . . Every such offender or offenders for every second offense shall forfeit ten pounds sterling or the value thereof . . . or, in case such offender or offenders shall not then have goods and chattels within this province sufficient for that purpose, . . . be publicly and severely whipped and imprisoned as before is expressed. . . . Every person . . . offending herein the third time shall . . . forfeit all his lands and goods and be forever banished and expelled out of this province. . . .

Whatsoever person or persons shall from henceforth upon any occasion of offense or otherwise in a reproachful manner or way declare, call, or denominate any person or persons whatsoever inhabiting, residing, trafficking, trading, or commercing within this province . . . "a heretic," "schismatic," "idolator," "Puritan," "Independent," "Presbyterian," "popish priest," "Jesuit," "Jesuited papist," "Lutheran," "Calvinist," "Anabaptist," "Brownist," "Antinomian," "Barrowist," "Roundhead," "Separatist," or any other name or term in a reproachful manner relating to a matter of religion, shall for every offense forfeit and lose the sum of ten shillings sterling . . . , the one half thereof to be forfeited and paid unto the person and persons of whom such reproachful words are or shall be spoken or uttered, and the other half to the Lord Proprietary. . . .

Every person and persons within this province that shall at any time profane the Sabbath or Lord's Day, called "Sunday," by frequent swearing, drunkenness, or by any uncivil or disorderly recreation, or by working on that day when absolute necessity doth not require it, shall for every first offense forfeit 2 shillings, 6 pence, sterling or the value thereof, and for the second offense 5 shillings . . . and for every time he shall offend in like manner afterwards 10 shillings. . . . In case such offender shall not have sufficient goods . . . , the party so offending shall for the first and second offense . . . be imprisoned till he or she shall publicly in open court before the chief commander, judge, or magistrate of that county, town, or precinct where such offense shall be committed, acknowledge the scandal and offense he hath in that respect given against God and the good and civil government of this province, and. . . for every time afterwards be publicly whipped.

And whereas the enforcing of the conscience in matters of religion hath frequently fallen out to be of dangerous consequence in those commonwealths where it hath been practiced, and for the more quiet and peaceful government of this province, and the better to preserve mutual love and amity among the inhabitants thereof, be it therefore also by the Lord Proprietary with the advice and consent of this Assembly ordained and enacted (except as in this present Act is before declared and set forth) that:

No person or persons whatsoever within this province . . . professing to believe in Jesus Christ shall from henceforth be in any way troubled, molested, or discountenanced for or in respect of his or her religion nor in the free exercise thereof within this province or the islands thereunto belonging nor any way compelled to the belief or exercise of any other religion against his or her consent, so as they be not unfaithful to the Lord Proprietary, or molest or conspire against the civil government established or to be established under him or his heirs. And that all . . . persons that shall presume contrary to this Act and the true intent and meaning thereof directly or indirectly either in person or estate willfully to wrong, disturb, trouble or molest any person whatsoever within this province professing to believe in Jesus Christ for or in respect of his or her religion or the free exercise thereof . . . other than is provided for in this Act: that such person or persons so offending shall be compelled to pay treble damages to the party so wronged or molested and for every such offense shall also forfeit 20 shillings sterling in money or the value thereof. . . . Or if the party so offending shall refuse or be unable to recompense the party so wronged, or to satisfy such fine or forfeiture, then such offender shall be severely punished by public whipping and imprisonment during the pleasure of the Lord Proprietary or his . . . chief Governor of this province for the time being without bail.

11 Thomas Paine, *The Rights of Man*

Thomas Paine (1739–1809), an Englishman who became a leading propagandist on the American side in the War for Independence, subsequently went to France and supported the early stages of the French Revolution. But when the French revolutionaries announced that they would tolerate religious diversity, Paine felt that they were arrogating power to themselves without justification. For Paine, the right to worship according to the dictates of conscience was so fundamental that no government should act as if that right could be granted or denied by the state.

QUESTIONS TO CONSIDER

1. What is the meaning and significance of Paine's statement that "before any human institutions of government were known in the world, there existed . . . a compact between God and man"? Compare and contrast this with Rousseau's concept of the "social contract" (see Reading 19).

2. Why does Paine believe that a variety of religious denominations is healthy and should be tolerated?

3. Why does Paine believe that state enforcement of religious beliefs would be detrimental to both the state and religion?

There is a single idea, which if it strikes rightly upon the mind, either in a legal or a religious sense, will prevent any man, or any body of men, or any government, from going wrong on the subject of religion; which is, that before any human institutions of government were known in the world, there existed, if I may so express it, a compact between God and man, from the beginning of time; and that as the relation and condition which man in his *individual person* stands in toward his Maker cannot be changed, or in any ways altered by any human laws or human authority, that religious devotion, which is a part of this compact, cannot so much as be made a subject of human laws; and that all laws must conform themselves to this prior existing compact, and not assume to make the compact conform to the laws, which, besides being human, are subsequent thereto. The first act of man, when he looked around and saw himself a creature which he did not make, and a world furnished for his reception, must have been devotion; and devotion must ever continue sacred to every individual man, *as it appears right to him;* and governments do mischief by interfering. . . .

With respect to what are called denominations of religion, if everyone is left to judge of his own religion, there is no such thing as a religion that is wrong; but if they are to judge of each other's religion, there is no such thing as a religion that is right; and therefore all the world is right, or all the world is wrong. But with respect to religion itself, without regard to names, and as directing itself from the universal family of mankind to the divine object of all adoration, *it is man bringing to his Maker the fruits of his heart;* and though these fruits may differ from each other like the fruits of the earth, the grateful tribute of every one is accepted. . . .

But as religion is very improperly made a political machine, and the reality of it is thereby destroyed, I will conclude this work with stating in what light religion appears to me:

If we suppose a large family of children, who, on any particular day, or particular occasion, make it a custom to present to their parents some token of their affection and gratitude, each of them would make a different offering, and most probably in a different manner.

Some would pay their congratulations in themes of verse and prose, by some little devices, as their genius dictated, or according to what they thought would please; and, perhaps the least of all, not able to do any of those things, would ramble into the garden, or the field, and gather what it thought the prettiest flower it could find, though, perhaps it might be but a simple weed. The parents would be more gratified by such a variety than if the whole of them had acted on a concerted plan, and each had made exactly the same offering. This would have the cold appearance of contrivance, or the harsh one of control. But of all unwelcome things, nothing would more afflict the parent than to know that the whole of them had afterwards gotten together by the ears, boys and girls, fighting, reviling, and abusing each other about which was the best or worst present.

Why may we not suppose that the great Father of all is pleased with variety of devotion; and that the greatest offense we can act is that by which we seek to torment and render each other miserable? For my own part I am fully satisfied that what I am now doing, with an endeavor to conciliate mankind, to render their condition happy, to unite nations that have hitherto been enemies, and to extirpate the horrid practice

From *Writings of Thomas Paine*, ed. Moncure D. Conway (New York: G.P. Putnam's Sons, 1894), pp. 354, n. 10, 326, 515–16.

of war and break the chains of slavery and oppression, is acceptable in His sight, and being the best service I can perform I act it cheerfully.

I do not believe that any two men, on what are called doctrinal points, think alike who think at all. It is only those who have not thought that appear to agree. . . .

12 Gotthold Ephraim Lessing, *Nathan the Wise Man*

Gotthold Ephraim Lessing (1729–1781), the foremost German playwright before Goethe and Schiller, was also one of the most articulate spokespersons for Enlightenment values in the German-speaking countries. The following speech from *Nathan the Wise Man* offers a parable about religious toleration. Nathan, a Jew, is presenting his case for the toleration of Jews before the Islamic Turkish Sultan Saladin.

QUESTIONS TO CONSIDER

1. What do the three rings in Nathan's speech represent?
2. What advice does the judge offer to the squabbling sons? Would that advice have been acceptable to Lord Baltimore (see Reading 10) or Thomas Paine (see Reading 11)?

Nathan: Countless years ago in the East there lived a man who possessed a ring of immeasurable worth, given to him by a loved one. Its stone was an opal which reflected a hundred beautiful colors and had the secret power of making anyone who wore it and believed in it pleasing to God and men. Is it any wonder then that this man in the East never took it from his finger and provided in his will and testament that it should never leave his family? He left the ring to the son he loved the most, providing that he in turn should will the ring to the one of his sons he loved the most and always the best-loved son, not necessarily the eldest, should be lord of the whole family through the sole power of the ring. . . .

The ring thus went from son to son, but finally came to the father of three sons, all of whom obeyed him equally well, so that he could not resist loving them all equally. It happened that this one from time to time, then that one, then the third one—just depending on which one was alone with him without the other two sharing in what came straight from his heart—seemed worthier of the ring to him, and in his soft-heartedness he would promise it to him. And so that went on as long as it could go on. The time came to die, and the kindly father was embarrassed painfully at having to grieve two of his sons, who were relying on his word. What to do? He sent it to an expert craftsman, placing an order for two others and telling him to spare neither cost

From Gotthold Ephraim Lessing, *Nathan der Weise*, act 3, scene 7. In *Lessings Werke*, Vol. 2, ed. Georg Witlowski (Leipzig: Bibliographisches Institut, n.d.), pp. 342–47. Trans. Henry A. Myers.

nor pains to make them altogether like the original. With cheer and joy he called his sons—each one separately—and gave each one his blessing individually and his ring. Then he died, . . . [but] he was hardly dead before each one came with his ring, and each one wanted to be lord of the family. Investigations, complaints, and fights followed to no avail: no proof could be found for the one true ring. . . .

The sons sued each other, each one swearing before the judge that he took his ring right from his father's hand, which was true, after having already had the promise of lordship through the ring from him for a long time—which was no less true. Each one swore that his father could not have played false with him. Before he would suspect his father of that he would have to accuse his brothers of foul play—however much he had previously been inclined to believe only the best about them—and before long he wanted the satisfaction of seeing the traitors identified and brought to justice. . . .

The Judge said: "If you don't soon produce your father for me, I will dismiss you from my court. Do you think that I am here to solve riddles? Or do you insist on waiting around until the ring opens its mouth? But wait! I have been hearing that the right ring has the miraculous power of making the wearer pleasing to God and men. That fact must be decisive, for the false rings will never be able to do that! Now tell me, whom do two of you love the most? Speak up now! You have nothing to say? Are the rings having an effect only on the wearer and no effect outside of him? Each of you loves only himself the most? Oh, then you are all three deceived deceivers! None of your three rings is real. The real ring must be assumed lost: to hide the loss, the father had three replacements made for it. . . .

"And so," the Judge continued, "if you want only my sentence but not my advice, just leave! But my advice to you is this: accept the matter just as it is. If each of you received his ring from his father, let each one sincerely believe his ring to be the real one. It is possible that the father no longer wanted to tolerate the tyranny of the ring in his household, which seems all the more likely since he loved all three of you and loved you equally to the extent that he could not ignore two of you in order to favor one. Go to it! Free of prejudice and corrupting influences, let each one of you pursue what he loves. Let each of you compete to demonstrate the power in his ring—whether this power assists you when you are gentle, when you gladly put up with the faults of others, when you do good works, or when your devotion to God is most sincere. And when the powers of this stone reveal themselves in your children's children, I summon you to appear a thousand times a thousand years from now before this bench. Then a wiser man than I will sit here and give you his verdict. Go!" These were the words of the knowing judge.

Early Modern Political Economy

Good and bad economic policies for states have furnished subject matter for writers on political theory since the time of Plato and Aristotle. From the end of the Renaissance to the mid-nineteenth century, such a concentration on economic themes was evident in political debates that experts or would-be experts in the field were generally called "political economists" rather than "political scientists." The issues that most concerned them related to developments in the advance of capitalism. These included how to bring about a favorable balance of trade; what to do about the displacement of rural people because of more efficient agricultural production and, later, their migration to work in urban factories; and what economic measures would ensure a loyal population, devoted to its society, and, related to this, what economic system promoted political and social stability.

A disproportionate number of the most influential political economists were seventeenth- and eighteenth-century Britons, probably because both the Puritan and Glorious Revolutions led to deep divisions over the proper nature of government and because England was progressing very rapidly from an agrarian to a commercial and then an industrial society. Their attempts to postulate rational explanations for economic phenomena and equally rational proposals for addressing their imbalances contributed to the problem-solving environment of the unfolding Enlightenment.

In the eighteenth century, "Enlightened Despotism" gave active kingship a new lease on life in Spain and Eastern Europe; however, in most of Western Europe what remained of popular enthusiasm for extensive monarchical government declined. Particularly in Britain and France, spokespersons for the middle class came to regard much royal regulation as unnecessary.

The political side of this attack on state power was, of course, phrased in terms of keeping governmental functions to the minimum necessary for protecting life, liberty, and property (see Reading 20). Those voicing the economic side of this argument indicted mercantilism for inefficiency and for placing burdens on the people as producers, consumers, and taxpayers for the benefit of special interests favored by government. Mercantilism was the theory that made government responsible for creating a favorable balance of trade, particularly through external tariffs against foreign imports, subsidies and grants of monopolies, and the acquisition of colonies to assure the mother country of steady supplies of cheap raw materials and markets for finished goods.

Leading the economic attack in France were Dr. François Quesnay, a physician who wrote in the 1750s and 1760s, and his followers. Known as "physiocrats" (from *physis,* "nature," and *-crat,* "ruler"), this group advocated letting nature rule in the economic sphere. They compared the free, unregulated, "natural" production and flow of goods with the flow of blood in the human body, with which it would be foolish to interfere. Although the physiocrats, who saw land and agriculture as the source of all proper wealth, were most concerned about productive land use, their phrases *laissez-faire* ("let things be made") and *laissez-passer* ("let things circulate") furthered the idea that capitalism need only be left alone for nature to take its course and usher in an era of general prosperity.

In England, the comparable aims were summarized simply as "free trade." Free-trade advocates were less concerned about land use than were the physiocrats. Instead, they particularly stressed the notion of enlightened self-interest—people working at what they did best for their own immediate good in a society respecting life, liberty, law, and property—as the means for assuring that goods of the best quality would be produced at the lowest possible prices for consumers throughout the world. Seeing the state as having a very limited role in the national economy, they attempted to show that mercantilistic policies were not only useless but counterproductive: Tariffs and monopolies raised prices for consumers; subsidies to bail out inefficient producers burdened taxpayers; and requiring overseas settlers to buy and sell at the mother country's direction was both unfair and indirectly costly to taxpayers, who had to provide the necessary revenue for enforcing trade restrictions overseas.

Free trade became a popular cause in Britain in considerable part because the British were more industrially advanced than most of their competitors and, with some justification, believed that they could win out in a completely unregulated framework of international trade.

13 James Harrington, *The Commonwealth of Oceana*

In 1656, James Harrington (1611–1677) published a description of the utopian state, "Oceana," in terms that he thought applied to England but that had a greater influence in the American colonies. Unlike John Locke (1632–1704), the later political philosopher for whom the House of Commons was the rightfully dominant branch of government, since for Locke it reflected the people's will, Harrington advocated a firm separation of powers into a senate of the most talented citizens, to propose legislation, and an assembly more representative of the common people, to approve or reject the senate's measures.

Harrington was convinced that a healthy republic or commonwealth is based on the support of large numbers of farmer-citizen-soldiers, whose ownership of small farms makes them identify with their government and society. To this end, following his perception of what made society stable in the early Roman Republic, he advocated "agrarian laws" to ensure widespread ownership of land. He approved of redistributive measures, which in our own day would be called "land reform," to keep the owners of large estates from swallowing up the holdings of their smaller neighbors. The idea that small landowners are the best citizens—sometimes called the "Jeffersonian myth," sometimes the "Harringtonian myth"—has enjoyed a long life in American political-economic thought. Its radical implication—that government should actively redistribute land to keep it in the hands of tillers of the soil—never gained much support on the North American continent, although it was rather much what General Douglas MacArthur (see Reading 77) put into effect in Japan after World War II.

QUESTIONS TO CONSIDER

1. Why is Harrington so convinced of the need for a government "of laws" and not "of men"?
2. What is Harrington's interest in "dividing and choosing" in the legislative process all about? Do our own bicameral legislatures work on this principle or on a different one?
3. Why does Harrington think that the Roman warlord Sulla effectively destroyed the Roman Republic by making a new kind of "agrarian law"?

Government (to define it *de jure* or according to ancient prudence) is an art whereby a civil society of men is instituted and preserved upon the foundation of common right or interest, or (to follow Aristotle and Livy) it is the empire of laws and not of men.

And government (to define it *de facto* or according to modern prudence) is an art whereby some man, or some few men, subject a city or a nation, and rule it according to his or their private interest; which may be said to be the empire of men and not of laws. . . .

Government, according to the ancients and their learned disciple Machiavelli, the only [analytical] politician of later ages, is of three kinds: the government of one man, or of the better sort, or of the whole people; which by their more learned names are called monarchy, aristocracy, and democracy. These, they hold, through their proneness to degenerate, to be all evil. For whereas they that govern should govern according to reason, if they govern according to passion, they do that which they should

From James Harrington, *The Commonwealth of Oceana*, introduced by James Morley (London: Routledge & Sons, 1887), pp. 15–16, 26–31, 48–49. Condensed and language slightly modernized by Allen C. Myers.

not do. Wherefore, as reason and passion are two things, so government by reason is one thing and the corruption of government by passion is another thing, but not always another government. . . . The corruption then of monarchy is called tyranny; that of aristocracy, oligarchy; and that of democracy, anarchy. But legislators, having found these three governments at best to be naught, have invented another consisting of a mixture of them all, which only is good. This is the doctrine of the ancients. . . .

To go mine own way, and yet to follow the ancients, the principles of governments are twofold: internal, or goods of the mind, and external, the goods of fortune. The goods of the mind are natural or acquired virtues, as wisdom, prudence and courage, etc. The goods of fortune are riches. . . . To the goods of the mind answers authority; to the goods of fortune, power or empire. . . .

To begin with riches, in regard that men are hung upon these, not of choice as upon the other, but of necessity and by the teeth: for as much as he who wants bread is the servant of the man who will feed him, if a man thus feeds a whole people, they are under his empire.

Empire is of two kinds, domestic and national, or foreign and provincial. Domestic empire is founded upon dominion. Dominion is property real or personal; that is to say in lands, or in money and goods. Lands, or the parts and parcels of territory, are held by the proprietor or proprietors, lord or lords of it, in some proportion; and such (except if it be in a city that has little or no land, and whose revenue is in trade) as is the proportion or balance of dominion or property in land, such is the nature of the empire.

If one man be sole landlord of a territory, or overbalance the people, for example, three parts in four, he is grand signor, for so the Turk is called for his property; and his empire is absolute monarchy. If the few or a nobility, or a nobility with the clergy be landlords, or overbalance the people in like proportion, it makes the Gothic balance and the empire is mixed monarchy, as that of Spain, Poland, and late of Oceana.

And if the whole people be landlords, or hold the lands so divided among them, that no one man nor group of men, within the compass of the few or aristocracy, overbalance them, the empire (without the interposition of force) is a commonwealth. . . .

Now government is no other than the soul of a nation or city; wherefore that which was reason in the debate of a commonwealth, being brought forth by the result, must be virtue; and for as much as the soul of a city or nation is the sovereign power, her virtue must be law. But the government whose law is virtue, and whose virtue is law, is the same whose empire is authority, and whose authority is empire.

Again, if the liberty of a man consists in the empire of his reason, the absence whereof would betray him unto the bondage of his passions; then the liberty of a commonwealth consists in the empire of her laws, the absence whereof would betray her to the lusts of tyrants; and these I conceive to be the principles upon which Aristotle and Livy have grounded their assertions that a commonwealth is an empire of laws and not of men. . . .

Seeing they that make the laws in commonwealths are but men, the main question seems to be how a commonwealth comes to be an empire of laws and not of men, or how the debate or result of a commonwealth is so sure to be according to reason, seeing they who debate and they who resolve be but men. . . .

[I]f the interest of popular government is right reason, a man does not look upon reason as it is right or wrong in itself, but as it works for him or against him. Unless you can show such orders of a government as, like those of God in nature, shall be able to constrain this or that creature to shake off that inclination which is more peculiar to it and take up that which regards the common good or interest, all this is to no more end than to persuade every man in a popular government not to carve himself of that which he desires most, but to be mannerly at the public table, and give the best from himself to decency and the common interest. But that such orders may be established as must give the upper hand in all cases to common right or interest, notwithstanding the nearness of that which sticks to every man in private, and this in a way of equal certainty and facility, is known even unto girls, being no other than those that are of common practice with them in many cases. For example, two of them have a cake yet undivided, to share between them. So that they may each have for themselves that which is due, "Divide," says one to the other, "and I will choose, or let me divide, and you can choose." If this be once agreed upon, it is enough; for one who divides unequally loses, in regard that the other takes the better half, so that she divides equally, and so both have right. *O the depth of the wisdom of God!* and yet *by the mouths of babes and sucklings hath he set forth his strength.* That which great philosophers dispute in vain is brought to light by two silly girls: even the whole mystery of a commonwealth, which lies only in dividing and choosing. God has not left so much to mankind to dispute upon as who shall divide and who shall choose, but distributed them forever into two orders: one with the right of dividing and the other with the right of choosing. For example:

A commonwealth is but a civil society of men. Let us take any number of men, as twenty, and with them make a commonwealth. Twenty men, if they be not all idiots—perhaps if they be—can never come so together without there being such a difference in them that about a third will be wiser, or at least less foolish, than the rest. These upon acquaintance will be discovered and lead the herd; for while the six, discoursing and arguing with one another, show their eminence, the fourteen discover things that they never thought on, or gain an understanding of many truths which had formerly perplexed them. In matters of common concernment, they hang upon the lips of the six as children upon their fathers, and the influence thus acquired by the six, the eminence of whose parts is found to be a stay and comfort to the fourteen, is *auctoritas patrum*, the authority of the fathers. This can be no other than a natural aristocracy diffused by God throughout the whole body of mankind to this end, and therefore such as the people have not only a natural but a positive obligation to make use of as their guides; as where the people of Israel are commanded to *take wise men understanding and known among their tribes, to be made rulers over them.*[1] The six then approved of are the senate, not by hereditary right, nor in regard of the greatness of their estates only, which would tend to such power as might coerce the people, but by election for their excellent parts, which tends to the advancement of the influence of their virtue or authority that leads the people.

The office of the senate is not to be commanders but counsellors of the people; and that which is proper for counsellors is first to debate the business whereupon they should give advice, and afterward to give advice in the business whereupon they have debated; whence the decrees of the senate are never laws, . . . the senate is no more than the debate of the commonwealth. But to debate is to discern, or put a difference between things that being alike are not the same, or it is separating and weighing this reason against that and that reason against this, which is dividing.

The senate then having divided, who shall choose? Ask the girls; for if she that divided must have chosen also, it had been little worse for the other, . . . [if] she had

---

[1]Deuteronomy, 1:13.

not divided at all, but kept the whole cake unto herself, in regard that being to choose too, she divided accordingly. Wherefore if the senate has any further power than to divide, the commonwealth can never be equal. But in a commonwealth consisting of a single council, there is no other to choose than that which divided; whence it is, that such a council does not fail to be factious, there being no other dividing of the cake in that case but among themselves; there is no remedy but to have another council to choose. . . .

Dividing and choosing, in the language of a commonwealth, is debating and resolving; and whatever upon debate of the senate is proposed unto the people, and resolved by them, is enacted by the authority of the fathers and the power of the people, which concurring make a law.

But the law being made, says Leviathan,[2] "is but words and paper without the hands and swords of men;" and as those two orders of a commonwealth, the senate and the people, are legislative, so of necessity there must be a third to be executive of the laws made, and this is the magistracy; in which order with the rest, being wrought up by art, the commonwealth consists of the senate proposing, the people resolving, and the magistracy executing, whereby partaking of the aristocracy as in the senate, the democracy as in the people, and the monarchy as in the magistracy, it is complete. . . .

. . . [I]t will be convenient in this place to speak a word unto such as go about to insinuate to the nobility or gentry a fear of the people, or into the people a fear of the nobility or gentry, as if their interests were each destructive to the other. . . ; this is a pernicious error. There is something first in the making of a commonwealth, then in the governing of her, and last of all in the leading of her armies, which, though there are great diviners, great lawyers, and great men in all professions, seems peculiar to the genius of a gentleman. For so it is in the universal series of stories, that if any man has founded a commonwealth, he was first a gentleman. Moses had his education by the daughter of Pharoah; Theseus and Solon, of noble birth, were held by the Athenians worthy to be kings; Lycurgus was of the blood-royal, Romulus and Numa princes, Brutus and Publicola patricians. . . .

THE SECOND PART OF THE PRELIMINARIES

I shall now endeavor to show the rise, progress, and declination of modern prudence. The date of this kind of policy is to be computed from those inundations of Goths, Vandals, and Huns that overwhelmed the Roman Empire. But as there is no appearance in the bulk or constitution of modern prudence that she should ever have been able to come up and grapple with the ancient, so something of necessity must have been interposed, whereby the latter came to be enervated and the former to receive strength and encouragement. And this was the detestable reign of the Roman emperors, taking rise from the arms of Caesar, in which storm the ship of the Roman commonwealth was forced to disburden herself of that precious freight, which never since could emerge or raise its head but in the Gulf of Venice.

It is said in scripture, "Thy evil is of thyself, O Israel," to which answers that of the moralists, "No man can be harmed except from within himself," as also the whole

---

[2]Reference to Thomas Hobbes, contemporary English political theorist, who defended absolute monarchy in his *Leviathan* on the basis of the "natural right," as opposed to the "divine right" of kings.

matter of the politics: at present this example of the Romans who, through a negligence committed in their agrarian laws, let in the sink of luxury, and forfeited the inestimable treasure of liberty for themselves and posterity.

Their agrarian laws were such whereby their lands ought to have been divided among the people. The lands assigned, or that ought to have been assigned, were of three kinds. Such as were taken from the enemy and distributed to the people; or such as were taken from the enemy and, under color of being reserved for the public use, were by stealth possessed by the nobility; or such as were bought with the public money to be distributed. Of the laws offered in these cases, those which divided the lands taken from the enemy, or purchased with the public money, never occasioned any dispute; but such as drove at dispossessing the nobility of their usurpations, and dividing the common purchase of the sword among the people, were never touched but caused earthquakes, nor could ever be obtained by the people or, being obtained, be observed by the nobility, who not only preserved their prey but, growing vastly rich upon it, bought the people quite out of those shares conferred upon them.

. . . [T]he nobility of Rome, under the conduct of Sulla, overthrew the people and the commonwealth; seeing Sulla first introduced that new balance, which was the foundation of the succeeding monarchy, in the plantation of military colonies, instituted by his distribution of the conquered lands—not now of enemies, but of citizens—unto forty-seven legions of his soldiers; so that how he came to be a perpetual dictator, or other magistrates to succeed him in like power, is no miracle.

14 Sir William Petty, *Political Arithmetic*

Sir William Petty (1623–1687) went to sea as a boy and spent some time in the Royal Navy, but when the English civil war began he went to Holland to study medicine. Later he was professor of anatomy at Oxford and a member of the informal science club there that was to become the Royal Society. Throughout his life, rather much in the tradition of the Enlightenment of the century to come, he combined an interest in natural science with one in the social sciences. In Ireland after the English civil war, he was both physician general of the British army and the originator of a massive survey of property in Ireland, done partly in connection with confiscating the estates of Irish landowners and partly in support of a plan to rejuvenate the Irish economy.

Petty is the first influential political economist to base his theories on statistical analysis. His basic orientation was that an examination of what produces revenue with what result leads to conclusions concerning beneficial and injurious taxes, and that sovereign powers should make their tax policy decisions on the basis of a cost-benefit analysis of these conclusions. Although he was still mercantilist enough to see ultimate value in "gold, silver, and jewels," he was basically in favor of free trade, but his real innovation is in concluding that agriculture—

"cow-keeping" in his condescending phrase—is not nearly so good a basis for supporting the ongoing prosperity of a country as manufacturing and shipping. In his discussion of the wealth generated by industry rather than by farming, he develops an embryonic labor theory of value, which John Locke and Karl Marx would develop in support of capitalism and communism respectively.

Petty evidently had a winning personality: Not only was he knighted by Charles II after the Restoration in spite of his career with the Commonwealth Army in Ireland, but he espoused the idea of "liberty of conscience" well before (and with fewer reservations than) John Locke with no ill results for his reputation. He drafted social engineering blueprints of gigantic proportions: Sensing that there would be some difficulty for Britain with the governmental forms being developed in New England, he let his research and analysis lead him to the conclusion that the best policy would be to rescue the New Englanders from the lackluster occupation of cow-keeping and use them to repopulate Ireland with industrious subjects still quite loyal to the Crown.

QUESTIONS TO CONSIDER

1. What policies of the Dutch does Petty think made them prosperous?
2. From the standpoint of the health of national economies, how does Petty differentiate beneficial taxes from damaging ones?
3. How does Petty justify his contempt of agriculture as a source of national wealth? Compare his assessment with James Harrington's (see Reading 13).

The method I take . . . is not very usual; for instead of using only comparative and superlative words, and intellectual arguments, I have taken the course of expressing myself in terms of *number, weight, and measure;* . . . and to consider only such causes as have visible foundations in nature. I leave those arguments that depend upon the mutable minds, opinions, appetites, and passions of particular men to the consideration of others. . . .

CHAPTER 1:[1]

That a Small Country and few People, by its *Situation, Trade,* and *Policy,* may be equivalent in *Wealth* and *Strength,* to a far greater people and territory: And particularly that conveniences for *Shipping, Water Carriage,* do most eminently and fundamentally conduce thereunto.

[1]In *Political Arithmetic* each heading is a "conclusion" reached in the chapter it introduces.

From Sir William Petty, *Political Arithmetic or a Discourse Concerning the Extent and Value of Lands, People, Buildings; Husbandry, Manufacture, Commerce, Fishery, Artizans . . . Shipping, Power at Sea &c.* (London: Robert Clavel, 1691), pp. 1–117, *passim.* Condensed and language slightly modernized by Allen C. Myers.

The first part of this conclusion needs little proof, for one acre of land may bear as much corn, and feed as many cattle, as twenty, by the difference of the soil. Likewise, some parcel of ground is naturally so defensible, that a hundred men possessing it can resist the invasion of five hundred; and bad land may be made good. Bog may by draining be made meadow; the same land being built upon may yield a hundred times the rent which it yielded as pasture; one man by art may do as much work as many without it: one man with a mill can grind as much corn as twenty can pound in a mortar. . . .

To clear the second, and more material part of this conclusion, that this difference in land and people arises principally from their situation, trade, and policy, I shall compare Holland and Zealand[2] with the kingdom of France. Holland and Zealand [combined] do not contain above one million acres, whereas the kingdom of France contains above eighty million.

[I]t is hard to say whether, when these places were first planted, an acre in France was better than the like quantity in Holland and Zealand. There is no reason to suppose, but that therefore upon the first plantation, the number of planters was in proportion to the quantity of land: wherefore, if the people are not in the same proportion as the land, this must be attributed to the situation of the land, and to the trade and policy of the people living upon it.

Holland and Zealand, at this day, are not only an eightieth part as rich and strong as France, but have advanced to about one-third. . . . The people of Amsterdam, are one-third of those in Paris. But the value of the buildings in Amsterdam may well be half that of Paris, by reason of the foundations, grafts, and bridges, which in Amsterdam are more numerous and sturdier than in Paris.

The value of shipping in Europe being about two million tons, I suppose the English have five hundred thousand, the Dutch nine hundred thousand, the French a hundred thousand. . . . So as the shipping in our case of France to that of Holland and Zealand, is about one to nine, which figures to be as eight hundred thousand pounds, to seven million two hundred thousand pounds. The Hollanders' capital in the East India Company is worth above three million, where the French as yet have little or nothing. . . .

Upon the whole it seems that though France be in people to Holland and Zealand as 13 to 1, and in quantity of good land, as 80 to 1; yet it is not 13 times richer or stronger, much less 80 times, nor much above 3 times, which was to be proved. I now aim to show that this difference of improvement in wealth and strength arises from the situation, trade and policy of the respective places, and in particular from conveniences for shipping and water carriage. Many writing on this subject magnify the Dutch as if they were more than men and all other nations less; making them angels and others fools. I take the foundation of their achievements to lie originally in the situation of the country, whereby they do things inimitable by others, and have advantages whereof others are incapable.

First, the soil of Holland and Zealand is low, rich and fertile; whereby it is able to feed many men, and so as that men may live near each other, for their mutual alliance in trade. . . . Secondly, Holland is a level country, so that in any part of it a windmill may be set up, and by its being moist and vaporous, there is always wind stirring over it, by which advantage the labor of many thousand hands is saved. . . ; the value

---

[2]Zealand is a small territory bordering the North Sea; now a province of the United Netherlands, in Petty's day it was autonomous.

of this convenience is near 150,000 pounds. Thirdly, there is much more to be gained by manufacture than agriculture, and by merchandising than manufacture: Holland and Zealand, being seated at the mouths of three long great rivers which pass through rich countries, do leave all the inhabitants upon the sides of those rivers to be farmers, while they themselves manufacture commodities, and ship them into all parts of the world. In short, they keep the keys of trade of those countries through which the said rivers pass. The value of this third convenience, I suppose to be 200,000 pounds. . . .

Those who have their situation thus towards the sea, and abound with fish at home, and having also the command of shipping, have by consequence the fishing trade . . . amounting to over three millions a year [for Europe]. In addition, those who predominate in shipping and fishing have more occasions than others to frequent all parts of the world, and to observe what is wanting or redundant everywhere; and what each people can do and what they desire. They then bring all native materials to be manufactured at home into commodities; and carry the same back, even to that country in which they grew. . . .

. . . [I]n all the ancient states and empires, those who had the shipping had the wealth. . . . The great and ultimate effect of trade is not wealth at large, but particularly abundance of silver, gold, and jewels, which are not perishable or mutable, but are wealth at all times and all places. . . .

I have omitted to mention that the Dutch were one hundred years ago a poor and oppressed people, living in a country naturally cold and unpleasant, and were persecuted for their heterodoxy in religion. From hence it necessarily follows that this people must labor hard, and set all hands to work: rich and poor, young and old, must study the art of number, weight, and measure; must fare hard, provide for impotents and orphans, out of hope to make a profit by their labors. . . . All these particulars, said to be the subtle artifices of the Hollanders, seem to me but what almost could not have been otherwise. Liberty of conscience, registry of shipping, small customs, banks, and law merchants, rise all from the same spring and tend toward the same sea. . . .

The Dutch do rid themselves of two trades, which are of greatest turmoil and danger, and yet of least profit; the first being that of the common soldier, for such they can hire from England, Scotland, and Germany, to venture their lives for six pence a day, while they themselves safely and quietly follow such trades, whereby the meanest of them gain six times as much. . . . The other trade of which the Dutch have rid their hands is the old patriarchal trade of being cow keepers, and in a great measure of plowing and sowing corn; they have put that employment upon the Danes and the Poles. . . .

CHAPTER 2:

That some kind of taxes and public levies may rather increase than diminish the wealth of the Kingdom.

If the money or other effects, levied from the people by way of tax, were destroyed and annihilated, then it is clear that such levies would diminish the commonwealth. Or if the same were exported out of the kingdom without any return, then the case would also be the same or worse. But if what is levied, as stated above, is transferred from one hand to another, then we are only to consider whether the said money or commodities are taken from an improving hand and given to an ill husband, or vice versa. For example, suppose that money by way of tax is taken from one who would spend it on superfluous eating and drinking, and delivered to another who would employ it in improving of land, fishing, manufacture, or the like. It is manifest, that such tax is an advantage to the state whereof the said persons are members. . . . On the contrary, if the stocks of laborious and ingenious men, who are not only beautifying the country by their labors and manners, but increasing the gold, silver, and jewels of the country, should be diminished by a tax, and given to such as do nothing but eat and drink, sing, play, and dance, nay to such as study metaphysics, or other such needless speculation, or employ themselves in any other way which produces no material thing or real use and value in the Commonwealth, then the wealth of the public is diminished. . . .

To know whether a tax will do good or harm, the state of the people and their employments must be known. One must know what part of the people are unfit by labor by their infancy or impotency, and also what part are exempt by reason of their wealth, function, or dignities, or by reason of their charge and employments; otherwise than in governing, directing, and preserving those, who are appointed to labor and arts. In the next place the computation must be made, of what part of men fit for labor are able to perform the work of the nation in its present state and measure. It is to be considered, whether the remainder can make any of those commodities that are imported from abroad. The remainder of this sort of people (if any be) may safely and without possible prejudice to the Commonwealth, be employed in arts and exercises of pleasure and ornament; the greatest whereof is the improvement of natural knowledge.

I come next to intimate that no part of Europe has paid so much by way of tax and public contribution as Holland and Zealand, for this last hundred years. And yet no country has, in the same time, increased their wealth comparably to them. And it is manifest, they have followed the general considerations mentioned above; for they tax meat and drink most heavily of all, to refrain the excessive expense of those things, which 24 hours wholly annihilates . . . nor do they tax according to what men gain, except in extraordinary cases, but always according to what they spend.

I conceive that in Ireland, where there are about 1.2 million people, and 300,000 hearths, it would be more tolerable for the people and more profitable for the king: that each head paid two shillings worth of flax than that each hearth should pay two shillings in silver. Ireland, being underpeopled, there being everywhere fish and fowl, and the people there able to build their houses and construct their farming tools by hand, can live and subsist in their present fashion without the use of gold and silver. Now it has been found, that from the uselessness rather than the want of money, that from 300,000 hearths, which should have yielded 30,000 pounds per year, not 15,000 pounds could be levied. It is easily imagined that four or five people dwelling in a cottage could easily plant the same value in flax, . . . Nor is there any skill requisite to this practice with which the country is not already familiar. . . .

It is observed by clothmakers, and others, who employ great numbers of poor people, that when corn is extremely plentiful, that the labor of the poor is extremely dear; and scarce to be had at all (so licentious are they who labor only to eat and drink). When so many acres sown with corn produce perhaps double to what is expected or necessary, it seems not unreasonable that this common blessing of God should be applied to the common good of all people, represented by their sovereign; much rather than the same should be abused, by the vile and brutish part of mankind. And consequently, such surplus of corn should be sent to public storehouses; from thence to be disposed of to the best advantage of the public. . . .

CHAPTER 5:

That the impediments to England's greatness are but contingent and removable.

The first impediment of England's greatness is that its territories are too far asunder, and divided by the sea into many several islands and countries. They are divided even into so many kingdoms and governments, that there are three distinct legislative powers in England, Scotland, and Ireland, which instead of uniting together, often cross one another's interest, putting bars and impediments upon one another's trades, not only as if they were foreigners to each other, but sometimes as enemies. . . . The government of New England so differs from that of his Majesty's other dominions, that it is hard to say what may be the consequence of it. . . .

Small, divided, remote governments are seldom able to defend themselves. The burden of protecting them all must lie upon the chief Kingdom, England; and so all the smaller kingdoms and dominions are diminutions rather than additions. This is remedied by making two grand councils, as may equally represent the whole empire, one to be chosen by the King, the other by the people. . . .

England, sometimes prohibiting the commodities of Ireland and Scotland, as of late it did the cattle and fish of Ireland, did not only make food, and consequently labor, dearer in England, but also forced the people of Ireland to fetch those commodities from France, Holland and other places, which was before sold them from England, to the great detriment of both nations. . . .

Nextly, in New England, there are vast numbers of able-bodied Englishmen, employed chiefly in the meanest part of farming (breeding of cattle), whereas Ireland would have contained all those persons, and at worst would have afforded them land on better terms than they have in America. . . . There is no doubt that the same people, widely dispersed, must spend more on their government than when living compactly and with no occasion to depend upon the wind, weather, and accidents of the sea. . . .

[Another] impediment is that Ireland, being a conquered country, and containing not the tenth part as many Irish natives, as there are English in both Kingdoms, that natural and firm union is not made between the two peoples. By transplantations, and proportional mixture, so as there may be but a tenth part of the Irish in Ireland and the same proportion in England, the necessity of maintaining an army in Ireland at the expense of a quarter of all the rents of that kingdom may be taken away. . . .

None of these impediments are natural, but did arise as the irregularity of buildings do, by being built partly at one time, partly at another . . . perhaps the practices we complain of are but the warpings of time, from the rectitude of the first institution.

As these impediments are contingent, so are they also removable. For may not the land of superfluous territories be sold, and the people with their belongings brought away? . . . May not the three kingdoms be united into one, and equally represented in Parliament? Might not the several species of the King's subjects be equally mixed in their habitations? . . . Might not dissenters in religion be indulged, as they pay a competent force to keep the public peace? I humbly venture to say all these things may be done, if it be thought fit by the sovereign power, because the like has been done already at several places and times.

CHAPTER 8:

That there are spare hands enough among the King of England's Subjects, to earn two million pounds a year more than they now do; and that there are also employments, ready, proper, and sufficient, for that purpose.

To prove this point we must inquire, how much all the people could earn if they were disposed, or necessitated to labor, and had work with which to employ themselves. We must then compare that sum with that of the total expense above mentioned, deducting the rents, and profits of their land and stock, which, properly speaking, saves so much labor. . . .

Now if there were spare hands to earn and save millions of millions, they signify nothing unless there were employment for them . . . therefore the more material point is to prove that there is two millions worth of work to be done, which at present the King's subjects do neglect.

For the proof of this there needs little more to be done, than to compute: 1. How much money is paid by the King of England's subjects to foreigners for freight and shipping, 2. How much the Dutch gain by their fishing trade practiced upon our seas, and 3. What the value is of all the commodities imported into, and spent in England, which might by diligence be produced, and manufactured here. To make short of this matter, upon perusal of the most authentic accounts relating to these several particulars, I affirm that this amounts to above five millions, whereas I propounded but two millions. . . .

Having handled these principal conclusions, I might go on with others, *ad infinitum*. But what has been already said, I look upon as sufficient to show what I mean by political arithmetic; and to show the uses of: 1. Knowing the true state of the people, land, stock, trade, etc. 2. [Demonstrating] that the king's subjects are not in so bad a condition as discontented men would make them. 3. Showing the great effect of Unity, Industry, and Obedience, in order to advance the common safety, and each man's particular happiness.

15 John Locke, *The Second Treatise of Civil Government*

John Locke (1632–1704) was an English philosopher of the Glorious Revolution period whose works had a great influence on the people of his own country, on French *philosophes* of the eighteenth-century Enlightenment, and on the colonists who became American revolutionaries. In his political writing, Locke was most concerned with demonstrating that consent of the governed alone bestows legitimacy and that an attempt to rule in defiance of the people's will was tyranny.

Locke's two-volume *Essay Concerning Human Understanding* anticipated scientific psychology with its analysis of how the human mind actually works. As a by-product of his conclusion that both cognition and belief are the results of sensations acting on the mind, he showed that persecuting people for religious beliefs was senseless. Locke believed that people couldn't "help" what went through their minds; therefore, regulating religious beliefs meant teaching people to lie about what they believed. Although even Locke had some reservations about full political rights for Roman Catholics, Muslims, and atheists, he generally advocated religious toleration.

Even though Locke contributed substantially to the later concept of separation of Church and state, he drew at times on medieval ideas concerning God, humans, and the state. Using the medieval idea that man was God's property, he refuted the notion that kings or other rulers could treat people as their own property. Under the protection of the God to whom they would always belong, the people formed a government to protect their God-given or natural rights of life, liberty, and property.

Locke's reasoning became a mainstay of *constitutionalism,* the theory that the people give authority to governments conditionally as part of a contract. When government officials no longer protect the natural rights of the people, these officials can be removed—by revolution, if no other means are available.

Locke's stress on property as an essential right of the individual makes him an early defender of capitalism in the context of his times. Just as people belong to God because God created them, individuals own what they create with their labor. In Locke's "labor theory of value," raw materials take on higher value as labor turns them into finished commodities. Locke thus gave the efforts of all individuals who aided production credit for creating new value and thus supported capitalistic individualism. Marx and the Marxists later modified this labor theory of value and directed it against the whole capitalist system.

The following excerpts are from Locke's best-known political work, *The Second Treatise of Civil Government.*

QUESTIONS TO CONSIDER

1. What motivation do people have for parting with the liberty that they enjoy in the state of nature?
2. Which rights from the state of nature do people always keep under government?
3. How is government appropriately divided into branches? Are these branches approximately equal in authority or not?
4. When is revolution justified? Who makes this judgment?

THE CONTRACT TO PRESERVE LIFE, LIBERTY, AND PROPERTY

To understand political power right and derive it from its origin, we must consider what state all men are naturally in, and that is a state of perfect freedom to order their actions and dispose of their possessions and persons as they think fit, within the bounds of the law of nature, without asking leave or depending upon the will of any other man. [This is a] state also of equality, wherein all the power and jurisdiction is reciprocal, no one having more than another.

Men being . . . by nature all free, equal, and independent, no one can be put out of this estate and subjected to the political power of another without his own consent. The only way whereby any one divests himself of his natural liberty and puts on the bonds of civil society is by agreeing with other men to join and unite into a community for their comfortable, safe, and peaceable living amongst one another, in a secure enjoyment of their properties and a greater security against any that are not of it. This any number of men may do, because it injures not the freedom of the rest; they are left as they were in the liberty of the state of nature. When any number of men have so consented to make one community or government, they are thereby presently incorporated and make one body politic wherein the majority have a right to act and conclude the rest. . . . And thus that which begins and actually constitutes any political society is nothing but the consent of any number of freemen capable of a majority to unite and incorporate into such a society. And this is that, and that only, which did or could give beginning to any lawful government in the world.

If man in the state of nature be so free . . ., and if he be absolute lord of his own person and possessions, equal to the greatest, and subject to nobody, why will he part with his freedom, why will he give up his empire and subject himself to the dominion and control of any other power? To which it is obvious to answer that though in the state of nature he has such a right, yet the enjoyment of it is very uncertain and constantly exposed to the invasion of others; for all being kings as much as he, every man his equal, and the greater part no strict observers of equity and justice, the enjoyment of the property he has in this state is very unsafe, very unsecure. This makes him willing to quit a condition which, however free, is full of fears and continual dangers; and it is not without reason that he seeks out and is willing to join in society with others who are already united, or have a mind to unite, for the mutual preservation of their lives, liberties, and estates, which I call by the general name "property."

The great and chief end, therefore, of men's uniting into commonwealths and putting themselves under government is the preservation of their property. . . . Though the earth and all inferior creatures be common to all men, yet every man has a property in his own person; this nobody has any right to but himself. The labor of his body and the work of his hands, we may say, are properly his. Whatsoever then he removes out of the state that nature has provided and left it in, he has mixed his labor with, and joined to it something that is his own, and thereby makes it his property. It being by him removed from the common state nature has placed it in, it has by this labor something annexed to it that excludes the common right of other men. For this labor being the unquestionable property of the laborer, no man but he can have a right to what that is once joined to, at least where there is enough and as good left in common for others . . . As much land as a man tills, plants, improves, cultivates, and can use the product of, so much is his property. He by his labor does, as it were, enclose it from the common.

From *Second Treatise*, in *Two Treatises of Civil Government by John Locke* (London: G. Routledge & Sons, 1884), pp. 244–79, *passim*. Spelling and punctuation slightly modified.

LAW-MAKING AND EXECUTIVE POWER

It is reasonable and just that I should have a right to destroy that which threatens me with destruction; for, by the fundamental law of nature . . . when all cannot be preserved, the safety of the innocent is to be preferred; and one may destroy a man who makes war upon him, or has discovered an enmity to his being, for the same reason that he may kill a wolf or a lion, because such men . . . have no other rule but that of force and violence, and so may be treated as beasts of prey. . . .

To avoid this state of war is one great reason of men's putting themselves into society and quitting the state of nature; for where there is an authority, a power on earth from which relief can be had by appeal, there the continuance of the state of war is excluded, and the controversy is decided by that power.

Whenever, therefore, any number of men are so united into one society as to quit every one his executive power of the law of nature and to resign it to the public, there and there only is a political or civil society.

Because it may be too great a temptation to human frailty, apt to grasp at power, for the same persons who have the power of making laws to have also in their hands the power to execute them, whereby they may exempt themselves from obedience to the laws they make, and suit the law, both in its making and execution, to their own private advantage, and thereby come to have a distinct interest from the rest of the community contrary to the end of society and government; therefore, in well ordered commonwealths, where the good of the whole is so considered as it ought, the legislative power is put into the hands of diverse persons who, duly assembled, have by themselves, or jointly with others, a power to make laws; which when they have done, being separated again, they are themselves subject to the laws they have made. . . .

But because the laws that are at once and in a short time made have a constant and lasting force and need a perpetual execution or an attendance thereunto; therefore, it is necessary there should be a power always in being which should see to the execution of the laws that are made and remain in force. And thus the legislative and executive power come often to be separated. There is another power in every commonwealth which . . . contains the power of war and peace, leagues and alliances, and all the transactions with all persons and communities without the commonwealth, and may be called "federative," if anyone pleases. So the thing be understood, I am indifferent as to the name.

Man, being born, as has been proved, with a title to perfect freedom and uncontrolled enjoyment of all the rights and privileges of the law of nature equally with any other man or number of men in the world, has by nature a power not only to preserve his property—that is, his life, liberty, and estate—against the injuries and attempts of other men, but to judge of and punish the breaches of that law in others as he is persuaded the offense deserves, even with death itself in crimes where the heinousness of the fact in his opinion requires it. Every man who has entered into civil society and become a member of any commonwealth has quitted his power to punish offenses against the law of nature in prosecution of his own private judgment. He has given a right to the commonwealth to employ his force for the execution of the judgments of the commonwealth, which, indeed, are his own judgments, they being made by himself or his representative. . . .

[The] end of law is not to abolish or restrain but to preserve and enlarge freedom; for in all the states of created beings capable of laws, where there is no law, there is no freedom. For liberty is to be free from restraint and violence from others, which cannot be where there is not law; but freedom is not, as we are told: a liberty for every man to do what he likes—for who could be free, when every other man's humor might domineer over him?—but a liberty to dispose and order . . . his person, actions, possessions, and his whole property, within the allowance of those laws under which he is, and therein not to be subject to the arbitrary will of another, but freely follow his own.

RIGHT TO REMOVE TYRANNICAL GOVERNMENT

Since it can never be supposed to be the will of the society that the legislative should have a power to destroy that which every one designs to secure by entering into society, and for which the people submitted themselves to legislators of their own making, whenever the legislators endeavour to take away and destroy the property of the people, or to reduce them to slavery under arbitrary power, they put themselves into a state of war with the people, who are thereupon absolved from any further obedience, and are left to the common refuge which God has provided for all men against force and violence. Whensoever, therefore, the legislative shall transgress this fundamental rule of society, and either by ambition, fear, folly, or corruption, endeavour to grasp themselves or put into the hands of any other an absolute power over the lives, liberties, and estates of the people, by this breach of trust they forfeit the power the people had put into their hands, for quite contrary ends, and it devolves to the people, who have a right to resume their original liberty, and by the establishment of the new legislative (such as they shall think fit) provide for their own safety and security, which is the end for which they are in society. What I have said here concerning the legislative in general, holds true also concerning the supreme executor, who having a double trust put in him, both to have a part in the legislative and the supreme execution of the law, acts against both when he goes about to set up his own arbitrary will as the law of the society. He acts also contrary to his trust when he employs the force, treasure, and offices of the society, to corrupt the representatives, and gain them to his purposes. . . .

   The end of government is the good of mankind, and which is best for mankind, that the people should be always exposed to the boundless will of tyranny, or that the rulers should be sometimes liable to be opposed when they grow exorbitant in the use of their power, and employ it for the destruction and not the preservation of the properties of their people?

   If a controversy arise between a prince and some of the people in a matter where the law is silent or doubtful, and the thing be of great consequence, I should think the proper umpire in such a case should be the body of the people. . . . But if the prince or whoever they be in the administration decline that way of determination, the appeal then lies nowhere but to heaven; force between either persons who have no known superior on earth, or which permits no appeal to a judge on earth, being properly a state of war, wherein the appeal lies only to heaven, and in that state the injured party must judge for himself when he will think fit to make use of that appeal and put himself upon it.

16 Adam Smith, *The Wealth of Nations*

In 1776, Adam Smith published *An Inquiry into the Nature and Causes of the Wealth of Nations,* an attack on government-regulated economy and a defense of free trade. Today this volume remains the classic work in its field. Although its publication did not have any direct relationship to the American Revolution, by that time many of the American colonists entertained similar notions about British mercantile policy.

QUESTIONS TO CONSIDER

1. Why is Smith convinced that free importing of agricultural products will not harm farmers at home?
2. How does Smith characterize the mentality of merchants and manufacturers, as opposed to that of country gentlemen and farmers?
3. How does Smith rate problems of economic dislocation among the working population if foreign imports are freely allowed?
4. In what exceptional circumstances, according to Smith, may government regulation of foreign trade be necessary?
5. How does Smith describe the effects of raising revenue through taxes on necessary commodities?
6. Is Adam Smith's approach to international trade workable in an international economy in which not all the trading countries practice laissez-faire economic policies?

THE CASE FOR FREE TRADE AND LOWER TAXES

By restraining, either by high duties, or by absolute prohibitions, the importation of such goods from foreign countries as can be produced at home, the monopoly of the home-market is more or less secured to the domestic industry employed in producing them. Thus the . . . high duties upon the importation of corn, which in times of moderate plenty amount to a prohibition, give a like advantage to the growers of that commodity. The prohibition of the importation of foreign woollens is equally favorable to the woollen manufacturers. The silk manufacture, though altogether employed upon foreign materials, has lately obtained the same advantage. The linen manufacture has not yet obtained it, but is making great strides towards it. Many other sorts of manufacturers have, in the same manner, obtained in Great Britain, either altogether or very nearly, a monopoly against their countrymen. . . .

That this monopoly of the home-market frequently gives great encouragement to that particular species of industry which enjoys it . . . cannot be doubted. But whether it tends either to increase the general industry of the society, or to give it the most advantageous direction, is not, perhaps, altogether so evident.

From Adam Smith, *An Inquiry into the Nature and Causes of the Wealth of Nations* (1776), ed. Edwin Cannan (London: Methuen, 1904), pp. 418–36, *passim.* Spelling and punctuation slightly modified.

The general industry of the society never can exceed what the capital of the society can employ. As the number of workmen that can be kept in employment by any particular person must bear a certain proportion to his capital, so the number of those that can be continually employed by all the members of a great society, must bear a certain portion to the whole capital of that society, and never can exceed that proportion. No regulation of commerce can increase the quantity of industry in any society beyond what its capital can maintain. It can only divert a part of it into a direction into which it might not otherwise have gone; and it is by no means certain that this artificial direction is likely to be more advantageous to the society than that into which it would have gone of its own accord.

Every individual is continually exerting himself to find out the most advantageous employment for whatever capital he can command. It is his own advantage, indeed, and not that of the society, which he has in view. But the study of his own advantage naturally, or rather necessarily, leads him to prefer that employment which is most advantageous to the society.

First, every individual endeavors to employ his capital as near home as he can, and consequently as much as he can in the support of domestic industry; provided always that he can thereby obtain . . . ordinary profits. . . .

Thus upon equal or nearly equal profits, every wholesale merchant naturally prefers the home-trade to the foreign trade of consumption. . . . In the home-trade his capital is never so long out of his sight as it frequently is in the foreign trade of consumption. He can know better the character and situation of the persons whom he trusts, and if he should happen to be deceived, he knows better the laws of the country from which he must seek redress. . . . Home is in this manner the center, if I may say so, round which the capitals of the inhabitants of every country are continually circulating, and towards which they are always tending, though by particular causes they may sometimes be driven off and repelled from it towards more distant employments. But a capital employed in the home-trade . . . necessarily puts into motion a greater quantity of domestic industry, and gives revenue and employment to a greater number of the inhabitants of the country, than an equal capital employed in the foreign trade of consumption: and one employed in the foreign trade of consumption has the same advantage over an equal capital employed in the carrying trade. Upon equal, or only nearly equal profits, therefore, every individual naturally inclines to employ his capital in the manner in which it is likely to afford the greatest support to domestic industry, and to give revenue and employment to the greatest number of people of his own country.

Secondly, every individual who employs his capital in the support of domestic industry, necessarily endeavors so to direct that industry, that its produce may be of the greatest possible value.

The produce of industry is what it adds to the subject or materials upon which it is employed. In proportion as the value of this produce is great or small, so will likewise be the profits of the employer. But it is only for the sake of profit that any man employs a capital in the support of industry; and he will always, therefore, endeavor to employ it in the support of that industry of which the produce is likely to be of the greatest value, or to exchange for the greatest quantity either of money or of other goods. . . .

As every individual, therefore, endeavors as much as he can both to employ his capital in the support of domestic industry, and so to direct that industry that its produce may be of the greatest value; every individual necessarily labors to render the annual revenue of the society as great as he can. He generally, indeed, neither intends to promote the public interest, nor knows how much he is promoting it. By preferring the support of domestic to that of foreign industry, he intends only his own security; and by directing that industry in such a manner as its produce may be of the greatest value, he intends only his own gain, and he is in this, as in many other cases, led by an invisible hand to promote an end which was no part of his intention. Nor is it always the worse for the society that it was no part of it. By pursuing his own interest he frequently promotes that of the society more effectually than when he really intends to promote it. I have never known much good done by those who affected to trade for the public good. It is an affectation, indeed, not very common among merchants, and very few words need be employed in dissuading them from it. . . .

To give the monopoly of the home-market to the produce of domestic industry, in any particular art or manufacture, is in some measure to direct private people in what manner they ought to employ their capitals, and must, in almost all cases, be either a useless or a hurtful regulation. If the produce of domestic can be brought there as cheap as that of foreign industry, the regulation is evidently useless. If it cannot, it must generally be hurtful. It is the maxim of every prudent master of a family, never to attempt to make at home what it will cost him more to make than to buy. The tailor does not attempt to make his own shoes, but buys them of the shoemaker. The shoemaker does not attempt to make his own clothes, but employs a tailor. The farmer attempts to make neither the one nor the other, but employs those different artificers. All of them find it for their interest to employ their whole industry in a way in which they have some advantage over their neighbors, and to purchase with a part of its produce, or what is the same thing, with the price of a part of it, whatever else they have occasion for. . . .

The natural advantages which one country has over another in producing particular commodities are sometimes so great, that it is acknowledged by all the world to be in vain to struggle with them. By means of glasses, hotbeds, and hotwalls, very good grapes can be raised in Scotland, and very good wine too can be made of them at about thirty times the expense for which at least equally good can be brought from foreign countries. Would it be a reasonable law to prohibit the importation of all foreign wines, merely to encourage the making of claret and burgundy in Scotland? But if there would be a manifest absurdity in turning towards any employment, thirty times more of the capital and industry of the country, than would be necessary to purchase from foreign countries an equal quantity of the commodities wanted, there must be an absurdity, though not altogether so glaring, yet exactly of the same kind, in turning towards any such employment a thirtieth, or even a three hundredth part more of either. . . . As long as the one country has those advantages, and the other wants them, it will always be more advantageous for the latter, rather to buy of the former than to make. It is an acquired advantage only, which one artificer has over his neighbor, who exercises another trade; and yet they both find it more advantageous to buy of one another, than to make what does not belong to their particular trades.

Merchants and manufacturers are the people who derive the greatest advantage from this monopoly of the home market. The prohibition of the importation of foreign cattle, and of salt provisions, together with the high duties upon foreign corn, which in times of moderate plenty amount to a prohibition, are not near so advantageous to the graziers and farmers of Great Britain, as other regulations of the same kind are to its merchants and manufacturers. Manufacturers, those of the finer kind especially, are more easily transported from one country to another than corn or cattle. It is in the fetching and carrying of manufacturers, accordingly, that foreign trade is chiefly employed. In manufactures, a very small advantage will enable foreigners to undersell our own workmen, even in the home market. It will require a very great one to enable them to do so in the rude produce of the soil. If the free importation of foreign manufacturers were permitted, several of the home manufacturers would probably suffer, and some of them, perhaps, go to ruin altogether, and a considerable part of the stock and industry at present employed in them, would be forced to find out some other employment. But the freest importation of the rude produce of the soil could have no such effect upon the agriculture of the country.

If the importation of foreign cattle, for example, were made ever so free, so few could be imported, that the grazing trade of Great Britain could be little affected by it. Live cattle are, perhaps, the only commodity of which the transportation is more expensive by sea than by land. By land they carry themselves to market. By sea, not only the cattle, but their food and their water too must be carried at no small expense and inconveniency. . . .

THE SOLE JUSTIFICATIONS FOR RESTRICTING TRADE

To prohibit by a perpetual law the importation of foreign corn and cattle, is in reality to enact, that the population and industry of the country shall at no time exceed what the rude produce of its own soil can maintain.

There seem, however, to be two cases in which it will generally be advantageous to lay some burden upon foreign, for the encouragement of domestic industry.

The first is when some particular sort of industry is necessary for the defense of the country. The defense of Great Britain, for example, depends very much upon the number of its sailors and shipping. The act of navigation, therefore, very properly endeavors to give the sailors and shipping of Great Britain the monopoly of the trade of their own country, in some cases, by absolute prohibitions, and in others by heavy burdens upon the shipping of foreign countries. . . .

The act of navigation is not favorable to foreign commerce, or to the growth of that opulence which can arise from it. The interest of a nation in its commercial relations to foreign nations is, like that of a merchant with regard to the different people with whom he deals, to buy as cheap and to sell as dear as possible. But it will be most likely to buy cheap, when by the most perfect freedom of trade it encourages all nations to bring to it the goods which it has occasion to purchase; and, for the same reason, it will be most likely to sell dear, when its markets are thus filled with the greatest number of buyers. The act of navigation, it is true, lays no burden upon foreign ships that come to export the produce of British industry. Even the ancient aliens duty, which used to be paid upon all goods exported as well as imported, has, by several subsequent acts, been taken off from the greater part of the articles of exportation. But if foreigners, either by prohibitions or high duties, are hindered from coming to sell, they cannot always afford to come to buy; because coming without a cargo, they must lose the freight from their own country to Great Britain. By diminishing the number of sellers, therefore, we necessarily diminish that of buyers, and are thus likely not only to buy foreign goods dearer, but to sell our own cheaper, than if there was a more perfect freedom of trade. As defense, however, is of much more importance than opulence, the act of navigation is, perhaps, the wisest of all the commercial regulations of England.

The second case, in which it will generally be advantageous to lay some burden upon foreign for the encouragement of domestic industry, is, when some tax is imposed at home upon the produce of the latter. In this case, it seems reasonable that an equal tax should be imposed upon the like produce of the former. This would not give the monopoly of the home market to domestic industry, nor turn towards a particular employment a greater share of the stock and labor of the country, than what would naturally go to it. It would only hinder any part of what would naturally go to it from being turned away by the tax, into a less natural direction, and would leave the competition between foreign and domestic industry, after the tax, as nearly as possible upon the same footing as before. . . .

THE EFFECTS OF TAXING NECESSITIES

Taxes imposed with a view to prevent, or even to diminish importation, are evidently as destructive of the revenue of the customs as of the freedom of trade. [Taxes] upon the necessaries of life have nearly the same effect upon the circumstances of the people as a poor soil and a bad climate. Provisions are thereby rendered dearer in the same manner as if it required extraordinary labor and expense to raise them. As in the natural scarcity arising from soil and climate, it would be absurd to direct the people in what manner they ought to employ their capitals and industry, so is it likewise in the artificial scarcity arising from such taxes. To be left to accommodate, as well as they could, their industry to their situation, and to find out those employments in which, notwithstanding their unfavorable circumstances, they might have some advantage either in the home or in the foreign market, is what in both cases would evidently be most for their advantage. To lay a new tax upon them, because they are already overburdened with taxes, and because they already pay too dear for necessaries of life, to make them likewise pay too dear for the greater part of other commodities, is certainly a most absurd way of making amends.

Such taxes, when they have grown up to a certain height, are a curse equal to the barrenness of the earth and the inclemency of the heavens; and yet it is in the richest and most industrious countries that they have been most generally imposed. No other countries could support so great a disorder. As the strongest bodies only can live and enjoy health, under an unwholesome regimen; so the nations only, that in every sort of industry have the greatest natural and acquired advantages, can subsist and prosper under such taxes.

Women's Rights and Democracy in the Enlightenment

Begun in the twilight years of the seventeenth century, the Enlightenment movement paralleled almost exactly the unfolding chronology of the eighteenth century. Enlightenment writers, who insisted that reason could be applied to politics, frequently wrote texts arguing that men had been given certain inalienable rights that all sovereigns must recognize, protect, and write into law. If monarchs such as the English King James II (r. 1685–1688) or King George III (r. 1760–1820) did not do so, then, following the arguments of writers such as John Locke (see Reading 15) or Thomas Paine (see Reading 11), men must secure their rights through resistance and, if necessary, revolution. None of the major male Enlightenment writers ever considered that women had inalienable rights, and few female writers in the eighteenth century challenged this view.

Women living in the eighteenth century accepted the prevailing patriarchal structures of society. Fathers were expected to rule over their daughters, and wives were expected to submit to their husbands. Throughout the Enlightenment, vocational choices for women were limited and predictable: Women could aspire to be wives or mothers, or in Catholic countries they could enter a convent. Very few women could live independent lives outside of marriage. Those women who did so, such as artisans, laborers, widows, or single women, all too frequently found themselves living so close to poverty that an illness or economic downturn could force them into petty thievery, smuggling, or more likely prostitution. Aristocratic women born to wealth and privilege enjoyed opportunities to learn from private tutors, travel abroad, attend concerts and theater, and join in polite society's robust social life. Most well-born women, however, were concerned with wealth, status, and privilege; only a few ever considered the possibility of claiming rights independent of their privileged position in society. Middle-class women enjoyed some of the opportunities afforded their aristocratic sisters, but they had fewer opportunities for education, travel, and leisure. As the wives and daughters of merchants, lawyers, or physicians, eighteenth-century middle-class women focused their energies on the domestic sphere, ensuring their households were well managed and their children well behaved. The majority of women living during the Enlightenment were peasants who invariably married farmers and were heavily engaged in domestic and agricultural responsibilities. Spring planting, summer tilling, and autumn harvesting were busy times when these women worked the fields alongside their husbands. But in addition to these heavy demands, peasant women were responsible for their children, the kitchen, and household chores. For women living during the Enlightenment two things were certain. First, the overwhelming majority had neither the education nor the leisure to read the major texts or to grasp such concepts as "rights." Second, even women such as Olympe de Gouges (see Reading 27), who were inclined to read John Locke or Thomas Paine, were not drawn to vague, abstract notions of rights. They were much more interested in specific guarantees of their right to an education, to own property, and to have legal protection from the arbitrary and capricious control of their fathers, their husbands, and the Church.

Jean-Jacques Rousseau, the author of the last two selections in this section, suggests the misogynist views inherent in the Enlightenment's view of women. With proper education, Rousseau believed, men could construct a democracy. Women, according to Rousseau, were born to please men; therefore, rather than troubling themselves about rights—natural, inherent, individual, legal, or political—women should focus their energies and talents on their true, natural, and only vocations: marriage, motherhood, and domesticity.

17 Sophia, *Woman Not Inferior to Man*

The politics of the Enlightenment were quite often the politics of gender. Despite the importance of women in advancing much of the Enlightenment's agenda, eighteenth-century Europe remained very much a man's world. Women such as Lady Mary Wortley Montagu (1689–1762) or Olympe de Gouges (see Reading 27), who wished to enter the professions of law or medicine or sought political equality, confronted enormous barriers because of their sex. Legal and medical authorities insisted that with the exception of a few well-born women such as empresses and queens, most women were biologically and intellectually inferior to men and therefore should not be invested with higher learning or permitted to wield political power. Not surprisingly, in spite of its professed commitment to use reason to remedy social ills, few men of the Enlightenment were willing to consider the advancement of women's rights as a reasonable cause. Women who challenged this view quite often wrote under a pseudonym to protect their families from retribution or to avoid the personal abuse that so often accompanied the discussion of women's rights. The unknown author who wrote this essay under the pseudonym of "Sophia, a Person of Quality" might well have been Lady Mary Wortley Montagu, although the evidence remains inconclusive.

QUESTIONS TO CONSIDER

1. How would you compare Sophia's views of women with Jean-Jacques Rousseau's *Sophie* (see Reading 18) and Olympe de Gouges (see Reading 27)? How do these three readings suggest the sexual politics of the Enlightenment?

2. How would you evaluate Sophia's argument that education, exercise, and impressions, not gender, are the key elements that ensure diversity?

3. Sophia insists that women, by their nature, have a special aptitude for oratory, rhetoric, medicine, and teaching. Is this true? Why? Why not?

4. How persuasive are her arguments with respect to women's role in education and in the military?

WHETHER WOMEN ARE INFERIOR TO MEN IN THE INTELLECTUAL CAPACITY, OR NOT

There can be no real diversity contracted from the body. All diversity then must come from education, exercise, and the impressions of those external objects which surround us in different circumstances.

The same Creator, by the same laws, unites the souls of women and men to their respective bodies. The same sentiments, passions, and propensions cement that union in both. And the soul operating in the same manner in the one and the other is capable of the very same functions in both.

To render this more evident, we need only consider the texture of the head, the seat of the sciences, and the part where the soul exerts itself most. All the researches of anatomy have not yet been able to show us the least difference in this part between men and women. Our brain is perfectly like theirs, we receive the impressions of sense as they do, we marshall and preserve ideas for imagination and memory as they do, and we have all the organs they have and apply them to the same purposes as they do. We hear with ears, see with eyes, and taste with a tongue as well as they. Nor can there be any difference between any of our organs and theirs, but that ours are more delicate, and consequently fitter to answer the ends they were made for, than theirs.

Even among the men it is universally observed, that the more gross and lumpish are commonly stupid; and the more delicate are, on the other hand, ever the most sprightly. The reason is plain: The soul, while confined to the body, is dependent on its organs in all its operations; and therefore the more free or clogged those organs are, the more or less must the soul be at liberty to exert itself. Now it is too well known to need any support, that the organs in our sex are of a much finer, and more delicate temperature than theirs; and therefore, had we the same advantages of study allowed us which the men have, there is no room to doubt but we should at least keep pace with them in the sciences and every useful knowledge.

It can only then be a mean dastardly jealousy in them to exclude us from those advantages, in which we have so natural a right to emulate them. Their pretext for so doing, that study and learning would make women proud and vicious, is pitiful and capricious. No: false knowledge and superficial learning only can produce so bad an effect. For true knowledge and solid learning must make women, as well as men, both more humble, and more virtuous. And it must be owned, that if a little superficial knowledge had rendered some of our sex vain, it equally renders many of theirs in-

From Sophia, a Person of Quality, *Women not Inferior to Man: Or a Short and Modest Vindication of the Natural Rights of the Fair-Sex to Perfect Equality of Power, Dignity, and Esteem with the Men* (London: John Hawkins, 1739), pp. 23–62, *passim.* Spelling, capitalization, and usage have been modernized.

supportable. But that is no reason why solid learning should be denied, or not instilled into, either; rather ought the greater pains to be taken to improve, in both, every disposition to the sciences into a true relish for, and the knowledge of, them; according to the advice of their brightest writers, as applicable to any science as to poetry. . . .

Besides, let it be observed, what a wretched circle this poor way of reasoning among the men draws them insensibly into. Why is *learning* useless to us? Because we have no share in public offices? And why have we no share in public office? Because we have no *learning*. They are sensible of the injustice they do to us, and therefore are reduced to the mean shift of cloaking it at the expense of their own reason. But let truth speak for once: Why are they so industrious to debar us from that learning we have an equal right to with themselves, but for fear of our sharing with, and outshining them in, those public offices they fill so miserably? The same sordid selfishness which urged them to engross all power and dignity to themselves, prompted them to shut up from us that knowledge which would have made us their competitors.

As nature seems to have designed the men for our drudges, I could easily forgive them the usurpation by which they first took the trouble of public employment off our hands, if their injustice were content with stopping there. But as one abyss calls on another, and vices seldom go single, they are not satisfied with engrossing all authority into their own hands, but are confident enough to assert that they possess it by right, because we were formed by nature to be under *perpetual* subjection to them, for want of abilities to share with them in *government* and *public offices*. To confute this mannish extravagance, it will be necessary to sap it from the foundation on which it is built. . . .

WHETHER WOMEN ARE NATURALLY CAPABLE OF TEACHING SCIENCES OR NOT

Of rhetoric, we must be allowed to be by nature designed mistresses and models. Eloquence is a talent so natural and peculiar to woman, that no one can dispute it in her. Women can persuade what they please; and can dictate, defend, or distinguish between right and wrong, without the help of laws. There are few judges, who have not proved them the most prevalent counsel; and few pleaders who have not experienced them to be the most clear-headed, equitable judges. When women speak on a subject, they handle it with so delicate a touch, that the men are forced to own they feel what the former say. All the oratory of the schools is not able to give the men that eloquence and ease of speech, which costs us nothing. And that, which their mean envy call loquacity in us, is only a readiness of ideas, and an ease of delivery, which they in vain labor, for years, to attain to.

With what hesitation, confusion, and drudgery, do not the men labor to bring forth their thoughts? And when they do utter something tolerable, with what insipid gestures, distortions, and grimaces, do they murder the few good things they say? Whereas when a woman speaks, her air is generally noble and presenting, her gesture free, and full of dignity, her action is decent, her words are easy and insinuating, her style is pathetic and winning, and her voice melodious, and tuned to her subject. She can soar to a level with the highest intellect without bombast, and with a complacency natural to the delicacy of her frame, descend to the meanest capacity without meanness. What is there we are unfit to reason upon which does not offend against decency? When we discourse of good or evil, it is well known we are capable of winning to the one, and weaning from the other, the most obstinate men, if they have but minds susceptible of reason and argument: And that character of integrity, which is imprinted on our countenances while we speak, renders our power of persuasion more prevalent. Sure then, if we are endowed with a more communicative eloquence than they are, we must be at least as well qualified as they to teach the sciences; and if we are not seen in university chairs, it cannot be attributed to our want of capacity to fill them, but to that violence with which the men support their unjust intrusion into our places; or, if not, at least to our greater modesty and less degree of ambition.

If we were to apply to the law, we should succeed in it at least as well as the men. The natural talent we have undisputed, of explaining and unraveling the most knotty intricacies, of stating our own and other people's pretensions, of discovering the grounds of a dispute, with the means to set it right, and of setting engines to work to do ourselves justice, is sufficient to prove that, were we to fill the offices of counsel, judges, and magistrates, we should show a capacity in business which very few men can boast of. But peace and justice is our study, and our pride is to make up those breaches which the corruption of that sex makes them but industrious to widen.

Our sex seems born to teach and practice medicine; to restore health to the sick, and preserve it to the well. Neatness, handiness, and compliance are one half of a patient's cure; and in this the men must yield to us. Indeed, we must yield to them in the art of inventing hard names, and puzzling the cure with a number, as well as adding to a patient's grievance with the costliness of remedies. But we can invent, and have invented, without the help of Galen, or Hippocrates, an infinity of reliefs for the sick, which they and their blind adherents could neither improve nor disapprove.[1] And an old woman's recipe, as it is termed, has often been known to remove an inveterate distemper which has baffled the researches of a college of graduates. In a word, the observations made by women in their practice have been so exact, and built upon such solid reason, as to show more than once the useless pedantry of the major part of school systems. . . .

WHETHER WOMEN ARE NATURALLY QUALIFIED FOR MILITARY OFFICES, OR NOT

The military art has no mystery in it beyond others, which women cannot attain to. A woman is as capable as a man of making herself, by means of a map, acquainted with the good and bad ways, the dangerous and safe passes, or the proper situations for encampment. And what should hinder her from making herself mistress of all the stratagems of war, of charging, retreating, surprising, laying ambushes, counterfeiting marches, feigning flights, giving false attacks, supporting real ones, animating the soldiery, and adding example to eloquence by being the first to mount a breach. Persuasion, heat and example are the soul of victory: And women can show as much eloquence, intrepidity, and warmth, where their honor is at stake, as is requisite to attack or defend a town. . . .

What has greatly helped to confirm the men in the prejudiced notion of a woman's natural weakness, is the common manner of expression which this very vulgar error gave birth to. When they mean to stigmatize a man with want of courage they call him *effeminate*, and when they would praise a woman for her courage they call her

[1]Galen and Hippocrates were two ancient Greek medical authorities. Hippocrates is considered the father of modern medicine.

manly. But as these, and such like expressions, are merely arbitrary and but a fulsome compliment which the men pass on themselves, they establish no truth. The real truth is, that humanity and integrity, the characteristics of our sex, make us abhor unjust slaughter, and prefer honorable peace to unjust war. And therefore to use these expressions with propriety, when a man possesses our virtues he should be called *effeminate* by way of the highest praise of his good nature and justice; and a woman who should depart from our sex by espousing the injustice and cruelty of the men's nature, should be called a *man*; that is, one whom no sacred ties can bind to the observation of just treaties, and whom no bloodshed can deter from the most cruel violence and rapine. . . .

Thus far I think it evidently appears, that there is no science, office or dignity which women have not an equal right to share in with the men. Since there can be no superiority, but that of brutal strength, shown in the latter, to entitle them to engross all power and prerogative to themselves: Nor in any incapacity proved in the former, to disqualify them of their right, but what is owing to the unjust oppression of the men, and might be easily removed. With regard, however, to the warlike employments, it seems to be a disposition of Providence that custom has exempted us from them. As sailors in a storm throw overboard their more useless lumber, so it is but fit that the men should be exposed to the dangers and hardships of war, while we remain in safety at home. They are, generally speaking, good for little else but to be our bulwarks, and our smiles are the most notable rewards which the bravest of them all ought to desire, or can deserve, for all the hazards they encounter, and for all the labors they go through for our defense, in the most tedious campaign. . . .

CONCLUSION

Thus then does it hitherto fully appear, how falsely we are deemed, by the men, wanting in that solidity of sense which they so vainly value themselves upon. Our right is the same with theirs to all public employments; we are endowed, by nature, with geniuses at least as capable of filling them as theirs can be; and our hearts are as susceptible of virtue as our heads are of the sciences. We neither want spirit, strength, nor courage, to defend a country, nor prudence to rule it. Our souls are as perfect as theirs, and the organs they depend on are generally more refined. However, if the bodies be compared to decide the right of excellence in either sex; we need not contend: The men themselves I presume will give it up. They cannot deny but that we have the advantage of them in the internal mechanism of our frames, since in us is produced the most beautiful and wonderful of all creatures: And how much have we not the advantage of them in outside? What beauty, comeliness, and graces, has not the heavens attached to our sex above theirs? I should blush with scorn to mention this, if I did not think it an indication of our souls being also in a state of greater delicacy. For I cannot help thinking that the wise author of nature suited our frames to the souls he gave us. And surely then the acuteness of our minds, with what passes in the inside of our heads, ought to render us at least equals to men, since the outside seldom fails to make us their absolute mistresses.

And yet I would have none of my sex build their authority barely on so slight a foundation. No: Good sense will outlast a handsome face: And the dominion gained over hearts by reason is lasting. I would therefore exhort all my sex to throw aside idle amusements, and to betake themselves to the improvement of their minds, that we may be able to act with that becoming dignity our nature has fitted us to;

and, without claiming or valuing it, show ourselves worthy something from them, as much above their bare esteem, as they conceit themselves above us. In a word, let us show them, by what little we do without aid of education, the much we might do if they did us justice; that we may force a blush from them, if possible, and compel them to confess their own baseness to us, and that the worst of us deserve much better treatment than the best of us receive.

18 Jean-Jacques Rousseau, *Sophie, or The Woman*

Much more traditional in the eighteenth century's view of women and their education is Jean-Jacques Rousseau (1712–1778). Although born in Geneva, Rousseau spent most of his life in France and was certainly influenced by French views of women. French jurists, for example, commonly ranked wives of fifth importance in a family's household, behind their husband, children, domestic servants, and any apprentices serving in the household. A woman charged with adultery received harsher penalties than a man. She could be beaten, stripped of her dowry, and sent to prison for two years' confinement. French playwrights, moralists, and theologians—with some notable exceptions—unhesitatingly subscribed to the notion that women were inferior, rebellious, and prisoners of their own passions. Strong discipline, even for noble women, was necessary to correct their erring ways. So, too, French church authorities viewed women as powerful sources of corruption who in large part were culpable for nearly all the sins of the flesh. In 1762, Rousseau published *Émile, or On Education,* which remains even today an influential treatise on educational pedagogy. Although Rousseau's primary concern in *Émile* is the education of men, the last part of his study, excerpted here, is focused on the education of women.

QUESTIONS TO CONSIDER

1. According to Rousseau, nature dictates that man was born strong and woman weak, and once "this principle being established, it follows that woman was specifically made to please man." Is this argument original with the eighteenth-century Enlightenment? Can you think of similar arguments before or after Rousseau?

2. Rousseau seems to suggest that the Supreme Being gave man reason to govern his passions but "in endowing woman with unlimited desires he [the Supreme Being] added modesty in order to restrain them." Can this view be considered enlightened? Why would the Age of Enlightenment accept this explanation?

3. Although Rousseau insists that man is the stronger sex, he also argues that man is dependent upon woman's good will and seems to beg the question who is really superior when he asks, "Is it weakness that yields to force or is it voluntary self-surrender?" What does he mean here?
4. How would you compare the argument and evidence of Sophia (see Reading 17) and Rousseau's *Sophie?* How do these two readings suggest the ideals and politics of the Enlightenment?
5. Do you see any connections between this reading's discussion of authority and Rousseau's *The Social Contract* (see Reading 19)?

In the union of the sexes, each alike contributes to the common end, though in different ways. From this diversity springs the first difference that may be observed between man and woman in their moral relations. One should be strong and active, the other weak and passive; one must necessarily have both the power and the will—it is sufficient for the other to offer little resistance.

This principle being established, it follows that woman was specifically made to please man. If man ought to please her in turn, the necessity is less direct. His merit lies in his power; he pleases simply because he is strong. I grant you this is not the law of love; but it is the law of nature, which is older than love itself.

If woman is made to please and to be subjugated to man, she ought to make herself pleasing to him rather than to provoke him; her particular strength lies in her charms; by their means she should compel him to discover his own strength and put it to use. The surest art of arousing this strength is to render it necessary by resistance. Thus pride reinforces desire and each triumphs in the other's victory. From this originates attack and defense, the boldness of one sex and the timidity of the other and finally the modesty and shame with which nature has armed the weak for the conquest of the strong.

Who can possibly suppose that nature has indifferently prescribed the same advances to the one sex as to the other and that the first to feel desire should also be the first to display it. What a strange lack of judgment! Since the consequences of the sexual act are so different for the two sexes, is it natural that they should engage in it with equal boldness? How can one fail to see that when the share of each is so unequal, if reserve did not impose on one sex the moderation that nature imposes on the other, the result would be the destruction of both and the human race would perish through the very means ordained for its continuance. Women so easily stir men's senses and awaken in the bottom of their hearts the remains of an almost extinct desire that if there were some unhappy climate on this earth where philosophy had introduced this custom, especially in warm countries where more women than men are born, the men tyrannized over by the women would at last become their victims and would be dragged to their deaths without ever being able to defend themselves.

Reprinted from *Women, the Family, and Freedom: The Debate in Documents.* Vol. 1, 1750–1880, pp. 44–49, *passim*, ed. Susan Groag Bell and Karen M. Offen with the permission of the Board of Trustees of the Leland Stanford Junior University.

If female animals do not have the same sense of shame, what do we make of that? Are their desires as boundless as those of women, which are curbed by shame? The desires of animals are the result of need; and when the need is satisfied the desire ceases; they no longer pretend to repulse the male, they do so in earnest. . . . They take on no more passengers after the ship is loaded. Even when they are free their seasons of receptivity are short and soon over; instinct pushes them on and instinct stops them. What would supplement this negative instinct in women when you have taken away their modesty? When the time comes that women are no longer concerned with men's well-being, men will no longer be good for anything at all.

The Supreme Being has deigned to do honor to the human race: in giving man unlimited desires, at the same time he provided the law that regulates them so he could be free and self-controlled; and while delivering him to these immoderate passions he added reason in order to govern them. In endowing woman with unlimited desires he added modesty in order to restrain them; moreover he has also given a reward for the correct use of their faculties, to wit, the taste one acquires for right conduct when one makes it the law of one's behavior. To my mind this is certainly as good as the instinct of the beasts.

Whether the woman shares the man's desires or not, whether or not she is willing to satisfy them, she always repulses him and defends herself, though not always with the same vigor and not, therefore, always with the same success. For the attacker to be victorious, the besieged must permit or direct the attack. How adroitly she can force the aggressor to use his strength. The freest and most delightful of all the acts does not admit any real violence; both nature and reason oppose it; nature, in that she has given the weaker party strength enough to resist if she chooses; reason, in that real violence is not only the most brutal of all acts but defeats its own ends, not only because man thus declares war against his companion and gives her the right to defend her person and her liberty even at the expense of the aggressor's life, but also because the woman alone is the judge of the situation and a child would have no father if any man might usurp a father's rights.

Thus the different constitution of the sexes leads us to a third conclusion, namely, that the strongest seems to be the master, but depends in fact on the weakest; this is not based upon a foolish custom of gallantry, nor upon the magnanimity of the protector but upon an inexorable law of nature. For nature, having endowed woman with more power to stimulate man's desire than he is able to satisfy, thus makes him dependent on woman's good will and compels him in turn to please her so that she may consent to yield to his superior strength. Is it weakness that yields to force or is it voluntary self-surrender? This uncertainty constitutes the chief delight of the man's victory, and the woman is usually cunning enough to leave him in doubt. In this respect women's minds exactly resemble their bodies; far from being ashamed of their weakness they revel in it. Their soft muscles offer no resistance; they pretend that they cannot lift the lightest loads; they would be ashamed to be strong. And why? This is not merely to appear delicate, they are too clever for that; they are providing themselves beforehand with excuses and with the right to be weak if need be. . . .

There is no parity between man and woman as to the importance of sex. The male is only a male at certain moments; the female all her life, or at least throughout her youth, is incessantly reminded of her sex and in order to carry out its functions she needs a corresponding constitution. She needs to be careful during pregnancy; she needs rest after childbirth; she needs a quiet and sedentary life while she nurses her children; she needs patience and gentleness in order to raise them; a zeal and affection that nothing can discourage. She serves as liaison between the children and their father. She alone wins the father's love for the children and gives him the confidence to call them his own. How much tenderness and care is required to maintain the entire family in unity! Finally all this should not be a matter of virtue but of inclination, without which the human species would soon be extinct.

The relative duties of the two sexes are not and cannot be equally rigid. When woman complains about the unjust inequalities placed on her by man she is wrong; this inequality is by no means a human institution or at least it is not the work of prejudice but of reason. She to whom nature has entrusted the care of the children must hold herself accountable for them. No doubt every breach of faith is wrong and every unfaithful husband who deprives his wife of the sole reward for the austere duties of her sex is an unjust and barbarous man. But the unfaithful wife is worse. She dissolves the family and breaks all the bonds of nature; by giving her husband children who are not his own she betrays both him and them and adds perfidy to faithlessness. . . .

Thus it is not enough that a wife should be faithful, but that she should be so judged by her husband, by her neighbors and by the world. She must be modest, devoted, reserved and she should exhibit to the world as to her own conscience testimony to her virtue. Finally, for a father to love his children he must esteem their mother. For these reasons the appearance of correct behavior must be among women's duties; it repays them with honor and reputation that are no less indispensable than chastity itself. From these principles derives, along with the moral difference of the sexes, a new motive for duty and propriety that prescribes to women in particular the most scrupulous attention to their conduct, manners, and behavior. To advance vague arguments about the equality of the sexes and the similarity of their duties is to lose oneself in vain declamation and does not respond to my argument.

Once it is demonstrated that man and woman are not, and should not be constituted the same, either in character or in temperament, it follows that they should not have the same education. In following the directions of nature they must act together but they should not do the same things; their duties have a common end, but the duties themselves are different and consequently also the tastes that direct them. After having tried to form the natural man, let us also see, in order not to leave our work incomplete, how the woman is to be formed who suits this man.

If you would always be well guided, follow the indications of nature. All that characterizes sexual difference ought to be respected or established by nature. You are always saying that women have faults that we men do not have. Your pride deceives you; they would be faults in you but they are virtues in them; things would go less well if they did not have them. Prevent these so-called faults from degenerating, but beware of destroying them.

Women, for their part, are always complaining that we raise them only to be vain and coquettish, that we keep them amused with trifles so that we may more easily remain their masters; they blame us for the faults we attribute to them. What stupidity! And since when is it men who concern themselves with the education of girls? Who is preventing the mothers from raising them as they please? There are no schools for girls—what a tragedy! Would God, there were none for boys! They would be raised more sensibly and more straightforwardly. Is anyone forcing your daughters to waste their time on foolish trifles? Are they forced against their will to spend half their lives on their appearance, following your example? Are you prevented from instructing them, or having them instructed according to your wishes? Is it our fault if they please us when they are beautiful, if their airs and graces seduce us, if the art they learn from you attracts and flatters us, if we like to see them tastefully attired, if we let them display at leisure the weapons with which they subjugate us? Well then, decide to raise them like men; the men will gladly agree; the more women want to resemble them, the less women will govern them, and then men will truly be the masters.

All the faculties common to the two sexes are not equally divided; but taken as a whole, they offset one another. Woman is worth more as a woman and less as a man; wherever she makes her rights valued, she has the advantage; wherever she wishes to usurp ours, she remains inferior to us. One can only respond to this general truth by citing exceptions in the usual manner of the gallant partisans of the fair sex.

To cultivate in women the qualities of the men and to neglect those that are their own is, then, obviously to work to their detriment. Shrewd women see this too clearly to be duped by it. In trying to usurp our advantages they do not abandon their own, but from this it comes to pass that, not being able to manage both properly on account of their incompatibility, they fall short of their own possibilities without attaining to ours, and thus lose half their value. Believe me, judicious mother, do not make a good man of your daughter as though to give the lie to nature, but make of her a good woman, and be assured that she will be worth more to herself and to us.

Does it follow that she ought to be raised in complete ignorance and restricted solely to the duties of the household? Shall man make a servant of his companion? Shall he deprive himself of the greatest charm of society? The better to reduce her to servitude, shall he prevent her from feeling anything or knowing anything? Shall he make of her a real automaton? Certainly not! Nature, who has endowed women with such an agreeable and acute mind, has not so ordered. On the contrary, she would have them think, and judge, and love, and know, and cultivate their minds as they do their faces: these are the weapons she gives them to supplement the strength they lack and to direct our own. They ought to learn many things, but only those which it becomes them to know.

Whether I consider the particular destination of the female sex or observe woman's inclinations, or take account of her duties, everything concurs equally to convince me of the form her education should take. Woman and man are made for each other, but their mutual dependence is not equal: men are dependent on women because of their desires; women are dependent on men because of both their desires and their needs. We men could subsist more easily without women than they could without us. In order for women to have what they need to fulfill their purpose in life, we must give it to them, we must want to give it to them, we must believe them worthy; they are dependent on our feelings, on the price we place on their merit, and on the opinion we have of their charms and of their virtues. By the very law of nature, women are at the mercy of men's judgments as much for themselves as for their children. It is not sufficient that they be thought estimable; they must also be esteemed. It is not sufficient that they be beautiful; they must please. It is not sufficient they be well behaved; they must be recognized as such. Their honor lies not only in their conduct but in their reputation. It is impossible for a woman who permits herself to be morally compromised ever to be considered virtuous. A man has no one but himself to consider, and so long as he does right he may defy public opinion; but when a woman does right, her task is only half finished, and what people think of her matters as much as what she really is. Hence it follows that the system of woman's education should in this respect be the opposite of ours: among men, opinion is the tomb of virtue; among women it is the throne.

19 Jean-Jacques Rousseau, *The Social Contract*

Like Locke (see Reading 15), but in a different way, Rousseau stressed the concept of a *contract* as the basis for a just political system. Although the period in which he wrote falls in the middle of the Enlightenment, his ideas had more in common with those of the Romantic period, which was soon to follow.

Like the Romantics, Rousseau rejected the idea that an increasingly complex civilization was making people better or happier. In his "Discourse on the Origin of Inequality" (1753), he portrays humankind as better off in simpler days before the artificiality and materialism of social institutions corrupted human nature. He consequently contributed to the notion of the "noble savage" (the person of very early society) as honest, faithful, and brave, in contrast with cynical, greedy, and apathetic modern humanity. Later, in *The Social Contract* (1762), he views the educated advances of modern times as potentially positive if people would only begin to control their political, social, and educational environments.

Whereas Locke and others of the early Enlightenment believed that individual freedom was the main goal to be pursued by improving political systems, the Romantics attached as much or more importance to demands made by groups (such as nations, classes, and religious denominations) on individuals. Rousseau thought that the sovereign people, united by a "general will," would rightfully dominate individuals, with their own "particular wills," in any issue involving societal interests.

Unlike Locke, who viewed representation as a guarantee that government would be responsive to the people, Rousseau was scornful of a people who delegated authority to representatives rather than constantly participating in legislative decision making themselves. In his own version of keeping government responsible, Rousseau drew a sharp line between the *state,* as the sovereign union of all citizens, and *government,* as the collective body of institutions and office holders responsible for implementing the state's laws.

Rousseau was passionately democratic, in the sense of desiring citizens to be constantly involved in political decision making. He was a bit weak in protecting individuals and minorities from the "general will" because he equated that will—at least when it was well informed—with public right-mindedness. He was convinced that when people were forced against their own particular wills to obey the general will, they were being led to do what they really would want to do if they understood the matter fully. Thus, for Rousseau there was no contradiction in at least occasionally forcing people to be free.

Although little attention was paid to the first edition of *The Social Contract,* by the 1780s Rousseau's work had become a well-known text. Once the French Revolution began in 1789, Rousseau's ideas became instrumental in shaping the politics and ideology of revolutionary France.

QUESTIONS TO CONSIDER

1. What does Rousseau mean when he states that in a good society (a) each member is able to obey only himself or herself and (b) any member who refuses to obey the general will should be forced to do so?
2. To what extent are private-property rights protected in the society that Rousseau describes?
3. Why does Rousseau think that using representatives is a sign of decadence in society?
4. In his discussion of civil religion, how could Rousseau insist that there is no contradiction between his recommendations that there be no religious intolerance—in fact, that religions with intolerant dogmas be banned—and that banishment and even the death penalty may be justified for offenses to the civil religion?
5. Edmund Burke (see Reading 29) once described Rousseau as "an insane Socrates." Why would Burke say this about Rousseau?
6. How would you compare Rousseau's approach to civil government with that of John Locke (see Reading 15)?

ORIGIN AND TERMS OF THE SOCIAL CONTRACT

Man was born free, but everywhere he is in chains. This man believes that he is the master of others, and still he is more of a slave than they are. How did that transformation take place? I don't know. How may the restraints on man become legitimate? I do believe I can answer that question. . . .

At a point in the state of nature when the obstacles to human preservation have become greater than each individual with his own strength can cope with . . . , an adequate combination of forces must be the result of men coming together. Still, each man's power and freedom are his main means of self-preservation. How is he to put them under the control of others without damaging himself . . . ?

This question might be rephrased: "How is a method of associating to be found which will defend and protect—using the power of all—the person and property of each member and still enable each member of the group to obey only himself and to remain as free as before?" This is the fundamental problem; the social contract offers a solution to it.

The very scope of the action dictates the terms of this contract and renders the least modification of them inadmissible, something making them null and void. Thus, although perhaps they have never been stated in so many words, they are the same everywhere and tacitly conceded and recognized everywhere. And so it follows that each individual immediately recovers his primitive rights and natural liberties whenever any violation of the social contract occurs and thereby loses the contractual freedom for which he renounced them.

From Jean-Jacques Rousseau, *Contrat social ou Principes du droit politique* (Paris: Garnier Frères, 1880), pp. 240–332, *passim*. Trans. Henry A. Myers.

The social contract's terms, when they are well understood, can be reduced to a single stipulation: the individual member alienates [gives] himself totally to the whole community together with all his rights. This is first because conditions will be the same for everyone when each individual gives himself totally, and secondly, because no one will be tempted to make that condition of shared equality worse for other men. . . .

Once this multitude is united this way into a body, an offense against one of its members is an offense against the body politic. It would be even less possible to injure the body without its members feeling it. Duty and interest thus equally require the two contracting parties to aid each other mutually. The individual people should be motivated from their double roles as individuals and members of the body, to combine all the advantages which mutual aid offers them. . . .

INDIVIDUAL WILLS AND THE GENERAL WILL

In reality, each individual may have one particular will as a man that is different from—or contrary to—the general will which he has as a citizen. His own particular interest may suggest other things to him than the common interest does. His separate, naturally independent existence may make him imagine that what he owes to the common cause is an incidental contribution—a contribution which will cost him more to give than their failure to receive it would harm the others. He may also regard the moral person of the State as an imaginary being since it is not a man, and wish to enjoy the rights of a citizen without performing the duties of a subject. This unjust attitude could cause the ruin of the body politic if it became widespread enough.

So that the social pact will not become meaningless words, it tacitly includes this commitment, which alone gives power to the others: Whoever refuses to obey the general will shall be forced to obey it by the whole body politic, which means nothing else but that he will be forced to be free. This condition is indeed the one which by dedicating each citizen to the fatherland gives him a guarantee against being personally dependent on other individuals. It is the condition which all political machinery depends on and which alone makes political undertakings legitimate. Without it, political actions become absurd, tyrannical, and subject to the most outrageous abuses.

Whatever benefits he had in the state of nature but lost in the civil state, a man gains more than enough new ones to make up for them. His capabilities are put to good use and developed; his ideas are enriched, his sentiments made more noble, and his soul elevated to the extent that—if the abuses in this new condition did not often degrade him to a condition lower than the one he left behind—he would have to keep blessing this happy moment which snatched him away from his previous state and which made an intelligent being and a man out of a stupid and very limited animal. . . .

PROPERTY RIGHTS

In dealing with its members, the State controls all their goods under the social contract, which serves as the basis for all rights within the State, but it controls them only through the right of first holder which individuals convey to the State. . . .

A strange aspect of this act of alienating [giving away] property rights to the state is that when the community takes on the goods of its members, it does not take these goods away from them. The community does nothing but assure its members of legitimate possession of goods, changing mere claims of possession into real rights and customary use into property. . . . Through an act of transfer having advantages for the public but far more for themselves they have, so to speak, really acquired everything they gave up. . . .

INDIVISIBLE, INALIENABLE SOVEREIGNTY

The first and most important conclusion from the principles we have established thus far is that the general will alone may direct the forces of the State to achieve the goal for which it was founded, the common good. . . . Sovereignty is indivisible . . . and is inalienable. . . . A will is general or it is not: it is that of the whole body of the people or only of one faction. In the first instance, putting the will into words and force is an act of sovereignty: the will becomes law. In the second instance, it is only a particular will or an administrative action; at the very most it is a decree.

Our political theorists, however, unable to divide the source of sovereignty, divide sovereignty into the ways it is applied. They divide it into force and will; into legislative power and executive power; into the power to tax, the judicial power, and the power to wage war; into internal administration and the power to negotiate with foreign countries. Now we see them running these powers together. Now they will proceed to separate them. They make the sovereign a being of fantasy, composed of separate pieces, which would be like putting a man together from several bodies, one having eyes, another arms, another feet—nothing more. Japanese magicians are said to cut up a child before the eyes of spectators, then throw the pieces into the air one after the other, and then cause the child to drop down reassembled and alive again. This is the sort of magic trick our political theorists perform. After having dismembered the social body with a trick worthy of a travelling show, they reassemble the pieces without anybody knowing how. . . .

If we follow up in the same way on the other divisions mentioned, we find that we are deceived every time we believe we see sovereignty divided. We find that the jurisdictions we have thought to be exercised as parts of sovereignty in reality are subordinate to the [one] sovereign power. They presuppose supreme wills, which they merely carry out in their jurisdictions. . . .

NEED FOR CITIZEN PARTICIPATION, NOT REPRESENTATION

It follows from the above that the general will is always in the right and inclines toward the public good, but it does not follow that the deliberations of the people always have the same rectitude. People always desire what is good, but they do not always see what is good. You can never corrupt the people, but you can often fool them, and that is the only time that the people appear to will something bad. . . .

If, assuming that the people were sufficiently informed as they made decisions and that the citizens did not communicate with each other, the general will would always be resolved from a great number of small differences, and the deliberation would always be good. But when blocs are formed, associations of parts at the expense of the whole, the will of each of these associations will be general as far as its members are concerned but particular as far as the State is concerned. Then we may say that there are no longer so many voters as there are men present but as many as there are associations. The differences will become less numerous and will yield less general results. Finally, when one of these associations becomes so strong that it dominates the others, you no longer have the sum of minor differences as a result but rather one single [unresolved] difference, with the result that there no longer is a general will, and the view that prevails is nothing but one particular view. . . .

But we must also consider the private persons who make up the public, apart from the public personified, who each have a life and liberty independent of it. It is very necessary for us to distinguish between the respective rights of the citizens and the sovereign and between the duties which men must fulfill in their role as subjects from the natural rights they should enjoy in their role as men.

It is agreed that everything which each individual gives up of his power, his goods, and his liberty under the social contract is only that part of all those things which is of use to the community, but it is also necessary to agree that the sovereign alone is the judge of what that useful part is.

All the obligations which a citizen owes to the State he must fulfill as soon as the sovereign asks for them, but the sovereign in turn cannot impose any obligation on subjects which is not of use to the community. In fact, the sovereign cannot even wish to do so, for nothing can take place without a cause according to the laws of reason, any more than according to the laws of nature [and the sovereign community will have no cause to require anything beyond what is of communal use]. . . .

Government . . . is wrongly confused with the sovereign, whose agent it is. What then is government? It is an intermediary body established between the subjects and the sovereign to keep them in touch with each other. It is charged with executing the laws and maintaining both civil and political liberty. . . . The only will dominating government . . . should be the general will or the law. The government's power is only the public power vested in it. As soon as [government] attempts to let any act come from itself completely independently, it starts to lose its intermediary role. If the time should ever come when the [government] has a particular will of its own stronger than that of the sovereign and makes use of the public power which is in its hands to carry out its own particular will—when there are thus two sovereigns, one in law and one in fact—at that moment the social union will disappear and the body politic will be dissolved.

Once the public interest has ceased to be the principal concern of citizens, once they prefer to serve the State with money rather than with their persons, the State will be approaching ruin. Is it necessary to march into combat? They will pay some troops and stay at home. Is it necessary to go to meetings? They will name some deputies and stay at home. Laziness and money finally leave them with soldiers to enslave their fatherland and representatives to sell it. . . .

Sovereignty cannot be represented. . . . Essentially, it consists of the general will, and a will is not represented: either we have it itself, or it is something else; there is no other possibility. The deputies of the people thus are not and cannot be its representatives. They are only the people's agents and are not able to come to final decisions at all. Any law that the people have not ratified in person is void, it is not a law at all.

SOVEREIGNTY AND CIVIL RELIGION

Now then, it is of importance to the State that each citizen should have a religion requiring his devotion to duty; however, the dogmas of that religion are of no interest to the State except as they relate to morality and to the duties which each believer is required to perform for others. For the rest of it, each person may have whatever opinions he pleases. . . .

It follows that it is up to the sovereign to establish the articles of a purely civil faith, not exactly as dogmas of religion but as sentiments of social commitment without which it would be impossible to be either a good citizen or a faithful subject. . . . While the State has no power to oblige anyone to believe these articles, it may banish anyone who does not believe them. This banishment is not for impiety but for lack of social commitment, that is, for being incapable of sincerely loving the laws and justice or of sacrificing his life to duty in time of need. As for the person who conducts himself as if he does not believe them after having publicly stated his belief in these same dogmas, he deserves the death penalty. He has lied in the presence of the laws.

The dogmas of civil religion should be simple, few in number, and stated in precise words without interpretations or commentaries. These are the required dogmas: the existence of a powerful, intelligent Divinity, who does good, has foreknowledge of all, and provides for all; the life to come; the happy rewards of the just; the punishment of the wicked; and the sanctity of the social contract and the laws. As for prohibited articles of faith, I limit myself to one: intolerance. Intolerance characterizes the religious persuasions we have excluded.

The Enlightenment in Russia

atherine II (r. 1762–1796), Empress of Russia, continued the Westernization begun by Peter the Great, encouraging the Russian nobility to adopt European customs, ideas, and fashions. Catherine the Great, as she became known, had been deeply interested in Enlightenment thought, corresponded with the most noted philosophers of the time, and wrote plays and essays advocating Enlightenment philosophy.

20 Catherine the Great, *The Instruction to the Commissioners for Composing a New Code of Laws*

In 1767, Catherine summoned more than five hundred deputies to Moscow to present to them *The Instruction to the Commissioners for Composing a New Code of Laws.* This document, had it been implemented, would have maintained Russia as an absolute monarchy but would have provided a uniform system of law for all free subjects of the empire, excluding serfs. The deputies spent four years working on a new legal code. Because of the war with Turkey and the Cossack and peasant revolt of 1773–1775, Catherine disbanded the commission before it completed its work. Moreover, the American and French Revolutions convinced Catherine of the danger of Enlightenment ideas, which she now attempted to suppress in Russia.

The tragic irony was that Russian nobles who had followed Catherine's directions and immersed themselves in Western enlightened thought were now ordered to cast off those ideas. Many educated noblemen, believing in their natural rights, resented the state's tyranny, as we see illustrated in the next reading. Thus began a process of opposition to the government that culminated in the Russian Revolution of 1917.

QUESTIONS TO CONSIDER

1. According to Catherine, "Russia is a European State." Is this true? What does she mean when she uses the word "equality"? Does she use "equality" in the same way it is used in other readings from the Enlightenment? (See Readings 17, 18, 26, and 27.)
2. What does this reading reveal about the Russian judicial system, the condition of the peasants, and Catherine's concerns about disease and public health?
3. Are there any comparisons between Catherine's reforms and those of Mikhail Gorbachev (see Reading 91)?

    6. Russia is a European State.
    7. This is clearly demonstrated by the following Observations: The Alterations which *Peter the Great* undertook in Russia succeeded with the greater Ease, because the Manners, which prevailed at that Time, and had been introduced amongst us by a Mixture of different Nations, and the Conquest of foreign Territories, were quite unsuitable to the Climate. *Peter the First*, by introducing the Manners and Customs of Europe among the European People in his Dominions, found at that Time such Means as even he himself was not sanguine enough to expect. . . .
    9. The Sovereign is absolute; for there is no other Authority but that which centers in his single Person, that can act with a Vigour proportionate to the Extent of such a vast Dominion.
    10. The Extent of the Dominion requires an absolute Power to be vested in that Person who rules over it. It is expedient so to be, that the quick Dispatch of Affairs, sent from distant Parts, might make ample Amends for the Delay occasioned by the great Distance of the Places.

From Catherine II, Empress of Russia. *The Grand Instructions to the Commissioners Appointed to Frame a New Code of Laws for the Russian Empire.* Trans. Michael Tatischeff (London: T. Jefferys, 1768), pp. 80–166.

11. Every other Form of Government whatsoever would not only have been prejudicial to Russia, but would even have proved its entire Ruin.

12. Another Reason is: That it is better to be subject to the Laws under one Master, than to be subservient to many.

13. What is the true End of Monarchy? Not to deprive People of their natural Liberty; but to correct their Actions, in order to attain the *supreme Good.*

14. The Form of Government, therefore, which best attains this End, and at the same Time sets less Bounds than others to natural Liberty, is that which coincides with the Views and Purposes of rational Creatures, and answers the End, upon which we ought to fix a steadfast Eye in the Regulations of civil Polity.

15. The Intention and the End of Monarchy, is the Glory of the Citizens, of the State, and of the Sovereign.

16. But, from this Glory, a Sense of Liberty arises in a People governed by a Monarch; which may produce in these States as much Energy in transacting the most important Affairs, and may contribute as much to the Happiness of the Subjects, as even Liberty itself. . . .

33. The Laws ought to be so framed, as to secure the Safety of every Citizen as much as possible.

34. The Equality of the Citizens consists in this; that they should all be subject to the same Laws.

35. This Equality requires Institutions so well adapted, as to prevent the Rich from oppressing those who are not so wealthy as themselves, and converting all the Charges and Employments entrusted to them as Magistrates only, to their own private Emolument. . . .

37. In a State or Assemblage of People that live together in a Community, where there are Laws, Liberty can only consist *in doing that which every One ought to do,* and *not to be constrained to do that which One ought not to do.*

38. A Man ought to form in his own Mind an exact and clear Idea of what Liberty is. *Liberty is the Right of doing whatsoever the Laws allow:* And if any one Citizen could do what the Laws forbid, there would be no more Liberty; because others would have an equal Power of doing the same.

39. The political Liberty of a Citizen is the Peace of Mind arising from the Consciousness, that every Individual enjoys his peculiar Safety; and in order that the People might attain this Liberty, the Laws ought to be so framed, that no one Citizen should stand in Fear of another; but that all of them should stand in Fear of the same Laws. . . .

193. The Torture of the Rack is a Cruelty established and made use of by many Nations, and is applied to the Party accused during the Course of his Trial, either to extort from him a Confession of his Guilt, or in order to clear up some Contradictions in which he had involved himself during his Examination, or to compel him to discover his Accomplices, or in order to discover other Crimes, of which, though he is not accused, yet he may *perhaps* be guilty.

194. (1) No Man ought to be looked upon as *guilty* before he has received his judicial Sentence; nor can the Laws deprive him of *their* Protection before it is proved that he has *forfeited all Right* to it. What Right therefore can Power give to any to inflict Punishment upon a Citizen at a Time when it is yet dubious whether he is innocent or guilty? Whether the Crime be known or unknown, it is not very difficult to gain a thorough Knowledge of the Affair by duly weigh-

ing all the Circumstances. If the Crime be known, the Criminal ought not to suffer any Punishment but what the Law ordains; consequently the Rack is quite unnecessary. If the Crime be not known, the Rack ought not to be applied to the Party accused; for this Reason, *That the Innocent ought not to be tortured;* and, in the Eye of the Law, every Person is innocent whose Crime is not yet *proved.* It is undoubtedly extremely necessary that no Crime, after it has been proved, should remain unpunished. The Party accused on the Rack, whilst in the Agonies of Torture, is not Master enough of himself to be able to declare the Truth. Can we give more Credit to a Man when he is light-headed in a Fever, than when he enjoys the free Use of his Reason in a State of Health? The Sensation of Pain may arise to such a Height that, after having subdued the whole Soul, it will leave her no longer the Liberty of producing any proper Act of the Will, except that of taking the shortest instantaneous Method, in the very twinkling of an Eye, as it were, of getting rid of her Torment. In such an Extremity, even an *innocent* Person will roar out that he is *guilty,* only to gain *some Respite* from his Tortures. Thus the very same Expedient, which is made use of to distinguish the *Innocent* from the *Guilty,* will take away the *whole Difference* between them; and the Judges will be as uncertain whether they have an *innocent* or a *guilty* Person before them, as they were before the Beginning of this *partial* Way of Examination. The Rack, therefore, is a sure Method of condemning an innocent person of a weakly Constitution, and of acquitting a *wicked Wretch,* who depends upon the Robustness of his Frame. . . .

196. (3) To make use of the Rack for discovering whether the Party accused has not committed *other Crimes,* besides *that* which he has been *convicted* of, is a certain Expedient to *screen every Crime from its proper* Punishment: For a Judge will always be discovering new Ones. Finally, this Method of Proceeding will be founded upon the following Way of reasoning: *Thou art guilty of one Crime, therefore, perhaps, thou hast committed an Hundred others: According to the Laws, thou wilt be tortured and tormented; not only because thou are guilty, but even because thou mayest be still more guilty.* . . .

220. A Punishment ought to be *immediate, analogous* to the *Nature* of the Crime, and *known* to the Public.

221. The *sooner* the Punishment succeeds to the Commission of a Crime, the *more useful* and *just* it will be. *Just;* because it will spare the Malefactor the torturing and useless Anguish of Heart about the *Uncertainty* of his Destiny. Consequently the Decision of an Affair, in a Court of Judicature, ought to be finished in as little Time as possible. *I have said before that Punishment immediately inflicted is most useful;* the Reason is because the smaller the Interval of Time is which passes between the Crime and the Punishment, the *more* the Crime will be esteemed as a *Motive* to the Punishment, and the Punishment as an *Effect* of the Crime. Punishment must be *certain* and *unavoidable.*

222. The most certain Curb upon Crimes is not the *Severity* of the Punishment, but the absolute Conviction in the People that Delinquents will be *inevitably* punished. . . .

264. *Of the Propagation of the human Species in a State.*

265. Russia is not only *greatly* deficient in the *number* of her Inhabitants; but at the same Time, extends her Dominion over *immense* Tracts of Land; which are neither peopled nor improved. And therefore, in a Country so circumstanced, *too much* Encouragement can never be given to the *Propagation* of the human Species.

266. The Peasants generally have twelve, fifteen, and even twenty Children by one Marriage; but it rarely happens that one *Fourth* of these ever attains to the *Age* of Maturity. There must therefore be some Fault, either in their Nouriture, in their Way of Living, or Method of Education, which occasions this *prodigious* Loss, and disappoints the *Hopes* of the Empire. How flourishing would the State of this Empire be if we could but ward off, or *prevent* this fatal Evil by proper Regulations!

267. You must add too to *this*, that two Hundred Years are now elapsed since a *Disease* unknown to our Ancestors was imported from America, and *hurried* on the Destruction of the human Race. This Disease spreads *wide its mournful* and *destructive* Effects in *many* of our Provinces. The utmost Care ought to be taken of the Health of the Citizens. It would be highly prudent, therefore, to stop the Progress of this Disease by the Laws.

21 A. N. Radishchev, *A Journey from St. Petersburg to Moscow*

Alexander Radishchev (1749–1801) was one of the young noblemen victimized by Catherine's change of mind. At the age of seventeen, he was sent by her, along with other promising young Russian noblemen, to study at the University of Leipzig. In 1790, he published *A Journey from St. Petersburg to Moscow,* in which he condemned serfdom and pleaded for the establishment of a society based on law, natural rights, and intellectual freedom. Outraged by the work, Catherine had Radishchev arrested, tried, and sentenced to death. She later commuted his sentence to exile in Eastern Siberia.

In the following selection, Radishchev uses a story told by a former judge to express his own condemnation of serfdom. He discusses the "right of first night": a lord's right to spend the first night with a virgin serf bride. He also expresses his enlightened views of civil and natural law.

QUESTIONS TO CONSIDER

1. What principles expressed in the *Instruction* were flagrantly violated, according to Radishchev?
2. What does Catherine's treatment of Radishchev indicate about her "enlightened" views?
3. Radishchev was a writer not a revolutionary, yet Catherine arrested him and exiled him to Siberia. What exactly was so threatening about Radishchev and this story that Catherine would do this?

"I have observed from a great many examples that the Russian people are very patient and long-suffering, but when they reach the end of their patience, nothing can restrain them from terrible cruelty. This is just what happened in the case of the assessor. The occasion for it was provided by the brutal and dissolute, or say rather the beastly act of one of his sons.

"In his village there was a good-looking peasant girl who was betrothed to a young peasant of the same village. The assessor's middle son took a liking to her and used every possible means to win her love for himself; but the girl remained true to the promise she had made to her sweetheart, a steadfastness rare but still possible among the peasantry. The wedding was to have taken place on a Sunday. In accordance with the custom current on many landed estates, the bridegroom's father went with his son to the manor house and brought two poods of bridal honey to his master. The young 'nobleman' decided to use this last moment for the gratification of his lust. He took both his brothers with him and, having summoned the bride to the courtyard by a strange boy, gagged her and carried her off to a shed. Unable to utter a sound, she struggled with all her strength against her young master's beastly purpose. At last, overcome by the three of them, she had to yield to force, and the vile monster was just about to carry out his long-cherished purpose when the bridegroom, returning from the manor, entered the yard, saw one of the young masters near the shed, and guessed their evil intention. He called his father to help him and flew faster than lightning to the shed. What a spectacle presented itself to him! Just as he got there they closed the doors of the shed, but the combined strength of the two brothers could not stem the onrush of the maddened bridegroom. Nearby he picked up a stake, ran into the shed, and hit the ravisher of his bride over the back with it. The others wanted to seize the bridegroom, but, seeing his father running with a stake to his assistance, they abandoned their prey, jumped out of the shed, and ran away. But the bridegroom caught up with one of them and broke his head with a blow of the stake. Bent on revenge for this injury, these evildoers went straight to their father and told him that they had met the bride while passing through the village and had jested with her, and that the bridegroom, seeing this, had straightway fallen upon them and beaten them, with the help of his father. As proof they showed him the one brother's wounded head. Infuriated by the wounding of his son, the father burst into a rage. He ordered the three evildoers—as he called the bridegroom, the bride, and the bridegroom's father—to be brought before him without delay. When they appeared before him, the first question he asked them was who had broken his son's head. The bridegroom did not deny that he had done it, and told him everything that had happened. 'How did you dare,' said the old assessor, 'to raise your hand against your master? Even if he had spent the night with your bride on the eve of your wedding, you should have been grateful to him. You shall not marry her. She shall be attached to my house, and you shall all be punished.' After this judgment, he turned the bridegroom over to his sons, and ordered them to flog him mercilessly with the cat-o'-nine-tails. He stood the scourging manfully and watched with indomitable fortitude as they began to subject his father to the same torture. But he could not endure it when he saw his master's children starting to take his bride into the house. The punishment was taking place in the yard. In an instant he snatched her from the hands of her abductors, and the two lovers, now free, ran away from the yard. Seeing this, the master's sons stopped beating the old man and started to pursue them. Seeing that they were catching up with him, the bridegroom snatched a rail out of the fence and prepared to defend himself. Meanwhile the noise attracted other peasants to

Reprinted by permission of the publisher from Aleksandr Nikolaevich Radishchev, *A Journey from St. Petersburg to Moscow*, trans. Leo Weiner, ed. Roderick Page Thaler (Cambridge, MA: Harvard University Press, 1958), pp. 96–99, 102–3. Copyright © 1958 by the President and Fellows of Harvard College.

the manor yard. They sympathized with the young peasant and, infuriated against their masters, they gathered around their fellow to defend him. Seeing all this, the assessor himself ran up, began to curse them, and struck the first man he met so violently with his cane that he fell senseless to the ground. This was the signal for a general attack. They surrounded their four masters and, in short, beat them to death on the spot. They hated them so much that not one wanted to miss the chance to take part in murdering them, as they themselves later confessed. Just at this time the chief of the country police of that district happened to come by with a detachment of soldiers. He was an eyewitness of part of what happened. He had the guilty persons—that is, half the village—put under guard, and instituted an investigation which ultimately reached the criminal court. The case was clearly established, and the guilty persons confessed everything, pleading in their defense only the barbarous acts of their masters, of which the whole province had been cognizant. In the course of my official duty it was incumbent upon me to pass the final sentence of death upon the guilty persons and to commute it to confiscation of property and lifelong penal servitude.

"Upon reviewing the case, I found no sufficient or convincing reason to condemn the offenders. The peasants who had killed their master were guilty of murder. But was it not forced upon them? Was not the murdered assessor himself the cause of it? If in arithmetic a third number follows invariably from two given ones, the consequence was equally inevitable in this case. The innocence of the defendants was, at least for me, a mathematical certainty. If I am going on my way and an evildoer falls upon me and raises a dagger over my head to strike me down, am I to be considered a murderer if I forestall him in his evil deed and strike him down lifeless at my feet? If a Mohock today, having won the universal contempt he deserves, wants to revenge himself for it on me, and, meeting me in a solitary place, attacks me with drawn sword to deprive me of life or at least to wound me, am I guilty if I draw by sword in self-defense and deliver society from a member who disturbs its peace? Can an act be considered prejudicial to the inviolable human rights of a fellow being if I do it to save myself, if it prevents my destruction, if without it my well-being would be forever undone? . . .

"Every man is born into the world equal to all others. All have the same bodily parts, all have reason and will. Consequently, apart from his relation to society, man is a being that depends on no one in his actions. But he puts limits to his own freedom of action, he agrees not to follow only his own will in everything, he subjects himself to the commands of his equals; in a word, he becomes a citizen. For what reason does he control his passions? Why does he set up a governing authority over himself? Why, though free to seek fulfillment of his will, does he confine himself within the bounds of obedience? For his own advantage, reason will say; for his own advantage, inner feeling will say; for his own advantage, wise legislation will say. Consequently, wherever being a citizen is not to his advantage, he is not a citizen. Consequently, whoever seeks to rob him of the advantages of citizenship is his enemy. Against his enemy he seeks protection and satisfaction in the law. If the law is unable or unwilling to protect him, or if its power cannot furnish him immediate aid in the face of clear and present danger, then the citizen has recourse to the natural law of self-defense, self-preservation, and well-being. For the citizen, in becoming a citizen, does not cease to be a man, whose first obligation, arising from his very nature, is his own preservation, defense, and welfare. By his bestial cruelty the assessor who was murdered by the peasants had violated their rights as citizens. At the moment when he abetted the violence of his sons, when he added insult to the heartfelt injury of the bridal pair, when he, seeing their opposition to his devilish tyranny, moved to punish them, then the law that protects a citizen fell into abeyance and its efficacy disappeared; then the law of nature was reborn, and the power of the wronged citizen, which the positive law cannot take from him when he has been wronged, comes into operation, and the peasants who killed the beastly assessor are not guilty before the law. On rational grounds my heart finds them not guilty, and the death of the assessor, although violent, is just. Let no one presume to seek in reasons of state or in the maintenance of public peace grounds for condemning the murderers of the assessor, who expired in the midst of his wickedness. No matter in what estate heaven may have decreed a citizen's birth, he is and will always remain a man; and so long as he is a man, the law of nature, as an abundant wellspring of goodness, will never run dry in him, and whosoever dares wound him in his natural and inviolable right is a criminal. Woe to him, if the civil law does not punish him. He will be marked as a pariah by his fellow citizens, and may whosoever has sufficient power exact vengeance against him for his evildoing."

22 Catherine the Great, "Instructions to Captain Joseph Billings"

Russia's interest in the North Pacific increased during the eighteenth century. In 1725, just before his death, Peter the Great had commissioned a Danish soldier, Vitus Bering, to explore the Kamchatka peninsula and to "discover where it is joined to America, and go as far as some town belonging to a European power; if you encounter some European ship, ascertain from it what is the name of the nearest coast, and write it down and go ashore personally and obtain firsthand information, locate it on a map and return here."[1] Peter's successors followed these directions explicitly and continued to press even more aggressively Russia's exploration of the North Pacific to the lands much farther to the east of the Kamchatka peninsula, the Kurile Islands, and Japan. In the following document, we get a glimpse of how Russia in the late eighteenth century attempted to gain a foothold in Alaska and North America. Catherine the Great instructs Captain Joseph Billings how to secure Russian control over Alaska and the North American coast.

QUESTIONS TO CONSIDER

1. Given the political realities of the fledgling American Republic and the British, French, and Spanish Empires in 1785, did Catherine's instructions for colonization have any chance of success?
2. What are some of the reasons that might explain why the Russian colonial imprint in North America remained so slight?

---

[1] "Instructions of Peter the Great to Vitus Bering, January 28, 1725," in *Russian Penetration of the North Pacific Ocean, 1700–1797: A Documentary Record,* ed. and trans., Basil Dmytryshyn, E.A.P. Crownhart-Vaughan, and Thomas Vaughan (Portland: Oregon Historical Society Press, 1988), p. 69.

When you bring newly discovered and independent lands and peoples under Russian suzerainty you are to observe the following instructions. Since such people have probably never been abused by any Europeans, your first responsibility is to see to it that they have a favorable opinion of the Russians. When you discover such a coast or island or promontory you are to send one or two baidaras,[1] with armed men, under the command of an experienced helmsman. Send interpreters and small gifts with them. Have them look for a harbor or bay where vessels may safely be anchored, then take soundings and proceed into these. However, if no harbor is to be found, then send baidaras or boats with part of your men ashore to see if there are inhabitants, forests, animals, etc. They are not all to put ashore together. A guard is to remain with the boats, and those who go ashore are to stay together, not to spread out.

If there are inhabitants, your men are to communicate with them through interpreters, but such persons are never to be sent ashore alone. They are always to be accompanied by men who are armed either secretly or openly. It has happened in the past that savages have killed interpreters or taken them prisoner, which is a great loss to the explorers.

The interpreter is to speak to them of your friendly intentions. To prove this, he is to allow them to choose presents, and invite them in a friendly manner to accept these gifts. He is to invite the chieftains on board the ships. To flatter these chieftains, they may be given medals to hang around their necks; you have been provided such medals for this purpose. Tell the savages that these medals are tokens of eternal friendship of the Russians. Ask them for tokens in return, and accept whatever they choose to give you. Persuade them to tell all their fellow inhabitants that the Russians wish to be their friends. Learn their [tribal] name and its origin or meaning. Discover whether their population is large, especially in men. Ask about their religion and their idols, and be careful that none of your men go near these idols or destroy them. Find out about their food and their crafts, where and how they travel, the names of the places they frequent and what their compass locations are, and whether these places are islands or on the mainland. When they point directions with their hands, observe secretly but accurately the compass directions and note in your journal how far distant these places are. If you do not understand their terms of measurement, ask how many days it takes to travel to these places, so that if you find it necessary to travel there by land or by sea, you will know how to set your course.

Ask if there are large bays on any of the islands or on the coast, and whether large ships with one or two or three masts and sails go there, or go to their own islands or those nearby, or to the coasts. If you see that they have any article of European or Asian workmanship, ask them how they came by it. Make all necessary observations so you can describe the place, and ask their permission to come ashore often. Learn how they greet one another, and greet them in that way when you meet.

---

[1]Baidara is a large open boat made of wooden framework covered with sea-mammal hides that could hold forty persons. Used by Aleutian Island natives, it was quickly adopted by Russian explorers.

From "Instructions from Catherine II and the Admiralty College to Captain Lieutenant Joseph Billings for His Expedition [1785–1794] to Northern Russia and the North Pacific Ocean," in *Russian Penetration of the North Pacific Ocean 1700–1797: A Documentary Record*, ed. and trans. Basil Dmytryshyn, E.A.P. Crownhart-Vaughan, and Thomas Vaughan (Portland: Oregon Historical Society Press, 1988), pp. 281–83, 285–86. Reprinted with the permission of the Oregon Historical Society.

When they come to like you because of your generosity and friendship, if you are certain they are not subject to any European power, tell them you wish to find other friends like them. Ask them to let you erect some mark on a high place on shore, as your friends in other places do, so you will be able to find again this place where the friends of the Russians live. This should be done in accordance with your own customary ceremonies. When they give permission for this, order that one of the posts you have had prepared at Okhotsk be marked with the arms of Russia and that letters be cut into it indicating the date of discovery, a brief account of the native people and of their voluntary submission to Russian suzerainty. State that this has been done by your efforts during the glorious reign of Catherine II, the Great.

If the islands and lands you discover have no name, you are authorized to name them. When the post is ready, let the inhabitants know that you are coming ashore to establish your mark, and do this with proper ceremony and caution. Afterward give the inhabitants small things of which they are fond. Give medals to the chieftains so they can hang them about their necks. Finally, persuade the inhabitants that if they elect to continue being friends of the Russians they are never to permit their own people or any others to remove or efface this marker. They are to preserve it whole, as well as the medals about their necks.

Such ceremonial proceedings are always effective with savages, and conquests made by these means are always the most enduring.

China's Sinocentric World

Imperial China's conduct of foreign relations was somewhat analogous to the way the two superpowers of the post–World War II era, the United States and the Soviet Union, dealt with their small allies. China was the Middle Kingdom in the center, and all the countries surrounding it were expected to behave as satellites in the Chinese orbit. By virtue of its imposing territorial expanse, military power, economic affluence, and brilliant old civilization, China developed an ethnocentric notion that it was the center of human civilization, in comparison to which it assumed all other non-Chinese peoples were ipso facto "barbarians," irresistibly attracted and willing to pay homage to the emperor of China, the "Son of Heaven." Such a Sinocentric world view of Imperial China was reflected in the tribute system that had been institutionalized since the early Ming dynasty (1368–1643) and lasted until the middle of the nineteenth century. Through this system, the reciprocal relationships of compassionate benevolence on the part of the Son of Heaven and humble submission of the junior members of the Sinitic world, such as Korea, Liuqiu (Liu-ch'iu or Ryukyu), Annam (Vietnam), Siam, Burma, Laos, and a host of other peripheral states in Southeast and Central Asia, were regulated and reassured. The Son of Heaven recognized the legitimacy of the rulers of the tributary states by sending imperial envoys to officiate at their investitures and by conferring on them the imperial patent of appointment. The imperial government also sent military and economic aid to the tributary states in times of foreign invasion or natural disasters. The tributary states sent periodic tribute missions to the imperial capital to renew their submission and their acknowledgment of the superiority of the celestial empire. Besides presenting the tribute and local products to the Son of Heaven, they performed the full ceremony of kowtow—three kneelings and nine knockings of the head on the ground—in the audience hall. Kowtow was a symbolic gesture of submission to the Chinese emperor, and this requirement annoyed the European envoys in the nineteenth century because they deemed it to be humiliating.

Trade was another important aspect of the tribute system, since a large number of traders accompanied the tributary mission and were allowed to engage in commercial transactions by the imperial government.

23 Ceremonial for Visitors: Court Tribute

The following excerpt shows the rules and protocols governing the tributary missions developed by the Ch'ing [Qing] government in 1764.

QUESTIONS TO CONSIDER

1. How analogous is China's tribute system to the Communist and Western alliance systems of post–World War II? What are the similarities and differences?
2. How do you relate this reading with Emperor Chien-lung's [Qianlong] letter to King George III of England (see Reading 25)?

> 1. "*As to the countries of the barbarians on all sides that send tribute to Court,* on the east is Korea; on the southeast, Liu-ch'iu and Sulu; on the south, Annam and Siam; on the southwest, Western Ocean, Burma, and Laos. (For the barbarian tribes of

From the 1764 Ch'ien-lung edition of the *Statutes* (Ch'ien-lung hui-tien 56.1–8b), in John K. Fairbank and Ssù-yu Teng, *Ch'ing Administration: Three Studies* (Cambridge: Harvard University Press, 1960), pp. 170–73. Copyright © 1960 by the Harvard-Yenching Institute. These rules and regulations set the standard for the last century and a half of the Qing dynasty (1644–1911).

the northwest, see under Court of Colonial Affairs.) All send officers as envoys to come to Court and present tributary memorials and pay tribute.

2. *"As to the imperial appointment of kings of (tributary) countries,* whenever the countries which send tribute to Court have a succession to the throne, they first send an envoy to request an imperial mandate at the Court. In the cases of Korea, Annam, and Liu-ch'iu, by imperial command the principal envoy and secondary envoy(s) receive the imperial patent (of appointment) and go (to their country) to confer it. As for the other countries, the patent (of appointment) is bestowed upon the envoy who has come (from his country) to take it back, whereupon an envoy is sent (from that country) to pay tribute and offer thanks for the imperial favor.

3. *"As to the king of Korea,* (the patent) is bestowed upon his wife the same as upon the king. When the son grows up, then he requests that it be bestowed upon him as the heir apparent. In all cases officials of the third rank or higher act as principal and secondary envoys. Their clothing and appearance, and ceremonial and retinue in each case are according to rank. In the cases of Annam and Liu-ch'iu, officials of the Hanlin Academy, the Censorate, or the Board of Ceremonies, of the fifth rank or below, act as principal and secondary envoys; (the Emperor) specially confers upon them 'unicorn' clothing of the first rank, in order to lend weight to their journey. In ceremonial and retinue they are all regarded as being of the first rank. When the envoys return, they hand back their clothing to the office in charge of it. . . .

6. *"As to tribute objects,* in each case they should send the products of the soil of the country. Things that are not locally produced are not to be presented. Korea, Annam, Liu-ch'iu, Burma, Sulu, and Laos all have as tribute their customary objects. Western Ocean and Siam do not have a customary tribute. . . .

7. *"As to the retainers* (who accompany an envoy), in the case of the Korean tribute envoy there are one attendant secretary, three chief interpreters, 24 tribute guards, 30 minor retainers who receive rewards, and a variable number of minor retainers who do not receive rewards. For Liu-ch'iu, Western Ocean, Siam, and Sulu, the tribute vessels are not to exceed three, with no more than 100 men per vessel; those going to the capital are not to exceed 20. When Annam, Burma, and Laos send tribute, the men are not to exceed 100, and those going to the capital are not to exceed 20. Those that do not go to the capital are to be retained at the frontier. The frontier officials give them a stipend from the government granary, until the envoy returns to the frontier, when he takes them back to their country.

[8. Presentation of tributary memorials, after arrival at Peking.]

9. *"As to the Court ceremony,* when a tribute envoy arrives at the capital at the time of a Great Audience or of an Ordinary Audience, His Majesty the Emperor goes to the T'ai Ho [Taihe] palace and, after the princes, dukes, and officials have audience and present their congratulations, the ushers lead in the tributary envoys and their attendant officers, each of them wearing his country's court dress. They stand in the palace courtyard on the west in the last place. When they hear (the command of) the ceremonial ushers they perform the ceremony of three kneelings and nine knockings of the head [the full kowtow]. They are graciously allowed to sit. Tea is imperially bestowed upon them. All this is according to etiquette (for details see under the Department of Ceremonies). If (a tribute envoy) does not come at the time of an Audience, he presents a memorial through the Board (of Ceremonies) asking for an imperial summons to Court. His Majesty the Emperor goes to a side hall of the palace . . . etc.

[10–13. There follow details concerning further ceremonies, with performances of the kowtow; banquets; and imperial escorts, including those provided for westerners because of their services as imperial astronomers.]

14. "*As to trade*,—when the tribute envoys of the various countries enter the frontier, the goods brought along in their boats or carts may be exchanged in trade with merchants of the interior (China); either they may be sold at the merchants' hongs in the frontier province or they may be brought to the capital and marketed at the lodging house (i.e., the Residence for Tributary Envoys). At the customs stations (lit. passes and fords) which they pass en route, they are all exempted from duty. As to barbarian merchants who themselves bring their goods into the country for trade,—for Korea on the border of Shêng-ching [Shengjing] [Fengtien province], and at Chung-chiang [Zhongjang] [northeast of Chengtu, Szechwan], there are spring and autumn markets, two a year; at Hui-ning [southeast of Lanchow, Kansu], one market a year; at Ch'ing-yüan [Qingyuan] [in Chihli, now Chao-hsien], one market every other year,—(each) with two Interpreters of the Board of Ceremonies, one Ninguta (Kirin) clerk, and one Lieutenant to superintend it. After twenty days the market is closed. For the countries beyond the seas, (the market) is at the provincial capital of Kwangtung [Guangdong]. Every summer they take advantage of the tide and come to the provincial capital (Canton). When winter comes they wait for a wind and return to their countries. All pay duties to the (local) officers in charge, the same as the merchants of the interior (China).

15. "*As to the prohibitions*,—when a foreign country has something to state or to request, it should specially depute an officer to bring a document to the Board (of Ceremonies), or in the provinces it may be memorialized on behalf (of the country) by the Governor-General and Governor concerned. Direct communication to the Court is forbidden. For a tribute envoy's entrance of the frontier and the tribute route which he follows, in each case there are fixed places. Not to follow the regular route, or to go over into other provinces, is forbidden. It is forbidden secretly (i.e., without permission) to buy official costumes which violate the regulations, or books of history, weapons, copper, iron, oil, hemp, or combustible saltpetre; or to take people of the interior or rice and grain out of the frontiers. There are boundaries separating the rivers and seas; to catch fish beyond the boundaries is forbidden. The land frontiers are places of defensive entrenchments where Chinese and foreign soldiers or civilians have established military colonies or signal-fire mounds, or cultivated rice-fields and set up huts; to abscond and take shelter (on either side) is forbidden. It is forbidden for civil or military officials on the frontier to communicate in writing with foreign countries not on public business. When commissioned to go abroad, to receive too many gifts, or when welcomed in coming and going, privately to demand the products of the locality (i.e., as "squeeze") is forbidden. Offenses against the prohibitions will be considered according to law.

[16. Charity and sympathy to be shown regarding foreign rulers' deaths, calamities, etc.]

17. "*As to the rescue* (of distressed mariners),—when ships of foreign merchants are tossed by the wind into the inner waters (of China), the local authorities should rescue them, report in a memorial the names and number of distressed barbarians, move the public treasury to give them clothing and food, take charge of the boat

and oars, and wait for a wind to send them back. If a Chinese merchant vessel is blown by the wind into the outer ocean, the country there can rescue it and give it aid, put a boat in order and send them (the merchants) back, or it may bring them along on a tribute vessel so as to return them. In all such cases an imperial patent is to be issued, praising the king of the country concerned; imperial rewards are to be given to the officers (of the tributary country) in different degrees."

24 Taisuke Mitamura, The Palace Eunuchs of Imperial China

One of the most bizarre practices in history was the emasculation of young males who served as attendants to kings, queens, sultans, and maharajas or as members of the Vatican choirs. Often this act of mutilation of the genitals was voluntary and was performed for various reasons, both spiritual and mundane. Although the exact origins for the existence of eunuchs cannot be determined, they are known to have existed for many centuries before the common era, in both the East and the West, and persisted, in some cases, down to the early twentieth century. Some suggest that the Assyrian queen Semiramis, who founded New Babylonia, was the first to institute the system. Herodotus wrote accounts of the selling and buying of eunuchs by the Greeks at Ephesus and Sardis. The Bible also makes many references to the activities of eunuchs. Some early Christians are said to have emasculated themselves as an act of devotion to God.

Perhaps no other country had as enduring a eunuch system as Imperial China. As an integral part of the imperial court, the system persisted for at least three thousand years, until the end of the Qing (Ch'ing) dynasty in 1912. Thousands of eunuchs performed a wide variety of duties, from the menial, such as gardening, water carrying, and sedan-chair bearing, to stage acting, taking charge of the imperial bed chambers, and acting as informal counselors and tutors to the emperor and princes. The following excerpts include a brief account of the duties of the eunuchs in charge of the imperial bed chambers.

QUESTIONS TO CONSIDER

1. Compare and contrast the eunuch system of Imperial China with that of another civilization.
2. What were the reasons for a person to become a eunuch?

Eunuchs participated in the nocturnal activities of the ruler. In the Ming dynasty, the office charged with the duty of looking after the Imperial bedchamber was called Ching Shih Fang, and the eunuch in charge was called the Ching Shih Fang T'ai Chien, or Chief of the Imperial Bedchamber. This office dealt exclusively with the nocturnal relations between the monarch and his consort and concubines.

When the Emperor had relations with the Empress, the date was recorded so that it would serve as proof in the case of conception. The procedure differed somewhat in the case of concubines. *Lu t'ou p'ai*, or nameplates painted green at the top, were prepared for the Emperor's favorite concubines. At dinner the eunuch in charge of the Imperial bedchamber would place as many as a score of these nameplates on a silver tray and take them to the Emperor with his meal. As soon as the Emperor finished eating, the eunuch would kneel before him, holding the silver tray high above his head, and await instructions. If the Emperor was not in the mood for love, he would dismiss the eunuch with a curt "Go." If he was interested he would pick up one of the nameplates and turn it over, face down. The eunuch would then hand the nameplate to the T'ai Chien in charge of carrying the concubines to his Majesty's bedchamber. When the time came, the T'ai Chien would strip the chosen concubine, wrap her in a feather garment, and carry her on his back to the Imperial bedchamber.

The eunuch in charge of the Imperial bedchamber and the T'ai Chien would then wait in front of the bedchamber a given length of time, at the end of which the T'ai Chien would shout, "Time is up" (*Shih shih Hou Le*). If the Emperor didn't reply, the call was repeated, and if he still did not reply after the words were repeated a third time, the eunuch would enter the bedchamber and carry off the concubine. He would only ask the Emperor if he wanted the concubine to bear his child. If the Emperor answered in the negative, the T'ai Chien would take proper contraceptive measures; if the Emperor answered in the affirmative, he would record the date so that it would later serve as proof. This was no small matter since a concubine's future position depended on whether or not she bore a child for the Emperor.

Exactly when this system was made official in the Ming dynasty is not known, but it was adopted in the Ching dynasty because, it is said, Emperor Shih Tsu believed its enforcement would keep his descendants from indulging excessively in sex. Also, the system was undoubtedly enforced in order to ensure succession in the autocratic system. Imperial life was more flexible at the Yuan Ming Yuan Detached Palace, where Emperor Ch'ien Lung was said to have stepped out frequently for a change of air.

It should be noted that, in the seraglio, the words of the Empress carried much weight. The Emperor, for instance, could not visit the chambers of his concubines whenever he felt the urge to do so. In such cases, the concubine of the Emperor's choice would first receive from the Empress a written notice to the effect that his Majesty would pay her a visit. Without the Empress' seal, the notice would not be valid, and without the notice the Emperor would be turned back.

The eunuchs were also in charge of the Emperor's sex education. In the Ming dynasty, several Buddhist statues were enshrined in the Inner Court. Of esoteric Lamaist origin, these strange images were in the form of men and women and beasts locked in carnal ecstasy. Buddhist, Taoist, and Lamaist halls, where eunuch Taoists and priests served, were also set up in the Imperial court. In preparation for the nuptials of the Emperor or Imperial princes, the eunuchs would have them worship these images and then, by intimately caressing the images, educate them in sexual love.

From Taisuke Mitamura, *Chinese Eunuchs, The Structure of Intimate Politics* (Rutland, VT: Charles E. Tuttle Co., 1970), pp. 111–15. Copyright © 1996, Chuo Koronsha, Tokyo, Japan.

Such intimate relations between the eunuchs and the rulers were established early in childhood. As soon as he was old enough to leave his nurse's side, an Imperial prince would be instructed in speech, table manners, deportment, etiquette, and knowledge by the eunuchs. In other words, he literally grew up with them. Emperor Wu Tsung of the Ming dynasty, who was profligate in his ways, always listened to his T'ai Chien, Wang Wei, although he never lent an ear to what his retainers had to say, because he had grown up with the eunuch, sharing the same desk and studying the same books. The Emperor called him *Pan Pan*, or friend.

25 Emperor Ch'ien-lung [Qianlong], Letter to King George III

London decided to send an official mission to Beijing on the occasion of the eighty-third birthday of Emperor Ch'ien-lung (r. 1735–1795), hoping to alleviate difficulties experienced by British merchants in Canton as a result of China's restrictive and cumbersome rules and regulations for foreign merchants and Chinese official irregularities.

The mission, headed by Lord Macartney, Baron of Lissanoure and a cousin of the Crown, was courteously received by the Chinese government because it was understood to be a tributary mission delivering felicitations from George III (r. 1760–1820). However, Macartney's mission failed to accomplish its real objectives, even the opening of discussions concerning trade extension and envoy exchange. The Ch'ing court considered Macartney's requests presumptuous and completely out of order. As far as the Ch'ing court was concerned, Macartney's mission had been completed after presenting gifts and offering felicitations to the emperor on his birthday. In the following letter to King George III, written in 1793, the ostentatious Emperor Ch'ien-lung flatly rejected all the requests presented by Macartney.

QUESTIONS TO CONSIDER

1. What reasons did Emperor Ch'ien-lung cite in his letter for outright rejection of the British demand for a diplomatic and trade relationship?
2. Compare and contrast the Western treaty system with China's tributary system.

You, O King, live beyond the confines of many seas, nevertheless, impelled by your humble desire to partake of the benefits of our civilisation, you have dispatched a mission respectfully bearing your memorial. Your Envoy has crossed the seas and paid his

From E. Backhouse and J.O.P. Bland, *Annals and Memoirs of the Court of Peking* (Boston: Houghton Mifflin, 1914), pp. 322–31, *passim.*

respects at my Court on the anniversary of my birthday. To show your devotion, you have also sent offerings of your country's produce.

I have perused your memorial: the earnest terms in which it is couched reveal a respectful humility on your part, which is highly praiseworthy. In consideration of the fact that your Ambassador and his deputy have come a long way with your memorial and tribute, I have shown them high favour and have allowed them to be introduced into my presence. To manifest my indulgence, I have entertained them at a banquet and made them numerous gifts. I have also caused presents to be forwarded to the Naval Commander and six hundred of his officers and men, although they did not come to Peking, so that they too may share in my all-embracing kindness.

As to your entreaty to send one of your nationals to be accredited to my Celestial Court and to be in control of your country's trade with China, this request is contrary to all usage of my dynasty and cannot possibly be entertained. It is true that Europeans, in the service of the dynasty, have been permitted to live at Peking, but they are compelled to adopt Chinese dress, they are strictly confined to their own precincts and are never permitted to return home. You are presumably familiar with our dynastic regulations. Your proposed Envoy to my Court could not be placed in a position similar to that of European officials in Peking who are forbidden to leave China, nor could he, on the other hand, be allowed liberty of movement and the privilege of corresponding with his own country; so that you would gain nothing by his residence in our midst.

Moreover, our Celestial dynasty possesses vast territories, and tribute missions from the dependencies are provided for by the Department for Tributary States, which ministers to their wants and exercises strict control over their movements. It would be quite impossible to leave them to their own devices. Supposing that your Envoy should come to our Court, his language and national dress differ from that of our people, and there would be no place in which to bestow him. It may be suggested that he might imitate the Europeans permanently resident in Peking and adopt the dress and customs of China, but, it has never been our dynasty's wish to force people to do things unseemly and inconvenient. Besides, supposing I sent an Ambassador to reside in your country, how could you possibly make for him the requisite arrangements? Europe consists of many other nations besides your own: if each and all demanded to be represented at our Court, how could we possibly consent? The thing is utterly impracticable. How can our dynasty alter its whole procedure and system of etiquette, established for more than a century, in order to meet your individual views? If it be said that your object is to exercise control over your country's trade, your nationals have had full liberty to trade at Canton for many a year, and have received the greatest consideration at our hands. Missions have been sent by Portugal and Italy, preferring similar requests. The Throne appreciated their sincerity and loaded them with favours, besides authorising measures to facilitate their trade with China. You are no doubt aware that, when my Canton merchant, Wu Chao-ping [Wu Zhaoping], was in debt to the foreign ships, I made the Viceroy advance the monies due, out of the provincial treasury, and ordered him to punish the culprit severely. Why then should foreign nations advance this utterly unreasonable request to be represented at my Court? Peking is nearly two thousand miles from Canton, and at such a distance what possible control could any British representative exercise?

If you assert that your reverence for Our Celestial dynasty fills you with a desire to acquire our civilisation, our ceremonies and code of laws differ so completely from your own that, even if your Envoy were able to acquire the rudiments of our civilisation, you could not possibly transplant our manners and customs to your alien soil. Therefore, however adept the Envoy might become, nothing would be gained thereby.

Swaying the wide world, I have but one aim in view, namely, to maintain a perfect governance and to fulfill the duties of the State: strange and costly objects do not interest me. If I have commanded that the tribute offerings sent by you, O King, are to be accepted, this was solely in consideration for the spirit which prompted you to dispatch them from afar. Our dynasty's majestic virtue has penetrated unto every country under Heaven, and Kings of all nations have offered their costly tribute by land and sea. As your Ambassador can see for himself, we possess all things. I set no value on objects strange or ingenious, and have no use for your country's manufactures. This then is my answer to your request to appoint a representative at my Court, a request contrary to our dynastic usage, which would only result in inconvenience to yourself. I have expounded my wishes in detail and have commanded your tribute Envoys to leave in peace on their homeward journey. It behoves you, O King, to respect my sentiments and to display even greater devotion and loyalty in future, so that, by perpetual submission to our Throne, you may secure peace and prosperity for your country hereafter. Besides making gifts (of which I enclose an inventory) to each member of your Mission, I confer upon you, O King, valuable presents in excess of the number usually bestowed on such occasions, including silks and curios—a list of which is likewise enclosed. Do you reverently receive them and take note of my tender goodwill towards you! A special mandate. . . .

[In the same letter, a further mandate to King George III dealt in detail with the British ambassador's proposals and the emperor's reasons for declining them.]

You, O King, from afar have yearned after the blessings of our civilisation, and in your eagerness to come into touch with our converting influence have sent an Embassy across the sea bearing a memorial. I have already taken note of your respectful spirit of submission, have treated your mission with extreme favour and loaded it with gifts, besides issuing a mandate to you, O King, and honouring you with the bestowal of valuable presents. Thus has my indulgence been manifested.

Yesterday your Ambassador petitioned my Ministers to memorialise me regarding your trade with China, but his proposal is not consistent with our dynastic usage and cannot be entertained. Hitherto, all European nations, including your own country's barbarian merchants, have carried on their trade with our Celestial Empire at Canton. Such has been the procedure for many years, although our Celestial Empire possesses all things in prolific abundance and lacks no product within its own borders. There was therefore no need to import the manufactures of outside barbarians in exchange for our own produce. But as the tea, silk and porcelain which the Celestial Empire produces, are absolute necessities to European nations and to yourselves, we have permitted, as a signal mark of favour, that foreign *hongs* [merchant firms] should be established at Canton, so that your wants might be supplied and your country thus participate in our beneficence. But your Ambassador has now put forward new requests which completely fail to recognise the Throne's principle to "treat strangers from afar with indulgence," and to exercise a pacifying control over barbarian tribes, the world over. Moreover, our dynasty, swaying the myriad races of the globe, extends the same benevolence towards all. Your England is not the only nation trading at Canton. If other nations, following your bad example, wrongfully importune my ear with further impossible requests, how will it be possible for me to treat them with easy indulgence? Nevertheless, I do not forget the lonely remoteness of your island, cut off from the world by intervening wastes of sea, nor do I overlook your excusable ignorance of the usages of our Celestial Empire. I have consequently commanded my Ministers to enlighten your Ambassador on the subject, and have ordered the departure of the mission. But I have doubts that, after your Envoy's return he may fail to acquaint you with my view in detail or that he may be lacking in lucidity, so that I shall now proceed . . . to issue my mandate on each question separately. In this way you will, I trust, comprehend my meaning. . . .

(3) Your request for a small island near Chusan, where your merchants may reside and goods be warehoused, arises from your desire to develop trade. As there are neither foreign *hongs* nor interpreters in or near Chusan, where none of your ships have ever called, such an island would be utterly useless for your purposes. Every inch of the territory of our Empire is marked on the map and the strictest vigilance is exercised over it all: even tiny islets and far-lying sand-banks are clearly defined as part of the provinces to which they belong. Consider, moreover, that England is not the only barbarian land which wishes to establish . . . trade with our Empire: supposing that other nations were all to imitate your evil example and beseech me to present them each and all with a site for trading purposes, how could I possibly comply? This also is a flagrant infringement of the usage of my Empire and cannot possibly be entertained.

(4) The next request, for a small site in the vicinity of Canton city, where your barbarian merchants may lodge or, alternatively, that there be no longer any restrictions over their movements at Aomen, has arisen from the following causes. Hitherto, the barbarian merchants of Europe have had a definite locality assigned to them at Aomen for residence and trade, and have been forbidden to encroach an inch beyond the limits assigned to that locality. . . . If these restrictions were withdrawn, friction would inevitably occur between the Chinese and your barbarian subjects, and the results would militate against the benevolent regard that I feel towards you. From every point of view, therefore, it is best that the regulations now in force should continue unchanged. . . .

(7) Regarding your nation's worship of the Lord of Heaven, it is the same religion as that of other European nations. Ever since the beginning of history, sage Emperors and wise rulers have bestowed on China a moral system and inculcated a code, which from time immemorial has been religiously observed by the myriads of my subjects. There has been no hankering after heterodox doctrines. Even the European (missionary) officials in my capital are forbidden to hold intercourse with Chinese subjects; they are restricted within the limits of their appointed residences, and may not go about propagating their religion. The distinction between Chinese and barbarian is most strict, and your Ambassador's request that barbarians shall be given full liberty to disseminate their religion is utterly unreasonable.

It may be, O King, that the above proposals have been wantonly made by your Ambassador on his own responsibility, or peradventure you yourself are ignorant of our dynastic regulations and had no intention of transgressing them when you expressed these wild ideas and hopes. . . . If, after the receipt of this explicit decree, you lightly give ear to the representations of your subordinates and allow your barbarian merchants to proceed to Chêkiang [Zhejiang] and Tientsin [Tianjin], with the object of landing and trading there, the ordinances of my Celestial Empire are strict in the extreme, and the local officials, both civil and military, are bound reverently to obey the law of the land. Should your vessels touch the shore, your merchants will assuredly never be permitted to land or to reside there, but will be subject to instant expulsion. In that event your barbarian merchants will have had a long journey for nothing. Do not say that you were not warned in due time! Tremblingly obey and show no negligence! A special mandate!

Part III

Revolutions and Rebellions

Men and Women in Revolution

The last decades of the eighteenth century ushered in an age of democratic revolution for many of the countries bordering the Atlantic Ocean. Because this age of revolution began first in America, documents such as the Declaration of Independence quickly became models for successive waves of revolution in the old European world and throughout Spanish America. Thomas Jefferson (1743–1826), the primary author of the Declaration of Independence, was feted in Paris, and his writings were read widely throughout France. The writings of other heroes of the American Revolution, such as James Madison (1751–1836), were also studied closely throughout the Atlantic world. This inspirational legacy of the American Revolution was one of its most important contributions to the age of democratic revolution.

Certainly the successful example of America's revolution, its heroes and their writings, inspired the people who steered the early course of the French Revolution, which broke upon France in the summer of 1789. On August 27, 1789, the new National Assembly issued the clearest statement of the goals of the French Revolution, the Declaration of the Rights of Man and of the Citizen, a document heavily influenced by the American Revolution. Despite the importance of this document and the earlier American declaration, neither specifically advanced or even recognized the rights of women. For at least one French woman, Olympe de Gouges (1748–1793), this omission had to be repaired. In 1791, she wrote a Declaration of the Rights of Woman and of the Female Citizen. Unfortunately for de Gouges, France's revolutionary leaders not only rejected her proposal but charged her with treason and ordered her executed.

Edmund Burke (1729–1797), a famous Irish statesman, closely observed both the French and the American Revolutions. He was sympathetic to the cause of the American colonists, and on the eve of their war for independence, he urged Parliament to consider a policy of conciliation; but he fervently denounced the French Revolution even before it had reached its radical phase. In 1790, Burke published his *Reflections on the Revolution in France,* in which he stressed the importance of historical institutions and traditions and outlined his views on government and society.

The unfolding drama of revolution in Philadelphia, Boston, and Paris was closely watched in Buenos Aires, Caracas, and Mexico City. By the late eighteenth century, a growing resentment of Spanish political and economic restrictions, coupled with the impact of the American and French Revolutions, inspired Spanish-American revolutionaries to challenge Spain's colonial control. The immediate cause of the Spanish-American revolutions was the French occupation of the Iberian peninsula in 1808. Napoleon's intervention there weakened Spain and provided revolutionary leaders in the New World with the opportunity to declare their independence and begin fighting for it. Many of these leaders looked to the U.S. Constitution in the hope of establishing democratic federal republics in Latin America. Others, such as Simón Bolívar (1783–1830), questioned whether the U.S. model would work in Spanish America.

26 The Declaration of Independence

After 1763, England adopted a new imperial policy, and some American colonists began to organize boycotts, to riot, and to resist. Even before the fighting started at Lexington and Concord, men such as Benjamin Franklin, Patrick Henry, and Samuel Adams had set their sights on independence. But most colonists feared revolution, and the risk of declaring independence held little appeal; consequently their claims against the British Crown increased only gradually. Thomas Paine's arguments in *Common Sense,* published on January 10, 1776, helped considerably to shape anti-British sentiment and create a popular demand for independence. On June 11, 1776, when the delegates to the Second Continental

Congress heard Richard Henry Lee formally propose a resolution calling for independence, they formed a committee to prepare a draft of a formal statement. Thomas Jefferson, the author of this draft, embodied the thoughts and aspirations of the Enlightenment more than any other man of his time in colonial America. With advice and revisions from John Adams, Benjamin Franklin, and others, he submitted the proposal that Congress adopted on July 4, 1776.

QUESTIONS TO CONSIDER

1. Are there any traces of John Locke (see Reading 15) and Jean-Jacques Rousseau (see Reading 19) in this document?
2. Are there any long-term implications to the grievance leveled at King George III that he "has endeavoured to bring on the inhabitants of our frontiers, the merciless Indian Savages, whose known rule of warfare, is an undistinguished destruction of all ages, sexes and conditions"?
3. In what way(s) does the Declaration of Independence conveniently ignore the impact of England's Glorious Revolution of 1688–1689 on the status of the monarchy in the British political system?
4. Although the Declaration of Independence has served well to justify the act of revolution as a people's rightful antidote for tyranny, which section(s) and phrase(s) seem to sternly warn against the act of revolution except as a last resort?
5. Examine the list of charges made against King George III of England. Which of those charges are meaningful only to those who understand the English political system? Which of those charges might be viewed as a broad condemnation of the monarchical form of governance?
6. Is the Declaration of Independence a broad condemnation of the monarchical form of government? Discuss.
7. Compare the Declaration of Independence with France's *Declaration of the Rights of Woman and of the Female Citizen* (see Reading 27). How does each of the documents define "natural rights"? Which of these documents provides the more expansive view of natural rights?
8. How might the Declaration of Independence be reworded to justify the revolution in Saint-Domingue that established Haiti's independence from France?

In Congress, July 4, 1776. *The unanimous Declaration of the thirteen united States of America.*

When in the Course of human events, it becomes necessary for one people to dissolve the political bands which have connected them with another, and to assume among the powers of the earth, the separate and equal station to which the Laws of

From James D. Richardson, ed., *A Compilation of the Messages and Papers of the Presidents, 1789–1902*, Vol. 1 (Washington, DC: Bureau of National Literature and Art, 1903), pp. 3–5.

Nature and of Nature's God entitle them, a decent respect to the opinions of mankind requires that they should declare the causes which impel them to the separation.—

We hold these truths to be self-evident, that all men are created equal, that they are endowed by their Creator with certain unalienable Rights, that among these are Life, Liberty and the pursuit of Happiness,—

That to secure these rights, Governments are instituted among Men, deriving their just powers from the consent of the governed,—

That whenever any Form of Government becomes destructive of these ends, it is the Right of the People to alter or to abolish it, and to institute new Government, laying its foundation on such principles and organizing its powers in such form, as to them shall seem most likely to effect their Safety and Happiness. Prudence, indeed, will dictate that Governments long established should not be changed for light and transient causes: and accordingly all experience hath shown, that mankind are more disposed to suffer, while evils are sufferable, than to right themselves by abolishing the forms to which they are accustomed. But when a long train of abuses and usurpations, pursuing invariably the same Object evinces a design to reduce them under absolute Despotism, it is their right, it is their duty, to throw off such Government, and to provide new Guards for their future security.—

Such has been the patient sufferance of these Colonies; and such is now the necessity which constrains them to alter their former Systems of Government. The history of the present King of Great Britain is a history of repeated injuries and usurpations, all having in direct object the establishment of an absolute Tyranny over these States. To prove this, let Facts be submitted to a candid world.—

He has refused his Assent to Laws, the most wholesome and necessary for the public good.—

He has forbidden his Governors to pass Laws of immediate and pressing importance, unless suspended in their operation till his Assent should be obtained; and when so suspended, he has utterly neglected to attend to them.—

He has refused to pass other Laws for the accommodation of large districts of people, unless those people would relinquish the right of Representation in the Legislature, a right inestimable to them and formidable to tyrants only.—

He has called together legislative bodies at places unusual, uncomfortable, and distant from the depository of their public Records, for the sole purpose of fatiguing them into compliance with his measures.—

He has dissolved Representative Houses repeatedly, for opposing with manly firmness his invasions on the rights of the people.—

He has refused for a long time, after such dissolutions, to cause others to be elected; whereby the Legislative powers, incapable of Annihilation, have returned to the People at large for their exercise; the State remaining in the mean time exposed to all the dangers of invasion from without, and convulsions within.—

He has endeavoured to prevent the population of these States; for that purpose obstructing the Laws for Naturalization of Foreigners; refusing to pass others to encourage their migrations hither, and raising the conditions of new Appropriations of Lands.—

He has obstructed the Administration of Justice, by refusing his Assent to Laws for establishing Judiciary powers.—

He has made Judges dependent on his Will alone, for the tenure of their offices, and the amount and payment of their salaries.—

He has erected a multitude of New Offices, and sent hither swarms of Officers to harrass our people, and eat out their substance.—

He has kept among us in times of peace, Standing Armies without the Consent of our legislatures.—

He has affected to render the Military independent of and superior to the Civil power.—

He has combined with others to subject us to a jurisdiction foreign to our constitution, and unacknowledged by our laws; giving his Assent to their Acts of pretended Legislation:—

For quartering large bodies of armed troops among us:—

For protecting them, by a mock Trial, from punishment for any Murders which they should commit on the Inhabitants of these States:—

For cutting off our Trade with all parts of the world:—

For imposing Taxes on us without our Consent:—

For depriving us in many cases, of the benefits of Trial by Jury:—

For transporting us beyond Seas to be tried for pretended offences:—

For abolishing the free System of English Laws in a neighbouring Province, establishing therein an Arbitrary government, and enlarging its Boundaries so as to render it at once an example and fit instrument for introducing the same absolute rule in these Colonies:—

For taking away our Charters, abolishing our most valuable Laws, and altering fundamentally the Forms of our Governments:—

For suspending our own Legislatures, and declaring themselves invested with power to legislate for us in all cases whatsoever.—

He has abdicated Government here, by declaring us out of his Protection and waging War against us.—

He has plundered our seas, ravaged our Coasts, burnt our towns, and destroyed the lives of our people.—

He is at this time transporting large Armies of foreign Mercenaries to compleat the works of death, desolation and tyranny, already begun with circumstances of Cruelty & perfidy scarcely paralleled in the most barbarous ages, and totally unworthy of the Head of a civilized nation.—

He has constrained our fellow Citizens taken Captive on the high Seas to bear Arms against their Country, to become the executioners of their friends and Brethren, or to fall themselves by their Hands.—

He has excited domestic insurrections amongst us, and has endeavoured to bring on the inhabitants of our frontiers, the merciless Indian Savages, whose known rule of warfare, is an undistinguished destruction of all ages, sexes and conditions.

In every stage of these Oppressions We have Petitioned for Redress in the most humble terms: Our repeated Petitions have been answered only by repeated injury. A Prince, whose character is thus marked by every act which may define a Tyrant, is unfit to be the ruler of a free people.

Nor have We been wanting in attentions to our British brethren. We have warned them from time to time of attempts by their legislature to extend an unwarrantable jurisdiction over us. We have reminded them of the circumstances of our emigration and settlement here. We have appealed to their native justice and magnanimity, and we have conjured them by the ties of our common kindred to disavow these usurpations, which would inevitably interrupt our connections and correspondence. They too have been deaf to the voice of justice and of consanguinity. We must, therefore, acquiesce in the necessity, which denounces our Separation, and hold them, as we hold the rest of mankind, Enemies in War, in Peace Friends.—

We, therefore, the Representatives of the united States of America, in General Congress, Assembled, appealing to the Supreme Judge of the world for the rectitude of our intentions, do, in the Name, and by Authority of the good People of these Colonies, solemnly publish and declare, That these United Colonies are, and of Right ought to be, Free and Independent States; that they are absolved from all Allegiance to the British Crown, and that all political connection between them and the State of Great Britain, is and ought to be totally dissolved; and that as Free and Independent States they have full Power to levy War, conclude Peace, contract Alliances, establish Commerce, and to do all other Acts and Things which Independent States may of right do.—

And for the support of this Declaration, with a firm reliance on the protection of divine Providence, we mutually pledge to each other our Lives, our Fortunes and our sacred Honor.

27 Olympe de Gouges, *Declaration of the Rights of Woman and of the Female Citizen*

In the summer of 1789, France exploded into revolution. The French government's inability to find new tax revenues without tampering with the privileged, tax-exempt status of the nobility had forced King Louis XVI (r. 1774–1792) to call representatives of the clergy, nobility, and Third Estate (all commoners who were not clergy) to assemble at Versailles as the Estates-General. For the first month little happened. Then, on June 17, the leadership of the Third Estate, along with representatives of the clergy and nobility, openly challenged Louis XVI by overturning the authority of the Estates-General and declaring themselves the National Assembly of France. On July 14, anxious Parisian crowds, driven by rumors of an aristocratic plot to starve the city, attacked the feared prison of the Bastille in search of weapons. At the same time, in widely scattered parts of rural France, peasants assaulted nobles and burned their chateaux. On August 27, 1789, the National Assembly issued *The Declaration of the Rights of Man and of the Citizen.* In large part because the seventeen articles of this document specified only the rights of men, Olympe de Gouges, a butcher's daughter, in 1791 wrote the seventeen articles in the following declaration. Her proposal called for a national assembly of women, emphasized the importance of education for all women, and suggested that women as well as men should vote. When the French Revolution moved into its most radical phase, called the "Terror" (1793–1794), women such as de Gouges pressed even harder for their rights. Fearful that any such recognition could undermine their own leadership and threaten the revolution, the National Convention charged Olympe de Gouges with treason. She was quickly arrested, tried, and on November 3, 1793, executed by the guillotine.

QUESTIONS TO CONSIDER

1. In light of articles 6, 7, 9, 10, and 12 of *The Declaration of the Rights of Woman and of the Female Citizen,* how would you define the political agenda of Olympe de Gouges?
2. What does article 11, along with Olympe de Gouges's reflections on marriage, suggest about the condition of women in eighteenth-century France?

Mothers, daughters, sisters and representatives of the nation demand to be constituted in a national assembly. Believing that ignorance, omission, or contempt for the rights of women are the only causes of public misfortune and the corruption of governments, we resolve to expose in a solemn declaration the natural, inalienable and sacred rights of woman so that this declaration, constantly exposed to all members of the society, may unceasingly remind them of their rights and duties; that the actions of women and the actions of men can at any moment harmonize with the goals of all political institutions; and that the demands of female citizens, founded on simple and incontestable principles, will always support the constitution, good morals, and the happiness of all.

Consequently, the sex superior in beauty and courageous in maternal sufferings recognizes and declares in the presence and under the auspices of the Supreme Being, the following Rights of Woman and of the Female Citizen:

1. Woman is born free and remains equal to man in rights. Social distinctions can be founded only on general utility.
2. The goal of all political association is the preservation of the natural and imprescriptible rights of Woman and Man: These rights are liberty, property, security, and above all resistance to oppression.
3. The source of all sovereignty resides in the nation, which is nothing but the union of Woman and Man: No body, no individual, may exercise any authority not emanating expressly therefrom.
4. Liberty and justice consist of returning all that belongs to another; thus, the only limits on the exercise of woman's natural rights are the perpetual tyranny wielded by men; these limits must be reformed by the law of nature and the law of reason.
5. The laws of nature and of reason prohibit all actions harmful to society: Anything not forbidden by these wise and divine laws, cannot be forbidden, and no one can be forced to do that which the law does not require.

From Olympe de Gouges, *La Nation à La Reine: Les Droits de la Femme* (Paris: Momoro, n.d.[1791]), pp. 6–13, 17–20. Trans. Philip F. Riley.

6. The law should be the expression of the general will; all female and male citizens should concur either personally or by their representatives in its formulation; it should be the same for all: All female and male citizens are equal in its eyes, and equally entitled to all honors, places and public employments according to their abilities without any other distinction than that of their virtues and their talents.

7. No woman is an exception; she is accused, arrested, and detained in cases determined by law. Women, like men, obey this rigorous law.

8. The law should only impose those penalties which are strictly and absolutely necessary, and one may be punished only by a law that has been established and promulgated prior to the offense and legally applied to women.

9. Once a woman has been declared guilty, the law should be applied rigorously.

10. No one is to be harassed for their fundamental beliefs; a woman has the right to mount the scaffold; she also has the right to mount the rostrum, providing that her actions do not threaten lawful public order.

11. Freedom of expression of thoughts and opinions is one of the most precious rights of woman, since this liberty assures the legitimate paternity of children. Each female citizen must be free to say I am the mother of this child which belongs to you, without being forced by barbarous prejudice to lie; however, lawful exceptions may be made, if this liberty is abused.

12. The guarantee of the rights of woman and the female citizen ensures a major advantage; this guarantee must be instituted for the advantage of all, and not for the particular utility of those to whom it is entrusted.

13. To maintain the public force and the expenses of administration, the contributions of woman and man are equal; she performs all the labor taxes, and all the painful duties; therefore she should have the same responsibilities, honors, and employment.

14. Female and male citizens have the right, either by themselves or by their representatives, to verify the necessity of the public tax. Women can do this if they are admitted to an equal share of the wealth, public administration, and permitted to determine the amount, basis, collection, and the duration of the tax.

15. The mass of women, joined for tax purposes with men, has the right to demand of each public agent an accounting of his administration.

16. Any society in which the guarantee of rights is not assured nor the separation of powers determined has no constitution at all; the constitution is invalid if the majority of individuals comprising the nation have not cooperated in its writing.

17. Property belongs to both sexes united or separate; for each property is an inviolable and sacred right; no one can be deprived of it, since it is the true patrimony of nature, except in cases of public necessity, verified by law, and on condition of a just and prior indemnity.

Woman, wake-up; the tocsin of reason is being heard in all the universe; discover your rights. Nature's powerful empire is no longer surrounded by lies, superstition, prejudice and fanaticism. The flame of truth has dissipated all the clouds of stupidity and usurpation. Enslaved man has multiplied his strength, but he needs your help to break his chains. Having become free, he has become unjust to his companion. Oh Women! Women, when will you cease being blind? What are the advantages you have received in this Revolution? More contempt? More disdain? In the centuries of corruption you ruled only over men's foibles. Your old empire is destroyed. How will it be restored? By convicting men's injustices. The reclamation of your patrimony must be based on the wise decrees of nature. Why should you fear such a fine venture? The *bon mot* of the Legislator of the wedding feast of Cana? Do you fear only that our French Legislators, correctors of a morality, long entangled by politics but now out of date, will ask you: women what do you have in common with us? Everything, you must respond. If they continue in their weakness, by permitting this absurdity to contradict their principles, you must courageously oppose the force of reason to the vain pretensions of superiority; unite under the banner of philosophy; deploy all the energy of your character, and you will see these arrogant fellows, not as sycophants groveling at your feet, but proud to share with you the treasures of the Supreme Being. Whatever the barriers before you, it is in your power to break them; you only have to want to break them. . . .

Marriage is a tomb of trust and love. A married woman can with impunity give bastards to her husband and give them also wealth that does not belong to them. An unmarried woman has only one feeble right: Ancient and inhuman laws deny·her children the name and the wealth of their father, and no new laws have corrected this. If it is considered a paradox on my part to try to give my sex an honorable and just consistency, I leave to men the glory of doing this; but, while waiting, we can prepare the way by national education, by restoring morality, and by conjugal conventions.

FORM FOR A SOCIAL CONTRACT BETWEEN MAN AND WOMAN

We, _____ and _____ , moved by our own will, unite ourselves for a lifetime, and for the duration of our mutual inclinations, under the following conditions: We intend and wish to put our wealth in common, while reserving the right to divide in favor of our children and whomever else we might select, recognizing that our property belongs to our children, from whatever bed they proceed, and that all our children have the right to carry the name of their fathers and mothers who have acknowledged them, and we agree to subscribe to the law which punishes those who deny their own blood. We are equally obliged, that in the case of separation, to divide our wealth, and to set aside a lawful portion for our children; and, in the case of perfect union, the spouse who dies first, will ensure that one-half of his property will pass to the children; and if there are no children the survivor will inherit this half-share unless the deceased spouse has made other arrangements.

That is the formula for marriage that I propose to execute. Upon reading this bizarre document, I see rising against me the hypocrites, the prudes, the clergy and all their infernal allies. But I believe this document offers to the wise the moral means of achieving the perfection of a happy government! . . .

I would also wish for a law that would assist widows and young women deceived by the false promises of a man to whom they were attached; I would like this law to force such a deceitful man to keep his promise of engagement, or to pay an indemnity equal to his wealth. I also believe this law should be rigorously applied against women, if it can be proven they have broken their word. I wish at the same time to reiterate a proposal I made in *Le Bonheur primitif de l'homme*, in 1788, that prostitutes be placed in designated quarters. Prostitutes do not contribute to the degradation of morality; it is the women of society. In regenerating the latter, the former will be improved. This chain of fraternal union will, at first, bring disorder, but over time it will be harmonious.

I offer an invincible means to elevate the soul of women; it is to join all the activities of men: If a man finds this impractical, let him share his fortune with a woman, not out of his whim but by the wisdom of the laws. Prejudice falls, morals are purified, and nature recaptures all her rights. Add to this the marriage of priests with the King firmly on his throne, and the French government cannot perish. . . .

28 James Madison, *The Federalist*, Number 10

The *Federalist* papers, written by Alexander Hamilton, James Madison, and John Jay in the campaign to gain adoption of the U.S. Constitution by New York State, are considered among the most important contributions to political thought in America. First published in New York newspapers, the essays defending the new Constitution appeared in book form in 1788. In *The Federalist*, Number 10, Madison discusses how the evil of faction and the danger of majority tyranny can be avoided in a republican union consisting of many diverse interests.

QUESTIONS TO CONSIDER

1. How does James Madison define *faction?* Why did he think the government outlined in the U.S. Constitution could deal with this problem?
2. Would James Madison agree with Rousseau's prescription for government (see Reading 19)?

Complaints are everywhere heard from our most considerate and virtuous citizens, equally the friends of public and private faith and of public and personal liberty, that our governments are too unstable, that the public good is disregarded in the conflicts of rival parties, and that measures are too often decided, not according to the rules of justice and the rights of the minor party, but by the superior force of an interested and overbearing majority. However anxiously we may wish that these complaints had no foundation, the evidence of known facts will not permit us to deny that they are in some degree true. It will be found, indeed, on a candid review of our situation, that some of the distresses under which we labor have been erroneously charged on the operation of our governments; but it will be found, at the same time, that other causes will not alone account for many of our heaviest misfortunes; and, particularly, for that prevailing and increasing distrust of public engagements and alarm for private rights which are echoed from one end of the continent to the other. These must be chiefly, if not wholly, effects of the unsteadiness and injustice with which a factious spirit has tainted our public administrations.

From *The Federalist* (New York: Colonial Press, 1901), pp. 44–51.

By a faction I understand a number of citizens, whether amounting to a majority or minority of the whole, who are united and actuated by some common impulse of passion, or of interest, adverse to the rights of other citizens, or to the permanent and aggregate interests of the community.

There are two methods of curing the mischiefs of faction: the one, by removing its causes; the other, by controlling its effects.

There are again two methods of removing the causes of faction: the one, by destroying the liberty which is essential to its existence; the other, by giving to every citizen the same opinions, the same passions, and the same interests.

It could never be more truly said than of the first remedy that it was worse than the disease. Liberty is to faction what air is to fire, an aliment without which it instantly expires. But it could not be a less folly to abolish liberty, which is essential to political life, because it nourishes faction than it would be to wish the annihilation of air, which is essential to animal life, because it imparts to fire its destructive agency.

The second expedient is as impracticable as the first would be unwise. As long as the reason of man continues fallible, and he is at liberty to exercise it, different opinions will be formed. As long as the connection subsists between his reason and his self-love, his opinions and his passions will have a reciprocal influence on each other; and the former will be objects to which the latter will attach themselves. The diversity in the faculties of men, from which the rights of property originate, is not less an insuperable obstacle to a uniformity of interests. The protection of these faculties is the first object of government. From the protection of different and unequal faculties of acquiring property, the possession of different degrees and kinds of property immediately results; and from the influence of these on the sentiments and views of the respective proprietors ensues a division of the society into different interests and parties.

The latent causes of faction are thus sown in the nature of men; and we see them everywhere brought into different degrees of activity, according to the different circumstances of civil society. A zeal for different opinions concerning religion, concerning government, and many other points, as well of speculation as of practice; an attachment to different leaders ambitiously contending for preeminence and power; or to persons of other descriptions whose fortunes have been interesting to the human passions, have, in turn, divided mankind into parties, inflamed them with mutual animosity, and rendered them much more disposed to vex and oppress each other than to cooperate for their common good. So strong is this propensity of mankind to fall into mutual animosities that where no substantial occasion presents itself the most frivolous and fanciful distinctions have been sufficient to kindle their unfriendly passions and excite their most violent conflicts. But the most common and durable source of factions has been the various and unequal distribution of property. Those who hold and those who are without property have ever formed distinct interests in society. Those who are creditors, and those who are debtors, fall under a like discrimination. A landed interest, a manufacturing interest, a mercantile interest, a moneyed interest, with many lesser interests, grow up of necessity in civilized nations, and divide them into different classes, actuated by different sentiments and views. The regulation of these various and interfering interests forms the principal task of modern legislation and involves the spirit of party and faction in the necessary and ordinary operations of the government.

From this view of the subject it may be concluded that a pure democracy, by which I mean a society consisting of a small number of citizens, who assemble and administer the government in person, can admit of no cure for the mischiefs of faction. A common passion or interest will, in almost every case, be felt by a majority of the whole; a communication and concert result from the form of government itself; and there is nothing to check the inducements to sacrifice the weaker party or an obnoxious individual. Hence it is that such democracies have ever been spectacles of turbulence and contention; have ever been found incompatible with personal security or the rights of property; and have in general been as short in their lives as they have been violent in their deaths. Theoretic politicians, who have patronized this species of government, have erroneously supposed that by reducing mankind to a perfect equality in their political rights, they would at the same time be perfectly equalized and assimilated in their possessions, their opinions, and their passions.

A republic, by which I mean a government in which the scheme of representation takes place, opens a different prospect and promises the cure for which we are seeking. Let us examine the points on which it varies from pure democracy, and we shall comprehend both the nature of the cure and the efficacy which it must derive from the Union.

The two great points of difference between a democracy and a republic are: first, the delegation of the government, in the latter, to a small number of citizens elected by the rest; secondly, the greater number of citizens and greater sphere of country over which the latter may be extended.

The effect of the first difference is, on the one hand, to refine and enlarge the public views by passing them through the medium of a chosen body of citizens, whose wisdom may best discern the true interest of their country and whose patriotism and love of justice will be least likely to sacrifice it to temporary or partial considerations. Under such a regulation it may well happen that the public voice, pronounced by the representatives of the people, will be more consonant to the public good than if pronounced by the people themselves, convened for the purpose. On the other hand, the effect may be inverted. Men of factious tempers, of local prejudices, or of sinister designs, may, by intrigue, by corruption, or by other means, first obtain the suffrage, and then betray the interests of the people. The question resulting is, whether small or extensive republics are most favorable to the election of proper guardians of the public weal; and it is clearly decided in favor of the latter by two obvious considerations.

In the first place it is to be remarked that however small the republic may be the representatives must be raised to a certain number in order to guard against the cabals of a few; and that however large it may be they must be limited to a certain number in order to guard against the confusion of a multitude. Hence, the number of representatives in the two cases not being in proportion to that of the two constituents, and being proportionally greatest in the small republic, it follows that if the proportion of fit characters be not less in the large than in the small republic, the former will present a greater option, and consequently a greater probability of a fit choice.

In the next place, as each representative will be chosen by a greater number of citizens in the large than in the small republic, it will be more difficult for unworthy candidates to practice with success the vicious arts by which elections are too often carried; and the suffrages of the people being more free, will be more likely to center on men who possess the most attractive merit and the most diffusive and established characters.

29   Edmund Burke, *Reflections on the Revolution in France*

Edmund Burke (1729–1797) was a leading voice of conservatism who denounced the French Revolution even before it had moved into its most radical phase. In 1790, he published *Reflections on the Revolution in France,* in which he condemned the destructiveness of the revolutionary movement and questioned whether the newly elected assembly could produce a better government and society.

QUESTIONS TO CONSIDER

1. What did Edmund Burke find so offensive about the leadership of the French Revolution? What elements of Burke's essay may be cited as the basis for modern political conservatism?
2. In light of Burke's attack on the French Revolution, how could he champion the rights of the American colonists to rebel against King George III?

France, by the perfidy of her leaders, has utterly disgraced the tone of lenient council in the cabinets of princes, and disarmed it of its most potent topics. She has sanctified the dark suspicious maxims of tyrannous distrust; and taught kings to tremble at (what will hereafter be called) the delusive plausibilities, of moral politicians. Sovereigns will consider those who advise them to place an unlimited confidence in their people, as subverters of their thrones; as traitors who aim at their destruction, by leading their easy good nature, under specious pretences, to admit combinations of bold and faithless men into a participation of their power. This alone (if there were nothing else) is an irreparable calamity to you and to mankind. . . .

Laws overturned; tribunals subverted; industry without vigor; commerce expiring; the revenue unpaid, yet the people impoverished; a church pillaged, and a state not relieved; civil and military anarchy made the constitution of the kingdom; every thing human and divine sacrificed to the idol of public credit, and national bankruptcy the consequence; and to crown all, the paper securities of new, precarious, tottering power, the discredited paper securities of impoverished fraud, and beggared rapine, held out as a currency for the support of an empire, in lieu of the two great recognised species that represent the lasting conventional credit of mankind, which disappeared and hid themselves in the earth from whence they came, when the principle of property, whose creatures and representatives they are, was systematically subverted.

Were all these dreadful things necessary? Were they the inevitable results of the desperate struggle of determined patriots, compelled to wade through blood and tumult, to the quiet shore of a tranquil and prosperous liberty? No! nothing like it. The fresh ruins of France, which shock our feelings wherever we can turn our eyes, are not the devastation of civil war; they are the sad but instructive monuments of rash

From Edmund Burke, *The Works of Edmund Burke*, Vol. 3 (Boston: Chas. C. Little and James Brown, 1839), pp. 57–62, 71–73, 81–83, 97–101, *passim.*

and ignorant counsel in time of profound peace. They are the display of inconsiderate and presumptuous, because unresisted and irresistible authority.

This unforced choice, this fond election of evil, would appear perfectly unaccountable, if we did not consider the composition of the national assembly; I do not mean its formal constitution, which, as it now stands, is exceptionable enough, but the materials of which, in a great measure, it is composed, which is of ten thousand times greater consequence than all the formalities in the world. If we were to know nothing of this assembly but by its title and function, no colors could paint to the imagination any thing more venerable. . . .

After I had read over the list of the persons and descriptions elected into the *Tiers Etat*, nothing which they afterwards did could appear astonishing. Among them, indeed, I saw some of known rank; some of shining talents; but of any practical experience in the state, not one man was to be found. The best were only men of theory. But whatever the distinguished few may have been, it is the substance and mass of the body which constitutes its character, and must finally determine its direction. . . .

Judge, sir, of my surprise, when I found that a very great proportion of the assembly (a majority, I believe, of the members who attended,) was composed of practitioners in the law. It was composed, not of distinguished magistrates, who had given pledges to their country of their science, prudence, and integrity; not of leading advocates, the glory of the bar; not of renowned professors in universities; but for the far greater part, as it must in such a number, of the inferior, unlearned, mechanical, merely instrumental members of the profession. There were distinguished exceptions; but the general composition was of obscure provincial advocates, of stewards of petty local jurisdictions, country attorneys, notaries, and the whole train of the ministers of municipal litigation, the fomenters and conductors of the petty war of village vexation. From the moment I read the list, I saw distinctly, and very nearly as it has happened, all that was to follow. . . .

Whenever the supreme authority is vested in a body so composed, it must evidently produce the consequences of supreme authority placed in the hands of men not taught habitually to respect themselves; who had no previous fortune in character at stake; who could not be expected to bear with moderation, or to conduct with discretion, a power, which they themselves, more than any others, must be surprised to find in their hands. . . .

Nothing is a due and adequate representation of a state, that does not represent its ability, as well as its property. But as ability is a vigorous and active principle, and as property is sluggish, inert and timid, it never can be safe from the invasions of ability, unless it be, out of all proportion, predominant in the representation. It must be represented too in great masses of accumulation, or it is not rightly protected. The characteristic essence of property, formed out of the combined principles of its acquisition and conservation, is to be *unequal*. . . .

The power of perpetuating our property in our families is one of the most valuable and interesting circumstances belonging to it, and that which tends the most to the perpetuation of society itself. It makes our weakness subservient to our virtue; it grafts benevolence even upon avarice. The possessors of family wealth, and of the distinction which attends hereditary possession (as most concerned in it) are the natural securities for this transmission. With us, the house of peers is formed upon this principle. It is wholly composed of hereditary property and hereditary distinction; and made therefore the third of the legislature; and in the last event, the sole judge of all property in all its subdivisions. The house of commons too, though not necessarily, yet in fact, is always so composed in the far greater part. Let those large proprietors be what they will, and they have their chance of being among the best, they are at the very worst, the ballast in the vessel of the commonwealth. For though hereditary wealth, and the rank which goes with it, are too much idolized by creeping sycophants, and the blind abject admirers of power, they are too rashly slighted in shallow speculations of the petulant, assuming, short-sighted coxcombs of philosophy. Some decent regulated preëminence, some preference (not exclusive appropriation) given to birth, is neither unnatural, nor unjust, nor impolitic.

It is said, that twenty-four millions ought to prevail over two hundred thousand. True; if the constitution of a kingdom be a problem of arithmetic. This sort of discourse does well enough with the lamp-post for its second: to men who *may* reason calmly, it is ridiculous. The will of the many, and their interest, must very often differ; and great will be the difference when they make an evil choice. A government of five hundred country attorneys and obscure curates is not good for twenty-four millions of men, though it were chosen by eight and forty millions; nor is it the better for being guided by a dozen persons of quality, who have betrayed their trust in order to obtain that power. At present, you seem in every thing to have strayed out of the high-road of nature. The property of France does not govern it. Of course property is destroyed, and rational liberty has no existence. All you have got for the present is a paper circulation, and a stockjobbing constitution: and as to the future, do you seriously think that the territory of France, upon the republican system of eighty-three independent municipalities (to say nothing of the parts that compose them) can ever be governed as one body, or can ever be set in motion by the impulse of one mind? When the national assembly has completed its work, it will have accomplished its ruin. . . .

Government is not made in virtue of natural rights, which may and do exist in total independence of it; and exist in much greater clearness, and in a much greater degree of abstract perfection: but their abstract perfection is their practical defeat. By having a right to every thing, they want every thing. Government is a contrivance of human wisdom to provide for human *wants*. Men have a right that these wants should be provided for by this wisdom. Among these wants is to be reckoned the want, out of civil society, of a sufficient restraint upon their passions. Society requires not only that the passions of individuals should be subjected, but that even in the mass and body as well as in the individuals, the inclinations of men should frequently be thwarted, their will controlled, and their passions brought into subjection. This can only be done *by a power out of themselves*; and not, in the exercise of its function, subject to that will and to those passions which it is its office to bridle and subdue. In this sense the restraints on men, as well as their liberties, are to be reckoned among their rights. But as the liberties and the restrictions vary with times and circumstances, and admit of infinite modifications, they cannot be settled upon any abstract rule; and nothing is so foolish as to discuss them upon that principle.

The moment you abate any thing from the full rights of men, each to govern himself, and suffer any artificial positive limitation upon those rights, from that moment the whole organization of government becomes a consideration of convenience. This it is which makes the constitution of a state, and the due distribution of its powers, a matter of the most delicate and complicated skill. It requires a deep knowledge of human nature and human necessities, and of the things which facilitate or obstruct the various ends which are to be pursued by the mechanism of civil institutions. The state is to have recruits to its strength, and remedies to its distempers. What is the use of discussing a man's abstract right to food or medicine? The question is upon the method of procuring and administering them. In that deliberation I shall always advise to call in the aid of the farmer and the physician, rather than the professor of metaphysics.

The science of constructing a commonwealth, or renovating it, or reforming it, is, like every other experimental science, not to be taught *a priori*. Nor is it a short experience that can instruct us in that practical science; because the real effects of moral causes are not always immediate; but that which in the first instance is prejudicial may be excellent in its remoter operation; and its excellence may arise even from the ill effects it produces in the beginning. . . .

The nature of man is intricate; the objects of society are of the greatest possible complexity: and therefore no simple disposition or direction of power can be suitable either to man's nature, or to the quality of his affairs. When I hear the simplicity of contrivance aimed at and boasted of in any new political constitutions, I am at no loss to decide that the artificers are grossly ignorant of their trade, or totally negligent of their duty. The simple governments are fundamentally defective, to say no worse of them. If you were to contemplate society in but one point of view, all these simple modes of polity are infinitely captivating. In effect each would answer its single end much more perfectly than the more complex is able to attain all its complex purposes. But it is better that the whole should be imperfectly and anomalously answered, than that, while some parts are provided for with great exactness, others might be totally neglected, or perhaps materially injured, by the overcare of a favorite member.

30 Simón Bolívar's Political Ideas

Simón Bolívar (1783–1830), inspired by the ideals and success of the North American and French Revolutions, led the struggle for independence in northern South America. After studying and traveling in Europe, he returned to Venezuela in 1807 to participate in the Caracas rebellion to liberate the area. In the subsequent decade, Bolívar led numerous military expeditions to end Spanish control. In 1819, he became president of the new republic of Gran Colombia, but he was unable to prevent the fragmentation of the state into Colombia, Venezuela, and Ecuador by 1830. Bolívar was important both as a military leader and as a political thinker. The following excerpts, reflecting many of his ideas on government, are from his message to the Congress of Angostura (1819), which had met to consider a proposed new constitution for Venezuela.

QUESTIONS TO CONSIDER

1. What advice did Bolívar offer to those forging new governments in Spanish America? Why did Bolívar's ideas appeal to those who advocated dictatorships as the best form of government for Latin America?

2.   According to Bolívar, what "civic virtues" were lacking in Latin America, in contrast to the United States, that made the brand of democracy and federalism in North America an inappropriate model for Spanish America?

America, in separating from the Spanish monarchy, found herself in a situation similar to that of the Roman Empire when its enormous framework fell to pieces in the midst of the ancient world. Each Roman division then formed an independent nation in keeping with its location or interests; but this situation differed from America's in that those members proceeded to reestablish their former associations. We, on the contrary, do not even retain the vestiges of our original being. We are not Europeans; we are not Indians; we are but a mixed species of aborigines and Spaniards. Americans by birth and Europeans by law, we find ourselves engaged in a dual conflict: we are disputing with the natives for titles of ownership, and at the same time we are struggling to maintain ourselves in the country that gave us birth against the opposition of the invaders. Thus our position is most extraordinary and complicated. But there is more. As our role has always been strictly passive and our political existence nil, we find that our quest for liberty is now even more difficult of accomplishment; for we, having been placed in a state lower than slavery, had been robbed not only of our freedom but also of the right to exercise an active domestic tyranny. Permit me to explain this paradox.

In absolute systems, the central power is unlimited. The will of the despot is the supreme law, arbitrarily enforced by subordinates who take part in the organized oppression in proportion to the authority that they wield. They are charged with civil, political, military, and religious functions; but, in the final analysis, the satraps of Persia are Persian, the pashas of the Grand Turk are Turks, and the sultans of Tartary are Tartars. China does not seek her mandarins in the homeland of Genghis Khan, her conqueror. America, on the contrary, received everything from Spain, who, in effect, deprived her of the experience that she would have gained from the exercise of an active tyranny by not allowing her to take part in her own domestic affairs and administration. This exclusion made it impossible for us to acquaint ourselves with the management of public affairs; nor did we enjoy that personal consideration, of such great value in major revolutions, that the brilliance of power inspires in the eyes of the multitude. In brief, Gentlemen, we were deliberately kept in ignorance and cut off from the world in all matters relating to the science of government.

Subject to the threefold yoke of ignorance, tyranny, and vice, the American people have been unable to acquire knowledge, power, or [civic] virtue. The lessons we received and the models we studied, as pupils of such pernicious teachers, were most destructive. We have been ruled more by deceit than by force, and we have been degraded more by vice than by superstition. Slavery is the daughter of Darkness: an ignorant people is a blind instrument of its own destruction. Ambition and intrigue abuse the credulity and experience of men lacking all political, economic, and civic knowledge; they adopt pure illusion as reality; they take license for liberty, treachery for patriotism, and vengeance for justice. This situation is similar to that of the robust

From Vicente Lecuna, comp., and Harold A. Bierck, Jr., ed., *Selected Writings of Bolívar*, Vol. 1 (Caracas: Banco de Venezuela, 1951), pp. 175–80, *passim*. Reprinted by permission.

blind man who, beguiled by his strength, strides forward with all the assurance of one who can see, but, upon hitting every variety of obstacle, finds himself unable to retrace his steps.

If a people, perverted by their training, succeed in achieving their liberty, they will soon lose it, for it would be of no avail to endeavor to explain to them that happiness consists in the practice of virtue; that the rule of law is more powerful than the rule of tyrants, because, as the laws are more inflexible, everyone should submit to their beneficent austerity; that proper morals, and not force, are the bases of law; and that to practice justice is to practice liberty. Therefore, Legislators, your work is so much the more arduous, inasmuch as you have to reeducate men who have been corrupted by erroneous illusions and false incentives. Liberty, says Rousseau, is a succulent morsel, but one difficult to digest. Our weak fellow-citizens will have to strengthen their spirit greatly before they can digest the wholesome nutriment of freedom. Their limbs benumbed by chains, their sight dimmed by the darkness of dungeons, and their strength sapped by the pestilence of servitude, are they capable of marching toward the august temple of Liberty without faltering? Can they come near enough to bask in its brilliant rays and to breathe freely the pure air which reigns therein?

Legislators, meditate well before you choose. Forget not that you are to lay the political foundation for a newly born nation which can rise to the heights of greatness that Nature has marked out for it if you but proportion this foundation in keeping with the high plane that it aspires to attain. Unless your choice is based upon the peculiar tutelary experience of the Venezuelan people—a factor that should guide you in determining the nature and form of government you are about to adopt for the well-being of the people—and, I repeat, unless you happen upon the right type of government, the result of our reforms will again be slavery. . . .

The more I admire the excellence of the federal Constitution of Venezuela, the more I am convinced of the impossibility of its application to our state. And, to my way of thinking, it is a marvel that its prototype in North America endures so successfully and has not been overthrown at the first sign of adversity or danger. Although the people of North America are a singular model of political virtue and moral rectitude; although the nation was cradled in liberty, reared on freedom, and maintained by liberty alone; and—I must reveal everything—although those people, so lacking in many respects, are unique in the history of mankind, it is a marvel, I repeat, that so weak and complicated a government as the federal system has managed to govern them in the difficult and trying circumstances of their past. But, regardless of the effectiveness of this form of government with respect to North America, I must say that it has never for a moment entered my mind to compare the position and character of two states as dissimilar as the English-American and the Spanish-American. Would it not be most difficult to apply to Spain the English system of political, civil, and religious liberty? Hence, it would be even more difficult to adapt to Venezuela the laws of North America. Does not [Montesquieu's] *L'Esprit des lois* state that laws should be suited to the people for whom they are made; that it would be a major coincidence if those of one nation could be adapted to another; that laws must take into account the physical conditions of the country, climate, character of the land, location, size, and mode of living of the people; that they should be in keeping with the degree of liberty that the Constitution can sanction respecting the religion of the inhabitants, their inclinations, resources, numbers, commerce, habits, and customs? This is the code we must consult, not the code of Washington!

America Asserts Itself

After the defeat of Napoleon, the victorious European powers joined together to preserve the postwar settlement agreed to at the Congress of Vienna in 1815. The suppression of a revolution in Spain and the restoration of the deposed king, Ferdinand VII, caused many to believe that the Europeans also hoped to restore Spanish authority in the Western Hemisphere, where the Latin American wars for independence had erupted. At the same time, Russia was extending her influence in the Western Hemisphere. In September 1821, the Tsar issued a decree claiming the west coast of North America down to the fifty-first degree of latitude and ordered foreign ships to stay away from the coastal area. Great Britain strongly objected because Russian claims threatened British interests in the northwest. In addition, the newly independent Latin American nations had opened their ports to ships of all nations, and the British were involved in a profitable trade that had formerly been a Spanish monopoly. The result was the promulgation of the Monroe Doctrine, which remained an integral part of U.S. foreign policy.

Apart from attempting to maintain the independence of the Western Hemisphere, the United States was influencing Europe in other ways. The American experiment with democracy appeared to reform-minded Europeans as worthy of at least selective imitation in the 1830s and 1840s. Alexis de Tocqueville, a very observant traveler to America, was a member of the French Chamber of Deputies and eventually joined the opposition to King Louis Philippe. He was active in French politics after the Revolution of 1848 until the coup d'état of Louis Napoleon Bonaparte restored the monarchy in a different form. In 1848, in the preface to the twelfth edition of his best-selling *Democracy in America,* he stressed the usefulness of the American model in some of its aspects for the new French Republic.

The American combination of democracy and capitalism appeared remarkably successful once again after its march had been interrupted by the American Civil War. Andrew Carnegie, as a prominent industrialist, was well qualified to extol the virtues of American progress, both in satisfying many material wants in man's pursuit of happiness and in making philanthropic projects possible on a grand scale through the sheer abundance of the wealth it produced.

31 The Monroe Doctrine

To exclude further British colonization in the Western Hemisphere, President James Monroe included in his annual message to Congress on December 2, 1823, two key ideas—noncolonization and separation of the New World from the Old. These two concepts and the reading that follows have become known as the Monroe Doctrine.

QUESTIONS TO CONSIDER

1. How did President Monroe's statements reflect a new sense of American confidence in foreign affairs?
2. Why did the British and French ignore the presidential statement for much of the nineteenth century?
3. How have subsequent U.S. presidents interpreted the Monroe Doctrine?

[T]he American Continents, by the free and independent condition which they have assumed and maintain, are henceforth not to be considered as subjects for future colonization by any European Powers. . . .

It was stated at the commencement of the last session, that a great effort was then making in Spain and Portugal, to improve the condition of the people of those countries, and that it appeared to be conducted with extraordinary moderation. It need scarcely be remarked that the result has been so far very different from what was then anticipated. Of events in that quarter of the globe, with which we have so much intercourse and from which we derive our origin, we have always been anxious and interested spectators. The citizens of the United States cherish sentiments the most friendly in favor of the liberty and happiness of their fellowmen on that side of the Atlantic. In the wars of the European powers in matters relating to themselves, we have never taken any part, nor does it comport with our policy, to do so. It is only when our rights are invaded or seriously menaced that we resent injuries or make preparation for our defense. With the movements in this Hemisphere we are of necessity more immediately connected, and by causes which must be obvious to all enlightened and impartial observers. The political system of the allied powers is essentially different in this respect from that of America. This difference proceeds from that which exists in their respective Governments; and to the defense of our own, which has been achieved by the loss of so much blood and treasure, and matured by the wisdom of their most enlightened citizens, and under which we have enjoyed unexampled felicity, this whole nation is devoted. We owe it, therefore, to candor and to the amicable relations existing between the United States and those powers to declare that we should consider any attempt on their part to extend their system to any portions of this Hemisphere as dangerous to our peace and safety. With the existing

From James D. Richardson, ed., *A Compilation of the Messages and Papers of the Presidents, 1789–1902,* Vol. 2 (Washington, DC: Bureau of National Literature and Art, 1903), pp. 209–19, *passim.*

colonies or dependencies of any European power we have not interfered and shall not interfere. But with the Governments who have declared their independence and maintained it, and whose independence we have, on great consideration and on just principles, acknowledged, we could not view any interposition for the purpose of oppressing them, or controlling in any other manner their destiny, by any European power in any other light than as the manifestation of an unfriendly disposition towards the United States. In the war between those new Governments and Spain we declared our neutrality at the time of their recognition, and to this we have adhered, and shall continue to adhere, provided no change shall occur which, in the judgement of the competent authorities of this Government, shall make a corresponding change on the part of the United States indispensable to their security. . . .

Our policy in regard to Europe, which was adopted at an early state of the wars which have so long agitated that quarter of the globe, nevertheless remains the same, which is, not to interfere in the internal concerns of any of its powers; to consider the government *de facto* as the legitimate government for us; to cultivate friendly relations with it, and to preserve those relations by a frank, firm and manly policy, meeting in all instances the just claims of every power, submitting to injuries from none. But in regard to those continents circumstances are eminently and conspicuously different. It is impossible that the allied powers should extend their political system to any portion of either continent without endangering our peace and happiness; nor can anyone believe that our southern brethren, if left to themselves, would adopt it of their own accord. It is equally impossible, therefore, that we should behold such interposition in any form with indifference. If we look to the comparative strength and resources of Spain and those new Governments, and their distance from each other, it must be obvious that she can never subdue them. It is still the true policy of the United States, to leave the parties to themselves, in the hope that other powers will pursue the same course.

32 Alexis de Tocqueville, *Democracy in America*

In 1831, Alexis de Tocqueville (1805–1859) was sent to the United States by the French government to study American prison and rehabilitation systems with the thought of applying some new concepts to prison reform in France. While traveling around the United States, then at the high point of Jacksonian democracy, de Tocqueville became intrigued by the variety of forces that made democracy function as it did in America. He was firmly convinced that democracy in America worked to assure that the will of majorities among the people prevailed and that it respected the rights of the population in general. His discussion of democracy in America amounts to a defense of it, in spite of his reservations about the role of the masses in American society and his frequently critical reaction to the behavior of particular Americans he spoke with. He was, after all, representing a constitutional monarchy in his official travels in the United States.

His classical education introduced de Tocqueville to the idea that humankind has the option of being governed by monarchical, aristocratic, or democratic principles—or some combination of these—and, in discussing French society, he writes as if choices among these systems were available on an ongoing basis; however, he is convinced that Americans will be prompted by the success of their own system to remain with democracy for the indefinite future.

QUESTIONS TO CONSIDER

1. What aspects of American democracy does de Tocqueville stress as worthy of imitation?
2. What price does de Tocqueville see a nation paying for adhering to democratic principles?
3. On what basis does de Tocqueville link American democracy with commercialism or capitalism?

In general, the laws of a democracy tend to benefit the greatest number of people, since they originate among a majority of all citizens, who might make mistakes but cannot desire anything contrary to their own interests.

Laws made by an aristocracy, by way of contrast, tend to concentrate wealth and power into the hands of a few, since an aristocracy by definition is always a minority. Thus it is correct to say that—all factors being equal—the aim of legislation in a democracy benefits the cause of humanity more than the aim of laws coming from an aristocracy.

An aristocracy is infinitely better at applying what it knows about legislation than can ever be true of a democracy. Always in command of itself, it is never subject to distractions of the moment but is able to make long-range plans, biding time with them until a favorable opportunity turns up for implementing them. An aristocracy knows what it is doing: it understands the art of making the combined force of its laws converge on the same point at the same time. . . .

How can we explain that in the United States, where people living there are recent arrivals; where they brought with them neither customs nor recollections [of political relevance], where they met each other for the first time . . . ; where, to put it briefly, patriotic feeling should hardly exist; how can we explain the fact that every individual takes as much interest in the affairs of his town, his country and his state as if they were his very own? The answer is that every single one takes an active part in governing society on some level. . . .

In the United States, the man on the street understands the impact of general prosperity on his own happiness. . . . Moreover, he is in the habit of giving himself credit for this prosperity. He identifies the public well-being with his own, and he works for the good of the state, motivated not only by duty and pride but by what I am almost tempted to call personal "greed."

From Alexis Charles . . . de Tocqueville. *De la démocratie en Amérique*, 15th ed. (Paris: Calmann Lévy frères, 1886). Vol. II, pp. 126–42. Trans. Henry A. Myers.

Since an American takes part in all his country's affairs, he comes to believe that it is up to him to defend it from all criticism, for in his mind it is not only his country which is being attacked: it is himself.

Nothing is more annoying in the behavior of Americans than their irritating patriotism. A foreigner may well be inclined to praise many things in the country, but he would have to ask permission to find fault with anything there without ever expecting actually to receive it. America is thus a country of liberty, where, to keep from hurting anyone, a foreigner dares not speak freely . . . about the state, or its citizens, or the authorities, or the public institutions or even the private enterprises or about anything else he finds there, except perhaps the climate and the soil. Even with these he will find Americans ready to defend them as if they had been co-planners at their creation.

In America, the man on the street has gotten a very good opinion of political rights because he enjoys those political rights. The people there do not undermine the rights of others, since they want to stay secure in their own rights. So that while in Europe a common man might well disobey the highest authority, an American submits to the authority of the least significant official without complaining.

[T]he political activity which prevails in the United States must be experienced first hand to be appreciated: hardly have you set foot on American soil before you find yourself confronted with a tumult of sorts. A confused clamor arises on all sides of you. A thousand voices reach your ear at the same time, each of them expressing some social need. Around you everything is in motion: here the people from one section of town are meeting to determine whether they should build a church there; there people are engaging in choosing a representative; a little farther over county commissioners are hurrying to the county seat to discuss some building projects. Elsewhere, local farmers have left their plows in order to discuss a proposed road or school. Citizens assemble for the sole purpose of expressing their disapproval of the way the government is being run, while others gather for no reason other than to honor incumbents as fathers of their country. Here you see even social organizations who—since they regard alcohol abuse as the chief evil threatening the state—unite in solemnly swearing to set an example of temperance. . . .

Having a hand in running society and being able to discuss government is an American's greatest concern and, in a way, his only pleasure. This reveals itself in every detail of American life: even women will attend public assemblies and seem to find political debate a welcome relief from household duties. To a certain extent political club activity is a substitute for theatrical entertainment. An American can carry on a discussion but not a conversation: his talk resembles a dissertation. He will speak to you as if he were addressing a meeting, and if his discussion heats up, he will say "Gentlemen," to you, his would-be conversation partner. . . .

[I]f an American were reduced to tending solely to his own affairs, he would be robbed of half his existence; he would feel a great void around him, and he would become incredibly unhappy. . . .

[C]ommon people cannot involve themselves in public affairs without expanding the framework of their vision or letting their minds escape the confines of routine. A common man who is given a minor role in government gains some self-respect in the process. Since he wields a bit of authority, other people of intelligence and education serve him with their talents. He is constantly pursued by people appealing to him with their special interests and, in trying to fool him they end up making him more knowledgeable in a thousand ways. He participates in political projects which he did not originate but which give him a taste for starting other projects. He discovers new improvements all the time in public property, which nurtures in him a desire to improve his own things.

Democracy does not give people the most efficient form of government; however, it brings about the very thing that the most efficient government is incapable of inducing most of the time: restless activity coursing through the whole social body, a superabundant force, an energy which cannot exist without it and which under the least favorable of circumstances may give birth to real wonders. Those are its true advantages. . . .

Do you want to raise the human spirit up a bit, leading it to confront the things of this world more openly and generously? Do you want to give men second thoughts about purely material things? Do you want to have them nourish deep convictions and prepare themselves for great commitments? Is it important to you that habits be refined, social graces be improved and the arts be cultivated? Do you like poetry, beauty and glory? Would your goals include mobilizing a people to exert a strong influence on all other nations? Would you have their destiny be one of grand undertakings, which, however they may turn out, will leave significant marks on history?

If all this appeals to you as the sum of goals towards which a society should be directed, do not choose democratic government, for it is not any sure means to your ends.

If, however, you think it is a good idea to steer human moral and intellectual activity towards raising the material standard of living and promoting general welfare; if you prefer straightforward reasoning to genius; if you would prefer to see habits of peace ingrained than heroic virtues; if you would rather put up with vice than crime and do not object to a reduction in noble deeds, providing that offenses can be reduced to the same extent; if you would rather have a high standard of living than a society distinguished by brilliance; and, finally, if you believe that the principal aim of a government is not to maximize the strength and glory of the whole body of the nation, but rather to provide for each individual in it a chance for greater happiness and exposure to less misery—go ahead and create conditions of equality: establish a democratic government.

Global Revolutionary Ferment

The second quarter of the nineteenth century witnessed revolutionary movements committed to the earlier goals of limiting monarchy or replacing it with a republic, as well as new ideas such as nationalism, which was a favorite cause of the Romantics (see Readings 36–40), and attempts to counteract abuses of the Industrial Revolution. In Britain, the problems of the industrial age were well publicized by reports of outrageous working conditions such as those described in "Women Miners in the English Coal Pits." In Britain, however, the tradition of parliamentary reform enabled that country to cope with the most obvious and compelling of workers' problems simply by passing new laws.

Marxism, which rejected parliamentary solutions of any sort, was very much a reaction to the abuses of the Industrial Revolution during this same period. Almost ignoring nationalism as an element in revolutionary discontent, Marxist theory established two models for future revolutions, one based on the self-destruction of capitalism, the other on pushing a backward regime over the brink with a coalition of all dissident forces. The models converge in their postrevolutionary stages: (1) dictatorship of the proletariat; (2) creation of a society of abundance; and (3) the withering away of the state.

The goals of the Taiping Rebellion in China, in contrast, evolved from the religious inspiration of its leader, Hung Hsiu-Ch'uan [Hong Xiuquan] as he met with increasing success. These included a commitment to social equality and to nationalism, specifically the aims of freeing native Chinese from the Manchus and—although this was not evident to Western observers at first—eliminating the dominance of Europeans in parts of China. The most constant element in the Taiping revolutionary message remained moral regeneration through the acceptance of Hung's interpretation of the divine will.

33 Women Miners in the English Coal Pits

Political revolution was not the only catalyst changing the global experience. Great Britain was the first country to undergo an industrial revolution, fueled in large part by the abundant coal deposits of Wales, Yorkshire, and Lancashire. Mining, like textile manufacture, was an occupation that exploited women and children. Not only did women and children work for less, their small bodies and nimble limbs permitted them to crawl the narrow tunnels to mine and haul the coal much more easily than men. Despite the clear economic advantages of using women and children in the English mines, by the 1840s there was a growing concern that the social and moral consequences of this exploitation were ruining the miners' family life. Agitation for reform in the mines compelled Parliament to investigate working conditions there and enact reform legislation to correct abuses. The following parliamentary reports printed in 1842 describe the working conditions for English women miners.

QUESTIONS TO CONSIDER

1. Why would so many women miners prefer to work in the mines without clothing? Why did the women need the heavy belts around their waists and chains between their legs?
2. What was the average workday of these female miners? What was their daily diet? What would be the social and familial cost for these female miners?
3. Karl Marx and Friedrich Engels (see Reading 34) argue that capitalism and industrialism are inherently exploitive of women so that "The bourgeois sees in his wife only an instrument of production." Based upon an analysis of this document, how would you respond to Marx and Engels's argument?

In England, exclusive of Wales, it is only in some of the colliery districts of Yorkshire and Lancashire that female Children of tender age and young and adult women are allowed to descend into the coal mines and regularly to perform the same kinds of underground work, and to work for the same number of hours, as boys and men; but in the East of Scotland their employment in the pits is general; and in South Wales it is not uncommon.

West Riding of Yorkshire: Southern Part.—In many of the collieries in this district, as far as relates to the underground employment, there is no distinction of sex, but the labour is distributed indifferently among both sexes, except that it is comparatively rare for the women to hew or get the coals, although there are numerous instances in which they regularly perform even this work. In great numbers of the coalpits in this district the men work in a state of perfect nakedness, and are in this state assisted in their labour by females of all ages, from girls of six years old to women of twenty-one, these females being themselves quite naked down to the waist.

"Girls," says the Sub-Commissioner [J. C. Symons], "regularly perform all the various offices of trapping, hurrying [Yorkshire terms for drawing the loaded coal corves],[1] filling, riddling,[2] tipping, and occasionally getting, just as they are performed by boys. One of the most disgusting sights I have ever seen was that of young females, dressed like boys in trousers, crawling on all fours, with belts round their waists and chains passing between their legs, at day pits at Hunshelf Bank, and in many small pits near Holmfirth and New Mills: it exists also in several other places. I visited the Hunshelf Colliery on the 18th of January: it is a day pit; that is, there is no shaft or descent; the gate or entrance is at the side of a bank, and nearly horizontal. The gate was not more than a yard high, and in some places not above 2 feet.

"When I arrived at the board or workings of the pit I found at one of the sideboards down a narrow passage a girl of fourteen years of age in boy's clothes, picking down the coal with the regular pick used by the men. She was half sitting half lying at her work, and said she found it tired her very much, and 'of course she didn't like it.' The place where she was at work was not 2 feet high. Further on were men lying on

---

[1]These were baskets to carry the hewn coal.
[2]Sifting and separating of the coal.

From Great Britain, *Parliamentary Papers*, 1842, Vol. XVI, pp. 24, 196.

their sides and getting. No less than six girls out of eighteen men and children are employed in this pit.

"Whilst I was in the pit the Rev Mr Bruce, of Wadsley, and the Rev Mr Nelson, of Rotherham, who accompanied me, and remained outside, saw another girl of ten years of age, also dressed in boy's clothes, who was employed in hurrying, and these gentlemen saw her at work. She was a nice-looking little child, but of course as black as a tinker, and with a little necklace round her throat.

"In two other pits in the Huddersfield Union I have seen the same sight. In one near New Mills, the chain, passing high up between the legs of two of these girls, had worn large holes in their trousers; and any sight more disgustingly indecent or revolting can scarcely be imagined than these girls at work—no brothel can beat it.

"On descending Messrs Hopwood's pit at Barnsley, I found assembled round a fire a group of men, boys, and girls, some of whom were of the age of puberty; the girls as well as the boys stark naked down to the waist, their hair bound up with a tight cap, and trousers supported by their hips. (At Silkstone and at Flockton they work in their shifts and trousers.) Their sex was recognizable only by their breasts, and some little difficulty occasionally arose in pointing out to me which were girls and which were boys, and which caused a good deal of laughing and joking. In the Flockton and Thornhill pits the system is even more indecent; for though the girls are clothed, at least three-fourths of the men for whom they "hurry" work *stark naked*, or with a flannel waistcoat only, and in this state they assist one another to fill the corves 18 or 20 times a day: I have seen this done myself frequently.

"When it is remembered that these girls hurry chiefly for men who are *not* their parents; that they go from 15 to 20 times a day into a dark chamber (the bank face), which is often 50 yards apart from any one, to a man working naked, or next to naked, it is not to be supposed but that where opportunity thus prevails sexual vices are of common occurrence. Add to this the free intercourse, and the rendezvous at the shaft or bullstake, where the corves are brought, and consider the language to which the young ear is habituated, the absence of religious instruction, and the early age at which contamination begins, and you will have before you, in the coal-pits where females are employed, the picture of a nursery for juvenile vice which you will go far and wide above ground to equal."

TWO WOMEN MINERS[3]

Betty Harris, age 37: I was married at 23, and went into a colliery when I was married. I used to weave when about 12 years old; can neither read nor write. I work for Andrew Knowles, of Little Bolton (Lancs), and make sometimes 7s a week, sometimes not so much. I am a drawer, and work from 6 in the morning to 6 at night. Stop about an hour at noon to eat my dinner; have bread and butter for dinner; I get no drink. I have two children, but they are too young to work. I worked at drawing when I was in the family way. I know a woman who has gone home and washed herself, taken to her bed, been delivered of a child, and gone to work again under the week.

I have a belt round my waist, and a chain passing between my legs, and I go on my hands and feet. The road is very steep, and we have to hold by a rope; and when

[3]From Great Britain, *Parliamentary Papers*, 1842, Vol. XV, p. 84, and ibid., Vol. XVII, p. 108.

there is no rope, by anything we can catch hold of. There are six women and about six boys and girls in the pit I work in; it is very hard work for a woman. The pit is very wet where I work, and the water comes over our clog-tops always, and I have seen it up to my thighs; it rains in at the roof terribly. My clothes are wet through almost all day long. I never was ill in my life, but when I was lying in.

My cousin looks after my children in the day time. I am very tired when I get home at night; I fall asleep sometimes before I get washed. I am not so strong as I was, and cannot stand my work so well as I used to. I have drawn till I have had the skin off me; the belt and chain is worse when we are in the family way. My feller (husband) has beaten me many a time for not being ready. I were not used to it at first, and he had little patience.

I have known many a man beat his drawer. I have known men take liberties with the drawers, and some of the women have bastards.

Patience Kershaw, age 17, Halifax: I go to pit at 5 o'clock in the morning and come out at 5 in the evening; I get my breakfast, porridge and milk, first; I take my dinner with me, a cake, and eat it as I go; I do not stop or rest at any time for the purpose, I get nothing else until I get home, and then have potatoes and meat, not every day meat.

I hurry in the clothes I have now got on—trousers and a ragged jacket; the bald place upon my head is made by thrusting the corves; I hurry the corves a mile and more under ground and back; they weigh 3 cwt. I hurry eleven a day. I wear a belt and chain at the workings to get the corves out. The getters that I work for are naked except their caps; they pull off all their clothes; I see them at work when I go up.

Sometimes they beat me if I am not quick enough, with their hands; they strike me upon my back. The boys take liberties with me sometimes; they pull me about. I am the only girl in the pit; there are about 20 boys and 15 men; all the men are naked. I would rather work in mill than in coal-pit.

Note by Sub-Commissioner Scriven: This girl is an ignorant, filthy, ragged, and deplorable looking object, and such a one as the uncivilized natives of the prairies would be shocked to look upon.

34   Karl Marx and Friedrich Engels, *Communist Manifesto*

As one of many responses to the suffering brought to European working classes by the Industrial Revolution, Karl Marx (1818–1883), a German radical writer who spent most of his life in France, Belgium, and England, formulated the philosophical and economic theories that still bear his name. In forecasting the downfall of capitalism, Marx proceeded from what he took to be demonstrable facts: (1) All new value comes from living labor. (2) In the material (or real) world, only physical labor (roughly what we would call "blue-collar labor") should be counted as productive living labor. (3) People who do not receive most of the value of what they produce are being cheated. (4) Laborers in a capitalistic system receive none of the new value of what they produce except for a mere subsistence wage. (5) Most of the new value that workers generate is taken from them by capitalists, who do no real work of their own. (6) Increasing unemployment will make the workers' lives unbearable, as competition leads capitalists to replace workers with machines.

Establishing these points as objectively true in his own mind, Marx concluded that capitalism is a system of highway robbery, which deserves not reformation but destruction. According to Marx, capitalism is plagued by a fatal contradiction in its very nature: Its efficient production generates vast quantities of goods, but its ceaseless drive to replace workers with machines renders the proletariat (working population) increasingly unemployed—thus unable to buy and consume these goods. Marx predicted that capitalism would be discredited and destroyed by a crisis of overproduction and underconsumption; mountains of machine-made goods would remain unbought in stores and warehouses, while unemployed workers would face deprivation without hope. Marx believed that the inevitable revolution would be violent because capitalists in most places would not allow capitalism to be voted out of existence and would use force to defend the remnants of their discredited system.

The *Communist Manifesto,* from which the following excerpts are taken, was the earliest comprehensive statement of Marx's economic, social, and political views; today this work remains the single most representative and influential document in the history of Marxism. Friedrich Engels (1820–1895), a German textile manufacturer whose family also owned a factory in England, assisted Marx in drafting the document. Despite his very bourgeois background, Engels collaborated for nearly forty years with Marx in producing works for publication. He also gave Marx financial support.

The *Manifesto* was written in 1847 and published early the following year to promulgate the ideas of a new group, which usually called itself the Communist League. (The term "Communist Party" was used only occasionally.) Previously, Marx and Engels had had some close associations with a group of German exiles called the League of the Just, which advocated a variety of democratic and collectivist principles. In effect, the more radical members of the League of the Just, influenced by Marx, became the nucleus of the Communist League. However, the Communist League was never very strong in members or influence and died of attrition in the early 1850s. In fact, those advocating the revolutionary theory of the *Manifesto*—including Marx and Engels themselves—were later forced by their small numbers to work with the labor reform movements they basically disliked.

It remained for Lenin in Russia to renounce the spirit of labor reform and return to advocating violent revolution as first proclaimed in the *Manifesto.*

QUESTIONS TO CONSIDER

1. Marx and Engels say there have always been class antagonisms. Why do they believe that the conflict between the bourgeoisie and the proletariat is different from previous class antagonisms?
2. What does the *Manifesto* mean by the statement that the bourgeoisie has forged the weapons that will be used against it?
3. What, according to Marx and Engels, make it neither possible nor desirable to reform capitalism?
4. Why do Marx and Engels predict so confidently that Communist society will be free of class antagonisms?
5. Why didn't Western European capitalism self-destruct in the manner predicted by the *Manifesto?*
6. Marx and Engels wrote their *Manifesto* for the industrialized First World rather than for the underdeveloped Third World. Ironically, Marx has had more appeal in nonindustrialized Third World countries of the late twentieth century than in the First World. Why?

CONFRONTATION BETWEEN CAPITALISM AND COMMUNISM

A specter is passing through Europe—the specter of Communism. All the powers of old Europe have joined in a holy crusade against this specter: Pope and Tsar, Metternich and Guizot, French radicals and German police. . . .

Bourgeoisie and Proletarians

The whole (written) history of society up to now has been the history of class struggles. . . .

Modern bourgeois society, rising from the ruins of feudal society, did not do away with class antagonisms. It only substituted new classes, new conditions of oppression and new forms of struggle for the old ones.

Our period, however, the bourgeois period, is distinguished by the fact that it has simplified class antagonisms. All society is splitting more and more into two great hostile camps, into two large classes opposing each other directly: bourgeoisie and proletariat. . . .

Large-scale industry established the world market for which the discovery of America had prepared the way. The world market has given unlimited development to commerce, navigation, and overland communication. This has had a reciprocal effect on the expansion of industry: the bourgeoisie has developed, increased its

From Karl Marx and Friedrich Engels, *Manifest der Kommunistischen Partei* (text of 1848; later clarifications by Engels are in parentheses). Berlin: Dietz Verlag, 1955, pp. 5–50, *passim.* Trans. Henry A. Myers.

funds for investment, and forced all the classes left over from the Middle Ages into obscurity to the same extent that commerce, shipping, and railroad construction have expanded.

We can thus see how the modern bourgeoisie is itself the product of a long chain of developments, a series of revolutions in the way production and trade have been carried on.

Each of these stages in the development of the bourgeoisie was accompanied by corresponding political progress (of that class). The bourgeoisie—as an oppressed class under the domination of feudal lords, as an armed and self-governing association in free cities, here in control of an independent urban republic, there serving as a monarchy's tax-paying Third Estate—served to balance the power of the nobility in semi-feudal or absolute monarchies with the growth of hand-tool industry and generally became the mainstay of the large monarchies. Finally, with the establishment of large industry and the world market the bourgeoisie conquered exclusive political domination for itself in modern states with representative governments. Those holding authority in modern states are only a committee looking out for the common class interests of the bourgeoisie.

The bourgeoisie has played a highly revolutionary role in history.

Wherever the bourgeoisie has taken over, it has destroyed all feudal, patriarchal, or idyllic relationships. It has relentlessly broken all those bright, multicolored feudal ties which bound men to their natural leaders, leaving no ties between man and man except naked interest, the bond of "cash payment" devoid of all feeling. It has drowned the holy ecstasies of religious fervor, of chivalrous enthusiasm, and even of top middle-class sentimentality in the ice-cold water of egotistical calculation. It has reduced personal importance to exchange value and substituted *one* single unscrupulous freedom for countless hard-earned and chartered freedoms. In a word, it has replaced exploitation veiled in religious and political illusions with open, shameless, direct and brutal exploitation.

The bourgeoisie has torn away the halo from every occupation regarded up to now with respect or awe. It has turned the physician, the attorney, the poet and the scientist into its own hired hands.

The bourgeoisie has ripped the ever so sentimental veil from family relationships and reduced them to purely monetary relations. . . .

By rapidly improving all instruments of production and by making communication infinitely easier, the bourgeoisie drags all, even the most barbarian, nations into civilization. The cheap prices of its commodities are the heavy artillery with which it levels all Chinese walls to the ground and with which it forces the most fervent hatred of barbarians for foreigners to give way. It compels all nations to adopt bourgeois methods of production if they want to survive. It forces them to introduce so-called civilization among themselves, that is, to become bourgeois. In short, the bourgeoisie creates a world in its own image.

The bourgeoisie has subjected the countryside to the rule of the city. It has raised enormous cities, greatly increasing the urban population numerically in relation to the rural one, and has thus rescued a significant part of the population from the idiocy of rural life. As it has made the countryside dependent on the city, it has also made barbarian and semi-barbarian peoples dependent on civilized peoples, agricultural populations on bourgeois ones, and the Orient on the Occident. . . .

During its class domination of scarcely one hundred years the bourgeoisie has created more colossal means of production and greater quantities of productive forces than have all past generations together. Subduing forces of nature, introducing machinery, steam navigation, railroads, and telegraphy, applying chemistry to industry and agriculture, clearing whole continents for cultivation, making rivers navigable, conjuring up whole populations to order—as if they were raising them out of the ground—what earlier century could have dreamed that such forces of production were asleep in the womb of associated labor? . . .

The weapons with which the bourgeoisie destroyed feudalism are now turned against the bourgeoisie itself.

The bourgeoisie, however, has not only forged the weapons of its own destruction but has also produced the men who will bear these weapons against them: the modern workers—the *proletarians.*

To the same extent to which the bourgeoisie—that is, capital—develops, the proletariat, the modern working class, also develops. Proletarians live only as long as they can find work, and they find work only as long as their work increases capital. These workers, who must sell themselves piecemeal, are a commodity like any other article of commerce and are therefore exposed to all the uncertainties of competition and to all the fluctuations of the market. . . .

Proletarians and Communists

What is the relationship of the Communists to the proletarians in general?

The Communists are no particular party to be contrasted with other workers' parties.

They have no interests separate from the whole proletariat.

They do not want to shape the proletarian movement in accordance with any special (sectarian) principles. The Communists are distinguished from the rest of the proletarian parties only by the fact that, on one hand, they strongly emphasize the common interests of the world proletariat independent of nationality considerations in the different national struggles of the proletarians and, on the other hand, they always represent the interests of the total movement in the different stages of development which the struggle between the proletariat and the bourgeoisie goes through.

The Communists are thus really the most committed part of workers' parties of all countries, the part which continually drives them further; their understanding of theory gives them insight into the conditions, the course, and the general outcomes of the proletarian movement in advance of the remaining mass of the proletariat.

The most immediate aim of the Communists is the same as that of all other proletarian parties: formation of the proletariat into a class, overthrow of bourgeois domination, and conquest of political power by the proletariat. . . .

On this subject, the Communists can sum up their theory in one phrase: abolition of private property.

We Communists have been accused of wanting to abolish that property which has been personally acquired through the owner's own efforts, property which is supposed to be the basis of all personal freedom, activity, and independence.

Property which has been worked for—acquired through the owner's own efforts! Are you talking about the property of the petty bourgeoisie or that of the small farmers which preceded bourgeois property? We don't need to abolish that: the development of industry has been abolishing it and is abolishing it every day.

Or are you talking about modern bourgeois private property?

Now, does the proletarian's work for wages create any property for him? In no way. It creates capital, i.e., property, which exploits wage labor and which can increase only under the condition that it produces a fresh supply of labor for wages, in order to exploit it in turn. Property in its current form is based on the antagonism of capital and wage labor. Let us observe the nature of this antagonism:

To be a capitalist means to occupy not only a purely personal but also a social position in production. Capital is a community product and can be put into motion only through the common activity of many members, indeed, in the final analysis, only through the common activity of all members of society.

Capital is thus not a personal force, but rather social power.

When capital is thus transformed into property belonging in common to all members of the community, personal property is not being changed into social property. Only the social character of property is changed. It loses its class character. . . .

In bourgeois society, living labor is only a means for increasing stored labor. In Communist society, stored labor is only a means for expanding, enriching, and improving the way workers live.

In bourgeois society, therefore, the past dominates the present; in Communist society, the present dominates the past. In bourgeois society, capital is individual and personal while the active individual person is dependent and depersonalized.

And the bourgeoisie calls the abolition of this relationship the abolition of individuality and freedom! And they are right. It is a question to be sure, of abolishing bourgeois individuality, independence, and freedom. . . .

Elimination of the family! Even the greatest radicals are horrified over this shameful intention of the Communists.

What is the basis of the present-day family, the bourgeois family? Capital, private gain. In its completely developed form, it exists only for the bourgeoisie; however, it requires two complements to maintain it: deprivation of proletarian family life and public prostitution.

The bourgeois family will naturally disappear with the disappearance of these complements to it, and both complements will disappear when capital disappears. . . .

All bourgeois sayings about family and education, about intimate relations of trust between parents and children, are becoming all the more disgusting as all family ties are torn apart for the proletarians by the development of big industry and their children are transformed into simple articles of trade and labor.

"But you Communists want to introduce the practice of holding women in common!" the whole bourgeoisie shouts back in chorus.

The bourgeois sees in his wife only an instrument of production. He hears that instruments of production are to be utilized for the common good, and naturally he can think of nothing other than that the fate of being common property will also fall to women.

He does not suspect that the real aim is to eliminate the position of women as mere instruments of production.

By the way, nothing is more ridiculous than the highly moral indignation of our bourgeois over the alleged official "community of women" of the Communists. The Communists do not need to introduce the community of women; it has almost always existed.

Our bourgeois men, not satisfied with the fact that the wives and daughters of their proletarians are at their disposal, to say nothing of public prostitution, take great pleasure in alternately seducing each other's wives.

Bourgeois marriage is in reality a community of married women. The most Communists can be accused of is a desire to introduce an official and open community of women, to take the place of a hypocritically concealed one. It goes without saying that with the abolition of the prevailing system of production the community of women arising from it, i.e., legal and illegal prostitution, will disappear.

Communists are further accused of wanting to abolish the fatherland and nationality.

Workers have no fatherland. We cannot take from them what they do not have. When the proletariat first takes over political rule and raises itself to the (leading) class of the nation, the proletariat will be constituting itself as the nation. It will then be "national" itself, although not at all in the bourgeois sense.

More and more national differences and antagonisms are disappearing already among the peoples due to the development of the bourgeoisie, freedom of trade, the world market, the uniformity of industrial production, and the living conditions corresponding with it.

Proletarian dominance will erase them even more. United action, among the civilized countries at least, is one of the basic preconditions for liberating the proletariat.

To the extent that the exploitation of one individual by another is eliminated, the exploitation of one nation by another will be eliminated.

The hostile stance of nations towards each other will disappear as the antagonism of classes inside the nation disappears.

The charges against Communism raised on religious, philosophical and ideological grounds in general do not deserve extensive discussion.

Does it require deep insight to grasp that when human living conditions—and with them social existences and relationships—change, their images, views, and concepts, in a word, their consciousness, will change as well?

What does the history of ideas prove other than that the output of the human mind changes itself to fit changes in material production? The ruling ideas of a period have always been only the ideas of the ruling class. . . .

In short, the Communists support every movement everywhere against existing social and political conditions.

In all these movements, they emphasize the property issue, regardless of how pronounced or faintly developed it is perceived to be, as the fundamental issue of the movement.

Finally, the Communists work everywhere for mutual understanding and support among the democratic parties of all countries.

The Communists scorn any concealment of their views and intentions. They declare openly that their goals can be reached only through the violent overthrow of all social structures which have existed previously. Let the ruling classes tremble at the prospect of a Communist Revolution. The proletarians have nothing to lose from it but their chains. They have a world to win.

Proletarians of all countries, unite!

35 The Taiping Rebellion

In the middle of the nineteenth century, China, under Manchu rule, was confronted with a dynastic crisis. British and French gunboats threatened China from the south, and the Russians encroached upon its territories from the north. Weakness, corruption, and rebellion spread across the land. By far the most serious rebellion was the Taiping Rebellion (1851–1864), started by Hung Hsiu-Ch'uan [Hong Xiuquan] (1814–1864).

The son of a farmer in southern China, Hung aspired to become an Imperial government official. After repeatedly failing the government service examinations, he fell ill in despair; in delirium he saw Jesus Christ, whom he called his Elder Brother. As the Heavenly Younger Brother of Christ, Hung came to believe that he was called to save humankind as the new messiah. His earlier contacts with the Reverend Issachar Roberts, an American Southern Baptist missionary, probably induced Hung's visions. By the late 1840s, his organization, called the God Worshippers' Society, had built a large following. Most of his followers were the frustrated and disaffected of southern China who were drawn to Hung's blend of Christian and Chinese ideology.

As his movement grew, it spread northward, defeating Imperial troops dispatched to crush the rebellion. In 1851, Hung bestowed upon himself the title of Heavenly King of the "Heavenly Kingdom of Great Peace" ("Taiping Tien-kuo [Taiping Dianquo]"). Within two years, his rebellion had captured Nanking [Nanjing], the second city of the empire, and had established a theocratic-military government. The policies of the Taiping leaders in the early period reflected their puritanical spirit. They prohibited opium-smoking, gambling, the use of tobacco and wine, polygamy, the sale of slaves, and prostitution. Their egalitarian ideas, including the equality of the sexes, were reflected in the abolition of footbinding and in the appointment of women as administrators and officers in the Taiping army. They also tried to abolish the private ownership of land and property, and they developed a program for the equal distribution of land. Many of the Taiping programs were thus quite unprecedented and revolutionary in nature. But the initial vigor and idealism were soon lost amid power struggles among the leaders, strategic blunders, poor diplomacy, and corruption. The rebellion faded by the summer of 1864.

The following excerpt is from the basic document of the Taiping Kingdom, called "The Land System of the Heavenly Kingdom." It is a sort of Taiping constitution. This document, first published in 1853, did not confine itself only to the land system but also included programs and policies related to military, civil, religious, financial, judicial, and educational institutions.

QUESTIONS TO CONSIDER

1. What were the egalitarian programs of the Taiping Kingdom?
2. How Christian was the Taiping ideology? How Chinese was it?
3. In what way was the Taiping Rebellion unique in the history of Chinese rebellions?
4. Compare the Taiping revolutionary programs with those of another revolutionary group.

All fields are to be divided into nine grades: every *mou*[1] of land, which during the two seasons, both early and late,[2] can produce 1,200 catties [of grain] shall be ranked as a superior field of the first class; every *mou* that produces 1,100 catties as a superior field of the second class; and every *mou* that produces 1,000 catties as a superior field of the third class. Every *mou* that produces 900 catties shall be considered as a medium field of the first class; every *mou* that produces 800 catties as a medium field of the second class; and every *mou* that produces 700 catties as a medium field of the third class. Every *mou* that produces 600 catties shall be considered as an inferior field of the first class; every *mou* that produces 500 catties as an inferior field of the second class; and every *mou* that produces 400 catties as an inferior field of the third class. One *mou* of superior field of the first class shall be considered equal to a *mou* and one-tenth of a superior field of the second class, and to a *mou* and two-tenths of a superior field of the third class; also to a *mou* and three-and-a-half tenths of a medium field of the first class, to a *mou* and five-tenths of a medium field of the second class, and to a *mou* and seven-and-a-half tenths of a medium field of the third class; also to two *mou* of an inferior field of the first class, to two *mou* and four-tenths of an inferior field of the second class, and to three *mou* of an inferior field of the third class.

The division of land must be according to the number of individuals, whether male or female; calculating upon the number of individuals in a household, if they be numerous, then the amount of land will be larger, and if few, smaller; and it shall be a mixture of the nine classes. If there are six persons in a family, then for three there shall be good land and for three poorer land, and of good and poor each shall have half. All the fields in the empire are to be cultivated by all the people alike. If the land is deficient in one place, then the people must be removed to another, and if the land is deficient in another, then the people must be removed to this place. All the fields throughout the empire, whether of abundant or deficient harvest, shall be taken as a whole: if this place is deficient, then the harvest of this abundant place must be removed to relieve it, and if that place is deficient, then the harvest of this abundant place must be removed in order to relieve the deficient place; thus, all the people in the empire may together enjoy the abundant happiness of the Heavenly Father, Supreme

[1]One acre equals 6.6 *mou*.
[2]I.e., a two-crop harvest.

From Franz Michael, *The Taiping Rebellion: History and Documents*, Vol. 2, *Documents and Comments* (Seattle: University of Washington Press, 1971), pp. 313–15, 319–20. © 1971 by the University of Washington Press. Reprinted by permission of the University of Washington Press.

Lord and Great God. There being fields, let all cultivate them; there being food, let all eat; there being clothes, let all be dressed; there being money, let all use it, so that nowhere does inequality exist, and no man is not well fed and clothed.

All men and women, every individual of sixteen years and upwards, shall receive land, twice as much as those of fifteen years of age and under. Thus, those sixteen years of age and above shall receive a *mou* of superior land of the first class, and those of fifteen years and under shall receive half that amount, five-tenths of a *mou* of superior land of the first class; again, if those of sixteen years and above receive three *mou* of inferior land of the third class, then those of fifteen years and below shall receive half that amount, one and one-half *mou* of inferior land of the third class.

Throughout the empire the mulberry tree is to be planted close to every wall, so that all women may engage in rearing silkworms, spinning the silk, and making garments. Throughout the empire every family should keep five hens and two sows, which must not be allowed to miss their proper season. At the time of harvest, every sergeant shall direct the corporals to see to it that of the twenty-five families under his charge each individual has a sufficient supply of food, and aside from the new grain each may receive, the remainder must be deposited in the public granary. Of wheat, pulse, hemp; flax, cloth, silk, fowls, dogs, etc., and money, the same is true; for the whole empire is the universal family of our Heavenly Father, the Supreme Lord and Great God. . . . For every twenty-five families there must be established one public granary, and one church where the sergeant must reside. Whenever there are marriages, or births, or funerals, all may go to the public granary; but a limit must be observed, and not a cash be used beyond what is necessary. Thus, every family which celebrates a marriage or a birth will be given one thousand cash and a hundred catties of grain. . . .

In every circle of twenty-five families, the work of the potter, the blacksmith, the carpenter, the mason, and other artisans must all be performed by the corporal and privates; when free from husbandry they are to attend to these matters. Every sergeant, in superintending marriages and funeral events in the twenty-five families, should in every case offer a eucharistic sacrifice to our Heavenly Father, the Supreme Lord and Great God; all corrupt ceremonies of former times are abolished.

In every circle of twenty-five families, all young boys must go to church every day, where the sergeant is to teach them to read the Old Testament and the New Testament, as well as the book of proclamations of the true ordained Sovereign. Every Sabbath the corporals must lead the men and women to the church, where the males and females are to sit in separate rows. There they will listen to sermons, sing praises, and offer sacrifices to our Heavenly Father, the Supreme Lord and Great God. . . .

In the creation of an army, for each 13,156 families there must first be a corps general; next there must be five colonels under the command of the corps general; next there must be five captains under the command of each colonel, altogether twenty-five captains; next each of the twenty-five captains must have under his command five lieutenants, altogether 125 lieutenants; next each of the 125 lieutenants must have under his command four sergeants, altogether 500 sergeants; next each of the 500 sergeants must have under his command five corporals, altogether 2,500 corporals; next each of the 2,500 corporals must have under his command four privates, altogether 10,000 privates, the entire army numbering altogether 13,156 men.

After the creation of an army, should the number of families increase, with the increase of five families there shall be an additional corporal; with the increase of twenty-six families there shall be an additional sergeant; with the increase of 105 families there shall be an additional lieutenant; with the increase of 526 families there shall be an additional captain; with the increase of 2,631 families there shall be an additional colonel; with the total increase of 13,156 families there shall be an additional corps general. Before a new corps general is appointed, the colonel and subordinate officers shall remain under the command of the old corps general; with the appointment of a corps general they must be handed over to the command of the new corps general.

Within [the court] and without, all the various officials and people must go every Sabbath to hear the expounding of the Holy Bible, reverently offer their sacrifices, and worship and praise the Heavenly Father, the Supreme Lord and Great God. On every seventh seven, the forty-ninth day, the Sabbath, the colonel, captains, and lieutenants shall go in turn to the churches in which reside the sergeants under their command and expound the Holy books, instruct the people, examine whether they obey the Commandments and orders or disobey the Commandments and orders, and whether they are diligent or slothful. On the first seventh seven, the forty-ninth day, the Sabbath, the colonel shall go to a certain sergeant's church, on the second seventh seven, the forty-ninth day, the Sabbath, the colonel shall then go to another sergeant's church, visiting them all in order, and after having gone the round he must begin again. The captains and lieutenants shall do the same.

Each man throughout the empire who has a wife, sons, and daughters amounting to three or four mouths, or five, six, seven, eight, or nine mouths, must give up one to be a soldier. With regard to the others, the widowers, widows, orphaned, and childless, the disabled and sick, they shall all be exempted from military service and issued provisions from the public granaries for their sustenance.

Throughout the empire all officials must every Sabbath, according to rank and position, reverently present sacrificial animals and offerings, sacrifice and worship, and praise the Heavenly Father, the Supreme Lord and Great God. They must also expound the Holy books; should any dare to neglect this duty, they shall be reduced to husbandmen. Respect this.

Nationalism and Romanticism

Although romanticism stressed a love of nature, the Romantics' view of what was natural and good differed from that held by most eighteenth-century intellectuals during the Enlightenment, who placed a high value on peace and tranquility. These intellectuals called the events in England in 1688–1689 the "Glorious Revolution" because it achieved constitutional government with so little apparent bloodshed and praised the American Revolution for *not* ushering in a period of class-based violence. Many Romantics, on the other hand, saw life itself as an endless struggle in which they were duty bound to participate on the side of justice.

We find Romantics entering into the class conflicts of the nineteenth century, usually on the side of the workers, and taking up such causes as the Greek war for liberation from the Turks.

Nationalism was fairly central to the thinking of most Romantics, who rejected the eighteenth-century notion that the universality of humankind overshadowed ethnic-group differences. They applied the idea that nature delighted in a splendid diversity of peoples and societies. This belief put them in a radical position after the Treaty of Vienna concluded the Napoleonic Wars and assigned many nationalities to multinational empires and effectively kept some other nationalities, notably the Germans and Italians, from moving toward national union. Even though Romantics generally backed armed conflict for idealistic causes, they did not condone war waged for the eighteenth-century reasons of dynastic succession or mere balance of power without regard for national identities or higher goals.

The word "nationalism" had first appeared in the French language in 1798, and its early meaning was closely bound up with the political ideology of the French Revolution. As the nineteenth century unfolded, a more universal definition of nationalism emerged, one that emphasized the importance of historical study to develop national consciousness; the insistence on a distinct and unique national character; the importance of a national homeland—one that could be celebrated by a national anthem and be represented by a national flag; and the promoting of a national language as the single best expression of national genius. This benign romantic character of early nationalism hardened after the revolutions of 1848 failed to achieve nationalist goals—or anything else—so that by the late nineteenth century, nationalism had become an explosive and quite often a militant force in European politics. This strident, aggressive-style nationalism was most commonly expressed in two ways. First, there was an irredentist (derived from the Italian word *irredentista*) form of nationalism that focused on the recovering of "unredeemed lands." Italian nationalists, for example, laid claim to parts of the Austrian-controlled territories of South Tyrol and the Dalmatian coast, especially those areas encompassing the cities of Trieste and Fiume. These territories, though separated from the Italian peninsula and ruled by a foreign power, were at least partly occupied by Italian-speaking peoples who considered themselves to be culturally and historically Italian. A second form of this new militant nationalism was focused not on the gathering-in of "lost lands," but on the freeing of an oppressed people from the yoke of a foreign power. Irish nationalism's Sinn Fein (in Gaelic meaning "we ourselves") movement is but one example of this strident, militant form of nationalism that was employed to resist and eventually overturn British rule in large parts of southern Ireland. Nationalistic sentiments were also expressed in the economic sphere. Advocates of economic nationalism argued for state protection of national economic interests by reviving the tariff and quota orientation of mercantilism on an "as-needed" basis. Friedrich List argued that newly emerging national economies such as those in Germany were ill equipped to compete with more developed economies, such as that in Great Britain.

36   Robert Southey, "The Battle of Blenheim"

Robert Southey (1774–1843), English poet, essayist, and historian, illustrates the Romantics' aversion to wars fought for abstract reasons of state or for the acquisition of seemingly random territory. The historical Battle of Blenheim, which took place about twenty-five miles from Augsburg in Bavaria, had been a major victory for the British, the Austrians, and their allies in the War of the Spanish Succession (1701–1714). In the recounting of the battle in Southey's poem, old Kaspar not only is ignorant of any idea why it was fought but has lost track of the fact that the main "heroes," the Duke of Marlborough and the Austrian Prince Eugene, were on the *other* side, fighting the French and Bavarian forces.

QUESTIONS TO CONSIDER

1. Why might a Romantic poet have condemned the War of the Spanish Succession as not worth the human sacrifices it demanded?
2. What is Southey's view of the sentiments of children in the poem? How do the words of Wilhelmine and Peterkin reflect the Romantics' view of children in general?
3. What, in Kaspar's view, made the victory at Blenheim a great one?

It was a summer evening,
Old Kaspar's work was done,
And he before his cottage door
Was sitting in the sun,
And by him sported on the green
His little grandchild Wilhelmine.

She saw her brother Peterkin
Roll something large and round,
Which he beside the rivulet
In playing there had found;
He came to ask what he found,
That was so large, and smooth, and round.

Old Kaspar took it from the boy,
Who stood expectant by;
And then the old man shook his head,
And, with a natural sigh,
" 'Tis some poor fellow's skull," said he,
"Who fell in the great victory."

"I find them in the garden,
For there's many here about;
And often when I go to plough,
The ploughshare turns them out!
For many thousand men," said he,
"Were slain in that great victory."

"Now tell us what 'twas all about,"
Young Peterkin, he cries;
And little Wilhelmine looks up
With wonder-waiting eyes;
"Now tell us all about the war;
And what they fought each other for."

"It was the English," Kaspar cried,
"Who put the French to rout;
But what they fought each other for,
I could not well make out;
But everybody said," quoth he,
"That 'twas a famous victory.

"My father lived at Blenheim then,
Yon little stream hard by;
They burnt his dwelling to the ground,
And he was forced to fly;
So with his wife and child he fled,
Nor had he where to rest his head.

From *Poems of Robert Southey*, ed. Maurice H. Fitzgerald (London: Henry Frowde, 1909), pp. 365–66 (first published 1798).

"With fire and sword the country round
Was wasted far and wide,
And many a childing mother then,
And new-born baby died;
But things like that, you know, must be
At every famous victory.

"They say it was a shocking sight
After the field was won;
For many thousand bodies here
Lay rotting in the sun;
But things like that, you know must be
After a famous victory.

"Great praise the Duke of Marlbro' won,
And our good Prince Eugene."
"Why 'twas a very wicked thing!"
Said little Wilhelmine.
"Nay . . . nay . . . my little girl," quoth he,
"It was a famous victory.

"And every body praised the Duke
Who this great fight did win."
"But what came of it at last?"
Quoth little Peterkin.
"Why that I cannot tell," said he,
"But 'twas a famous victory."

37 Friedrich List, *National System of Political Economy*

Typical of the nineteenth century's new economic nationalism was the German-born Friedrich List (1789–1846), who in 1825 emigrated to Pennsylvania, where he tried his hand at journalism, coal mining, and railroading. In 1832, he returned to Germany to become one of the prime organizers of a North German railway company. As a young man, List had admired Adam Smith and the Enlightenment thinkers advocating free-trade economics, but his commercial experiences in America and Germany convinced him that unbridled free trade did not always work. In 1841, List published his *National System of Political Economy,* which was not so much an attack on Adam Smith and the free traders as it was a comprehensive analysis of national economic development. List distrusted Smith's assertion that individual merchants led by "the invisible hand" of supply and demand could promote the common good in a complex industrialized society. List argued that Smith's metaphor of the "invisible hand" was never verified and that Smith's eighteenth-century examples of the farmer, the tailor, and the shoemaker did not reflect the new economic realities of industrialized countries; furthermore, Adam Smith had failed to take into account that in industrialized economies organizations, not individuals, create wealth. Although critical of Smith's arguments, List remained committed to the long-term value of free trade and actively sought to remove trade barriers; nonetheless, he argued that national economies mature at different rates and that free trade is not necessarily the best economic policy for all countries at all times. In fact, List argued, new, emerging national economies, such as those of his (not yet politically united) Germany, were ill equipped to compete with more developed economies, such as that of Great Britain and therefore needed certain economic safeguards to protect fledgling industries. Although highly critical of Adam Smith, he was not an advocate of central economic planning, nor did he suggest any form of socialism. Much like his slightly earlier American counterpart, Alexander Hamilton, he argued that government and industry should not view each other as natural adversaries but should work together to promote economic growth.

QUESTIONS TO CONSIDER

1. Friedrich List argues that as a class, merchants are too short-sighted and too selfish to direct an economy and that "legislative and administrative power" must guide the national economy if it is to succeed in an industrialized world economy. Is this argument accepted in capitalist countries today? Why? Why not? (See Reading 96.)

2. List argues that economies mature at different rates and that different nations will have different forms of capitalism; for example, Japanese capitalism differs from American capitalism, which, in turn, differs from German capitalism. Therefore, argues List, "free trade," even between capitalist countries, is not always "free" nor always fair. Is this correct?

3. List criticizes Adam Smith not only for failing to explain how the metaphor of the "invisible hand" regulates the market but also for emphasizing consumption rather than economic development to the point of wrongly assuming that a market economy driven by "free trade" will always advance the common good. Are List's criticisms of Adam Smith valid (see Reading 16)?

ADAM SMITH

The doctrine of Adam Smith in regard to international commerce, is but a continuation of that of the physiocrats. Like the latter, it disregards nationality; it excludes almost entirely politics and government; it supposes the existence of perpetual peace and universal association; it depreciates the advantages of national manufacturing industry, as well as the means of acquiring it; it demands absolute free trade.

Adam Smith, following the traces of the physiocrats, has committed the capital fault of considering absolute free trade as a dictate of reason, and of neglecting to study profoundly the historical development of that idea.

It is obvious that Adam Smith regarded this idea of free trade as the basis upon which he was to found his literary reputation. It is natural that he should exert himself in his work, to set aside, and to combat every obstacle to that idea; that regarding himself as the champion of absolute free trade he should write under the influence of this preconception.

With such prepossessions how could he appreciate facts and men, history and statistics, the measures of governments and their authors, from any point of view than that of their conformity or discrepancy with his principle? . . .

This system regards everything from a commercial point of view. The value of things is wealth: to acquire values was to obtain wealth. The development of productive power is abandoned by it to hazard, nature, or Providence, as it may happen. As for the government, it has no part in the matter, and as for public policy, it has no concern in the accumulation of values. Merchants always desire to purchase in the cheapest market; heavy importations may ruin the manufacturers of the country; it is of no consequence. If foreign nations grant premiums of exportation on their manufactured products, so much the better, their goods come so much the cheaper. Only those who produce exchangeable values are producers in their eyes. The advantages in detail of the division of labor are understood, but the division of labor which applies to the nation is not perceived. It is only by the way of individual saving that capital is increased, that business is increased or extended. As to the development of productive power produced by the establishment of manufacture, by external trade, and by that national vigor which is the result, no value whatever attaches to it. The future of a nation is of no importance, provided that individuals of which it consists acquire exchangeable values. Of land, the rent is alone deemed worthy of notice; the value of the soil is not considered. . . .

PRIVATE AND NATIONAL ECONOMY

It is obvious that this is not a system of national economy, but a system of individual economy, such as might occur without the intervention or protection of governments, without war, without hostile measures of unfriendly countries. It cannot explain by what means nations now flourishing have attained their actual degree of prosperity and power, and by what causes others have lost their former prosperity and power. It shows how, in private industry, the natural agents, viz., labor and cap-

From Friedrich List, *National System of Political Economy*, trans. G. A. Mathie and Henri Richelot (Philadelphia: J.B. Lippincott & Co., 1856), pp. 420–25; 253–61, *passim*.

ital, concur in producing for the market many valuable articles, and how these articles are distributed and consumed among men. But it does not show how to bring into activity and to give value to the natural power at the disposition of a whole people, how to conduct a poor or feeble nation to prosperity and power: it does not enter into such considerations, because the School,[1] repelling absolutely all public intervention, remains in ignorance of the particular condition of different nations, and seeks only the prosperity of all mankind. When the subject is international trade, the School always opposes the inhabitants of the country to foreigners; it borrows all its examples from the special relations of merchants; it always treats of merchandise in general, without making any distinction between agricultural and manufactured products, to show that it is indifferent whether imports and exports be of the precious metals, of raw materials, or manufactured articles, and whether they are or are not in equilibrium. . . .

The School admits no distinction between nations which have reached a superior degree of economical development, and those which yet occupy a lower scale. It excludes everywhere the interference of the State; for every individual must be capable of production in proportion as government leaves him to his own resources. If that doctrine be true, the most active and the richest producers of the globe should be the savages, for nowhere is the individual liberty greater, nowhere is the intervention of government less than in the savage state.

Statistics and history teach, on the contrary, that the action of legislative and administrative power becomes everywhere more necessary in proportion as the national economy is developed. As individual liberty is generally desirable only so far as it is not inconsistent with the public good; so private industry can reasonably claim an unrestrained liberty or action, only to the extent that such action is consistent with the general prosperity of a nation. But if this free action of individuals is useless or positively hurtful to the public, the nation has the right to turn this lost industry, this wasted power, to the support of the collective power of the country; or at least those concerned or engaged in this ill-directed industry should, for the sake of their own interests, submit to such public regulations as would enure to their own benefit as well as the public advantage. In representing free competition of producers as the surest means for developing the prosperity of mankind, the School is perfectly right, considering the point of view from which it regards the subject. In the hypothesis of universal association, every restriction upon honest trade between different countries would seem unreasonable and injurious. But as long as some nations will persist in regarding their special interests as of greater value to them than the collective interests of humanity, it must be folly to speak of unrestricted competition between inhabitants of the same country. A great nation must consequently endeavor to form a complete whole, which may maintain relations with other similar unities within the limits which its particular interest as a society may prescribe; now these social interests are known to differ immensely from the private interests of all the individuals of a nation, if each individual be taken separately and not as a member of the national association, if, as with Smith and Say,[2] individuals are regarded merely as producers and consumers, and not as citizens of a nation.

---

[1]Adam Smith and the "School" of free trade economists.
[2]Jean-Baptiste Say (1767–1832), a French economist, who, like Adam Smith, was committed to free trade.

38 Program of the Serb Society of National Defense [*Narodna Odbrana*]

Certainly one of the most violent national movements throughout the nineteenth and twentieth centuries, one that combined both the irredentist and militant strains of nationalism, was Balkan nationalism. "Balkan" is the Turkish word for mountain, and the rugged topography of the Balkan peninsula of southeastern Europe contributed mightily to the development of Balkan nationalism. Serbia, the largest of all the Balkan states, long considered itself the natural leader of all Balkan peoples and bitterly resented the interference of Austria-Hungary and Ottoman Turkey in Balkan affairs. After nearly five centuries of subjugation, Serbia gained its independence from Turkey in 1878 and aggressively sought to assert its hegemony over the entire Balkan peninsula. Early in the twentieth century, the executive committee of a Serbian patriotic society, the Society of National Defense, published its program for Serbian nationalism. Unlike many abstract, theoretical statements of nationalism, this document is a practical step-by-step blueprint for igniting Serbian nationalism to resist continued foreign interference and to prepare for a greater Serbian role in Balkan politics.

QUESTIONS TO CONSIDER

1. Scholars have both praised and criticized the Serbs for celebrating June 28, the battle of Kossowo, one of their greatest defeats, as their national holiday. What does this choice of national holiday, commemorating a defeat in the fourteenth century, tell us about Serbian nationalism?

2. Why would the Society of National Defense choose the present tense to describe the significance of the battle of Kossowo, a battle that took place in 1389? What does this insistence upon using the present tense and avenging the battle of Kossowo suggest about the character and spirit of Serbian nationalism?

3. As a part of its plan to develop Serbian nationalism, the Society of National Defense lists the following five elements: national consciousness, physical development, new methods of work, rifle clubs, and gymnastic societies. Which of these elements do you think is most important for the development of Serbian nationalism? Why?

4. How would you compare the Society of National Defense's definition of nationalism with that of Fustel de Coulanges (see Reading 40)?

5. Even though this document was written nearly a century ago, do you see any contemporary implications in the Program of the Serb Society of National Defense? What are they?

It is quite wrong to think Kossowo[1] once existed, is past, and that today it must simply be avenged. Kossowo is still among us, or, to put it differently, we are today in the middle of Kossowo, and we are not avenging it but fighting on its battlefield.

The Serbian people are always fighting the battle of Kossowo, only the battlefield changes form. Our present Kossowo is the darkness and ignorance in which the Serbs live. Barbarism of every kind, unhygienic conditions, lack of national consciousness, party and other feuds—these are the Turks of today against whom we must set out to a new Kossowo. These internal causes of a new Kossowo are considerable; there are external causes too, however, beyond our boundaries in the north and west— the Germans, the Austrians, and the Swabians with their drive toward our Serb and Slavic south. Darkness and ignorance among our people within and the German invasion from outside are the new Turks whom we must meet today on the Serb battlefield of Kossowo and with whom we have to resume the struggle for the Serbian name and Serbian freedom.

The freedom of a people is just as incomplete when it is in bondage to ignorance as when it is in physical bondage. Man can be enserfed also to errors, prejudices, ignorance, love of drink, barbarism. War must be waged against all these evils. Just as we once rebelled against the Turks, we must now rebel against these evil national conditions and fight for freedom from them.

The view that there is war only when the guns thunder and the rifles crack is a false one. Among nations there is never peace, but always a condition of war; life goes forward under the sign of struggle. Even today in the middle of peace the Serbs are waging a desperate war. Woe to him who does not know it. This war is our present fight for our soil, our health, civilization, knowledge, schools, physical culture—as we have described it already in the section "The New Contemporary *Narodna Odbrana*."

The *Narodna Odbrana*, convinced of this conception of our present position, expects that it will find among the unknown teachers and priests, among the students, merchants, and other modest workers displaying private initiative in all directions, new heroes such as are demanded by today's Kossowo, today's war for our freedom. Milosch Obilitsch fought his way through Turkish swords and lances to the tent of Mured to murder him. Our new contemporary hero, whether teacher or priest or some other national worker, must make his way through insults, humiliations, and injustice in order to drive darkness and ignorance from the soul of the people. Singjelitsch in the defense of the newly created Serbia blew himself and his companions up along with the breastwork. The national worker today must often sacrifice his personal happiness and his family in order to agitate day by day for the freeing of our society from the sins of disease, poverty, lack of national consciousness, and so on.

---

[1]The Turks crushed the Serbian-Albanian-Croatian army at Kossowo (also spelled as Kosovo or Kossovo) in 1389 and conquered the country, but Milosch Obilitsch, a Serb hero of the battle, succeeded in penetrating the Turkish line and slaying the Turkish sultan. The anniversary of the battle and of the assassination has been commemorated on June 28, a Serbian national holiday.

Narodna Odbrana Izdanje Stredisnog Odbora Odbrane (Belgrade, 1911), translated into German and printed in *Die Kriegsschuldfrage* (Berlin, 1927), V, 192–225 in *Europe in the Nineteenth Century: A Documentary Analysis of Change and Conflict*, ed., Eugene N. Anderson. Stanley J. Pinceti, Jr., and Donald J. Ziegler 2:329–31; 316–22. Reprinted by permission of Prentice-Hall, Inc., Upper Saddle River, NJ.

1. THE STRENGTHENING OF NATIONAL CONSCIOUSNESS

As its first, most sacred, and most important goal the *Narodna Odbrana* undertakes the awakening, unfolding, strengthening, and developing of Serbian nationalism from city to city, from village to village, from house to house, from man to man, and from greybeard to child. Our goal is a nationally conscious and proud Serbia. We wish to create such a Serbia as quickly as possible. Only such a country is worthy to bear the name Serbia; only such a country will have the power to withstand all the difficulties which rise up around us; only a country proud of its Serbian identity and highly conscious of it will be able to bear the sacrifices demanded in freeing and uniting an entire people.

Only when Serbian national consciousness bursts into flame can the popular will be kindled for all the other tasks of the *Narodna Odbrana.* Therefore the society places before all else the task of strengthening the national consciousness.

2. FURTHERING PHYSICAL DEVELOPMENT

From such experiences as those we have had with mustering, we know that our youth is largely deficient physically as a result of our great indifference toward bodily development.

While among other peoples in all places, on Sundays and holidays and even on work days the crack of rifles and the joyful cry of the Sokol resound, our effeminate society hardly bothers about physical or military exercise and spends its entire free time sitting in the coffee houses or dozing at home. Many of our villages and towns have no sport organization at all. Only a very few Serbs of either sex are members of sport groups; likewise, only a few of our wealthy people are founders and patrons of patriotic organizations. Weakness and indifference to the common good have overcome all classes of our society.

We know that a people able to meet the struggles facing Serbia cannot be created out of young people with pale faces and narrow chests who look like old men, and such young people we meet everywhere. Yet we are not concerned about the fatal results of our lack of action. Officers, priests, teachers, professors, and other officials are far too little interested in physical exercise, as are businessmen, industrial leaders, and others. Not only do they avoid sports; they ridicule those who disturb our sleepy world and who want to spur us on to exercise.

The annexation found us unprepared in everything, most lamentably of all in the field of physical conditioning.[2] The honor of Serbian physical culture was almost at an end! In as short a time as possible this situation must be changed by means of enthusiastic, well thought-through, and persistent effort.

The *Narodna Odbrana* will fight with all available means for the development and the progress of physical improvement in Serbia, and especially of the shooting and gymnastic groups. This will be its second main task. Its activity will develop in two directions: one part influencing society and the people by arousing a feeling for sports and by founding sport organizations even in the smallest Serbian villages; the

---

[2]In 1908, Austria-Hungary abruptly annexed the two Balkan provinces of Bosnia-Herzegovina, thereby deeply humiliating Serbia amongst the Balkan peoples and, at the same time, reaffirming Serbia's determination to gain control of the two "lost provinces" and drive Austria out of the Balkans.

other affecting the state, the government, and the national parliament, from which must be demanded the introduction of compulsory military education into all schools, and material aid to private initiative.

Parallel with these efforts in behalf of physical culture, agitation for the creation of a strong army must also be spread among the masses. A love for the military profession must be aroused, as well as love and a spirit of sacrifice for the fatherland. In special sections in this book we shall speak again of the close connection between the *Narodna Odbrana* and separate branches of physical exercise.

3. THE INTRODUCTION OF NEW METHODS OF WORK

The difficult conditions in which our people finds itself, and of which we have been seriously conscious only since the annexation, demand of us the deepest earnestness in fulfilling the tasks which various organizations and committees offer to individual initiative. To work for physical education and other goals cannot be a subject merely of conversation and must not serve to satisfy our vanity or provide a means of distraction. We must not concern ourselves with it only temporarily, but must show the enthusiasm and seriousness suitable for this great, important, and holy work.

We must not be ashamed to speak of Sokols, shooting societies, and popular gatherings; we must personally sacrifice time and money for this by giving up many pleasures. We must not avoid the small villages and cities but be proud to go there in order to serve the rebirth of our people. The *Narodna Odbrana* demands of the members of the groups and committees that they assume not just places of honor but the actual responsibility of accomplishing the work to be done. For an educated Serb the worthiest and best spot, the first to which every young Serb must devote himself and to which he must remain true late into life, is contact with the people in the lowest ranks, in the farthest villages, in the smallest towns where folk knowledge and national progress have progressed least. There he must work as a teacher, religious leader, county or municipal official. By means of promoting an effort of this kind for the commonweal, by popularizing these ideas among wide ranks of the people through lectures and meetings, through simultaneously arousing equal enthusiasm for all kinds of activity, the *Narodna Odbrana* transplants into our social order completely new methods of developing the work of private initiative.

4. RIFLE CLUBS AND THE *NARODNA ODBRANA*

Struggles between nations and states are always eventually decided by wars, and the wars are conducted with firearms.

The firing of weapons is today one of the most important means of carrying on warfare. Thus all peoples, all states, all thinking men in the entire world devote the greatest care to this matter. In the countries which have the greatest cultural development and the longest period of military service, practice in shooting is most common. Although the period of military service lasts only two or three years in such countries, everywhere there are shooting clubs where young and old may practice. From examples given elsewhere, everyone can see for himself how much is sacrificed throughout the world for the sake of practice in shooting.

If this is the situation in other countries, we are right in demanding that even more be done here for shooting practice than is done elsewhere, because we live in a country of peasants where the term of military service is only six months and where enemies surround us. The *Narodna Odbrana* demands that there be no Serb in Serbia who is not a member of a shooting club, that no hamlet be without a shooting society. Compulsory rifle practice is to be introduced into all schools, and the state must support the shooting clubs in such numbers as to make Serbia into one great rifle center, where on Sundays and holidays the Serbian rifle shot will echo from mountain to mountain and from one end of Serbia to the other.

5. GYMNASTIC SOCIETIES [SOKOLS]

Like all other forms of life, peoples too are defeated in the struggle for existence if they do not have the strength to endure. Everything which is weak and unhealthy is destroyed in competition, and only what is healthy, strong, and adaptable lives on. The history of those peoples which have disappeared and of those which still survive a people first began when immorality and indolence appeared, when good customs and a sound way of life were abandoned.

The history of the Serbian and Turkish peoples confirms this law. The Turks, better organized militarily, stronger in numbers, and fanatic in belief, destroyed the Serbian state when it was weakened internally and broken by the conflicts between Serbian feudal lords. But how do the Turks fare today? Once the strongest people in the world, the Turks today are the "sick man" of the Bosporus. This the Turks have become because they lacked the ability to endure the struggle with more powerful, healthier, more advanced peoples. What has all this to do with the Serbian Sokol?

In the south the old Turks are already retreating; only a part of our peoples still groans under their yoke; but from the north come new Turks, more fearsome and dangerous than the old ones. Culturally superior and economically strong, our northern enemies turn upon us. They want to rob us of freedom and language, tread upon us, destroy us. Already we perceive signs of the coming struggle; the Serbian people face the question: "To be or not to be?" And now the time has come for the institution of the Serbian Sokols. That is the demand of the hour, the order of national defense.

Only a sound, powerful, nationally conscious, and well-organized people is capable of defense, of war, and of victory.

This truth the Serbian Sokols have written on their flags and they announce it to the people. This truth they want to translate into fact.

The Serbian Sokol movement wants to strengthen everyone who joins—all Serbian brothers and sisters. It wants to awaken in each Serb pride in and consciousness of our national strength, so that we may embark upon the struggle as a powerful and conscious people with confidence in national victory and without fear for the future of the nation. That is what the Serbian Sokols want; that is their goal. . . .

The idea of the Serbian Sokol is the idea of the Serbian people. The Sokol idea coincides in its aims with the aims of the Serbian people. In the ideal of the Sokol the Serbian ideal becomes realized, because it unites in this ideal all its members irrespective of where they live. It is a powerful weapon which must be extended to all groups of the people.

Without troubling themselves about the political and religious convictions of their members, without paying attention to class or rank, the Sokols draw in young Serbs, both male and female, for the purpose of physical and moral training in the interest of national cultural development.

The Sokols' goal in promoting physical exercise is not the further holding of exhibitions to arouse wonder at the skill displayed; the exercises and entire organization of the Sokols exist instead to develop strong and hardy men and women, beautiful in growth and form, of free, courageous, and independent spirit—good patriots, who not only love their country but also are able to defend it in the hour of need.

The Serbian Sokol ideal is a great one because it is the national ideal. To make it a reality all Serbs must rally to the Sokols. Our people are in danger. We all must harness our strength, must develop every muscle, must illuminate every part of the brain. Through the tireless effort of us all, the Serbian Sokols will give the Serbian people a healthy, strong, nationally conscious, and well-organized nation, a nation that will not be defeated but will triumph in the struggle for national survival.

Thus the realization of the ideal of the Serbian Sokols is one of the first goals of national defense rightly understood.

39 Irish National Identity and Destiny: Three Views

Although once independent, from the early twelfth to the early twentieth centuries Ireland was governed by Great Britain. For more than four hundred years, the bitter tensions between the oppressed Irish Catholic majority and the dominant English-Protestant ruling minority frequently erupted in grim scenes of bloody, sectarian violence. In 1912, while the British Parliament was seriously considering greater internal autonomy for Ireland (Home Rule), the powerful Ulster Unionist Party, representing the Protestant majority of the six northern counties of Ireland, declared its unalterable opposition to Home Rule. Fearing that the British government's proposed Home Rule of 1912 would threaten their political and religious rights, the Ulster Unionist leaders declared September 12, 1912, "Ulster Day." In imitation of their seventeenth-century Presbyterian ancestors who pledged to establish the Presbyterian creed in England and Ireland, about 450,000 men and women signed this document (some with their own blood) denouncing Home Rule for Ireland's Catholic majority.

The outbreak of World War I in 1914 temporarily shelved the issue of Home Rule for Ireland until 1916 when the Sinn Fein ("we ourselves") movement vigorously resisted British military recruitment in Ireland for the fighting in France and urged an immediate reopening of the stalled debate on Home Rule. During Easter week 1916, Sinn Fein led a bloody, week-long rebellion in Dublin protesting British rule, culminating in the Declaration of a Provisional Government for an Irish Republic. The Easter Rising was brutally suppressed, but the political agitation, violence, and fighting among Irish Republicans, Ulster Unionists, and the British troops continued until a truce was signed on December 6, 1921, recognizing the twenty-six counties of southern Ireland as the Irish Free State within the British Commonwealth of Nations. During that Easter-week rising, four hundred people were killed and one thousand wounded. This event, perhaps more than any other, sealed the connections between militant Irish nationalism and the future Irish Republic.

The six counties of Northern Ireland (Ulster) withdrew from this Irish Free State and chose to remain part of the United Kingdom. In 1937, the Irish Free State changed its name to Érie and in 1947, Érie ceased to be a member of the British Commonwealth. Unfortunately, these political arrangements did not end the bloodshed or the violence. The outlawed Irish Republican Army (IRA) has advanced its goal of unity for the two Irelands by attacking British military units in Northern Ireland and by terror-bombing its political enemies throughout the United Kingdom. So, too, the political authorities of Northern Ireland, supported by the British military government, have a well-established record of denying the Catholic minority of Northern Ireland civic, political, and economic rights and have used brutality and torture in interrogating IRA suspects and their supporters.

The last statement in the following reading was made by Eamon De Valera (1882–1975), who served as the Republic of Ireland's (Érie) prime minister for twenty-one years. In a radio broadcast beamed to the United States on February 12, 1933, Lincoln's birthday, he explained his views on Irish nationalism and his dream of a united Ireland.

QUESTIONS TO CONSIDER

1. How does the first document suggest the historic fault lines of religion and politics in the shaping of Irish nationalism?
2. Why would the Ulster Unionists choose to title their pledge a "Solemn League and Covenant"?
3. Why would the Provisional Government cite the "exiled children in America" but omit mentioning "Great Britain" or "King George V"?
4. How would you compare this definition of Irish nationalism with the documents on Serbian and French nationalism (see Readings 38 and 40)?
5. In light of centuries of sectarian violence between Catholics and Protestants, how persuasive is De Valera's argument that Ireland is simply too small a country for two separate governments?
6. De Valera argues that the erection of the six counties of Ulster "was a purely arbitrary act, inspired solely by considerations of British imperial policy and contrary to every interest of the Irish people." In light of the 1912 "Ulster's Solemn League and Covenant," is this true?

IRISH DECLARATION OF INDEPENDENCE

The Provisional Government of the Irish republic to the people of Ireland

Irishmen and Irishwomen: In the name of God and of the dead generations from which she receives her old tradition of nationhood, Ireland, through us, summons her children to her flag and strikes for her freedom.

Having organized and trained her manhood through her secret revolutionary organization, the Irish Republican Brotherhood, and through her open military organizations, the Irish Volunteers, and the Irish Citizen Army, having patiently perfected her discipline, having resolutely waited for the right moment to reveal itself, she now seizes that moment, and, supported by her exiled children in America and by gallant allies in Europe, but relying in the first on her own strength, she strikes in full confidence of victory.

We declare the right of the people of Ireland to the ownership of Ireland, and to the unfettered control of Irish destinies, to be sovereign and indefeasible. The long usurpation of that right by a foreign people and government has not extinguished the right, nor can it ever be extinguished except by the destruction of the Irish people. In every generation the Irish people have asserted their right to national freedom and sovereignty; six times during the past three hundred years they have asserted it in arms. Standing on that fundamental right and again asserting it in arms in the face of the world, we hereby proclaim the Irish republic as a sovereign independent state, and we pledge our lives and the lives of our comrades-in-arms to the cause of its freedom, of its welfare, and of its exaltation among the nations.

The Irish republic is entitled to, and hereby claims, the allegiance of every Irishman and Irishwoman. The republic guarantees religious and civil liberty, equal rights and equal opportunities to all its citizens, and declares its resolve to pursue the happiness and prosperity of the whole nation and of all its parts, cherishing all the children of the nation equally, and oblivious of the differences carefully fostered by an alien government, which have divided a minority from the majority in the past.

Until our arms have brought the opportune moment for the establishment of a permanent national government, representative of the whole people of Ireland, and elected by the suffrages of all her men and women, the Provisional Government, hereby constituted, will administer the civil and military affairs of the republic in trust for the people. We place the cause of the Irish republic under the protection of the Most High God, whose blessing we invoke upon our arms, and we pray that no one who serves that cause will dishonour it by cowardice, inhumanity, or rapine. In this supreme hour the Irish nation must, by its valour and discipline, and by the readiness of its children to sacrifice themselves for the common good, prove itself worthy of the august destiny to which it is called.

Signed on behalf of the provisional government,

THOMAS J. CLARKE, SEAN MACDIARMADA, THOMAS MACDONAGH, P.H. PEARSE, EAMONN CEANNT, JAMES CONNOLLY, JOSEPH PLUNKETT.

First part from *The Times*, May 1, 1916; second part from *The Times*, September 20, 1912; third part from Maurice Moynihan, ed., *Speeches and Statements by Eamon De Valera, 1917–1973*, p. 234. Copyright © Maurice Moynihan. Reprinted by permission of St. Martin's Press, Incorporated.

ULSTER'S SOLEMN LEAGUE AND COVENANT

Being convinced in our consciences that Home Rule would be disastrous to the material well-being of Ulster, as well as of the whole of Ireland, subversive of our civil and religious freedom, destructive of our citizenship, and perilous to the unity of the Empire, we, whose names are underwritten, men of Ulster, loyal subjects of His Gracious Majesty King George V, humbly relying on the God Whom our fathers in the days of stress and trial confidently trusted, do hereby pledge ourselves in solemn Covenant throughout this our time of threatened calamity to stand by one another in defending for ourselves and our children our cherished position of equal citizenship in the United Kingdom and in using all means which may be found necessary to defeat the present conspiracy to set up a home rule parliament in Ireland. And in the event of such a Parliament being forced upon us we further and mutually pledge ourselves to refuse to recognize its authority. In sure confidence that God will defend the right, we hereto subscribe our names. And further we individually declare that we have not already signed this Covenant. God Save the King.

EAMON DE VALERA ON IRISH NATIONALISM

Ireland is more than a political union of states. It has been a nation from the dawn of history, united in traditions, in political institutions, in territory. The island is too small to be divided; it does not need and cannot afford two governments, with all the duplication of services and expenses which that involves. The pretext that partition was necessary to save a minority of Irishmen from religious persecution at the hands of the majority was an invention without any basis in the facts of our time or in the history of the past. No nation respects the rights of conscience more than Ireland, whose people too long bore persecution themselves to desire to inflict it on others. But British policy was not even consistent with the pretext invented to justify it; on the plea of saving one religious minority, it created two; on the plea of protecting the rights of a powerful and well-organised Protestant minority of twenty-five per cent, it split that minority, leaving part of it as a helpless remnant scattered through twenty-six counties.

Partition has no political or economic justification. The six counties cut off from the rest of Ireland had never been a political or administrative unit, and they could never hope to be in any measure an economic entity. They did not even comprise the whole of Ulster; that province itself, which British politicians affect to regard as holy ground, was not spared from mutilation. The erection of this six-county area into a petty state, under the ultimate control of the British Parliament and subsidised by the British Treasury, was a purely arbitrary act, inspired solely by considerations of British imperial policy and contrary to every interest of the Irish people. Imposed by force and maintained by subsidies, partition is the worst of all the many crimes committed by British statesmen against the Irish people during the last 750 years.

The area that Ireland has lost contains many of her holiest and most famous places. There is Armagh, the See of St Patrick; Downpatrick, his burial place, where lies also the body of Brian, who drove out the Danish invaders; Bangor, the site of one of the greatest of Ireland's ancient schools; Derry of St Columcille; Tyrone of the O'Neills; MacArt's Fort, where Wolfe Tone swore to work for Irish freedom; Belfast, the birthplace of the Irish Republican movement.[1] Ireland never can abandon the hope of regaining a territory hallowed by so many memories, the scene of so many of the most heroic incidents of her history. The efforts of her people will inevitably be bent upon the undoing of partition until all the land within her four seas is once more united.

"Ireland not free merely but Gaelic as well," wrote Pádraig Pearse, who died before partition was effected. "Ireland not free and Gaelic merely but united also"—that is the objective of the Irish people today, and it will remain their unshakable resolve until it has been finally attained.

40 Fustel de Coulanges, "What Is a Nation?" A Reply to Mr. Mommsen, Professor in Berlin

An expression of French nationalism, incorporating both elements of nineteenth-century nationalism, was written by Fustel de Coulanges in the early autumn of 1870. In the midst of the Franco-Prussian War, de Coulanges, a French historian teaching in Alsace at the University of Strasbourg, wrote an open letter to the German historian Theodor Mommsen explaining why the French-controlled province of Alsace should remain French and not become part of any new German state. Prussia defeated France, and despite de Coulanges's arguments, the two French provinces of Alsace and Lorraine were taken from France in 1871 and appended to a new, united Germany. In 1919, as part of the Treaty of Versailles, Alsace and Lorraine were returned to France. In many ways, the arguments of de Coulanges, though focused on two small provinces, exemplified the contentious spirit and emotional fervor of late-nineteenth-century European nationalism.

QUESTIONS TO CONSIDER

1. Why does Fustel de Coulanges argue that language is not the proper basis of nationality? According to de Coulanges, what is the proper basis of nationality?
2. Why does de Coulanges reject the legitimacy of Louis XIV's seventeenth-century conquest of Alsace and, instead, invoke the French Revolution as the basis of Alsace's affiliation with France?
3. According to de Coulanges, what is the definition of a nation?

---

[1]Theobald Wolf Tone (1763–1798), a Protestant, was one of the key Irish revolutionary leaders in the failed Irish revolt of 1798.

PARIS, OCTOBER 27, 1870

Sir:

You have lately addressed three letters to the Italian people. These letters, which were first published in Milan newspapers and were afterwards brought together in a pamphlet, are a real manifesto against our nation. You have relinquished your historical studies to drive an attack upon France; I therefore leave mine in order to reply. . . .

This past August, you indicated with perfect clarity that the true bone of contention between France and Prussia is Alsace and Lorraine. Bismarck [the Prussian premier] has not made this pronouncement as yet. He has not admitted that you are making war to take Alsace and Lorraine, but you are a discerning prophet and you have revealed the intentions and the goal of Prussia. You have clearly announced that it will be the object of this new war against our nation. Today no one can ignore that the issue that has engaged the young men of Germany and of France is clearly the question: Does Alsace belong to France or to Germany?

Prussia is determined to resolve this question by force, but force alone will not suffice for there is also the question of what is right. While your armies invade Alsace and bombard Strasbourg, you strive to prove that it is legitimate and lawful to control Alsace and Strasbourg. Alsace, according to you, is a German country: therefore she should belong to Germany. She was part of Germany in times past; from there you conclude that she should be handed back. She uses the German language, and you draw inferences now that Prussia may seize her. You call that the principle of nationality.

It is on this score that I want to reply because it is true that in this horrible duel, we know that right is not on the same side as force. It is also true that we know that Alsace has been wronged and that she is defending herself because Prussia has bombarded Strasbourg. You invoke the principle of nationality, but you understand it much differently than the rest of Europe. According to you, this principle would allow a powerful state to take hold of a province by force on the sole condition that this province is inhabited by the same race as that state. But according to Europe and to common sense, nationalism would also allow for a population or a province to refuse to submit to a foreign master against her will. I shall explain this by an example: the principle of nationality did not allow Piedmont to conquer by force Milan and Venice; but it authorized Milan and Venice to free themselves from Austria and join voluntarily to Piedmont. You see the difference. This principle may well give Alsace the right, but it does not give you any upon her.

I beg you to examine this question maturely, loyally! By what do you distinguish nationality? By what do you recognize the fatherland?

You believe you have proved that Alsace is of German nationality because its population is of Germanic race and because its language is German. But I am surprised that a historian like you feigns to ignore that it is neither race nor language that makes nationality.

It is not race. Have a look at Europe, and you will see that the people are almost never constituted after their primitive origins. Geographical conveniences, political or commercial interests are those which have brought populations together and founded states. Each nation has thus slowly been formed, each fatherland has taken shape without taking in account these ethnographical factors that you would like to bring into fashion. Your theory of race is contrary to the present state of Europe. If

From Fustel de Coulanges, *Questions historiques revues et completées d'après les notes de l'auteur par Camille Jullian* (Paris: Librarie Hachette, 1893), pp. 505–11. Trans. G. de Bertier de Sauvigny and Philip F. Riley.

nations only corresponded to race, Belgium would belong to France, Portugal would belong to Spain, and Holland would belong to Prussia. By the same token, Scotland should detach itself from England to whom she has been closely tied for a century and one-half. And Russia and Austria should each divide into three or four pieces; Switzerland should be split into two parts, and most assuredly Poznan (a Polish-speaking city) should not be controlled by Berlin. If your idea would prevail the entire world would have to be reformed.

Language is no more a characteristic sign of nationality. Five languages are spoken in France, and nevertheless no one would dare challenge our national unity. Three languages are spoken in Switzerland. Is Switzerland less of a nation, and would you say she is lacking in patriotism? Americans speak English: do you think that the United States should reestablish ties with England? You take pride in noting that in the city of Strasbourg German is spoken, but it is also true that it was in Strasbourg that one heard for the first time our *Marseillaise*.

What distinguishes nations is neither race nor language. Men feel in their hearts that they belong to a same people when they have a community of ideas, of interests, of affections, of memories and hopes. This is what makes a fatherland. This is why men want to march together, work together, live and die for one another. The fatherland is what one loves. It may be that Alsace is German by race and language. But by nationality and the sentiment of fatherland she is French. And do you know what has made Alsace French? It was not the conquests of Louis XIV, but it was our Revolution of 1789. Since that moment, Alsace has followed our destinies and lived our life. Everything that we have thought, she has thought. All that we have felt, she has felt. She has been part of our victories and part of our defeats, part of our success and part of our mistakes, part of all of our joys and all of our sorrows. She has nothing in common with you. For Alsace the fatherland is France, and Germany is the foreigner.

All the reasoning in the world will change nothing. It might be impressive to invoke ethnology and philology, but we are not in a university classroom. We are at the very center of the human heart. Your reasoning and your arguments insist that Alsace should have a German heart, but my eyes and my ears assure me that her heart is French. You insist that for a long time Alsace has harbored a spirit of provincial opposition to France, but based upon my close examination here of men from all classes, religions and political parties, I have never encountered this spirit of opposition to France. You insinuate that Alsatians have a great antipathy to Parisians, but I find that they are warmly welcomed here. In its heart and in its spirit, Alsace is one of the most Francophile of all our provinces. The Strasbourgers have, as we all do, two fatherlands: their native city, and then above all France. No thought is given to Germany because she is not considered a fatherland.

You are certainly an eminent historian, but when we speak of the present let us not fix our eyes only on the past. Race is part of history, but it is of the past. Language is certainly part of history, but it remains a sign of the distant past. That which is present and living are the aspirations, the ideas, the interests and the affections. History tells you perhaps that Alsace is a German country; but the present proves that she is a French country. It would be childish to assert she must return to Germany because she was part of it some centuries ago. Are we going to reinstate all that was in past times? If so, I ask, what Europe shall we go back to? That of the eighteenth century or that of the fifteenth century, or to that time when old Gaul possessed the whole of the Rhine, and when Strasbourg, Saverne, and Colmar were Roman cities?

Let us live in our times. We have today something better than history to guide us. We have in the nineteenth century a principle of public law which is infinitely clearer and more indisputable than your pretended principle of nationality. Our principle is that a population can be governed only by the institutions it accepts freely and that it must be part of a state only by its will and free consent. This is the modern principle. It is today the only foundation of order, and it is to this that must rally whoever is at the same time friend of peace and supporter of progress of mankind. Whether Prussia wishes it or not this principle will triumph. If Alsace remains French it is because she wishes to be. You can only make her German if she herself wishes to be German.

Racism

In their anthropology and what would soon be called "sociology," the early Romantics stressed a positive appreciation of differences among ethnic groups. As we saw in the last section, this led them to reject the eighteenth-century notion of the universality of the human race and to advocate nationalism. At first, this emphasis on difference had a benign form. Early Romantics, such as Johann G. von Herder (1744–1803), wrote at length on the advantage to humankind of having different peoples or races with diverse talents contribute to world civilization—rather much like a global version of what our own age calls "multiculturalism."

By the 1840s, however, the idea that the human race had diversity within it was replaced by theories that fit individual races into a hierarchy ranging from superior to inferior. Charles Darwin is most famous for this tendency: The title of his *On the Origin of Species by Means of Natural Selection, or The Preservation of Favoured Races in the Struggle for Life* sums up this thought succinctly. Darwin was preceded by less-well-known writers, whose ideas he drew upon apart from using his own research. Although the *Origin of Species* did not appear until 1959, that it was sold out on the very day of its publication attests to the growing interest in survival-of-the-fittest evolutionary theories. Thus, what began pleasantly enough as encouragement in appreciating national and racial diversity became the idea that some ethnic groups or races were superior to others largely based on their ability to win out in struggles and become dominant—notions that in the later nineteenth century were used to justify imperialism and in the twentieth century, ethnic cleansing in both limited versions and genocide (see Readings 64, 70, 71, and 72).

41 Heinrich von Treitschke, *A Word About the Jews Among Us*

Heinrich von Treitschke (1834–1896) typifies the nationalistic orientation of the later Romantic period, in which the earlier notion of a harmonious symphony of the talents of all nationalities gave way to strident assertions of the superiority of the writer's own culture. Treitschke was a professor of history and writer of historical works most of his life and used history effectively in support of political ideology. Elected to the new German Reichstag in 1871, he supported the Bismarckian order of things wholeheartedly, including the *Kulturkampf* (Cultural Struggle) with which Bismarck sought to unify German cultural and religious feeling by stressing Protestantism as a source of German national identity and by combating Catholic influence. Treitschke portrayed the subjection of state interests to religious leadership as decadent and typical of the Orient, where, in his mind, the other-worldly aspects of religions such as Hinduism and Buddhism kept people from mastering worthwhile knowledge and achieving progress.

For Treitschke, as for many European nationalists as the nineteenth century wore on, Jews are Semites and Semites are "Orientals," which means that they have a negative influence on national culture. Apart from that, Treitschke reveals impatience with the Jews in their desire to maintain some separate identity inside their "host" nations.

QUESTIONS TO CONSIDER

1. Treitschke presents "the Jews are our misfortune" as what people are saying rather than as his own statement. From the tone of his writing, do you get the impression that the distance he places between himself and the enemies of the Jews is real? Or is this distance a veil for anti-Semitism on his part?
2. For Treitschke, the solution Felix Mendelssohn found to problems of being a Jew in Germany was very satisfactory. Would you have felt comfortable recommending this example to Jews of that time (or later)? Why or why not?

"THE JEWS ARE OUR MISFORTUNE"

Among the symptoms of that great change in mood now coming over our people, nothing seems as alienating as the passionate movement against everything Jewish. . . . By now we have reached the point where a majority of registered voters in the city of Breslau—obviously not in a state of wild excitement but rather with calm premeditation—pledged not to elect a Jew to the state legislature (*Landtag*) under any

First part from Heinrich von Treitschke, *Ein Wort über unser Judenthum* (Berlin: G. Reimer, 1889), pp. 1–4, *passim*; second part from his *Deutsche Geschichte im neunzehnten Jahrhundert*, Part IV, 6th ed. (Leipzig: S. Hirzel, 1913), pp. 454–55. Trans. Henry A. Myers.

circumstances[Anti-Semitic associations are being formed, "the Jewish question" is discussed in meetings full of excitement, and a rising tide of anti-Jewish booklets is flooding the book market.]There is all too much dirt and vulgarity in what is happening here, and it is impossible not to be revolted by it. . . .

But are lower-class vulgarity and business envy the only things at work in these frantic cries of alarm? Are these outbursts of a deep, long-suppressed anger really only a fleeting welling-up of feeling . . . ? No, the instinct of the masses has actually identified a severe danger, a threat to the new life of Germans and one to be taken quite seriously. When people talk about the German Jewish problem, they are not tossing empty words around. . . .

[The number of Jews in Western Europe is so small that it cannot make Jewish influence felt on the national way of life; however, our Eastern border delivers year in, year out, a swarm of young men from that ever-full Polish cradle who are content for now to sell trousers but whose children and grandchildren will run stock exchanges and newspapers.] Immigration grows before our eyes, and the question of how we can melt this alien folk element together with our own keeps getting more serious. . . .

There is no German commercial city but what includes many honorable, praiseworthy[Jewish firms; however, there can be no doubt that Semitic influence plays a large part in the promotion of lies, deceit and greed in sordid business manipulations, and it reveals an accomplice's guilt in the despicable materialism of our age, which regards all work as profit-driven and threatens to smother the old easy-going and nurturing joy in work once felt by our people.]In thousands of German small towns sits a Jew ready to buy out his neighbors with the profits of usury. . . .

[The most dangerous result of all this comes from the unacceptable preponderance of Jewish influence in the daily press—a fateful result of our past, narrow-minded laws denying entrance to most of the learned professions to Israelites. For a full ten years, Jewish pens "made" official opinion in many German cities. . . . The necessary backlash against this unnatural state of affairs is the current impotence of the press. The man on the street cannot be talked out of his conviction that the Jews write the newspapers: for just that reason, he does not want to believe them anymore.

[The German-Jewish writer Ludwig] Börne first introduced into our journalism the peculiarly shameless stance of putting down the fatherland with no respect at all, writing as an outsider who has no feeling of belonging to it—as if contempt for Germany did not stab painfully and deep into the heart of each individual German. To this must be added that unhappy, many-sided pushiness which always seems to accompany such writing and which does not hesitate to use authoritative-sounding, corrective criticism in discussing internal affairs of Christian churches. What Jewish journalists have allowed themselves to write against Christianity with their articles full of contempt and their would-be humor is absolutely outrageous, particularly when such blasphemies are presented to our people in their own language as the very newest achievement of "German" enlightenment. . . .

If we survey this total situation—and how much we could add here!—the loud agitation of the moment emerges as a brutal, but natural, reaction of German folk feeling against a foreign element which has begun to take up too much space. . . . Let us not deceive ourselves: the movement is deep and strong, and jokes about the platitudes coming from Christian-social stump speakers will not make it go away. Even in the highest-educated circles, among men who would denounce every thought of religious intolerance or national arrogance, the words resound with a single voice: "The Jews are our misfortune!"

"FELIX MENDELSSOHN WENT UP IN GERMANY"

Felix Mendelssohn. . . had grown up in the spoiled circles of Berlin wealth, but his unspoiled, worthy personality took on only the good and productive characteristics from those typical of Berliners: many-sided education, open-mindedness, adaptable social skills, and a talent for skillful and easy communication. A German from the crown of his head down to his toes, he did not feel right spending his time indefinitely under the magic spell of the southern landscape: of all the foreigners he came in contact with, only the Germanic English understood him completely. His oratorio, "Saint Paul," gave new life to the genre among Protestants, and he gave a deep and festive musical expression to song-composition in Germany. Almost as successful as his written works, which raised him far above all contemporary composers, was his activity in concert halls.

As a youth of twenty, Mendelssohn was the first to risk putting on Johann Sebastian Bach's forgotten "Saint Matthew's Passion," and afterwards he labored ceaselessly to make the noble, and truly German artistic genres of symphony, oratorio and sonata accessible and dear to educated people. He prepared the nation to understand the works of Bach and Handel, as well as the symphonies of Beethoven, which had been written off as unenjoyable for a long time. After he had been waving his conductor's baton in Berlin, Düsseldorf, Frankfurt and Leipzig long enough to gain recognition and support everywhere in Germany, music, which had sunk nearly to the level of a pastime, was again honored as a great art. The Germans can thank Mendelssohn for the fact that a nucleus of uncorrupted good taste remained in musical audiences, even when the forces of anarchy broke in upon opera composition. Thus a German of Jewish descent led our educated society back to the old heritage of national artistic expression, even in those days when the German Jews in Paris were committing such sins against the culture of our people. Mendelssohn's noble and great influence proved forever that a German Jew can earn true renown if indeed he is totally willing to go up in German life without any reservations.[1]

42 *Enfumades* in French Algeria: Three Reports

Determined to teach the *Dey* (ruler) of Algiers a lesson for striking the French consul with his flywhisk, on July 5, 1830, 30,000 French soldiers descended upon Algeria and stormed the city of Algiers. By 1848, France had captured all of Algeria, but it was not an easy conquest. The Berber and Arab inhabitants of Algeria, whom the French invariably called "Arabs," strenuously resisted French rule.

---

[1]The double meaning of "to go up": (1) "to rise or ascend" and (2) "to be dissolved or destroyed," as in "to go up in smoke or flames" is the same in German and English but more used in conscious ambiguities in the latter. Treitschke probably means here that a German Jew could *rise* in German society only when, apart from his talents and abilities, he was willing to let his Jewish identity *dissolve*.

One of the most ardent promoters of the French conquest of Algeria was Alexis de Tocqueville, author of *Democracy in America.* De Tocqueville had published his "Letter on Algeria" in 1837 and, after visiting Algeria in 1841, published his major study *Work on Algeria.* Based upon his study of Islam and Arabic culture, de Tocqueville argued that the Arabs were heavily dependent upon commerce and trade. Therefore, in order to colonize Algeria, the French military must disrupt their commerce. Furthermore, argued de Tocqueville, because Arabs were not Europeans, the rules of European warfare need not apply in Algeria. "I have often heard in France," he wrote, "from men I respect but do not agree with, that we should not burn their crops, destroy their granaries, or seize their men. I believe these unfortunate tactics must be used when one is forced to make war against Arabs."[1] As a champion of French Algeria, de Tocqueville enthusiastically endorsed the French army's tactic of raiding *(razzia)* Algerian villages, insisting that "all means of desolating these Arabs should be used. I make an exception only for what is forbidden by international law and humanity."[2]

De Tocqueville's tough prescriptions for dealing with Arabs were welcomed by the French military fighting in Algeria, especially by Marshal Thomas Robert Bugeaud, the governor-general responsible for conquering Algeria. Commanding a force of more than 100,000 French, Moroccan, and Arab soldiers, Bugeaud proved to be a ruthless officer who brought to Algeria the brutal tactics the French army had learned from the Spanish guerrillas in Napoleon's failed Spanish campaign of 1807–1815. He divided his forces into lightly armed, mobile raiding parties that attacked Algerian villages, burned their crops, and disrupted their trade. By the 1840s, Bugeaud's soldiers had hit upon the tactic of driving the Algerians from their villages and forcing them into the mountains where they had little food or water. Quite often, to escape from the French, the Algerians sought refuge in caves. Many of these caves had multiple entrances and could hold more than one thousand men, women, and children, along with all of their cattle, goats, and sheep. When Bugeaud's soldiers were unable to convince the Algerians to leave the caves and surrender, they would start fires at the cave's entrance and fill the caves with smoke. These "smokings" or "gassings" (in French the word is *enfumade*) proved to be a devastating terror tactic, resulting in the deaths of hundreds, perhaps thousands, of people. In the 1840s, several large-scale *enfumades* occurred in the Dahra region of northern Algeria. These were reported in the British and French press and vigorously condemned in the French legislature.

[1]Alexis de Tocqueville, *De la colonie en algérie,* ed. Tzvetan Todorov (Paris: Éditions complexe, 1988), 77.
[2]Ibid., 77–78.

QUESTIONS TO CONSIDER

1. Based upon your study of nineteenth-century contacts between Western armies and the indigenous peoples of Africa, America, India, and China, were these *enfumades* typical or atypical of colonial policy?

2. There seems to be a difference in the tone in the reporting between the first two eyewitness accounts of Marshal Canrobert and Colonel Pélissier and the final account of Colonel de Saint-Arnaud. How would you account for this difference in tone, particularly as expressed in Saint-Arnaud's last sentence?

3. Colonel Pélissier insists in his report of his *enfumade* at Dahra that he did everything possible to negotiate with the Algerians, but they refused. Furthermore, he suggests that because the Algerians suffered only "slight damage" from the first day's fires, they elected to remain in the caves and thereby "were totally unprepared for the fires," resulting in their deaths. Is Colonel Pélissier correct in his assessment? Why? Why not?

4. Were these *enfumades* spontaneous decisions or planned events?

5. Frantz Fanon (see Reading 80) was a twentieth-century Algerian who wrote a good deal about French colonial policy. Would Fanon agree with de Tocqueville's, Pélissier's, and Saint-Arnaud's descriptions of Algerians? Why? Why not?

MARSHAL CANROBERT'S REPORT OF AN *ENFUMADE* IN 1844 AND COLONEL PÉLISSIER'S *ENFUMADE* AT DAHRA OF JUNE 18, 1845

I attended the first affair of the grottoes [*enfumade*] in 1844 when I was with my battalion under the command of [Colonel] Cavaignac. We set out by column to punish the Sbéahs [a rebel tribe], who had attacked our French colonists and our Arab administrators. For two days we pursued the Sbéahs until we came upon a high perpendicular cliff. At the base of the cliff were piles of boulders and blocks of stone that protected the entrance to a huge cave. As we pressed forward the Arabs, who were hiding behind the boulders and stones, were forced to retire inside the cave. We tried to negotiate with them, but they responded by shooting at us. Captain de Jouvencourt, one of my dearest comrades, stood up and walked alone to the mouth of the cave. He wanted to show the Arabs his moral authority, win their respect, obtain their surrender, stop the fighting, and save their lives. But as soon as he began to speak, several shots rang out and Jouvencourt was killed.

Because the Arabs would not negotiate with us, we opened fire on the mouth of the cave. We also began to collect bundles of brush and firewood. In the evening we placed the firewood near the entrance of the cave and ignited the bundles. The next

From Germain Bapst, *Le Maréchal Canrobert: Souvenirs d'un siècle*. (Paris: Librairie Plon, 1899), 1: 418–22. Trans. Philip F. Riley. (François Canrobert (1809–1895) served in Algeria between 1835 and 1839 and again between 1841 and 1850.)

morning several Arabs came to the mouth of the cave and offered to surrender. They told us that many of their comrades, their wives, and their children were dead. Our medics and some of our soldiers attended to the wounded and gave them water. That evening our battalion returned to Orléansville. This *enfumade* received little attention because Colonel Cavaignac never spoke of it. Certainly he never told anyone the number of Arabs who suffocated in this *enfumade*.

But the next year (1845) there was a real row in Paris in the chambers of peers, in some of the French press, and in the English newspapers over another *enfumade*. This time Colonel Pélissier was in command of a column pursuing rebels of the Ouled-Rias tribe. The morning of June 18, 1845, the anniversary of the battle of Waterloo, was beautiful. The sun shone brightly on our troops that had been marching since dawn. Colonel Pélissier was in the lead and at his side rode his trustworthy Arab interpreter, Chief Adji-el-Kain. Preceding our column was our advanced guard of Moroccan Cavalry. Suddenly the Moroccans stopped and fired their rifles into the air. We could see in the distance a gigantic white line cutting across the horizon like a line of chalk. Adji-el-Kain turned to Pélissier and announced, "Look, there are the Ouled-Rias's caves." Our column halted and we sent patrols to reconnoiter and guard all entrances to the caves. Our Arab allies approached the entrances to the caves and urged the Ouled-Rias to surrender. Shots were fired and two of our allies were killed. Later, three Ouled-Rias came out from the caves and told us they were fearful that if they surrendered they would be imprisoned in the Stork Tower at Mostaganem [a feared prison in the French garrison town]. No matter what we said, they were convinced we were determined to imprison the entire tribe in the Stork Tower.

Colonel Pélissier instructed his negotiators to tell the Arabs that no harm would come to them if they surrendered and left the caves immediately. In about an hour the Arabs announced they would leave the caves but only after we [the French] had retired from the field first. Pélissier now ordered his troops to cut all the brushwood and straw and stack it into fagots [bundles of wood]. Again, he warned the Arabs that unless they surrendered he would ignite the fagots, filling the cave with smoke, and then he would seal all the exits to the cave. Still, Pélissier gave one last try at negotiations. He approached the mouth of the cave and ordered the Arabs to leave, but they shot at him and killed one of our infantrymen. That night we ignited the fagots. The next morning, at the mouth of the cave, we saw blackened skeletons and half-dead bodies. The fire had produced a terrible effect.

Pélissier ordered our engineers to enter the cave, but the smoke and acrid odor that filled the cave prevented anyone from doing so. Slowly, as the air cleared, we entered the cave and came upon piles of cadavers with blackened faces and twisted limbs. Some of the Arabs were still alive. We attempted to aid them, but they died before we could give them first aid. Our glimmering lanterns revealed more than five hundred cadavers stretched in the subterranean passageways throughout the cave. Even if we had sent in three hundred men, we could not have rescued the living. Our comrades, walking with their heads down in the cave, would have trampled over each other. Pélissier made only one mistake. He writes too well and has gained too much notoriety as an author. He knows this but he could not resist the temptation to write an eloquent and realistic report of this *enfumade*. His report is much too realistic in describing the Arab cadavers laying thick upon the ground and in depicting the piles of bodies burned to a crisp and in suggesting the final tortures the unfortunate children, women, and elders had to endure.

COLONEL PÉLISSIER'S REPORT OF HIS *ENFUMADE* AT DAHRA OF JUNE 18, 1845

M. Marshal,

. . . As I reported earlier, I set up camp at Oued Bel Amia in the heartland of the Ouled Rias tribe. As soon as I set foot in their country, they fired at us from their hillside positions. I halted the column and ordered my Moroccans to cut down their orchards, search their homes, and then to destroy them. . . . Despite all precautions [as we approached the caves], five of my soldiers were wounded: A sergeant lost his left eye, another sergeant, a corporal, and an infantryman were grievously wounded, and an artillery soldier suffered a shoulder wound. At the entrance of the caves, hidden in the surrounding trees, we found several Kabyles [rebels]. To force them to retreat I shelled them with my artillery and drove them back into the cave. I tried to enter negotiations with them; they responded by shooting at us, although this had little effect. Some of my Moroccan cavaliers attempted to sneak up a ravine to entreat with the Arabs but they were unsuccessful.

At this point I followed your advice and gathered bundles of firewood into fagots and soon a great fire was ablaze at the main entrance to the cave. This fire lasted for the entire day. Meanwhile, I fortified my position and tightened control of all entrances to the cave. Thanks to a full moon and the placement of my patrols, I knew that no one could escape. Although it was quiet that night, we did capture one of the rebels who had sneaked out of the cave in search of water. From this captive we learned that the Arabs inside were without water and that some were thirsty enough to listen to our surrender terms. Because I was on high ground, I decided to throw more firewood on the fire and ordered my troops to gather wood and straw and to cut down all the trees near each of the entrances to the caves below.

I ordered my troops to suspend immediately all of their duties and concentrate on gathering firewood. I also continued to seek negotiations with the Arabs. When an Arab negotiator appeared, he asked that in return for surrender none of the Arabs be made a prisoner and that absolutely no one would be sent, as other rebels had been, to Mostaganem. I agreed to these two conditions, which I offered to put in writing, if they would disarm and surrender. Throughout negotiations I learned that they were deathly afraid of being imprisoned in the Stork Tower [a feared prison in Mostaganem]; indeed, this fear was repeatedly expressed in the most vivid terms. I sought to reassure them of our intentions but I could not convince them to surrender.

Our discussions lasted a little less than three hours. I gave them repeated assurances that they must surrender and leave the caves, but they insisted they would leave only if we would leave first and give up our siege of the caves. This was entirely unacceptable. I instructed my interpreter to tell them explicitly, as we had twenty times before, "No man, woman, or child would be imprisoned at Mostaganem." If they left the cave, they could retire in peace and would be free to go home. I also reminded them that we had kept our truce for three hours, but now they had one quarter of an hour to accept these terms or I would use all my power to dislodge them

From "Rapport du Colonel Pélissier au Maréchal Bugeaud, governeur-général de l'algérie, 22 juin 1845," in Raoul Busquet, "L'affaire de grottes du Dahra," *Revue Africaine: Journal des travaux de la société historique algérienne* 51 (1907): 145–54. Trans. Philip F. Riley. (Colonel Aimable Jean-Jacques Pélissier (1794–1864) served in Algeria between 1839 and 1851.)

from the caves. I told them that my men would stack fagots at all the entrances and then it would be too late to change anything. Again, they demanded that we evacuate our positions. I warned them that the time limit of a quarter of an hour was nearly over and repeated my earlier warning. At the same time I ordered all my firewood teams to duty stations.

It was now ten o'clock. Scarcely had I assembled all my men when a bullet from the cave wounded one of my cavalrymen. By one o'clock all was set for the igniting of the fagots, but I gave negotiation one more try. As my emissary, I sent an Arab [rebel], who along with his brother had recently escaped from the cave. He entered the cave through a small, inconspicuous opening and remained inside for more than an hour and a quarter, but he could not convince the Arabs to surrender. I was now at the limits of my patience.

At about fifty meters from the main entrance to the cave, I made a barricade of biscuit boxes filled with earth and also positioned a howitzer battery, thereby ensuring no one could exit from this entrance. At three o'clock I ignited the fires that burned all night. They were not extinguished until one hour before daylight. The heat from the fires was so intense that it caused large parts of the interior ceilings of the caves to collapse, thereby setting off frightful explosions resembling artillery fire within the cave. The explosions must have killed all of their cattle that had gathered near the caves' entrances. Once the fires and explosions began, I was powerless to extinguish the fires or to prevent what was underway below where the fires ensured that all would die of asphyxiation. I could only imagine the unfolding chaos. At daybreak I sent a scout into the cave to reconnoiter. He returned with seven men who were barely breathing. Immediately I sent another patrol to assist survivors, but they found only fifty Arabs alive. The smoke, dust, and acrid air in the cave prevented us from rendering any further assistance that day, although throughout the day several stragglers continued to stumble out of the cave. A strange thing happened at this point: From inside the cave some of the Arabs shot at those escaping, many of whom were women. The next day the air inside the cave had cleared and I sent in patrols to reconnoiter. We found one hundred and ten people alive; nine of these died before we could aid them, and the rest we eventually sent home. Throughout the cave we found more than five hundred dead lying in the most horrible condition.

Certainly such operations, M. Marshal, are undertaken when one is forced to, but I pray to God that I never have to do this again. It is a terrible lesson that their stubbornness, obstinacy, and determination to stay in the caves was based upon a misreading of the slight damage resulting from the first day's fires. They were totally unprepared for the fires that ignited their baggage and set off the explosions dislodging the ceiling fragments, which fell on their gunpowder, setting off the explosions we mistakenly thought were firefights among the Arabs themselves. Although most of their weapons were destroyed, we captured sixty rifles, a dozen sabers, a few pistols, and some old bayonets. All of the survivors were permitted to recover their belongings spared by the fires and to remove the bodies of their comrades, but no one, Arab or Frenchman, was permitted to return to the cave.

COLONEL DE SAINT-ARNAUD'S REPORT OF HIS *ENFUMADE* AT DAHRA OF AUGUST 12, 1845

Really, my brother, what do you think of our good French press? I would have done exactly what Pélissier did. If in eight days I find myself in such a position I would attack the Sbéahs in their caves and wipe out as many as possible so as to save my own troops.

My soldiers always come first. Would you prefer to read in *L'Akhbar* [an Algerian newspaper] that Colonel Pélissier and two hundred of his soldiers had been killed before the caves of Ouled-Rias and that the enemy had escaped with his arms? . . . As for me, I am disgusted and indignant. Here we are in Africa, ruining our health, working all the time for the glory of France, and now are vilified and insulted. . . . I am so tired and feverish. For the past twenty-four hours I have been on my horse.

I can only provide you with a brief summary of what happened. You recall that I had directed my three columns of troops to attack and surprise the enemy. Indeed I was able to drive Bou Maza [a rebel leader] off the hills at Ténès and Mostaganem, but he was able to slip between our lines with only thirty-four casualties. I did, however, learn that he had retreated into a subterranean cave two hundred meters deep that had five separate entrances.

When we approached the cave, they fired at us and, even though it was not my custom, I returned fire. On August 9th, I began the siege by blocking its main entrance and laying a string of mines at its mouth. For the next three days the enemy fired at us, swore at us, and took casualties from our fire. On August 11th, one rebel left the cave and urged his comrades to join him but no one escaped. On August 12th, eleven Arabs surrendered but we continued to receive fire from the Arabs in the cave. Now I decided to seal all five entrances and light the fires we had prepared at the entrances. By smoke and by sealing all the entrances I created a vast cemetery where the corpses of these fanatics will rest forever. I was the only one to enter the caves. Only I knew that they contain five hundred rebels who will never again cut the throats of Frenchmen. In a confidential letter to Marshal [Bugeaud], I told him everything quite simply and without dwelling upon the terrible poetry of the scene I confronted. Brother, by taste and nature, no one is more inclined to kindness than I. From the 8th to the 12th, I have been ill, but my conscience has not troubled me. I have done my duty as a commander and tomorrow I shall begin again, but I have begun to loathe Africa.

43 Count Arthur de Gobineau, *The Inequality of Human Races*

Sometimes given the title of dubious distinction "Father of Racism," Joseph Arthur de Gobineau (1816–1882) at the very least shaped and promoted the idea of superior and inferior races into much more of a geopolitical force than it had been. He was a very marginal member of the French aristocracy—there is some question about the legitimacy of his assuming the prefix "Conte de" before the surname "Gobineau" he was born with—but this may well have made him all the more determined to defend the rights of groups asserting the naturalness of their claims to

From "Letters to Louis Adolphe de Saint-Arnaud, 26 July and 15 August 1845," in *Lettres du Maréchal de Saint-Arnaud, 1832–1854* (Paris: Michel Lévy, 1864), 2: 24–27. Trans. Philip F. Riley. (Armand-Jacques Le Roy de Saint-Arnaud (1801–1854) served in Algeria between 1837 and 1848. He had witnessed Pélissier's *enfumade* of June 19, 1845. On July 20, 1845, Marshal Bugeaud wrote to Saint-Arnaud, advising: "It is certainly to be presumed that the Sbéah will not withdraw into the caves, but if they do it is necessary to have resolved to employ in a crisis and as a last resort, the tactic used by Colonel Pélissier.")

privilege and domination over others. In his early years before racism came to dominate his mental world, he was befriended by Alexis de Toqueville (see Reading 32), who recognized his energy and literary skills. When Louis Napoleon Bonaparte made de Toqueville his foreign minister in 1849, de Tocqueville named Gobineau as his official secretary, and whereas de Tocqueville was soon out of his ministerial office, Gobineau supported himself for much of the rest of his life as a French foreign service official, which brought him into contact with exotic peoples and places, enabling him to speak with what seemed like authority about races and cultures.

Later he was befriended by the German composer Richard Wagner, an ardent Germanic racist himself. Gobineau's racial theory placed the white race at the top of the global categories and the "Aryan" at the apex of the white pyramid, although it took the influence of Wagner and the proto-Nazis to make "Aryan," a term originally designating the ancient Indo-European conquerors of India into simply "Nordic." Although Gobineau favored northern Europeans in his racial categories, thinking basically of the inhabitants of northern France as well as those of England, Holland, Belgium, northern Germany, and the Scandinavian countries as a group, his theories were never so popular anywhere as in the new Germany. In France, the idea that northern Frenchmen were superior to southern Frenchmen was dead on arrival among the quite large numbers of Frenchmen who thought of themselves as descending from Gauls and Romans; however, in the newly united Germany (1871) the idea that "Germanic" meant "Nordic," which, in turn, meant "superior," had considerable appeal, even if it involved the mental feat of making non-Nordic central and southern Germans into "Nordic," as Hitler was subsequently able to do for his own south German—and not noticeably Nordic—physical person.

Wagner and Gobineau differed on the issue of what could be done to stop racial degeneration: Gobineau was convinced the situation was hopeless and had no proposals to do anything about it. Wagner, like Hitler later, thought that indeed something could be done about it. When the Gobineau Society was founded twelve years after the man's death, its members had no difficulty in using Gobineau's volumes of anecdotal material posing as research in order to promote their political agenda.

QUESTIONS TO CONSIDER

1. How does Gobineau think that the utilization of sense perception separates the main races? What other criteria does he use?
2. What are for him the pros and cons of "hybridization"?
3. As editors, we had much discussion over whether or not to include this piece in *The Global Experience.* Do you think it belongs in a book like this? Is it so offensive that this fact outweighs including it because of its strong influence on shaping European racial attitudes?

4. Have you yourself heard any ideas concerning the ranking of races? How do they compare with Gobineau's ideas?

THE RESPECTIVE CHARACTERISTICS OF THE THREE GREAT RACES; THE SUPERIORITY OF THE WHITE TYPE, AND, WITHIN THIS TYPE, OF THE ARYAN FAMILY

I have shown the unique place in the organic world occupied by the human species, the profound physical, as well as moral, differences separating it from all other kinds of living creatures. Considering it by itself, I have been able to distinguish, on physiological grounds alone, three great and clearly marked types, the black, the yellow, and the white. However uncertain the aims of physiology may be, however meagre its resources, however defective its methods, it can proceed thus far with absolute certainty.

The negroid variety is the lowest, and stands at the foot of the ladder. The animal character, that appears in the shape of the pelvis, is stamped on the negro from birth, and foreshadows his destiny. His intellect will always move within a very narrow circle. He is not however a mere brute, for behind his low receding brow, in the middle of his skull, we can see signs of a powerful energy, however crude its objects. If his mental faculties are dull or even non-existent, he often has an intensity of desire, and so of will, which may be called terrible. Many of his senses, especially taste and smell, are developed to an extent unknown to the other two races.

The very strength of his sensations is the most striking proof of his inferiority. All food is good in his eyes, nothing disgusts or repels him. What he desires is to eat, to eat furiously, and to excess; no carrion is too revolting to be swallowed by him. It is the same with odours; his inordinate desires are satisfied with all, however coarse or even horrible. To these qualities may be added an instability and capriciousness of feeling, that cannot be tied down to any single object, and which, so far as he is concerned, do away with all distinctions of good and evil. We might even say that the violence with which he pursues the object that has aroused his senses and inflamed his desires is a guarantee of the desires being soon satisfied and the object forgotten. Finally, he is equally careless of his own life and that of others: he kills willingly, for the sake of killing; and this human machine, in whom it is so easy to arouse emotion, shows, in the face of suffering, either a monstrous indifference or a cowardice that seeks a voluntary refuge in death.

The yellow race is the exact opposite of this type. The skull points forward, not backward. The forehead is wide and bony, often high and projecting. The shape of the face is triangular, the nose and chin showing none of the coarse protuberance that mark the negro. There is further a general proneness to obesity, which, though not confined to the yellow type, is found there more frequently than in the others. The yellow man has little physical energy, and is inclined to apathy; he commits none of the strange excesses so common among negroes. His desires are feeble, his will-power rather obstinate than violent; his longing for material pleasures, though constant, is kept within bounds. A rare glutton by nature, he shows far more discrimination in his choice of food. He tends toward mediocrity in everything; he understands easily

From Conte Joseph Arthur de Gobineau, *The Inequality of Human Races*, trans. Adrian Collins. (New York: G.P. Putnam & Sons, 1915), pp. 205–11.

enough anything not too deep or sublime. He has a love of utility and a respect for order, and knows the value of a certain amount of freedom. He is practical, in the narrowest sense of the word. He does not dream or theorize; he invents little, but can appreciate and take over what is useful to him. His whole desire is to live in the easiest and most comfortable way possible. The yellow races are thus clearly superior to the black. Every founder of a civilization would wish the backbone of his society, his middle class, to consist of such men. But no civilized society could be created by them; they could not supply its nerve-force, or set in motion the springs of beauty and action.

We come now to the white people. These are gifted with reflective energy, or rather with an energetic intelligence. They have a feeling for utility, but in a sense far wider and higher, more courageous and ideal, than the yellow races; a perseverance that takes account of obstacles and ultimately finds a means of overcoming them; a greater physical power, an extraordinary instinct for order, not merely as a guarantee of peace and tranquility, but as an indispensable means of self-preservation. At the same time, they have a remarkable, and even extreme, love of liberty, and are openly hostile to the formalism under which the Chinese are glad to vegetate, as well as to the strict despotism which is the only way of governing the negro.

The white races are, further, distinguished by an extraordinary attachment to life. They know better how to use it, and so as it would seem, set a greater price on it; both in their own persons and those of others, they are more sparing of life. When they are cruel, they are conscious of their cruelty; it is very doubtful whether such a consciousness exists in the negro. At the same time, they have discovered reasons why they should surrender this busy life of theirs, that is so precious to them. The principal motive is honour, which under various names has played an enormous part in the ideas of the race from the beginning. I need hardly add that the word honour, together with all the civilizing influences connoted by it, is unknown to both the yellow and the black man.

On the other hand, the immense superiority of the white peoples in the whole field of the intellect is balanced by an inferiority in the intensity of their sensations. In the world of the senses, the white man is far less gifted than the others, and so is less tempted and less absorbed by considerations of the body, although in physical structure he is far the most vigorous.

Such are the three constituent elements of the human race. I call them secondary types, as I think myself obliged to omit all discussion of the Adamite man. From the combination, by intermarriage, of the varieties of these types come the tertiary groups. The quaternary formations are produced by the union of one of these tertiary types, or of a pure-blooded tribe, with another group taken from one of the two foreign species.

Below these categories others have appeared—and still appear. Some of these are very strongly characterized, and form new and distinct points of departure, coming as they do from races that have been completely fused. Others are incomplete, and ill-ordered, and one might even say, anti-social, since their elements, being too numerous, too disparate, or too barbarous, have had neither the time nor the opportunity for combining to any fruitful purpose. No limits, except the horror excited by the possibility of infinite intermixture, can be assigned to the number of these hybrid and chequered races that make up the whole of mankind.

It would be unjust to assert that every mixture is bad and harmful. If the three great types had remained strictly separate, the supremacy would no doubt have always been in the hands of the finest of the white races, and the yellow and black varieties would have crawled forever at the feet of the lowest of whites. Such a state is so far [only an] ideal [one], since it has never been beheld in history; and we can imagine it only by recognizing the undisputed superiority of those groups of the white races which have remained the purest.

It would not have been all gain. The superiority of the white race would have been clearly shown, but it would have been bought at the price of certain advantages which have followed the mixture of blood. Although these are far from counter-balancing the defects they have brought in their train, yet they are sometimes to be commended. Artistic genius, which is equally foreign to each of the three great types, arose only after the intermarriage of white and black. Again, in the Malayan variety, a human family was produced from the yellow and black races that had more intelligence than either of its ancestors. Finally, from the union of white and yellow, certain intermediary peoples have sprung, who are superior to the purely Finnish tribes as well as to the negroes.

I do not deny that these are good results. The world of art and great literature that comes from the mixture of blood, the improvement and ennoblement of inferior races—all these are wonders for which we must needs be thankful. The small have been raised. Unfortunately, the great have been lowered by the same process; and this is an evil that nothing can balance or repair. Since I am putting together the advantages of racial mixtures, I will also add that to them is due the refinement of manners and beliefs, and especially the tempering of passion and desire. But these are merely transitory benefits, and if I recognize that the mulatto, who may become a lawyer, a doctor, or a business man, is worth more than his Negro grandfather, who was an absolute savage and fit for nothing, I must also confess that the Brahmans of primitive India, the heroes of the Iliad and the Shahnameh, the warriors of Scandinavia—the glorious shades of noble races that have disappeared—give us a higher and more brilliant idea of humanity, and were more active, intelligent, and trusty instruments of civilization and grandeur than the people, hybrid a hundred times over, of the present day. And the blood even of these was no longer pure.

However it has come about, the human races, as we find them in history, are complex; and one of the chief consequences has been to throw into disorder most of the primitive characteristics of each type. The good as well as the bad qualities are seen to diminish in intensity with repeated intermixture of blood; but they also scatter and separate off from each other, and are often mutually opposed. The white race originally possessed the monopoly of beauty, intelligence, and strength. By its union with other varieties, hybrids were created, which were beautiful without strength, strong without intelligence, or, if intelligent, both weak and ugly. Further, when the quantity of white blood was increased to an indefinite amount by successive infusions, and not by a single admixture, it no longer carried with it its natural advantages, and often merely increased the confusion already existing in the racial elements. Its strength, in fact, seemed to be its only remaining quality, and even its strength served only to promote disorder. The apparent anomaly is easily explained. Each stage of a perfect mixture produces a new type from diverse elements, and develops special faculties. As soon as further elements are added, the vast difficulty of harmonizing the whole creates a state of anarchy. The more this increases, the more do even the best and richest of the new contributions diminish in value, and by their mere presence add fuel to an evil which they cannot abate. If mixtures of blood are, to a certain extent, beneficial to the mass of mankind, if they raise and ennoble it, this is merely at the expense of mankind itself, which is stunted, abased, enervated, and humiliated in the persons of its noblest sons. Even if we admit that it is better to turn a myriad of degraded beings into mediocre men than to preserve the race of princes whose blood is adulterated and impoverished by being made to suffer this dishonourable change, yet there is still the unfortunate fact that the change does not stop here; for when the mediocre men are once created at the expense of the greater, they combine with other mediocrities, and from such unions, which grow ever more and more degraded, is born a confusion which, like that of Babel, ends in utter impotence, and leads societies down to the abyss of nothingness whence no power on earth can rescue them.

Such is the lesson of history. It shows us that all civilizations derive from the white race, that none can exist without its help, and that a society is great and brilliant only so far as it preserves the blood of the noble group that created it, provided that this group itself belongs to the most illustrious branch of our species.

Of the multitude of peoples which live or have lived on the earth, ten alone have risen to the position of complete societies. The remainder have gravitated round these more or less independently, like planets round their suns. If there is any element of life in these ten civilizations that is not due to the impulse of the white races, any seed of death that does not come from the inferior stocks that mingled with them, then the whole theory on which this book rests is false. On the other hand, if the facts are as I say, then we have an irrefragable proof of the nobility of our own species. Only the actual details can set the final seal of truth on my system, and they alone can show with sufficient exactness the full implications of my main thesis, that peoples degenerate only in consequence of the various admixtures of blood which they undergo; that their degeneration corresponds exactly to the quantity and quality of the new blood, and that the rudest possible shock to the vitality of a civilization is given when the ruling elements in a society and those developed by racial change have become so numerous that they are clearly moving away from the homogeneity necessary to their life, and it therefore becomes impossible for them to be brought into harmony and so acquire the common instincts and interests, the common logic of existence, which is the sole justification for any social bond whatever.

NOTE. The "ten civilizations" mentioned in the last paragraph are as follows. . . . :

I. The Indian civilization, which reached its highest point round the Indian Ocean, and in the north and east of the Indian Continent, southeast of the Brahmaputra. It arose from a branch of a white people, the Aryans.

II. The Egyptians, round whom collected the Ethiopians, the Nubians, and a few smaller peoples to the west of the oasis of Ammon. This society was created by an Aryan colony from India, that settled in the upper valley of the Nile.

III. The Assyrians, with whom may be classified the Jews, the Phoenicians, the Lydians, the Carthaginians, and the Hymiarites. They owed their civilizing qualities to the great white invasions which may be grouped under the name of the descendants of Shem and Ham. The Zoroastrian Iranians, who ruled part of Central Asia under the names of Medes, Persians, and Bactrians, were a branch of the Aryan family.

IV. The Greeks, who came from the same Aryan stock, as modified by Semitic elements.

V. The Chinese civilization, arising from a cause similar to that operating in Egypt. An Aryan colony from India brought the light of civilization to China also. Instead, however, of becoming mixed with black peoples, as on the Nile, the colony became absorbed in Malay and yellow races, and was reinforced, from the northwest, by a fair number of white elements, equally Aryan but no longer Hindu.

VI. The ancient civilization of the Italian peninsula, the cradle of Roman culture. This was produced by a mixture of Celts, Iberians, Aryans, and Semites.

VII. The Germanic races, which in the fifth century transformed the Western mind. These were Aryans.

VIII.–X. The three civilizations of America, the Alleghanian, the Mexican, and the Peruvian.

Of the first seven civilizations, which are those of the Old World, six belong, at least in part, to the Aryan race, and the seventh, that of Assyria, owed to this race the Iranian Renaissance, which is, historically, its best claim to fame. Almost the whole Continent of Europe is inhabited at the present time by groups of which the basis is white, but in which the non-Aryan elements are the most numerous. There is no civilization among the European peoples, where the Aryan branch is not predominant.

In the above list no negro race is seen as the initiator of a civilization. Only when it is mixed with some other can it even be initiated into one. Similarly, no spontaneous civilization is to be found among the yellow races; and when the Aryan blood is exhausted stagnation supervenes.

44 Chinese Exclusion Acts, 1882, 1892

Among all the immigrant groups in the United States during the nineteenth century, the Chinese were perhaps one of the most mistreated and were the targets of institutionalized racial discrimination. In the mid-nineteenth century, when the United States experienced such momentous historical events as victory in the Mexican war (1846–1848), the annexation of California in 1848, the California gold rush in 1849, and the building of the transcontinental railroad, a small number of Chinese laborers began reaching the shores of Hawaii and the West Coast. At first, Chinese laborers were not only welcomed but sought after by American entrepreneurs and policy makers because of their reputation as obedient, quick-learning hard workers who made few demands. But by the late 1860s and early 1870s, while more Chinese workers continued arriving, the economic conditions in the United States became unstable; many Californians and others, including recent arrivals from Europe, began scapegoating the Chinese. Fanned by racist demagogues and agitators who believed that "white-only America" was being threatened by the new wave of immigrants from across the Pacific, anti-Chinese sentiments were steadily spreading to the rest of the country where there were few or no Chinese. In 1880, the Chinese population in California was estimated at 75,000, which constituted a mere 0.002 percent of the U.S. population. Chinese immigrants were subjected to vicious verbal as well as physical attacks, including lynching, disembowelment, dismemberment, and being burned alive.

Under mounting pressure from the intensely color-conscious members of Congress from California and other racists, the U.S. Congress enacted a series of laws restricting Chinese immigration. Through these congressional acts, the door to Chinese immigration was systematically shut. All new immigration of Chinese laborers was suspended; naturalized citizenship was denied to those Chinese already living in the United States; and the reentry of Chinese laborers formerly residing in the United States was denied. In 1888, prohibitions formerly limited to Chinese laborers were broadened to include all persons of Chinese descent with the exception of Chinese officials, teachers, students, tourists, and businesspersons. Furthermore, Chinese residents were the only people who were required to carry with them at all times certificates attesting to their right to reside in the United States, or they would risk imprisonment at hard labor followed by deportation. Immigrants from other Asian countries did not fare any better than the Chinese.

The following selection includes two of the key Chinese exclusion laws enacted in 1882 and 1892. In 1943, at the height of the war against Japan, which was also the enemy of China, President Franklin D. Roosevelt requested that Congress repeal these laws to "correct a historic mistake." The new law provided an annual quota for Chinese immigration whereby only 105 Chinese would be allowed to enter the United States and the right of naturalized citizenship was extended to them.

QUESTIONS TO CONSIDER

1. What were the reactions of the three American presidents, Chester Arthur, Grover Cleveland, and Benjamin Harrison, who served during the period of the Chinese exclusion controversy? What other reasons besides race do you see for their acquiescence or active support for such legislation?
2. What were the economic conditions of California and the United States in the late 1860s and early 1870s? How seriously did Chinese immigrant laborers threaten the jobs of white Americans? In your opinion, did the immigrant laborers recently arrived from Ireland or Poland have more rights than their Chinese counterparts in obtaining employment? Why?
3. In 1943, President Roosevelt urged Congress "to be big enough" to acknowledge an error of the past by the repeal of the Chinese exclusion laws. Why do you think he took such a step?
4. Do you see any connections among Arthur de Gobineau's *The Inequality of Human Races* (see Reading 43), *Enfumades* in French Algeria: Three Reports (see Reading 42), and the Chinese Exclusion Acts? What are they?

CHINESE EXCLUSION ACTS MAY 6, 1882, AND MAY 5, 1892

Whereas, in the opinion of the Government of the United States the coming of Chinese laborers to this country endangers the good order of certain localities within the territory thereof: Therefore,

Be it enacted by the Senate and House of Representatives of the United States of America in Congress assembled, That from and after the expiration of ninety days next after the passage of this act, and until the expiration of ten years next and after the passage of this act, the coming of Chinese laborers to the United States be, and the same is hereby, suspended; and during such suspension it shall not be lawful for any Chinese laborer to come, or, having so come after the expiration of said ninety days, to remain within the United States. . . .

Sec. 13. That this act shall not apply to diplomatic and other officers of the Chinese Government traveling upon the business of that government, whose credentials shall be taken as equivalent to the certificate in this act mentioned, and shall exempt them and their body and household servants from the provisions of this act as to other Chinese persons.

Sec. 14. That hereafter no State court or court of the United States shall admit Chinese to citizenship; and all laws in conflict with this act are hereby repealed.

Sec. 15. That the words "Chinese laborers," wherever used in this act, shall be construed to mean both skilled and unskilled laborers and Chinese employed in mining.

Approved, May 6, 1882.

* * *

Be it enacted by the Senate and House of Representatives of the United States of America in Congress assembled, That all laws now in force prohibiting and regulating the coming into this country of Chinese persons and persons of Chinese descent are hereby continued in force for a period of ten years from the passage of this act. . . .

Sec. 2. That any Chinese person or person of Chinese descent, when convicted and adjudged under any of said laws to be not lawfully entitled to be or remain in the United States, shall be removed from the United States to China, unless he or they shall make it appear to the justice, judge, or commissioner before whom he or they are tried that he or they are subjects or citizens of some other country, in which case he or they shall be removed from the United States to such country: Provided, That in any case where such other country of which such Chinese person shall claim to be a citizen or subject shall demand any tax as a condition of the removal of such person to that country, he or she shall be removed to China.

Sec. 3. That any Chinese person of Chinese descent arrested under the provisions of this act or the acts hereby extended shall be adjudged to be unlawfully within the United States unless such person shall establish, by affirmative proof, to the satisfaction of such justice, judge, or commissioner, his lawful right to remain in the United States.

Sec. 4. That any such Chinese person or person of Chinese descent convicted and adjudged to be not lawfully entitled to be or remain in the United States shall be

From *Statutes at Large of the United States* (Washington, DC: Government Printing Office, 1883), Vol. 22, pp. 58–61; 1893, Vol. 27, pp. 25–26.

imprisoned at hard labor for a period of not exceeding one year and thereafter removed from the United States, as hereinafter provided.

Sec. 5. That after the passage of this act on application to any judge or court of the United States in the first instance for a writ of habeas corpus, by a Chinese person seeking to land in the United States, to whom that privilege has been denied, no bail shall be allowed, and such application shall be heard and determined promptly without unnecessary delay.

Sec. 6. And it shall be the duty of all Chinese laborers within the limits of the United States at the time of the passage of this act, and who are entitled to remain in the United States, to apply to the collector of internal revenue of their respective districts, within one year after the passage of this act, for a certificate of residence, and any Chinese laborer, within the limits of the United States, who shall neglect, fail, or refuse to comply with the provisions of this act, or who after one year from the passage hereof, shall be found within the jurisdiction of the United States without such certificate of residence, shall be deemed and adjudged to be unlawfully within the United States, and may be arrested, by any United States customs official, collector of internal revenue or his deputies, United States marshal or his deputies, and taken before a United States judge, whose duty it shall be to order that he be deported from the United States as hereinbefore provided, unless he shall establish clearly to the satisfaction of said judge, that by reason of accident, sickness or other unavoidable cause, he has been unable to procure his certificate, and to the satisfaction of the court, and by at least one credible white witness, that he was a resident of the United States at the time of the passage of this act; and if upon the hearing, it shall appear that he is so entitled to a certificate, it shall be granted upon his paying the cost. Should it appear that said Chinaman had procured a certificate which has been lost or destroyed, he shall be detained and judgment suspended a reasonable time to enable him to procure a duplicate from the officer granting it, and in such cases, the cost of said arrest and trial shall be in the direction of the court. And any Chinese person other than a Chinese laborer, having a right to be and remain in the United States, desiring such certificate as evidence of such right may apply for and receive the same without charge. . . .

Approved, May 5, 1892

Part IV

Empires and Upheavals

England's Imperial March

Imperialism—one country's dominating the economic or political affairs of a weaker country—was certainly not new to the nineteenth century; however, its explosive character and global scale were new. In the eighteenth century, European colonists (with the exception of the United States) had been content to occupy the coastlines of Africa, India, China, and the New World. But by the mid-nineteenth century, a more aggressive imperialism, equipped with new tools of empire, sought a deeper and more permanent penetration of the non-European world. Of all the imperialistic countries in the nineteenth century, Great Britain was the most successful one.

The British gained footholds in India, particularly in Bengal in northeast India, through the British East India Company, a privately owned "joint stock company" founded for conducting trade. Supported from time to time by British military strength, the Company took on many of the characteristics of a colonial government in the areas it controlled during the last half of the eighteenth century. The governor-general of the Company was appointed in large part to carry out the policies of the British Prime Minister and Parliament, which established a Board of Control in 1784 to direct the Company's political activities.

In strengthening the British economic and military position in India, Company officials first attempted to leave Muslim and Hindu religious laws intact; however, high Company officials found some native religious customs intolerable. For example, the practice of infanticide was tolerated by Hindu custom, but it was a crime by British standards, and consequently the East India Company prohibited it. A highly symbolic case for the Company and its board was that of *sati* (or *suddhee*), a custom of higher Hindu castes that required widows to burn themselves on their husbands' funeral pyres. By the 1820s, some officials of the Company were not only repulsed by *sati* but had become convinced that it was no longer necessarily a voluntary religious act. This was a clear reflection of the cultural side of British imperialism. Civilizing non-Europeans by shouldering the "white man's burden" was perceived by British imperialists as being just as important as political and economic controls of the non-Western world.

The English East India Company engaged in smuggling a very large volume of opium into China by violating China's laws against opium importation in an attempt to increase its profits through reversal of the balance of trade, which had been running in favor of China. In response, China made desperate attempts to stop the opium inflow. In turn, this eventually led to the Opium War, 1839–1842, which humilated China.

45 Lord William Bentinck, Comments on Ritual Murder and the Limits of Religious Toleration

The pros and cons of intervening in these cases are weighed in the following selection by Lord William Bentinck (1774–1839), who was appointed governor-general of the East India Company in 1828.

QUESTIONS TO CONSIDER

1. Why does Bentinck think it advisable and necessary for the Company to abolish the custom of *sati?*
2. What does *sati* have to do with the British policy of religious toleration?
3. What reaction does Bentinck expect from the Hindus if *sati* is abolished?
4. If *sati* is abolished, what advice does he give for handling possible violations?
5. Would you have approached this situation in the same way as Bentinck, or would you have used different reasoning?

Whether the question be to continue or to discontinue the practice of *sati*, the decision is equally surrounded by an awful responsibility. To consent to the consignment year after year of hundreds of innocent victims to a cruel and untimely end, when the power exists of preventing it, is a predicament which no conscience can contemplate without horror. But, on the other hand, if heretofore received opinions are to be considered of any value, to put to hazard by a contrary course the very safety of the British Empire in India, and to extinguish at once all hopes of those great improvements—affecting the condition not of hundreds and thousands but of millions—which can only be expected from the continuance of our supremacy, is an alternative which even in the light of humanity itself may be considered as a still greater evil. It is upon this first and highest consideration alone, the good of mankind, that the tolerance of this inhuman and impious rite can in my opinion be justified on the part of the government of a civilized nation. While the solution of this question is appalling from the unparalleled magnitude of its possible results, the considerations belonging to it are such as to make even the stoutest mind distrust its decision. On the one side, Religion, Humanity, under the most appalling form, as well as vanity and ambition—in short, all the most powerful influences over the human heart—are arrayed to bias and mislead the judgment. On the other side, the sanction of countless ages, the example of all the Mussulman conquerors, the unanimous concurrence in the same policy of our own most able rulers, together with the universal veneration of the people, seem authoritatively to forbid, both to feeling and to reason, any interference in the exercise of their natural prerogative. In venturing to be the first to deviate from this practice it becomes me to show that nothing has been yielded to feeling, but that reason, and reason alone, has governed the decision.

It must be first observed that of the 463 *satis* occurring in the whole of the Presidency of Fort William, 420 took place in Bengal, Behar, and Orissa, or what is termed the Lower Provinces, and of these latter 287 in the Calcutta Division alone.

It might be very difficult to make a stranger to India understand, much less believe, that in a population of so many millions of people as the Calcutta Division includes, and the same may be said of all the Lower Provinces, so great is the want of courage and of vigour of character, and such the habitual submission of centuries, that insurrection or hostile opposition to the will of the ruling power may be affirmed to be an impossible danger. . . .

If, however, security was wanting against extensive popular tumult or revolution, I should say that the Permanent Settlement, which, though a failure in many other respects and in its most important essentials, has this great advantage at least, of having created a vast body of rich landed proprietors deeply interested in the continuance of the British Dominion and having complete command over the mass of the people. . . .

Were the scene of this sad destruction of human life laid in the Upper instead of the Lower Provinces, in the midst of a bold and manly people, I might speak with less confidence upon the question of safety. In these Provinces the *satis* amount to forty-three only upon a population of nearly twenty millions. It cannot be expected that any general feeling, where combination of any kind is so unusual, could be excited in defense of a rite in which so few participate, a rite also notoriously made too often subservient to views of personal interest on the part of the other members of the family. . . .

From "Lord William Bentinck on the Suppression of *Sati*, 8 November 1829," in *Speeches and Documents on Indian Policy, 1750–1921*, ed. Arthur B. Keith (Oxford: Oxford University Press, 1922), Vol. 1, pp. 208–26.

But I have taken up too much time in giving my own opinion when those of the greatest experience and highest official authority are upon our records. In the report of the Nizamat Adalat for 1828, four out of five of the Judges recommended to the Governor-General in Council the immediate abolition of the practice, and attest its safety. The fifth Judge, though not opposed to the opinions of the rest of the Bench, did not feel then prepared to give his entire assent. In the report of this year the measure has come up with the unanimous recommendation of the Court. . . . No documents exist to show the opinions of the public functionaries in the interior, but I am informed that nine-tenths are in favour of the abolition. . . .

Having made inquiries, also, how far *satis* are permitted in the European foreign settlements, I find from Dr. Carey that at Chinsurah no such sacrifices had ever been permitted by the Dutch Government. That within the limits of Chandarnagar itself they were also prevented, but allowed to be performed in the British territories. The Danish Government of Serampur has not forbidden the rite, in conformity to the example of the British Government.

It is a very important fact that, though representations have been made by the disappointed party to superior authority, it does not appear that a single instance of direct opposition to the execution of the prohibitory orders of our civil functionaries has ever occurred. How, then, can it be reasonably feared that to the Government itself, from whom all authority is derived, and whose power is now universally considered to be irresistible, anything bearing the semblance of resistance can be manifested? Mr. Wilson also is of opinion that no immediate overt act of insubordination would follow the publication of the edict. The Regulation of Government may be evaded, the police may be corrupted, but even here the price paid as hush money will operate as a penalty, indirectly forwarding the object of Government.

I venture, then, to think it completely proved that from the native population nothing of extensive combination, or even of partial opposition, may be expected from the abolition. . . .

I have now to submit for the consideration of Council the draft of a regulation enacting the abolition of *satis*. . . . It is only in the previous process, or during the actual performance of the rite, when the feelings of all may be more or less roused to a high degree of excitement, that I apprehend the possibility of affray or of acts of violence through an indiscreet and injudicious exercise of authority. It seemed to me prudent, therefore, that the police, in the first instance, should warn and advise, but not forcibly prohibit, and if the *sati*, in defiance of this notice, were performed, that a report should be made to the magistrate, who would summon the parties and proceed as in any other case of crime. . . .

The first and primary object of my heart is the benefit of the Hindus. I know nothing so important to the improvement of their future condition as the establishment of a purer morality, whatever their belief, and a more just conception of the will of God. The first step to this better understanding will be dissociation of religious belief and practice from blood and murder. They will then, when no longer under this brutalizing excitement, view with more calmness acknowledged truths. They will see that there can be no inconsistency in the ways of Providence, that to the command received as divine by all races of men, "No innocent blood shall be spilt," there can be no exception; and when they shall have been convinced of the error of this first and most criminal of their customs, may it not be hoped that others, which stand in the way of their improvement, may likewise pass away, and that, thus emancipated from those chains and shackles upon their minds and actions, they may no longer continue, as they have done, the slaves of every foreign conqueror, but that they may assume their first places among the great families of mankind? I disown in these remarks, or in this measure, any view whatever to conversion to our own faith. I write and feel as a legislator for the Hindus, and as I believe many enlightened Hindus think and feel.

Descending from these higher considerations, it cannot be a dishonest ambition that the Government of which I form a part should have the credit of an act which is to wash out a foul stain upon British rule, and to stay the sacrifice of humanity and justice to a doubtful expediency; and finally, as a branch of the general administration of the Empire, I may be permitted to feel deeply anxious that our course shall be in accordance with the noble example set to us by the British Government at home, and that the adaptation, when practicable to the circumstances of this vast Indian population, of the same enlightened principles, may promote here as well as there the general prosperity, and may exalt the character of our nation.

46 Lin Tse-hsü [Lin Zexu], Letter of Moral Admonition to Queen Victoria

Although the English East India Company's trade with China was profitable, the overall balance of trade had remained in China's favor until the early decades of the nineteenth century. European traders bought tea, silk, rhubarb, and other goods from China, but the Chinese found little need for Western goods. A reversal in the trade balance came in the 1830s, and opium importation was one of the most important factors. Opium, forbidden in China, was smuggled into the country from India in ever-increasing quantities, primarily by English East India Company ships through the port of Canton [Guanzhou]. During the years of 1838–1839 alone, more than five million pounds of opium were imported illegally by East India Company ships.

The effects of the illicit trade on Chinese morality and health, as well as on the economy, were so deleterious that Emperor Tao-kuang [Daoguang] (r. 1821–1850) was gravely concerned. He searched for an official who would be able to deal with the opium menace effectively and resolutely. In Lin Tse-hsü [Lin Zexu] he found such a person. A high official in the Imperial government, Lin had enjoyed a wide reputation for his competence and integrity and for his hard-line approach toward the proliferation of opium. In December 1838, he was appointed imperial commissioner at Canton, with full power to stop the Canton opium traffic.

Lin Tse-hsü arrived in Canton in March 1839 and immediately began to stamp out the opium traffic; however, it became clear to him that the solution was to stop the supply at its source. The following selection is his letter to Queen Victoria, appealing to the British conscience and demanding an end to the opium trade. The letter was written in the summer of 1839, only a few months before the outbreak of the Opium War in November 1839. The fact that Lin Tse-hsü refers to

Queen Victoria as "king" might suggest how knowledgeable the Chinese government was of English politics.

QUESTIONS TO CONSIDER

1. What moral arguments did Commissioner Lin present against the British importation of opium into China?
2. On the basis of Lin's letter to Queen Victoria and Emperor Ch'ien-lung's letter to King George III (see Reading 25), describe China's view of the West, especially of Great Britain. Contrast these views with those expressed by Rudyard Kipling in "The White Man's Burden" (see Reading 47).

A communication: magnificently our great Emperor soothes and pacifies China and the foreign countries, regarding all with the same kindness. If there is profit, then he shares it with the peoples of the world; if there is harm, then he removes it on behalf of the world. This is because he takes the mind of heaven and earth as his mind.

The kings of your honorable country by a tradition handed down from generation to generation have always been noted for their politeness and submissiveness. We have read your successive tributary memorials saying, "In general our countrymen who go to trade in China have always received His Majesty the Emperor's gracious treatment and equal justice," and so on. Privately we are delighted with the way in which the honorable rulers of your country deeply understand the grand principles and are grateful for the Celestial grace. For this reason the Celestial Court in soothing those from afar has redoubled its polite and kind treatment. The profit from trade has been enjoyed by them continuously for two hundred years. This is the source from which your country has become known for its wealth.

But after a long period of commercial intercourse, there appear among the crowd of barbarians both good persons and bad, unevenly. Consequently there are those who smuggle opium to seduce the Chinese people and so cause the spread of the poison to all provinces. Such persons who only care to profit themselves, and disregard their harm to others, are not tolerated by the laws of heaven and are unanimously hated by human beings. His Majesty the Emperor, upon hearing of this, is in a towering rage. He has especially sent me, his commissioner, to come to Kwangtung, and together with the governor-general and governor jointly to investigate and settle this matter.

~All those people in China who sell opium or smoke opium should receive the death penalty. If we trace the crime of those barbarians who through the years have been selling opium, then the deep harm they have wrought and the great profit they have usurped should fundamentally justify their execution according to law. We take into consideration, however, the fact that the various barbarians have still known how to repent their crimes and return to their allegiance to us by taking the 20,183 chests of opium from their storeships and petitioning us, through their consular officer [superintendent of trade], Elliot, to receive it. It has been entirely destroyed and this has

Reprinted by permission of the publisher from *China's Response to the West: A Documentary Survey*, 1839–1923 by Ssu-yu Teng and John K. Fairbank, Cambridge, Mass.: Harvard University Press, pp. 24–27. Copyright © 1954 by the President and Fellows of Harvard College; Copyright © renewed 1982 by Ssu-yu Teng and John K. Fairbank, Copyright © for new preface 1979 by the President and Fellows of Harvard College.

been faithfully reported to the Throne in several memorials by this commissioner and his colleagues.

Fortunately we have received a specially extended favor from His Majesty the Emperor, who considers that for those who voluntarily surrender there are still some circumstances to palliate their crime, and so for the time being he has magnanimously excused them from punishment. But as for those who again violate the opium prohibition, it is difficult for the law to pardon them repeatedly. Having established new regulations, we presume that the ruler of your honorable country, who takes delight in our culture and whose disposition is inclined towards us, must be able to instruct the various barbarians to observe the law with care. It is only necessary to explain to them the advantages and disadvantages and then they will know that the legal code of the Celestial Court must be absolutely obeyed with awe.

We find that your country is sixty or seventy thousand *li* [three *li* make one mile] from China. Yet there are barbarian ships that strive to come here for trade for the purpose of making a great profit. The wealth of China is used to profit the barbarians. That is to say, the great profit made by barbarians is all taken from the rightful share of China. By what right do they then in return use the poisonous drug to injure the Chinese people? Even though the barbarians may not necessarily intend to do us harm, yet in coveting profit to an extreme, they have no regard for injuring others. Let us ask, where is your conscience? I have heard that the smoking of opium is very strictly forbidden by your country; that is because the harm caused by opium is clearly understood. Since it is not permitted to do harm to your own country, then even less should you let it be passed on to the harm of other countries—how much less to China! Of all that China exports to foreign countries, there is not a single thing which is not beneficial to people: they are of benefit when eaten, or of benefit when used, or of benefit when resold; all are beneficial. Is there a single article from China which has done any harm to foreign countries? Take tea and rhubarb, for example; the foreign countries cannot get along for a single day without them. If China cuts off these benefits with no sympathy for those who are to suffer, then what can the barbarians rely upon to keep themselves alive? Moreover the woolens, camlets, and longells [i.e., textiles] of foreign countries cannot be woven unless they obtain Chinese silk. If China, again, cuts off this beneficial export, what profit can the barbarians expect to make? As for other food-stuffs, beginning with candy, ginger, cinnamon, and so forth, and articles for use, beginning with silk, satin, chinaware, and so on, all the things that must be had by foreign countries are innumerable. On the other hand, articles coming from the outside to China can only be used as toys. We can take them or get along without them. Since they are not needed by China, what difficulty would there be if we closed the frontier and stopped the trade? Nevertheless our Celestial Court lets tea, silk, and other goods be shipped without limit and circulated everywhere without begrudging it in the slightest. This is for no other reason but to share the benefit with the people of the whole world.

The goods from China carried away by your country not only supply your own consumption and use, but also can be divided up and sold to other countries, producing a triple profit. Even if you do not sell opium, you still have this threefold profit. How can you bear to go further, selling products injurious to others in order to fulfill your insatiable desire?

Suppose there were people from another country who carried opium for sale to England and seduced your people into buying and smoking it; certainly your honorable ruler would deeply hate it and be bitterly aroused. We have heard heretofore that your honorable ruler is kind and benevolent. Naturally you would not wish to give unto others what you yourself do not want. We have also heard that the ships coming to Canton have all had regulations promulgated and given to them in which it is stated that it is not permitted to carry contraband goods. This indicates that the administrative orders of your honorable rule have been originally strict and clear. Only because the trading ships are numerous, heretofore perhaps they have not been examined with care. Now after this communication has been dispatched and you have clearly understood the strictness of the prohibitory laws of the Celestial Court, certainly you will not let your subjects dare again to violate the law.

We have further learned that in London, the capital of your honorable rule, and in Scotland (Su-ko-lan), Ireland (Ai-lun), and other places, originally no opium has been produced. Only in several places of India under your control such as Bengal, Madras, Bombay, Patna, Benares, and Malwa has opium been planted from hill to hill, and ponds have been opened for its manufacture. For months and years work is continued in order to accumulate the poison. The obnoxious odor ascends, irritating heaven and frightening the spirits. Indeed you, O King, can eradicate the opium plant in these places, hoe over the fields entirely, and sow in its stead the five grains [i.e., millet, barley, wheat, etc.]. Anyone who dares again attempt to plant and manufacture opium should be severely punished. This will really be a great, benevolent government policy that will increase the common weal and get rid of evil. For this, Heaven must support you and the spirits must bring you good fortune, prolonging your old age and extending your descendants. All will depend on this act.\

As for the barbarian merchants who come to China, their food and drink and habitation are all received by the gracious favor of our Celestial Court. Their accumulated wealth is all benefit given with pleasure by our Celestial Court. They spend rather few days in their own country but more time in Canton. To digest clearly the legal penalties as an aid to instruction has been a valid principle in all ages. Suppose a man of another country comes to England to trade, he still has to obey the English laws; how much more should he obey in China the laws of the Celestial Dynasty?

Now we have set up regulations governing the Chinese people. He who sells opium shall receive the death penalty and he who smokes it also the death penalty. Now consider this: if the barbarians do not bring opium, then how can the Chinese people resell it, and how can they smoke it? The fact is that the wicked barbarians beguile the Chinese people into a death trap. How then can we grant life only to these barbarians? He who takes the life of even one person still has to atone for it with his own life; yet is the harm done by opium limited to the taking of one life only? Therefore in the new regulations, in regard to those barbarians who bring opium to China, the penalty is fixed at decapitation or strangulation. This is what is called getting rid of a harmful thing on behalf of mankind.

Moreover we have found that in the middle of the second month of this year [April 9] Consul [Superintendent] Elliot of your nation, because the opium prohibition law was very stern and severe, petitioned for an extension of the time limit. He requested a limit of five months for India and its adjacent harbors and related territories, and ten months for England proper, after which they would act in conformity with the new regulations. Now we, the commissioner and others, have memorialized and have received the extraordinary Celestial grace of His Majesty the Emperor, who has redoubled his consideration and compassion. All those who within the period of the coming one year (from England) or six months (from India) bring opium to China by mistake, but who voluntarily confess and completely surrender their opium, shall be exempt from their punishment. After this limit of time, if there are still those who bring opium to China then they will plainly have committed a willful violation and shall at once be executed according to law, with absolutely no clemency or pardon. This may be called the height of kindness and the perfection of justice.

Our Celestial Dynasty rules over and supervises the myriad states, and surely possesses unfathomable spiritual dignity. Yet the Emperor cannot bear to execute people without having first tried to reform them by instruction. Therefore he especially promulgates these fixed regulations. The barbarian merchants of your country, if they wish to do business for a prolonged period, are required to obey our statutes respectfully and to cut off permanently the source of opium. They must by no means try to test the effectiveness of the law with their lives. May you, O King, check your wicked and sift your vicious people before they come to China, in order to guarantee the peace of your nation, to show further the sincerity of your politeness and submissiveness, and to let the two countries enjoy together the blessings of peace. How fortunate, how fortunate indeed! After receiving this dispatch will you immediately give us a prompt reply regarding the details and circumstances of your cutting off the opium traffic. Be sure not to put this off. The above is what has to be communicated. [Vermilion endorsement:] This is appropriately worded and quite comprehensive.

47 Rudyard Kipling, "The White Man's Burden"

No single statement better represents the justification for British imperialism than "The White Man's Burden," written by Rudyard Kipling (1865–1936).

QUESTIONS TO CONSIDER

1. Why would this poem appeal to religious and scientific sentiment in Victorian England?
2. Compare and contrast Kipling's view of native, nonwhite people with that of Frantz Fanon (see Reading 80).

> Take up the White Man's burden—
> Send forth the best ye breed—
> Go bind your sons to exile
> To serve your captives' need;
> To wait in heavy harness,
> On fluttered folk and wild—
> Your new-caught, sullen peoples,
> Half-devil and half-child.
>
> Take up the White Man's burden—
> In patience to abide,
> To veil the threat of terror
> And check the show of pride;

From Rudyard Kipling, *Verse*, inclusive ed. (New York: Doubleday and Page, 1920), pp. 371–72.

By open speech and simple,
An hundred times made plain
To seek another's profit,
And work another's gain.

Take up the White Man's burden—
The savage wars of peace—
Fill full the mouth of Famine
And bid the sickness cease;
And when your goal is nearest
The end for others sought,
Watch sloth and heathen Folly
Bring all your hopes to nought.

Take up the White Man's burden—
No tawdry rule of kings,
But toil of serf and sweeper—
The tale of common things.
The ports ye shall not enter,
The roads ye shall not tread,
Go mark them with your living,
And mark them with your dead.

Take up the White Man's burden—
And reap his old reward:
The blame of those ye better,
The hate of those ye guard—
The cry of hosts ye humour
(Ah, slowly!) toward the light:—
"Why brought he us from bondage,
Our loved Egyptian night?"

Take up the White Man's burden—
Ye dare not stoop to less—
Nor call too loud on Freedom
To cloke your weariness;
By all ye cry or whisper,
By all ye leave or do,
The silent, sullen peoples
Shall weigh your gods and you.

Take up the White Man's burden—
Have done with childish days—
The lightly proferred laurel,
The easy, ungrudged praise.
Comes now, to search your manhood
Through all the thankless years,
Cold, edged with dear-bought wisdom,
The judgment of your peers!

Japan: Tradition and Transformation

Tokugawa Japan's self-imposed isolation, which had lasted for more than two hundred years, finally came to an end in 1854. In that year, an American, Commodore Matthew C. Perry, brought to Japan from President Millard Fillmore a message expressing his desire to open relations with that country. This resulted in the signing of the Treaty of Kanagawa with the shogunal government in Edo. This abandonment of the two-hundred-year-old seclusion policy represented a severe blow to the prestige of the shogunal government in the eyes of the Japanese people. This event ushered in a new era in modern Japanese history, marking the beginning of the final collapse of the old order, which was replaced by a modern Japan under the government of Emperor Meiji in 1868.

In 1858, four years after the Kanagawa treaty, Townsend Harris, the first consul general of the United States, signed a more substantial commercial treaty with the Japanese, the Treaty of Amity and Commerce between the United States and Japan. In accordance with its guidelines, the ratified treaty was to be exchanged in Washington, D.C. This provided Japan with the opportunity to send her envoys to America for the first time ever. The seventy-seven-member entourage of Japan's first embassy reached Washington, D.C., and exchanged the ratified treaty on May 22, 1860. President James Buchanan received the embassy in the White House. This occasion was an important eye-opener for the members of the Japanese embassy.

In Japan itself, a handful of dedicated leaders of the Meiji Restoration rallied around Emperor Meiji (1867–1912) and launched sweeping political, social, economic, and intellectual reforms. They studied Western institutions carefully, adopting the best features without abandoning Japan's traditional ideals and virtues. This was best exemplified in their effort to enact a constitution. Within the lifetime of Emperor Meiji, Japan experienced the transition from a backward, agrarian, and feudal state into a powerful, modern, industrial, and constitutional monarchy. After having successfully transformed internally, Japan began to embark on imperialistic adventures abroad. Before the end of the Meiji era, Japan fought two successful wars against two big powers of the world, China and Russia, and joined the rank of the major world powers.

Despite the modern transformation of Japan during the Meiji period, many old institutions continued to endure. One of these was the institution of the geisha. The profession of geisha is one of the better-known traditional Japanese entertainment occupations, about which Westerners often have misconceptions.

48 Geisha: *Glimpse of Unfamiliar Japan*

The term "geisha" was first used in the middle of the eighteenth century during the Tokugawa period (1600–1868), and the first geisha were male entertainers. But in time, women came to dominate the profession. Aspiring geisha had to have good looks and, more important, good training in various traditional arts such as classical dancing, playing a stringed instrument called the samisen, singing, games, and flirtatious conversation. Some of the ambitious geisha were even trained in the tea ceremony, flower arranging, calligraphy, and painting. Training began early for girls—often as young as eight or nine—from poor families who were adopted into geisha houses and worked as maid servants for a few years as part of their early apprenticeship. When they reached the age of about thirteen, they were admitted to full apprenticeship, which lasted about five years. Upon successful completion of the apprenticeship, these girls had to pass an examination of their artistic skills at their local geisha registry before the senior members of the geisha union. Successful geisha candidates then registered at the local registry and were ready to receive assignments. They were hired to entertain customers at dinner parties or at certain restaurants. In recent decades, the profession of geisha has suffered a decline as a result of the inroad of the Western-style bar hostesses. But the geisha house today still enjoys the special favor of the Japanese politicians who prefer to conduct political negotiations at a geisha house rather than at Western-style restaurants.

The following excerpt is an account of the Japanese geisha and a geisha party described by Lafcadio Hearn (1850–1904), an Anglo-Irish-Greek who went to Japan in 1890 and became a Japanese citizen, taking the Japanese name Koizumi Yagumo. He became one of the most popular Western writers on Japan at the turn of the century.

QUESTIONS TO CONSIDER

1. How do you compare geisha with women in a comparable entertainment profession in the West?

2. Why do you think Japanese politicians generally prefer geisha houses to Western-style restaurants for conducting political negotiations?
3. Why would a woman become a geisha?

The robed guests take their places, quite noiselessly and without speech, upon the kneeling-cushions. The lacquered services are laid upon the matting before them by maidens whose bare feet make no sound. For a while there is only smiling and flitting, as in dreams. You are not likely to hear any voices from without, as a banqueting-house is usually secluded from the street by spacious gardens. At last the master of ceremonies, host or provider, breaks the hush with the consecrated formula: "*O-somatsu degozarimasu ga!—dōzo o-hashi!*" whereat all present bow silently, take up their hashi (chopsticks), and fall to. But hashi, deftly used, cannot be heard at all. The maidens pour warm saké into the cup of each guest without making the least sound; and it is not until several dishes have been emptied, and several cups of sake absorbed, that tongues are loosened.

Then, all at once, with a little burst of laughter, a number of young girls enter, make the customary prostration of greeting, glide into the open space between the ranks of the guests, and begin to serve the wine with a grace and dexterity of which no common maid is capable. They are pretty; they are clad in very costly robes of silk; they are girdled like queens; and the beautifully dressed hair of each is decked with mock flowers, with wonderful combs and pins, and with curious ornaments of gold. They greet the stranger as if they had always known him; they jest, laugh, and utter funny little cries. These are the geisha,[1] or dancing-girls, hired for the banquet.

Samisen[2] tinkle. The dancers withdraw to a clear space at the farther end of the banqueting-hall, always vast enough to admit of many more guests than ever assemble upon common occasions. Some form the orchestra, under the direction of a woman of uncertain age; there are several samisen, and a tiny drum played by a child. Others, singly or in pairs, perform the dance. It may be swift and merry, consisting wholly of graceful posturing,—two girls dancing together with such coincidence of step and gesture as only years of training could render possible. But more frequently it is rather like acting than like what we Occidentals call dancing,—acting accompanied with extraordinary waving of sleeves and fans, and with a play of eyes and features, sweet, subtle, subdued, wholly Oriental. There are more voluptuous dances known to geisha, but upon ordinary occasions and before refined audiences they portray beautiful old Japanese traditions, like the legend of the fisher Urashima, beloved by the Sea God's daughter; and at intervals they sing ancient Chinese poems, expressing a natural emotion with delicious vividness by a few exquisite words. And always they pour the wine,—that warm, pale yellow, drowsy wine which fills the veins with soft contentment, making a faint sense of ecstasy, through which, as through some poppied sleep, the commonplace becomes wondrous and blissful, and the geisha Maids of Paradise, and the world much sweeter than, in the natural order of things, it could ever possibly be.

[1]The Kyōto word is *maiko*.
[2]Guitars of three strings.

From Lafcadio Hearn, *Glimpse of Unfamiliar Japan*, Vol. II (Boston: Houghton Mifflin and Co., 1894), pp. 525–33.

The banquet, at first so silent, slowly changes to a merry tumult. . . .

Notwithstanding all this apparent comradeship, a certain rigid decorum between guest and geisha is invariably preserved at a Japanese banquet. However flushed with wine a guest may have become, you will never see him attempt to caress a girl; he never forgets that she appears at the festivities only as a human flower, to be looked at, not to be touched. The familiarity which foreign tourists in Japan frequently permit themselves with geisha or with waiter-girls, though endured with smiling patience, is really much disliked, and considered by native observers an evidence of extreme vulgarity.

For a time the merriment grows; but as midnight draws near, the guests begin to slip away, one by one, unnoticed. Then the din gradually dies down, the music stops; and at last the geisha, having escorted the latest of the feasters to the door, with laughing cries of *Sayōnara*, can sit down alone to break their long fast in the deserted hall.

Such is the geisha's rôle. But what is the mystery of her? What are her thoughts, her emotions, her secret self? What is her veritable existence beyond the night circle of the banquet lights, far from the illusion formed around her by the mist of wine? . . .

The girl begins her career as a slave, a pretty child bought from miserably poor parents under a contract, according to which her services may be claimed by the purchasers for eighteen, twenty, or even twenty-five years. She is fed, clothed, and trained in a house occupied only by geisha; and she passes the rest of her childhood under severe discipline. She is taught etiquette, grace, polite speech; she has daily lessons in dancing; and she is obliged to learn by heart a multitude of songs with their airs. Also she must learn games, the service of banquets and weddings, the art of dressing and looking beautiful. Whatever physical gifts she may have are carefully cultivated. Afterwards she is taught to handle musical instruments: first, the little drum (*tsudzumi*), which cannot be sounded at all without considerable practice; then she learns to play the samisen a little, with a plectrum of tortoise-shell or ivory. At eight or nine years of age she attends banquets, chiefly as a drum-player. She is then the most charming little creature imaginable, and already knows how to fill your wine-cup exactly full, with a single toss of the bottle and without spilling a drop, between two taps of her drum.

Thereafter her discipline becomes more cruel. Her voice may be flexible enough, but lacks the requisite strength. In the iciest hours of winter nights, she must ascend to the roof of her dwelling-house, and there sing and play till the blood oozes from her fingers and the voice dies in her throat. The desired result is an atrocious cold. After a period of hoarse whispering, her voice changes its tone and strengthens. She is ready to become a public singer and dancer.

In this capacity she usually makes her first appearance at the age of twelve or thirteen. If pretty and skillful, her services will be much in demand, and her time paid for at the rate of twenty to twenty-five sen (Japanese cent) per hour. Then only do her purchasers begin to reimburse themselves for the time, expense, and trouble of her training; and they are not apt to be generous. For many years more all that she earns must pass into their hands. She can own nothing, not even her clothes.

At seventeen or eighteen she has made her artistic reputation. She has been at many hundreds of entertainments, and knows by sight all the important personages of her city, the character of each, the history of all. Her life has been chiefly a night life; rarely has she seen the sun rise since she became a dancer. She has learned to drink wine without ever losing her head, and to fast for seven or eight hours without ever feeling the worse. She has had many lovers. To a certain extent she is free to smile upon whom she pleases; but she has been well taught, above all else, to use her power of charm for her own advantage. She hopes to find Somebody able and willing to buy her freedom,—which Somebody would almost certainly thereafter discover many new and excellent meanings in those Buddhist texts that tell about the foolishness of love and the impermanency of all human relationships.

49 President Fillmore, "Letter to the Emperor of Japan"

Millard Fillmore, the thirteenth president of the United States (1850–1853), sent a letter to the emperor of Japan seeking friendly commercial relations between the two countries. For this historic mission, Commodore Matthew C. Perry of the U.S. Navy was chosen. He led three steam frigates and five other ships—a quarter of the American navy—to Japan. The following is President Fillmore's letter dated November 13, 1852.

QUESTIONS TO CONSIDER

1. Why was it necessary for the United States among other Western nations to spearhead and open Japan, which had been following a policy of self-imposed isolationism for over two centuries?
2. Why did the Tokugawa government in Edo succumb to the American pressure without any resistance and abandon its two-centuries'-old seclusion policy? What were the significant consequences of Tokugawa's signing of the Treaty of Kanagawa with the United States?

LETTER OF THE PRESIDENT OF THE UNITED STATES TO THE EMPEROR OF JAPAN

Great and Good Friend!

I send you this public letter by Commodore Matthew C. Perry, an officer of highest rank in the Navy of the United States, and commander of the squadron now visiting Your Imperial Majesty's dominions.

I have directed Commodore Perry to assure Your Imperial Majesty that I entertain the kindest feelings toward Your Majesty's person and government, and that I have no other object in sending him to Japan but to propose to Your Imperial Majesty that the United States and Japan should live in friendship and have commercial intercourse with each other.

The constitution and laws of the United States forbid all interference with the religious or political concerns of other nations. I have particularly charged Commodore

Roger Pineau, ed., *The Japan Expedition, 1852–1854. The Personal Journal of Commodore Matthew C. Perry* (Washington, DC: Smithsonian Institution Press, 1968), pp. 220–21.

Perry to abstain from every act which could possibly disturb the tranquility of Your Imperial Majesty's dominions.

The United States of America reach from ocean to ocean, and our territory of Oregon and state of California lie directly opposite to the dominions of Your Imperial Majesty. Our steamships can go from California to Japan in eighteen days.

Our great state of California produces about sixty millions of dollars in gold every year, besides silver, quicksilver, precious stones, and many other valuable articles. Japan is also a rich and fertile country and produces many very valuable articles. Your Imperial Majesty's subjects are skilled in many of the arts. I am desirous that our two countries should trade with each other for the benefit both of Japan and the United States.

We know that the ancient laws of Your Imperial Majesty's government do not allow of foreign trade except with the Dutch. But as the state of the world changes, and new governments are formed, it seems to be wise from time to time to make new laws. There was a time when the ancient laws of Your Imperial Majesty's government were first made.

About the same time America, which is sometimes called the New World, was first discovered and settled by the Europeans. For a long time there were but a few people, and they were poor. They have now become quite numerous; their commerce is very extensive; and they think that if your Imperial Majesty were so far to change the ancient laws as to allow a free trade between the two countries, it would be extremely beneficial to both.

If Your Imperial Majesty is not satisfied that it would be safe, altogether, to abrogate the ancient laws which forbid foreign trade, they might be suspended for five or ten years, so as to try the experiment. If it does not prove as beneficial as was hoped, the ancient laws can be restored. The United States often limits its treaties with foreign states to a few years, and then renew them or not, as they please.

I have directed Commodore Perry to mention another thing to Your Imperial Majesty. Many of our ships pass every year from California to China, and great numbers of our people pursue the whale fishery near the shores of Japan. It sometimes happens in stormy weather that one of our ships is wrecked on Your Imperial Majesty's shores. In all such cases we ask and expect that our unfortunate people should be treated with kindness, and that their property should be protected till we can send a vessel and bring them away. We are very much in earnest in this.

Commodore Perry is also directed by me to represent to Your Imperial Majesty that we understand that there is a great abundance of coal and provisions in the empire of Japan. Our steam ships, in crossing the great ocean, burn a great deal of coal, and it is not convenient to bring it all the way from America. We wish that our steam ships and other vessels should be allowed to stop in Japan and supply themselves with coal, provisions, and water. They will pay for them in money, or anything else Your Imperial Majesty's subjects may prefer, and we request Your Imperial Majesty to appoint a convenient port in the southern part of the empire where our vessels may stop for this purpose. We are very desirous of this.

These are the only objects for which I have sent Commodore Perry with a powerful squadron to pay a visit to Your Imperial Majesty's renowned city of Edo: friendship, commerce, a supply of coal, and provisions and protection for our shipwrecked people.

We have directed Commodore Perry to beg Your Imperial Majesty's acceptance of a few presents. They are of no great value in themselves, but some of them may serve as specimens of the articles manufactured in the United States, and they are intended as tokens of our sincere and respectful friendship.

May the Almighty have Your Imperial Majesty in his great and holy keeping!

In witness whereof I have caused the great seal of the United States to be hereunto affixed, and have subscribed the same with my name, at the city of Washington in America, the seal of my government, on the thirteenth day of the month of November, in the year one thousand eight hundred and fifty-two.

Your good friend,
Millard Fillmore

By the President
Edward Everett
Secretary of State

50 Ito Hirobumi, "Reminiscences on the Drafting of the New Constitution"

The leading architect of a constitutional government in Japan was Ito Hirobumi (1841–1909). Entrusted by the emperor with a mission to investigate the workings of European countries, Ito spent eighteen months in Europe from 1882 to 1883. He admired Bismarck's Germany and became convinced that—in form at least—the German imperial constitution of 1871 was best suited for Japan; but he insisted that the spirit behind the constitution should be Japanese. Among other factors, he was determined to see the emperor remain the source of political power in the new constitutional order. His liberal critics were fearful of creating an authoritarian government, whereas conservatives were afraid that the constitution would be too progressive.

The constitution was promulgated on February 11, 1889, the anniversary of the founding of the nation in 660 B.C., as an imperial gift to the people. It provided for a bicameral parliament or Diet, the first of its kind east of the Suez. The following memoir was written by Ito Hirobumi, the four-time premier, just before his death in 1909. The document reflects the author's views on the importance of adopting the Western concept of popular participation in government without sacrificing Japanese political traditions.

QUESTIONS TO CONSIDER

1. What aspects of Western political institutions, particularly those of Germany, were attractive to Ito Hirobumi?

2. What were the native political institutions that the author valued most in framing the constitution?
3. Was the Meiji constitution a democratic document?

DRAFT OF THE NEW CONSTITUTION

It was in the month of March, 1882, that His Majesty ordered me to work out a draft of a constitution to be submitted to his approval. No time was to be lost, so I started on the 15th of the same month for an extended journey to different constitutional countries to make as thorough a study as possible of the actual workings of different systems of constitutional government, of their various provisions, as well as of theories and opinions actually entertained by influential persons on the actual stage itself of constitutional life. I took young men with me, who all belonged to the élite of the rising generation, to assist and to cooperate with me in my studies. I sojourned about a year and a half in Europe, and having gathered the necessary materials, in so far as it was possible in so short a space of time, I returned home in September, 1883. Immediately after my return I set to work to draw up the Constitution. I was assisted in my work by my secretaries, prominent among whom were the late Viscount K. Inouyé, and the Barons M. Itō and K. Kanéko, and by foreign advisers, such as Professor Roesler, Mr. Piggott, and others.

PECULIAR FEATURES OF THE NATIONAL LIFE

It was evident from the outset that mere imitation of foreign models would not suffice, for there were historical peculiarities of our country which had to be taken into consideration. For example, the Crown was, with us, an institution far more deeply rooted in the national sentiment and in our history than in other countries. It was indeed the very essence of a once theocratic State, so that in formulating the restrictions on its prerogatives in the new Constitution, we had to take care to safeguard the future realness or vitality of these prerogatives, and not to let the institution degenerate into an ornamental crowning piece of the edifice. At the same time, it was also evident that any form of constitutional régime was impossible without full and extended protection of honor, liberty, property, and personal security of citizens, entailing necessarily many important restrictions on the powers of the Crown.

EMOTIONAL ELEMENTS IN SOCIAL LIFE
OF PEOPLE

On the other hand, there was one peculiarity of our social conditions that is without parallel in any other civilized country. Homogeneous in race, language, religion, and sentiments, so long secluded from the outside world, with the centuries-long traditions and inertia of the feudal system, in which the family and quasi-family ties permeated and formed the essence of every social organization, and moreover with such moral and religious tenets as laid undue stress on duties of fraternal aid and mutual succor, we had during the course of our seclusion unconsciously become a vast village community where cold intellect and calculation of public events were always restrained and even often hindered by warm emotions between man and man. . . .

It must, of course, be admitted that this social peculiarity is not without beneficial influences. It mitigates the conflict, serves as the lubricator of social organisms, and tends generally to act as a powerful lever for the practical application of the moral principle of mutual assistance between fellow citizens. But unless curbed and held in restraint, it too may exercise baneful influences on society, for in a village community, where feelings and emotions hold a higher place than intellect, free discussion is apt to be smothered, attainment and transference of power liable to become a family question of a powerful oligarchy, and the realization of such a régime as constitutional monarchy to become an impossibility, simply because in any representative régime free discussion is a matter of prime necessity, because emotions and passions have to be stopped for the sake of the cool calculation of national welfare, and even the best of friends have often to be sacrificed if the best abilities and highest intellects are to guide the helm. Besides, the dissensions between brothers and relatives, deprived as they usually are of safety-valves for giving free and hearty vent to their own opinions or discontents, are apt to degenerate into passionate quarrels and overstep the bounds of simple differences of opinion. The good side of this social peculiarity had to be retained as much as possible, while its baneful influences had to be safeguarded. These and many other peculiarities had to be taken into account in order to have a constitution adapted to the actual condition of the country.

CONFLICT BETWEEN THE OLD AND NEW THOUGHTS

Another difficulty equally grave had to be taken into consideration. We were just then in an age of transition. The opinions prevailing in the country were extremely heterogeneous, and often diametrically opposed to each other. We had survivors of former generations who were still full of theocratic ideas, and who believed that any attempt to restrict an imperial prerogative amounted to something like high treason. On the other hand, there was a large and powerful body of the younger generation educated at the time when the Manchester theory was in vogue, and who in consequence were ultra-radical in their ideas of freedom. Members of the bureaucracy were prone to lend willing ears to the German doctrinaires of the reactionary period, while, on the other hand, the educated politicians among the people having not yet tasted the bitter significance of administrative responsibility, were liable to be more influenced by the dazzling words and lucid theories of Montesquieu, Rousseau, and other similar French writers. A work entitled *History of Civilization*, by Buckle, which denounced every form of government as an unnecessary evil, became the great favorite of students of all the higher schools, including the Imperial University. On the other hand, these same students would not have dared to expound the theories of Buckle before their own conservative fathers. At that time we had not yet arrived at the stage of distinguishing clearly between political opposition on the one hand, and treason to the established order of things on the other. The virtues necessary for the smooth working of any constitution, such as love of freedom of speech, love of publicity of proceedings, the spirit of tolerance for opinions opposed to one's own, etc., had yet to be learned by long experience.

DRAFT OF THE CONSTITUTION COMPLETED

It was under these circumstances that the first draft of the Constitution was made and submitted to His Majesty, after which it was handed over to the mature deliberation of the Privy Council. The Sovereign himself presided over these deliberations, and he had full opportunities of hearing and giving due consideration to all the conflicting opinions above hinted at. I believe nothing evidences more vividly the intelligence of our august Master than the fact that in spite of the existence of strong undercurrents of an ultra-conservative nature in the council, and also in the country at large, His Majesty's decisions inclined almost invariably towards liberal and progressive ideas, so that we have been ultimately able to obtain the Constitution as it exists at present.

51 Russo-Japanese War, 1904–1905, *Imperial Rescript*

During the Meiji period (1868–1912), Japan enjoyed phenomenal success as it transformed from a small, obscure, feudal, agrarian island-state into a modern industrial and imperial power. After having successfully modernized its government, economy, society, and military, Japan began to turn its attention abroad and show its expansionistic impulses. The first major victims of Japan's imperialistic thrust into the Asian continent were the Chinese Empire, which had been in steady decline since the Opium War (1839–1842), and its small neighbor, the Kingdom of Korea. China was humiliated and shocked by its defeat at the hands of such a small insular nation in the Sino-Japanese War (1894–1895). Invigorated by easy victory, Japan stepped up its expansionism against Manchuria, a northeastern province of China, and against Korea. Here, Japan's expansionism collided with tsarist Russia's territorial ambitions. Impatient with the impasse of bilateral negotiations, Japan declared war on Russia on February 10, 1904, two days after it had launched devastating naval attacks on Russian warships at Inchon, Korea, and Port Arthur in Manchuria. After an eighteen-month-long bitter fight, the Russo-Japanese War came to an end when the two powers signed the Portsmouth Treaty in 1905. American President Theodore Roosevelt acted as mediator at the negotiation for peace at Portsmouth, New Hampshire. Through this victory, Japan was catapulted into the ranks of the world powers. The following excerpts are from Japan's declaration of war against Russia, and Russia's communiqué in response.

QUESTIONS TO CONSIDER

1. What were the underlying and immediate causes of the war? Was the war avoidable? How? Evaluate the Russian response to Japan's war declaration. What were the important consequences of the war?

2. Define the word "imperialism" in your own words and illustrate it by citing one or two specific historical examples (see Readings 45 and 46).

3. Why did Russia, the largest country in the world, lose the war to one of the smallest countries in the world, the newly emerging, modern state of Japan? What role did American President Theodore Roosevelt play at the peace talks between Japan and Russia in Portsmouth, New Hampshire?

4. How would you compare the Japanese attack on the Russian naval base at Port Arthur on February 8, 1904, with the Japanese attack on the American naval base at Pearl Harbor on December 7, 1941? In what ways were they similar? How did they differ?

DECLARATION OF WAR ON RUSSIA: *IMPERIAL RESCRIPT*

The Japanese Imperial Rescript, countersigned by all the members of the Cabinet, and declaring war against Russia, read as follows:—

"We, by the Grace of Heaven, the Emperor of Japan, seated on the Throne occupied by the same dynasty from time immemorial, do hereby make proclamation to all our loyal and brave subjects:—

"We hereby declare war against Russia. We command our army and navy to carry on hostilities against her with all their strength, and we also command all our officials to make effort, in pursuance of their duties and in accordance with their powers, to attain the national aim, with all the means within the limits of the law of nations.

"We deem it essential to international relations, and make it our constant aim, to promote the pacific progress of our Empire in civilization, to strengthen our friendly ties with other States, and thereby to establish a state of things which would maintain enduring peace in the East, and assure the future security of our Empire without injury to the rights and interests of other Powers. Our officials also perform their duties in obedience to our will, so that our relations with all Powers grow steadily in cordiality.

"It is thus entirely against our wishes that we have unhappily come to open hostilities against Russia.

"The integrity of Korea has long been a matter of the gravest concern to our Empire, not only because of the traditional relations between the two countries, but because the separate existence of Korea is essential to the safety of our Empire. Nevertheless, Russia, despite her explicit treaty pledges to China and her repeated assurances to other Powers, is still in occupation of Manchuria, and has consolidated and strengthened her hold upon it, and is bent upon its final absorption,. Since the possession of Manchuria by Russia would render it impossible to maintain the integrity of Korea, and would, in addition, compel the abandonment of all hope for peace in the Far East, we expected, in these circumstances, to settle the question by negotiations

From K. Asakawa, *The Russo-Japanese Conflict: Its Causes and Issues* (Port Washington, NY: Kennikat Press, 1904), pp. 346–49.

and secure thereby a permanent peace. With this object in view, our officials by our order made proposals to Russia, and frequent conferences were held during the last half year. Russia, however, never met such proposals in a spirit of conciliation, but by her prolonged delays put off the settlement of the pending question, and, by ostensibly advocating peace on the one hand, and on the other secretly extending her naval and military preparations, sought to bring about our acquiescence. It is not possible in the least to admit that Russia had from the first a sincere desire for peace. She has rejected the proposals of our Empire; the safety of Korea is in danger; the interests of our Empire are menaced. At this crisis, the guarantees for the future which the Empire has sought to secure by peaceful negotiations can now only be sought by an appeal to arms.

"It is our earnest wishes that, by the loyalty and valor of our faithful subjects, peace may soon be permanently restored and the glory of our Empire preserved."[1]

OFFICIAL RESPONSE FROM RUSSIA

On February 18, the Russian Government issued the following official *communiqué:*—

"Eight days have now elapsed since all Russia was shaken with profound indignation against an enemy who suddenly broke off negotiations, and, by a treacherous attack, endeavored to obtain an easy success in a war long desired. The Russian nation, with natural impatience, desires prompt vengeance, and feverishly awaits news from the Far East. The unity and strength of the Russian people leave no room for doubt that Japan will receive the chastisement she deserves for her treachery and her provocation of war at a time when our beloved Sovereign desired to maintain peace among all nations.

"The conditions under which hostilities are being carried on compel us to wait with patience for news of the success of our troops, which cannot occur before decisive actions have been fought by the Russian army. The distance of the territory now attacked and the desire of the Czar to maintain peace were causes of the impossibility of preparations for war being made a long time in advance. Much time is now necessary in order to strike at Japan blows worthy of the dignity and might of Russia, and, while sparing as much as possible the shedding of blood of her children, to inflict just chastisement on the nation which has provoked the struggle.

"Russia must await the event in patience, being sure that our army will avenge that provocation a hundred-fold. Operations on land must not be expected for some time yet, and we cannot obtain early news from the theatre of war. The useless shedding of blood is unworthy of the greatness and power of Russia. Our country displays such unity and desire for self-sacrifice on behalf of the national cause that all true news from the scene of hostilities will be immediately due to the entire nation."[2]

---

[1]The English translation was slightly altered to bring it nearer to the original language by K. Asakawa. London *Times*, February 12, 1904, p. 3.
[2]The London *Times*, February 19, 1904, p. 3.

U.S. Expansion: Two Perspectives

U.S. involvement in Latin America sharply increased after the Spanish-American War of 1898 when the United States helped Cuba achieve its independence from Spain. A few years later, during Theodore Roosevelt's administration, the United States aided the Panamanian revolutionaries in their effort to secede from Colombia. Cuba and Panama included in their new constitutions the right of American intervention to guarantee their independence and enhance stability. When the United States began to build a canal through the Isthmus of Panama, both that nation and Cuba became virtual American protectorates, and U.S. influence spread extensively throughout Central America and the Caribbean.

Meanwhile, in the Latin American nations, powerful landholding interests and local militias collaborated to suppress rebellions and reforms; civil wars rather than legitimate elections became institutionalized as a mechanism for transferring power. Because of this chronic instability, Roosevelt announced, as a "corollary" to the Monroe Doctrine, that the United States had the right to intervene to prevent "chronic wrongdoing" and European interference. Although the United States hoped to encourage political stability in the area by supervising elections and enacting financial reforms, the most controversial "remedy" for instability was U.S. military intervention, which frequently occurred at the request of an incumbent regime. For nearly three decades, these interventions helped to stabilize governments in Nicaragua, Cuba, the Dominican Republic, Haiti, and Mexico. In most cases, however, one of the most important legacies of U.S. involvement was a U.S.-trained local militia or National Guard, which remained aligned with conservative interests to block reforms and suppress revolutionary movements.

The selection by Francisco García Calderón reflects the reaction of Latin American intellectuals toward U.S. expansionism at the turn of the century. He was a prominent Peruvian diplomat who represented his nation at the Paris Peace Conference in 1918 and in the League of Nations.

52 The Roosevelt Corollary

In his message to Congress on December 6, 1904, Theodore Roosevelt was, at least in part, responding to the crisis that had developed when the Dominican Republic defaulted on its financial obligations to foreign creditors and European warships arrived in the Caribbean to support the claims of their citizens. In addition, the International Court of Justice at the Hague (Netherlands) had recently ruled that claims of blockading powers should have priority over those of other nations; clearly, this seemed to sanction armed intervention for the collection of debts. These developments greatly disturbed the president and prompted him to announce a new interpretation of the Monroe Doctrine, which became known as the Roosevelt Corollary.

QUESTIONS TO CONSIDER

1. President Roosevelt notes that "the adherence of the United States to the Monroe Doctrine may force the United States, however reluctantly, in flagrant cases of such wrongdoing or impotence, to the exercise of an international police power." Based on your reading of the Monroe Doctrine (see Reading 31), is this a proper inference?
2. Would you agree that the U.S. national interest required a form of "benevolent intervention" to prevent non-American intervention? Had the national interests of the United States changed since 1823? Explain why or why not.
3. Contrast Roosevelt's statement that "our interests and those of our southern neighbors are in reality identical" with the views expressed by Francisco García Calderón (see Reading 53) and Simón Bolívar (see Reading 30).

The Monroe Doctrine should be the cardinal feature of the foreign policy of all the nations of the two Americas, as it is of the United States. Just seventy-eight years have passed since President Monroe in his annual message announced that "The American continents are henceforth not to be considered as subjects for future colonization by any European power." In other words, the Monroe Doctrine is a declaration that there must be no territorial aggrandizement by any non-American power at the expense of any American power on American soil. It is in no wise intended to give cover to any aggression by one New World at the expense of any other. It is simply a step, and a long step, toward assuring the universal peace of the world by securing the possibility of permanent peace on this hemisphere.

During the past century other influences have established the permanence and independence of the smaller states of Europe. Through the Monroe Doctrine we hope

From *Fifty-Seventh Congress, 1st session, 1901–1902, House Documents,* Vol. 1, No. 1, *Foreign Relations,* No. 4268; *Fifty-Eighth Congress, 3rd session, 1904–1905, House Documents,* Vol. 1, No. 1, *Foreign Relations,* No. 4780.

to be able to safeguard like independence and secure like permanence for the lesser among the New World nations.

This doctrine has nothing to do with the commercial relations of any American power, save that it in truth allows each one of them a guaranty of the commercial independence of the Americas. We do not ask under this doctrine for any exclusive commercial dealings with any other American state. We do not guarantee any state against punishment if it misconducts itself, provided that punishment does not take the form of the acquisition of territory by any non-American power.

Our attitude in Cuba is sufficient guaranty of our own good faith. We have not the slightest desire to secure any territory at the expense of any of our neighbors. We wish to work with them hand in hand so that all of us may be uplifted together, and we rejoice over the good fortune of any of them, we gladly hail their material prosperity, and political stability, and are concerned and alarmed if any of them fall into industrial or political chaos. We do not wish to see any Old World military power grow up on this continent, or to be compelled to become a military power ourselves. The peoples of the Americas can prosper best if left to work out their own salvation in their own way. . . . It is not true that the United States feels any land hunger or entertains any projects as regards the other nations of the Western Hemisphere save such as are for their welfare. All that this country desires is to see the neighboring countries stable, orderly, and prosperous. Any country whose people conduct themselves well can count upon our hearty friendship. If a nation shows that it knows how to act with reasonable efficiency and decency in social and political matters, if it keeps order and pays its obligations, it need fear no interference from the United States. Chronic wrongdoing, or an impotence which results in a general loosening of the ties of civilized society, may in America as elsewhere, ultimately require intervention by some civilized nation, and in the Western Hemisphere, the adherence of the United States to the Monroe Doctrine may force the United States, however reluctantly, in flagrant cases of such wrongdoing or impotence, to the exercise of an international police power. If every country washed by the Caribbean Sea would show the progress in stable and just civilization which, with the aid of the Platt Amendment, Cuba has shown since our troops left the island, and which so many of the republics in both Americas are constantly and brilliantly showing, all questions of interference by this Nation with their affairs would be at an end.[1] Our interests and those of our southern neighbors are in reality identical. They have great natural riches, and if within their borders the reign of law and justice obtains, prosperity is sure to come to them. While they thus obey the primary laws of civilized nations they may rest assured that they will be treated by us in a spirit of cordial and helpful sympathy. We would interfere with them only in the last resort, and then only if it became evident that their inability or unwillingness to do justice at home and abroad had violated the rights of the United States or had invited foreign aggression to the detriment of the entire body of American nations. It is a mere truism to say that every nation, whether in America or anywhere else, which desires to maintain its freedom, its independence, must ultimately realize that the rights of such independence cannot be separated from the responsibility of making good use of it.

---

[1] The Platt Amendment (1901) gave the United States the right to intervene in Cuba to protect American lives and property; it also gave the United States the right to oversee Cuban diplomatic relations and the right to maintain an American naval base at Guantánamo Bay.

In asserting the Monroe Doctrine, in taking such steps as we have taken in regard to Cuba, Venezuela, and Panama, and in endeavoring to circumscribe the theatre of the war in the Far East, and to secure the open door in China, we have acted in our own interest as well as in the interest of humanity at large.

53 Francisco García Calderón, "The North American Peril"

In this selection, Francisco García Calderón, a Peruvian diplomat and writer, sharply criticizes U.S. policy and private commercial interests for exploiting Latin Americans. He also warns of the dangers of cultural imperialism.

QUESTIONS TO CONSIDER

1. Would you agree with García Calderón's statement that "interventions [in Latin America] have become more frequent with the expansion of frontiers"? Why does he warn about the dangers of the U.S. shift from the "tradition of the Pilgrim fathers" to that of the "morality of Wall Street"?
2. According to the author, what were some of the differences that divided the two Americas? Were his judgments valid, or were they based on false assumptions? How have these differences exacerbated U.S. relations with Latin America?
3. Why did García Calderón regard the United States as a threat to Latin America's cultural identity? Were his concerns justified?
4. Compare Calderón's views of the American character with those expressed by Alexis de Tocqueville (see Reading 32). Are there similarities? If so, what are they, and why do they exist? Also, compare his beliefs with Simón Bolívar's (see Reading 30).

Against the policy of respect for Latin liberties are ranged the instincts of a triumphant plutocracy. The center of North American life is passing from Boston to Chicago; the citadel of the ideal gives way to the material progress of the great porcine metropolis. There is a conflict of dissimilar currents of morality. The Puritan tradition of New England seems useless in the struggle of the Far West; the conquest of the desert demands another morality; the morality of conflict, aggression and success. The trusts raise their heads above the impotent clamor of the weak. The conflict between the new-comers is tumultuous and brutal; as in the time of imperial Rome, the latter-day republicans are becoming aware of their defeat by a new caste, animated by an im-

From Francisco García Calderón, *Latin America: Its Rise and Progress* (London: T.F. Unwin, 1913), pp. 300–12, *passim*.

petuous love of conflict. It is the struggle between idealism and plutocracy, between the tradition of the Pilgrim Fathers and the morality of Wall Street; the patricians of the Senate and the bosses of Tammany Hall.

The great historical parties are divided; while the democrats do not forget the ideal of Washington and Lincoln, the republicans think only of imperialism.

Will a generous elite succeed in withstanding this racial tendency? Perhaps, but nothing can check the onward march of the United States. Their imperialism is an unavoidable phenomenon.

The nation which was peopled by nine millions of men in 1820 now numbers eighty millions—an immense demographic power; in the space of ten years, from 1890 to 1900, this population increased by one-fifth. By virtue of its iron, wheat, oil, and cotton, and its victorious industrialism, the democracy aspires to a world-wide significance of destiny; the consciousness of its powers is creating fresh international duties. Yankee pride increases with the endless multiplication of wealth and population, and the patriotic sentiment has reached such an intensity that it has become transformed into imperialism.

The United States buy the products they themselves lack from tropical nations. To rule in these fertile zones would to them appear the geographical ideal of a northern people. Do not their industries demand new outlets in America and Asia? So to the old mystic ambition are added the necessities of utilitarian progress. An industrial nation, the States preach a practical Christianity to the older continents, to Europe, and to lands yet barbarous; as to South America, they profess a doctrine of aggressive idealism, a strange fusion of economic tendencies and Puritan fervor. The Christian Republic imposes its tutelage upon inferior races, and so prepares them for self-government. . . .

Interventions have become more frequent with the expansion of frontiers. The United States have recently intervened in the territory of Acre,[1] there to found a republic of rubber gatherers; at Panama, there to develop a province and construct a canal; in Cuba, under the cover of the Platt Amendment,[2] to maintain order in the interior; in San Domingo, to support the civilizing revolution and overthrow the tyrants; in Venezuela, and in Central America, to enforce upon these nations, torn by internecine disorders, the political and financial tutelage of the imperial democracy. In Guatemala and Honduras the loans concluded with the monarchs of North American finance have reduced the people to a new slavery. Supervision of the customs and the dispatch of pacificatory squadrons to defend the interests of the Anglo-Saxon have enforced peace and tranquility: such are the means employed. The *New York American* announces that Mr. Pierpont Morgan proposes to encompass the finances of Latin America by a vast network of Yankee banks. Chicago merchants and Wall Street financiers created the Meat Trust in the Argentine. The United States offer millions for the purpose of converting into Yankee loans the moneys raised in London in the last century by the Latin American States; they wish to obtain a monopoly of credit. It has even been announced, although the news hardly appears probable, that a North American syndicate wished to buy enormous belts of land in Guatemala, where the English tongue is the obligatory language. The fortification of

---

[1]Territory between Brazil and Bolivia very rich in natural rubber trees; after its people tried to set up an independent republic, it was annexed by Brazil (1903).

[2]Putting Cuba under the military protection of the United States.

the Panama Canal, and the possible acquisition of the Galapagos Islands in the Pacific, are fresh manifestations of imperialistic progress.

The Monroe Doctrine takes an aggressive form with Mr. Roosevelt, the politician of the "big stick," and intervention *a outrance*. Roosevelt is conscious of his sacred mission: he wants a powerful army and a navy majestically sailing the two oceans. . . .

He recognizes the fact that the progress accomplished by the United States is not of a nature to tranquillize the South American; "that the Yankee believes that his Southern neighbors are trivial and childish peoples, and above all incapable of maintaining a proper self-government." He thinks the example of Cuba, liberated "from the rule of Spain, but not from internal troubles, will render the American of the States skeptical as to the aptitude of the Latin-American populations of mixed blood to govern themselves without disorder," and recognizes that the "pacific penetration" of Mexico by American capital constitutes a possible menace to the independence of that Republic, were the death of Diaz to lead to its original state of anarchy and disturb the peace which the millionaires of the North desire to see untroubled.

Warnings, advice, distrust, invasion of capital, plans of financial hegemony—all these justify the anxiety of the southern peoples. . . .

For geographical reasons, and on account of its very inferiority, South America cannot dispense with the influence of the Anglo-Saxon North, with its exuberant wealth and its industries. South America has need of capital, of enterprising men, of bold explorers, and these the United States supply in abundance. The defense of the South should consist in avoiding the establishment of privileges or monopolies, whether in favor of North Americans or Europeans.

It is essential to understand not only the foundations of North American greatness, but also the weaknesses of the Anglo-Saxon democracy, in order to escape from the dangers of excessive imitation.

The Anglo-Saxons of America have created an admirable democracy upon a prodigious expanse of territory. A caravan of races has pitched its tents from the Atlantic to the Pacific, and has watered the desert with its impetuous blood. Dutch, French, Anglo-Saxons, and Germans, people of all sects, Quakers, Presbyterians, Catholics, Puritans, all have mingled their creed in a single multiform nation. At the contact of new soil men have felt the pride of creation and of living. Initiative, self-assertion, self-reliance, audacity, love of adventure, all the forms of the victorious will are united in this Republic of energy. A triumphant optimism quickens the rhythm of life; an immense impulse of creation builds cities in the wilderness, and founds new plutocracies amidst the whirlpool of the markets. Workshops, factories, banks; the obscure unrest of Wall Street; the architectural insolence of the skyscraper; the many-colored, material West; all mingle perpetually in the wild, uncouth hymn which testifies the desperate battle of will and destiny, of generation against death. . . .

But this civilization, in which men of strong vitality win wealth, invent machines, create new cities, and profess a Christianity full of energy and accomplishment, has not the majesty of a harmonious structure. It is the violent work of a people of various origin, which has not yet been ennobled by the *patina* of tradition and time. In the cities which restless workers hastily raise on barren soil, one can as yet perceive no definitive unity. Race antagonism disturbs North America; the Negroes swarm in the South; Japanese and Orientals aspire to the conquest of the West. Neo-Saxon civilization is still seeking its final form, and in the meantime it is piling up wealth amid the prevailing indiscipline. "We find in the United States," says M. André Chevrillon, "a political system, but not a social organization."The admirable traditions of Hamilton and Jefferson have been subjected to the onslaught of new influences, the progress of plutocracy, the corruption of the administrative functions, the dissolution of parties, the abuse of the power of monopolies. The axis of the great nation is becoming displaced towards the West, and each step in advance marks the triumph of vulgarity.

An octopus of a city, New York, might be taken as the symbol of this extraordinary nation; it displays the vertigo, the audacity, and all the lack of proportion that characterize American life. Near the poverty of the Ghetto and the disturbing spectacle of Chinatown you may admire the wealth of Fifth Avenue and the marble palaces which plagiarize the architecture of the Tuscan cities. Opposite the obscure crowds of emigrants herded in the docks you will see the refined luxury of the plutocratic hotels, and facing the majestic buildings of Broadway, the houses of the parallel avenues, which are like the temporary booths of a provincial fair. Confusion, uproar, instability—these are the striking characteristics of the North American democracy. Neither irony nor grace nor skepticism, gifts of the old civilizations, can make way against the plebeian brutality, the excessive optimism, the violent individualism of the people.

All these things contribute to the triumph of mediocrity; the multitude of primary schools, the vices of utilitarianism, the cult of the average citizen, the transatlantic M. Homais, and the tyranny of opinion noted by Tocqueville; and in this vulgarity, which is devoid of traditions and has no leading aristocracy, a return to the primitive type of the redskin, which has already been noted by close observers, is threatening the proud democracy. From the excessive tension of wills, from the elementary state of culture, from the perpetual unrest of life, from the harshness of the industrial struggle, anarchy and violence will be born in the future. In a hundred years men will seek in vain for the "American soul," the "genius of America," elsewhere than in the undisciplined force or the violence which ignores moral laws.

Among the Anglo-Saxon nations individualism finds its limits in the existence of a stable home; it may also struggle against the State, according to the formula consecrated by Spencer, "the man versus the State." It defends its jealous autonomy from excessive legislation, from the intervention of the Government in economic conflicts or the life of the family. And it is precisely the family spirit which is becoming enfeebled in North America, under the pressure of new social conditions. The birth-rate is diminishing, and the homes of foreign immigrants are contributing busily to the formation of the new generations; the native stock inheriting good racial traditions would seem to be submerged more and more by the new human tide. A North American official writes that "the decrease in the birth-rate will lead to a complete change in the social system of the Republic." From this will result the abandonment of the traditional austerity of the race, and the old notions of sacrifice and duty. The descendants of alien races will constitute the nation of the future. The national heritage is threatened by the invasion of Slavs and Orientals, and the fecundity of the negroes; a painful anxiety weighs upon the destinies of the race.

The family is unstable, and divorces are increasing at an extraordinary rate. Between 1870 and 1905 the population doubled; during the same period the divorces increased sixfold and the marriages decreased. There is no fixity in the elements of variety, and the causes of this state of transition will not disappear, as they are intimately allied with the development of the industrial civilization which has brought with it a new ideal of happiness. By emancipating men and women from the old moral principles it has modified sexual morality; by accelerating social progress it has brought an additional bitterness into the social melee, a greater egoism into human conflict.

Excessive and heterogenous immigration prevents any final crystallization; in the last ten years 8,515,000 strangers have entered into the great hospitable Union. They came from Germany, Ireland, Russia, or Southern Italy. It is calculated that the United States are able to assimilate 150,000 to 200,000 immigrants each year, but they certainly cannot welcome such an overwhelming host without anxiety.

Criminality increases; the elaboration of a common type among these men of different origin is proceeding more slowly. Doubtless beneath the shelter of the political federation of the various States a confused agglomeration of races is forming itself, and this justifies the query of Professor Ripley: "The Americans of the North," he says, "have witnessed the disappearance of the Indians and the buffalo, but can they be certain today that the Anglo-Saxons will survive them?"

In seeking to imitate the United States we should not forget that the civilization of the peoples of the North presents these symptoms of decadence.

Europe offers the Latin-American democracies what the latter demand of Anglo-Saxon America, which was formed in the school of Europe. We find the practical spirit, industrialism, and political liberty in England; organization and education in Germany; and in France inventive genius, culture, wealth, great universities, and democracy. From these ruling peoples the new Latin world must indirectly receive the legacy of Western civilization.

Essential points of difference separate the two Americas. Differences of language and therefore of spirit; the difference between Spanish Catholicism and the multiform Protestantism of the Anglo-Saxons; between the Yankee individualism and the omnipotence of the State natural to the nations of the South. In their origin, as in their race, we find fundamental antagonisms; the evolution of the North is slow and obedient to the lessons of time, to the influences of custom; the history of the southern peoples is full of revolutions, rich with dreams of an unattainable perfection.

The people of the United States hate the half-breed, and the impure marriages of whites and blacks which take place in southern homes; no manifestation of Pan-Americanism could suffice to destroy the racial prejudice as it exists north of Mexico. The half-breeds and their descendants govern the Ibero-American democracies, and the Republic of English and German origin entertains for the men of the tropics the same contempt which they feel for the slaves of Virginia whom Lincoln liberated.

In its friendship for them there will always be disdain; in their progress, a conquest; in their policy, a desire of hegemony. It is the fatality of blood, stronger than political affinities or geographical alliances.

Instead of dreaming of an impossible fusion the Neo-Latin peoples should conserve the traditions which are proper to them. The development of the European influences which enrich and improve them, the purging of the nation from the strain of miscegenation, and immigration of a kind calculated to form centers of resistance against any possibilities of conquest, are the various aspects of this Latin Americanism.

Part V
An Era of Global Violence

World War I

World War I (1914–1918) was the second most destructive war in modern history, and the Battle of the Somme (July 1 to November 18, 1916), fought on the chalky scrublands of northwestern France, was the bloodiest battle ever fought by the British army. On the first day of the battle, the British army suffered 57,470 casualties: 19,240 dead, 35,493 wounded, 2,152 missing, and 585 captured. In the first ten minutes of the attack, one German observer estimated that 14,000 British soldiers fell to the deadly German machine-gun and artillery fire; and in the first twenty-four hours of battle, the British army counted more dead than the combined British deaths of the Crimean, Boer, and Korean wars.

Nothing in the first two years of fighting had prepared the soldiers for these huge losses. In the summer of 1916, British and German soldiers—separated by a desolate, shell-ravaged no-man's-land—peered at each other from zigzagged lines of trenches. Both armies had adjusted to the troglodyte horrors of trench warfare, where the best weapons often were "clubs, ax handles, daggers, medieval man traps, and crossbows, primitive catapults."[1] But even then death came slowly and painfully. Philip Gibbs of the *Daily Telegraph* reported that "the horrors of the first aid post were standard—men hold their intestines in both hands, broken bones tearing the flesh,

---

[1] From Michael Kernan, "Day of Slaughter on the Somme." *The Washington Post,* June 27, 1976, p. C1.

209

arteries spurting blood, maimed hands, empty eye sockets, pierced chests, skin hanging down in tatters from the burned face, missing lower jaws . . . men with chunks of steel in their lungs and bowels vomiting great gobs of blood, men with legs and arms torn from their trunks, men without noses and their brains throbbing through open scalps. . . ."[2]

Survivors of battle sought safety and refuge in their trenches. But here the horror of combat only continued: "the incredible mud, into which horses and men sometimes sank clear out of sight, the stench of excrement and rotted flesh and explosives and mustard gas, the maggots that writhed underfoot and oozed up from the cracks in the dried mud, the rats, gorged on human meat (they preferred eyes and livers), some of them as big as terriers and as bold as cats, the churned-up battlefields lost and won and lost again, a dozen times since 1914, in which the earth itself seemed to be composed of dead bodies, where arms and legs and heads protruded through trench walls and had to be covered with empty sandbags or chopped off with shovels and buried."[3]

To break the deadlock of two years of immobility, the British High Command ordered the Somme offensive to crack open the Western Front and break the German army's hold on northern France. However, slaughter rather than victory awaited the 120,000 British soldiers who attacked the German lines on July 1, 1916, the first day of the Somme offensive.

Diplomatic efforts to end World War I began in earnest in 1915 and continued through the Treaty of Brest-Litovsk of March 3, 1918, between Russia and Germany; the Armistice of November 11, 1918, between the Allies and Germany; and the comprehensive peace treaties of 1919. But European diplomats, concerned with ending the war on terms favorable to their own nations, often gave scant regard to the national aspirations of other peoples. For example, Arab leaders who sought to establish independent states had to accept vague promises from Great Britain and France. The Chinese were shocked to learn, after the Treaty of Versailles in 1919, that the Western powers had assigned German colonial rights in China to Japan.

By the time the Western diplomats assembled in Versailles, the enthusiasm that had greeted President Woodrow Wilson's Fourteen Points peace

[2]Cited in ibid.
[3]Ibid.

proposal had melted away. The Allied powers did not permit Germany to participate in the Versailles deliberations; however, they did assign to Germany and her allies full responsibility for causing the war and insisted that Germany pay for damages incurred during the fighting. The United States refused to join the new League of Nations, and Wilson's plea for dismantling the Western colonial empires went unheeded.

The following selections suggest some of the global effects of the diplomacy of World War I.

54 Slaughter on the Somme

The following are excerpts from the diaries of three British soldiers who participated in the Battle of the Somme.

QUESTIONS TO CONSIDER

1. What do the diary entries reveal about the soldiers' views of authority, the enemy, and the press?
2. What do the diary entries reveal about the soldiers' sense of duty?

DIARY OF PRIVATE TOM EASTON

A beautiful summer morning, though we'd had a bit of rain earlier. The skylarks were just singing away. Then the grand mine went up, it shook the earth for nearly a minute, and we had to wait for the fallout. The whistles blew and we stepped off one yard apart going straight forward. We were under orders not to stop or look or help the wounded. Carry on if you're fit, it was. . . .

Men began to fall one by one. . . . One officer said we were OK, all the machine-guns were firing over our heads. This was so until we passed our own front line and started to cross No Man's Land. Then trench machine-guns began the slaughter from the La Boiselle salient [German positions]. Men fell on every side screaming. Those who were unwounded dare not attend to them, we must press on regardless. Hundreds lay on the German barbed wire which was not all destroyed and their bodies formed a bridge for others to pass over and into the German front line.

There were few Germans, mainly in machine-gun posts. These were bombed out, and there were fewer still of us, but we consolidated the lines we had taken by

From Michael Kernan, "Day of Slaughter on the Somme," *The Washington Post*, June 27, 1976, pp. C1, C5, *passim*. © 1976, The Washington Post. Reprinted by permission.

preparing firing positions on the rear of the trenches gained, and fighting went on all morning and gradually died down as men and munitions on both sides became exhausted.

When we got to the German trenches we'd lost all our officers. They were all dead, there was no question of wounded. About 25 of us made it there. . . .

Yes, as we made our way over the latter stages of the charge, men dropped all around like ninepins. Apart from machine-guns, the German artillery was also very active, great sheets of earth rose up before one. Every man had to fend for himself as we still had to face the Germans in their trenches when we got there.

I kept shouting for my MOTHER to guide me, strange as it may seem. Mother help me. Not the Virgin Mother but my own maternal Mother, for I was then only 20 years of age.

DIARY OF CAPTAIN REGINALD LEETHAM

I got to my position and looked over the top. The first thing I saw in the space of a tennis court in front of me was the bodies of 100 dead or severely wounded men lying there in our own wire. . . . I sent my runner 200 yards on my right to get into touch with our right company, who should have been close beside me. He came back and reported he could find nothing of them. It subsequently transpired that they never reached the front line as their communication trenches had caught it so much worse than mine, and the communication trench was so full of dead and dying, that they could not get over them. . . . Those three battalions [2500 men] who went over were practically annihilated. Every man went to his death or got wounded without flinching. Yet in this war, nothing will be heard about it, the papers have glowing accounts of great British success. . . . 60 officers went out, lots of whom I knew. I believe 2 got back without being wounded. . . .

The dead were stretched out on one side [of the trench], one on top of the other, six high. . . . To do one's duty was continually climbing over corpses in every position. . . . Of the hundreds of corpses I saw I only saw one pretty one—a handsome boy called Schnyder of the Berkshires who lay on our firestep shot through the heart. There he lay with a sandbag over his face: I uncovered it as I knew he was an officer. I wish his Mother could have seen him—one of the few whose faces had not been mutilated.

The 2nd Middlesex came back with 22 men out of 600. . . .

DIARY OF SUBALTERN EDWARD G.D. LIVEING

There was the freshness and splendor of a summer morning over everything. . . .

Just in front the ground was pitted by innumerable shellholes. . . . More holes opened suddenly every now and then. Here and there a few bodies lay about. Farther away, before our front line and in No Man's Land, lay more. In the smoke one could distinguish the second line advancing. One man after another fell down in a seemingly natural manner, and the wave melted away. In the background, where ran the remains of the German lines and wire, there was a mask of smoke, the red of the shrapnel bursting amid it. As I advanced I felt as if I was in a dream, but I had all my wits about me. We had been told to walk. Our boys, however, rushed forward with splendid impetuosity. . . .

A hare jumped up and rushed towards me through the dry yellowish grass, its eyes bulging with fear. . . . At one time we seemed to be advancing in little groups. I was at the head of one for a moment or two only to realize shortly afterwards that I was alone. I came up to the German wire. Here one could hear men shouting to one another and the wounded groaning above the explosion of shells and bombs and the rattle of machine-guns. . . .

Suddenly I cursed. I had been scalded in the left hip. A shell, I thought, had blown up in a waterlogged crump hole and sprayed me with boiling water. Letting go of my rifle, I dropped forward full length on the ground. My hip began to smart unpleasantly, and I felt a curious warmth stealing down my left leg. I thought it was the boiling water that had scalded me. Certainly my breeches looked as if they were saturated with water. I did not know they were saturated with blood.

55 "World War I: A Frenchman's Recollections"

Not all the casualties were on the battlefield. Certainly one of the most devastating aspects of World War I was its effect upon the civilian populations, particularly in the small towns and villages. This particular account is from the recollections of François Carlotti (1907–   ), who draws upon his boyhood memories to describe the effects of the Great War upon the French town of Auneau, located fifteen kilometers west of the cathedral city of Chartres.

QUESTIONS TO CONSIDER

1. Does this set of recollections suggest anything about the quality of civilian morale in France during the Great War?
2. Do these recollections coupled with the diary entries (see Reading 54) help to explain the appeal of fascism (see Reading 63) to some of the men and women who survived the battles and devastation of World War I?

The first leaves fell at the end of October. After the defeat at the frontiers, the retreat, the miracle of the Marne, the stabilization of the line in the trenches was necessary to give France time to recover her balance.

And then the High Command and government, appalled by the losses that surpassed imagining, probably found themselves little disposed to reveal the truth.

Up to this point we had only bad news of those wounded who, evacuated to the interior, had succeeded in getting a letter or a message through, and they were not many. One had lost a leg and another had been hit in the stomach. We had showed them much sympathy, them and their families. We should soon envy them.

François Carlotti, "World War I: A Frenchman's Recollections," *The American Scholar* 57:2 (Spring 1988), pp. 286–88. Copyright © 1988 by the author. By permission of the publishers.

When the two gendarmes who had stayed at headquarters started to go on their rounds with the official notices, "Died on the field of Honor," a terrified silence fell on the town, the villages, and the hamlets.

Gustave was killed, the little clerk who had once worked for my father and who had looked so handsome in his cavalryman's uniform.

Arsène, Alcide, Jules, Léon, Kléber, Maurice, Rémi, Raoul—all killed. Georges, the son of the fat ironmonger in the marketplace, who had studied in Paris and come back with advanced ideas—talking English, putting up little hurdles in the field to jump over as he ran, teaching the boys to play with a queer sort of ball that wasn't even round—killed.

Alphonse, Clothaire, Emile, Etienne, Firmin, Marceau, Raymond, Victor—killed, killed. . . .

The grief was often the more terrible because in most cases it was an only son.

And then there were the three Cochon brothers.

The Cochons were one of those families of small market-gardeners who grew their crops by the banks of the river. Every morning, the wife threaded on her shoulder straps, took up the shafts of the enormous wheelbarrow, and set out through the town to sell her mountain of fresh vegetables while her husband stayed home working in the garden.

Tall, spare, bony, mother Cochon was always the first to set out and the last to return. She had four men in the house.

The eldest daughter, married to an employee of the railway from far away, had made her home with him there in the Capdenac region where he had a good job.

The father remained at home with his three sons, who had been born one after the other within the space of five years. The three boys had all done very well at school, while also giving a helping hand at home when required. They had passed their leaving certificates before rejoining their father to toil with him from dawn to dusk.

Yet, despite all their work, their plot of land did not suffice to provide a livelihood for the whole family, and, in turn, one or two of the boys went to work for wages. They were not living as lodgers, like Belgians or Bretons who, at St. Jean, poured from the trains in serried ranks with their round hats and their clogs, their working boots slung round their necks—no, they worked as neighbors who were well favored, eating at their master's table. These Cochons were good boys who would never have worked less than their father.

Happy lads, not bothered by jokes on their name, always the first to sound the trumpet and bang the drum of the town band, first over the parallel bars or the vaulting horse, or leaders at the dance in the *mairie* on holidays.[1]

The father died while the eldest boy was away doing his training. The other two boys slaved away in the garden, working all the harder because the first born did not return home when the youngest son left. And after his three years' service, this youngest son faced mobilization and war.

When the gendarmes arrived that morning, Mme. Cochon received them standing, with the one word: "Which?" "Auguste," replied one of them and laid the little notice on the table.

"Ah, Auguste, my first born, my strongest and my bravest." A slow shudder passed across her face, but she didn't flinch.

And then, as the gendarmes stood their ground, shifting from one foot to the other, she looked them full in the face, till one of them, gathering all his courage, man-

---

[1] In French *cochon* means pig. The *mairie* was the town hall.

aged to say, "And Désiré," putting the official notification on the table as he left. "Désiré, my most handsome, my most gentle, the golden-haired one." Now she trembled from head to foot, murmuring. "Auguste . . . Désiré . . . Auguste . . . Désiré . . . ," ever more softly, as though she was clasping them.

When the gendarmes returned, a month later, she turned towards them from her seat in the corner of the fireplace without looking at them and asked: "Is it Marcel?" They bowed their heads, unable to speak.

"Ah, Marcel, my baby, my last, my dearest, O Marcel." And then suddenly a terrible cry rent the air and carried down to the river. "Marcel, Marcel. Now there are no more Cochons."

Without hearing, the gendarme forced himself to read the paper. "Cochon, Marcel, sergeant, infantry . . . heroic conduct . . . citation . . . *croix de guerre.*"[2] She repeated her crazy, despairing threnody, "No more Cochons, no more Cochons."

From that day she hardly ever went out except to walk to her husband's grave. Those who met her would often hear her muttering. "No more Cochons . . . there are no more." But no one ever saw her cry.

She died at the onset of winter.

And there were still four years of war to come. The long hopeless agonies in the military hospitals, the boys of *classe 16*,[3] called up at eighteen, who would never see their twentieth year, men who were wounded three times, bandaged up, nursed and healed, who returned yet again to the line never to return, the atrocious deaths in the gas attacks. There was the terrible winter of 1916–17 when even wild animals were frozen to death; and the insane spring offensives of 1917 when for a moment one thought oneself back in the bloodiest days of the summer of 1914, when training regiments were rushed into the line to plug the yawning gaps that held fast, never bending under the shells and the hail of the machine guns. The Americans arrived, the diabolical long-range guns shelled Paris, the last great German offensive began, which again reached the Marne, and the final victorious counter-offensive was launched.

There was the great Roger who fell on November 8.

When it was all ended and there was no family left to ask for the return of their corpses, they remained on their battlefields—the three brothers, with the vast army of shadows in the great military cemeteries, neat and orderly where they rest, hidden forever, the bravery, the gaiety, the youth of this people of France, who were—like the men of Athens before them—the adornment of the world.

56 Sir Henry McMahon, Letter to Ali Ibn Husain

Sir Henry McMahon, the British high commissioner in Egypt, and Ali Ibn Husain, the sherif of Mecca, exchanged ten letters from 1915 to 1916. The following excerpt from a letter written October 24, 1915, shows Britain's aim—to enlist Arab support against Britain's enemy Turkey in return for hints of British support of an independent Arab state.

[2]French military decoration for valor in battle.
[3]This was the draft levy of 1916.

QUESTIONS TO CONSIDER

1. Do the suggestions made in the McMahon letter provide a perspective on the contemporary political problems in the Middle East (see Readings 83 and 84)?
2. Did the British government have the legal and moral authority to promise the birth of an Arab state?

As for those regions lying within those frontiers wherein Great Britain is free to act without detriment to the interests of her ally, France, I am empowered in the name of the Government of Great Britain to give the following assurances and make the following reply to your letter:

1. Subject to the above modifications, Great Britain is prepared to recognise and support the independence of the Arabs in all the regions within the limits demanded by the Sherif of Mecca.

2. Great Britain will guarantee the Holy Places against all external aggression and will recognise their inviolability.

3. When the situation admits, Great Britain will give to the Arabs her advice and will assist them to establish what may appear to be the most suitable forms of government in those various territories.

4. On the other hand, it is understood that the Arabs have decided to seek the advice and guidance of Great Britain only, and that such European advisers and officials as may be required for the formation of a sound form of administration will be British.

5. With regard to the vilayets [provinces] of Bagdad and Basra, the Arabs will recognise that the established position and interests of Great Britain necessitate special administrative arrangements in order to secure these territories from foreign aggression, to promote the welfare of the local populations and to safeguard our mutual economic interests.

I am convinced that this declaration will assure you beyond all possible doubt of the sympathy of Great Britain towards the aspirations of her friends the Arabs and will result in a firm and lasting alliance, the immediate results of which will be the expulsion of the Turks from the Arab countries and the freeing of the Arab peoples from the Turkish yoke, which for so many years has pressed heavily upon them.

57 The Balfour Declaration

To enlist Jewish support for the war, British Foreign Secretary, Arthur James Balfour wrote the following letter to Lord Rothschild, a prominent Jewish leader, and had it printed in *The Times.* The letter contains the official statement that soon became known as the Balfour Declaration.

From Great Britain, *Parliamentary Papers,* 1939, Misc. No. 3, Cmd. 5957.

QUESTIONS TO CONSIDER

1. Why did the British government wait until 1917 to publicly support the desire of the Jewish people for a state?
2. What are the contemporary implications of Lord Balfour's statement: ". . . it being clearly understood that nothing shall be done which may prejudice the civil and religious rights of existing non-Jewish communities in Palestine"?

Foreign Office
November 2nd, 1917

Dear Lord Rothschild:

I have much pleasure in conveying to you, on behalf of His Majesty's Government, the following declaration of sympathy with Jewish Zionist aspirations which has been submitted to, and approved by, the Cabinet:

> His Majesty's Government view with favor the establishment in Palestine of a national home for the Jewish people, and will use their best endeavors to facilitate the achievement of this object, it being clearly understood that nothing shall be done which may prejudice the civil and religious rights of existing non-Jewish communities in Palestine, or the rights and political status enjoyed by Jews in any other country.

I should be grateful if you would bring this declaration to the knowledge of the Zionist Federation.

Yours,

Arthur James Balfour

58 Woodrow Wilson, "Speech on the Fourteen Points"

On January 8, 1918, U.S. President Woodrow Wilson, speaking before a joint session of Congress, put forth his Fourteen Points proposal for ending the war. In this speech, he established the basis of a peace treaty and the foundation of a League of Nations.

From *The Times* (London), November 9, 1917.

QUESTIONS TO CONSIDER

1. What was the political impact of the Fourteen Points on the peoples living under colonial rule? Was Wilson's idea of self-determination for colonial peoples to decide their own fate?
2. An underlying assumption of the Fourteen Points is that America should use its power to ensure that the world "be made fit and safe to live in." Is this the proper policy of the United States? Why? Why not?

We entered this war because violations of right had occurred which touched us to the quick and made the life of our own people impossible unless they were corrected and the world secured once and for all against their recurrence. What we demand in this war, therefore, is nothing peculiar to ourselves. It is that the world be made fit and safe to live in; and particularly that it be made safe for every peace-loving nation which, like our own, wishes to live its own life, determine its own institutions, be assured of justice and fair dealing by the other peoples of the world as against force and selfish aggression. All the peoples of the world are in effect partners in this interest, and for our own part we see very clearly that unless justice be done to others it will not be done to us. The programme of the world's peace, therefore, is our programme; and that programme, the only possible programme, as we see it, is this:

I. Open covenants of peace, openly arrived at, after which there shall be no private international understanding of any kind but diplomacy shall proceed always frankly and in the public view.
II. Absolute freedom of navigation upon the seas, outside territorial waters, alike in peace and in war, except as the seas may be closed in whole or in part by international action for the enforcement of international covenants.
III. The removal, so far as possible, of all economic barriers and the establishment of an equality of trade conditions among all the nations consenting to the peace and associating themselves for its maintenance.
IV. Adequate guarantees given and taken that national armaments will be reduced to the lowest point consistent with domestic safety.
V. A free, open-minded, and absolutely impartial adjustment of all colonial claims, based upon a strict observance of the principle that in determining all such questions of sovereignty the interests of the populations concerned must have equal weight with the equitable claims of the government whose title is to be determined.
VI. The evacuation of all Russian territory and such a settlement of all questions affecting Russia as will secure the best and freest cooperation of the other nations of the world in obtaining for her an unhampered and unembarrassed opportunity for the independent determination of her own political development and national policy and assure her a sincere welcome into the society of free nations under institutions of her own choosing; and, more than a welcome, assistance also of every kind that she may need and may herself desire. The treatment accorded Russia by her sister nations in the months to come will be the acid test of

From Woodrow Wilson, "Speech on the Fourteen Points," *Congressional Record*, 65th Congress, 2nd Session, 1918, pp. 680–81.

their good will, of their comprehension of her needs as distinguished from their own interests, and of their intelligent and unselfish sympathy.

VII. Belgium, the whole world will agree, must be evacuated and restored, without any attempt to limit the sovereignty which she enjoys in common with all other free nations. No other single act will serve as this will serve to restore confidence among the nations in the laws which they have themselves set and determined for the government of their relations with one another. Without this healing act the whole structure and validity of international law is forever impaired.

VIII. All French territory should be freed and the invaded portions restored, and the wrong done to France by Prussia in 1871 in the matter of Alsace-Lorraine, which has unsettled the peace of the world for nearly fifty years, should be righted, in order that peace may once more be made secure in the interest of all.

IX. A readjustment of the frontiers of Italy should be effected along clearly recognizable lines of nationality.

X. The peoples of Austria-Hungary, whose place among the nations we wish to see safeguarded and assured, should be accorded the freest opportunity of autonomous development.

XI. Rumania, Serbia, and Montenegro should be evacuated; occupied territories restored; Serbia accorded free and secure access to the sea; and the relations of the several Balkan states to one another determined by friendly counsel along historically established lines of allegiance and nationality; and international guarantees of the political and economic independence and territorial integrity of the several Balkan states should be entered into.

XII. The Turkish portions of the present Ottoman Empire should be assured a secure sovereignty, but the other nationalities which are now under Turkish rule should be assured an undoubted security of life and an absolutely unmolested opportunity of autonomous development, and the Dardanelles should be permanently opened as a free passage to the ships and commerce of all nations under international guarantees.

XIII. An independent Polish state should be erected which should include the territories inhabited by indisputably Polish populations, which should be assured a free and secure access to the sea, and whose political and economic independence and territorial integrity should be guaranteed by international covenant.

XIV. A general association of nations must be formed under specific covenants for the purpose of affording mutual guarantees of political independence and territorial integrity to great and small states alike.

Bolshevik Utopian Dreams and Stalin's Revolution

Joseph Vissarionovich Dzhugashvili (1879–1953), much better known as "Stalin" (man of steel), the cover name he assumed as a Bolshevik revolutionary, was a native of Russian Georgia who arose from modest peasant origins to become probably the twentieth century's most successful dictator.

Stalin gained Vladimir Lenin's (1870–1924) trust in Bolshevik affairs through his unwavering support of Lenin in all controversies against all critics. With Lenin's backing, Stalin became the first editor of *Pravda,* the Bolshevik (and later Communist Party) newspaper, in 1912. Although Stalin logged an adventurous revolutionary career as a young man, leading robberies on wagon trains to get funds for the Bolsheviks, for example, he had considerable literary talent, particularly when it came to marshaling unwieldy facts and fictions in the service of politically useful conclusions. After the 1917 October Revolution bringing the Bolsheviks to power, Stalin took on the routine sort of desk work that the higher-profile Bolsheviks found dull and distasteful. He soon headed the ministry that checked the new Soviet bureaucracy for inefficiency, and in 1922 he became general secretary of the Communist Party, a post that enabled him to put his friends and supporters in higher offices.

Stalin's crudeness and inclination to brutality offended Lenin before the latter died in 1924, but within a few years after Lenin's death, Stalin was firmly in control of both the Communist Party and the Soviet government. Holding firm to the reins of police-state power, Stalin eliminated personal opponents by the hundreds, real or imagined ideological opponents by the thousands, and "class enemies" by the millions. His program of industrializing Russia at the expense of agriculture and consumer-goods production was successful enough to provide the Russians with armaments to resist the German invasion during World War II, but his insistence on thoroughly collectivizing agriculture left Soviet farmers without much motivation to produce and led to decades of regular and severe food shortages in the same country that had, under the tsars, exported agricultural surpluses.

Unlike Adolf Hitler, Stalin was very patient. He took his time killing off opposition, and he waited for international opportunities to ripen before seizing them with great speed and skill. Stalin's revolution did not put an end to the Bolshevik dreams that had inspired the 1917 October Revolution, which had brought the Bolsheviks to power. Highly idealistic notions inherited from Lenin concerning what communism was to become flourished not only among the Party faithful in the USSR but among many intellectuals in the Western world as well. Travelers from Western Europe and the United States in the 1930s would frequently report on (particularly young) people there as aflame with the sort of enthusiasm that Lenin had urged aspiring

Communists to adopt for themselves and that Lenin's wife, Krupskaya, elaborated on after Lenin's declining health had forced him to lessen his public activities. Some Western idealists chose to join those committed to building a better life in the Soviet Union. The idealism of young American college student–welder John Scott and the desperation of terror victim Nadezhda Mandelstam simply illustrate different aspects of Stalin's revolution.

59 Nadezhda K. Krupskaya, "What a Communist Ought to Be Like"

Nadezhda Konstantinova Krupskaya (1869–1939), a Russian social worker who married Lenin in 1898, aided Lenin in his revolutionary program as long as he lived and supported Bolshevik programs as his legacy after he died. From 1900 to 1917, she served as the secretary of the Bolshevik wing of the Social Democratic Party in Russia, which after the Revolution became the Communist Party of the USSR. (It was later as "General" Secretary of the Communist Party's Central Committee that Stalin ruled the Soviet Union; Krupskaya's long secretaryship was of a more conventional nature.) Stalin's rude treatment of Krupskaya not long before her husband's death provoked the stroke-weakened Lenin into a rebuke of the future dictator, but Krupskaya had no inclination to publicize their differences and subsequently treated Stalin as Lenin's more or less rightful successor. In the following selection, she elaborates on Lenin's discussion of Communist ethics and morality.

QUESTIONS TO CONSIDER

1. Why does Krupskaya find well-developed social instincts to characterize most workers most of the time but to be rare among capitalists?
2. What are some of the areas in which Communists should acquire extensive knowledge?
3. What are some aspects of a Communist's personal life, according to Krupskaya?

A communist is, first and foremost, *a person involved in society*, with strongly developed social instincts, who desires that all people should live well and be happy.

Communists can come from all classes of society, but most of all they are workers by birth. Why? Because the conditions of workers' lives are such as to nurture in them social instincts: collective labor, the success of which depends on the separate efforts of each; the same conditions of labor; common experiences; the common struggle for humane conditions of existence. All this brings workers closer together and unites them with the bonds of class solidarity. Let us take the capitalist class. The conditions of life for this class are completely different. Competition forces each capitalist to see another capitalist primarily as an opponent, who has to be tripped up. In the worker the capitalist sees only "worker's hands" which must labor for the creation of his, the capitalist's, profits. Of course, the common struggle against the working class unites capitalists, but that internal unity, that formation into a collective which we see among workers—they have nothing to divide among themselves—does not exist in the capitalist class, where solidarity is corroded by competition. That is why in the working class the person with well-developed social instincts is the rule, while among the capitalists such a person is the exception.

Social instinct means a great many things. Often it offers a clue for finding a way out of a situation, for choosing the correct path. That is why during the purge of the RKP [Russian Communist Party], attention was paid to whether this or that member of the party had been born in a working family or not. He who comes from a worker's background will more easily straighten himself out. The Russian intelligentsia, seeing how easily a worker, thanks to this class instinct, comprehends that which an intellectual, for example, perceives only with great difficulty, was inclined, in the end of the nineties and in the first half of the first decade of the twentieth century (1896–1903) to exaggerate the significance of class instinct. *Rabochaya Mysl' [Workers' Thought]*, one of the underground Social Democratic newspapers, even came to the conclusion that no one other than people from workingman backgrounds could be accepted as socialists. Since Marx and Engels were not workers, *Rabochaya Mysl'* wrote "We don't need Marx and Engels!"

Class instinct, which among workers coincides with a social one, is a necessary condition for being a communist. Necessary, but not sufficient.

A communist must also *know* quite a lot. First, he must understand what is happening around him, and must gain an understanding of the existing system. When the workers' movement began to develop in Russia, Social Democrats were concerned from the very first with the widespread distribution of such pamphlets as Dikshtein's "Who Lives by What," "Worker's Day," etc. But it is not enough to understand the mechanics of the capitalist system. The communist must also study the laws of the development of human society. He must know the history of the development of economic forms, of the development of property, of division into classes, of the development of state forms. He must understand their interdependence and know how religious and moral notions will develop out of a particular social structure. Understanding the laws of the development of human society, the communist must clearly picture to himself where social development is heading. Communism must be seen by him as not only a desired system, where the happiness of some will not be based on the misfortune of others; he must further understand that communism is that very system toward which mankind is moving, and that communists must clear a path to this system, and promote its speedy coming.

In workers' circles at the dawn of the workers' movement in Russia, commonly studied courses were, on the one hand, political economy, which had the aim of explaining the structure of contemporary society, and the history of culture (the history of culture was usually opposed to the regular exposition of history, which often presented just a set of heterogeneous historical data). That is why in the circles of those days they read the first volume of Marx's *Capital* and F. Engels' *The Origins of the Family, Property and State.*

In 1919, in one of the villages of Nizhny Novgorod province, in the village of Rabotki, I happened to come across this phenomenon. Teachers told me that in the intermediate school they taught political economy and the history of culture; that the students unanimously demanded the introduction of these subjects into the curriculum of the intermediate school.

Where could such a desire, and such a definitely formulated one, have come from among peasant youth in a Volga village whose population was occupied exclusively with Volga river trades and agriculture? Obviously, interest in political economy and the history of culture was brought into Rabotki by some worker, who at one time had attended some circle and who explained to the children what they needed to know.

However, at the present moment the Russian communist must know not only that. The October Revolution opened for Russia an opportunity for widespread building in the direction of communism. But in order to utilize these possibilities it is necessary to know what one can do at the moment in order to make at least one first step toward communism, and what one cannot, and it is necessary to know how to build a new life. It is necessary first and foremost to know thoroughly that sphere of work which you have undertaken, and then to master the method of a communist *approach* to the matter. Let us take an example. In order to organize correctly medical affairs in the country, it is first necessary to know the situation itself, secondly, how it was organized earlier in Russia and is currently organized in other states, and thirdly, how to approach the problem in a communist manner, namely, to conduct agitation among wide strata of workers, to interest them, to attract them to work, to create with their efforts a powerful organization in regard to medical affairs. It is necessary not only to know how to do all this, but to be able to *do* it. Thus it follows that a communist must know not only what communism is and why it is inevitable, but also know his own affairs well, and be able to approach the masses, influence them, and convince them.

In his personal life, a communist must always conduct himself in the interests of communism. What does this mean? It means, for example, that however nice it might be to stay in a familiar, comfortable home environment, that if for the sake of the cause, for the success of the communist cause, it is necessary to abandon everything and expose oneself to danger, the communist will do this. It means that however difficult and responsible the task the communist is called upon to perform, he will take it upon himself and try to carry it out to the best of his strength and skill, whether it is at the front, during the confiscation of valuables, etc. It means that the communist puts his personal interests aside, subordinates them to the common interest. It means that the communist is not indifferent to what is happening around him and that he actively struggles with that which is harmful to the interests of the toiling masses, and that he on the other hand actively defends these interests and makes them his own. . . .

Who was discarded during the purging of the party? (a) the self-seekers and their adherents, that is, those who put their personal interests above the communist cause; (b) those who were indifferent to communism, who did nothing to help it make headway, who stood far from the masses and made no efforts to draw closer to them; (c) those who did not enjoy the respect and love of the masses; (d) those who were distinguished by a coarse manner, conceit, insincerity and other such characteristics.

Thus, in order to be a communist: (1) it is necessary to know what is bad about the capitalist system, where social development is heading and how to promote the speediest coming of the communist system; (2) it is necessary to know how to apply one's knowledge to the cause; and (3) it is necessary to be spiritually and physically devoted to the interests of the working masses and to communism.

60 John Scott, *Behind the Urals*

In 1932, John Scott (1912–1976), a twenty-year-old American college student, left the United States to work as a welder in the Soviet Union. Disturbed by the conditions of the American depression, Scott hoped that the Russian Revolution of 1917 had destroyed social inequality and injustice and that a better society was being created. Soviet reality turned out to be quite different from his expectations, but Scott remained in the Soviet Union for five years and eventually returned to the United States with a Russian wife. In *Behind the Urals,* he offers a vivid description of life in Magnitogorsk, Russia's new city of steel, located on the eastern slopes of the Ural Mountains. These were the years of the first Five-Year Plan, whose two major goals were industrialization and collectivization of the countryside. Scott lived and worked in the harsh, freezing conditions along with Soviet workers—some of whom had been sent there as punishment for being rich peasants (*kulaks*). He vividly describes the chronic shortages of everything from bread to welding rods; the frequent, often fatal, accidents of inexperienced, underfed workers; and the ever-present bureaucratic red tape. Yet Scott also was a witness to the hope, optimism, and commitment of many of these people who believed that their personal sacrifices would benefit all humankind. This work offers a detached and penetrating documentation of the tensions, problems, and heroic tasks confronting the men and women engaged in attempting to erect the first Communist society.

QUESTIONS TO CONSIDER

1. According to John Scott's observations, what were some of the social problems encountered in trying to meet the goals for industrialization set by the first Five-Year Plan?
2. In the process of collectivization, how did the peasants and the Communist Party decide who were the rich peasants? What was their fate?

The big whistle on the power house sounded a long, deep, hollow six o'clock. All over the scattered city-camp of Magnitogorsk, workers rolled out of their beds or bunks and dressed in preparation for their day's work.

From John Scott, *Behind the Urals: An American Worker in Russia's City of Steel* (Bloomington: Indiana University Press, 1973), pp. 9–10, 15–21, *passim.*

I climbed out of bed and turned on the light. I could see my breath across the room as I woke my roommate, Kolya. Kolya never heard the whistle. Every morning I had to pound his shoulder for several seconds to arouse him.

We pushed our coarse brown army blankets over the beds and dressed as quickly as we could—I had good American long woolen underwear, fortunately; Kolya wore only cotton shorts and a jersey. We both donned army shirts, padded and quilted cotton pants, similar jackets, heavy scarves, and then ragged sheepskin coats. We thrust our feet into good Russian "valinkis"—felt boots coming up to the knee. We did not eat anything. We had nothing on hand except tea and a few potatoes, and there was no time to light a fire in our little home-made iron stove. We locked up and set out for the mill.

It was January, 1933. The temperature was in the neighborhood of thirty-five below. A light powdery snow covered the low spots on the ground. The high spots were bare and hard as iron. A few stars cracked in the sky and some electric lights twinkled on the blast furnaces. Otherwise the world was bleak and cold and almost pitch-dark.

It was two miles to the blast furnaces, over rough ground. There was no wind, so our noses did not freeze. I was always glad when there was no wind in the morning. It was my first winter in Russia and I was not used to the cold. . . .

By the time the seven o'clock whistle blew, the shanty was jammed full of riggers, welders, cutters, and their helpers. It was a varied gang, Russians, Ukrainians, Tartars, Mongols, Jews, mostly young and almost all peasants of yesterday, though a few, like Ivanov, had long industrial experience. There was Popov, for instance. He had been a welder for ten years and had worked in half a dozen cities. On the other hand, Khaibulin, the Tartar, had never seen a staircase, a locomotive, or an electric light until he had come to Magnitogorsk a year before. His ancestors for centuries had raised stock on the flat plains of Kazakhstan. They had been dimly conscious of the Czarist government; they had had to pay taxes. Reports of the Kirghiz insurrection in 1916 had reached them. They had heard stories of the October Revolution; they even saw the Red Army come and drive out a few rich landlords. They had attended meetings of the Soviet, without understanding very clearly what it was all about, but through all this their lives had gone on more or less as before. Now Shaimat Khaibulin was building a blast furnace bigger than any in Europe. He had learned to read and was attending an evening school, learning the trade of electrician. He had learned to speak Russian, he read newspapers. His life had changed more in a year than that of his antecedents since the time of Tamerlane. . . .

I took my mask and electrodes and started out for No. 3. On the way I met Shabkov, the ex-kulak; a great husky youth with a red face, a jovial voice, and two fingers missing from his left hand.

"Well, Jack, how goes it?" he said, slapping me on the back. My Russian was still pretty bad, but I could carry on a simple conversation and understood almost everything that was said.

"Badly," I said. "All our equipment freezes. The boys spend half their time warming their hands."

"Nichevo, that doesn't matter," said the disfranchised rigger's brigadier. "If you lived where I do, in a tent, you wouldn't think it so cold here."

"I know you guys have it tough," said Popov, who had joined us. "That's what you get for being kulaks."

Shabkov smiled broadly. "Listen, I don't want to go into a political discussion, but a lot of the people living down in the special section of town are no more kulaks than you."

Popov laughed. "I wouldn't be surprised. Tell me, though, how did they decide who was to be dekulakized?"

"Ah," said Shabkov, "that's a hell of a question to ask a guy that's trying to expiate his crimes in honest labor. Just between the three of us, though, the poor peasants of the village get together in a meeting and decide: 'So-and-so has six horses; we couldn't very well get along without those in the collective farm; besides he hired a man last year to help on the harvest.' They notify the GPU, and there you are. So-and-so gets five years. They confiscate his property and give it to the new collective farm. Sometimes they ship the whole family out. When they came to ship us out, my brother got a rifle and fired several shots at the GPU officers. They fired back. My brother was killed. All of which, naturally, didn't make it any better for us. We all got five years, and in different places. I heard my father died in December, but I'm not sure." . . .

Popov and I set about welding up a section of the bleeder pipe on the blast furnace. He gave me a break and took the outside for the first hour. Then we changed around. From the high scaffolding, nearly a hundred feet above the ground, I could see Kolya making the rounds of his thirty-odd welders, helping them when they were in trouble, swearing at them when they spent too much time warming their hands. People swore at Kolya a good deal too, because the scaffolds were unsafe or the wages bad.

It was just about nine-fifteen when I finished one side of the pipe and went around to start the other. The scaffold was coated with about an inch of ice, like everything else around the furnaces. The vapor rising from the large hot-water cooling basin condensed on everything and formed a layer of ice. But besides being slippery, it was very insecure, swung down on wires, without any guys to steady it. It swayed and shook as I walked on it. I always made a point of hanging on to something when I could. I was just going to start welding when I heard someone sing out, and something swished down past me. It was a rigger who had been working up on the very top.

He bounced off the bleeder pipe, which probably saved his life. Instead of falling all the way to the ground, he landed on the main platform about fifteen feet below me. By the time I got down to him, blood was coming out of his mouth in gushes. He tried to yell, but could not. There were no foremen around, and the half-dozen riggers that had run up did not know what to do. By virtue of being a foreigner I had a certain amount of authority, so I stepped in and said he might bleed to death if we waited for a stretcher, and three of us took him and carried him down to the first-aid station. About halfway there the bleeding let up and he began to yell every step we took.

I was badly shaken when we got there, but the two young riggers were trembling like leaves. We took him into the little wooden building, and a nurse with a heavy shawl over her white gown showed us where to put him. "I expect the doctor any minute," she said; "good thing, too, I wouldn't know what the hell to do with him."

The rigger was gurgling and groaning. His eyes were wide open and he seemed conscious, but he did not say anything. "We should undress him, but it is so cold in here that I am afraid to," said the nurse. Just then the doctor came in. I knew him. He had dressed my foot once when a piece of pig iron fell on it. He took his immense sheepskin off and washed his hands. "Fall?" he asked, nodding at the rigger.

"Yes," I said.

"How long ago?"

"About ten minutes."

"What's that?" asked the doctor, looking at the nurse and indicating the corner of the room with his foot. I looked and for the first time noticed a pair of ragged valinkis sticking out from under a very dirty blanket on the floor.

"Girder fell on his head," said the nurse.

"Well," said the doctor, rolling up his sleeves, "let's see what we can do for this fellow." He moved over toward the rigger, who was lying quietly now and looking at the old bearded doctor with watery blue eyes. I turned to go, but the doctor stopped me.

"On your way out, please telephone the factory board of health and tell them I simply must have more heat in this place," he said.

I did the best I could over the telephone in my bad Russian, but all I could get was, "Comrade, we are sorry, but there is no coal."

I was making my way unsteadily back to the bleeder pipe on No. 3 when Kolya hailed me. "Don't bother to go up for a while, the brushes burnt out on the machine you were working on. They won't be fixed for half an hour or so." I went toward the office with Kolya and told him about the rigger. I was incensed and talked about some thorough checkup on scaffoldings. Kolya could not get interested. He pointed out there was not enough planking for good scaffolds, that the riggers were mostly plowboys who had no idea of being careful, and that at thirty-five below without any breakfast in you, you did not pay as much attention as you should.

"Sure, people will fall. But we're building blast furnaces all the same, aren't we?" and he waved his hand toward No. 2 from which the red glow of flowing pig iron was emanating. He saw I was not satisfied. "This somewhat sissified foreigner will have to be eased along a little," he probably said to himself. He slapped me on the back. "Come on in the office. We are going to have a technical conference. You'll be interested."

61 Nadezhda Mandelstam, *Hope Against Hope*

In the 1930s, Nadezhda Mandelstam (1899–1980) experienced the Soviet terror. Her husband, Osip Mandelstam (1891–1938), recognized today as the greatest Russian poet of the twentieth century, was persecuted because he portrayed Stalin as a tyrant in one of his poems. He was sentenced in 1938 to five years of hard labor in a camp in Vladivostok, but he died within the first year. Nadezhda first learned that her husband had died when a package she had sent him was returned, and she was told that the addressee was dead.

QUESTIONS TO CONSIDER

1. What was the justification given in Stalin's Russia for the arrest, imprisonment, and execution of "enemies of the state"?
2. How did those who had not been arrested behave during Stalin's terror?
3. What are the long-term consequences for the Soviet Union of Stalin's mass murders (see Readings 78 and 91)?

When I used to read about the French Revolution as a child, I often wondered whether it was possible to survive during a reign of terror. I now know beyond doubt that it is impossible. Anybody who breathes the air of terror is doomed, even if nominally he manages to save his life. Everybody is a victim—not only those who die, but also all the killers, ideologists, accomplices and sycophants who close their eyes or wash their hands—even if they are secretly consumed with remorse at night. Every section of the population has been through the terrible sickness caused by terror, and none has so far recovered, or become fit again for normal civic life. It is an illness that is passed on to the next generation, so that the sons pay for the sins of the fathers and perhaps only the grandchildren begin to get over it—or at least it takes on a different form with them.

Who was it who dared say that we have no "lost generation" here? The fact that he could utter such a monstrous untruth is also a consequence of terror. One generation after another was "lost" here, but it was a completely different process from what may have happened in the West. Here people just tried to go on working, struggling to maintain themselves, hoping for salvation, and thinking only about their immediate concerns. In such times your daily round is like a drug. The more you have to do, the better. If you can immerse yourself in your work, the years fly by more quickly, leaving only a gray blur in the memory. Among the people of my generation, only a very few have kept clear minds and memories. In M.'s generation, everybody was stricken by a kind of sclerosis at an early stage.

True as this is, however, I never cease to marvel at our hardiness. After Stalin's death my brother Evgeni said to me: "We still do not realize what we have been through." Not long ago, as I was traveling in an overcrowded bus, an old woman pushed up against me and I found my arm was bearing the whole weight of her body. "That must be killing you," she said suddenly. "No," I replied, "we're as tough as the devil." "As tough as the devil?" she said, and laughed. Somebody nearby also laughingly repeated the phrase, and soon the whole bus was saying it after us. But then the bus stopped and everybody started to push toward the exit, jostling each other in the usual way. The little moment of good humor was over. . . .

When life becomes absolutely intolerable, you begin to think the horror will never end. In Kiev during the bombardment I understood that even the unbearable can come to an end, but I was not yet fully aware that it often does so only at death. As regards the Stalinist terror, we always knew that it might wax or wane, but that it might end—this we could never imagine. What reason was there for it to end? Everybody seemed intent on his daily round and went smilingly about the business of carrying out his instructions. It was essential to smile—if you didn't, it meant you were afraid or discontented. This nobody could afford to admit—if you were afraid, then you must have a bad conscience. Everybody who worked for the State—and in this country even the humblest stall-keeper is a bureaucrat—had to strut around wearing a cheerful expression, as though to say: "What's going on is no concern of mine, I have very important work to do, and I'm terribly busy. I am trying to do my best for the State, so do not get in my way. My conscience is clear—if what's-his-name has been arrested, there must be good reason." The mask was taken off only at home, and then not

Excerpted from *Hope Against Hope: A Memoir* by Nadezhda Mandelstam, pp. 297–98, 304–05, 316–17, 369–71. Translated from the Russian by Max Hayward with introduction by Clarence Brown. Copyright © 1970 Atheneum Publishers. English translation copyright © 1970 Atheneum Publishers. Introduction copyright © 1970 Atheneum Publishers. Reprinted with the permission of Scribner, a Division of Simon & Schuster.

always—even from your children you had to conceal how horror-struck you were; otherwise, God save you, they might let something slip in school. . . . Some people had adapted to the terror so well that they knew how to profit from it—there was nothing out of the ordinary about denouncing a neighbor to get his apartment or his job. But while wearing your smiling mask, it was important not to laugh—this could look suspicious to the neighbors and make them think you were indulging in sacrilegious mockery. We have lost the capacity to be spontaneously cheerful, and it will never come back to us. . . .

I think he exaggerated the extent to which our secret police went in for ordinary detective work. They were not in the least bit interested in *real* facts—all they wanted were lists of people to arrest, and these they got from their network of informers and the volunteers who brought them denunciations. To meet their quotas, all they needed were names of people, not details about their comings and goings. During interrogations they always, as a matter of routine, collected "evidence" against people whom they had no intention of arresting—just in case it was ever needed. I have heard of a woman who heroically went through torture rather than give "evidence" against Molotov! A man was asked for evidence against Liuba Ehrenburg, whom he had never even met. He managed to send word about this from the forced-labor camp, and Liuba was warned—apparently Akhmatova passed on the message to her. Liuba could not believe it: "What Spasski? I don't know him." She was still naïve in those days, but later she understood everything.

In the torture chambers of the Lubianka they were constantly adding to the dossiers of Ehrenburg, Sholokhov, Alexei Tolstoi, and others whom they had no intention of touching. Dozens, if not hundreds of people were sent to camps on a charge of being involved in a "conspiracy" headed by Tikhonov and Fadeyev! Among them was Spasski. Wild inventions and monstrous accusations had become an end in themselves, and officials of the secret police applied all their ingenuity to them, as though reveling in the total arbitrariness of their power. Their basic principle was just what Furmanov had told us at the end of the twenties: "Give us a man, and we'll make a case." On the day we had spent at Stenich's apartment, his name was almost certainly already on a list of persons due to be arrested—his telephone number would have been found in Diki's address book, and no further information about him was needed.

The principles and aims of mass terror have nothing in common with ordinary police work or with security. The only purpose of terror is intimidation. To plunge the whole country into a state of chronic fear, the number of victims must be raised to astronomical levels, and on every floor of every building there must always be several apartments from which the tenants have suddenly been taken away. The remaining inhabitants will be model citizens for the rest of their lives—this will be true for every street and every city through which the broom has swept. The only essential thing for those who rule by terror is not to overlook the new generations growing up without faith in their elders, and to keep on repeating the process in systematic fashion. Stalin ruled for a long time and saw to it that the waves of terror recurred from time to time, always on an even greater scale than before. But the champions of terror invariably leave one thing out of account—namely, that they can't kill everyone, and among their cowed, half-demented subjects there are always witnesses who survive to tell the tale. . . .

The only link with a person in prison was the window through which one handed parcels and money to be forwarded to him by the authorities. Once a month, after waiting three or four hours in line (the number of arrests was by now falling off, so this was not very long), I went up to the window and gave my name. The clerk behind the window thumbed through his list—I went on days when he dealt with the letter "M"—and asked me for my first name and initial. As soon as I replied, a hand stretched out of the window and I put my identity papers and some money into it. The hand then returned my papers with a receipt and I went away. Everybody envied me because I at least knew that my husband was alive and where he was. It happened only too often that the man behind the window barked: "No record. . . . Next!" All questions were useless—the official would simply shut his window in your face and one of the uniformed guards would come up to you. Order was immediately restored and the next in line moved up to the window. If anybody ever tried to linger, the guard found ready allies among the other people waiting.

There was generally no conversation in the line. This was the chief prison in the Soviet Union, and the people who came here were a select, respectable and well-disciplined crowd. There were never any untoward events, unless it was a minor case of someone asking a question—but persons guilty of such misconduct would speedily retreat in embarrassment. The only incident I saw was when two little girls in neatly starched dresses once came in. Their mother had been arrested the previous night. They were let through out of turn and nobody asked what letter their name began with. All the women waiting there were no doubt moved by pity at the thought that their own children might soon be coming here in the same way. Somebody lifted up the elder of the two, because she was too small to reach the window, and she shouted through it: "Where's my mummy?" and "We won't go to the orphanage. We won't go home." They just managed to say that their father was in the army before the window was slammed shut. This could have been the actual case, or it could have meant that he had been in the secret police. The children of Chekists were always taught to say that their father was "in the army"—this was to protect them from the curiosity of their schoolmates, who, the parents explained, might be less friendly otherwise. Before going abroad on duty, Chekists also made their children learn the new name under which they would be living there. . . . The little girls in the starched dresses probably lived in a government building—they told the people waiting in line that other children had been taken away to orphanages, but that they wanted to go to their grandmother in the Ukraine. Before they could say any more, a soldier came out of a side door and led them away. The window opened again and everything returned to normal. As they were being led away, one woman called them "silly little girls," and another said: "We must send ours away before it's too late."

These little girls were exceptional. Children who came and stood in line were usually as restrained and silent as grown-ups. It was generally their fathers who were arrested first—particularly if they were military people—and they would then be carefully instructed by their mothers on how to behave when they were left completely alone. Many of them managed to keep out of the orphanages, but that depended mainly on their parents' status—the higher it had been, the less chance the children had of being looked after by relatives. It was astonishing that life continued at all, and that people still brought children into the world and had families. How could they do this, knowing what went on in front of the window in the building on Sophia Embankment?

Fascism: Three Faces

Fascism, the only new comprehensive political philosophy of the twentieth century, appeared in every industrialized country in the 1920s or 1930s.

In Japan, Kita Ikki (1885–1937) was the foremost proponent of national socialist reform, and his book *Outline for the Reconstruction of Japan* (1919) became the bible of Japanese fascists. Kita advocated a complete reorganization of Japanese polity: a military takeover of the government to free the emperor from his selfish and weak advisers; nationalization of land and capital; and an aggressive, expansionist foreign policy, especially on the Asian mainland, to help solve Japan's shortage of natural resources, relieve the population pressure, and free Asia from Western influence.

European fascists, on the other hand, generally tended to avoid rigorous, positive definitions of their programs, concentrating instead on the political and economic failures of democracy and communism. Of all the fascist leaders, Benito Mussolini (1883–1945) has made, perhaps, the clearest and most complete theoretical statement of the fascist ideology. Mussolini denounced the class war and celebrated the fascist cult of violence and death. Adolf Hitler (1889–1945), though heavily influenced by Mussolini, emphasized propaganda and the special role of race in the development of his National Socialist (Nazi) form of German fascism.

62 Kita Ikki, *Outline for the Reconstruction of Japan*

Following World War I, Japan experimented with parliamentary democracy at home and pursued internationalism abroad. But Japanese radicals, both right- and left-wing, had little confidence in parliamentary solutions for social problems. Radical nationalists, particularly ultranationalistic young army officers, found inspiration for the future in the thought and writings of Kita Ikki (1885–1937). This advocate of national socialism was implicated in the abortive military coup d'état of February 26, 1936, and was executed in 1937.

QUESTIONS TO CONSIDER

1. Why would Kita Ikki urge that the study of English be abolished?
2. Are there any parallels between Kita Ikki's and Mussolini's views of war and violence (see Reading 63)?
3. Compare and contrast national social socialism advocated by Adolf Hitler with Kita's ideas of restructuring Japan (see Reading 64).

THE EMPEROR OF THE PEOPLE

Suspension of the Constitution: In order to establish a firm base for national reorganization, the Emperor, with the aid of the entire Japanese nation and by invoking his imperial prerogatives, shall suspend the Constitution for a period of three years, dissolve the two houses of the Diet, and place the entire country under martial law.

The true significance of the Emperor: We must make clear the fundamental principle that the Emperor is the sole representative of the people and the pillar of the state. . . .

Abolition of the peerage system: By abolishing the peerage system, we shall be able to remove the feudal aristocracy which constitutes a barrier between the Emperor and the people. In this way the spirit of the Meiji Restoration shall be proclaimed.

The House of Peers shall be replaced by the Deliberative Council which shall review decisions made by the House of Representatives. The Deliberative Council may reject for a single time only any decisions of the House of Representatives.

The members of the Deliberative Council shall consist of men distinguished in various fields of activities, elected by each other or appointed by the Emperor.

Popular election: All men twenty-five years of age and above shall have the right to elect and be elected to the House of Representatives, exercising their rights with full equality as citizens of Great Japan. Similar provisions shall apply to all local self-governing bodies. No women shall be permitted to participate in politics.

Restoration of people's freedom: Existing laws which restrict people's freedom and circumvent the spirit of the constitution shall be abolished. These laws include the civil service appointment ordinance, peace preservation law, press act, and publication law.

National reorganization Cabinet: A national reorganization Cabinet shall be formed during the time martial law is in effect. In addition to the existing ministries, the Cabinet shall establish such ministries of industries as described below and add a number of ministers without portfolio. Members of the reorganization Cabinet shall be selected from outstanding individuals throughout the country, avoiding those who are presently connected with military, bureaucratic, financial, or party cliques. . . .

Granting of imperial estate: The Emperor shall set a personal example by granting to the state, the lands, forests, shares and similar properties held by the Imperial Household. The expenses of the Imperial Household shall be limited to thirty million yen per annum appropriated from the national treasury. However, the Diet may authorize additional expenditure if the need arises.

From David John Lu, *Sources of Japanese History,* Vol. 2 (New York: McGraw-Hill, 1974), pp. 131–36. Reprinted by permission.

LIMITATION ON PRIVATE PROPERTY

Limitation on private property: No Japanese family shall possess property in excess of one million yen. A similar limitation shall apply to Japanese citizens holding property overseas. No one shall be permitted to make a gift of property to those related by blood or to others, or to transfer his property by other means with the intent of circumventing this limitation.

Nationalization of excess amount over limitation on private property: Any amount which exceeds the limitation on private property shall revert to the state without compensation. No one shall be permitted to resort to the protection of present laws in order to avoid remitting such excess amount. Anyone who violates these provisions shall be deemed a person thinking lightly of the example set by the Emperor and endangering the basis of national reorganization. As such, during the time martial law is in effect, he shall be charged with the crimes of endangering the person of the Emperor and engaging in internal revolt and shall be punished by death.

THREE PRINCIPLES FOR DISPOSITION OF LANDS

Limitation on private landholding: No Japanese family shall hold land in excess of 100,000 yen in current market value. . . .

Lands held in excess of the limitation on private landholding shall revert to the state. . . .

Popular ownership of lands reverted to state: The state shall divide the lands granted by the Imperial Household and the lands reverted to it from those whose holdings exceed the limitation and distribute such lands to farmers who do not possess their own lands. These farmers shall gain title to their respective lands by making annual installment payments to the state. . . .

Lands to be owned by the state: Large forests, virgin lands which require large capital investment, and lands which can best be cultivated in large lots shall be owned and operated by the state.

CONTROL OF LARGE CAPITAL

Limitation on private property: No private industry shall exceed the limit of 10,000,000 yen in assets. A similar limitation shall apply to private industries owned by Japanese citizens overseas.

Nationalization of industries exceeding the limitation: Any industry whose assets exceed the limitation imposed on private industry shall be collectivized and operated under state control. . . .

INDUSTRIAL ORGANIZATION OF THE STATE

No. 1. Ministry of Banking: The assets of this ministry shall come from the money expropriated from large banks whose assets exceed the limitation on private industry and from individuals whose net worth exceeds the limitation on private property. . . .

No. 2. Ministry of Navigation: Ships and other assets expropriated from private lines in excess of the limitation on private property shall be utilized mainly for transoceanic voyages in order to attain supremacy of the seas. [The ministry shall also] engage in shipbuilding (naval and commercial) and other activities. . . .

No. 3. Ministry of Mines: Large mines whose assets or market values exceed the limitation on private industry shall be expropriated and operated by this ministry. . . .

No. 4. Ministry of Agriculture: Management of nationally owned lands; management of Taiwan sugar industry and forestry; development of Taiwan, Hokkaido, Karafuto (Southern Sakhalin), and Chōsen (Korea); development of South and North Manchuria and colonies to be acquired in the future; and management of large farms when acquired by the state.

No. 5. Ministry of Industries: Various large industries expropriated by the state shall be reorganized, unified, and expanded to form a truly large industrial combine through which all types of industries may acquire competitive advantages now possessed by comparable foreign industries. The ministry shall also operate industries urgently needed by the nation but not undertaken by private parties. Naval Steel Works and Military Ordnance Factories shall be placed under this ministry's jurisdiction and be operated by it. . . .

Railways whose assets do not exceed the limitation on private industry shall be open to private operation.

Vast income of the national treasury: The vast income realized by the industrial ministries shall be sufficient for the expenditures of various service ministries and guarantee adequate living conditions for the people as described below. Therefore, with the exception of basic income taxes, all other inequitable taxes shall be abolished. Without exception, all industrial ministries shall be taxed in a manner similar to all private industries. . . .

RIGHTS OF WORKERS

Functions of the Ministry of Labor: A Ministry of Labor shall be established within the Cabinet to protect the rights of all workers employed by state-owned and privately owned industries. Industrial disputes shall be submitted to the Ministry of Labor for arbitration in accordance with a law to be enacted independently. . . .

Working hours: Working hours shall be uniformly set at eight hours a day. Wages shall be paid for Sundays and holidays when no work is performed. Farm workers shall receive additional wages for the overtime work performed during the busy farming seasons.

Distribution of profits to workers: One half of the net profits of private industries shall be distributed to workers employed in such industries. All workers, mental and physical, shall participate in the profit distribution proportionate to their salaries or wages. Workers shall elect their own representatives to participate in the industry's management planning and bookkeeping. Similar provisions shall apply to farm workers and landlords.

Workers employed in state-owned industries shall receive semi-annual bonuses in lieu of the profit distribution. . . .

Establishment of employee-shareholder system: Every private corporation shall set up a provision under which physical and mental workers in their employment shall have the right to become stockholders of the corporation.

Protection of tenant farmers: The state shall enact a separate law, based on the basic human rights, to protect tenant farmers tilling the lands owned by small landlords whose holdings do not exceed the limitation on private lands.

Women's labor: Women's labor shall be free and equal to that of men. However, after the reorganization, the state shall make it a matter of national policy that the burden of labor shall not rest on the shoulders of women. In order to prepare women to replace men in providing needed labor in a national emergency, women shall receive education equal to that of men.

PEOPLE'S RIGHT TO LIVE

Children's right to live: Children under fifteen years of age without both parents or father, having rights as children of the state, shall be uniformly supported and educated by the state. . . .

Support of the aged and disabled: The state shall assume the responsibility of supporting those men and women sixty years of age or over who are poor and not having their natural born or adopted sons. Similar support shall be given to those disabled and crippled persons who are poor, unable to work, and without fathers and sons.

Rights to education: National (compulsory) education shall last for a period of ten years from ages six to sixteen. Similar education shall be given to both male and female. There shall be instituted a fundamental reform in the educational system. . . .

English shall be abolished and Esperanto shall become the second language. . . .

RIGHTS OF THE STATE

Continuation of the conscript system: The state, having rights to existence and development among the nations of the world, shall maintain the present conscript system in perpetuity. . . .

Positive right to start war: In addition to the right to self-defense, the state shall have the right to start a war on behalf of other nations and races unjustly oppressed by a third power. (As a matter of real concern today, the state shall have the right to start a war to aid the independence of India and preservation of China's integrity.)

As a result of its own development, the state shall also have the right to start a war against those nations who occupy large colonies illegally and ignore the heavenly way of the co-existence of all humanity. (As a matter of real concern today, the state shall have the right to start a war against those nations which occupy Australia and Far Eastern Siberia for the purpose of acquiring them.)

63 Benito Mussolini, "The Political and Social Doctrine of Fascism"

Capitalizing on the economic and political unrest of Italy following World War I, Benito Mussolini (1883–1945) came to power after his black-shirted fascists marched on Rome in 1922. In 1932, Mussolini, with the help of Giovanni Gentile, wrote the following definition of Italian fascism.

QUESTIONS TO CONSIDER

1. How did Mussolini view democracy, socialism, and pacifism?
2. Why would Mussolini's passionate embrace of heroism and violence appeal to so many Italians (and others) in the 1920s?

The years which preceded the March to Rome were years of great difficulty, during which the necessity for action did not permit research of or any complete elaboration of doctrine. The battle had to be fought in the towns and villages. There was much discussion, but—what was more important and more sacred—men died. They knew how to die. Doctrine, beautifully defined and carefully elucidated, with headlines and paragraphs, might be lacking; but there was to take its place something more decisive—Faith. Even so, anyone who can recall the events of the time through the aid of books, articles, votes of congresses, and speeches of great and minor importance— anyone who knows how to research and weigh evidence—will find that the fundamentals of doctrine were cast during the years of conflict. It was precisely in those years that Fascist thought armed itself, was refined, and began the great task of organization. The problem of the relation between the individual citizen and the State; the allied problems of authority and liberty; political and social problems as well as those specifically national—a solution was being sought for all these while at the same time the struggle against Liberalism, Democracy, Socialism, and the Masonic bodies was being carried on, contemporaneously with the "punitive expedition." But, since there was inevitably some lack of system, the adversaries of Fascism have disingenuously denied that it had any capacity to produce a doctrine of its own, though that doctrine was growing and taking shape under their very eyes, even though tumultuously; first, as happens to all ideas in their beginnings, in the aspect of a violent and dogmatic negation, and then in the aspect of positive construction which has found its realization in the laws and institutions of the regime as enacted successively in the years 1926, 1927 and 1928.

Fascism is now a completely individual thing, not only as a regime, but as a doctrine. And this means that today Fascism, exercising its critical sense upon itself and upon others, has formed its own distinct and peculiar point of view, to which it can refer and upon which, therefore, it can act in the face of all problems, practical or intellectual, which confront the world.

And above all, Fascism, the more it considers and observes the future and the development of humanity quite apart from political considerations of the moment, believes neither in the possibility nor the utility of perpetual peace. It thus repudiates the doctrine of Pacifism—born of a renunciation of the struggle and an act of cowardice in the face of sacrifice. War alone brings up to its highest tension all human energy and puts the stamp of nobility upon the peoples who have the courage to meet it. All other trials are substitutes, which never really put men into the position where they have to make the great decision—the alternative of life or death. Thus a doctrine which is founded upon this harmful postulate of peace is hostile to Fascism. And thus hostile to the spirit of Fascism, though accepted for what use they can be in dealing with particular political situations, are all the international leagues and societies which, as history

From Benito Mussolini, "The Political and Social Doctrine of Fascism," *International Conciliation*, 306 (January 1935), pp. 5–17, *passim*. Reprinted by permission of the Carnegie Endowment for International Peace.

will show, can be scattered to the winds when once strong national feeling is aroused by any motive—sentimental, ideal, or practical. This anti-pacifist spirit is carried by Fascism even into the life of the individual; the proud motto of the Squadrista, *"Me ne frego"* (I do not fear), written on the bandage of the wound, is an act of philosophy not only stoic, the summary of a doctrine not only political—it is the education to combat, the acceptance of the risks which combat implies, and a new way of life for Italy. Thus the Fascist accepts life and loves it, knowing nothing of and despising suicide: he rather conceives of life as duty and struggle and conquest, life which should be high and full, lived for oneself, but above all for others—those who are at hand and those who are far distant, contemporaries, and those who will come after.

This "demographic" policy of the regime is the result of the above premise. Thus the Fascist loves in actual fact his neighbor, but this "neighbor" is not merely a vague and undefined concept, this love for one's neighbor puts no obstacle in the way of necessary educational severity, and still less to differentiation of status and to physical distance. Fascism repudiates any universal embrace, and in order to live worthily in the community of civilized peoples watches its contemporaries with vigilant eyes, takes good note of their state of mind and, in the changing trend of their interests, does not allow itself to be deceived by temporary and fallacious appearances.

Such a conception of life makes Fascism the complete opposite of that doctrine, the base of the so-called scientific and Marxian Socialism, the materialist conception of history; according to which the history of human civilization can be explained simply through the conflict of interests among the various social groups and by the change and development in the means and instruments of production. That the changes in the economic field—new discoveries of raw materials, new methods of working them, and the inventions of science—have their importance no one can deny; but that these factors are sufficient to explain the history of humanity excluding all others is an absurd delusion. Fascism, now and always, believes in holiness and in heroism; that is to say, in actions influenced by no economic motive, direct or indirect. And if the economic conceptions of history be denied, according to which theory men are no more than puppets, carried to and fro by the waves of chance, while the real directing forces are quite out of their control, it follows that the existence of an unchangeable and unchanging class war is also denied—the natural progeny of the economic conception of history. And above all Fascism denies that class war can be the preponderant force in the transformation of society. These two fundamental concepts of Socialism being thus refuted, nothing is left of it but the sentimental aspiration—as old as humanity itself—towards a social convention in which the sorrows and sufferings of the humblest shall be alleviated. But here again Fascism repudiates the conception of "economic" happiness, to be realized by Socialism and, as it were, at a given moment in economic evolution to assure to everyone the maximum of well-being. Fascism denies the materialist conception of happiness as a possibility, and abandons it to its inventors, the economists of the first half of the nineteenth century: that is to say, Fascism denies the validity of the equation, well-being = happiness, which would reduce men to the level of animals, caring for one thing only—to be fat and well-fed—and would thus degrade humanity to a purely physical existence.

After Socialism, Fascism combats the whole complex system of democratic ideology, and repudiates it, whether in its theoretical premises or in its practical application. Fascism denies that the majority, by the simple fact that it is a majority, can direct human society; it denies that numbers alone can govern by means of a periodical consultation, and it affirms the immutable, beneficial, and fruitful inequality of mankind, which can never be permanently leveled through the mere operation of a mechanical process such as universal suffrage. The democratic regime may be defined as from time to time giving the people the illusion of sovereignty, while the real effective sovereignty lies in the hands of other concealed and irresponsible forces. Democracy is a regime nominally without a king, but it is ruled by many kings—more absolute, tyrannical, and ruinous than one sole king, even though a tyrant. This explains why Fascism, having first in 1922 (for reasons of expediency) assumed an attitude tending towards republicanism, renounced this point of view before the March to Rome; being convinced that the question of political form is not today of prime importance, and after having studied the examples of monarchies and republics past and present reached the conclusion that monarchy or republicanism are not to be judged, as it were, by an absolute standard; but that they represent forms in which the evolution—political, historical, traditional, or psychological—of a particular country has expressed itself.

64 Adolf Hitler, *Mein Kampf*

Adolf Hitler (1889–1945) became chancellor of Germany in 1933 and ruled Germany until 1945. In 1943, in the midst of World War II, the U.S. State Department translated and published the following extract of Hitler's National Socialist (Nazi) program, which was originally published in the first volume of Hitler's book, *Mein Kampf (My Struggle)*.

QUESTIONS TO CONSIDER

1.   What were Hitler's views on the racial characteristics of Germans?
2.   According to Hitler, what was the function of propaganda?
3.   Based upon this text, to whom was Hitler's message directed?

The basic racial elements are differently situated, not only territorially but also in individual cases within the same territory. Nordic men exist side by side with Eastern types; Easterners, with Dinarics; both of these types, with Westerners; and everywhere among them are mixed types. On the one hand this is a great disadvantage: The German folk lacks that sure instinct of the herd which has its roots in the unity of blood and, especially in moments when great danger threatens, preserves the nation from collapse, in as much as with such a folk all small internal distinctions will then immediately disappear and the common enemy will be faced with the closed front of the uniform herd. In the existence side by side of our most varied component racial elements, which have remained unmixed, lies the foundation of that which we designate with the

From Raymond Murphy, *National Socialism: Basic Principles. Their Application by the Nazi Party's Foreign Organization, and the Use of Germans Abroad for Nazi Aims* (Washington, DC: Government Printing Office, 1943), pp. 845–49, *passim*.

word superindividualism. In peaceful times it may sometimes perform good services for us, but, considered all in all, it has deprived us of world supremacy. If the German folk, in its historical development, had possessed that herdlike unity which other peoples have enjoyed, the German Reich would today be mistress of the globe. World history would have taken another course, and no one can tell whether in this way that might not have been attained which so many deluded pacifists are hoping today to wheedle by moaning and whining: A peace supported not by the palm branches of tearful pacifistic female mourners but founded by the victorious sword of a master race (Herrenvolk) which places the world in the service of a higher culture. . . .

PROPAGANDA

In this regard one proceeded from the very correct principle that the size of the lie always involves a certain factor of credibility, since the great mass of a people will be more spoiled in the innermost depths of its heart, rather than consciously and deliberately bad. Consequently, in view of the primitive simplicity of its mind it is more readily captivated by a big lie than by a small one, since it itself often uses small lies but would be, nevertheless, too ashamed to make use of big lies. Such an untruth will not even occur to it, and it will not even believe that others are capable of the enormous insolence of the most vile distortions. Why, even when enlightened, it will still vacillate and be in doubt about the matter and will nevertheless accept as true at least some cause or other. Consequently, even from the most impudent lie something will always stick.

To whom must propaganda appeal? To the scientific mind or to the less educated masses?

The task of propaganda does not lie in a scientific education of the individual but in pointing out to the masses definite facts, processes, necessities, etc., the significance of which in this way is first to be brought within the masses' range of vision.

The art lies exclusively therein, to do this in such an excellent way that a universal conviction arises of the reality of a fact, of the necessity of a process, of the correctness of something necessary, etc. Since it is not and cannot be necessary in itself, since its task, just as in the case of a placard, consists of bringing something before the attention of the crowd and not in the instruction of those who are scientifically trained or are seeking education and insight, its efficacy must always be oriented more to the emotions and only in a very restricted way to the so-called "intellect."

All propaganda has to appeal to the people and its intellectual level has to be set in accordance with the receptive capacities of the most-limited persons among those to whom it intends to address itself. The larger the mass of men to be reached, the lower its purely intellectual level will have to be set. . . .

The art of propaganda lies precisely therein, that, comprehending the great masses' world of emotions and imagination, it finds the way, in a psychologically correct form, to the attention and, further, to the hearts of the great masses.

The receptive capacity of the great masses is very restricted, its understanding small. On the other hand, however, its forgetfulness is great. On account of these facts all effective propaganda must restrict itself to very few points and impress these by slogans, until even the last person is able to bring to mind what is meant by such a word. . . .

In general the art of all truly great popular leaders at all times consists primarily in not scattering the attention of a people but rather in concentrating it always on one single opponent. The more unified this use of the fighting will of a people, the greater will be the magnetic attractive force of a movement and the more powerful the force of its push. It is a part of the genius of a great leader to make even quite different opponents appear as if they belonged only to one category, because the recognition of different enemies leads weak and unsure persons only too readily to begin doubting their own cause.

When the vacillating masses see themselves fighting against too many enemies, objectivity at once sets in and raises the question whether really all the others are wrong and only one's own people or one's own movement is right.

Therewith, however, appears already the first weakening of one's own force. Consequently, a number of intrinsically different opponents must always be comprehended together, so that in the view of the masses of one's own adherents the fight is only being carried on against one enemy alone. This strengthens the faith in one's own cause and increases the bitterness toward the aggressor against this cause.

In all cases in which there is a question of the fulfillment of apparently impossible demands or tasks, the entire attention of a people must be concentrated only on this one question, in such a way as if being or non-being actually depends on its solution. Only in this way will one make a people willing and capable of really great accomplishments and exertions.

World War II: Asia and Europe

As a solution to post–World War I Japanese economic and security problems, the Japanese military in Manchuria, known as the Kwangtung Army,[1] without prior approval of the Tokyo government seized control of Mukden, a key administrative center in Manchuria in September 1931. Within a few months, the Kwangtung Army had placed all of Manchuria under its military control by driving out the Chinese military and creating the "puppet state" of Manchukuo in 1932. The Japanese invasion of Manchuria marked the beginning of a decade and a half of military domination by the Japanese government, and it put Japan on a collision course with the United States. To protect Manchuria, the Japanese military continued to nibble away at Chinese territory adjacent to Manchukuo. Continued Japanese encroachment of Chinese sovereignty finally led to an all-out war with China on July 7, 1937. Quite unexpectedly, the war with China dragged on and the Nationalist Chinese government in Nanking refused to surrender even after Japan sealed the entire coastal provinces of China.

---

[1]Three northeastern provinces of China are often known as Manchuria. As part of the peace settlement following Japan's defeat of Russia in 1905, Japan took over the Russian leasehold in the Liaotung Peninsula in southern Manchuria and tsarist railway and economic rights in Manchuria. A Japanese governor-general administered the leased territory, including the railway zone. The Japanese army stationed in Liaotung Peninsula to guard the Japanese interest in Manchuria was known as the Kwangtung Army.

From the beginning of the conflict, the Japanese military targeted Chinese civilians for special treatment. Japanese aircraft bombed and strafed Chinese cities. By late November, Japanese troops had captured Beijing and Shanghai and were besieging Nanking. On December 13, 1937, Japanese forces captured Nanking and initiated a horrifying policy of massacre, rape, and genocide resulting in the death of more than 300,000 civilians. The first reading in this section documents this atrocity.

Isolated internationally, Japan desperately sought an end to further expansion of the seemingly endless war in China, trying to resort to a war of attrition, but unable to do so on its own terms. Increasingly Japan blamed the Soviet Union, the United States, and Great Britain for China's continuing resistance. The United States showed its displeasure with Japan's aggression toward China by adopting a series of economic sanctions. In the summer of 1938, Washington placed an embargo on shipments of aircraft, arms, and other war material to Japan; in July 1939, it abrogated a commercial treaty with Japan; and in the fall of 1940, the embargo was expanded to include scrap iron and steel. In July 1941, the export of American oil to Japan was banned. Great Britain, the British Commonwealth, and the Dutch East Indies joined the oil embargo. This cut Japan's oil imports by 90 percent and compelled Japan to make a crucial decision between giving up China, including Manchuria, or invading the oil-rich Dutch East Indies and risking war with the United States, Britain, China, and the Dutch. With Nazi Germany and fascist Italy on its side, the Japanese government chose the road to war.[2] This led to the Pearl Harbor attack on December 7, 1941.

The war in Europe began when Adolf Hitler pushed Germany into declaring war on Poland on September 1, 1939. Hitler's new "lightning war" (*Blitzkrieg*) in Poland was followed by German victories in Denmark, Norway, Holland, and Belgium; the climax was the stunning defeat of France on June 17, 1940. Hitler's quick victories whetted the appetites for war of his Axis allies—Italy and Japan. On June 10, 1940, Italy pounced on France; after the defeat of France, Japan accelerated its timetable for Pacific expansion by occupying northern French Indochina on September 22, 1940.

Surprisingly, despite the Axis alliance among Berlin, Rome, and Tokyo (1940), there was little effort devoted to coordinating war plans. In part, this

[2]Impressed by the German military successes in Europe, the Japanese government signed a Tripartite Pact with Germany and Italy and became a member of the Axis alliance in September 1940.

lack of effort stemmed from the personality of Adolf Hitler. Hitler, like all politicians, changed his mind and altered plans, but by 1937 he had become convinced that Germany could achieve greatness only through war. Hitler wanted a short war: First Germany would win key battles in the west, then turn east and defeat the Soviet Union, establishing a European continental empire. Despite the size and reputation of the French army, Hitler held France in contempt. Although he respected England, he did not believe that England would fight once France was defeated. An isolated Soviet Union, Hitler believed, would be an easy prey for his *Blitzkrieg* style of war.

Hitler miscalculated. His diagnosis of France was correct, but he misread Winston Churchill (1874–1965), England's wartime prime minister, and he severely underestimated the resiliency and military power of the Soviet Union. Though suffering huge losses throughout the war, the Soviet Union destroyed more than 600 German divisions; the Battle of Stalingrad (1942) marked the end of *Blitzkrieg* and turned the tide against Germany. Hitler also underestimated the economic and military capacity of the United States. Inexplicably but fatefully, he declared war on the United States on December 11, 1941.

The following documents describe the horrors of the Japanese occupation of Nanking, outline Hitler's plans for war in 1937, detail America's peacetime commitment to help Great Britain resist Hitler, and present Tojo's defense of Japan's aggression.

65 John Rabe, *The Diaries of the Nanking Massacre*

The fall of Nanking [Nanjing] to the invading Japanese army occurred on December 13, 1937. During the first six weeks of Japanese occupation of Nationalist China's capital, the people of Nanking experienced one of the bloodiest horrors in history—mass killings, systematic arson, tortures, and wholesale rape. Tens of thousands of Chinese prisoners of war in the battle of Nanking were executed in the most brutal ways, and women of Nanking were subjected to large-scale rape and murder. The death toll reached nearly a third of a million people.

The horror of Nanking could have been worse had it not been for the intercession of a handful of courageous American and European residents of Nanking. They were businesspeople, educators, and Christian missionaries. Shortly before the onslaught of the Japanese army on the capital, these brave foreigners formed the International Committee for the Nanking Safety Zone. They created a neutral zone in the center of the city to save the lives of those civilians who were caught in the crossfire between the invaders and the defenders of the capital. Of these brave foreigners, the heroic efforts of one man were particularly noteworthy. He was John Rabe, a German businessman who headed the Nanking branch of Siemens, a German electrical engineering firm. Rabe was elected chairman of the International Committee for the Nanking Safety Zone. Given that Germany was an ally of Japan and, moreover, that he was a leader of the National Socialist German Workers' Party (NSDAP or simply Nazi) in Nanking, Rabe's swastika armband often helped him shield fear-stricken Chinese refugees in the safety zone from the guns, bayonets, and sexual attacks of rampaging Japanese soldiers. Risking his life, he saved the lives of a quarter of a million Chinese who had poured into the safety zone that was only two and a half square miles. Furthermore, he opened his private residence to more than six hundred Chinese men, women, and children. For his heroic acts, John Rabe is often called China's Oskar Schindler, the man credited with saving hundreds of Jews from the Nazis. The grateful refugees of Nanking called him "the Living Buddha." The following excerpts are from his diaries, which were posthumously published in Germany as recently as 1997 under the title *Gute Deutsche von Nanking.*

QUESTIONS TO CONSIDER

1. What is genocide? Did the Japanese army in Nanking commit genocide? How do Japanese revisionist historians view the "rape of Nanking"? Discuss fully.
2. Compare and contrast Oskar Schindler's story with that of John Rabe in Nanking. Why did both men risk their own lives to save others? Were they heroes? How do you define a hero?
3. Choose one or two cases of genocide from Readings 69, 70, 71, and 72 and compare and contrast them with the brutality perpetrated by Japan's invading army in Nanking in 1937.
4. Do you see any new historic trend or improvement in humankind's inhumanity in times of war? Is punishment for war crimes an effective deterrent to wartime atrocities?

21 SEPTEMBER 1937

Many Americans and Germans have departed as well.[1] I've been seriously considering the matter from all sides these last few nights. It wasn't because I love adventure that

---

[1]Many foreigners along with rich and better off Chinese had left Nanking, which was the capital of the Nationalist China, before the arrival of the invading army of Japan.

From Edwin Wickart, ed., and John Woods, trans., *The Good Man of Nanking: The Diaries of John Rabe,* pp. 4–5, 28–29, 67, 77, 78–79, 84–85, *passim.* Copyright © 1998 by Alfred A. Knopf, Inc. Endpaper maps copyright © 1998 by David Lindroth, Inc. Used by permission of Alfred A. Knopf, a division of Random House, Inc.

I returned here from the safety of Peitaiho, but primarily to protect my property and to represent Siemens's interests. Of course the company can't—nor does it—expect me to get myself killed here on its behalf. Besides, I haven't the least desire to put my life at risk for the sake of either the company's or my own property; but there is a question of morality here, and as a reputable Hamburg businessman, so far I haven't been able to side-step it.

Our Chinese servants and employees, about 30 people in all including immediate families, have eyes only for their "master." If I stay, they will loyally remain at their posts to the end. I saw the same thing happen before in the wars up north. If I run, then the company and my own house will not just be left deserted, but they will probably be plundered as well. Apart from that, and as unpleasant as that would be, I cannot bring myself for now to betray the trust these people have put in me. And it is touching to see how they believe in me, even the most useless people whom I would gladly have sent packing during peacetime. I gave Mr. Han, my assistant, an advance on his salary so that he could send his wife and two children to safety in Taianfu. He quite frankly admits: "Where you stay, I stay too. If you go, I go along!"

Under such circumstances, can I, may I, cut and run? I don't think so. Anyone who has ever sat in a dugout and held a trembling Chinese child in each hand through the long hours of an air raid can understand what I feel.

Finally—subconsciously—there's a last, and the not least important, reason that makes my sticking it out here seem simply a matter of course. I am a member of the NSDAP, and temporarily even held the office of local deputy leader.

22 NOVEMBER

Five P.M. meeting of the International Committee for Establishing a Neutral Zone for Noncombatants in Nanking. They elect me chairman. My protests are to no avail. I give in for the sake of a good cause. I hope I prove worthy of the post, which can very well become important. The German ambassador, to whom I introduce Dr. Smythe shortly before he leaves to board his ship, gives his consent to the text of a telegram to be sent to the Japanese ambassador by way of the American consulate general in Shanghai, which has a wireless. We already have the permission of the English and American ambassadors. . . . The text of the telegram reads in part as follows:

> An international committee composed of nationals of Denmark, Germany, Great Britain, and the United States, desires to suggest to the Chinese and Japanese authorities the establishment of a Safety Zone for Civilian Refugees in the unfortunate event of hostilities at or near Nanking. The International Committee will undertake to secure from the Chinese authorities specific guarantees that the proposed "Safety Zone" will be made free and kept free from military establishments and offices, including those of communications; from the presence of armed men other than civilian police with pistols; and from the passage of soldiers or military officers in any capacity. The International Committee would inspect and observe the Safety Zone to see that these undertakings are satisfactorily carried out. . . .

The International Committee earnestly hopes that the Japanese authorities may find it possible for humanitarian reasons to respect the civilian character of this Safety Zone.

13 DECEMBER

The Japanese march through the city in groups of ten to twenty soldiers and loot the shops. If I had not seen it with my own eyes I would not have believed it. They smash open windows and doors and take whatever they like. Allegedly because they're short of rations. I watched with my own eyes as they looted the café of our German baker Herr Kiessling. Hempel's hotel was broken into as well, as was almost every shop on Chung Shang and Taiping Road. Some Japanese soldiers dragged their booty away in crates, others requisitioned rickshas to transport their stolen goods to safety.

Of the perhaps one thousand disarmed soldiers that we had quartered at the Ministry of Justice, between 400 and 500 were driven from it with their hands tied. We assume they were shot since we later heard several salvos of machine-gun fire. These events have left us frozen with horror.

We may no longer enter the Foreign Ministry, where we took wounded soldiers. Chinese doctors and nursing personnel are not allowed into the building, either.

We manage quickly to find lodging in some vacant buildings for a group of 125 Chinese refugees, before they fall into the hands of the Japanese military. Mr. Han says that three young girls of about 14 or 15 have been dragged from a house in our neighborhood. Doctor Bates reports that even in the Safety Zone refugees in various houses have been robbed of their few paltry possessions. At various times troops of Japanese soldiers enter my private residence as well, but when I arrive and hold my swastika armband under their noses, they leave.[2] There's no love for the American flag. A car belonging to Mr. Sone, one of our committee members, had its American flag ripped off and was then stolen.

17 DECEMBER

Two Japanese soldiers have climbed over the garden wall and are about to break into our house. When I appear they give the excuse that they saw two Chinese soldiers climb over the wall. When I show them my party badge they return the same way they came.

In one of the houses in the narrow street behind my garden wall, a woman was raped, and then wounded in the neck with a bayonet. I manage to get an ambulance so we can take her to Kulou Hospital. There are about 200 refugees in the garden now. They fall to their knees when you walk by, even though in all this misery we barely know up from down ourselves. One of the Americans put it this way: "The Safety Zone has turned into a public house for the Japanese soldiers."

That's very close to the truth. Last night up to 1,000 women and girls are said to have been raped, about 100 girls at Ginling Girls College alone. You hear of nothing but rape. If husbands or brothers intervene, they're shot. What you hear and see on all sides is the brutality and bestiality of the Japanese soldiery.

[2]Nazi Germany was a military ally of Japan during World War II.

At 6 P.M. I bring 60 straw mats to my refugees in the garden. Great joy! Four Japanese soldiers scramble over the garden wall again. I catch three of them on the spot and chase them off. The fourth works his way through the rows of refugees as far as the main iron gate, where I nab him and politely escort him out the door. No sooner are these fellows outside than they take off at a run. They don't want to tangle with a German.

Usually all I have to do is shout "Deutsch" and "Hitler" and they turn polite, whereas the Americans have real trouble getting their way. Our letter of protest directed to the Japanese embassy has apparently made a lasting impression on Mr. Kiyoshi Fukui, the 2nd secretary. At any rate he promised that he would pass the letter on at once to the highest level of army command.

18 DECEMBER

6:00 P.M.

I arrive home just in time to meet up with a pair of Japanese soldiers who had entered by way of the garden wall. One of the two has already taken off his uniform and sidearm and is about to violate one of the girls among the refugees, when I come up and demand that he return at once the same way he came. The other fellow is already sitting astraddle the wall when he spots me and a gentle push sends him on his way.

At 8 o'clock Herr Hatz shows up in a truck with a Japanese police commissioner and a whole battery of gendarmes, who are supposed to guard Ginling College tonight. Our protest at the Japanese embassy already seems to have helped a little.

I open the gate at our Committee Headquarters at Ninhai Lu No. 5 in order to let in a number of women and children who have fled to us. The wailing of these poor women and children echoes in my ears for hours afterward. The 5,500 square feet in my garden and grounds keep filling up with more and more refugees. There must be about 300 people living here with me now. My house is considered the safest spot. When I'm at home that's probably true, for I physically remove each intruder, but when I'm gone the safety doesn't amount to much. Japanese notices pasted on doors do little good. The soldiers pay no attention to them. Most climb over the garden wall anyway. Chang's wife became so ill during the night that we had to take her to Kulou Hospital early this morning. Unfortunately several nurses at Kulou Hospital have been raped as well.

21 DECEMBER

The Americans are indeed in a bad way. While I succeed in making a suitable impression by pompously pointing to my swastika armband and party badge, and at the German flags in my house, the Japanese have no regard whatever for the American flag.

66 Adolf Hitler, The Obersalzberg Speech

On August 22, 1939, Adolf Hitler invited his chief military commanders and commanding generals, including Air Marshall Hermann Göring, to his Bavarian retreat high in the Obersalzberg. Here in the rarified mountain air, he informed his military commanders of his plans for war. No complete text of this speech survives, so what we have here is a collation of notes of the generals who were in attendance. Although no one disputes the overall outline and argument of this speech, some historians caution that the graphic language attributed to Hitler in this speech, for example, his identification with Genghis Khan and such phrases as "Chamberlain or some other such pig of a fellow," might have been inserted afterward by his dissident generals, who wanted to portray Hitler as brutally as possible. This florid language, if inserted by a dissident, could have been used to alert his adversaries, such as British Prime Minister Neville Chamberlain, or the French Premier Édouard Daladier, that by August 1939, Hitler was determined to go to war immediately. Yet, one cannot dismiss entirely the authenticity of this speech. Hitler was quite unpredictable, and the sensational and vulgar rhetoric of this text can be found in many of his other speeches. Despite the emotional character and questions of attribution, the Obersalzberg speech remains important because it provides a good insight into Hitler's grasp of history and his strategic thinking just on the eve of his September 1, 1939, attack on Poland. Similar versions of this speech have been printed in the principal documents of the Nuremberg War Trials (1945–1946), as well as in the official U.S. and British government documents on Hitler and the coming of World War II.

QUESTIONS TO CONSIDER

1. What does Hitler think of Stalin, his Italian and Japanese allies, and the leaders of Britain, France, and Turkey?
2. Hitler asks, "Who after all is today speaking about the destruction of the Armenians?" What does this suggest about his views of the twentieth century's first large-scale genocide?
3. How does Hitler view the coming war? What does he plan for Poland and the Polish people? How closely did he follow these plans?

Decision to attack Poland was arrived at in spring. Originally there was fear that because of the political constellation we would have to strike at the same time against England, France, Russia and Poland. This risk too we should have had to take. Göring had demonstrated to us that his Four-Year Plan is a failure and that we are at the end of our strength, if we do not achieve victory in a coming war.

From *Documents on British Foreign Policy, 1919–1939*, ed. E.L. Woodward and Rohan Butler, 3rd series (London: HMSO, 1954), 7:258–60.

Since the autumn of 1938 and since I have realised that Japan will not go with us unconditionally and that Mussolini is endangered by that nitwit of a King and the treacherous scoundrel of a Crown Prince, I decided to go with Stalin. After all there are only three great statesmen in the world, Stalin, I and Mussolini. Mussolini is the weakest, for he has been able to break the power neither of the crown nor of the Church. Stalin and I are the only ones who visualise the future. So in a few weeks hence I shall stretch out my hand to Stalin at the common German-Russian frontier and with him undertake to re-distribute the world.

Our strength lies in our quickness and in our brutality; Genghis Khan has sent millions of women and children into death knowingly and with a light heart. History sees in him only the great founder of States. As to what the weak Western European civilisation asserts about me, that is of no account. I have given the command and I shall shoot everyone who utters one word of criticism, for the goal to be obtained in the war is not that of reaching certain lines but of physically demolishing the opponent. And so for the present only in the East I have put my death-head formations[1] in place with the command relentlessly and without compassion to send into death many women and children of Polish origin and language. Only thus we can gain the living space that we need. Who after all is today speaking about the destruction of the Armenians?

Colonel-General von Brauchitsch has promised me to bring the war against Poland to a close within a few weeks. Had he reported to me that he needs two years or even only one year, I should not have given the command to march and should have allied myself temporarily with England instead of Russia for we cannot conduct a long war. To be sure a new situation has arisen. I experienced those poor worms Daladier and Chamberlain in Munich. They will be too cowardly to attack. They won't go beyond a blockade. Against that we have our autarchy and the Russian raw materials.

Poland will be depopulated and settled with Germans. My pact with the Poles was merely conceived of as a gaining of time. As for the rest, gentlemen, the fate of Russia will be exactly the same as I am now going through with in the case of Poland. After Stalin's death—he is a very sick man—we will break the Soviet Union. Then there will begin the dawn of the German rule of the earth.

The little States cannot scare me. After Kemal's death Turkey is governed by "*cretins*" and half idiots. Carol of Roumania is through and through the corrupt slave of his sexual instincts. The King of Belgium and the Nordic kings are soft jumping jacks who are dependent upon the good digestions of their over-eating and tired peoples.

We shall have to take into the bargain the defection of Japan. I gave Japan a full year's time. The Emperor is a counterpart to the last Czar—weak, cowardly, undecided. May he become a victim of the revolution. My going together with Japan never was popular. We shall continue to create disturbances in the Far East and in Arabia. Let us think as "gentlemen" and let us see in these peoples at best lacquered half maniacs who are anxious to experience the whip.

The opportunity is as favourable as never before. I have but one worry, namely that Chamberlain or some other such pig of a fellow ("Saukerl") will come at the last moment with proposals or with ratting ("Umfall"). He will fly down the stairs, even if I shall personally have to trample on his belly in the eyes of the photographers.

---

[1]The S.S. Death's Head formations were principally employed in peacetime in guarding concentration camps. With the S.S. Verfügungstruppen, they formed the nucleus of the Waffen S.S.

No, it is too late for this. The attack upon and the destruction of Poland begins Saturday early. I shall let a few companies in Polish uniform attack in Upper Silesia or in the Protectorate. Whether the world believes it is quite indifferent ("scheissegal"). The world believes only in success.

For you, gentlemen, fame and honour are beginning as they have not since centuries. Be hard, be without mercy, act more quickly and brutally than the others. The citizens of Western Europe must tremble with horror. That is the most human way of conducting a war. For it scares the others off.

The new method of conducting war corresponds to the new drawing of the frontiers. A war extending from Reval, Lublin, Kaschau to the mouth of the Danube. The rest will be given to the Russians. Ribbentrop has orders to make every offer and to accept every demand. In the West I reserve to myself the right to determine the strategically best line. Here one will be able to work with Protectorate regions, such as Holland, Belgium and French Lorraine.

And now, on to the enemy, in Warsaw we will celebrate our reunion.

The speech was received with enthusiasm. Göring jumped on a table, thanked blood-thirstily and made bloodthirsty promises. He danced like a wild man. The few that had misgivings remained quiet. (Here a line of the memorandum is missing in order no doubt to protect the source of information.)

67 The Atlantic Charter

President Franklin D. Roosevelt's concern over the war in Europe sharply increased in 1940 with the collapse of France and the potential expansion of Hitler's empire to the New World if Britain fell. In September, Roosevelt tried to strengthen Britain's ability to resist by exchanging American destroyers for the right to lease naval and air bases in British Commonwealth territories. The following spring, although the United States was technically neutral, Roosevelt urged the passage of the Lend-Lease Act to provide war materials to those nations fighting the Axis powers. While taking these important steps on the road to war, President Roosevelt outlined his objectives and the national interest in his 1941 State of the Union Address, which became known as his "Four Freedoms" speech.

Later that summer, Roosevelt and Churchill met for a shipboard conference off Argentia, Newfoundland, and forged a closer alignment with their joint statement of war aims known as the Atlantic Charter.

QUESTIONS TO CONSIDER

1. Why would the influential Japanese newspaper *Asahi* regard the Atlantic Charter, particularly its fourth article, as a de facto declaration of war by the United States and Great Britain (see Reading 62)?
2. Would Woodrow Wilson approve of this charter? Why? Why not? (See Reading 58.)

Joint declaration of the President of the United States of America and the Prime Minister, Mr. Churchill, representing His Majesty's Government in the United Kingdom, being met together, deem it right to make known certain common principles in the national policies of their respective countries on which they base their hopes for a better future for the world.

First, their countries seek no aggrandizement, territorial or other;

Second, they desire to see no territorial changes that do not accord with the freely expressed wishes of the peoples concerned;

Third, they respect the right of all peoples to choose the form of government under which they will live; and they wish to see sovereign rights and self-government restored to those who have been forcibly deprived of them;

Fourth, they will endeavor, with due respect for their existing obligations, to further the enjoyment by all states, great or small, victor or vanquished, of access, on equal terms, to the trade and to the raw materials of the world which are needed for their economic prosperity;

Fifth, they desire to bring about the fullest collaboration between all nations in the economic field with the object of securing, for all, improved labor standards, economic advancement, and social security;

Sixth, after the final destruction of the Nazi tyranny, they hope to see established a peace which will afford to all nations the means of dwelling in safety within their own boundaries, and which will afford assurance that all the men in all the lands may live out their lives in freedom from fear and want;

Seventh, such a peace should enable all men to traverse the high seas and oceans without hindrance;

Eighth, they believe that all the nations of the world, for realistic as well as spiritual reasons, must come to the abandonment of the use of force. Since no future peace can be maintained if land, sea, or air armaments continue to be employed by nations which threaten, or may threaten, aggression outside of their frontiers, they believe, pending the establishment of a wider and permanent system of general security, that the disarmament of such nations is essential. They will likewise aid and encourage all other practicable measures which will lighten for peace-loving peoples the crushing burden of armaments.

Franklin D. Roosevelt
Winston S. Churchill

From U.S. Department of State, *Peace and War: United States Foreign Policy, 1931–1941,* Publication 1983 (Washington, DC: Government Printing Office, 1943), pp. 718–19.

68 "Tojo Makes Plea of Self Defense"

Soon after Japan's defeat in World War II, twenty-eight Japanese leaders[1] who had held high posts in the Japanese government and military between 1928 and 1945 were apprehended by the U.S. occupation authorities and charged with fifty-five counts of war crimes, which were grouped in three categories: (1) crimes against peace (first 36 counts), namely, the planning, preparation, initiation, or waging of a declared or undeclared war of aggression, or a war in violation of international law, treaties, agreements, or assurances, or participation in a common plan, or conspiring for the accomplishment of any of the foregoing; (2) murder (counts 37 through 52); and (3) conventional war crimes, namely, violations of the laws or customs of war, and crimes against humanity, namely, murder, extermination, enslavement, deportation, and other inhumane acts committed before or during the war (counts 53, 54, and 55).[2] They were tried by the International Military Tribunal for the Far East (I.M.T.F.E.), which was created on January 19, 1946, by the Supreme Commander of the Allied Powers in Japan in accordance with the directive of the U.S. Joint Chiefs of Staff. The Supreme Commander of the Allied Powers, General Douglas MacArthur, appointed eleven justices to the bench, one from each of the eleven victorious nations.[3] After nearly two and a half years of trial, despite a vigorous defense by the defense counsels, the defendants themselves and the jurists, including one of the justices, on the grounds that they had acted in self-defense of their nation, all twenty-five defendants were found guilty.[4] Seven of them–former Prime Minister General Hideki Tojo, former Foreign Minister Koki Hirota, and five generals–received death sentences by hanging, and the remaining eighteen received various prison terms, ranging from seven years to life. Eight of the eleven justices supported the judgment of the tribunal. Justice Radhabinod Pal of India, the leading dissenter, questioned, among other things, the justness of the victors' deciding whether or not the vanquished resorted to war in self-defense. Justice Pal was apprehensive that the notion that "might makes right" would become an accepted rule in the international system. On December 23, 1948, the seven defendants were hanged at Sugamo Prison in Tokyo.

[1]Among them were four former prime ministers, four former foreign ministers, five former war ministers, two former navy ministers, four former ambassadors, and four field commanders.

[2]Charter of the International Military Tribunal for the Far East, Section II, Article 5 in Richard H. Minear, *Victor's Justice, The Tokyo War Crimes Trial* (Princeton, NJ: Princeton University Press, 1971), pp. 186–87.

[3]The eleven nations were the United States, the Republic of China, the United Kingdom, the Soviet Union, Australia, Canada, France, the Netherlands, New Zealand, India, and the Philippines.

[4]Of the original twenty-eight defendants, two had died during the trial and one had been determined mentally unfit and dismissed.

During the trial, General Hideki Tojo, leader of the hawkish ultranationalistic faction of the Imperial Army of Japan, who became prime minister in October 1941, less than two months before the Pearl Harbor attack, and remained in that post until July 1944, justified what he and Japan did in the name of national survival and anticommunism. In a 60,000-word written testimony, he accused the United States and Britain of forcing Japan into war and accepted full responsibility for his and Japan's actions. He also strongly defended Emperor Hirohito's innocence in starting the war. The following excerpts are an edited version of a *New York Times* report of the trial.

QUESTIONS TO CONSIDER

1. Was the judgment at the Tokyo trial an exercise in victors' justice, as alleged by some jurists? Why? Why not?
2. How valid was the argument put up by Tojo and other defendants at the trial that Japan was forced by the United States and Britain into war?
3. Should a sovereign nation retain complete freedom of action concerning questions vital to its existence?

Defiantly the 63 year old career soldier who attempted suicide two years ago on the heels of the Japanese surrender, told the eleven-nation court that the Western Allies maneuvered so as to force Japan to fire the first shot "in self-defense" to preserve her "national existence."

Japan's leaders, including Emperor Hirohito, Tojo testified, went to war reluctantly and only after peaceful means of settlement had been exhausted. Economic pressure had brought the nation in 1941 "to the point of annihilation," he asserted. But Japan attempted to fight the war honorably, Tojo implied.

His government had no intention of making the Pearl Harbor attack a sneak affair, Tojo said. . . .

The treatment of prisoners, he indicated, could in part be explained by Japanese psychology.

As for the Doolittle fliers[1] who were caught after the attack on Tokyo in April 1942, their execution, he asserted, followed "the atrocities they committed in violation of international law and regulations" in the bombing of civilian population.

Tojo, the last but one of the remaining twenty-five top war leaders of Japan to open his defense, gave his testimony in a 60,000-word affidavit. A defense attorney began reading the document to the court while Tojo sat erect in the witness box, earphones clamped to his head. . . .

In effect a long bill of indictment against the Allied nations, restating in much detail Japan's pre-war charges of blockade, encirclement, bad faith and aid to a "hos-

---

[1]James H. Doolittle, an American general, then lieutenant colonel, led the first daring air raid on Tokyo with 16 B-25 bombers that took off from the U.S.S. Hornet on April 18, 1942, at the height of World War II.

From "Tojo Makes Plea of Self Defense" by Lindsey Parrot, *The New York Times*, December 26, 1947. Copyright © 1947 by The New York Times Company. Reprinted by permission.

tile" China. Tojo's affidavit roundly attacked the prosecution's main contention that the Japanese leaders formed a conspiracy for war.

"I fail utterly to understand the reasoning of the prosecution in this fantastic accusation," Tojo wrote.

Under the Japanese imperial system with its "fundamental and unchangeable administrative processes," he asserted, such a conspiracy, continuing over a long period and involving many changes of administration was "unthinkable to persons of reason and intelligence."

For Japan's defeat in the war Tojo said he as Premier accepted full responsibility, but he challenged the "legal or criminal" responsibility that the Allied prosecutors attach to him.

"Never at any time did I ever conceive that the waging of this war would or could be challenged by the victors as an international crime," his affidavit concluded, "or that regularly constituted officials of the vanquished nation would be charged individually as criminals under any recognized international law or under alleged violations of treaties between nations."

In one long passage of the affidavit Tojo made vigorous effort to exculpate Emperor Hirohito from all blame for the war as a sovereign who constantly pressed his Ministers to seek other means of settlement but who eventually was powerless to alter the course of events.

"Even though some explanation of this point has previously been given by me, further exposition should be made so that, with regard to the Emperor's position, there be no possibility of misconstruction," Tojo wrote. "That to me is quite important."

"The Emperor had no free choice in the governmental structure setting up the Cabinet and Supreme Command. He was not in a position to reject the recommendations and advice of the Cabinet and the High Command."

Although Hirohito might have advanced personal "hopes and wishes" through Marquis Koichi Kido, Lord Keeper of the Privy Seal, Tojo said, even such imperial expressions were subject to Cabinet and military examination.

"The recommendations and suggestions after this careful examination had to be approved by the Emperor and never to be rejected," the statement said. "That was the position of the Emperor beforehand during this most perplexing period in the history of the Japanese Empire."

"These facts being what they are," this part of the argument concluded, "it was solely upon the Cabinet and the Supreme Command that responsibility lay for the political, diplomatic and military affairs of the nation. Accordingly, full responsibility for the decision of Dec. 1, 1941 for war is that of the Cabinet Ministers and members of the High Command and absolutely not the responsibility of the Emperor."

Tojo asserted two main factors forced Japan into war, first "pressure" by Britain and the United States and second national fear of communism.

While the United States and Britain, he wrote, would have been content with nothing less than Japan's evacuation of China and abandonment by the Japanese of all advantages they had gained there in almost ten years of warfare, Japan feared the "bolshevization of Asia" would be the result. To this thesis Tojo reverted several times.

In the Konoye Cabinet of 1939 in which he served as War Minister, Tojo said he expressed this viewpoint regarding the "unconditional withdrawal" from China as sought by the United States.

"Chinese contempt for Japan will expand if we retire from China unconditionally because of United States duress. Relations between Japan and China will grow worse coupled with the thorough-going resistance against Japan maintained by the

Communists in China. Certainly China Incident No. 2 and China Incident No. 3 would result, and the repercussions at our loss of prestige would be keenly felt in Manchuria and Korea."

During his own Premiership (Oct. 18, 1941 to July 22, 1944) and up to the end of the war, Tojo asserted, Japan's policy was to preserve peace with Russia despite urgings from Germany, although the Soviet Union after Yalta[2] "actually had pledged itself to enter the war against Japan on the promise of territorial gains even while the (nonaggression) treaty was still valid and that nation actually attacked Japan while the agreement still was in force."

Japan has always been deeply concerned over communism in Asia, Tojo said.

"She realized that the activities of the Chinese Communist party were among the important causes preventing the establishment of peace between Japan and China in the China Incident," he went on. "Thus she made the joint prevention of communism one of the conditions for settlement of the Incident and also made prevention of communism an essential policy among the independent states of East Asia.

"This was all done with a view to saving East Asia from the danger of bolshevization and at the same time to making herself a barrier against world bolshevization. The present condition of the world two years after the end of World War II eloquently tells how important these barriers were for the peace of the world."

Tojo used a large part of his affidavit to set out what he argued was a "cold war" waged by Britain and the United States against Japan in the Nineteen Thirties and which, he argued, forced upon Japan nearly every step she took outside her borders, including her understanding with the Berlin-Rome Axis.

On more than one occasion, after Japan was cut off from food, rubber and petroleum by Allied economic measures after her credits had been frozen and after the United States began on a tremendously expanding arms program, Tojo said Japanese leaders feared armed attack in the Pacific.

"We did not anticipate at the time (1940–41) that America was so directing the war as to force Japan to make the first overt act," he wrote.

Such measures as the construction of air bases in French Indo-China, to which the Allies objected as presaging aggression, Tojo said were "protection against attacks from the south." From this direction, Japan's leaders thought, he said, might come an "onslaught by the 'have' nations against the Japanese Empire."[3]

Patterns of Genocide

Large-scale murders of the vanquished by victors have occurred at intervals throughout most of the history of civilization, but genocide—literally, "species-killing," the systematic attempt to eradicate whole ethnic groups seen as alien, hostile, and inferior—has been a more modern phenomenon, beginning with Turkish attempts to eliminate Armenians in

---

[2]In February 1945, three Allied leaders, Franklin D. Roosevelt, Winston Churchill, and Joseph Stalin, met at Yalta to confer on the execution of the war and the postwar settlement.

[3]"Have" nations refer, in this case, particularly to the United States and Britain.

territories under Turkish control after World War I. Indeed, the Armenian genocide of 1915, resulting in the death of more than a million Armenians, set the pattern for later twentieth-century genocides.

It was, however, the racially motivated Nazi mass murders that gave the most notoriety to the term "genocide." Adolf Hitler and his Nazi followers were determined to exterminate "racially inferior" Europeans—especially Jews from Nazi-occupied Europe. Between 1939 and 1945, 3 million Poles; uncounted thousands of Slavs, Gypsies, and Russians; and at least 7 million Jews were killed.

Genocidal efforts in the Balkans and in Rwanda have not yet approached the numbers of people killed by the Nazis in absolute terms, but in terms of population percentages the number of victims has been very high. Recurring instances of an inflamed desire to kill off members of an "enemy" ethnic group, with whom the group doing the killing has lived in peace for centuries, may well prove to be one of the most serious problems of the twentieth century inherited by the twenty-first.

69 Roupen of Sassoun, Eyewitness to Armenia's Genocide

All the belligerents in World War I had internal political problems, but the Turkish Empire had special problems with its large minority populations. Fearful that its huge Armenian population would be too sympathetic to its enemy, Russia, in the spring of 1915, the Turkish military authorities decided to remove Armenians from eastern Turkey and march them south to the city to Aleppo, where they would be sent into the Syrian desert or marched east into the Tigris-Euphrates valley. On April 24, 1915, the first roundup of Armenians began. Throughout the spring and summer of 1915, large elements of the Armenian population were removed from their homes, stripped of their property, and marched into the desert; in many cases, they were killed in their villages. Although the exact numbers are difficult to determine, it is likely that more than a million Armenians were slaughtered in 1915. Mr. Roupen, an Armenian resident of Sassoun District, provided this eyewitness account of the 1915 summer massacres in an interview with Mr. A.S. Safrastian. In his account, he refers to the Kurds, another minority under Turkish rule, who were frequently used by the Turks to attack the Armenians.

QUESTIONS TO CONSIDER

1. How would you compare this eyewitness account of "ethnic cleansing" with other accounts in this section? Are there any common characteristics?

2. Why would the Turkish military use Kurdish troops against Armenians?
3. Are Armenian women targeted for any special treatment? Why would women be a special target in genocide (see Reading 70)?
4. Were the Turkish concerns about Armenians supporting Russians justified? Why? Why not?

Early in July, the authorities ordered the Armenians to surrender their arms, and pay a large money ransom. The leading Armenians of the town and the headmen of the villages were subjected to revolting tortures. Their finger nails and then their toe nails were forcibly extracted; their teeth were knocked out, and in some cases their noses were whittled down, the victims being thus done to death under shocking, lingering agonies. The female relatives of the victims who came to the rescue were outraged in public before the very eyes of their mutilated husbands and brothers. The shrieks and death-cries of the victims filled the air, yet they did not move the Turkish beast. The same process of disarmament was carried out in the large Armenian villages of Khaskegh, Franknorshen, etc., and on the slightest show of resistance men and women were done to death in the manner described above. On the 10th July, large contingents of troops, followed by bands of criminals released from the prisons, began to round up the able-bodied men from all the villages. In the 100 villages of the plain of Moush most of the villagers took up any arms they possessed and offered a desperate resistance in various favourable positions. In the natural order of things the ammunition soon gave out in most villages, and there followed what is perhaps one of the greatest crimes in all history. Those who had no arms and had done nothing against the authorities were herded into various camps and bayoneted in cold blood.

In the town of Moush itself the Armenians, under the leadership of Gotoyan and others, entrenched themselves in the churches and stone-built houses and fought for four days in self-defense. The Turkish artillery, manned by German officers, made short work of all the Armenian positions. Every one of the Armenians, leaders as well as men, was killed fighting; and when the silence of death reigned over the ruins of churches and the rest, the Moslem rabble made a descent upon the women and children and drove them out of the town into large camps which had already been prepared for the peasant women and children. The ghastly scenes which followed may indeed sound incredible, yet these reports have been confirmed from Russian sources beyond all doubt.

The shortest method for disposing of the women and children concentrated in the various camps was to burn them. Fire was set to large wooden sheds in Alidjan, Megrakom, Khaskegh, and other Armenian villages, and these absolutely helpless women and children were roasted to death. Many went mad and threw their children away; some knelt down and prayed amid the flames in which their bodies were burning; others shrieked and cried for help which came from nowhere. And the executioners, who seem to have been unmoved by this unparalleled savagery, grasped infants by one leg and hurled them into the fire, calling out to the burning mothers: "Here are your lions." Turkish prisoners who had apparently witnessed some of these scenes were horrified and maddened at remembering the sight. They told the Russians that the stench of the burning human flesh permeated the air for many days after.

From The Treatment of Armenians in the Ottoman Empire: Documents Presented to Viscount Grey of Fallodon, Secretary of State for Foreign Affairs, with a Preface by Viscount Bryce (London: HMSO, 1916), pp. 85–87.

Under present circumstances it is impossible to say how many Armenians, out of a population of 60,000 in the plain of Moush, are left alive; the one fact which can be recorded at present is that now and then some survivors escape through the mountains and reach the Russian lines to give further details of the unparalleled crime perpetrated in Moush during July.

The Massacres in Sassoun.—While the "Butcher" battalions of Djevdet Bey and the regulars of Kiazim Bey were engaged in Bitlis and Moush, some cavalry were sent to Sassoun early in July to encourage the Kurds who had been defeated by the Armenians at the beginning of June. The Turkish cavalry invaded the lower valley of Sassoun and captured a few villages after stout fighting. In the meantime the reorganized Kurdish tribes attempted to close on Sassoun from the south, west, and north. During the last fortnight of July almost incessant fighting went on, sometimes even during the night. On the whole, the Armenians held their own on all fronts and expelled the Kurds from their advanced positions. However, the people of Sassoun had other anxieties to worry about. The population had doubled since their brothers who had escaped from the plains had sought refuge in their mountains; the millet crop of the last season had been a failure; all honey, fruit, and other local produce had been consumed, and the people had been feeding on unsalted roast mutton (they had not even any salt to make the mutton more sustaining); finally, the ammunition was in no way sufficient for the requirements of heavy fighting. But the worst had yet to come. Kiazim Bey, after reducing the town and the plain of Moush, rushed his army to Sassoun for a new effort to overwhelm these brave mountaineers. Fighting was renewed on all fronts throughout the Sassoun district. Big guns made carnage among the Armenian ranks. Roupen tells me that Gorioun, Dikran, and twenty other of their best fighters were killed by a single shell, which burst in their midst. Encouraged by the presence of guns, the cavalry and Kurds pushed on with relentless energy.

The Armenians were compelled to abandon the outlying lines of their defence and were retreating day by day into the heights of Antok, the central block of the mountains, some 10,000 feet high. The non-combatant women and children and their large flocks of cattle greatly hampered the free movements of the defenders, whose number had already been reduced from 3,000 to about half that figure. Terrible confusion prevailed during the Turkish attacks as well as the Armenian counterattacks. Many of the Armenians smashed their rifles after firing the last cartridge and grasped their revolvers and daggers. The Turkish regulars and Kurds, amounting now to something like 30,000 altogether, pushed higher and higher up the heights and surrounded the main Armenian position at close quarters. Then followed one of those desperate and heroic struggles for life which have always been the pride of mountaineers. Men, women and children fought with knives, scythes, stones, and anything else they could handle. They rolled blocks of stone down the steep slopes, killing many of the enemy. In a frightful hand-to-hand combat, women were seen thrusting their knives into the throats of Turks and thus accounting for many of them. On the 5th August, the last day of the fighting, the blood-stained rocks of Antok were captured by the Turks. The Armenian warriors of Sassoun, except those who had worked round to the rear of the Turks to attack them on their flanks, had died in battle. Several young women, who were in danger of falling into the Turks' hands, threw themselves from the rocks, some of them with their infants in their arms. The survivors have since been carrying on a guerilla warfare, living only on unsalted mutton and grass. The approaching winter may have disastrous consequences for the remnants of the Sassounli Armenians, because they have nothing to eat and no means of defending themselves.

70 Marie Claude Vaillant-Couturier, Testimony on the Gassing at Auschwitz

Although the Nazis did experiment with mass shootings to kill *Untermenschen* (subhumans), they eventually adopted a form of killing that used Cyclon-B gas in their extermination camps. The following account is part of an exchange between Charles Debost, the French deputy prosecutor at the Nuremberg War Crimes Tribunal (1945–1946) and Marie Claude Vaillant-Couturier, a thirty-three-year-old French woman who was arrested by the Nazis for her work in the French Resistance. Mme. Vaillant-Couturier spent more than three years in the concentration camp at Auschwitz.

QUESTIONS TO CONSIDER

1. What parts of Mme. Vaillant-Couturier's testimony suggest the mechanistic, industrialized, and thorough approach of the Nazis' genocide?
2. What ploys did the Nazis use to deceive the prisoners and mask the true purpose of the camps?
3. Why were women and children special targets of Hitler's genocide? Is this always the case?

MME. VAILLANT-COUTURIER: . . . [W]e saw the unsealing of the cars and the soldiers letting men, women, and children out of them. We then witnessed heart-rending scenes; old couples forced to part from each other, mothers made to abandon their young daughters, since the latter were sent to the camp, whereas mothers and children were sent to the gas chambers. All these people were unaware of the fate awaiting them. They were merely upset at being separated, but they did not know that they were going to their death. To render their welcome more pleasant at this time—June–July 1944—an orchestra composed of internees, all young and pretty girls dressed in little white blouses and navy blue skirts, played during the selection, at the arrival of the trains, gay tunes such as "The Merry Widow," the "Barcarolle" from "The Tales of Hoffman," and so forth. They were then informed that this was a labor camp and since they were not brought into the camp they saw only the small platform surrounded by flowering plants. Naturally, they could not realize what was in store for them. Those selected for the gas chamber, that is, the old people, mothers, and children, were escorted to a red-brick building.

M. DUBOST: These were not given an identification number?

VAILLANT-COUTURIER: No.

DUBOST: They were not tattooed?

From International Military Tribunal, *Trial of the Major War Criminals Before the International Military Tribunal, Nuremberg, 14 November 1945–1 October 1946*, 42 vols. (Nuremberg: International Military Tribunal, 1947), 6: 215–18.

VAILLANT-COUTURIER: No. They were not even counted.

DUBOST: You were tattooed?

VAILLANT-COUTURIER: Yes, look. [*The witness showed her arm.*] They were taken to a red brick building, which bore the letters "Baden," that is to say "Baths." There, to begin with, they were made to undress and given a towel before they went into the so-called shower room. Later on, at the time of the large convoys from Hungary, they had no more time left to play-act or to pretend; they were brutally undressed, and I know these details as I knew a little Jewess from France who lived with her family at the "Republique" district.

DUBOST: In Paris?

VAILLANT-COUTURIER: In Paris. She was called "little Marie" and she was the only one, the sole survivor of a family of nine. Her mother and her seven brothers and sisters had been gassed on arrival. When I met her she was employed to undress the babies before they were taken into the gas chamber. Once the people were undressed they took them into a room which was somewhat like a shower room, and gas capsules were thrown through an opening in the ceiling. An SS man would watch the effect produced through a porthole. At the end of 5 or 7 minutes, when the gas had completed its work, he gave the signal to open the doors; and men with gas masks—they too were internees—went into the room and removed the corpses. They told us that the internees must have suffered before dying, because they were closely clinging to one another and it was very difficult to separate them.

After that a special squad would come to pull out gold teeth and dentures; and again, when the bodies had been reduced to ashes, they would sift them in an attempt to recover gold.

At Auschwitz there were eight crematories but, as from 1944, these proved insufficient. The SS had large pits dug by the internees, where they put branches, sprinkled with gasoline, which they set on fire. Then they threw the corpses into the pits. From our block we could see after about three-quarters of an hour or an hour after the arrival of a convoy, large flames coming from the crematory, and the sky was lighted up by the burning pits.

One night we were awakened by terrifying cries. And we discovered, on the following day, from the men working in the Sonderkommando—the "Gas Kommando"—that on the preceding day, the gas supply having run out, they had thrown the children into the furnaces alive.

DUBOST: Can you tell us about the selections that were made at the beginning of winter?

VAILLANT-COUTURIER: . . . During Christmas 1944—no, 1943, Christmas 1943—when we were in quarantine, we saw, since we lived opposite Block 25, women brought to Block 25 stripped naked. Uncovered trucks were then driven up and on them the naked women were piled, as many as the trucks could hold. Each time a truck started, the infamous Hessler. . . ran after the truck and with his bludgeon repeatedly struck the naked women going to their death. They knew they were going to the gas chamber and tried to escape. They were massacred. They attempted to jump from the truck and we, from our own block, watched the trucks pass by and heard the grievous wailing of all those women who knew they were going to be gassed. Many of them could very well have lived on, since they were suffering only from scabies and were, perhaps, a little too undernourished. . . .

Since the Jewesses were sent to Auschwitz with their entire families and since they had been told that this was a sort of ghetto and were advised to bring all their goods and chattels along, they consequently brought considerable riches with them. As for the Jewesses from Salonika, I remember that on their arrival they were given picture postcards bearing the post office address of "Waldsee," a place which did not exist; and a printed text to be sent to their families, stating, "We are doing very well here; we have work and we are well treated. We await your arrival." I myself saw the cards in question; and the Schreiberinnen, that is, the secretaries of the block, were instructed to distribute them among the internees in order to post them to their families. I know that whole families arrived as a result of these postcards.

71 Ethnic Cleansing in Northwestern Bosnia: Three Witnesses

The dissolution of Yugoslavia, which began in 1991, resulted in great physical destruction. The once resplendent cities of Dubrovnik and Sarajevo are now battered, shell shocked, and strewn with rubble. By 1996 between 200,000 and 500,000 people were killed in the fighting, more than 3 million were refugees, and between 20,000 and 50,000 Bosnian Muslim women were raped.[1]

Ethnic, religious, and national rivalries in the Balkans run very deep. Certainly the animosity between the Muslim and the Christian populations in the Balkans stretches back over six hundred years of bloodied history. These ethnic and religious tensions came to a flash point in the years immediately following the death of Communist Party leader Marshal Tito, who had ruled Yugoslavia with considerable skill between 1945 and 1980. To assuage the ethnic rivalries after the death of Tito, the seat of government of Yugoslavia in the 1980s rotated among the six autonomous republics of Serbia, Croatia, Bosnia-Herzegovina, Macedonia, Slovenia, and Montenegro. But this system of rotation soon proved unworkable, and in 1991 Croatia and Slovenia declared their independence from Yugoslavia. Serbia, the largest of the republics, tried to forestall further dissolution, but the Republic of Bosnia-Herzegovina also declared its independence from Yugoslavia.

Of the six former Yugoslav republics, Bosnia is the most ethnically and religiously diverse. It is the only republic not established on a purely ethnic or religious basis. It was not until 1971 that the Muslims in Bosnia gained official separate recognition in the Yugoslav census. Prior to 1971, Muslims were identified as "Yugoslav" or "other." This distinction underscores the difficulty of defining precisely who and what a Bosnian is, because Muslims, Serbs, and Croats all lay claim to this designation. At the time of the 1992 referendum on independence,

[1] Sabrina Petra Ramet, "Europe's Painful Transition," *Current History* 95 (March 1996), p. 97; and Lenard J. Cohen, "Bosnia and Herzegovina: Fragile Peace in a Segmented State," ibid., p. 112.

the 4 million Bosnians were divided approximately into a population that was 44 percent Muslim, 31 percent Serbian, 17 percent Croatian, with the remainder being Gypsies, Albanians, and other Balkan or Western European people. This religious and ethnic division was further complicated by the fact that large concentrations of Serbs live in western Bosnia close to the Croatian border and large concentrations of Muslims live in eastern Bosnia close to the Serbian Republic. Beginning in the spring of 1992, brutal internecine fighting broke out among the Muslim, Serbian, and Croatian populations in Bosnia. The practice of "ethnic cleansing," or the forced removal (or annihilation) of a targeted population from its homes, villages, and cities, has been used by all groups against their enemies throughout this war. The following accounts are the statements of three Muslim survivors of Serbian ethnic cleansing in former Muslim-occupied areas of northwestern Bosnia-Herzegovina who were later interrogated in Zagreb, Croatia, and Wifferfuerth, Germany.

QUESTIONS TO CONSIDER

1. How do you account for the brutality suggested in these statements, particularly since in many cases the oppressor and victim had, until recently, been neighbors and whose people had lived in the same community for hundreds of years?
2. It has been estimated that between 20,000 and 50,000 Bosnian Muslim women have been raped in this ethnic conflict. Why would rape become one of the preferred tactics of ethnic cleansing? Why would the woman in the second account admit that after seeing her uncle in Zagreb, "Immediately after we exchanged greetings, he said he was inclined to kill me"?
3. Do you see any connections between the Serbian "Program of the Society of National Defense" (see Reading 38) and these accounts of Serbian ethnic cleansing?
4. How would these readings compare to the other accounts of genocide in this section?

A WITNESS FROM THE OMARSKA AND TRNOPOLJE CAMPS (NEAR PRIJEDOR); MUSLIM, BORN 1931, MALE

After the occupation of Kozarac, on May 27, 1992, I was imprisoned for the first time in Ciglane (the Brickyards) near Prijedor. I spent two days and three nights there. Then I was transferred to the "Keraterm" camp and after three days, I spent another

From Ante Beljo, ed., *Bosnia-Herzegovina: Genocide: Ethnic Cleansing in Northwestern Bosnia* (Zagreb: Croatian Information Centre, 1993), pp. 43–44, 77–79, 94–95. Reprinted by permission of the Croatian Information Centre.

six days in the Omarska camp. The last camp I was taken to was Trnopolje. The total number of days spent in various camps is one month and twenty days.

We heard that they took away children from their mothers and that the children were never returned. Women were separated from men. People slept on the concrete floor under the eaves of the brickyard. People would urinate at a spot ten meters away from the rest of the prisoners. The people imprisoned there were mostly from the village of Kozarac, the surrounding area of Prijedor and even from Bosanski Novi.

They caught us in such a manner that they used the Red Cross emblem and shouted into a megaphone: "Surrender, the Red Cross is waiting for you, you will be protected." There were twenty-one buses on the road and in front of them they separated women and children. We had to keep our heads lowered in the bus. Some buses drove straight through the woods and into Trnopolje, the others went to Ciglane (the Brickyards).

They would take people to Ciglane by night. Then machine-gun fire would be heard and that person never returned. I saw how they tortured a reserve policeman. First they broke his bones and then they put a piece of clothing into his mouth, drenched him in gas and set him on fire.

In Omarska they battered and interrogated people. I think that I saved myself by my persistent claim that I have no brothers or children. I did not betray anyone for being in battle or having arms. The camp was on the Banja Luka-Bosanski Novi railroad. There was also a mine with screening towers 20 meters high. Inside the towers there were bins (10×6 square meters) each containing some 300 people. These bins were used for screening ore. Each bin had four floors and there were 8,000 people in six rooms. We could not sleep but maybe doze on somebody's shoulder. There was no light. At last, after three days, we got one loaf of bread to share among six people. We urinated inside the same room we occupied. My two brothers were there and one of them died on the second floor. I did not dare look at him and I did not know that he died until I came to Trnopolje and was told so by some people. Approximately thirty-five or forty people died in six days. We got bread once every three days. Later we even got some beans. They would come to the door, and we would form a circle and take our food in a piece of cardboard or a milk pack that we found there. Every day they would give us as much water as we could catch in a piece of cardboard. On several occasions they put a hose through a steel mesh platform which separated each floor. The camp was divided into three sections: A, B and C. No one survived in the C section. I know that because later nobody from the C section came to Trnopolje. Three men from the village of Kozarac committed suicide. Two of them got out through the drain and the guards outside killed them. Besides the towers, there were also prisoners in the storage building. There were only thirty women in the camp. Interrogations were carried out every night. They put a gun barrel into my mouth and thus I lost seven teeth. Many did not return after the interrogation. Interrogators were educated Serbs. I know three of them. Two of them were Mladen Mitrović, our neighbor, and Slobodan Kuruzović, a local teacher. They were both some sort of commanders in the camp. They wore caps with the Chetnik insignia.[1] They beat camp prisoners. They used to tell us that they would kill thirty Muslims for each Serb killed.

I was the only one from the C section to mount a bus with forty-five men, mostly older in age. Young men would come to the camp, and the older ones would leave. Boys and young men did not stand a chance.

---

[1]Chetnik originally described the partisan guerrilla fighters who fought against the Germans in World War II, but in the context of the current ethnic cleansing it has come to refer to the Bosnian Serb military.

We arrived in the Trnopolje camp at 5:00 P.M. It was as if we were free at last. We were happy for being able to lie on the concrete. Upon my arrival, there were some 4,500 people in the central fenced-in area surrounded by guards. However, the entire village of Trnopolje was a camp, and seen from this angle it contained 10,000 prisoners. Some women were allowed to go home escorted by Chetniks and prepare meals. On the one side of the camp there was a highway, and on the other side there was a railroad where people were hurled into cattle wagons for the purpose of ethnic cleansing. From the cinema where I spent my first night, Bakir Mahić was taken out. They entered every night and took away people in succession, not according to any list or bill of indictment. They would take boys to a macadam road and tread on them. However, less people died here than in Omarska because there was some food. In the entire central camp area there was one school and one outdoor toilet. We got enough drinking water and A.V. would pass us a hose over the fence.

Once the camp commander gave me permission to go home for a visit and after 2.5 kilometers the guards caught us, forced us into a van (seven people on top of another seven people, etc., like logs), and then they returned us to the camp. They filed us in the clinic and there I saw captured Muslim doctors. In front of the clinic I saw how Chetniks carved the Chetnik insignia (four cyrillic S) into S.K.'s chest. He was a big thirty-one year old man. After that they cut the sinews on his legs. They threw another man on the ground and cut his spine in half with a knife so that his legs were instantly paralyzed. The Chetniks who call themselves Rambos did such things. Those particular members of irregular units had various details to their uniform such as reticular masks on their faces, black gloves, and black ribbons on their foreheads. They were not Bosnian Serbs because they talked in Ekavian dialect (used in Serbia) and they often used the word "bre" (Serbian dialect). Through an open window I could hear women crying from twenty meters away. One girl was saying through tears: "People, leave me alone, I was operated only a month ago." "Do you have a mama?," they asked her, and then they brought her parents to her. They raped her mother in front of her and her father. Once they took five thirteen-year-old girls to Mirsad's house and returned them the following day in such a state that S.P., a medic, managed to sew up two of them, while the other three had to be transferred to the Prijedor hospital. At least they said that they took them there. Ten women were raped under a poplar tree. Some thirty Chetniks were standing guard in shifts. Doctor P. told me how Zeljko Sikora from Prijedor, Czech by nationality, was mutilated. He also worked in the hospital as a medic. They chopped off his testicles and gouged out his eyes. He was falsely accused that he had castrated 300 Serbian children before the war.

After one month and twenty days spent in camps, I left Bosnia with a convoy of refugees.

Zagreb, July 31, 1992

A WITNESS TELLS OF THE INTERROGATION METHODS IN THE OMARSKA CONCENTRATION CAMP (NEAR PRIJEDOR); MUSLIM, BORN 1966, FEMALE

I finished electrotechnical school in 1985. Because of difficulties in finding employment, I was forced to work as a waitress for an entrepreneur in his restaurant. I worked there until September 1, 1991, when the restaurant was sold. I had to wait four months, until January 1, 1992, when I started working at a grill for the same owner. Our boss did not want to send us to the employment office to wait, because the restaurant was in the process of being built and he would need us at any time. I worked at the grill in shifts until April 30, 1992, when the government changed overnight. I was working the second shift and while walking through the city I saw armed persons in uniforms. I did not understand anything. At that point I was unaware of these events. At work I asked what was going on and they told me to be quiet and work. On the same day a curfew was proclaimed. Because of my grave financial situation I had to keep working. At work there were constant provocations, people would play around with weapons, but I put up with it thinking that it would pass. I heard them saying that all Croats and Muslims were going to be slaughtered and killed, but I never believed that would actually happen. They often asked me if I was a little "Ustasha," and gave me that nickname.[2] All of this was more or less normal for me until they came to my place. First they told me that they would set all of my things on fire, that it all had to burn because it was Muslim, and after all of these provocations they took me to jail. At the Internal Affairs Office they hit me and yelled at me and looked for a Serbian flag to nail it on my head. They even said that they would carve it in my forehead. I spent the night in jail and in the morning I was taken to the Omarska camp. The drive to Omarska was horrible. They taunted me and hit me sometimes, and told me that I would never again return to Prijedor, and that they wanted an ethnically clean Greater Serbia. They drove me through Kozarac. At every one of their checkpoints they stopped and took me out with the intention of shooting me right on the spot. They told me to take a good look at Kozarac, which no longer existed and never again would. I could only see destroyed and burned houses. They told me that this was no longer Kozarac, that it was now Radmilovo. There were two militiamen with me in the car, Bato Kovačević and a certain Jančević. Both of them took some writing pads on this trip. When I arrived in Omarska, they said that I was an extreme case and that I had to be watched closely. First they took all my money and turned my pockets inside out. Several times they hit me over the back with automatic guns and they struck me with a cane twice. Then they took me to the interrogation room. While they were questioning me, they extinguished cigarettes on my legs because I could not answer their questions. I ended up with two open wounds. After the interrogation they locked me up with the other women. Here I was able to see the elite of Prijedor society. These people had had it all, and now they were poor and pathetic. Every day we watched what they did to our men. Prisoners had to lie out in the sun on their stomachs all day, while the guards danced on them. The worst was night time. They often came and took me out somewhere and raped me. In the morning Commander Željko Mejakić would call me and ask me how I had spent the night and if I had slept well. I could not say anything because they hit me a few more times with their fists or rifle-butts with the warning to shut up. This same commander knew what was happening because he was one of them. Every day I counted and looked to see where the men were taken after interrogation, either to another room or out in the field. When they took a man out we knew that there was one person less. Every morning and evening a truck came by and took all of those that were out in the field. They even came with a dredger to pick them

---

[2]"Ustasha" is a reference to the Ustashi military forces, recruited from Croats and Muslims by the Germans in World War II to exterminate the Serbian partisan guerrillas.

up. In the course of the day they often took me to their office to clean up the blood. When I came in they would tell me whose blood it was and how they were beaten.

One day I was cleaning Asaf Kapetanović's blood and on the way back to my room I saw that they were taking Idriz Jakupović in for questioning. They were hitting him and yelling at him, and they threw him against the wall so that he broke his arm. This whole scene and all of these images are always in my head. These two are no longer alive, but they are not the only ones. Muhamed Čehaić, Abdulah Puškar, Nedžad Šerić, Ziko and Osman Mahmuljin, Ado Begić and many others were killed in front of me. The way they killed men was to beat them to the point when they could no longer get up, so that they would lie there and rot. They would just throw them outside and let them die. This is very hard for me to write, because every moment that I spent in that camp is like an open wound. My writing about it only scratches the surface. I spent fifty-six days in this camp. Every night I listened to the people crying and moaning, begging and pleading for their torturers to stop, trying to convince them of their innocence. They were guilty on only one charge: for being Croatian or Muslim. Then the Serbs brought in the people from my hill (Bišćani). They beat and killed them. At the same time, members of the Serbian Red Cross arrived, and among them was a Mića from the medical center. He did not have a hand, but he was able to beat and kill people. Then they beat up and killed Ratih Kadirić, who worked as a driver at the medical center. There was a Zoran, called Zoka, who distributed the sour and moldy food, who was also one of the killers, and Kole, who carried an extension cord, Krle, Dražen Kačavenda, Mite, Drago, Živko who would not let us have our bread, Čkalja, who watched these scenes with pleasure, and many others whose names I do not know. After fifty-six days I was taken to Trnopolje with twenty-eight other women. I stayed there for three days and then I was released. I remained in the city, because I could not get to my house in the village. I knew nothing of my family. The people in my village were either forced out or killed. I stayed in the city for two weeks and then I left with a convoy for Travnik. Just as we departed, after a few kilometers, they began with the looting. Every few kilometers they stopped and looked for money, German Marks, jewelry and other things. They also took various pendants, nail-clippers, pencils, lighters, etc. Sometimes they took someone's child and said that they would kill him/her if they did not get a set amount of German Marks.

Subsequently they even stripped us of our clothes and shook us to make sure we hid nothing. In this way they stripped us of all we had, and in the end, on Vlašić Mountain, they took out 250 young and strong men and killed them. They took fifteen men out of the truck that I was in. In Travnik, after three months, I finally met up with my parents. They told me everything that had happened to them. I do not know anything about my brother. After several days I received an affidavit of support from Germany so I left for Zagreb with my parents. I stayed there a few days and had a medical check-up. This was a gynecological check-up. A friend of mine who had also been in the camp and was the only person who knew what I had been through got a telephone number that I could refer to. The wounds on my legs had gotten worse. Because of a lack of any kind of hygiene they got infected and I had to see a doctor about this as well. Because of fear I did not tell the doctor what had happened. After a month and a half the wounds healed, but still I have two scars. After a few days in Zagreb my uncle came for me and my family. Immediately after we exchanged greetings, he said he was inclined to kill me. Because of this vile treatment from him and his wife, I did not tell them any of the things I had experienced. Surely more provocations would have followed. After twenty days they threw my parents and me out. While I was going through all of these medical procedures I applied for a room from social services. This room was 13 square meters, but my uncle did not even like that, and he wanted to have me taken out of there as well. My aunt is German, so that the people from social services believed her more than me, but after all of these problems I am still here. I now have psychological problems and sometimes I ask myself what to do. I have not found work yet, and I do not know what to do because I am still afraid of any contact with men. Sometimes I wish I could work at anything just so that I do not have time to think about it all. This is about everything, in summary. I survived all of this and I have to keep on living.

Wipperfuerth, December 1992

A VICTIM OF RAPE IN THE VILLAGE OF RIZVANOVIĆI (PRIJEDOR COUNTY); MUSLIM, BORN 1977, FEMALE

After the attack on my village, I witnessed the massacre of civilians as the worst tragedy. At that point I did not know that something much worse than death was yet to come. My sister gave birth to a child in the basement where we hid, during the mortar attacks on the village. After the village of Rizvanovići fell, and after the Chetniks came, I saw dead children, three to eight years of age near my house. I saw the destroyed mosque, and men who were taken away. Some more prominent men were singled out from the column and taken away. They shot them in the head. They fell down and remained lying there in grotesque positions. There was chaos, panic and death. My grandfather was accused of killing a Serb, and they executed him on the threshold of his house. A certain number of women and children remained in the village. We hid in the basements of the destroyed houses. Our house was intact. That day, several Chetniks arrived. They searched for valuable things and men who hid in the nearby forest. One of the Chetniks, thirty years of age, ordered me to accompany him into the house. I had to go. I was terrified, but I did not comprehend what was going to happen to me. I knew that I would endanger the lives of the members of my family if I resisted.

When we entered the house, he searched for money, jewelry and other valuable objects. He could take everything he wanted. He ordered me to confess where the men were hidden. I did not answer. Then he ordered me to take off my clothes. I was horrified. I took off my clothes silently, and everything fell apart in me. Under my naked skin I felt I was dying. I closed my eyes. I could not bear look at him. He hit me with his fist and I fell down on the floor. Then he jumped on the top of me. He raped me. I cried, and squirmed, and bled a lot. I was a virgin. He ordered me to get up. I wanted to pick up my clothes and cover my naked and disfigured body, but he told me not to touch them. He ordered me to stand still and wait. He said I better be careful of what I did, because I am responsible for the fate of my family. He went out, turned around to make sure nobody saw him and then invited another two Chetniks to come in. I felt lost. I did not feel anything when they left. I do not know how long I was lying on the floor. My mother came in and found me lying there. And her seeing me in such a humiliating state was even worse than everything that had happened to me. I suddenly realized what had happened. I realized that I had been depraved, raped, deformed forever. My mother knew what was happening inside of me. That was the saddest moment in our lives. We both cried, screamed. She covered me. Together, we went back to the basement. I remember all that was happening to me later on through some sort of mist, some distorted dream. We were transported to Trnopolje, and then went on foot to Travnik over the Vlašić Mountain, some thirty kilometers away. It was in Travnik that I emerged from this dreamy, confused state. Now, I sometimes find myself wondering if all this ever happened to me. To me of all people. My mother helped me tremendously. I want to become a mother one day. Only how? For me, men represent a horrible picture of violence and pain. I know that not all of them are like that, but this feeling of horror is stronger than my sense of reason. I cannot help myself.

In Zagreb, July 1992

72 Alain Destexhe, *Rwanda and Genocide in the Twentieth Century*

In the spring of 1994, the Western media reported "tribal warfare" of unusual ferocity in Rwanda, a small central African country with Zaire on its west, Uganda on its north, and Kenya on its east. Together with its southern neighbor, Burundi, Rwanda had been a German colony from 1885 to World War I and a Belgian mandate from 1925 to 1962. In 1994, the majority Hutus seemed intent on killing as many of the minority Tutsis, who had formerly enjoyed something of an elite status, as they could. In the summer months of the same year, the Rwandan Patriotic Front (RPF), a group composed largely of Tutsis in exile in Uganda, with some Hutus hostile to the regime, led an invasion that succeeded in toppling almost the entire Hutu government. The leadership of the fallen regime encouraged Hutus to flee the country, and hundreds of thousands did so, huge numbers ending up in a sprawling refugee camp in Goma, just across the Zairian border.

Alain Destexhe is an experienced observer of African affairs and the former secretary general of *Médecins sans Frontières* (Doctors Without Borders), a worldwide relief and health organization very active in Africa. In his work, excerpted here, he traces how the Tutsis, who raised cattle and acquired wealth and status separating them from the Hutus, who were mostly crop farmers and laborers, became the objects of murderous resentment.

QUESTIONS TO CONSIDER

1. How would *you* define "genocide"? Do you think that Destexhe is correct in indicting the Hutu leadership for this crime?
2. In the refugee camp at Goma at least tens of thousands and possibly several hundred thousand Hutus died, largely from cholera, which swept the area in epidemic fashion. Several media sources applied the term "genocide" to the tragedy at Goma, but Destexhe finds it inappropriate. What do you think?

3. Destexhe finds only three *bona fide* cases of genocide in the twentieth cen-
    tury. Apart from the Nazis killing Jews and Hutus killing Tutsis, discussed here,
    what do you suppose his third example is? Would you add a third one? Do
    you think there is a valid conceptual border between genocide and generic
    mass murder? Why or why not?

HUTU RACIST IDEOLOGY

It took exactly fifty years . . . *it* or something very like *it* has indeed happened again.
Just as Hitler's grand plan was founded on an ingrained European anti-Semitism
which he played on by singling out the Jews as the source of all Germany's ills, the
Hutu radicals are inheritors of the colonial lunacy of classifying and grading different
ethnic groups in a racial hierarchy. While the Jews were described by Nazis as "ver-
min," the Tutsis were called *invenzi* ("the cockroaches that have to be crushed"). Anti-
Tutsi propaganda presented them as a "minority, well-off and foreign"—so similar to
the image developed to stigmatize the Jews—and thus an ideal scapegoat for all
Rwanda's problems.

In a country which receives virtually no information from the outside world, local media, particularly the radio, play an essential role. For a large part of the population, a transistor radio is the only source for information and therefore has the potential for exerting a powerful influence. Rwandan radio broadcasts are in two languages,
French and the national language, Kinyarwanda, which is spoken by all Rwandans.
Less than a year before the genocide began, two close associates of President Habyarimana set up the "private" radio station, known as Radio *Mille Collines* (Thousand
Hills). Assured of a large audience thanks to regular programs of popular music, the
programs in Kinyarwanda broadcast unceasing messages of hate, such as "The grave
is only half full. Who will help us fill it?" Christened "the radio that kills" by its opponents, it was the basic instrument of propaganda for the Hutu extremists, and the
militias rallied in support of its slogans.

On 6 April 1994 the plane carrying President Habyarimana and President Cy-
prien Ntariyamira of Burundi was shot down by rocket fire. Although it is not yet
known who was behind this assassination, it is clear that it acted as the fuse for the
eruption of violence which led to the greatest tragedy in the history of the country.

As the stereotypes of physical characteristics do not always provide sufficient
identification—and can even be totally misleading—it was the identity cards demanded at the roadblocks set up by the militias that acted as the signature of a death
warrant for the Tutsis. As control of the road could not alone ensure that no Tutsi escaped, the militia leaders divided up the territory under their control so that one man
was allocated for every ten households in order to systematically search for Tutsis in
their immediate localities. In this way every Tutsi family could be denounced by somebody who knew the members personally: pupils were killed by their teachers, shop
owners by their customers, neighbor killed neighbor and husbands killed wives in

From Alain Destexhe, *Rwanda and Genocide in the Twentieth Century,* trans. by Alison Marschner (New
York: New York University Press, 1995), pp. 28, 30, 31–32, 33, 37–38, 43, 47, 49, 61–62, 70, *passim.* Used
by permission.

order to save them from a more terrible death. Churches where Tutsis sought sanctuary were particular targets and the scene of some of the worst massacres: 2,800 people in Kibungo, 6,000 in Cyahinda, 4,000 in Kibeho, to give just a few examples. In Rwanda, the children of mixed marriages take the ethnic group of the father and, although many of the Hutu killers—including some militia leaders—had Tutsi mothers, so effective was the indoctrination program, that even this apparently counted for nothing. Radio *Mille Collines* encouraged the violence with statements such as that made at the end of April 1994, "By 5 May, the country must be completely cleansed of Tutsis." Even the children were targeted: "We will not repeat the mistake of 1959. The children must be killed too." The media directly influenced Hutu peasants, convincing them that they were under threat and encouraging them to "make the Tutsis smaller" by decapitating them. In the northern areas occupied by the RPF, the peasants were astonished that the Tutsi soldiers did not have horns, tails and eyes that shone in the dark as they had been described in radio programs.

The genocide spread rapidly to cover the whole country under the control of the government army. By the end of April, it was estimated that 100,000 people had been killed. There are aspects of this genocide which are new and contemporary; others we have seen before. The use of propaganda, the way control was exercised over the administration: these are all reflections of the modern era. So too are the extreme racist ideology and the radical determination to exterminate all Tutsis in one all-encompassing blow. It would be a mistake to think that the killings were carried out in an archaic manner: the reality is that they were meticulously well organized. However, the means used to accomplish them were primitive in the extreme: for example, the use of machetes and *unfunis* (wooden clubs studded with metal spikes). Unfortunately, the media eclipsed the first aspect of its preoccupation with the second.

Nobody really knows the exact origin of the Hutu, Tutsi and Twa peoples (the Twa represent only one percent of the population and have never played a significant role in the region). The three groups speak the same language, share the same territory and follow the same traditions. By all definitions, this should qualify Rwanda as a nation in the true sense.

The first Europeans to reach Rwandan territory described the people and their way of life in terms very much influenced by the scientific ideas of their time. Until the beginning of the nineteenth century, the origin of Africa's many peoples was regarded by Europeans as rooted in the biblical story of Ham, Noah's son. The book of Genesis tells how Ham and his descendants were cursed throughout all generations after he had seen his father naked. The "Blacks" were believed to be descendants of Ham, their color a result of that curse. At the beginning of the nineteenth century, linguistic studies, archaeological research and rational thinking led to a questioning of this theory, which was subsequently replaced with a system of classifying people according to their physical characteristics: skin color, type of hair, shape of the skull, etc. Those who were then classified as "blacks" were regarded as "another" kind of human being, not descended from Noah. Yet this classification did not cover the whole population of the African continent. Explorers in the region we now know as Niger and the areas of the Zambezi and the Upper Nile, came across people that did not correspond to the caricature of the negro.

So it was that German, and later Belgian, colonizers developed a system of categories for different "tribes" that was largely a function of aesthetic impressions. Individuals were categorized as Hutu or Tutsi according to their degree of beauty, their pride, intelligence and political organization. The colonizers established a distinction between those who did not correspond to the stereotype of a negro (the Tutsi) and those who did (the Hutu). The first group, "superior Africans," were designated Hamites or "white coloreds" who represented a "missing link" between the "whites" and the "blacks." Also included in this group were the Galla peoples of Ethiopia and Somalia. "Any quality attributed to an African group must be read as a sign of inter-breeding with 'non-negro' cultures":[1] this "hamitic" ideology translates into the hypothesis, for which there is no serious proof, that a migration of the Galla took place in the seventeenth century, thus explaining the similarities between the Galla and the Tutsi.

The Belgians also favored the Tutsi students and the main priority of Rwanda's schools was their education. As this was, inevitably, also the policy at the tertiary level, the educated elite at the country's university, Astrida, the future administrative and technical backbone of the country, were very largely Tutsi. The colonizers blamed the imbalance in the schools and resulting low social standing of the Hutu on Hutu passivity, making no acknowledgement of their own role in the situation. The legacy of this theory continues even today. The missionaries also supported the Tutsi power structure, using it to evangelize from the top down. The Tutsi chiefs, once they had become Christian, then felt a moral obligation to convert the Hutu masses. The seminaries were more open to the Hutu than the schools. Although, after 1959, the educated Tutsi sometimes backed the theory of the mono-ethnic origins of the population following the removal from power of the Tutsi aristocracy . . . the myth of Egyptian origins and Hamitic superiority was supported by many among the Tutsi people. Some Hutu discovered the extent to which they, the "native" people of the region, had been "despoiled" and developed their own theory of the "Ethiopian invaders," categorizing the Tutsi as colonizers, the same as the Belgians. Rwandan Tutsis were from now on treated as immigrants and the 1959 "revolutionaries" called for "the return to Ethiopia of the Tutsi colonizers." The Hutu had begun to believe that they alone were the native people of Rwanda.

Belgium, criticized at the UN for a colonial policy that ensured that only a handful of the local population in their colonies received sufficient training for them to eventually be promoted to the higher levels of their national administrations—a policy aimed at ensuring that they would not think they were capable of running their own country—gradually ceded power to the small Hutu elite. The democratic principle of majority rule was cited as justification for the removal of the Tutsi from their previous positions of influence; a complete reversal of previous political policy. The Hutu became the "good guys" who "have been dominated for so long by the Tutsi" and the Belgians now expressed "sympathy for the cause of the suppressed masses."

In 1959, a series of riots directed against the authority of the Tutsi chiefs were allowed by the Belgians to escalate into a revolution accompanied by massacres which killed more than 20,000 Tutsi. What happened in Rwanda illustrates a situation where the coexistence of different social groups or castes metamorphosed into an ethnic problem with an overwhelmingly racist dimension. The caricature of physical stereotypes, although they did not always hold true and were probably due to the principle of endogamy practiced by each group despite the number of mixed marriages, was manipulated to provide proof of the racial superiority of one group over the other.

---

[1]This hypothesis originated with the British explorer J.H. Speke; references to it continued as late as 1945. Jean-Pierre Chretien, *Burundi: l'histoire retrouvée* (Paris: Karthala, 1993).

Archaic political divisions were progressively transformed into racial ideologies and repeated outbreaks of violence resulting from the colonial heritage which was absorbed by local elites who then brought it into the political arena. The present generation has internalized this ethnological colonial model, with some groups deliberately choosing to play the tribal card. The regimes that have ruled Rwanda and Burundi since independence have shown that they actually *need* ethnic divisions in order both to reinforce and justify their positions. Finally, however, it was the ethnic classification registered on identity cards introduced by the Belgians that served as the basic instrument for the genocide of the Tutsi people who were "guilty" on three counts: they were a minority, they were a remainder of a feudal system and they were regarded as colonizers in their own country.

Day by day, as the death toll increased in the spring of 1994, the reality that a genocide was underway became clearer. By the end of April, it was estimated that 100,000 people had been killed, by mid-May 200,000, and by the end of May half a million. Although nobody really knew the actual death toll, the signs of massacres were everywhere and the River Nyaborongo carried thousands of corpses towards Lake Victoria along what Hutu propaganda described as "the shortest way back to Ethiopia."

Taking humanitarian, rather than political, action is one of the best ways for a developed country to avoid facing up to its responsibilities in the wake of a disaster such as Rwanda. Another way is language. Employing a particular vocabulary can cast doubt on the actual causes of the massacre and foster confused images of the guilty and the victims. "Warring parties," "belligerents" and "civil war" on one hand, and "aggression," "massacre" and "genocide" on the other, are all strong words—but they are not synonyms in meaning. Under the cover of a supposed objectivity, to suggest that "both parties" have committed atrocities can often be seen as an underhand way of giving them the same status. To speak of tribal disputes when an armed majority perpetrates a genocide against an unarmed minority is patronizing and meaningless. The aggression against the Bosnians and the genocide of the Tutsis both exceed civil war. In the case of Rwanda, to compare the RPF with the Rwandan Armed Forces (FAR) is at best a display of ignorance, at worst propaganda. The FAR have committed a genocide and the RPF have carried out exactions: the two things cannot be compared. If a distinction is not made, then genocide is reduced to the status of common murder—but murder is *not* the same as genocide. They differ both in nature and in degree, a fact that needs to be constantly emphasized if the crimes committed in Rwanda are not to be pushed to the back of international consciousness.

The racist philosophy of the previous Hutu government and the dangers of trivializing, and even forgetting, the events of last summer are summed up perfectly in a remarkable interview with François Karera, the former mayor of Kigali, now living comfortably with his family in Zaire, just a few miles from the misery of the refugee camps (one of which he is responsible for). According to Karera, "The Tutsis are originally bad. They are murderers. The Tutsis have given the white people their daughters. Physically they are weak—look at their arms and legs. No Tutsi can build: they are too weak . . . they just command. . . . The others work. If the reasons are just, the massacres are justified. In war you don't consider the consequences, you consider the causes."[2]

[2] *International Herald-Tribune*, 16 August 1994.

The perpetrators of genocide should permanently lose any legitimacy as rulers of their people. They should be outlawed by the international community and brought to trial for their crimes. In the case of Rwanda, no attempt should be made to negotiate with those responsible for the genocide of the Tutsis: they are not only directly responsible for this worst possible crime against humanity, but also for the exodus from Rwanda and the catastrophic events in Goma which followed. When the new Allied forces won victory in 1945, there was never any question of providing a role for the Nazi party in the new Germany, nor of considering just how small a fraction of the population it really represented. The Nazis were banned outright and the authors of genocide then, as should happen in Rwanda today, lost any right to participate in public life.

Part VI
The Later Twentieth Century

The Cold War

As World War II drew to a close, the United States and the Soviet Union rapidly emerged as the arbiters of the world; their mutual suspicions about each other's designs deepened, and their relationship became increasingly confrontational. The postwar world, which was envisioned and shaped by the Allied leaders during wartime at such conferences as Cairo, Yalta, and Potsdam, did not turn out as these leaders had hoped—at least as far as the United States, China, and Great Britain were concerned. In the first two years of the postwar period, the world became increasingly polarized. Despite the pledges made at the Yalta Conference in February 1945 that "free and unfettered elections" would be held in liberated Poland, Stalin imposed a Communist regime. Soon, all of Central and Eastern Europe was swept into the Russian orbit.

But nowhere else were the tensions between the United States and the Soviet Union more clearly present than in the two bisected nations, Korea and Germany—particularly the former. During the war, at the Cairo Conference, the Allied leaders issued a declaration that Korea, which had been a colony of Japan since 1910, would become free and independent. Two days after the first atomic bomb was dropped on Hiroshima and six days before Japan's surrender, the Soviet Union finally declared war on Japan, as agreed at Yalta, and the Red Army crossed into Korea three weeks before the Americans. By then, President Harry S Truman had had second thoughts about the need for Soviet participation in the war against Japan. To prevent the rapidly advancing

Red Army from overrunning the Korean peninsula, the United States proposed to the Soviets a line at the thirty-eighth parallel, dividing the U.S. troops in the south from those of the Soviet Union in the north. This line, which was casually drawn in the last days of the war, has continued to be a source of international conflict and enormous suffering for the Korean people.

Meanwhile, the Soviet Union's expansionistic designs in northern Iran and Turkey and its support of the insurgency in Greece were being countered by the U.S. containment policy. In 1947, President Truman declared that the United States would provide military and economic support to any country threatened by Communist aggression. In accordance with this "Truman Doctrine," money and supplies poured into Greece, and the insurgency was crushed by 1949. This move by the United States is usually regarded as the start of the cold war. The Truman Doctrine led to the Marshall Plan, aimed at rebuilding Europe, as well as to the policy of military defense and collective security provided by the North Atlantic Treaty Organization (NATO), which went into operation in August 1949. After the French defeat in Indochina in 1954, John Foster Dulles, Secretary of State under President Dwight D. Eisenhower, took the initiative to extend the collective security system to Southeast Asia.

After the death of Joseph Stalin (1879–1953), the new Soviet leadership asserted that a less rigid foreign and domestic policy was needed. Coexistence—rather than confrontation—would be the new theme in foreign policy, whereas domestic policy was aimed at relaxing controls and improving the standard of living in the Soviet Union and throughout Eastern Europe.

From the late 1980s into 1991, the failure of Marxist economic systems in Eastern Europe to provide a good standard of living and the failure of political systems there to win even the grudging approval of the bulk of the populations led to the collapse of one Communist regime after another. Even the USSR under Mikhail Gorbachev abandoned many basic Marxist principles. In 1991, it was dissolved, leaving Russia still a huge country but giving independence to the other states or republics of the former union. Although the forces of democracy and capitalism did not reverse their earlier defeats in China, Cuba, and much of Indochina, adversarial relations between the two major groups ended. Before it underwent dissolution, the USSR agreed to German unification, ending a Marxist East Germany. The

NATO countries began massive food aid to combat severe shortages in the USSR during its final years and to the successor states after that. There was even some coordination by the old adversaries to counteract the Iraqi occupation of Kuwait in 1990–1991. All these events and many similar ones indicated that the cold war had passed into history at least in Europe and former Soviet Asia.

73 The Truman Doctrine

By 1947, Greece was in the midst of a civil war that appeared to Washington to be a Communist-led revolution, which, if successful, would threaten Turkey, the Middle East, Africa, and all of Europe. When the British notified Washington that they could no longer guarantee stability in the eastern Mediterranean, President Harry S Truman asked the U.S. Congress for military and economic aid for both Greece and Turkey. With strong bipartisan support, Congress approved the funds and implemented the Truman Doctrine, which declared the U.S. determination to pursue a policy of containment by aiding nations attempting to resist Communist pressure. In the following address, given to Congress on March 12, 1947, President Truman outlined the nature of the crisis in Greece and Turkey as well as U.S. responsibilities in the postwar era.

QUESTIONS TO CONSIDER

1. Why did President Truman believe that the governments of Greece and Turkey were unable to resolve their internal problems and needed assistance? Why did he recommend that the United States, rather than the United Nations, provide economic and military aid to Greece and Turkey? What were the "broad implications" of extending that aid?
2. Why did President Truman believe that the national security of the United States was at stake in Greece and Turkey?
3. Are there similarities between President Truman's ideals and goals and those expressed by Woodrow Wilson in his "Fourteen Points" address to Congress (see Reading 58) and the Atlantic Charter (see Reading 67)?
4. Although the Truman Doctrine was directed at problems in Greece and Turkey, President Truman asserted that "it must be the policy of the United States to support free peoples who are resisting attempted subjugation by armed minorities or by outside pressures." What were the cold war implications of this assertion?

The gravity of the situation which confronts the world today necessitates my appearance before a joint session of the Congress.

The foreign policy and the national security of this country are involved.

One aspect of the present situation, which I wish to present to you at this time for your consideration and decision, concerns Greece and Turkey. . . .

The very existence of the Greek state is today threatened by the terrorist activities of several thousand armed men, led by Communists, who defy the Government's authority at a number of points, particularly along the northern boundaries. A commission appointed by the United Nations Security Council is at present investigating disturbed conditions in northern Greece and alleged border violations along the frontier between Greece on the one hand and Albania, Bulgaria, and Yugoslavia on the other.

Meanwhile, the Greek Government is unable to cope with the situation. The Greek Army is small and poorly equipped. It needs supplies and equipment if it is to restore the authority of the Government throughout Greek territory.

Greece must have assistance if it is to become a self-supporting and self-respecting democracy.

The United States must supply this assistance. We have already extended to Greece certain types of relief and economic aid but these are inadequate.

There is no other country to which democratic Greece can turn.

No other nation is willing and able to provide the necessary support for a democratic Greek Government.

The British Government, which has been helping Greece, can give no further financial or economic aid after March 31. Great Britain finds itself under the necessity of reducing or liquidating its commitments in several parts of the world, including Greece.

We have considered how the United Nations might assist in this crisis. But the situation is an urgent one requiring immediate action, and the United Nations and its related organizations are not in a position to extend help of the kind that is required.

It is important to note that the Greek Government has asked for our aid in utilizing effectively the financial and other assistance we may give to Greece, and in improving its public administration. It is of the utmost importance that we supervise the use of any funds made available to Greece, in such a manner that each dollar spent will count toward making Greece self-supporting, and will help to build an economy in which a healthy democracy can flourish.

No government is perfect. One of the chief virtues of a democracy, however, is that its defects are always visible and under democratic processes can be pointed out and corrected. The Government of Greece is not perfect. Nevertheless it represents 85 percent of the members of the Greek Parliament who were chosen in an election last year. Foreign observers, including 692 Americans, considered this election to be a fair expression of the views of the Greek people.

The Greek Government has been operating in an atmosphere of chaos and extremism. It has made mistakes. The extension of aid by this country does not mean that the United States condones everything that the Greek Government has done or will do. We have condemned in the past, and we condemn now, extremist measures of the right or the left. We have in the past advised tolerance, and we advise tolerance now.

Greece's neighbor, Turkey, also deserves our attention.

From U.S. Congress, *Congressional Record.* 80th Congress, 1st Session, 1947, XCIII, 1980–1981.

The future of Turkey as an independent and economically sound state is clearly no less important to the freedom-loving peoples of the world than the future of Greece. The circumstances in which Turkey finds itself today are considerably different from those of Greece. Turkey has been spared the disasters that have beset Greece. And during the war, the United States and Great Britain furnished Turkey with material aid.

Nevertheless, Turkey now needs our support.

Since the war, Turkey has sought financial assistance from Great Britain and the United States for the purpose of effecting that modernization necessary for the maintenance of its national integrity.

That integrity is essential to the preservation of order in the Middle East.

The British Government has informed us that, owing to its own difficulties, it can no longer extend financial or economic aid to Turkey.

As in the case of Greece, if Turkey is to have the assistance it needs, the United States must supply it. We are the only country able to provide that help.

I am fully aware of the broad implications involved if the United States extends assistance to Greece and Turkey, and I shall discuss these implications with you at this time.

One of the primary objectives of the foreign policy of the United States is the creation of conditions in which we and other nations will be able to work out a way of life free from coercion. This was a fundamental issue in the war with Germany and Japan. Our victory was won over countries which sought to impose their will, and their way of life, upon other nations.

To insure the peaceful development of nations, free from coercion, the United States has taken a leading part in establishing the United Nations. The United Nations is designed to make possible lasting freedom and independence for all its members. We shall not realize our objectives, however, unless we are willing to help free peoples to maintain their free institutions and their national integrity against aggressive movements that seek to impose upon them totalitarian regimes. This is no more than a frank recognition that totalitarian regimes imposed on free peoples, by direct or indirect aggression, undermine the foundations of international peace and hence the security of the United States.

The peoples of a number of countries of the world have recently had totalitarian regimes forced upon them against their will. The Government of the United States has made frequent protests against coercion and intimidation, in violation of the Yalta agreement, in Poland, Rumania, and Bulgaria. I must also state that in a number of other countries there have been similar developments.

At the present moment in world history nearly every nation must choose between alternative ways of life. The choice is too often not a free one.

One way of life is based upon the will of the majority, and is distinguished by free institutions, representative government, free elections, guarantees of individual liberty, freedom of speech and religion, and freedom from political oppression.

The second way of life is based upon the will of a minority forcibly imposed upon the majority. It relies upon terror and oppression, a controlled press and radio, fixed elections, and the suppression of personal freedoms.

I believe that it must be the policy of the United States to support free peoples who are resisting attempted subjugation by armed minorities or by outside pressures.

I believe that we must assist free peoples to work out their own destinies in their own way.

I believe that our help should be primarily through economic and financial aid, which is essential to economic stability and orderly political processes.

The world is not static and the status quo is not sacred. But we cannot allow changes in the status quo in violation of the Charter of the United Nations by such methods as coercion, or by such subterfuges as political infiltration. In helping free and independent nations to maintain their freedom, the United States will be giving effect to the principles of the Charter of the United Nations.

It is necessary only to glance at a map to realize that the survival and integrity of the Greek nation are of grave importance in a much wider situation. If Greece should fall under the control of an armed minority, the effect upon its neighbor, Turkey, would be immediate and serious. Confusion and disorder might well spread throughout the entire Middle East.

Moreover, the disappearance of Greece as an independent state would have a profound effect upon those countries in Europe whose peoples are struggling against great difficulties to maintain their freedoms and their independence. . . .

It would be an unspeakable tragedy if these countries, which have struggled so long against overwhelming odds, should lose that victory for which they sacrificed so much. Collapse of free institutions and loss of independence would be disastrous not only for them but for the world. Discouragement and possibly failure would quickly be the lot of neighboring peoples striving to maintain their freedom and independence.

Should we fail to aid Greece and Turkey in this fateful hour, the effect will be far reaching to the West as well as to the East.

We must take immediate and resolute action.

I therefore ask the Congress to provide authority for assistance to Greece and Turkey in the amount of $400,000,000 for the period ending June 30, 1948. In requesting these funds, I have taken into consideration the maximum amount of relief assistance which would be furnished to Greece out of the $350,000,000 which I recently requested that the Congress authorize for the prevention of starvation and suffering in countries devastated by the war.

In addition to funds, I ask the Congress to authorize the detail of American civilian and military personnel to Greece and Turkey, at the request of those countries, to assist in the tasks of reconstruction, and for the purpose of supervising the use of such financial and material assistance as may be furnished. I recommend that authority also be provided for the instruction and training of selected Greek and Turkish personnel.

Finally, I ask that the Congress provide authority which will permit the speediest and most effective use, in terms of needed commodities, supplies, and equipment, of such funds as may be authorized.

If further funds, or further authority, should be needed for purposes indicated in this message, I shall not hesitate to bring the situation before the Congress. On this subject the executive and legislative branches of the Government must work together.

This is a serious course upon which we embark.

I would not recommend it except that the alternative is much more serious.

The United States contributed $341,000,000,000 toward winning World War II. This is an investment in world freedom and world peace.

The assistance that I am recommending for Greece and Turkey amounts to little more than one-tenth of 1 percent of this investment. It is only common sense that we should safeguard this investment and make sure that it was not in vain.

The seeds of totalitarian regimes are nurtured by misery and want. They spread and grow in the evil soil of poverty and strife. They reach their full growth when the hope of a people [dies].

We must keep that hope alive.

The free peoples of the world look to us for support in maintaining their freedoms.

If we falter in our leadership, we may endanger the peace of the world—and we shall surely endanger the welfare of our own Nation.

Great responsibilities have been placed upon us by the swift movement of events. I am confident that the Congress will face these responsibilities squarely.

74 Korea: The Thirty-eighth Parallel

On August 9, 1945, the Soviet Union declared war on Japan, and soon afterwards the Soviet Red Army crossed into Manchuria and Korea. The United States, whose armed forces were hundreds of miles away from Korea, had to draw up a military demarcation line across the Korean peninsula to prevent the Russians from over-running the entire region. On August 11, the State-War-Navy Coordinating Committee ordered two former Rhodes scholars, Colonels Dean Rusk and Charles H. Bonesteel III, to determine a line within thirty minutes. They recommended the thirty-eighth parallel as a division between U.S. and Soviet occupation zones. By the time American troops entered Korea on September 8, the Russians were already entrenched along the thirty-eighth parallel. This line had been intended merely as a temporary military line to expedite the disarming of the Japanese troops in Korea. On August 14, Japan surrendered and Japanese rule in Korea ended; however, Korea found itself bisected and a focal point of intense rivalry between the United States and the Soviet Union. The following excerpt provides a detailed account of who actually drew the line and why.

QUESTIONS TO CONSIDER

1. How do you assess the behind-the-scenes decision for the containing of the Soviet advance in the Korean peninsula? Was the decision to divide Korea at the thirty-eighth parallel a wise one? Would another approach have been feasible?
2. How did the decision to divide Korea shape the course of Korean history and influence the cold war?

At Potsdam, the chief of the Russian General Staff told General Marshall that Russia would attack Korea after declaring war on Japan. He asked whether the Americans could operate against Korean shores in co-ordination with this offensive. General Marshall told him that the United States planned no amphibious operation against

From James F. Schnabel, *United States Army in the Korean War. Policy and Direction: The First Year* (Washington, DC: Office of the Chief of Military History, Untied States Army, 1972), pp. 8–11.

Korea until Japan had been brought under control and Japanese strength in South Korea was destroyed. Although the Chiefs of Staff developed ideas concerning the partition of Korea, Manchuria, and the Sea of Japan into U.S. and USSR zones, these had no connection with the later decisions that partitioned Korea into northern and southern areas.

Russian entry into the war against Japan on 9 August, and signs of imminent Japanese collapse on 10 August 1945 changed U.S. Army planning from defeating Japan to accepting its surrender. Military planners in the War Department Operations Division began to outline surrender procedures in General Order No. 1, which General MacArthur would transmit to the Japanese Government after its surrender. The first paragraph of the order specified the nations and commands that were to accept the surrender of Japanese forces throughout the Far East.

The Policy Section of the Strategy and Policy Group in the Operations Division drafted the initial version of the order.

Under pressure to produce a paper as quickly as possible, members of the Policy Section began work late at night on 10 August. They discussed possible surrender zones, the allocation of American, British, Chinese, and Russian occupation troops to accept the surrender in the zones most convenient to them, the means of actually taking the surrender of the widely scattered Japanese military forces, and the position of Russia in the Far East. They quickly decided to include both provisions for splitting up the entire Far East for the surrender and definitions of the geographical limits of those zones.

The Chief of the Policy Section, Col. Charles H. Bonesteel, had thirty minutes in which to dictate Paragraph 1 to a secretary, for the Joint Staff Planners and the State-War-Navy Coordinating Committee were impatiently awaiting the result of his work. Colonel Bonesteel [along with Colonel Dean Rusk] thus somewhat hastily decided who would accept the Japanese surrender. His thoughts, with very slight revision, we incorporated into the final directive.

Bonesteel's prime consideration was to establish a surrender line as far north as he thought the Soviets would accept. He knew that Russian troops could reach the southern tip of Korea before American troops could arrive. He knew also that the Russians were on the verge of moving into Korea, or were already there. The nearest American troops to Korea were on Okinawa, 600 miles away. His problem therefore was to compose a surrender arrangement which, while acceptable to the Russians, would at the same time prevent them from seizing all of Korea. If they refused to confine their advance to North Korea, the United States would be unable to stop them.

At first Bonesteel had thought of surrender zones conforming to the provincial boundary lines. But the only map he had in his office, which was a small National Geographic map, a 1942 Gilbert Grosvenor Edition of "Asia and Adjacent Areas," was hardly adequate for this sort of distinction. The 38th Parallel, he noted, cut Korea approximately through the middle. If this line was agreeable to President Truman and to Generalissimo Stalin, it would place Seoul and a nearby prisoner of war camp in American hands. It would also leave enough land to be apportioned to the Chinese and British if some sort of quadripartite administration became necessary. Thus he decided to use the 38th Parallel as a hypothetical line dividing the zones within which Japanese forces in Korea would surrender to appointed American and Russian authorities. . . .

When Bonesteel's draft paper reached the Joint Planners in the predawn hours of 11 August, Admiral M.B. Gardner suggested moving the surrender line north to the 39th Parallel, a recommendation that the planners believed the Navy Secretary, James C. Forrestal, favored. Gardner pointed out that the 39th Parallel would place Dairen in the military zone to be occupied by the Americans. General Lincoln, however, felt that the Russians would hardly accept a surrender line that barred them from Dairen and other parts of the Liaotung Peninsula; besides, American units would have great difficulty reaching the Manchurian port ahead of the Russians. Calling Assistant Secretary of State James Dunn, Lincoln ascertained that his opinion was shared. Mr. Dunn believed that Korea was more important politically to the United States than Dairen, and he felt this to be the view of Secretary of State James F. Byrnes. As a result, the 38th Parallel remained in the draft when the Joint Planners handed the general order to the State-War-Navy Coordinating Committee.

While General Lincoln was shepherding the document through the State-War-Navy Coordinating Committee on 11 and 12 August, the Russians invaded Korea, landing on the northeast coast near Rashin. Russian troops then poured out of the maritime provinces of Siberia, down the Korean peninsula, and into the Kaesong-Ch'unch'on area above Seoul, where they looted much equipment, including locomotives and rolling stock. Reports of the Russian troop movements reaching Washington underscored the need for concurrence in the proposed general order. Otherwise, the Russian advance would render academic the American acceptance of the Japanese surrender in southern Korea. At the same time, swift Russian troop movements into key areas of southern Manchuria eliminated the possibility of including Dairen in the American surrender zone.

Between 11 and 14 August, the State-War-Navy Coordinating Committee and the Joint Chiefs of Staff discussed the wording of the surrender instrument. Meanwhile, General MacArthur informed the Joint Chiefs of Staff that he would adhere to three priorities for the use of the forces under his command. After the Japanese surrender, the occupation of Japan would come first, Korea second, China third.

In Washington, the War Department Operations Division rephrased General Order No. 1 to the satisfaction of the Joint Chiefs of Staff and the heads of the State, War, and Navy Departments. On 15 August 1945, clean copies of the draft order were sent to Fleet Admiral William D. Leahy's White House office. Within a few hours President Truman gave his approval, directing at the same time that General Order No. 1 be sent also to the capitals of Great Britain and the USSR with requests for concurrence by the heads of those states. . . .

Among the items it specified, General Order No. 1 stated that Japanese forces north of the 38th Parallel in Korea would surrender to the Russian commander, while those south of the parallel would surrender to the commanding general of the U.S. expeditionary forces. As Washington waited for the Moscow reaction to President Truman's message, there was a short period of suspense. Russian troops had entered Korea three days before the President accepted the draft of General Order No. 1. If the Russians failed to accept the proposal, and if Russian troops occupied Seoul, General Lincoln suggested that American occupation forces move into Pusan.

Stalin replied to President Truman on 16 August 1945. He said nothing specifically about the 38th Parallel but offered no objection to the substance of the President's message.

75 Chong K. Yoon, The Korean War: A Personal Account

Although Korea was freed from a thirty-five-year long colonial rule under the Japanese at the end of World War II in August 1945, it did not gain independence as one nation. At the conclusion of the war, two of the victors, the United States and the Soviet Union, agreed to divide Korea along the thirty-eighth parallel line in order to facilitate the surrender of Japanese troops (see Reading 74). The U.S. troops occupied the southern half of Korea, and Soviet troops occupied the northern half. Soon, the line that had originally been established as a temporary demarcation became solidified and was quickly turned into a line of confrontation between the two superpowers and their client states. By the early autumn of 1948, two distinct and ideologically irreconcilable rival governments under the watchful eyes of the Soviet Union in the North and the United States in the South had emerged. The Communist government in the North was known as the Democratic People's Republic of Korea (DPRK) in Pyongyang, and in the South, a marginally democratic anti-Communist government called the Republic of Korea (ROK) in Seoul was formed. Sporadic border clashes at the thirty-eighth parallel line intensified between the North, which was heavily armed mostly with Soviet weapons, and the American-equipped South. Finally, in the early dawn hours of June 25, 1950, the Korean People's Army (KPA) of the Communist North, reinforced by scores of heavy T-3-class Soviet-made tanks, launched an all-out invasion of the South across the thirty-eighth parallel line, which was defended by the marginally armed South Korean army. Thus began the tragic three-year-long fratricidal Korean War, which involved some sixteen UN member nations on the side of the South in accordance with the UN Security Council Resolution calling for the repulse of the aggressors, and the Communist Chinese army on the northern side. The United States assumed a major military role in the execution of the war. The following is a personal account of the first three months of the war, tracing the memories back more than fifty years.

QUESTIONS TO CONSIDER

1. North and South Korea blame each other for the start of the war. Which side was the guilty party?
2. Why did the Soviet Union fail to exercise its veto power when the UN Security Council adopted the resolution to assist South Korea in repelling North Korean invaders?
3. How do you assess the Korean War? What did it achieve? Why is Korea still a divided nation?

It was around noon on a warm, humid Sunday afternoon. I had joined with several friends from my high school oratory and debate club to celebrate the arrival of the carefree, lazy, dog-days of summer. We were getting ready for a picnic at a park overlooking the central part of Seoul, the capital of South Korea. The guys and I had just opened bottles of chilled cider and were engaged in light-hearted chatter, friendly banter, adolescent cajoling, and boyish horseplay when we were suddenly interrupted by blaring siren sounds emanating from one of the city's towers. Initially, we figured there was probably a major fire somewhere in the city. But no one could see billowing smoke or raging flames anywhere. The siren went off repeatedly and continued as if it were eager to tell the people of the city that some impending disaster was in the making.

Within a few minutes, a police car was driving around the park, and people were being ordered to go home. The reason was that North Korean communist troops, known as the Korean People's Army, or KPA, had launched a full-fledged armed attack all along the 38th parallel. What was more ominous was that they had been steadily pushing southward since the crack of dawn that day. Since Seoul is located only about 30 miles south of the 38th parallel line, we knew that this was certainly a dire emergency. But we also wondered why no one had heard about the situation on the radio. We suspected that the Seoul government was deliberately keeping the people of the capital city in the dark in order to prevent possible widespread panic. It was a tragic day for the Korean people—June 25, 1950. Thus began what would become a three-year-long fratricidal war between Koreans in the southern half of the country, and those in the northern half. Most of us at the picnic bitterly condemned North Korea for starting the war, but as usual, there were a few skeptics who weren't so sure about exactly who the guilty party was. Sporadic border skirmishes between the north and the south had escalated sharply for many months before the outbreak of the war. The Seoul government of Syngman Rhee may not have been totally innocent as far as occasional and localized border clashes were concerned. But the way the South Korean border defenses collapsed within the first hour of war made it quite obvious that despite North Korean propaganda to the contrary, South Korea was simply unprepared to launch an all-out invasion of the north. At any rate, I was saddened by the folly of the fratricidal war in which Koreans would kill other Koreans, using arms supplied by foreign powers. Gripped by sinking fear and uncertainty about the future, we hurriedly left the park and scattered in different directions toward our homes.

Seoul was a city of more than a million and a half people, bustling with government officials, shoppers, students, foreign diplomats, and cars before the war. Now, an unusual and eerie quietness had descended upon Seoul, interrupted only by speeding military vehicles whizzing through the streets carrying heavily armed, grim-faced soldiers and policemen with their chin strips fastened. The entire city was under an extraordinary martial law. Everything, including the government, schools, banks, stores, and public transportation, was shut down. The only exceptions were occasional small "Mom-n-Pop" shops that had chosen to remain open. Newspapers stopped publishing and rumors were rampant.

As hours went by, faint thunder-like sounds from the not-so-distant north grew louder and more distinct. Like an impending thunderstorm, the booms and bangs not

From Chong K. Yoon, *The Korean War Memoir*, typescript, to be published. Reprinted by permission.

only increased, but became clearer and more frequent. These were the unmistakable sounds of artillery. The invaders were drawing ever closer to Seoul. People all around me looked nervous.

On the second day of the war, Youngchol, a good friend of mine who lived a few blocks away came to see me. Looking sad and worried, he dropped in to say goodbye—hopefully only a temporary goodbye. His parents had already decided that they were not going to take any chances. Hence they planned to quietly slip out of the city's southern edge, past the Han River, which in a serpentine fashion hugs the southern end of Seoul. Youngchol's father had served as the second-highest ranking man in the South Korean police, an institution that was hated most by the communists. He and his family had obviously received more "insider" information than most residents on the discouraging development of the war. I was filled with mixed emotions about Youngchol's family's decision. I was sad that my good school buddy was leaving and going into an uncertain future, and at the same time, I could not but feel contempt toward the government leaders who were fleeing the city while keeping the residents of the capital in the dark.

On the third day of the war, the KPA swept down and captured Seoul. Incessant sounds of machine gun fire, artillery, loud echoing explosions, and passing heavy Russian-made tanks kept city residents awake the entire night. Luckily however, the much dreaded street-to-street battles were confined to a few pockets of the city. Overall, it looked as though the capital escaped massive destruction and bloodbath, thanks ironically to the pathetically unprepared and weak South Korean military defenders. As a typical teenage male, fearless and filled with curiosity, I joined some neighborhood buddies and walked about three miles to the central government square to steal a glimpse of those KPA soldiers. I heard rumors that Russian military advisors were coming in with the KPA invaders. I was curious about what those so-called "liberators" from the north looked like. As we neared the square, we detected the smell of gasoline, diesel oil, and explosives hanging in the air. To our horror, right in the middle of the very street leading to the central plaza lay three partially charred bodies strewn on the ground, alongside a couple of badly crushed and burned South Korean government jeeps. Apparently some high-ranking South Korean government officials, perhaps police or security officials making last-minute attempts to flee Seoul early that morning, had met violent deaths. Later that day, I learned that the twin Han River bridges had been blown up during the night by the hastily retreating South Korean army in an attempt to slow the advancing communist army from the north. This pair of bridges, one for trains and the other for motor vehicles and pedestrians, had been the only vital links between the city proper and the southern suburbs. Unfortunately, the destruction of these bridges had the most disastrous effects on the officials of the Seoul government and the people who attempted to flee the city, instead of on the KPA troops. Perhaps hundreds, if not tens, of thousands of residents of Seoul were trapped.

We ventured past the scene toward the front lawn of the central government building. There stood several large, intimidating-looking Russian T-3 tanks. On the other side of the building, several large anti-aircraft guns were positioned on the rooftop. Before we knew it, what looked like a regiment of KPA troops in two columns was entering the square, lingering there briefly, and then moving on toward the South Gate. An ironic scene we captured was what appeared to be a very high-ranking KPA commanding officer with a soldier chauffeur entering the square behind those KPA troops. They were riding in an American-made Packard sedan, which had perhaps been appropriated from somewhere in the city. It was amusing to me that a communist general loved the comfort of a capitalist sedan. As the KPA troops passed by, a man in his mid-twenties wearing a red armband suddenly shouted, "Don't just look! Let's welcome our liberators!" and shouted "Long live the People's Army!" He might very well have been a member of the fifth column, which had been operating underground. Not wishing to be suspected of being hostile, everybody in the crowd followed his cue politely but with little enthusiasm. Although the soldiers' uniforms and weapons looked strange and foreign, their faces were unmistakably Korean faces, and not those of the Russians. Despite heavy northern provincial accents, their language was most definitely Korean. They were Koreans by any measure, but Koreans from the other side of the fence. I lamented the true tragedy of the fratricidal war.

At the western end of the central square plaza, bursts of cheers went up from a jubilant crowd. The individuals gathered there were still decked in prison garb. I soon learned that during the previous night, North Korean communist commandos smashed the gate of Sodaemun Prison, the largest prison in Korea where many communists and communist sympathizers had been imprisoned by the South Korean authorities. With their arms around the shoulders of the fellow marchers, these pale-faced freed prisoners marched down the boulevard singing the "Communist International," and intermittently shouting and chanting "Long live Marshal Kim Il-Song!" and "Long live the People's Army." With their time in prison as badges of honor, these freed prisoners, I was sure, would soon wear red armbands and look for their former tormentors.

On the way back home, I heard a sudden commotion in a nearby alley where there was a crowd of about a dozen people. Two armed men in soldiers' uniforms, perhaps the feared communist partisans, accompanied by one plain-clothed man with a red armband, were chasing after a man who was running for his life. The scene was reminiscent of a pack of hungry lions charging a gazelle in an African safari. The man being chased had obviously been flushed from a hideout. His hair was covered with spider webs and dust. His fate was quickly sealed when he ran into a dead-end alley. The excited plain-clothed man shouted that the one being cornered was a "notorious Seoul police torturer who tormented and maimed fellow communist comrades." As he desperately begged for his life with an ashen expression, one of the soldiers knocked him to the ground with a rifle butt. The other soldier stood over him and pumped two bullets into his head and shouted in a shrill voice, "The enemy of the people is thus punished." For the first time in my life I had witnessed one person taking the life of another in the most cold-blooded way. I regretted that I had witnessed such a horror. I hurried home as swiftly as I could, but the scene of that horror lingered in my mind and I was unable to sleep for many nights. I wondered just how many others had been executed summarily in that fashion elsewhere in the city. It was then that I fully realized that a bloody reign of terror had really descended upon Korea.

The communist occupation of Seoul had barely taken hold when communist authorities started rounding up former South Korean government officials who were trapped in the city. These were the so-called "running dogs of American imperialism and its puppet government of Syngman Rhee," and included members of the National Assembly, wealthy businessmen, bank and insurance executives, absentee landlords living in Seoul, leaders of civic organizations that were regarded as anti-communist, and even church leaders. In fact, some of our neighbors, and many of my friends' fathers, uncles, and brothers belonged to such categories. Many, including one of my uncles who was a Methodist minister, were taken away for interrogation by communist security officials with the help of local collaborators and informers and never returned home again. By this time, widespread fear enveloped the residents of the capital.

The day after the military occupation of Seoul, I ran errands to procure essential food supplies at a market near the city's East Gate. As I hurried briskly past the city zoo, my eyes fell upon at least a dozen South Korean soldiers' bodies in blood-soaked uniforms that had been shoved to the side of the road. There, I saw an old stooped man carrying a large burlap bag over his shoulder. He was walking slowly by the dead bodies, carefully inspecting each. I thought to myself that he must have been looking for a missing son who might have been one of those ill-fated defenders of the capital. But to my dismay and disbelief, I saw him bending down, removing wrist watches and blood-stained combat boots from the dead soldiers, and then depositing them one by one in his sack. It was indeed a pathetic scene.

A few days later in early July, for the first time, I saw three small U.S. warplanes that appeared in the skies over the southern end of the city. They were bombing some targets that might have been oil storage facilities or perhaps a bridge. Such bombings did not seem to make much of a dent on the communist military's drive south, at least in the early stages of the war. Yet the appearance of those warplanes was clear evidence that the U.S. had entered the war, at least from the air, in support of the badly mauled South Korean military. As time passed, increasing numbers of U.S. warplanes began to fill the skies overhead. Now, ever so often, I heard the echoes of the sounds of U.S. aerial bombings. However, it was a discouraging sign that the sounds of artillery and small arms fire from the south had become increasingly fainter. It was apparent that the South Korean defenses were being pushed further and further south, away from Seoul. It was discouraging for those who had hoped for the quick return of the South Korean army, which had supposedly made a tactical retreat just south of the Han River to gain time to regroup for a major counter offensive. Apparently, it was wishful thinking. I knew that the next few months were going to be a long, hot summer.

About a week into the war, I saw about two dozen unshaven, exhausted-looking U.S. soldiers flanked by submachine-gun-toting KPA guards. As they paraded down the main Chongno boulevard in the heart of Seoul, two American soldiers walking in front carried a large banner printed in both Korean and English. It read, "Down With U.S. Imperialism!" The crowd on the sidewalks stood silently, neither jeering nor applauding. These soldiers were apparently the first group of American POWs in the Korean War. My earlier doubts about U.S. willingness to send ground troops to Korea were completely dispelled. I thought that Kim Il-Song must have been caught off guard by the quick entry into the war by the U.S. military, both in the air and on the ground.

As life in Seoul became increasingly uncertain and tense, and rumors spread that all able-bodied young people would be forced into the so-called youth volunteer army and shipped to the war front, I concluded that staying in Seoul as a young person was unsafe. Moreover, our family's food reserves were running low. After having given careful consideration to these lurking problems, my parents came to a painful decision. All the young members of the family—my two older brothers, myself, and a cousin who stayed with us and was a first-year student at the same high school I attended— were to leave the city. For the duration of the war, we would go to our ancestral home, where our uncle and his family lived, in a small rural town some fifty miles southeast of Seoul. My oldest brother, a third-year medical student, decided to take his chances and remain in Seoul to take care of our parents despite my parents' advice. After bidding a very painful farewell to my parents, who prayed to God for our safe journey, we three young men set out on foot. My brother, a second-year engineering student at Seoul National University, assumed the leadership role. As a safety precaution, we avoided main highways although they were a tempting shortcut. Highways were known to be primary targets of aerial attacks from U.S. warplanes during daylight hours, to deter the KPA's southward movement. After dark, these highways became busy with KPA troop movements. We followed narrow, rugged, country backroads. Every day we walked from early morning to dusk, braving the scorching mid-summer sun. Along the road, we appreciated the rustic beauty of the rugged countryside and were gratified to find that rural folks had not lost their innocence. They were so trusting and hospitable that we did not have to worry about food and lodging, almost always free at the courtesy of these kind rural people.

At the end of the third day, we finally managed to reach our ancestral town. Despite our extreme fatigue and hunger, we felt reenergized upon seeing the town. It seemed peaceful and quiet, almost as though the whole town was empty. We breathed sighs of relief. And yet, how deceiving looks can be. Were we like swimmers in calm clear waters where a shark was just around a nearby coral reef? About a half mile from my uncle's home, a half-drunken KPA officer emerged from the town's deserted winery accompanied by a soldier. The officer barked at us to stop. He pulled out a Soviet-made pistol from his holster in a quite intimidating manner. Spewing out alcohol-laden breath, he sat down upon the steps of the winery and questioned what and who we were, where we were from, and where we were headed. We answered that we were students from Seoul who had come to visit our uncle and relatives who lived in the town since school had been closed indefinitely back in Seoul. The soldier began shuffling through our backpacks, one by one. When he got to my backpack, he pulled out a notebook where I kept a diary in English. He immediately called the officer's attention to it. Obviously, the officer was unable to read English because he stepped closer to me and demanded to know what the notebook was all about. I responded that it was a journal I kept as part of a requirement for my high school English class. Next, he asked me why I was studying English instead of Russian. I thought the question was a simple but very stupid one. Yet, with the full realization that my life was in his hands, I answered in a very apologetic and humble voice that Russian was unfortunately not offered at my high school. He then tried to convince me that Russian was the language of the future. I was sure that this guy was some half-baked communist ideologue, and that he might have been a political commissar in the KPA unit. I could not believe how persistent this officer was. Next he raised yet another question. He wished to know if our parents and grandparents belonged to the bourgeoisie or landlord class. His reasoning was that our being students at Seoul's premier high school and university meant that we belonged to the socioeconomic class that communist revolutionaries hated the most. We hesitated for a few seconds and then replied that we were self-supporting, struggling students in Seoul. Upon hearing this, the officer gestured with his hands to a passerby, an elderly village woman, to come over. He asked her whether our ancestors were rich landlords who lived off the rents from tenant farmers and peasants. Seeing our nervous look, the woman told him haltingly that our ancestors had been very affluent a couple of generations ago but that their family fortune had slipped and declined sharply and that they had become poor. As we listened, we were quietly pleased and thankful for her adroit, quick-thinking, and favorable response about us. We were all scared and wondered what the officer's next question would be. He then asked if we knew the difference between the proletariat and bourgeoisie. We tried to answer. Just at that time, as dusk was settling in on the area, a low-pitched bugle sounded from somewhere nearby. Another soldier came running over to tell the officer that it was time to resume their move. We realized that a unit of KPA soldiers had been resting somewhere in town during the day and was now ready to resume its southward move under the cover of darkness. Before rejoining his unit, the officer gave us a quick stern lecture that we as learned young men should help awaken the rural people about the loftiness of the war of liberation. He warned that he would come back to check on us to ensure we were truly doing so. We assured him of our support and wished him luck. How glad we were to see him disappear into the darkness!

For three young people, the months of July through October proved to be a long and hot summer. It was no easy task to live life as forced hermits. It was downright difficult being completely cut off from the rest of the world. We had no mail service, no newspaper, no electricity, and no radio. I must admit that the hearty appetites of three young males were probably hard on my uncle's food reserves. Luckily, potatoes and zucchinis from a several-acre mini-farm combined with the forced diet of only two meals per day rather than three helped ease the food situation somewhat. Our daily routine was simple and monotonous: eating, reading, and playing chess. We devoured whatever reading materials we could get our hands on. But after about a month, we had exhausted everything in print that was available in the house despite the fact that my uncle's household probably had more books and reading materials than any other household in that town. We went through our uncle's dusty bookshelves and to our delight, discovered among other books, Johann Wolfgang von Goethe's collected works in Japanese translation. Among others, I loved reading Goethe's *The Sorrows of Young Werther* and *Faust*. My brother loved Leo Tolstoy's *War and Peace*.

Slowly but surely, our boredom and feelings of restlessness reached a critical stage; however, we were helpless and there were no alternatives. The high expectations we had held that the war's tide would soon change in favor of the South Korean military with the support of the United States dimmed fast. However, by mid-September, strange things were happening. We heard continuously reverberating faint sounds of explosions of bombs and heavy artillery. Oddly though, and quite unexpectedly I might add, these noises were coming from a northwesterly direction rather than the usual southern direction where the main battles were supposedly taking place. At the same time, on the north-south highway that went through our town, we began to see refugees coming from the north and moving southward. These refugees broke the news that war was raging in the Inchon-Seoul corridor. We were in disbelief! We had been led to believe that the KPA, which had swept south like a tidal wave, was nearly completing its "war of liberation" in the southeastern corner around Pusan. Soon, we confirmed that the U.S. Marines had made a successful amphibious landing at Inchon, a gateway to Seoul, and were advancing rapidly toward the capital. We rejoiced and believed that we were finally seeing the light at the end of tunnel. The communist defense of Inchon and Seoul was crumbling fast before the rapidly advancing U.S. Marines joined by the South Korean troops. Seoul was recaptured on September 28, exactly three months after its fall to the KPA. General Douglas MacArthur's brilliant strategy for the Inchon landing caught the North Korean military totally off guard. The rear of the tens of thousands of the best North Korean troops fighting deep down in the south had been cut, and they were hopelessly trapped. Kim Il-Song's dream of unifying Korea by military means was completely shattered. This American general was my own hero and liberator! Today, fifty years later, I still often ponder what my life might have been like had there not been such a hero and liberator as General MacArthur, notwithstanding the criticisms leveled at him by some quarters that he was a hawkish general who had a propensity to rattle atomic bombs.

In late October after three months of self-imposed exile, the three of us decided to return to Seoul. We wondered with apprehension whether or not our parents and brother were well and if our house was still standing. We set out for our return trip on foot as before, because there was no available public transportation. Along the way, we noticed that not a single bridge stood completely undamaged. This time, the U.S. Army engineers were busy building temporary bridges. As we approached the capital

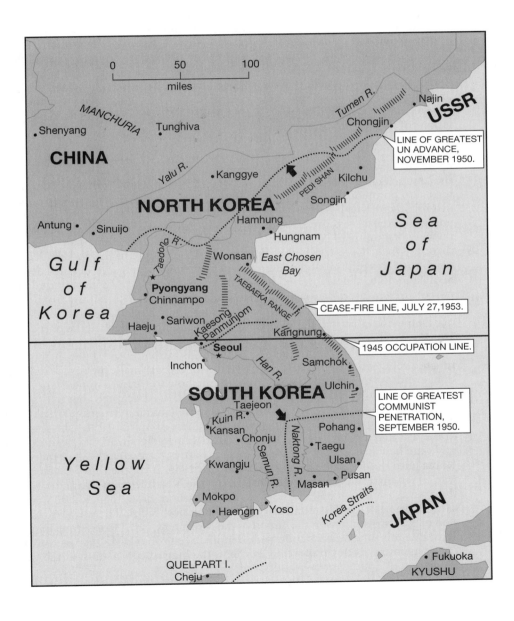

city, the lingering smells of war were still fresh and the scars of battles were ever present. The hopelessly mangled tangle of massive steel bridges over the Han River, the early major structural casualties of the war, were still standing as if they were living symbols of the brutal war. And yet, we were happily surprised that Seoul had escaped total ruin. It had not been turned into a sea of death or heaps of ashes, thanks to the speedy retreat of the communist occupiers of Seoul. Evidently, the communists were so totally caught off guard by the Inchon landing that they abandoned the city in a hurry, not bothering to put up much fight. Now, soldiers of South Korea and other friendly nations were visible everywhere, and military vehicles of all types filled the streets. None of the theaters, schools, banks, postal services, or department stores were open. Only a few street vendors selling baked sweet potatoes and roasted chestnuts were visible. We were delighted to spot our house in the distance and it was standing undamaged. The moment that we stepped into our house quickly turned into a joyous and emotional family reunion, full of laughter as well as a good share of tears. We were all safe and alive, even though we had all become thinner and pale from all the tribulations of the past few months.

Our optimism was short lived. About three weeks after our return to Seoul, we learned in disbelief that the South Korean army and UN forces, which had just swept up all the way to the Manchurian border just south of the Yalu River, also known as the "Amnokkang" in Korean, which separated North Korea from China, were in full retreat. Communist China had entered the war to save the nearly collapsed communist regime of North Korea and sent hundreds of thousands of so-called Chinese volunteer fighters across the frozen river into North Korea sometime in late October or the very beginning of November. It sounded like a tidal wave that had reversed its direction. Once again, fear and anxiety gripped the people of Seoul. Like most of our neighbors, this time all of the members of our family, young and old, decided to leave Seoul and go to the southernmost city of Pusan, hundreds of miles south, before the visit of arctic winter. We also wanted to avoid possible chaos resulting from a mass exodus. This time, I did not have to travel on foot. On a truck loaded and filled only with our family essentials, we all traveled for a week and finally reached the port city of Pusan. We had become refugees in our own country.

Despite all the frustrations and tribulations I experienced, I deeply felt how fortunate a refugee I was in Pusan. The brutality of the war made me realize more keenly than ever how fragile life was, yet it taught me how to treasure mine everyday. About a month after we settled there, on January 4, 1951, we learned that Seoul fell once again to the communists—this time, the Chinese Communist Army, which later was driven out of Seoul by the UN forces in the middle of March 1951. The seesaw phase of the war had already begun. Alas, the American soldiers who had been expected to go home by Christmas, faced even bloodier battles for two-and-a-half more years in Korea until the armistice was signed in July 27, 1953. After the thirty-seven months of war, which involved nineteen nations, two on the North Korean side and seventeen on the South, more than 830,000 soldiers died, of whom more than 45,000 were Americans, as well as countless number of civilians on both sides. The war created destruction of epic proportions in the "Land of the Morning Calm." Korea remained divided, separated this time by a 2.5-mile-wide demilitarized zone (DMZ) across Korea instead of the infamous 38th parallel line. Perhaps, the biggest consolation of the war is that the nation of South Korea has survived.

76 Henry A. Myers, "East Berliners Rise Up Against Soviet Oppression," A Personal Account

After Stalin's death in March 1953, the less-threatening plural leadership in the USSR probably expected the people of Eastern Europe under Soviet control to look for some increase in political freedom and perhaps improvements in their standards of living. Those leaders seem *not* to have expected that a willingness on their part to listen to complaints would be taken as a sign of weakness and would lead to revolt.

In the early postwar period, East Germany appeared to have the native regime most obedient to the USSR and the most passive population in Soviet-occupied Eastern Europe. Yet even there demands for change rose in the spring of 1953. Student groups hoped for some freedom of the press. Workers sought improvements in pay and length of the workweek: A particular complaint was the regime's insistence on "voluntary," that is, unpaid, Saturday afternoon work of clearing away rubble at sites still not repaired or rebuilt since the end of the war—this following regular Saturday-morning work in the forty-five-hour workweek.

The Eisenhower-Nixon campaign for the American presidency in 1952 had stressed "rolling back the tide of communism in Eastern Europe" as a foreign policy objective along with an honorable end to the Korean War. Many East German students and workers took this to mean that if Eastern Europeans rose up against their Soviet occupiers, the new president would send American troops to help them. In June 1953, American-sponsored radio broadcasts did not promise American aid, but by reporting news of snowballing protests in major East German cities and Soviet inaction, these broadcasts did much to encourage dissidents to press their demands. By June 16, crowds in moods of rebellion appeared to be in control of main streets in many cities, most of all in East Berlin.

The author of the following piece, then a nineteen-year-old U.S. student in West Berlin, enjoyed a pleasantly exciting morning on June 17, the peak of revolutionary activity in East Berlin, when protesters spoke enthusiastically of the American support they thought was coming. In the afternoon, however, when Russian troops systematically put down the uprising with tanks followed by soldiers with submachine guns and others with bayonets, separating the massive crowds into manageable clusters, it became evident that the demonstrating, rock-throwing opponents of the regime were on their own.

QUESTIONS TO CONSIDER

1. Before 1953 the (West) German Federal Republic had no holidays commemorating national personages or events. Why was there a certain logic in celebrating June 17 as "Day of German Unity"?

2. Why do you suppose that although the June Uprising was generally applauded in Western Europe and the United States, there were some less than enthusiastic responses there also?

3. What lessons do you think other Eastern Europeans in the Soviet bloc drew (or failed to draw) from the June Uprising and the American response?

Stretched across Berlin's broadest avenue, with massive bomb-scarred columns towering 40 feet above the street, stands a stone arch, the Brandenburger Tor. A red flag, large enough to be seen flapping miles away, flies day and night from the roof of the arch here on the border between East and West Berlin. The red flag is a symbol of Soviet control in East Germany, a control that for eight years has gone unquestioned and untested.

With the last subway to cross the East-West border before the anti-Soviet uprising shut down all means of transportation, I arrived at Alexanderplatz, Soviet Berlin's main business section, on the morning of June 17. Scattered crowds of protestors had been gathering since the evening before and now a full-scale riot was breaking out. The streets were jammed with Berliner workers by the thousands, who were jeering in chorus at the trucks of Russian troops being driven by to intimidate them. A week before, an open complaint against the puppet government (which clamors its single-minded purpose of running a "workers' government" while in reality exploiting the workers with extra long hours under the worst of working conditions coupled with high prices out of the workers' reach in the government-owned stores) could never have been heard on the street where giant posters of government bosses Pieck, Grotewohl, and Ulbricht,[1] stared from every flat wall surrounded by banners and slogans, and patrols of carbine-carrying "Vopos," German "People's Police," who do the dirty work of the Russian occupation, policed the streets. But that morning the defiant mob had ripped every poster within reach into pieces and trampled the fragments along with the red flags on the muddy cobblestones. As the troop-trucks of Russian soldiers continued to roll by, the demonstrators chanted in unison "Down with the clique of pointed beards," meaning Ulbricht and his hirelings, and "Bread! Free elections! A united Germany!" There was a mixture of surprise and anger on the faces of the Russian soldiers as if a workers' uprising against a "workers' government" just couldn't be. Some of them attempted to laugh it off and waved their hats with broad grins at the fist-shaking mob, who cleared up any doubts by showering the soldiers with stone fragments and yelling "Go home!" in German and Russian.

As the last troop truck rolled by, the crowd pressed into the street and surrounded several cars that were trying to make their way through. Car doors were ripped open and bureaucrats yanked out and thrown against the curb, while workers tore up and scattered their party-record books and wrecked their cars. One wrinkled little man clung fast to his steering wheel and pleaded with the crowd: "But I'm a worker!" "A worker!" shouted an exasperated young hausfrau, "If you were a worker, you wouldn't have a car to drive." Finally the little man produced papers to show that he was only a messenger for the film industry and was allowed to drive away on four wheels. Others weren't so lucky. A little farther down the street we came to a battered

---

[1]Wilhelm Pieck held the largely symbolic office of president of the German Democratic Republic, Otto Grotewohl was its prime minister, and Walter Ulbricht headed the Socialist Unity Party, which was for all intents and purposes the East German Communist Party.

From *The Daily Mail*, Vol. CXXV, No. 148 (Hagerstown, Maryland: June 25, 1953), pp. 1–2. Reprinted by permission. Footnotes added.

door, then a tire-rim followed by a battery and an inner-tube and finally a burning heap of unclassified rubbish. "What's that?" I asked. The answer was prompt but calm, "Oh, they found a real Bonzen [government boss] driving it."

Soon a parade of demonstrators, thousands strong, was headed for the headquarters of the hated Vopos. The crowd collected bricks from nearby ruins and began to heave them through the windows, when suddenly the Vopos swarmed out of the building and began beating the crowd back with riot clubs. Part of the crowd stampeded and we were forced through the narrow gateway of a courtyard opposite the headquarters. From the street we heard pistol volleys from the Vopos and a rain of brick fragments in answer, but it was not until we were able to push out of the courtyard again that we saw what had really happened. The Vopos had been driven back into their building by the enraged demonstrators who were helping some of their badly beaten wounded away. Four huge black squad cars lay on their side engulfed in flames.

The uprising was in full sway. Back at Alexanderplatz, children climbed to the top of the "Monument to German Soviet Friendship" and tore loose the wooden decorations and glass-framed pictures of Stalin, smashing them on the sidewalk below. By this time the panic-stricken government had sent out a general alarm. Help came in the form of Russian troops and Vopos, heavy tanks and gun wagons. At Alexanderplatz, a man was brutally smashed by a tank as the reenforcements rolled by. The groups of demonstrators were cut off from each other as the tanks zigzagged down the streets, churning up the cobblestones as they collided with the sidewalks. A Russian officer stood in the turret of the lead tank and directed the panzers with a pretentious sweep of his cane. Squads of soldiers sprang from the trucks and advanced on the demonstrators with fixed bayonets, firing machine gun bursts over their heads.

Yet the workers were far from finished. On the parade street "Unter den Linden," they reassembled and even erected a crude wooden cross where one of their members had been shot by a Vopo. An hour before, two East Berliners had scrambled atop the Brandenburger Tor and thrown down the symbolic red flag into a crowd on the West Berlin side, where it was burned under the arch. Now the East Berliners organized for a last march past the Soviet panzers and Vopo troops, down the parade street, and through the Brandenburger Tor into the West. We joined the ranks, which had been considerably thinned through the Soviet maneuvers, behind two young workers carrying the black, gold, and red German flag. Suddenly over the street-corner loudspeakers came a sharp announcement: "By order of the Soviet Commander, East Berlin has been placed under martial law. Curfew is declared from 9 P.M. until 5 A.M. Gatherings of more than three persons are strictly forbidden." Suddenly the demonstrators broke into a run. As the first ranks passed through under the arch into the free West, the marchers struck up a chorus of "Deutschland über alles,"[2] which was taken up by the waiting crowd on the other side.

---

[2]The Romantic poet Heinrich Hoffman von Fallersleben wrote *"Deutschland, Deutschland über alles"* ("Germany, Germany above Everything") in 1841 to urge German unification. Decades later, after unification took place, it became the national anthem. During both World Wars the Allies related its message to German conquests rather than unification; after World War II it was banned, although its less-threatening–seeming third verse, beginning "Unity, Justice and Freedom for the German Fatherland" became the West German and much later the all-German anthem. The 1950s uprisings in East Germany, Poland, and Hungary all suffered from a lack of fitting revolutionary songs. In the June 1953 East German revolt, demonstrators against the Soviet occupation occasionally sang songs of Communist origin, such as "Brothers, to the Sun, to Freedom . . . !" and "Arise, ye Prisoners of Starvation . . . !" (The *Internationale*) simply because they had heard their revolutionary words on the state-run radio often enough to know their first verses, which they repeated over and over.

A few minutes later, several young demonstrators appeared on the roof of the arch and fastened three flags to the huge mast. Others followed after them, bringing flags and emblems of all sorts. A tall blond girl stood in the middle of the assemblage on the roof and waved the black, gold, and red flag as the cheers from below reached a climax. Suddenly the little group stiffened and as the crowd looked on in silent horror, the girl walked to the West edge of the arch-roof and dropped the flag over the side. We soon learned why. From the East side of the arch, a Russian gun wagon had pulled up and focused its MGs on the arch-roof. Machine-gun bursts methodically strafed the small staircase leading down from the roof. Only with the aid of a long pole and a rope were the six able to reach the street on the western side where they were carried on the shoulders of the crowd and bestowed with presents of cigarettes—a tribute which in postwar Germany was no meager honor.

That evening as Russian troop trucks and tanks were still stationed behind the Brandenburger Tor and the East Berlin horizon was still discolored with smoke from burning government-owned booths and stands throughout the city, the Russians removed the rebellious German flags and hoisted a new red one over the arch. But the new flag was little more than half the size of the monstrous red banner Berliners were used to and looked conspicuously bare on the huge mast. Berliners on the way home could feel that, unconscious though it was, the change in the size of the red flag behind them also marked a whittling down of Soviet confidence as the Russians reviewed their control in East Germany and counted on its support in the Cold War.

77 General Douglas MacArthur, Report to Congress, April 19, 1951: "Old Soldiers Never Die"

General of the Army Douglas MacArthur (1880–1964), who was much respected by the World War II generation of Americans as the successful Allied Supreme Commander of forces in the Pacific and then head of the military government of Japan, opposed "containment" as too passive at best and as "appeasement" at worst. Appointed as commander of UN forces at the outbreak of the Korean War, MacArthur's disagreements with President Truman over how aggressively the United States should pursue the Korean War led to his dismissal in April 1951. In possession of a substantial following among Americans, MacArthur was invited to address a joint session of Congress to report on the situation in the Far East, an occasion he used to advocate widening the scope of war measures against communism there. The ballad that he cites near the end gave the speech a familiar name. No less than five recording companies issued releases of the song, which became an immediate hit, at least one version including a new final verse, which began:

Washington and Grant and Lee were all tried and true,
Eisenhower, Bradley, [pause] *and MacArthur too!*

QUESTIONS TO CONSIDER

1. In a speech to the Texas legislature some three months after his Report to Congress, MacArthur called the Truman administration's policy "appeasement on the battlefield, whereunder we soften our blows, withhold our power, and surrender military advantages, in apparent hope that some nebulous way by doing so a potential enemy be coerced to desist from attacking us."[1] Did Truman's policy or MacArthur's—outlined below—make more sense in the conflict in Korea? Was "containment" really "appeasement"? Did it tend to leave the initiative for international action with Communist adversaries during the cold war? Was it ultimately successful?

2. How does MacArthur allude to the relationship between China and Taiwan (Formosa)? How would you assess his proposed Taiwan policies and predictions half a century later?

3. Some forceful rhetoric in April 1951, including slogans on placards and bumper stickers, called for the impeachment of President Truman for his firing of MacArthur. How much chance do you think impeachment proceedings really had?

I address you with neither rancor nor bitterness in the fading twilight of life with but one purpose in mind—to serve my country.

The issues are global and so interlocked that to consider the problem of one sector, oblivious to those of another, is but to court disaster of the whole. . . .

The Communist threat is a global one. Its successful advance in one sector threatens the destruction of every other sector. You cannot appease or otherwise surrender to communism in Asia without simultaneously undermining our efforts to halt its advance in Europe.

Beyond pointing out these simple truisms, I shall confine my discussion to the general areas of Asia. Before one may objectively assess the situation now existing there, he must comprehend something of Asia's past and the revolutionary changes which have marked her course up to the present. Long exploited by the so-called colonial powers, with little opportunity to achieve any degree of social justice, individual dignity, or a higher standard of life such as guided our own noble administration of the Philippines, the peoples of Asia found their opportunity in the war just past to throw off the shackles of colonialism, and now see the dawn of new opportunity, a heretofore unfelt dignity and the self-respect of political freedom.

Mustering half of the earth's population and 60 percent of its natural resources, these peoples are rapidly consolidating a new force, both moral and material, with

---

[1] In *A Soldier Speaks: Public Papers and Speeches of General of the Army Douglas MacArthur,* ed. Vorin E. Whan, Jr. (New York: Praeger, 1965), p. 264.

From United States Congressional Record, "Address of General of the Army Douglas MacArthur," 82nd Congress, 1st Session, 19 April 1951, pp. 4123–25.

which to raise the living standard and erect adaptations of the design of modern progress to their own distinct cultural environments. . . .

Our strategic frontier [has] shifted to embrace the entire Pacific Ocean, which became a vast moat to protect us as long as we hold it. Indeed, it acts as a protective shield for all of the Americas and all free lands of the Pacific Ocean area. We control it to the shores of Asia by a chain of islands extending in an arc from the Aleutians to the Mariannas held by us and our free allies.

From this island chain we can dominate with sea and air power every Asiatic port from Vladivostok to Singapore and prevent any hostile movement into the Pacific. Any predatory attack from Asia must be an amphibious effort. No amphibious force can be successful without control of the sea lanes and the air over those lanes in its avenue of advance. With naval and air supremacy and modest ground elements to defend bases, any major attack from continental Asia toward us or our friends of the Pacific would be doomed to failure. . . .

The holding of this littoral defense line in the western Pacific is entirely dependent upon holding all segments thereof, for any major breach of that line by an unfriendly power would render vulnerable to determined attack every other major segment. This is a military estimate as to which I have yet to find a military leader who will take exception. For that reason I have strongly recommended in the past as a matter of military urgency that under no circumstances must Formosa fall under Communist control. Such an eventuality would at once threaten the freedom of the Philippines and the loss of Japan, and might well force our western frontier back to the coasts of California, Oregon, and Washington. . . .

At the turn of the century, . . . efforts toward greater homogeneity produced the start of a nationalist urge [in China]. This was further and more successfully developed under the leadership of Chiang Kai-shek, but has been brought to its greatest fruition under the present regime, to the point that it has now taken on the character of a united nationalism of increasingly dominant aggressive tendencies.

Through these past fifty years, the Chinese people have thus become militarized in their concepts and in their ideals. They now constitute excellent soldiers with competent staffs and commanders. This has produced a new and dominant power in Asia which for its own purposes is allied with Soviet Russia, but which in its own concepts and methods has become aggressively imperialistic with a lust for expansion and increased power normal to this type of imperialism. There is little of the ideological concept either one way or another in the Chinese make-up. The standard of living is so low and the capital accumulation has been so thoroughly dissipated by war that the masses are desperate and avid to follow any leadership which seems to promise the alleviation of local stringencies.

I have from the beginning believed that the Chinese Communists' support of the Koreans was the dominant one. Their interests are at present parallel to those of the Soviet, but I believe that the aggressiveness recently displayed not only in Korea, but also in Indochina and Tibet, and pointing potentially toward the south, reflects predominantly the same lust for the expansion of power which has animated every would-be conqueror since the beginning of time.

The Japanese people since the war have undergone the greatest reformation recorded in modern history. With a commendable will, eagerness to learn, and marked capacity to understand, they have, from the ashes left in war's wake, erected in Japan an edifice dedicated to the primacy of individual liberty and personal dignity, and in the ensuing process there has been created a truly representative government committed to the advance of political morality, freedom of economic enterprise, and social justice. Politically, economically and socially Japan is now abreast of many free nations of the earth and will not again fail the universal trust. . . .

I sent all four of our occupation divisions to the Korean battlefront without the slightest qualms as to the effect of the resulting power vacuum upon Japan. The results fully justified my faith. I know of no nation more serene, orderly and industrious—nor in which higher hopes can be entertained for future constructive service in the advance of the human race. . . .

On Formosa, the government of the Republic of China has had the opportunity to refute by action much of the malicious gossip which so undermined the strength of its leadership on the Chinese mainland. The Formosan people are receiving a just and enlightened administration with majority representation on the organs of government; and politically, economically, and socially they appear to be advancing along sound and constructive lines.

With this brief insight into the surrounding areas I now turn to the Korean conflict. While I was not consulted prior to the President's decision to intervene in support of the Republic of Korea, that decision, from a military standpoint, proved a sound one as we hurled back the invader and decimated his forces. Our victory was complete and our objectives within reach when Red China intervened with numerically superior ground forces. This created a new war and an entirely new situation—a situation not contemplated when our forces were committed against the North Korean invaders—a situation which called for new decisions in the diplomatic sphere to permit the realistic adjustment of military strategy. Such decisions have not been forthcoming.

While no man in his right mind would advocate sending our ground forces into continental China, and such was never given a thought, the new situation did urgently demand a drastic revision of strategic planning if our political aim was to defeat this new enemy as we had defeated the old.

Apart from the military need as I saw it to neutralize the sanctuary protection given the enemy north of the Yalu, I felt that military necessity in the conduct of the war made mandatory:

1. The intensification of our economic blockade against China;
2. The imposition of a naval blockade against the China coast;
3. Removal of restrictions on air reconnaissance of China's coastal areas and of Manchuria;
4. Removal of restrictions on the forces of the Republic of China on Formosa with logistical support to contribute to their effective operations against the common enemy.

For entertaining these views, all professionally designed to support our forces committed to Korea and bring hostilities to an end with the least possible delay and at a saving of countless American and Allied lives, I have been severely criticized in lay circles, principally abroad, despite my understanding that from a military standpoint the above views have been fully shared in the past by practically every military leader concerned with the Korean campaign, including our own Joint Chiefs of Staff.

I called for reinforcements, but was informed that reinforcements were not available. I made clear that if not permitted to destroy the [enemy] build-up bases north of the Yalu; if not permitted to utilize the friendly Chinese force of some 600,000 men on Formosa; if not permitted to blockade the China coast to prevent the Chinese Reds from getting succor from without; and if there were to be no hope of major reinforcements, the position of the command from the military standpoint forbade victory. We could hold in Korea by constant maneuver and at an approximate area where our supply line advantages were in balance with the supply line disadvantages of the enemy, but we could hope at best for only an indecisive campaign, with its terrible and constant attrition upon our forces if the enemy utilized his full military potential.

I have constantly called for the new political decisions essential to a solution. Efforts have been made to distort my position. It has been said, in effect, that I am a warmonger. Nothing could be further from the truth. I know war as few other men now living know it, and nothing to me is more revolting. I have long advocated its complete abolition as its very destructiveness on both friend and foe has rendered it useless as a means of settling international disputes. . . .

There are some who for varying reasons would appease Red China. They are blind to history's clear lesson; for history teaches with unmistakable emphasis that appeasement but begets new and bloodier war. It points to no single instance where the end has justified that means—where appeasement has led to more than a sham peace. Like blackmail, it lays the basis for new and successively greater demands, until, as in blackmail, violence becomes the only other alternative.

Why, my soldiers asked of me, surrender military advantages to an enemy in the field? I could not answer. Some may say to avoid spread of the conflict into an all-out war with China; others, to avoid Soviet intervention. Neither explanation seems valid. For China is already engaging with the maximum power it can commit and the Soviets will not necessarily mesh its actions with our moves. Like a cobra, any new enemy will more likely strike whenever it feels that the relativity in military or other potential is in its favor on a worldwide basis.

The tragedy of Korea is further heightened by the fact that as military action is confined to its territorial limits, it condemns that nation, which it is our purpose to save, to suffer the devastating impact of full naval and air bombardment, while the enemy's sanctuaries are fully protected from such attack and devastation. Of the nations of the world, Korea alone, up to now, is the sole one which has risked its all against communism. The magnificence of the courage and fortitude of the Korean people defies description. They have chosen to risk death rather than slavery. Their last words to me were "Don't scuttle the Pacific."

I have just left your fighting sons in Korea. They have met all tests there and I can report to you without reservation they are splendid in every way. It was my constant effort to preserve them and end this savage conflict honorably and with the least loss of time and a minimum sacrifice of life. Its growing bloodshed has caused me the deepest anguish and anxiety. Those gallant men will remain often in my thoughts and in my prayers always.

I am closing my fifty-two years of military service. When I joined the Army, even before the turn of the century, it was the fulfillment of all my boyish hopes and dreams. The world has turned over many times since I took the oath on the plain at West Point, and the hopes and dreams have long since vanished. But I still remember the refrain of one of the most popular barrack ballads of that day which proclaimed most proudly that "Old soldiers never die. They just fade away."

And like the old soldier of that ballad, I now close my military career and just fade away—an old soldier who tried to do his duty as God gave him the light to see that duty.

Goodbye.

China and Soviet Russia Go Separate Ways

A
lthough linked by Marxism-Leninism as a common ideological norm, Russia and China grew far apart in the 1950s as the result of different interests in their regions and different perceptions of leadership. Whereas Russia took a softer line of peaceful coexistence and internal relaxation of control, China remained committed to stricter policies under Mao Zedong.

In 1956, Nikita Khrushchev, the new Communist Party first secretary (1953–1964), shocked the Twentieth Party Congress by denouncing the "cult of the individual" and the crimes of Joseph Stalin. Unintentionally, his speech, designed to tighten his control over the party apparatus, contributed to further unrest in Eastern Europe. By saluting the special case of Yugoslavian communism, Khrushchev hinted that differing styles of communism within Eastern Europe were acceptable. But in 1956, when rioting and political unrest erupted in Poland and Hungary, Khrushchev sent in the Red Army to restore control. Despite the blatant crushing of these revolts, Soviet leadership under Leonid I. Brezhnev (1964–1982) permitted a relaxation of political controls within Eastern Europe. Even in Hungary there was a thaw; but it was in 1968 in Czechoslovakia that the most daring attempts to democratize government were made. The Soviets responded to the Czech rebellion with strong military force and justified their actions with the policy known as the Brezhnev Doctrine, which stated that no secessions from the "Socialist" camp of countries would be tolerated.

Khrushchev had made it plain that peaceful coexistence was not exactly peace. While he, and Brezhnev after him, ruled out warfare between the USSR and the industrial countries of the West, he defended Soviet aid to groups waging civil wars or "wars of national liberation." Soviet policy remained one of giving aid to movements hostile to Western influence, and countries of the West generally advocated a policy of containing communism. The West gave half-hearted encouragement but no military assistance to anti-Communist resistance in Eastern Europe.

As a result, the cold war was characterized by adversarial relations between the USSR and Western countries, but the actual wars waged between forces fighting in the name of Marxist revolution and their opponents were regional ones in the Third World. Twice, in Korea and Vietnam, the United

States fought with its own troops in regional Asian wars, while in 1979 the USSR intervened in Afghanistan with the Soviet Army, but Soviet forces were never in direct combat against those of the United States or any other NATO country, and the geographical sphere of the fighting remained almost completely confined to the countries where the wars had begun.

Until his death in 1976, Mao Tse-tung was the supreme figure, reminiscent of the old Chinese emperor, in the People's Republic of China (PRC). He was one of the dozen who gave birth to the Communist Party of China in Shanghai in 1921. He emerged as the sole "survivor" among the original members of the party. The rest left the party for one reason or another, including purges, defections, resignations, or deaths. His rise to the leadership of the Chinese Communist Party, which was dominated in its early years by the Moscow-trained and urban-oriented Chinese Communists, was through rather unorthodox means. He carefully built his power base in the countryside, believing that the peasants, rather than the urban proletariat, were the mainstay of the Communist revolution. He spent more than twenty years in rural China organizing and leading peasants and the peasant army, the forerunner of the People's Liberation Army. He presided over the Communist insurgent government (known as the Chinese Soviet Republic) in a mountainous region of south-central China from 1931 to 1934. After the collapse of this "Red Republic" in 1935, during the six-thousand-mile Long March, harassed by pursuing Chiang Kai-shek's Nationalist troops, Mao emerged as the undisputed leader in the Communist Party by eclipsing the Moscow-oriented party leadership, which had lost its urban base to Chiang Kai-shek. His leadership of the party was formalized in 1943 when he was elected chairman of the Central Committee and the Politburo of the Communist Party of China. In Yenan [Yan'an], the new hinterland base of operations of the Communists from 1936 to 1947, Mao enjoyed not only unchallenged leadership in the Chinese Communist movement, but he also emerged as a Communist theoretician by adapting Marxism-Leninism to the unique socioeconomic and political conditions within China. He produced a number of theoretical works, including "On Practice," "On Contradiction," and "Problems of Strategy in China's Revolutionary War."

78 Nikita S. Khrushchev, Address to the Twentieth Party Congress

On February 28, 1956, in an address to the Twentieth Congress of the Soviet Communist Party, Nikita Khrushchev provided a long list of the crimes of the late Joseph Stalin. Khrushchev's rough, earthy humor did not mask the fact that Stalin had perpetrated an immense reign of terror against the Russian people. The detailed indictment confirmed long-held Western views that between 1928 and 1953 Stalin imprisoned, deported, and killed millions of Russians (see Reading 61). Khrushchev's address to the Party Congress inadvertently raised the hope of reform in Eastern Europe.

QUESTIONS TO CONSIDER

1. What steps did Khrushchev propose to eradicate the "cult of the individual" in the Soviet Union?
2. How did Khrushchev employ the legacy of Lenin to attack his predecessor?
3. Are there any connections between Khrushchev's attacks on Stalin and Mikhail Gorbachev's policies of *Perestroika* (see Reading 91)?

When we analyze the practice of Stalin in regard to the direction of the party and of the country, when we pause to consider everything which Stalin perpetrated, we must be convinced that Lenin's fears were justified. The negative characteristics of Stalin, which, in Lenin's time, were only incipient, transformed themselves during the last years into a grave abuse of power by Stalin, which caused untold harm to our party.

We have to consider seriously and analyze correctly this matter in order that we may preclude any possibility of a repetition in any form whatever of what took place during the life of Stalin, who absolutely did not tolerate collegiality in leadership and in work, and who practiced brutal violence, not only toward everything which opposed him, but also toward that which seemed to his capricious and despotic character, contrary to his concepts.

Stalin acted not through persuasion, explanation, and patient cooperation with people, but by imposing his concepts and demanding absolute submission to his opinion. Whoever opposed this concept or tried to prove his viewpoint, and the correctness of his position—was doomed to removal from the leading collective and to subsequent moral and physical annihilation. This was especially true during the period following the 17th party congress, when many prominent party leaders and rank-and-file party workers, honest and dedicated to the cause of communism, fell victim to Stalin's despotism. . . .

Lenin's traits—patient work with people; stubborn and painstaking education of them; the ability to induce people to follow him without using compulsion, but rather through the ideological influence on them of the whole collective—were entirely foreign to Stalin. He (Stalin) discarded the Leninist method of convincing and educating;

From U.S. Congress, *Congressional Record*, 84th Congress, 2nd Session, 1956, CII, pp. 9389–403, *passim*.

he abandoned the method of ideological struggle for that of administrative violence, mass repressions, and terror. He acted on an increasingly larger scale and more stubbornly through punitive organs, at the same time often violating all existing norms of morality and of Soviet laws. . . .

During Lenin's life party congresses were convened regularly; always when a radical turn in the development of the party and the country took place Lenin considered it absolutely necessary that the party discuss at length all the basic matters pertaining to internal and foreign policy and to questions bearing on the development of party and government. . . .

Were our party's holy Leninist principles observed after the death of Vladimir Ilyich?

Whereas during the first few years after Lenin's death party congresses and central committee plenums took place more or less regularly; later, when Stalin began increasingly to abuse his power, these principles were brutally violated. This was especially evident during the last 15 years of his life. Was it a normal situation when 13 years elapsed between the 18th and 19th party congresses, years during which our party and our country had experienced so many important events? These events demanded categorically that the party should have passed resolutions pertaining to the country's defense during the patriotic war and to peacetime construction after the war. Even after the end of the war a congress was not convened for over 7 years.

Central committee plenums were hardly ever called. It should be sufficient to mention that during all the years of the patriotic war not a single central committee plenum took place. . . .

In practice Stalin ignored the norms of party life and trampled on the Leninist principle of collective party leadership. . . .

Facts prove that many abuses were made on Stalin's orders without reckoning with any norms of party and Soviet legality. Stalin was a very distrustful man. . . . He could look at a man and say: "Why are your eyes so shifty today?" or "Why are you turning so much today and avoiding to look me directly in the eyes?" The sickly suspicion created in him a general distrust even toward eminent party workers whom he had known for years. Everywhere and in everything he saw enemies, "two-facers" and spies.

Possessing unlimited power he indulged in great willfulness and choked a person morally and physically. A situation was created where one could not express one's own will. . . .

The willfulness of Stalin showed itself not only in decisions concerning the internal life of the country but also in the international relations of the Soviet Union.

The July plenum of the Central Committee studied in detail the reasons for the development of conflict with Yugoslavia. It was a shameful role which Stalin played here. The "Yugoslav affair" contained no problems which could not have been solved through party discussions among comrades. There was no significant basis for the development of this "affair"; it was completely possible to have prevented the rupture of relations with that country. This does not mean, however, that the Yugoslav leaders did not make mistakes or did not have shortcomings. But these mistakes and shortcomings were magnified in a monstrous manner by Stalin, which resulted in a break of relations with a friendly country.

I recall the first days when the conflict between the Soviet Union and Yugoslavia began artificially to be blown up. Once, when I came from Kiev to Moscow, I was invited to visit Stalin who, pointing to the copy of a letter lately sent to Tito, asked me, "Have you read this?"

Not waiting for my reply he answered, "I will shake my little finger and there will be no more Tito. He will fall."

We have dearly paid for this "shaking of the little finger." This statement reflected Stalin's mania for greatness, but he acted just that way: "I shall shake my little finger and there will be no Kossior"; "I will shake my little finger once more and Postyshev and Chubar will be no more"; "I will shake my little finger again and Voznesensky, Kuznetsov and many others will disappear."

But this did not happen to Tito. No matter how much or how little Stalin shook, not only his little finger but everything else that he could shake, Tito did not fall. Why? The reason was that, in this case of disagreement with the Yugoslav comrades, Tito had behind him a state and a people who had gone through a severe school of fighting for liberty and independence, a people which gave support to its leaders.

You see to what Stalin's mania for greatness led. He had completely lost consciousness of reality; he demonstrated his suspicion and haughtiness not only in relation to individuals in the U.S.S.R., but in relation to whole parties and nations.

We have carefully examined the case of Yugoslavia and have found a proper solution which is approved by the peoples of the Soviet Union and of Yugoslavia as well as by the working masses of all the people's democracies and by all progressive humanity. The liquidation of the abnormal relationship with Yugoslavia was done in the interest of the whole camp of socialism, in the interest of strengthening peace in the whole world. . . .

If we are to consider this matter as Marxists and as Leninists, then we have to state unequivocally that the leadership practice which came into being during the last years of Stalin's life became a serious obstacle in the path of Soviet social development.

Stalin often failed for months to take up some unusually important problems concerning the life of the party and of the state whose solution could not be postponed. During Stalin's leadership our peaceful relations with other nations were often threatened, because one-man decisions could cause and often did cause great complications.

In the last years, when we managed to free ourselves of the harmful practice of the cult of the individual and took several proper steps in the sphere of internal and external policies, everyone saw how activity grew before their very eyes, how the creative activity of the broad working masses developed, how favorably all this acted upon the development of economy and of culture. [Applause.]

Some comrades may ask us: Where were the members of the Political Bureau of the Central Committee? Why did they not assert themselves against the cult of the individual in time? And why is this being done only now?

First of all we have to consider the fact that the members of the Political Bureau viewed these matters in a different way at different times. Initially, many of them backed Stalin actively because Stalin was one of the strongest Marxists and his logic, his strength, and his will greatly influenced the cadres and party work. . . .

Later, however, abusing his power more and more, [Stalin] began to fight eminent party and government leaders and to use terroristic methods against honest Soviet people. . . .

It is clear that such conditions put every member of the Political Bureau in a very difficult situation. And when we also consider the fact that in the last years the Central

Committee plenary sessions were not convened, and that the sessions of the Political Bureau occurred only occasionally, from time to time, then we will understand how difficult it was for any member of the Political Bureau to take a stand against one or another unjust or improper procedure, against serious errors and shortcomings in the practices of leadership. . . .

Comrades, we must abolish the cult of the individual decisively, once and for all; we must draw the proper conclusions concerning both ideological-theoretical and practical work.

It is necessary for this purpose:

First, in a Bolshevik manner to condemn and to eradicate the cult of the individual as alien to Marxism-Leninism and not consonant with the principles of party leadership and the norms of party life, and to fight inexorably all attempts at bringing back this practice. . . .

Secondly, to continue systematically and consistently the work done by the party's central committee during the last years, a work characterized by minute observation in all party organizations, from the bottom to the top, of the Leninist principles of party leadership, characterized, above all, by the main principle of collective leadership, characterized by the observation of the norms of party life described in the statutes of our party, and, finally, characterized by the wide practice of criticism and self-criticism.

Thirdly, to restore completely the Leninist principles of Soviet Socialist democracy, expressed in the constitution of the Soviet Union, to fight willfulness of individuals abusing their power. The evil caused by acts violating revolutionary Socialist legality which have accumulated during a long time as a result of the negative influence of the cult of the individual has to be completely corrected. . . .

We are absolutely certain that our party, armed with the historical resolutions of the 20th Congress, will lead the Soviet people along the Leninist path to new successes, to new victories. [Tumultuous, prolonged applause.]

Long live the victorious banner of our party—Leninism. [Tumultuous, prolonged applause ending in ovation. All rise.]

79 Mao Tse-tung [Mao Zedong], "The People's Democratic Dictatorship"

Following Japan's defeat in World War II in August 1945 and the subsequent Communist victory over Chiang Kai-shek's Nationalist forces in the bitterly fought four-year civil war, on October 1, 1949, twenty-eight years after the formation of the Communist Party of China, Mao Tse-tung stood on the Gate of Heavenly Peace (Tiananmen) in Beijing (Peking) to proclaim the birth of the People's Republic of China. Mao now was the leader of the world's most populous Communist state. He gave the following speech earlier that year on June 30, 1949, in commemoration of the Chinese Communist Party's twenty-eighth anniversary.

QUESTIONS TO CONSIDER

1. What meaning does Mao give to the term "democratic"? How does he make this term consistent with the term "dictatorship"?
2. What is Mao's attitude toward the Soviet Union? Did he remain constant in this attitude?

Communists the world over are wiser than the bourgeoisie, they understand the laws governing the existence and development of things, they understand dialectics and they can see farther. The bourgeoisie does not welcome this truth because it does not want to be overthrown.

As everyone knows, our Party passed through these twenty-eight years not in peace but amid hardships, for we had to fight enemies, both foreign and domestic, both inside and outside the Party. We thank Marx, Engels, Lenin and Stalin for giving us a weapon. This weapon is not a machine-gun, but Marxism-Leninism. . . .

The Russians made the October Revolution and created the world's first socialist state. Under the leadership of Lenin and Stalin, the revolutionary energy of the great proletariat and labouring people of Russia, hitherto latent and unseen by foreigners, suddenly erupted like a volcano, and the Chinese and all mankind began to see the Russians in a new light. Then, and only then, did the Chinese enter an entirely new era in their thinking and their life. They found Marxism-Leninism, the universally applicable truth, and the face of China began to change. . . .

There are bourgeois republics in foreign lands, but China cannot have a bourgeois republic because she is a country suffering under imperialist oppression. The only way is through a people's republic led by the working class. . . .

Twenty-four years have passed since Sun Yat-sen's death, and the Chinese revolution, led by the Communist Party of China, has made tremendous advances both in theory and practice and has radically changed the face of China. Up to now the principal and fundamental experience the Chinese people have gained is twofold:

1. Internally, arouse the masses of the people. That is, unite the working class, the peasantry, the urban petty bourgeoisie and the national bourgeoisie, form a domestic united front under the leadership of the working class, and advance from this to the establishment of a state which is a people's democratic dictatorship under the leadership of the working class and based on the alliance of workers and peasants.
2. Externally, unite in a common struggle with those nations of the world which treat us as equals and unite with the peoples of all countries. That is, ally ourselves with the Soviet Union, with the People's Democracies and with the proletariat and the broad masses of the people in all other countries, and form an international united front.

"You are leaning to one side." Exactly. The forty years' experience of Sun Yat-sen and the twenty-eight years' experience of the Communist Party have taught us to

From Mao Tse-tung, Speech "In Commemoration of the 28th Anniversary of the Communist Party of China, June 30, 1949," in *Selected Works*, Vol. 5 (New York: International Publishers, n.d.), pp. 411–23.

lean to one side, and we are firmly convinced that in order to win victory and consolidate it we must lean to one side. In the light of the experiences accumulated in these forty years and these twenty-eight years, all Chinese without exception must lean either to the side of imperialism or to the side of socialism. Sitting on the fence will not do, nor is there a third road. We oppose the Chiang Kai-shek reactionaries who lean to the side of imperialism, and we also oppose the illusions about a third road.

"You are too irritating." We are talking about how to deal with domestic and foreign reactionaries, the imperialists and their running dogs, not about how to deal with anyone else. With regard to such reactionaries, the question of irritating them or not does not arise. Irritated or not irritated, they will remain the same because they are reactionaries. Only if we draw a clear line between reactionaries and revolutionaries, expose the intrigues and plots of the reactionaries, arouse the vigilance and attention of the revolutionary ranks, heighten our will to fight and crush the enemy's arrogance can we isolate the reactionaries, vanquish them or supersede them. We must not show the slightest timidity before a wild beast.

"Victory is possible even without international help." This is a mistaken idea. In the epoch in which imperialism exists, it is impossible for a genuine people's revolution to win victory in any country without various forms of help from the international revolutionary forces, and even if victory were won, it could not be consolidated. This was the case with the victory and consolidation of the great October Revolution, as Lenin and Stalin told us long ago.

"We need help from the British and U.S. governments." This, too, is a naive idea in these times. Would the present rulers of Britain and the United States, who are imperialists, help a people's state? Why do these countries do business with us and, supposing they might be willing to lend us money on terms of mutual benefit in the future, why would they do so? Because their capitalists want to make money and their bankers want to earn interest to extricate themselves from their own crisis—it is not a matter of helping the Chinese people.

"You are dictatorial." My dear sirs, you are right, that is just what we are. All the experience the Chinese people have accumulated through several decades teaches us to enforce the people's democratic dictatorship, that is, to deprive the reactionaries of the right to speak and let the people alone have that right.

"Who are the people?" At the present stage in China, they are the working class, the peasantry, the urban petty bourgeoisie and the national bourgeoisie. These classes, led by the working class and the Communist Party, unite to form their own state and elect their own government; they enforce their dictatorship over the running dogs of imperialism—the landlord class and bureaucrat-bourgeoisie, as well as the representatives of those classes, the Kuomintang reactionaries and their accomplices—suppress them, allow them only to behave themselves and not to be unruly in word or deed. If they speak or act in an unruly way, they will be promptly stopped and punished. Democracy is practised within the ranks of the people, who enjoy the rights of freedom of speech, assembly, association and so on. The right to vote belongs only to the people, not to the reactionaries. The combination of these two aspects, democracy for the people and dictatorship over the reactionaries, is the people's democratic dictatorship.

"Why must things be done this way?" The reason is quite clear to everybody. If things were not done this way, the revolution would fail, the people would suffer, the country would be conquered.

"Don't you want to abolish state power?" Yes, we do, but not right now; we cannot do it yet. Why? Because imperialism still exists, because domestic reaction still exists, because classes still exist in our country. Our present task is to strengthen the people's state apparatus—mainly the people's army, the people's police and the people's courts—in order to consolidate national defense and protect the people's interests. Given this condition, China can develop steadily, under the leadership of the working class and the Communist Party, from an agricultural into an industrial country and from a new-democratic into a socialist and communist society, can abolish classes and realize the Great Harmony. The state apparatus, including the army, the police and the courts, is the instrument by which one class oppresses another. It is an instrument for the oppression of antagonistic classes; it is violence and not "benevolence." "You are not benevolent!" Quite so. We definitely do not apply a policy of benevolence to the reactionaries and towards the reactionary activities of the reactionary classes. Our policy of benevolence is applied only within the ranks of the people, not beyond them to the reactionaries or to the reactionary activities of reactionary classes. . . .

Here, the method we employ is democratic, the method of persuasion, not of compulsion. When anyone among the people breaks the law, he too should be punished, imprisoned or even sentenced to death; but this is a matter of a few individual cases, and it differs in principle from the dictatorship exercised over the reactionaries as a class.

As for the members of the reactionary classes and individual reactionaries, so long as they do not rebel, sabotage or create trouble after their political power has been overthrown, land and work will be given to them as well in order to allow them to live and remould themselves through labour into new people. If they are not willing to work, the people's state will compel them to work. . . .

Such remoulding of members of the reactionary classes can be accomplished only by a state of the people's democratic dictatorship under the leadership of the Communist Party. When it is well done, China's major exploiting classes, the landlord class and the bureaucrat-bourgeoisie (the monopoly capitalist class), will be eliminated for good. There remain the national bourgeoisie; at the present stage, we can already do a good deal of suitable educational work with many of them. When the time comes to realize socialism, that is, to nationalize private enterprise, we shall carry the work of educating and remoulding them a step further. The people have a powerful state apparatus in their hands—there is no need to fear rebellion by the national bourgeoisie. . . .

The people's democratic dictatorship is based on the alliance of the working class, the peasantry and the urban petty bourgeoisie, and mainly on the alliance of the workers and the peasants, because these two classes comprise 80 to 90 per cent of China's population. These two classes are the main force in overthrowing imperialism and the Kuomintang reactionaries. The transition from New Democracy to socialism also depends mainly upon their alliance.

The people's democratic dictatorship needs the leadership of the working class. For it is only the working class that is most farsighted, most selfless and most thoroughly revolutionary. The entire history of revolution proves that without the leadership of the working class revolution fails. In the epoch of imperialism, in no country can any other class lead any genuine revolution to victory. This is clearly proved by the fact that the many revolutions led by China's petty bourgeoisie and national bourgeoisie all failed. . . .

To sum up our experience and concentrate it into one point, it is: the people's democratic dictatorship under the leadership of the working class (through the Communist Party) and based upon the alliance of workers and peasants. This dictatorship must unite as one with the international revolutionary forces. This is our formula, our principal experience, our main programme. . . .

The Communist Party of the Soviet Union is our best teacher and we must learn from it. The situation both at home and abroad is in our favour, we can rely fully on the weapon of the people's democratic dictatorship, unite the people throughout the country, the reactionaries excepted, and advance steadily to our goal.

Decolonization: Africa, Latin America, and India

Changes in the developing countries of Africa, Latin America, and Asia have shaped much of the history of the second half of the twentieth century. In the first two decades following World War II, one-third of the world's population threw off colonial rule. Between 1945 and 1980, more than ninety new nations joined the ranks of independent countries. For some new nations, the transition was relatively easy; others found the process painful, deceptive, and fraught with bloodshed and economic failure.

Events in Africa paralleled those in Asia, where revolutionary independence movements assaulted the colonial rule of the leading Western powers. When transitions to independence were relatively peaceful, they were often followed by internal revolutions.

France and Great Britain, the Western powers that built the largest colonial empires in the nineteenth century, saw their empires collapse in the decades following World War II. This was attributable in part to the costs of fighting the war. By 1945, Britain was nearly bankrupt, and France, though nominally a victor, was afflicted with the psychological wounds of defeat and the stigma of having collaborated with German occupiers. The last day of the European war, May 8, 1945, marked the first day of French-controlled Algeria's struggle for independence—a struggle that continued for seventeen years at a cost of 750,000 lives. A year later, in 1946, Ho Chi Minh broke off negotiations with France, and for the next eight years he directed a guerrilla insurgency that won independence for North Vietnam in 1954 at a cost of hundreds of thousands of Vietnamese lives and more than 90,000 soldiers of the French Indochina Army.

The following selections suggest some of the differing perspectives on general decolonization in Africa and the struggle over apartheid in South Africa.

In *The Wretched of the Earth,* the Algerian psychiatrist Frantz Fanon puts the colonial presence and anticolonial struggle in a new black-and-white set of terms. He saw no redeeming features in European civilization. He did not try to persuade his audience that the natives in the colonies had the same democratic values that Europeans had: He did not believe that this was necessary or even relevant.

South Africa differed from the rest of Africa in that its problems of ethnic-group relations began well before nineteenth-century colonialism. It also differed from the rest of sub-Saharan Africa in having a much larger white minority in relation to the black majority, with some of this group tracing family origins back to Dutch settlers of the seventeenth century. Dominating much of urban life and agriculture after three centuries, they no longer thought of themselves as settlers. In the late 1940s, they sensed fearfully that the British government might be moving toward a one-man, one-vote system in the Union of South Africa or that the British might grant South Africa independence in a way that would put political power into the hands of its black majority. As a result, the white minority, which continued to exercise political control of the country, used its power to enact *apartheid* (literally "apartness"), a set of policies designed to heighten the existing segregation of races with the goal of retaining South Africa as a place run by whites. Apartheid engendered a great deal of international attention because it opposed integration and increasing attempts to promote equality in most of the world from the 1950s to the 1980s. Mercifully, it came to a gradual but total end roughly at the time the cold war ended in the late 1980s and early 1990s. In 1994, Nelson Mandela, the foremost leader of the militantly anti-apartheid African National Congress who had spent more than twenty-seven years in prison for planning acts of sabotage against the regime, was duly elected the first black president of a new South Africa, apparently determined to overcome his country's past history of racial animosities.

Although most Latin American nations achieved independence in the early nineteenth century, colonial institutions and values remained deeply ingrained in many countries. The Mexican Revolution provided a model for potential change for some nationalists who hoped to reform their nations and also achieve greater independence from the influence of the United States. American presidents focused their postwar attention on Europe and Asia and tended to favor authoritarian regimes that offered stability and were strongly anti-Communist. After World War II, Guatemala was one of the most important nations in the region undergoing significant change and re-form, and Presidents Harry S Truman and Dwight D. Eisenhower viewed the country as a potential area of Soviet expansion and a threat to hemispheric security. In 1954, the U.S. government helped overthrow a popular left-ori-ented government and install a pro-U.S. regime. About the same time, Fidel Castro was organizing and training Cuban exiles to overthrow the dictatorial government of Cuba. The Cuban Revolution became the most dramatic event in Latin American history: It brought Castro to power in 1959 and chal-lenged the United States' traditional hemispheric hegemony.

80 Frantz Fanon, *The Wretched of the Earth*

One of the most articulate spokespersons for decolonization in the Third World was the French-educated Algerian psychiatrist Frantz Fanon (1925–1961). Fanon's writings, coupled with his struggle against French colonial rule in Algeria, ensured that he would become one of the most celebrated leaders of decolonization in the 1960s.

QUESTIONS TO CONSIDER

1. Are there any parallels between Frantz Fanon's diagnosis of colonialism and Francisco García Calderón's discussion of "The North American Peril" (see Reading 53)?
2. Fanon describes the colonial world as a "Manichean world." Would Rudyard Kipling agree (see Reading 47)? Why? Why not?

The colonial world is a world cut in two. The dividing line, the frontiers are shown by barracks and police stations. In the colonies it is the policeman and the soldier who are the official, instituted go-betweens, the spokesmen of the settler and his rule of op-pression. . . . In the capitalist countries a multitude of moral teachers, counselors and "bewilderers" separate the exploited from those in power. In the colonial countries, on the contrary, the policeman and the soldier, by their immediate presence and their fre-quent and direct action maintain contact with the native and advise him by means of rifle butts and napalm not to budge. It is obvious here that the agents of government speak the language of pure force. The intermediary does not lighten the oppression, nor seek to hide the domination; he shows them up and puts them into practice with the clear conscience of an upholder of the peace; yet he is the bringer of violence into the home and into the mind of the native.

The zone where the natives live is not complementary to the zone inhabited by the settlers. The two zones are opposed, but not in the service of a higher unity. Obedient to the rules of pure Aristotelian logic, they both follow the principle of reciprocal exclusivity. No conciliation is possible, for of the two terms, one is superfluous. The settlers' town is a strongly built town, all made of stone and steel. It is a brightly lit town; the streets are covered with asphalt, and the garbage cans swallow all the leavings, unseen, unknown and hardly thought about. The settler's feet are never visible, except perhaps in the sea; but there you're never close enough to see them. His feet are protected by strong shoes although the streets of his town are clean and even, with no holes or stones. The settler's town is a well-fed town, an easygoing town; its belly is always full of good things. The settlers' town is a town of white people, of foreigners.

The town belonging to the colonized people, or at least the native town, the Negro village, the medina, the reservation, is a place of ill fame, peopled by men of evil repute. They are born there, it matters little where or how; they die there, it matters not where, nor how. It is a world without spaciousness; men live there on top of each other, and their huts are built—one on top of the other. The native town is a hungry town, starved of bread, of meat, of shoes, of coal, of light. The native town is a crouching village, a town on its knees, a town wallowing in the mire. It is a town of niggers and dirty Arabs. The look that the native turns on the settler's town is a look of lust, a look of envy; it expresses his dreams of possession—all manner of possession: to sit at the settler's table, to sleep in the settler's bed, with his wife if possible. The colonized man is an envious man. And this the settler knows very well; when their glances meet he ascertains bitterly, always on the defensive, "They want to take our place." It is true, for there is no native who does not dream at least once a day of setting himself up in the settler's place. . . .

The violence which has ruled over the ordering of the colonial world, which has ceaselessly drummed the rhythm for the destruction of native social forms and broken up without reserve the systems of reference of the economy, and the customs of dress and external life, that same violence will be claimed and taken over by the native at the moment when, deciding to embody history in his own person, he surges into the forbidden quarters. To wreck the colonial world is henceforward a mental picture of action which is very clear, very easy to understand and which may be assumed by each one of the individuals which constitute the colonized people. To break up the colonial world does not mean that after the frontiers have been abolished lines of communication will be set up between the two zones. The destruction of the colonial world is no more and no less than the abolition of one zone, its burial in the depths of the earth or its expulsion from the country.

The natives' challenge to the colonial world is not a rational confrontation of points of view. It is not a treatise on the universal, but the untidy affirmation of an original idea propounded as an absolute. The colonial world is a Manichean world. It is not enough for the settler to delimit physically, that is to say with the help of the army and the police force, the place of the native. As if to show the totalitarian character of colonial exploitation the settler paints the native as a sort of quintessence of evil. Native society is not simply described as a society lacking in values. It is not enough for the colonist to affirm that those values have disappeared from, or still better never existed in, the colonial world. The native is declared insensible to ethics; he represents not only the absence of values, but also the negation of values. He is, let us dare to admit, the enemy of values, and in this sense he is the absolute evil. He is the corrosive element, destroying all that comes near him; he is the deforming element, disfiguring all that has to do with beauty or morality; he is the depository of maleficent powers, the unconscious and irretrievable instrument of blind forces.

81 Desmond Tutu, "The Question of South Africa"

Desmond Tutu (1931–   ) was elected the first black Archbishop of Cape Town in 1986. In recognition of his leadership in seeking racial justice in South Africa, he was awarded the Nobel Peace Prize in 1984. Shortly after receiving the Nobel Prize, Tutu gave the following speech, attacking South Africa's racial policies, to the United Nations Security Council. Although he commended South African President P. W. Botha for signing the nonaggression pact (the Nkomati Accords of 1984) between South Africa and Mozambique, he was not as sanguine about the future of race relations within South Africa.

QUESTIONS TO CONSIDER

1. What specific steps did Archbishop Tutu urge to overcome apartheid?
2. Did the apartheid laws apply only to black South Africans? What other groups are affected by these laws? Why?

I speak out of a full heart, for I am about to speak about a land that I love deeply and passionately; a beautiful land of rolling hills and gurgling streams, of clear starlit skies, of singing birds, and gamboling lambs; a land God has richly endowed with the good things of the earth, a land rich in mineral deposits of nearly every kind; a land of vast open spaces, enough to accommodate all its inhabitants comfortably; a land capable of feeding itself and other lands on the beleaguered continent of Africa, a veritable bread-basket; a land that could contribute wonderfully to the material and spiritual development and prosperity of all Africa and indeed of the whole world. It is endowed with enough to satisfy the material and spiritual needs of all its peoples.

And so we would expect that such a land, veritably flowing with milk and honey, should be a land where peace and harmony and contentment reigned supreme. Alas, the opposite is the case. For my beloved country is wracked by division, by alienation, by animosity, by separation, by injustice, by avoidable pain and suffering. It is a deeply fragmented society, ridden by fear and anxiety, covered by a pall of despondency and a sense of desperation, split up into hostile, warring factions.

It is a highly volatile land, and its inhabitants sit on a powder-keg with a very short fuse indeed, ready to blow us all up into kingdom-come. There is endemic unrest, like a festering sore that will not heal until not just the symptoms are treated but the root causes are removed.

South African society is deeply polarized. Nothing illustrates this more sharply than the events of the past week. While the black community was in the seventh heaven of delight because of the decision of that committee in Oslo, and while the world was congratulating the recipient of the Nobel Peace Prize, the white government and most white South Africans, very sadly, were seeking to devalue that prize. An event that should have been the occasion of uninhibited joy and thanksgiving revealed a sadly divided society.

From Bishop Desmond Tutu. "The Question of South Africa," *Africa Report*, 30 (January–February 1985), pp. 50–52. Originally a statement to the United Nations Security Council, October 23, 1984.

Before I came to this country in early September to go on sabbatical, I visited one of the trouble-spots near Johannesburg. I went with members of the Executive Committee of the South African Council of Churches, which had met in emergency session after I had urged Mr. P.W. Botha to meet with church leaders to deal with a rapidly deteriorating situation. As a result of our peace initiative, we did get to meet with two cabinet ministers, demonstrating thereby our concern to carry out our call to be ministers of reconciliation and ambassadors of Christ.

In this black township, we met an old lady who told us that she was looking after her grandchildren and the children of neighbors while they were at work. On the day about which she was speaking, the police had been chasing black schoolchildren in that street, but the children had eluded the police, who then drove down the street past the old lady's house. Her wards were playing in front of the house, in the yard. She was sitting in the kitchen at the back, when her daughter burst in, calling agitatedly for her. She rushed out into the living room. A grandson had fallen just inside the door, dead. The police had shot him in the back. He was six years old. Recently a baby, a few weeks old, became the first white casualty of the current uprisings. Every death is one too many. Those whom the black community has identified as collaborators with a system that oppresses them and denies them the most elementary human rights have met cruel death, which we deplore as much as any others. They have rejected these people operating within the system, whom they have seen as lackies and stooges, despite their titles of town councilors, and so on, under an apparently new dispensation extending the right of local government to the blacks.

Over 100,000 black students are out of school, boycotting—as they did in 1976—what they and the black community perceive as an inferior education designed deliberately for inferiority. An already highly volatile situation has been ignited several times and, as a result, over 80 persons have died. There has been industrial unrest, with the first official strike by black miners taking place, not without its toll of fatalities among the blacks.

Some may be inclined to ask: But why should all this unrest be taking place just when the South African government appears to have embarked on the road of reform, exemplified externally by the signing of the Nkomati accord and internally by the implementation of a new constitution which appears to depart radically from the one it replaces, for it makes room for three chambers: one for whites, one for Coloureds, and one for Indians; a constitution described by many as a significant step forward?

I wish to state here, as I have stated on other occasions, that Mr. P.W. Botha must be commended for his courage in declaring that the future of South Africa could no longer be determined by whites only. That was a very brave thing to do. The tragedy of South Africa is that something with such a considerable potential for resolving the burgeoning crisis of our land should have been vitiated by the exclusion of 73 percent of the population, the overwhelming majority in the land.

By no stretch of the imagination could that kind of constitution be considered to be democratic. The composition of the committees, in the ratio of four whites to two Coloureds to one Indian, demonstrates eloquently what most people had suspected all along—that it was intended to perpetuate the rule of a minority. The fact that the first qualification for membership in the chambers is racial says that this constitution was designed to entrench racism and ethnicity. The most obnoxious features of apartheid would remain untouched and unchanged. The Group Areas Act, the Population Registration Act, separate educational systems for the different race groups; all this and more would remain quite unchanged.

This constitution was seen by the mainline English-speaking churches and the official white opposition as disastrously inadequate, and they called for its rejection in the whites-only referendum last November. The call was not heeded. The blacks overwhelmingly rejected what they regarded as a sham, an instrument in the politics of exclusion. Various groups campaigned for a boycott of the Coloured and Indian elections—campaigned, I might add, against very great odds, by and large peacefully. As we know, the authorities responded with their usual iron-fist tactics, detaining most of the leaders of the United Democratic Front (UDF) and other organizations that had organized the boycott—and we have some of them now holed up in the British Consulate in Durban, causing a diplomatic contretemps. . . .

As blacks we often run the gauntlet of roadblocks on roads leading into our townships, and these have been manned by the army in what are actually described as routine police operations. When you use the army in this fashion, who is the enemy?

The authorities have not stopped stripping blacks of their South African citizenship. Here I am, 53 years old, a bishop in the church, some would say reasonably responsible; I travel on a document that says of my nationality that it is "undeterminable at present." The South African government is turning us into aliens in the land of our birth. It continues unabated with its vicious policy of forced population removals. It is threatening to remove the people of Kwa Ngema. It treats carelessly the women in the KTC squatter camp near Cape Town whose flimsy plastic coverings are destroyed every day by the authorities; and the heinous crime of those women is that they want to be with their husbands, with the fathers of their children.

White South Africans are not demons; they are ordinary human beings, scared human beings, many of them; who would not be, if they were outnumbered five to one? Through this lofty body I wish to appeal to my white fellow South Africans to share in building a new society, for blacks are not intent on driving whites into the sea but on claiming only their rightful place in the sun in the land of their birth.

We deplore all forms of violence, the violence of an oppressive and unjust society and the violence of those seeking to overthrow that society, for we believe that violence is not the answer to the crisis of our land.

We dream of a new society that will be truly non-racial, truly democratic, in which people count because they are created in the image of God.

We are committed to work for justice, for peace, and for reconciliation. We ask you, please help us; urge the South African authorities to go to the conference table with the . . . representatives of all sections of our community. I appeal to this body to act. I appeal in the name of the ordinary, the little people of South Africa. I appeal in the name of the squatters in crossroads and in the KTC camp. I appeal on behalf of the father who has to live in a single-sex hostel as a migrant worker, separated from his family for 11 months of the year. I appeal on behalf of the students who have rejected this travesty of education made available only for blacks. I appeal on behalf of those who are banned arbitrarily, who are banished, who are detained without trial, those imprisoned because they have had a vision of this new South Africa. I appeal on behalf of those who have been exiled from their homes.

I say we will be free, and we ask you: Help us, that this freedom comes for all of us in South Africa, black and white, but that it comes with the least possible violence, that it comes peacefully, that it comes soon.

82 Fidel Castro, Second Declaration of Havana

Fidel Castro's interest in the rest of Latin America became evident soon after he gained control of the Cuban government. In 1959 and 1960, he frequently spoke of the need for revolutionary changes in other nations of the region, and he saw them using the Cuban example. What changed from his initial months in office was the political ideology he hoped to use in enacting reforms. Instead of developing democratic processes, constitutional procedures, and elections as he had suggested before 1959, Castro turned to the Communist Party and adopted Marxism-Leninism as the official doctrine of the nation. Under Castro's personalistic leadership, the party became the vehicle to organize Cubans and challenge the United States in the Western Hemisphere. This was clearly expressed in Castro's Second Declaration of Havana delivered on February 4, 1962, soon after he officially adopted Marxism-Leninism.

QUESTIONS TO CONSIDER

1. Prior to this address, Castro rejected charges that he was exporting revolution and included the statement, "Revolutions are not exported; they are made by the peoples." Discuss this idea. Are there historical precedents to support this statement?
2. Why was this address a significant turning point in Cuban policy toward the United States and the rest of the Western Hemisphere? What were some of the consequences of this new Cuban initiative?
3. Why was Castro's call for reforms and/or revolution appealing to some people in Latin America and other underdeveloped countries?

What is Cuba's history but that of Latin America? What is the history of Latin America but the history of Asia, Africa, and Oceania? And what is the history of all these peoples but the history of the cruelest exploitation of the world by imperialism?

At the end of the last century and the beginning of the present, a handful of economically developed nations had divided the world among themselves, subjecting two thirds of humanity to their economic and political domination. Humanity was forced to work for the dominating classes of the group of nations which had a developed capitalist economy.

The historic circumstances which permitted certain European countries and the United States of North America to attain a high industrial development level put them in a position which enabled them to subject and exploit the rest of the world.

From *Fidel Castro's Personal Revolution in Cuba: 1959–1973*, pp. 264–68, by James Nelson Goodsell. Copyright © 1974 by Alfred A. Knopf, Inc. Reprinted by permission of Alfred A. Knopf, a Division of Random House, Inc.

What motives lay behind this expansion of the industrial powers? Were they moral, "civilizing" reasons, as they claimed? No. Their motives were economic.

The discovery of America sent the European conquerors across the seas to occupy and to exploit the lands and peoples of other continents; the lust for riches was the basic motivation for their conduct. America's discovery took place in the search for shorter ways to the Orient, whose products Europe valued highly.

A new social class, the merchants and the producers of articles manufactured for commerce, arose from the feudal society of lords and serfs in the latter part of the Middle Ages.

The lust for gold promoted the efforts of the new class. The lust for profit was the incentive of their behavior throughout its history. As industry and trade developed, the social influence of the new class grew. The new productive forces maturing in the midst of the feudal society increasingly clashed with feudalism and its serfdom, its laws, its institutions, its philosophy, its morals, its art, and its political ideology. . . .

Since the end of the Second World War, the Latin American nations are becoming pauperized constantly. The value of their capita income falls. The dreadful percentages of child death rate do not decrease, the number of illiterates grows higher, the peoples lack employment, land, adequate housing, schools, hospitals, communication systems and the means of subsistence. On the other hand, North American investments exceed 10 billion dollars. Latin America, moreover, supplies cheap raw materials and pays high prices for manufactured articles. Like the first Spanish conquerors, who exchanged mirrors and trinkets with the Indians for silver and gold, so the United States trades with Latin America. To hold on to this torrent of wealth, to take greater possession of America's resources and to exploit its long-suffering peoples: this is what is hidden behind the military pacts, the military missions and Washington's diplomatic lobbying. . .

As to the accusation that Cuba wishes to export its revolution, we reply: Revolutions are not exported; they are made by the peoples.

What Cuba can give and has already given to the peoples is its example.

And what does the Cuban Revolution teach: that revolution is possible, that the peoples can make it, that in today's world there is no force strong enough to impede the peoples' liberation movements.

Our victory would never have been possible if the revolution itself had not been inexorably destined to arise from the conditions which existed in our economic-social reality, a reality which pertains even to a greater degree in a goodly number of Latin American countries.

It happens inevitably that in those countries where Yankee monopolist control is strongest, where exploitation by the reigning few is most unrestrained and where the conditions of the masses of workers and peasants are most unbearable, the political power becomes more vicious, states of siege become habitual, all expression of mass discontent is suppressed by force, and the democratic channels are closed off, thereby revealing more plainly than ever the kind of brutal dictatorship assumed by the dominating classes. That is when the peoples' revolutionary breakthrough becomes inevitable.

And while it is true that in America's underdeveloped countries the working class is in general relatively small, there is a social class which because of the sub-human conditions under which it lives constitutes a potential force which—led by the workers and the revolutionary intellectuals—has a decisive importance in the struggle for national liberation: the peasantry.

In our countries two circumstances are joined: underdeveloped industry and an agrarian regime of a feudal character. That is why no matter how hard the living conditions of the workers are, the rural population lives under even more horrible conditions of oppression and exploitation. But, with few exceptions, it also constitutes the absolute majority, sometimes more than 70 percent of Latin American populations. . . .

Wherever roads are closed to the peoples, where repression of workers and peasants is fierce, where the domination of Yankee monopolies is strongest, the first and most important lesson is to understand that it is neither just nor correct to divert the peoples with the vain and fanciful illusion that the dominant classes can be uprooted by legal means which do not and will not exist. The ruling classes are entrenched in all positions of state power. They monopolize the teaching field. They dominate all means of mass communication. They have infinite financial resources. Theirs is a power which the monopolies and the ruling few will defend by blood and fire with the strength of their police and their armies.

The duty of every revolutionary is to make revolution. We know that in America and throughout the world the revolution will be victorious. But revolutionaries cannot sit in the doorways of their homes to watch the corpse of imperialism pass by. The role of Job does not behoove a revolutionary. Each year by which America's liberation may be hastened will mean millions of children rescued from death, millions of minds freed for learning, infinitudes of sorrow spared the peoples. Even though the Yankee imperialists are preparing a bloodbath for America they will not succeed in drowning the peoples' struggle. They will evoke universal hatred against themselves. This will be the last act of their rapacious and cave-man system.

No one people of Latin America is weak, because all are part of a family of 200 million brothers who suffer the same miseries, harbor the same sentiments, face the same enemy. All dream alike of a happier fate, and all can count on the solidarity of all honorable men and women throughout the world.

The epic of Latin America's independence struggles was great, and that fight was a heroic one. But today's generation of Latin Americans is summoned to write a greater epic, one even more decisive for humanity. The earlier fight was to free ourselves from Spanish colonial power, from a decadent Spain which had been invaded by Napoleon's armies. Today the liberation struggle confronts the strongest imperial land in all the world, the most significant power of the world imperialist system. Thus we perform an even greater service for humanity than did our ancestors.

This struggle, more than the first, will be conducted by the masses, by the peoples. The people will play a far more important role than they did then. Individual leaders matter less in this fight than in that.

This epic we have before us will be written by the hungry masses of Indians, of landless peasants, of exploited workers. It will be written by the progressive masses, the honest and brilliant intellectuals of whom we have so many in these suffering lands of Latin America. A battle of masses and of ideas, an epic borne onward by our peoples who have been ignored until today and who now are beginning to make imperialism lose its sleep. They thought us to be an impotent, submissive herd, but now they are beginning to fear that herd. It is a thundering herd of 200 million Latin Americans among whom Yankee monopoly capital already spies its gravediggers. . . .

The Middle East: Politics and Upheaval

I n the second half of the twentieth century, the Middle East has been tormented by the agonies of war and the explosive politics of religious violence. Although the causes of these upheavals are deeply rooted and complex, three central, and intertwined, episodes have shaped the politics of this region: the birth of the state of Israel; the quest for a Palestinian state; and, in the wake of the Iranian Revolution (1979), the emergence of religious fundamentalism in Islamic politics.

Israel's Proclamation of Independence in 1948 placed the new state on a collision course with its Arab neighbors, resulting in four major wars and the displacement of more than 2 million Palestinians from their homeland. Despite the wars, five decades of guerrilla attacks and reprisals, active interventions by the United Nations, and Israel's recognition of an independent Palestinian state, deep hostilities still exist between Israel, its Arab and Palestinian neighbors, and the Palestinians who continue to live in areas controlled by Israel.

These hostilities—especially between the Palestinians and Israelis—have been complicated by a destructive civil war in Lebanon (beginning in 1975), the Iranian Revolution (1979), the inconclusive war between Iran and Iraq (1980–1988), and the Persian Gulf War (1991). The near-destruction of the state of Lebanon, coupled with the Israeli occupation of south Lebanon, not only deepened Arab-Israeli hostility but also signaled the emergence of Syria, Iraq, and Iran as powers in the region, further complicating the search for peace.

83 Israel's Proclamation of Independence

One day before the termination of the British mandate for Palestine, the Provisional State Council (a forerunner of the Israeli Parliament) declared the independence of Israel on May 14, 1948. The following selection is an excerpt from this official announcement.

QUESTIONS TO CONSIDER

1. Can the historic and religious ties of the Jewish people to Israel accommodate the fact that for nearly two thousand years Israel was also the dwelling place of Arabs and other non-Jewish populations?

2. **How does Israel's Proclamation of Independence suggest the influence of European and American history in this area (see Reading 57)?**

The Land of Israel was the birthplace of the Jewish people. Here their spiritual, religious and national identity was formed. Here they achieved independence and created a culture of national and universal significance. Here they wrote and gave the Bible to the world.

Exiled from the Land of Israel the Jewish people remained faithful to it in all the countries of their dispersion, never ceasing to pray and hope for their return and the restoration of their national freedom.

Impelled by this historic association, Jews strove throughout the centuries to go back to the land of their fathers and regain their statehood. In recent decades they returned in their masses. They reclaimed the wilderness, revived their language, built cities and villages, and established a vigorous and ever-growing community, with its own economic and cultural life. They sought peace, yet were prepared to defend themselves. They brought the blessings of progress to all inhabitants of the country and looked forward to sovereign independence.

In the year 1897 the First Zionist Congress, inspired by Theodor Herzl's vision of the Jewish State, proclaimed the right of the Jewish people to national revival in their own country.

This right was acknowledged by the Balfour Declaration of November 2, 1917, and re-affirmed by the Mandate of the League of Nations, which gave explicit international recognition to the historic connection of the Jewish people with Palestine and their right to reconstitute their National Home.

The recent holocaust, which engulfed millions of Jews in Europe, proved anew the need to solve the problem of the homelessness and lack of independence of the Jewish people by means of the re-establishment of the Jewish State, which would open the gates to all Jews and endow the Jewish people with equality of status among the family of nations.

The survivors of the disastrous slaughter in Europe, and also Jews from other lands, have not desisted from their efforts to reach Eretz-Yisrael, in face of difficulties, obstacles and perils; and have not ceased to urge their right to a life of dignity, freedom and honest toil in their ancestral land.

In the second World War the Jewish people in Palestine made their full contribution to the struggle of the freedom-loving nations against the Nazi evil. The sacrifices of their soldiers and their war effort gained them the right to rank with the nations which founded the United Nations.

On November 29, 1947, the General Assembly of the United Nations adopted a Resolution requiring the establishment of a Jewish State in Palestine. The General Assembly called upon the inhabitants of the country to take all the necessary steps on their part to put the plan into effect. This recognition by the United Nations of the right of the Jewish people to establish their independent State is unassailable.

It is the natural right of the Jewish people to lead, as do all other nations, an independent existence in its sovereign State.

ACCORDINGLY WE, the members of the National Council, representing the Jewish people in Palestine and the World Zionist Movement, are met together in solemn assembly today, the day of termination of the British Mandate for Palestine; and by virtue of the natural and historic right of the Jewish people and of the Resolution of the General Assembly of the United Nations.

WE HEREBY PROCLAIM the establishment of the Jewish State in Palestine, to be called Medinath Yisrael (The State of Israel).

WE HEREBY DECLARE that, as from the termination of the Mandate at midnight, the 14th–15th May, 1948, and pending the setting up of the duly elected bodies of the State in accordance with a Constitution, to be drawn up by the Constituent Assembly not later than the 1st October, 1948, the National Council shall act as the Provisional State Council, and that the National Administration shall constitute the Provisional Government of the Jewish State, which shall be known as Israel.

THE STATE OF ISRAEL will be open to the immigration of Jews from all countries of their dispersion; will promote the development of the country for the benefit of all its inhabitants; will be based on the principles of liberty, justice and peace as conceived by the Prophets of Israel; will uphold the full social and political equality of all its citizens, without distinction of religion, race, or sex; will guarantee freedom of religion, conscience, education and culture; will safeguard the Holy Places of all religions; and will loyally uphold the principles of the United Nations Charter.

THE STATE OF ISRAEL will be ready to co-operate with the organs and representatives of the United Nations in the implementation of the Resolution of the Assembly of November 29, 1947, and will take steps to bring about the Economic Union over the whole of Palestine.

We appeal to the United Nations to assist the Jewish people in the building of its State and to admit Israel into the family of nations.

In the midst of wanton aggression, we yet call upon the Arab inhabitants of the State of Israel to preserve the ways of peace and play their part in the development of the State, on the basis of full and equal citizenship and due representation in all its bodies and institutions—provisional and permanent.

84 Palestinian Declaration of Independence

Forty years after the state of Israel declared its independence, the Palestine National Council, meeting in Algiers, further revised its 1964 charter and on November 15, 1988, proclaimed this Declaration of Independence for the Palestinian people.

QUESTIONS TO CONSIDER

1. After a half century of bitter warfare between Palestinians and Israelis, can the Palestinian Declaration of Independence be reconciled with the state of Israel's concerns about national security? Can the two peoples ever find a way to live in peace?

2. In its Declaration of Independence, the Palestinian National Council "calls upon the United Nations to bear special responsibility for the Palestinian Arab people and its homeland." Do you believe that the UN should "bear a special responsibility" for ensuring the security of a Palestinian state? How should the UN exercise this responsibility?

In the name of God, the Compassionate, the Merciful.

Palestine, the land of the three monotheistic faiths, is where the Palestinian Arab people was born, on which it grew, developed, and excelled. The Palestinian people was never separated from or diminished in its integral bonds with Palestine. Thus the Palestinian Arab people ensured for itself an everlasting union between itself, its land, and its history. . . .

Despite the historical injustice inflicted on the Palestinian Arab people resulting in their dispersion and depriving them of their right to self-determination, following upon UN General Assembly Resolution 181 (1947), which partitioned Palestine into two states, one Arab, one Jewish, yet it is this resolution that still provides those conditions of international legitimacy that ensure the right of the Palestinian Arab people to sovereignty and national independence. . . .

In Palestine and on its perimeters, in exile distant and near, the Palestinian Arab people never faltered and never abandoned its conviction in its rights of return and independence. Occupation, massacres, and dispersion achieved no gain in the unabated Palestinian consciousness of self and political identity, as Palestinians went forward with their destiny, undeterred and unbowed. And from out of the long years of trial in evermounting struggle, the Palestinian political identity emerged further consolidated and confirmed. And the collective Palestinian national will forge itself in a political embodiment, the Palestine Liberation Organization, its sole, legitimate representative, recognized by the world community as a whole, as well as by related regional and international institutions. . . .

The massive national uprising, the *intifadah*, now intensifying in cumulative scope and power on occupied Palestinian territories, as well as the unflinching resistance of the refugee camps outside the homeland, have elevated consciousness of the Palestinian truth and right into still higher realms of comprehension and actuality. Now at last the curtain has been dropped around a whole epoch of prevarication and negation. The Intifadah has set siege to the mind of official Israel, which has for too long relied exclusively upon myth and terror to deny Palestinian existence altogether. Because of the Intifadah and its revolutionary irreversible impulse, the history of Palestine has therefore arrived at a decisive juncture.

Whereas the Palestinian people reaffirms most definitely its inalienable rights in the land of its patrimony:

Now by virtue of natural, historical, and legal rights and the sacrifices of successive generations who gave of themselves in defense of the freedom and independence of their homeland;

From Palestine National Council, "Palestinian Declaration of Independence," Algiers, November 15, 1988. *The Journal of Palestine Studies* 70 (Winter 1989), pp. 213–16. Copyright © Journal of Palestine Studies. Reprinted by permisison.

In pursuance of resolutions adopted by Arab summit conferences and relying on the authority bestowed by international legitimacy as embodied in the resolutions of the United Nations Organization since 1947;

And in exercise by the Palestinian Arab people of its rights to self-determination, political independence, and sovereignty over its territory;

The Palestine National Council, in the name of God, and in the name of the Palestinian Arab people, hereby proclaims the establishment of the State of Palestine on our Palestinian territory with its capital Jerusalem (Al-Quds Ash-Sharif).

The State of Palestine is the state of Palestinians wherever they may be. The state is for them to enjoy in it their collective national and cultural identity, theirs to pursue in it a complete equality of rights. In it will be safeguarded their political and religious convictions and their human dignity by means of a parliamentary democratic system of governance, itself based on freedom of expression and the freedom to form parties. The rights of minorities will duly be respected by the majority, as minorities must abide by decisions of the majority. Governance will be based on principles of social justice, equality and nondiscrimination in public rights on grounds of race, religion, color, or sex under the aegis of a constitution which ensures the role of law and an independent judiciary. Thus shall these principles allow no departure from Palestine's age-old spiritual and civilizational heritage of tolerance and religious co-existence.

The State of Palestine is an Arab state, an integral and indivisible part of the Arab nation, at one with that nation in heritage and civilization, with it also in its aspiration for liberation, progress, democracy, and unity. The State of Palestine affirms its obligation to abide by the Charter of the League of Arab States, whereby the coordination of the Arab states with each other shall be strengthened. It calls upon Arab compatriots to consolidate and enhance the emergence in reality of our State, to mobilize potential, and to intensify efforts whose goal is to end Israeli occupation.

The State of Palestine proclaims its commitment to the principles and purposes of the United Nations, and to the Universal Declaration of Human Rights. It proclaims its commitment as well to the principles and policies of the Non-Aligned Movement.

It further announces itself to be a peace-loving state, in adherence to the principles of peaceful co-existence. It will join with all states and peoples in order to assure a permanent peace based upon justice and the respect of rights so that humanity's potential for well-being may be assured, an earnest competition for excellence be maintained, and in which confidence in the future will eliminate fear for those who are just and for whom justice is the only recourse.

In the context of its struggle for peace in the land of love and peace, the State of Palestine calls upon the United Nations to bear special responsibility for the Palestinian Arab people and its homeland. It calls upon all peace- and freedom-loving peoples and states to assist it in the attainment of its objectives, to provide it with security, to alleviate the tragedy of its people, and to help to terminate Israel's occupation of the Palestinian territories.

The State of Palestine herewith declares that it believes in the settlement of regional and international disputes by peaceful means, in accordance with the UN Charter and resolutions. Without prejudice to its natural right to defend its territorial integrity and independence, it therefore rejects the threat or use of force, violence, and terrorism against its territorial integrity, or political independence, as it also rejects their use against the territorial integrity of other states.

Therefore, on this day unlike all others, 15 November, 1988, as we stand at the threshold of a new dawn, in all honor and modesty we humbly bow to the sacred spirits of our fallen ones, Palestinian and Arab, by the purity of whose sacrifice for the homeland our sky has been illuminated and our land given life. . . .

Therefore, we call upon our great people to rally to the banner of Palestine, to cherish and defend it, so that it may forever be the symbol of our freedom and dignity in that homeland, which is a homeland for the free, now and always.

In the name of God, the Compassionate, the Merciful.

America and the Second Indochina War

The Geneva Agreements of July 1954, which ended the First Indochina War (1946–1954) between France and Ho Chi Minh's Viet Minh, provided for (1) a temporary division of Vietnam into two parts at the seventeenth parallel; (2) general elections to be held no later than 1956 to decide upon Vietnamese reunification; (3) the creation of free and independent states of Laos and Cambodia; and (4) the end of the French empire in Indochina. Although the United States did not sign the Geneva Agreements, it did agree "to refrain from the threat of the use of force to disturb them" and that it "would view any renewal of the aggression . . . with grave concern and as seriously threatening international peace and security."[1]

The expected general elections of 1956 were never held, and Vietnam remained divided. Ho Chi Minh governed the Democratic Republic of Vietnam (North Vietnam) from Hanoi, and in 1955 Ngo Dinh Diem was elected president of the Republic of Vietnam (South Vietnam), which he governed from Saigon.

Between 1955 and 1975, the United States assisted South Vietnam in establishing its government and in attacking a political-military insurgency that in 1960 identified itself as the National Front for the Liberation of South Vietnam (NLF). The more familiar label for this insurgency was Viet Cong, a shorthand term for Vietnamese Communist. By the early 1960s, the NLF, organized and operating in South Vietnam, was receiving instructions and supplies from Ho Chi Minh's Communist government of North Vietnam. By the spring of 1963, the NLF insurgency in the countryside and the Buddhist-led antigovernment demonstrations in the key cities

---

1Quoted in Marvin E. Gettleman, ed., *Vietnam: History, Documents, and Opinions on a Major World Crisis* (New York: New American Library, 1970), pp. 184–85.

of Hue and Saigon posed severe military and political problems for President Diem. On November 1, 1963, three weeks before U.S. President John F. Kennedy's death, a South Vietnamese military junta seized power from Diem and killed him and his brother. Diem's assassination ushered in a period of political instability and an acceleration of the NLF insurgency, prompting President Lyndon B. Johnson to increase America's role in fighting the Viet Cong.

On April 30, 1970, President Richard Nixon announced that U.S. forces were invading Cambodia to destroy North Vietnamese and NLF targets and thereby shorten the war in Vietnam. This Cambodian incursion, though lasting only two months, had two immediate effects. First, the American antiwar movement exploded: Student demonstrations at Kent State University resulted in four deaths, and two students were killed at Jackson State University. A second consequence of the incursion was the dramatic growth of the Khmer Rouge Communist insurgency inside Cambodia. By 1975, the Khmer Rouge were strong enough to capture all of Cambodia and begin the systematic killing of Cambodians deemed "enemies of the people." Although Congress never formally declared war, 2 million Americans served in Vietnam, and U.S. combat troops remained there until 1973. During this Second Indochina War (ca. 1957–1975), America spent more than $239 billion fighting the war, suffered 296,000 casualties, and lost more than 57,000 lives.

The sudden collapse of South Vietnam, followed by the rapid and unexpectedly easy North Vietnamese takeover of the South in May 1975, left a bewildering legacy of confusion, doubt, and frustration for many Americans and Vietnamese.

85 Views of a Viet Cong Official

Truong Nhu Tang was a founder of the National Liberation Front (NLF) and a minister of justice in the NLF's Provisional Revolutionary Government. In 1982, he gave the following account of the Viet Cong movement and the collapse of South Vietnam. The 1968 Tet offensive he refers to was a failed North Vietnamese and Viet Cong campaign against South Vietnamese cities. This occurred while General Thieu, Truong Nhu Tang's captor, was president of South Vietnam.

QUESTIONS TO CONSIDER

1. According to Truong Nhu Tang, was the Tet offensive a military victory for the insurgency? Why did the American public perceive Tet as an American defeat?
2. As a southerner in the NLF, what was Truong Nhu Tang's attitude toward the North Vietnamese? Did American policy take into account this division in the NLF ranks?

The North Vietnamese on their part never indicated that they wanted to impose communism on the South. On the contrary, they knew, they said, that the South must have a different program altogether, one that embodied our aspirations not just for independence but also for internal political freedom. I believe, in addition, that the Northern leadership would have the wisdom to draw from the experiences—both good and bad—of other communist countries, and especially of North Vietnam, and that they could avoid the errors made elsewhere. North Vietnam was, as Ho Chi Minh often declared, a special situation in which nationalists and communists had combined their efforts. Clearly South Vietnam was no less special, and the newly constituted NLF Permanent Committee felt a certain amount of confidence in working with our Northern compatriots. . . .

The great majority of our troops then were Southern resistance fighters many of whom were veterans of the French colonial wars. Others were peasants who joined us when the NLF was formed. Almost all of this latter group still lived at home. During the day they were loyal citizens of South Vietnam; at night they became Viet Cong.

For the most part these guerrillas cared nothing about Marxist-Leninism or any other ideology. But they despised the local officials who had been appointed over them by the Saigon dictatorship. Beyond this, joining the Viet Cong allowed them to stay clear of the ARVN draft and to remain near their families. They were treated as brothers by the NLF, and although Viet Cong pay was almost nonexistent, these peasant soldiers were loyal and determined fighters. Moreover, they had the support of much of the population: people in the countryside and even in the cities provided food and intelligence information and protected our cadres. Although South Vietnamese propaganda attacked us as communists and murderers, the peasants believed otherwise. To them we were not Marxist-Leninists but simply revolutionaries fighting against a hated dictatorship and foreign intervention.

Because it was a people's war, the Viet Cong cadres were trained carefully to exploit the peasants' sympathies. But our goals were in fact generally shared by the people. We were working for Southern self-determination and independence—from Hanoi as well as from Washington. While we in the Viet Cong were beholden to Hanoi for military supplies and diplomatic contacts, many of us still believed that the North Vietnamese leadership would respect and support the NLF political program, that it would be in their interest to do so.

From Truong Nhu Tang, "Myth of a Liberation," *The New York Review of Books*, 39, no. 16 (October 21, 1982), pp. 31–36, *passim*. Reprinted with permission from *The New York Review of Books*. Copyright © 1982 Nyrev, Inc.

As early as the 1968 Tet offensive, after I was released from Thieu's prisons, I protested to the communist leaders about the atrocities committed by North Vietnamese troops in Hue, where many innocent people were murdered and about a dozen American prisoners were shot. It was explained to me that these were political executions and also that a number of "errors" had been made. I managed to persuade myself then that no such "errors" would be necessary once the war was over.

Unfortunately the Tet offensive also proved catastrophic to our plans. It is a major irony of the Vietnamese war that our propaganda transformed this military debacle into a brilliant victory, giving us new leverage in our diplomatic efforts, inciting the American antiwar movement to even stronger and more optimistic resistance, and disheartening the Washington planners.

The truth was that Tet cost us half of our forces. Our losses were so immense that we were simply unable to replace them with new recruits. One consequence was that the Hanoi leadership began to move unprecedented numbers of troops into the South, giving them a new and much more dominant position in the NLF deliberations. The Tet failure also retarded the organization of the Alliance of National, Democratic, and Peace Forces, an opposition coalition that had formed around thirty prominent South Vietnamese intellectuals and opinion makers. . . .

The Hanoi leadership knew all this and orchestrated their position toward us accordingly. They accepted and supported the NLF platform at every point, and gave the firmest assurances of respect for the principle of South Vietnamese self-determination. Later, of course we discovered that the North Vietnamese communists had engaged in a deliberate deception to achieve what had been their true goal from the start, the destruction of South Vietnam as a political or social entity in any way separate from the North. They succeeded in their deception by portraying themselves as brothers who had fought the same battles we were fighting and by exploiting our patriotism in the most cynical fashion. Nevertheless, the eventual denouement would not have taken place except for several wholly unpredictable developments.

After the Paris peace agreement was signed in 1973, most of us were preparing to create a neutralist government, balanced between Northern leftists and Southern rightists. We hoped that America and other signers would play an active role in protecting the agreement. Certainly no one expected Watergate and Nixon's resignation. No one expected America's easy and startlingly rapid abandonment of the country. I myself, the soon-to-be minister of justice, was preparing a reconciliation policy that specifically excluded reprisals. But the sudden collapse of the South Vietnamese regime (caused partly by the hasty departure of many top Saigon leaders) together with the abandonment by the Americans left me and other "independent socialists" with no counterweight to the huge influx of Northern communists.

It is important to note that our views were not based solely on naivete. During the Sixties neither the NLF leaders nor the Politburo ever hoped for total military victory against the Americans and their clients. Our entire strategy was formulated with the expectation that eventually we would be involved in some kind of coalition government. Such a government would have been immune to outright North Vietnamese domination and could have expected substantial international support. . . .

Unfortunately when the war did end, North Vietnamese vindictiveness and fanaticism blossomed into a ferocious exercise of power. Hundreds of thousands of former officials and army officers of the Saigon regime were imprisoned in "re-education camps." Literally millions of ordinary citizens were forced to leave their homes and settle in so-called New Economic Zones.

86 An American Prisoner of War

Congressional Medal of Honor winner and retired Vice Admiral James Bond Stockdale was a prisoner of war in Vietnam for eight years. In 1992, he was Ross Perot's running mate for the U.S. vice presidency. In the following essay, he recounts some of his experiences in Vietnam and offers his views on the lessons to be learned from the war.

QUESTIONS TO CONSIDER

1. President Ronald Reagan described the Vietnam War as a "noble crusade." James B. Stockdale describes it "as a misguided experiment of the Harvard Business School crowd." Which description do you believe to be correct? Why?
2. What do the accounts of Truong Nhu Tang and James B. Stockdale suggest about the ambiguities and frustrations of the Second Indochina War (see Reading 85)?

My viewpoint of the Vietnam War was that Eisenhower's domino theory was probably valid: that if North Vietnam took over the south, a chain reaction could be expected to proceed to the southwest. I also knew that South Vietnam was not really like the western democracy our government tried to pretend it was. I knew there was a formidable framework of a Communist infrastructure in the south that would have to be burned out. I also knew how militantly doctrinaire and disciplined the North Vietnamese were. Putting all this together, I thought, during the war, after it, and still today, that Barry Goldwater had the only sensible outlook: either move quickly against Hanoi with repeated high impact non-nuke hammer blows from the air or forget it. Vietnam was no place for the Army.

So how do I classify the tragedy of Vietnam, if not a crusade, a mistake, a crime or a conspiracy? I classify it as a misguided experiment of the Harvard Business School crowd—the "whiz kids"—in achieving foreign policy objectives by so-called rational game theory, while ignoring the reality and obstinacy of human nature.

These were some of the policy lessons of Vietnam: You can't finesse human nature, human will, or human obstinacy, with economic game theory. And you should never let those who think you can, call the shots in a war! . . .

The central strategy of the North Vietnamese prison system was extortion pressure—pressure to get us to contribute to what turned out to be their winning propaganda campaign beamed at the American man on the street, pressure to get us to inform on one another. These ideas were tied together as integral parts of the whole and were to be extracted by the imposition of loneliness, fear and guilt—fear of pain, guilt at having betrayed a fellow prisoner. . . .

From James B. Stockdale, *A Vietnam Experience: Ten Years of Reflection* (Stanford, CA: Hoover Institution, 1984), pp. 109, 122–28. This material originally appeared in "The Most Important Lesson of Vietnam: Power of the Human Spirit," *San Jose Mercury News*, January 3, 1982, copyright 1982 by *The San Diego Union*; and "Dignity and Honor in Vietnam," *The Wall Street Journal*, April 16, 1982. Reprinted by the kind permission of James Bond Stockdale, *The San Diego Union*, and *The Wall Street Journal*.

Chivalry was dead in my prison. Its name was Hoa Lo, meaning "fiery furnace," located in downtown Hanoi, a prison the French built in 1895.

I arrived there, a prisoner of war in North Vietnam, in the late morning of a rainy Sunday in September 1965, a stretcher case. I had a broken leg (which my welcoming party, a street mob of civilians, had inflicted), a broken back (which I charge off to my carelessness in not having had the presence of mind to brace myself correctly before ejecting into low altitude, high-speed air from a tumbling airplane), and a gunshot wound in my good leg (which an irate farmer had pumped into my stretcher during my first night on the ground, an act I credit as morally neutral just to keep the score balanced). The North Vietnamese officer who presided over my arrival after three days in the back of a truck was about my age (42 at the time), also a career military man.

I asked him for medical attention for my broken bones and open wounds. "You have a medical problem and you have a political problem," he said. "In this country we handle political problems first, and if they are satisfactorily resolved, that is, if you demonstrate a proper understanding of the American war of imperialist aggression in Vietnam and take concrete actions to stop it, we will attend to your medical problems." That was the last time the subject of medical attention for me ever came up in my next eight years as a prisoner of war. . . .

These prisons are all the same; the name of the game is to unstring their victims with fear and polarize them with guilt. There are always more rules than can practically be obeyed, always a tripwire system to snare you in a violation that the jailers can brand as moral turpitude—and there is always an escape valve, a way to make amends if you repent.

The tripwire in Hanoi was based on the "no communication" rule. As with all tripwires, the prisoner had a choice to make and he stood to lose either way. If he obeyed and did not communicate with his comrades, he accrued the conscience problems of betraying his fellows and at the same time sentenced himself to a desperate loneliness which would likely get to him after a year or two. If he communicated, and this was the only way to go for loyalty, for a feeling of self-worth, for dignity, he would periodically be caught and tortured under the charge of ingratitude for the "humane and lenient treatment" he was being given.

(Incidentally, communication grew to be a very refined, high-volume, high-speed, highly accurate though dangerous art. We used the same code Koestler's fictional Commissar N.S. Rubashov used during his Moscow trial and execution period in the late 1930's.)

By torture, I don't mean leg irons or handcuffs or isolation. We were always careful to remind ourselves that those were just inconveniences, not to panic. By torture we meant the intentional imposition of pain and claustrophobia over as short a time as necessary to get the victim to "submit."

In my experience this is best done by heavily slapping the prisoner, seating him on the brick floor, reeving his upper arms with ropes, and while standing barefoot on his back cinching up the elaborate bindings by jerks, pulling his shoulders together while stuffing his head down between his feet with the heel of your foot. Numb arms under contorted tension produce an excruciating pain and a gnawing but sure knowledge that a clock is ticking while your blood is stopped and that the longer you wait before submitting the longer useless arms will dangle at your sides (45 minutes of blood stoppage usually cost about six months of dangle). The claustrophobia also concentrates the mind wonderfully.

How long to submission for a good man? About 30 minutes. Why not hold your silence and die? You can't just will yourself dead and have it happen—especially in that position. Why not just give them what they want and be done with it? Reasons that come to mind include dignity, self-esteem, contempt for B-grade pageants. They can make you tell them most anything they know you know. The trick is, year in and year out, never to level with your captors, never let them really know what you know. . . .

The political prison experience is an emotional experience in that you learn that your naked, most inner self is in the spotlight, and that any detected shame or deep fear, any chink in your moral armor is a perfect opening for the manipulative crowbar. And once the manipulator gets it into you, he can put you out front working for him because he has something on you of which you are genuinely ashamed; he has the means to destroy your reputation if you fail him. Fates like that are what prison nightmares are made of, not the fear of pain. . . .

Americans in Hanoi learned fast. They made no deals. They learned that "meeting them half way" was the road to degradation. My hypothetical young prison mate soon learned that impulses, working against the grain, are very important in political prisons, that one learns to enjoy fighting city hall, to enjoy giving the enemy upside-down logic problems, that one soon finds himself taking his lumps with pride and not merely liking but loving that tapping guy next door, the man he never sees, the man he bares his soul to after each torture session, until he realizes he is thereby expiating all residual guilt. Then he realizes he can't be hurt and he can't be had as long as he tells the truth and clings to that forgiving band of brothers who are becoming his country, his family.

This is the power of comradeship and high mindedness that ultimately springs up among people of good will under pressure in mutual danger. It is a source of power as old as man, one we forget in times of freedom, of affluence, of fearful pessimism—like now.

Eight years in a Hanoi prison, survival and dignity. What does it all come down to? It does not come down to coping or supplication or hatred or strength beyond the grasp of any normal person. It comes down to unselfish comradeship, and it comes down to pride, dignity, an enduring sense of self-worth and to that enigmatic mixture of conscience and egoism called personal honor.

87 Teeda Butt Mam, Worms from Our Skin

Pol Pot, the leader of the Cambodian Khmer Rouge Communist Party, created another genocidal terror when he implemented one of the most theoretical and brutal Communist revolutions of the twentieth century. Convinced that the Khmer Rouge Communists could achieve a Cambodian worker's paradise immediately, one of its officers told the Cambodian head of state, Prince Norodom Sihanouk: "We want to have our name in history as the ones who can reach total communism with one leap forward. . . . We want to be known as the only communist party to communize a country without a step-by-step policy, without going through socialism."[1] To achieve this goal, between 1975 and 1979 the Khmer Rouge liquidated more than a million Cambodians.

Once the Khmer Rouge took the Cambodian capital city of Phnom Penh in April 1975, they started to move people out of the cities into the countryside for a massive reeducation program. At the same time, the Angkar (the "Higher Committee") began the systematic killing of those Cambodians associated with the governments of Lon Nol and Norodom Sihanouk. But, in addition to these political killings, the Khmer Rouge started to annihilate any Cambodian man, woman, or child who threatened the revolution or refused to obey orders. Between 1975 and 1979, more than a million Cambodians, out of a population of 7 million, fell in the Khmer Rouge killing fields.

To punish Cambodia for its close relations with China and its defiance of Vietnam, in 1979, battle-hardened Vietnamese troops swept into Cambodia, set up their own puppet government, and forced Pol Pot to seek refuge deep in the jungles of northwestern Cambodia, where he remained an unrepentant fugitive until his death in April 1998. Arguably one of the most brutal killers of the twentieth century, Pol Pot also remains one of the century's greatest enigmas.

Teeda Butt Mam was a fifteen-year-old girl when the Khmer Rouge came to power. For four years she endured the Khmer Rouge's murderous rule of her country. When the Vietnamese Communists invaded Cambodia and drove Pol Pot from power in 1979, she fled Cambodia and immigrated to the United States, where she wrote this memoir.

QUESTIONS FOR CONSIDERATION

1. What was Teeda Butt Mam's "crime" that could convince the Khmer Rouge soldiers to kill her?
2. While this genocide was in progress, many human rights activists insisted that the United States and European countries had an obligation to intervene and stop the killing in Cambodia. Should the United States or European countries have intervened to end the killing? Why? Why not?
3. How would you compare this genocide with the Armenian and Nazi genocides (see Readings 69 and 70)? In what ways were they similar? How exactly did they differ?

We were seduced into returning to our hometowns in the villages so they could reveal our true identities. Then the genocide began. First, it was the men.

[1]Marlowe Hood, "The Lesser Evil: An Interview with Norodom Sihanouk," *The New York Review of Books,* March 14, 1985, p. 24.

They took my father. They told my family that my father needed to be reeducated. Brainwashed. But my father's fate is unknown to this day. We can only imagine what happened to him. This is true for almost all Cambodian widows and orphans. We live in fear of finding out what atrocities were committed against our fathers, husbands, brothers. What could they have done that deserved a tortured death?

Later the Khmer Rouge killed the wives and children of the executed men in order to avoid revenge. They encouraged children to find fault with their own parents and spy on them. They openly showed their intention to destroy the family structure that once held love, faith, comfort, happiness, and companionship. They took young children from their homes to live in a commune so that they could indoctrinate them.

Parents lost their children. Families were separated. We were not allowed to cry or show any grief when they took away our loved ones. A man would be killed if he lost an ox he was assigned to tend. A woman would be killed if she was too tired to work. Human life wasn't even worth a bullet. They clubbed the back of our necks and pushed us down to smother us and let us die in a deep hole with hundreds of other bodies.

They told us we were VOID. We were less than a grain of rice in a large pile. The Khmer Rouge said that the Communist revolution could be successful with only two people. Our lives had no significance to their great Communist nation, and they told us, "To keep you is no benefit, to destroy you is no loss."

They accomplished all of this by promoting and encouraging the "old" people, who were the villagers, the farmers, and the uneducated. They were the most violent and ignorant people, and the Khmer Rouge taught them to lead, manage, control, and destroy. These people took orders without question. The Khmer Rouge built animosity and jealousy into them so the killings could be justified. They ordered us to attend meetings every night where we took turns finding fault with each other, intimidating those around us. We survived by becoming like them. We stole, we cheated, we lied, we hated ourselves and each other, and we trusted no one.

The people on the Khmer Rouge death list were the group called the city people. They were the "new" people. These were any Cambodian men, women, girls, boys, and babies who did not live in their "liberated zones" before they won the war in 1975. Their crime was that they lived in the enemy's zone, helping and supporting the enemy.

The city people were the enemy, and the list was long. Former soldiers, the police, the CIA, and the KGB. Their crime was fighting in the civil war. The merchants, the capitalists, and the businessmen. Their crime was exploiting the poor. The rich farmers and the landlords. Their crime was exploiting the peasants. The intellectuals, the doctors, the lawyers, the monks, the teachers, and the civil servants. These people thought, and their memories were tainted by the evil Westerners. Students were getting education to exploit the poor. Former celebrities, the poets. These people carried bad memories of the old, corrupted Cambodia.

The list goes on and on. The rebellious, the kind-hearted, the brave, the clever, the individualists, the people who wore glasses, the literate, the popular, the complainers, the lazy, those with talent, those with trouble getting along with others, and those with soft hands. These people were corrupted and lived off the blood and sweat of the farmers and the poor.

Very few of us escaped these categories. My family were not villagers. We were from Phnom Penh. I was afraid of who I was. I was an educated girl from a middle-class family. I could read, write, and think. I was proud of my family and my roots. I was scared that they would hear my thoughts and prayers, that they could see my dreams and feel my anger and disapproval of their regime.

I was always hungry. I woke up hungry before sunrise and walked many kilometers to the worksite with no breakfast. I worked until noon. My lunch was either rice porridge with a few grains or boiled young bananas or boiled corn. I continued working till sunset. My dinner was the same as lunch. I couldn't protest to Angkar, but my stomach protested to me that it needed more food. Every night I went to sleep dirty and hungry. I was sad because I missed my mom. I was fearful that this might be the night I'd be taken away, tortured, raped, and killed.

I wanted to commit suicide but I couldn't. If I did, I would be labeled "the enemy" because I dared to show my unhappiness with their regime. My death would be followed by my family's death because they were the family of the enemy. My greatest fear was not my death, but how much suffering I had to go through before they killed me.

They kept moving us around, from the fields into the woods. They purposely did this to disorient us so they could have complete control. They did it to get rid of the "useless people." Those who were too old or too weak to work. Those who did not produce their quota. We were cold because we had so few clothes and blankets. We had no shoes. We were sick and had little or no medical care. They told us that we "volunteered" to work fifteen hours or more a day in the rain or in the moonlight with no holidays. We were timid and lost. We had to be silent. We not only lost our identities, but we lost our pride, our senses, our religion, our loved ones, our souls, ourselves.

The Khmer Rouge said they were creating a utopian nation where everyone would be equal. They restarted our nation by resettling everyone and changing everything back to zero. The whole nation was equally poor. But while the entire population was dying of starvation, disease, and hopelessness, the Khmer Rouge was creating a new upper class. Their soldiers and the Communist party members were able to choose any woman or man they wanted to marry. In addition to boundless food, they were crazed with gold, jewelry, perfume, imported watches, Western medicine, cars, motorcycles, bicycles, silk, and other imported goods.

My dear friend Sakon was married to a handicapped Khmer Rouge veteran against her will. He was mentally disturbed and also suffered from tetanus. At night he woke up from his sleep with nightmares of his crimes and his killings. After that, he beat her. One night, he stabbed my friend to death and injured her mother.

Near my hut there was a woman named Chamroeun. She watched her three children die of starvation, one at a time. She would have been able to save their lives had she had gold or silk or perfume to trade for food and medicine on the black market. The Khmer Rouge veterans and village leaders had control of the black market. They traded rice that Chamroeun toiled over for fancy possessions. The Khmer Rouge gave a new meaning to corruption.

The female soldiers were jealous of my lighter skin and feminine figure. While they were enjoying their nice black pajamas, silk scarves, jewelry, new shoes, and perfume, they stared at me, seeing if I had anything better than they did. I tried to appear timid with my ragged clothes, but it was hard to hide the pride in my eyes.

In January 1979 I was called to join a district meeting. The district leader told us that it was time to get rid of "all the wheat that grows among the rice plants." The city people were the wheat. The city people were to be eliminated. My life was saved because the Vietnamese invasion came just two weeks later.

When the Vietnamese invasion happened, I cried. I was crying with joy that my life was saved. I was crying with sorrow that my country was once again invaded by our century-old enemy. I stood on Cambodian soil feeling that I no longer belonged to it. I wanted freedom. I decided to escape to the free world.

I traveled with my family from the heart of the country to the border of Thailand. It was devastating to witness the destruction of my homeland that had occurred in only four years. Buddhist temples were turned into prisons. Statues of Buddha and artwork were vandalized. Schools were turned into Khmer Rouge headquarters where people were interrogated, tortured, killed, and buried. School yards were turned into killing fields. Old marketplaces were empty. Books were burned. Factories were left to rust. Plantations were without tending and bore no fruit.

This destruction was tolerable compared to the human conditions. Each highway was filled with refugees. We were refugees of our own country. With our skinny bodies, bloated stomachs, and hollow eyes, we carried our few possessions and looked for our separated family members. We asked who lived and didn't want to mention who died. We gathered to share our horrifying stories. Stories about people being pushed into deep wells and ponds and suffocating to death. People were baked alive in a local tile oven. One woman was forced to cook her husband's liver, which was cut out while he was still alive. Women were raped before execution. One old man said, "It takes a river of ink to write our stories."

In April 1979, the Buddhist New Year, exactly four years after the Khmer Rouge came to power, I joined a group of corpselike bodies dancing freely to the sound of clapping and songs of folk music that defined who we were. We danced under the moonlight around the bonfire. We were celebrating the miracles that saved our lives. At that moment, I felt that my spirit and my soul had returned to my weak body. Once again, I was human.

Africa in the Later Twentieth Century

In the nineteenth century, all of Africa except Liberia and Ethiopia came under colonial rule of one sort or another. From the 1950s to the 1980s, nearly all that colonial rule disappeared (see Readings 80 and 81). Some African states retained fairly close ties to the former "mother country": Many former British and French colonies entered the British Commonwealth or the French Union. Others opted for complete independence. In the early years of the decolonization period, many African leaders hoped that the common bond of struggling against colonialism would result in a unified Africa.

Just *how* unified Africa was to be was a different matter. Kwame Nkrumah, an articulate advocate of independence and undisputed leader of the new Ghana for its first decade, advocated a strong federation of African states and stressed the parallel between the American colonists fighting for independence and unifying soon afterward into the United States with the opportunity presented to the newly independent African states. In the early postcolonial period, African leaders were so critical of the way colonial powers had drawn arbitrary lines with no regard for tribal or religious differences or similarities among the people assigned to the various colonies that it seemed likely that many of the ex-colonies would not last as new states. A continent brought together under the Organization of African Unity appeared as a real alternative; redivisions along tribal lines appeared to be a more difficult alternative. In the final analysis, however, most African leaders attempted to keep intact the old colonial boundaries they had inherited as national boundaries.

This meant confronting the problems of diverse ethnic groups living in close proximity to one another. Some leaders, such as Jomo Kenyatta in Kenya and Samora Machel in Mozambique tried to counter tribal hostilities with either an active policy of getting the tribes to work together (Kenyatta) or "killing tribalism" (Machel). Apart from tribal relations, there was the matter of black-white relations—which, to the surprise of nearly everyone, turned out to be one of the least problematic of the African ethnic-group issues to deal with—and friction between black Africans and Asians, particularly Indians in East Africa. Uganda had made a promising beginning in the 1960s with a constitution guaranteeing equal rights and a government of checks and balances. Under the regime of Idi Amin, however, conflicts exploded that suspended government under law and led to the East Indian population taking the brunt of built-up resentments.

Apart from ethnic-group conflict, political or pseudo-political warfare raged for years after independence, particularly in the large former Portuguese colonies of Angola and Mozambique. There was a strong cold war involvement in the anticolonial struggles there, with the USSR supporting the anti-Portuguese guerrillas, who won in 1975. In both countries, the victorious leaders attempted to implement Marxist political and economic ideas as they understood them. Their attempts at collectivization ran the economies of both countries into the ground, giving rise to prolonged and devastating civil wars between the new Marxist governments supported by the USSR and the nationalist guerrillas supported by some of the NATO countries and South Africa. A by-product of the end of the cold war was a corresponding end to support for surrogate Marxists and nationalists in their warfare against each other in Africa and other parts of the Third World.

Although military aid from NATO and Warsaw Pact countries had stopped by the end of the 1980s, Western powers continue to provide aid to Africa for development and relief. The former colonial powers, particularly Britain, France, and Portugal, have often supplied aid to their former colonies. The United States, which had, at most, a paternalistic interest in Liberia, and Germany, which ceded its African colonies to several of the victorious Allies after World War I, have been spreading their aid more evenly around the continent. Much of the aid, however, is supplied by nongovernmental organizations (NGOs) from all continents, frequently those with a Christian orientation, such as World Vision.

Present-day Africa has many features that outsiders find attractive. In African villages, visitors are often struck by the level of cooperation in work and celebration among age groups. Children, young adults, and old people still till the soil, herd animals, and perform songs, rituals, and dances together much as in ages past. Hospitality toward strangers and mutual respect among generations remain striking aspects of African life. Many African American leaders refer to Africa as a source of inspiration for blacks in the United States, who, until the second half of the twentieth century, were not encouraged to take much of an interest in their heritage. Still, Africa has its depressing side, as the journalist Keith Richburg points out, and NGOs today have difficulty in recruiting and retaining African Americans for their posts in Africa.

88 Kwame Nkrumah, *I Speak of Freedom: A Statement of African Ideology*

Kwame Nkrumah (1909–1972) led the former British colony of the Gold Coast to become the independent country of Ghana in 1957. Until he was overthrown by a coup d'état in 1966, Kwame Nkrumah was one of Africa's most influential leaders.

QUESTIONS TO CONSIDER

1. Why have Kwame Nkrumah's dreams of African unity had so little appeal for many modern African political leaders?
2. Is the dream of African unity too idealistic? Why? Why not?

For centuries, Europeans dominated the African continent. The white man arrogated to himself the right to rule and to be obeyed by the non-white; his mission, he claimed was to "civilise" Africa. Under this cloak, the Europeans robbed the continent of vast riches and inflicted unimaginable suffering on the African people.

All this makes a sad story, but now we must be prepared to bury the past with its unpleasant memories and look to the future. All we ask of the former colonial powers is their goodwill and co-operation to remedy past mistakes and injustices and to grant independence to the colonies in Africa. . . .

It is clear that we must find an African solution to our problems, and that this can only be found in African unity. Divided we are weak; united, Africa could become one of the greatest forces for good in the world.

Although most Africans are poor, our continent is potentially extremely rich. Our mineral resources, which are being exploited with foreign capital only to enrich foreign investors, range from gold and diamonds to uranium and petroleum. Our forests contain some of the finest woods to be grown anywhere. Our cash crops include cocoa, coffee, rubber, tobacco and cotton. As for power, which is an important factor in any economic development, Africa contains over 40% of the total potential water power of the world, as compared with about 10% in Europe and 13% in North America. Yet so far, less than 1% has been developed. This is one of the reasons why we have in Africa the paradox of poverty in the midst of plenty, and scarcity in the midst of abundance.

Never before have a people had within their grasp so great an opportunity for developing a continent endowed with so much wealth. Individually, the independent states of Africa, some of them potentially rich, others poor, can do little for their people. Together, by mutual help, they can achieve much. But the economic development of the continent must be planned and pursued as a whole. A loose confederation designed only for economic cooperation would not provide the necessary unity of purpose. Only a strong political union can bring about full and effective development of our natural resources for the benefit of our people.

The political situation in Africa today is heartening and at the same time disturbing. It is heartening to see so many new flags hoisted in place of the old; it is disturbing to see so many countries of varying sizes and at different levels of development, weak and, in some cases, almost helpless. If this terrible state of fragmentation is allowed to continue it may well be disastrous for us all.

There are at present some 28 states in Africa, excluding the Union of South Africa, and those countries not yet free. No less than nine of these states have a population of less than three million. Can we seriously believe that the colonial powers meant these countries to be independent, viable states? The example of South America, which has as much wealth, if not more than North America, and yet remains weak and dependent on outside interests, is one which every African would do well to study.

Critics of African unity often refer to the wide differences in culture, language and ideas in various parts of Africa. This is true, but the essential fact remains that we are all Africans, and have a common interest in the independence of Africa. The difficulties presented by questions of language, culture and different political systems are not insuperable. If the need for political union is agreed by us all, then the will to create it is born; and where there's a will there's a way.

The present leaders of Africa have already shown a remarkable willingness to consult and seek advice among themselves. Africans have, indeed, begun to think continentally. They realise that they have much in common, both in their past history, in their present problems and in their future hopes. To suggest that the time is not yet ripe for considering a political union of Africa is to evade the facts and ignore realities in Africa today.

The greatest contribution that Africa can make to the peace of the world is to avoid all the dangers inherent in disunity, by creating a political union which will also by its success, stand as an example to a divided world. A union of African states will project more effectively the African personality. It will command respect from a world that has regard only for size and influence. The scant attention paid to African opposition to the French atomic tests in the Sahara, and the ignominious spectacle of the U.N. in the Congo quibbing about constitutional niceties while the Republic was tottering into anarchy, are evidence of the callous disregard of African Independence by the Great Powers.

We have to prove that greatness is not to be measured in stock piles of atom bombs. I believe strongly and sincerely that with the deep-rooted wisdom and dignity, the innate respect for human lives, the intense humanity that is our heritage, the African race, united under one federal government, will emerge not as just another world bloc to flaunt its wealth and strength, but as a Great Power whose greatness is indestructible because it is built not on fear, envy and suspicion, nor won at the expense of others, but founded on hope, trust, friendship and directed to the good of all mankind.

The emergence of such a mighty stabilising force in this strife-worn world should be regarded not as the shadowy dream of a visionary, but as a practical proposition, which the peoples of Africa can, and should, translate into reality. There is a tide in the affairs of every people when the moment strikes for political action. Such was the moment in the history of the United States of America when the Founding Fathers saw beyond the petty wranglings of the separate states and created a Union. This is our chance. We must act now. Tomorrow may be too late and the opportunity will have passed, and with it the hope of free Africa's survival.

89 Theresa Andrews, *Letters from a 1990s Bush Doctor*

Theresa Andrews (1958–   ) is a physician with World Vision in Africa. Having served in Mozambique from 1990 to 1994 and in Zaire (Democratic Republic of the Congo) and Sierra Leone since then, she has documented the complexity of African survival and development struggles in letters to her organization, family, and friends. In the following excerpt, Andrews recalls what it felt like to be caught with her husband, Tim, and their three-year-old son, Joseph, in the middle of a violent coup in Freetown, capital of Sierra Leone.

Sierra Leone's transition to independence from Britain in 1961 was peaceful, but an increasingly corrupt government in the 1970s led to coups in the 1980s and 1990s, sometimes resulting in military rule. In the interior of the country, the rebel Revolutionary United Front (RUF), a group interested largely in its own power and access to wealth, particularly Sierra Leone's rich diamond-mining area, made sure that villagers would be too afraid to resist its forces by terrorizing them with massacres and mutilations—usually chopping off hands—and the resulting efforts of the government in Freetown to cope with them led to an ongoing civil war. In democratic elections, a former UN employee, Ahmed Kabbah, was elected president, but his administration was so ineffective and so unpopular with the military that an alliance of the RUF with disaffected military forces led to a coup on May 25, 1997, which toppled his government.

QUESTIONS TO CONSIDER

1. Why does Andrews think that *friendship* has a stronger meaning among Africans than in normal English usage?
2. Strong religious influences, as well as those of secular ideologies, are still very much a force in the later twentieth century. How do Andrews's Christian convictions compare with the Marxist convictions of Fidel Castro (see Reading 82)? Is the role of strong opposing, demonic forces comparable for both of them?
3. How did the Andrewses cope with potential looters? How would you have coped with them?

Isata, Joseph's nanny, woke us at 6:30 AM on Sunday to report that the prisoners had been released from Pademba prison. She had no more information than that, but was clearly frightened as she lives quite close to Pademba. I headed back to bed to tell Tim about the call when suddenly gunfire erupted about a mile or two down the mountain. Something was up—but the whole thing seemed so unreal. Just yesterday we'd had a lovely picnic at a small beach south of Freetown. Trying to confront the new reality around us, we went outside to talk to our night guards; they have hand-held radio sets and are our best sources of news at times like these.

Our house was just across the street from the Minister of Works. This normally worked to our advantage, as that particular minister controlled the city's electricity supply, and our area had the best supply of electricity in Freetown. Now it was a problem. Government ministers (along with Kabbah's police) are prime targets of both the RUF and the military. The military still grumbles about last year's democratic elections, which "robbed" them of their country leadership status. Kabbah made things worse recently by reducing soldiers' wages from $18 and four bags of rice per month to $16 and two bags of rice. As the military are so closely associated with the RUF, they

From Theresa M. Andrews, MD, *Letters from a 1990s Bush Doctor* (Churchville, VA: POETA Books, 1998), pp. 239–55. Reprinted with permission.

are nicknamed "sobels" or "soldiers by day—rebels by night." Our neighboring Minister of Works and three colleagues appeared on the veranda as we spoke, looking in the direction of the gunfire.

The phone rang, bringing us back inside. Angie, our finance manager, had called to tell us that a military coup had been sprung. She'd heard that a group of low-ranking military officials released some political prisoners (military officers arrested for a coup attempt some months before) to gain momentum for this month's attempted overthrow of the president. We did not know that 700 criminals, many of them in jail for rape and murder, had been released as well. We also did not know that the military was handing out uniforms and AK47s to beach boys, street gangs and anybody who was willing to "join the cause." A gun is pure gold to the deprived person who must fight, steal or cajole for a daily living. Guns represent free passage to as many looted goods as can be handled, a veritable lifetime of wealth. "The cause" did not interest these people in the least. But the idea of quick money did. The street recruits and prisoners turned out to be the coup's most motivated and effective fighting branch.

About ten minutes after we saw them on the veranda, the minister and his colleagues left their house—on foot. When a wealthy man leaves his house like that during armed conflict, he knows he's losing everything in his house—and he's fleeing for his life. They left none too soon. Within minutes, Tim and I were watching a truckload of soldiers force its way through the minister's gate. Shooting guns in the air, they ran to the house, surrounded it, then blasted their way through the doors. For the next 5 hours, Tim and I had a privileged "front row seat" via our kitchen window of the looting that ensued. I could not watch it for any length of time as it gave me a sick feeling in the pit of my stomach. Somebody's orderly, established house was being entered by violent men with no respect. A strong sense of violation welled up within me as I watched this family's household being entered by strangers who took as much pleasure in destroying the goods as they did in stealing them. The greater reason for my sick stomach, however, was the knowledge that our house was only several yards from the minister's front lawn. I faintly hoped that the focus of the looting would be on the political "big shots." But I knew deep down that Africans in general, and Sierra Leonean soldiers in particular, would not be so discriminating in their taste for "lootable" houses.

As the soldiers began serious looting they momentarily forgot about shooting, and Tim and I took the opportunity to venture out onto our balcony. A soldier appeared at our gate with a gun slung on his back. Our night guard and SSD approached him to explain that while many of the houses in our neighborhood belonged to ministers or other wealthy individuals, this was a World Vision house. They described with great flourish how we were helping the country of Sierra Leone by giving food to families displaced by war and seeds to farmers returning to their fields after having lost everything. These seemed like weak words to a poor soldier with potential access to the wealth of our house, but the soldier smiled graciously and said he was merely looking for moral support (i.e. money). As it happened, Tim and I only had about $60 in the house. We gave the soldier $10. He grinned, apparently happy with this, and left waving what looked like the two-fingered peace sign (we learned later that it stood for "Love 2"—the name of this coup; the previous unsuccessful coup had been dubbed "Love 1"). The soldier assured us that we would be safe. Tim and I knew enough of Africa not to believe this—the lone soldier probably had no real plan or power to protect us, but we were happy to have averted an immediate incident.

The gunfire picked up, this time with heavier artillery and grenades. I glanced out the window to see a truckload of soldiers heading down our street. There was little time to think as the gunfire seemed to surround us and we headed for the hallway. The shots were extremely loud and shook our house again. We realized after localizing the sounds that soldiers were forcing their way into the other side of our duplex where a British lady pediatrician lives with her husband and two children. The woman is a wonderful person who spends much of her time giving free clinical care to those who cannot afford it—including the children of the military who live in the barracks just down the street from us. Her manner is pleasant though reserved, almost stoic. Dramatic shows of emotion are not part of her repertoire. When we heard her scream through the wall, we were shaken to the core. We heard considerable scuffling, voices, and a few more shots. Then a car drove off. We could only listen with horror at the sound of furniture being dragged through doors that were too small and air conditioners being dropped.

More than once the question of how to rely on God's grace came to mind. I've thought about this before—hearing tales of Christian martyrs and having personally experienced smaller gunfire episodes in other countries. I firmly believe that God gives us the grace to face any situation to which he calls us. I wondered how this grace was going to manifest itself today. I was getting too shaky to function—it felt like my mind was sort of shutting down and I started to wonder whether a mental "blackout" was going to be God's way of letting me cope.

When it seemed I could not tolerate the fear and pressure any longer, the phone rang—our American friend Trish called to see how we were. She seemed to be holding up, and urged us to read Psalm 91. I knew Psalm 91 well, having memorized it several years before to combat fear during a prolonged stay in Johannesburg (the murder capital of the world). I wondered whether reading it again would accomplish much, but Tim and I had very few options, so we sat down together and read it out loud several times. Then we prayed. We praised God for who He was and we sang praises to Him. As we did, an amazing sense of God's reality overwhelmed us. The more we prayed and sang, the more real His presence became and I was filled with the conviction that the reality we were experiencing—what seemed to be a piece of God's kingdom—was more "real" than the war going on around us. No matter how audible and tangible the gunshots were, the real battles of this world are fought in the realm of the spirit, and Jesus had gotten the victory there nearly 2,000 years ago.

A neighbor of ours, Ali, lives with his wife, four children and several cousins in a tiny two-room shack just beyond our driveway. His four-year old daughter (Cumba) and Joseph became such close friends over the past 6 months that Cumba had become a regular part of our family—coming over to play as soon as Joseph got home from nursery school, joining us for our beach and hotel outings, and returning home around bedtime each night. Ali came to our house looking extremely worried. This was the worst coup he'd been through in his forty years. I asked the obvious, just to clear the air. "Do you think we'll be looted?" Ali grimaced, then frowned and was quiet for some minutes, as if fighting an inner battle. Finally, he spoke with great resolve: "You are my friends. To hurt you and your house is to hurt me. I must go for help." Ali knew two "good" soldiers from his home tribe in Kono (northwestern Sierra Leone). He also knew the risks of seeking them out and the risks of siding with or protecting an expatriate family—but he'd counted the cost and headed out our gate.

After several hours, Ali returned with two heavily armed soldiers. They looked kindly enough. After all we'd seen that day, I found it hard to develop an immediate trust. The soldiers seemed to feel the same, but Ali broke the ice, explaining that he'd known one of the soldiers for 20 years. They were "brothers" by merit of being from the same village. He went on with great eloquence to explain to the soldiers the nobility of their task: to protect foreigners who are helping their country, and more importantly, to protect his friends. In Africa, friendship and family outweigh just about everything. It leads to considerable trouble in government, where friends and family are appointed to high level posts regardless of qualifications or popular sentiment. This time both friendship and family worked to protect us. The soldier was Ali's "family" and was bound as such not to betray him. We were Ali's friends—a concept for which there is no equivalent term in the States. We were not acquaintances or just nice neighbors. We were people for which Ali was risking his life. Despite the temptation they must have felt to forget their friendships and loot our house, their respect for Ali, and by association for us, held firm.

Somewhere in the late afternoon, a very loud single gunshot rattled our doors and windows. I peered out our bedroom window, seeing our soldiers wave a friendly "good-bye" to a group of military exiting our back yard. It turned out that an intruder had shot through the garage door to gain entry. Upon seeing the cars, he recognized mine (this soldier lived near the tennis courts where he'd seen me playing). Taking advantage of the familiarity, our soldiers persuaded the intruder and his cohorts to "do the noble thing" and leave us alone. Our soldiers were proud of the accomplishment, but asked if we couldn't donate a bottle of whiskey to boost the morale of the next visitors. Whiskey was not in our store of supplies, but they knew where it could be readily purchased at the bargain price of $2.50, even during the coup. Perhaps I should have struggled a bit more with the morality of supplying whiskey to looters who were already a bit crazy, but so far the soldiers were handling things well. I deferred to their understanding of their own culture, and handed over the cash.

Around nightfall, while I was packing in the bedroom, I heard shouting and scuffles that brought me back to the front of the house. A large military truck was parked outside our gate and numerous soldiers were milling around in our driveway. I knew what the truck meant. Large vehicles are reserved for houses anticipated to contain a large amount of lootable goods. It was difficult to sort out the figures in the darkness, but it was clear that there were more looters than our two military. The looters were heavily armed, including rocket launchers. I peered out the porch window where our guard was standing. "They want money." We'd already been contacted by friends who'd had to pay hundreds of dollars to threatening looters. After our first bribe, a $20 down payment to our friendly soldiers, and the bottle of whiskey, we were left with about $25. How could this appease the multitude of hungry looters in our courtyard? I sent the guard around to Tim, who was controlling the money that day, and kept watch behind the curtain. To my amazement, I saw the group become quiet. Then one by one, seven soldiers filed sullenly out our gate, started their truck up and left. How my heart lifted! I abandoned reason for a moment and went out to find Tim and speak to the soldiers. Everyone was shaken. They'd held Mohammed, who cooks for the guards, at gunpoint, claiming that as cook he must have keys. As Sam tried to defend him, they turned their guns at Sam saying "We're going to kill you." Sam, also from Kono, realized his advantage: "Would you kill your brother from Kono?" he said and they backed off. I was afraid our group of guards and soldiers was becoming discouraged. How can they justify risking their lives for the meager salary of $35 per month? But as they told their stories, I could see that this victory had invigorated them. "God is helping us," said Mohammed, beaming.

The victory was sweet, but it added somberness to the evening. The night was young, and looting in Africa (perhaps everywhere) gets more aggressive and violent as the night wears on. What will we be facing? Tim and I lay in our bed, fully clothed. We did not even pull the mosquito net in case of the need for sudden flight. I braced myself for a sleepless night, and asked the Lord to steady me for the visitors that would be coming. I could hardly believe or understand the peace and comfort that enveloped me. I felt like a baby wrapped securely in a warm blanket. God was saying, "You'll have no more visitors. Go to sleep."

90 Keith B. Richburg, *A Black Man Confronts Africa*

Keith B. Richburg was born in Detroit in 1958, graduated from the University of Michigan in 1980, and completed a master's degree in international relations at the London School of Economics in 1983. He then began a career in journalism with the *Washington Post* and from 1991 to 1994 was based in Nairobi as the paper's African bureau chief. Richburg won the National Association of Black Journalists' foreign reporting award in 1993 for his coverage of the civil war and famine in Somalia and has received other awards for his coverage of African affairs. Whereas some black Americans in search of their roots and ethnic and cultural identity turn to Africa, Richburg, who was black, found little to identify with while living there. In the following selection, he provides an interesting perspective on the turbulent continent.

QUESTIONS TO CONSIDER

1. In addition to his job of reporting, the author writes that he was also searching for his "ancestral homeland." What caused him to declare, "I am an American, a black American, and I feel no connection to this strange and violent place"?
2. Richburg also lived in Washington, D.C., and New York City, and after residing in both cities, he claims that he and many other black Americans have consistently been made to "feel like strangers in our own land." What caused him to develop these feelings?
3. Compare and contrast Richburg's account of living in Africa with the views expressed by Theresa Andrews (see Reading 89).

It's been a long journey now, and I'll be leaving Africa soon. I'm beaten down, weary, ready to leave all of these lurid images behind me, ready to go home. I've seen too much death, too much misery, too much hatred, and I find I no longer care.

From Keith B. Richburg, *Out of America: A Black Man Confronts Africa* (New York: Basic Books, 1997), pp. 225–29. Reprinted by permission.

Africa. Birthplace of civilization. My ancestral homeland. I came here thinking I might find a little bit of that missing piece of myself. But Africa chewed me up and spit me back out again. It took out a machete and slashed into my brain the images that have become my nightmares. I close my eyes now and I am staring at a young woman atop a pile of corpses. I see an old man on the side of the road imploring me for a last drop of water before he dies in the dirt. I see my friends surrounded by an angry mob as they try to fend off the stones that rain down to crush their skulls. I see the grotesquely charred body of a young man set on fire. I see a church altar desecrated by the blood of the dead, and bullet holes forming a halo around Christ's likeness on the cross. Then I see Ilaria, beautiful Ilaria, bleeding to death in her car on the side of the road. There is an old man, broken and bent, who still limps from the pain of the torture that destroyed his limbs. There are the limbless beggars pressing their bloodied stumps against a car window. There is a child, smiling at me, while he aims his loaded grenade launcher at my passing car.

My eyes snap open, but I remain frightened of these ghosts that I know are out there, in the darkness, in Africa. I tried my best to get to know this place, to know the people. But instead I am sitting here alone in my house in Nairobi, frightened, staring into the blackness of the African night. It's quiet outside and I'm feeling scared and lonely. I am surrounded by a high fence and protected by two large dogs. I have a paid security guard patrolling the perimeter, a silent alarm system, and a large metal door with a sliding bolt that I keep firmly closed, all to prevent Africa from sneaking across my front yard and bashing into my brains with a panga knife for the two hundred dollars and change I keep in my top desk drawer.

It wasn't supposed to turn out this way. I really did come here with an open mind, wanting to love the place, love the people. I would love to end this journey now on a high note, to see hope amid the chaos. I'd love to talk about the smiles of the African people, their generosity and perseverance, their love of life, their music and dance, their respect for elders, their sense of family and community. I could point out the seeds of democracy, the formation of a "civil society," the emergence of an urban middle class, the establishment of independent institutions, and the rule of law. I wish I could end my story this way, but it would all be a lie.

How can anyone talk about democracy and constitutions and the rule of law in places where paramilitary security forces firebomb the offices of opposition newspapers? Where entire villages get burned down and thousands of people made homeless because of competing political loyalties? Where whole chunks of countries are under the sway of armed guerrillas? And where traditional belief runs so deep that a politician can be arrested and charged with casting magic spells over poor villagers to force them to vote for him?

My language may seem dark and disturbing, but that's what the reality was for me—almost all dark and disturbing. More than three years here have left me bitter and largely devoid of hope, and largely drained of compassion.

Now when I hear the latest reports of the latest African tragedy—a tribal slaughter in Burundi, perhaps, a riot in a refugee camp in a remote corner of Zaire, maybe a new flood of refugees streaming across a border in Uganda or Sierra Leone—I can watch with more than casual interest because I have been there. I feel sorrow for the victims. I shake my head in frustration at the continent's continuing anguish. I might even rush off a contribution to the Red Cross or one of the other aid agencies struggling to help. But I feel nothing more.

Maybe I would care more if I had not been here myself, if I had not seen the suffering up close, if I hadn't watched the bodies tumbling over the waterfall, smelled the rotting flesh. Yes, perhaps from a different vantage point, I would still have the luxury of falling back on the old platitudes. Maybe if I had never set foot here, I could celebrate my own blackness, my "African-ness." Then I might feel a part of this place, and Africa's pain might be my own. But while I know that "Afrocentrism" has become fashionable for many black Americans searching for identity, I know it cannot work for me. I have been here, I have lived here and seen Africa in all its horror. I am an American, a black American, and I feel no connection to this strange and violent place.

You see? I just wrote "black American." I couldn't even bring myself to write "African American." It's a phrase that, for me, doesn't roll naturally off the tongue: "African American." Is that what we really are? Is there anything really "African" left in the descendants of those original slaves who made the torturous journey across the Atlantic? Are white Americans whose ancestors sailed west across the same ocean as long ago as the slaves still considered "English Americans" or "Dutch Americans"? And haven't the centuries on America's shores erased all those ancient connections, so that we descendants of Africa and England and Holland and Ireland and China are now simply "Americans"?

If you want to establish some kind of ethnic pecking order, based on the number of years in the New World, then blacks would be at the top of the list; the first slaves from Africa arrived in Virginia before the Mayflower even set sail. Black influence today is visible in so many aspects of American culture, from jazz to basketball to slang time to poetry. Spaghetti and dim sum and sushi have all become part of the American culinary scene, but what can be more American than down-home southern cooking—fried chicken and biscuits, barbecued spare ribs, grits and greens—and in the big houses of the old South, there was invariably a black face in the back, preparing the meals.

Yet despite our "American-ness," despite the black contributions to the culture America claims as its own, black Americans have consistently been made to feel like strangers in our own land, the land where we have lived for some four hundred years. I know, because I have felt that way too. It's subtle sometimes, that sense of not belonging. But in ways large and small, most black people in America would probably say they feel it every day.

I myself feel it whenever I'm "dressed down," not wearing a suit and tie, in a well-worn pair of old jeans and a T-shirt perhaps, and I walk into a department store or a corner shop. I can feel the store detective's eyes following me through the aisles, making sure I'm not there to shoplift the merchandise. And if I have a newspaper under my arm when I enter the store, I make a point of waving it openly to the sales clerk, just so she doesn't think later that I'm trying to pilfer it off the rack.

I feel it when I'm standing on a street corner in Washington or New York, trying to hail a taxi. If I'm on the way home from work, I remember to open my overcoat so the cab driver can see my dress shirt and necktie, so he will think: This is not some street thug who might rob me; this is a respectable black man on the way home from the office. And if I am in Washington and it's night, and I'm going west of Rock Creek Park, to Georgetown or one of the city's more affluent "white" neighborhoods, I make sure to stand on the correct side of the street so I am not mistaken for a black man heading east, to the black neighborhoods, to the areas where I know taxi drivers, even black ones, fear to tread.

I feel it, too, when I'm driving a car in America, anywhere in America. If I am pulled over by the police, I keep my hands clearly visible on the steering wheel; if I am wearing sunglasses, I remove them. Because I know I am a black man in America and I might be seen as a threat, a danger.

Part VII
The Twenty-First Century

From *Perestroika* to a New Russia

Soon after Mikhail Gorbachev (1931–   ) assumed leadership in the Soviet Union in 1985, he announced his policy of *perestroika* (restructuring), which initiated a powerful process of revolutionary renovation and presented a provocative challenge to many—in both the USSR and the West. Numerous changes, both internally and abroad, generated great debate. Gorbachev's economic policies included an effort to reduce the role of central planning in the Soviet economy and allowed greater authority for the managers of the nation's enterprises. An effort was also made to encourage more autonomy for private businesses as well as cooperative ventures with Western firms. Politically, Gorbachev's reforms included a loosening of centralized controls internally as well as in the satellite states of Eastern Europe. This permitted a resurgence of national consciousness that led to the liberation of Eastern Europe, the dismantling of the Berlin Wall, and the unification of Germany—historic events signifying the end of the cold war. Some of Gorbachev's reforms were met from the first with suspicion, cynicism, and strong opposition within Soviet officialdom. As late as the spring of 1991, he appeared to have consolidated his power, but as a leader he did not long survive the dissolution of the Soviet Union into Russia and the other successor states. It remains an open question whether his *perestroika* hastened the demise of the Soviet Union, as his Russian critics predicted, or whether there was a possibility that his reforms could have succeeded—if their timing had been different—in preserving much of the Communist Party's regime in the Soviet Union in a way comparable to the success of Deng Xiaoping in salvaging Communist Party control in China (see Reading 95).

91 Mikhail Gorbachev, *Perestroika*

This selection, taken from *Perestroika: New Thinking for Our Country and the World,* explains Mikhail Gorbachev's thoughts behind the urgent need for reforms.

QUESTIONS TO CONSIDER

1. What is the meaning of *perestroika,* and what prompted the idea? What domestic and international examples of *perestroika* occurred under Gorbachev's leadership?
2. What does "restructuring" mean for the history of socialism? Were there foreseeable dangers in encouraging economic but not political reforms? What historic examples are there to illustrate the implications of such "unequal" changes?
3. Which changes advocated by Gorbachev were indicative of a greater openness to Western-style democracy and market capitalism, a break from the isolation of the Soviet Union, and perhaps an end to the cold war?
4. Compare Gorbachev's reforms with those initiated by Catherine the Great (see Reading 20).

What is perestroika? What prompted the idea of restructuring? What does it mean in the history of socialism? What does it augur for the peoples of the Soviet Union? How might it influence the outside world? All these questions concern the world public and are being actively discussed. Let me begin with the first one.

PERESTROIKA—AN URGENT NECESSITY

I think one thing should be borne in mind when studying the origins and essence of perestroika in the USSR. Perestroika is no whim on the part of some ambitious individuals or a group of leaders. If it were, no exhortations, plenary meetings or even a party congress could have rallied the people to the work which we are now doing and which involves more and more Soviet people each day.

Perestroika is an urgent necessity arising from the profound processes of development in our socialist society. This society is ripe for change. It has long been yearning for it. Any delay in beginning perestroika could have led to an exacerbated internal situation in the near future, which, to put it bluntly, would have been fraught with serious social, economic and political crises.

We have drawn these conclusions from a broad and frank analysis of the situation that has developed in our society by the middle of the eighties. This situation and the problems arising from it presently confront the country's leadership, in which new people have gradually appeared in the last few years. I would like to discuss here the main results of this analysis, in the course of which we had to reassess many things and look back at our history, both recent and not so recent.

Russia, where a great Revolution took place seventy years ago, is an ancient country with a unique history filled with searchings, accomplishments and tragic events. It has given the world many discoveries and outstanding personalities.

However, the Soviet Union is a young state without analogues in history or in the modern world. Over the past seven decades—a short span in the history of human civilization—our country has traveled a path equal to centuries. One of the mightiest powers in the world rose up to replace the backward semi-colonial and semi-feudal Russian Empire. Huge productive forces, a powerful intellectual potential, a highly advanced culture, a unique community of over one hundred nations and nationalities, and firm social protection for 280 million people on a territory forming one-sixth of the Earth—such are our great and indisputable achievements and Soviet people are justly proud of them.

I am not saying this to make my land appear better than it was or is. I do not want to sound like an apologist for whom "mine" means best and unquestionably superior. What I have just said is actual reality, authentic fact, the visible product of the work of several generations of our people. And it is equally clear that my country's progress became possible thanks to the Revolution. It is the product of the Revolution. It is the fruit of socialism, the new social system, and the result of the historical choice made by our people. Behind them are the feats of our fathers and grandfathers and millions of working people—workers, farmers and intellectuals—who seventy years ago assumed direct responsibility for the future of their country.

I would like the reader to contemplate all this: otherwise it would be hard to see what had happened and is happening in our society. I shall return to the historical aspects of our development later. Let me first explain the far-from-simple situation which had developed in the country by the eighties and which made perestroika necessary and inevitable.

At some stage—this became particularly clear in the latter half of the seventies—something happened that was at first sight inexplicable. The country began to lose momentum. Economic failures became more frequent. Difficulties began to accumulate and deteriorate, and unresolved problems to multiply. Elements of what we call stagnation and other phenomena alien to socialism began to appear in the life of society. A kind of "braking mechanism" affecting social and economic development formed. And all this happened at a time when a scientific and technological revolution opened up new prospects for economic and social progress.

Something strange was taking place: the huge fly-wheel of a powerful machine was revolving, while either transmission from it to work places was skidding or drive belts were too loose.

Analyzing the situation, we first discovered a slowing economic growth. In the last fifteen years the national income growth rates had declined by more than a half and by the beginning of the eighties had fallen to a level close to economic stagnation. A country that was once quickly closing on the world's advanced nations began to lose one position after another. Moreover, the gap in the efficiency of production, quality of products, scientific and technological development, the production of advanced technology and the use of advanced techniques began to widen, and not to our advantage.

The gross output drive, particularly in heavy industry, turned out to be a "top-priority" task, just an end in itself. The same happened in capital construction, where a sizable portion of the national wealth became idle capital.

There were costly projects that never lived up to the highest scientific and technological standards. The worker or the enterprise that had expended the greatest amount of labor, material and money was considered the best. It is natural for the producer to "please" the consumer, if I may put it that way. With us, however, the consumer found himself totally at the mercy of the producer and had to make do with what the latter chose to give him. This was again a result of the gross output drive.

It became typical of many of our economic executives to think not of how to build up the national asset, but of how to put more material, labor and working time into an item to sell it at a higher price. Consequently, for all "gross output," there was a shortage of goods. We spent, in fact we are still spending, far more on raw materials, energy and other resources per unit of output than other developed nations. Our country's wealth in terms of natural and manpower resources has spoilt, one may even say corrupted, us. That, in fact, is chiefly the reason why it was possible for our economy to develop extensively for decades.

Accustomed to giving priority to quantitative growth in production, we tried to check the falling rates of growth, but did so mainly by continually increasing expenditures: we built up the fuel and energy industries and increased the use of natural resources in production.

As time went on, material resources became harder to get and more expensive. On the other hand, the extensive methods of fixed capital expansion resulted in an artificial shortage of manpower. In an attempt to rectify the situation somehow, large, unjustified, i.e., in fact unearned, bonuses began to be paid and all kinds of undeserved incentives introduced under the pressure of this shortage, and that led, at a later stage, to the practice of padding reports merely for gain. Parasitical attitudes were on the rise, the prestige of conscientious and high-quality labor began to diminish and a "wage-leveling" mentality was becoming widespread. The imbalance between the measure of work and the measure of consumption, which had become something like the linchpin of the braking mechanism, not only obstructed the growth of labor productivity, but led to the distortion of the principle of social justice.

So the inertia of extensive economic development was leading to an economic deadlock and stagnation.

The economy was increasingly squeezed financially. The sale of large quantities of oil and other fuel and energy resources and raw materials on the world market did not help. It only aggravated the situation. Currency earnings thus made were predominantly used for tackling problems of the moment rather than on economic modernization or on catching up technologically.

Declining rates of growth and economic stagnation were bound to affect other aspects of the life of Soviet society. Negative trends seriously affected the social sphere.

This led to the appearance of the so-called "residual principle" in accordance with which social and cultural programs received what remained in the budget after allocations to production. A "deaf ear" sometimes seemed to be turned to social problems. The social sphere began to lag behind other spheres in terms of technological development, personnel, know-how and most importantly, quality of work.

Here we have more paradoxes. Our society has ensured full employment and provided fundamental social guarantees. At the same time, we failed to use the full potential of socialism to meet the growing requirements in housing, in quality and sometimes quantity of foodstuffs, in the proper organization of the work of transport, in health services, in education and in tackling other problems which, naturally, arose in the course of society's development.

An absurd situation was developing. The Soviet Union, the world's biggest producer of steel, raw materials, fuel and energy, has shortfalls in them due to wasteful or inefficient use. One of the biggest producers of grain for food, it nevertheless has to buy millions of tons of grain a year for fodder. We have the largest number of doctors and hospital beds per thousand of the population and, at the same time, there are shortcomings in our health services. Our rockets can find Halley's comet and fly to Venus with amazing accuracy, but side by side with these scientific and technological triumphs is an obvious lack of efficiency in using scientific achievements for economic needs, and many Soviet household appliances are of poor quality.

This, unfortunately, is not all. A gradual erosion of the ideological and moral values of our people began.

It was obvious to everyone that the growth rates were sharply dropping and that the entire mechanism of quality control was not working properly; there was a lack of receptivity to the advances in science and technology; the improvement in living standards was slowing down and there were difficulties in the supply of foodstuffs, housing, consumer goods and services.

On the ideological plane as well, the braking mechanism brought about ever greater resistance to the attempts to constructively scrutinize the problems that were emerging and to the new ideas. Propaganda of success—real or imagined—was gaining the upper hand. Eulogizing and servility were encouraged; the needs and opinions of ordinary working people, of the public at large, were ignored. In the social sciences scholastic theorization was encouraged and developed, but creative thinking was driven out from the social sciences, and superfluous and voluntarist assessments and judgments were declared indisputable truths. Scientific, theoretical and other discussions, which are indispensable for the development of thought and for creative endeavor, were emasculated. Similar negative tendencies also affected culture, the arts and journalism, as well as the teaching process and medicine, where mediocrity, formalism and loud eulogizing surfaces, too.

The presentation of a "problem-free" reality backfired: a breach had formed between word and deed, which bred public passivity and disbelief in the slogans being proclaimed. It was only natural that this situation resulted in a credibility gap: everything that was proclaimed from the rostrums and printed in newspapers and textbooks was put in question. Decay began in public morals; the great feeling of solidarity with each other that was forged during the heroic times of the Revolution, the first five-year plans, the Great Patriotic War and postwar rehabilitation was weakening; alcoholism, drug addiction and crime were growing; and the penetration of the stereotypes of mass culture alien to us, which bred vulgarity and low tastes and brought about ideological barrenness increased.

Party guidance was relaxed, and initiative lost in some of the vital social processes. Everybody started noticing the stagnation among the leadership and the violation of the natural process of change there. At a certain stage this made for a poorer performance by the Politburo[1] and the Secretariat[2] of the CPSU Central Committee, by the government and throughout the entire Central Committee and the Party apparatus, for that matter.

Political flirtation and mass distribution of awards, titles and bonuses often replaces genuine concern for the people, for their living and working conditions, for a favorable social atmosphere. An atmosphere emerged of "everything goes," and fewer and fewer demands were made on discipline and responsibility. Attempts were made to cover it all up with pompous campaigns and undertakings and celebrations of numerous anniversaries centrally and locally. The world of day-to-day realities and the world of feigned prosperity were diverging more and more.

The need for change was brewing not only in the material sphere of life but also in public consciousness. People who had practical experience, a sense of justice and commitment to the ideals of Bolshevism criticized the established practice of doing things and noted with anxiety the symptoms of moral degradation and erosion of revolutionary ideals and socialist values.

Workers, farmers and intellectuals, Party functionaries centrally and locally, came to ponder the situation in the country. There was a growing awareness that things could not go on like this much longer. Perplexity and indignation welled up that the great values born of the October Revolution and the heroic struggle for socialism were being trampled underfoot.

All honest people saw with bitterness that people were losing interest in social affairs, that labor no longer had its respectable status, that people, especially the young, were after profit at all cost. Our people have always had an intrinsic ability to discern the gap between word and deed. No wonder Russian folk tales are full of mockery aimed against people who like pomp and trappings; and literature, which had always played a great role in our country's spiritual life, is merciless to every manifestation of injustice and abuse of power. In their best works writers, film-makers, theater producers and actors tried to boost people's belief in the ideological achievements of socialism and hope for a spiritual revival of society and, despite bureaucratic bans and even persecution, prepared people morally for perestroika.

By saying all this I want to make the reader understand that the energy for revolutionary change has been accumulating amid our people and in the Party for some time. And the ideas of perestroika have been prompted not just by pragmatic interests and considerations but also by our troubled conscience, by the indomitable commitment to ideals which we inherited from the Revolution and as a result of a theoretical quest which gave us a better knowledge of society and reinforced our determination to go ahead.

---

[1]*Politburo of the CPSU Central Committee*—the collective leadership body of the CSPU Central Committee, which is selected at a plenary meeting of the Central Committee to guide the Party work between the plenary meetings of the CPSU Central Committee.

[2]*Secretariat of the CPSU Central Committee*—body of the CPSU Central Committee, which is elected at a plenary meeting of the Central Committee to supervise the Party's day-to-day work, mainly in selecting the cadres and organizing the verification of the fulfillment of the decisions adopted.

Human Rights and International Relations

After World War II, the establishment of the United Nations' Commission on Human Rights reflected international concern over the violation of human rights, defined in part as the right to life, liberty, and the integrity of the individual. Although the U.S. government appeared ready to make the protection of human rights an important aspect of its foreign policy immediately after World War II, the issue became increasingly politicized as ideological disagreements over defining human rights were reinforced by cold war tensions. Throughout the 1950s and most of the 1960s, the relatively small numbers of human rights activists were generally viewed as naive and unrealistic.

By the 1970s, however, the human rights movement began to revive. Representatives from thirty-five nations met in Helsinki, Finland, for a two-year conference that focused on issues of security, human rights, and cooperation in Europe. The Helsinki Accords was an agreement signed on August 1, 1975. In the United States, the human rights movement began to revive, and pressure mounted to make it an important component of American foreign policy, especially in dealing with Third World nations. The U.S. Congress passed legislation requiring the State Department to assess the status of human rights in various nations. The law also called for the possible curtailment of U.S. foreign aid if a nation were found in gross violation of those rights or if insufficient progress had occurred to reflect improvement.

After President Jimmy Carter's inauguration in 1977, the issue of human rights quickly became a high priority in foreign policy decisions, especially toward Latin American nations where violence escalated and violations of human rights appeared unusually severe and increasing in numbers. As a result the Carter administration withheld economic and military aid to the military regimes of Guatemala, Argentina, and Chile, and in early 1979, the government of Anastasio Somoza in Nicaragua.

In pursuit of the containment policy against communism, the United States, as well as some other NATO countries, was apt to favor authoritarian regimes guilty of human rights violations by their military and police as the lesser of two evils. The greater perceived evil was a takeover in those countries by Marxist revolutionaries who, with the support of the USSR or mainland

China, would establish a totalitarian regime that would not only make short work of human rights but function as an international enemy of the West as well. American support of such lesser-evil dictatorships was often—in the case of Cuba and Nicaragua—less than wholehearted, and yet it did serve to mute governmental criticism of human rights abuses on the part of anti-Communist military regimes until the mid-1980s. With the collapse of the USSR and of Marxism as a geopolitical force, the dilemma of having to support unsavory, anti-Communist strongmen has disappeared, although there are many such figures making it on their own and making life miserable for their citizens in the ways chronicled by Carolyn Forché.

In China, pro-independence demonstrations by the Tibetans, ethnic minorities in China, were brutally suppressed by the Chinese troops. The Dalai Lama, the Tibetans' exiled religious and secular leader, has been leading a firm but nonviolent resistance movement against the Chinese oppression.

92 The United Nations Declaration of Human Rights

On December 10, 1948, the General Assembly of the United Nations adopted *The Universal Declaration of Human Rights.* Those composing and voting for this declaration were, of course, aware that the rights enumerated in it were being violated in numerous places around the globe. The authors set down a standard by which governments could be judged on the basis of this mid-twentieth-century consensus.

QUESTIONS TO CONSIDER

1. What is the aim of the Preamble? Do the writers consider their principles to be based on self-evident truths? Are they attempting to demonstrate something more or different from the truth of their propositions?
2. In the rest of the document, what seems close in language and spirit to the American Declaration of Independence (see Reading 26)? To the English or American Bill of Rights? To the French Revolution declarations (see Reading 27)?
3. Do you think this UN declaration has had some effect? If so, what and where? Is it likely to be more or less observed as a standard in the twenty-first century? Why?

PREAMBLE

Whereas recognition of the inherent dignity and of the equal and inalienable rights of all members of the human family is the foundation of freedom, justice and peace in the world,

Whereas disregard and contempt for human rights have resulted in barbarous acts which have outraged the conscience of mankind, and the advent of a world in which human beings shall enjoy freedom of speech and belief and freedom from fear and want has been proclaimed as the highest aspiration of the common people,

Whereas it is essential, if man is not to be compelled to have recourse, as a last resort, to rebellion against tyranny and oppression, that human rights should be protected by the rule of law,

Whereas it is essential to promote the development of friendly relations between nations,

Whereas the peoples of the United Nations have in the Charter reaffirmed their faith in fundamental human rights, in the dignity and worth of the human person and in the equal rights of men and women and have determined to promote social progress and better standards of life in larger freedom,

Whereas Member States have pledged themselves to achieve, in co-operation with the United Nations, the promotion of universal respect for and observance of human rights and fundamental freedoms,

Whereas a common understanding of these rights and freedoms is of the greatest importance for the full realisation of this pledge,

Now therefore

THE GENERAL ASSEMBLY PROCLAIMS

This Universal Declaration of Human Rights as a common standard of achievement for all peoples and all nations, to the end that every individual and every organ of society, keeping this Declaration constantly in mind, shall strive by teaching and education to promote respect for these rights and freedoms and by progressive measures, national and international, to secure their universal and effective recognition and observance, both among the peoples of Member States themselves and among the peoples of territories under their jurisdiction.

Article 1. All human beings are born free and equal in dignity and rights. They are endowed with reason and conscience and should act towards one another in a spirit of brotherhood.

Article 2. Everyone is entitled to all the rights and freedoms set forth in this Declaration, without distinction of any kind, such as race, colour, sex, language, religion, political or other opinion, national or social origin, property, birth or other status. Furthermore, no distinction shall be made on the basis of the political, jurisdictional or international status of the country or territory to which a person belongs, whether it be independent, trust, non-self-governing or under any other limitation of sovereignty.

From *Text: The Universal Declaration of Human Rights.* United Nations Publication No. 63.1.13. (New York: The United Nations, 1963), pp. 33–38.

Article 3. Everyone has the right to life, liberty and security of person.

Article 4. No one shall be held in slavery or servitude; slavery and the slave trade shall be prohibited in all their forms.

Article 5. No one shall be subjected to torture or to cruel, inhuman or degrading treatment or punishment.

Article 6. Everyone has the right to recognition everywhere as a person before the law.

Article 7. All are equal before the law and are entitled without any discrimination to equal protection of the law. All are entitled to equal protection against any discrimination in violation of this Declaration and against any incitement to such discrimination.

Article 8. Everyone has the right to an effective remedy by the competent national tribunals for acts violating the fundamental rights granted him by the constitution or by law.

Article 9. No one shall be subjected to arbitrary arrest, detention or exile.

Article 10. Everyone is entitled in full equality to a fair and public hearing by an independent and impartial tribunal, in the determination of his rights and obligations and of any criminal charge against him.

Article 11. (1) Everyone charged with a penal offence has the right to be presumed innocent until proved guilty according to law in a public trial at which he has had all the guarantees necessary for his defence.

(2) No one shall be held guilty of any penal offence on account of any act or omission which did not constitute a penal offence, under national or international law, at the time when it was committed. Nor shall a heavier penalty be imposed than the one that was applicable at the time the penal offence was committed.

Article 12. No one shall be subjected to arbitrary interference with his privacy, family, home or correspondence, nor to attacks upon his honour and reputation. Everyone has the right to the protection of the law against such interference or attacks.

Article 13. (1) Everyone has the right to freedom of movement and residence within the borders of each state.

(2) Everyone has the right to leave any country, including his own, and to return to his country.

Article 14. (1) Everyone has the right to seek and to enjoy in other countries asylum from persecution.

(2) This right may not be invoked in the case of prosecutions genuinely arising from non-political crimes or from acts contrary to the purposes and principles of the United Nations.

Article 15. (1) Everyone has the right to a nationality.

(2) No one shall be arbitrarily deprived of his nationality nor denied the right to change his nationality.

Article 16. (1) Men and women of full age, without any limitation due to race, nationality or religion, have the right to marry and to found a family. They are entitled to equal rights as to marriage, during marriage and at its dissolution.

(2) Marriage shall be entered into only with the free and full consent of the intending spouses.

(3) The family is the natural and fundamental group unit of society and is entitled to protection by society and the State.

Article 17. (1) Everyone has the right to own property alone as well as in association with others.

(2) No one shall be arbitrarily deprived of his property.

Article 18. Everyone has the right to freedom of thought, conscience and religion; this right includes freedom to change his religion or belief, and freedom, either alone or in community with others and in public or private, to manifest his religion or belief in teaching, practice, worship and observance.

Article 19. Everyone has the right to freedom of opinion and expression; this right includes freedom to hold opinions without interference and to seek, receive and impart information and ideas through any media and regardless of frontiers.

Article 20. (1) Everyone has the right to freedom of peaceful assembly and association.

(2) No one may be compelled to belong to an association.

Article 21. (1) Everyone has the right to take part in the government of his country, directly or through freely chosen representatives.

(2) Everyone has the right of equal access to public service in his country.

(3) The will of the people shall be the basis of the authority of government; this will shall be expressed in periodic and genuine elections which shall be by universal and equal suffrage and shall be held by secret vote or by equivalent free voting procedures.

Article 22. Everyone, as a member of society, has the right to social security and is entitled to realisation, through national effort and international co-operation and in accordance with the organisation and resources of each State, of the economic, social and cultural rights indispensable for his dignity and the free development of his personality.

Article 23. (1) Everyone has the right to work, to free choice of employment, to just and favourable conditions of work and to protection against unemployment.

(2) Everyone, without any discrimination, has the right to equal pay for equal work.

(3) Everyone who works has the right to just and favourable remuneration insuring for himself and his family an existence worthy of human dignity, and supplemented, if necessary, by other means of social protection.

(4) Everyone has the right to form and to join trade unions for the protection of his interests.

Article 24. Everyone has the right to rest and leisure, including reasonable limitation of working hours and periodic holidays with pay.

Article 25. (1) Everyone has the right to a standard of living adequate for the health and well-being of himself and of his family, including food, clothing, housing and medical care and necessary social services, and the right to security in the event of unemployment, sickness, disability, widowhood, old age or other lack of livelihood in circumstances beyond his control.

(2) Motherhood and childhood are entitled to special care and assistance. All children, whether born in or out of wedlock, shall enjoy the same social protection.

Article 26. (1) Everyone has the right to education. Education shall be free, at least in the elementary and fundamental stages. Elementary education shall be compulsory. Technical and professional education shall be made generally available and higher education shall be equally accessible to all on the basis of merit.

(2) Education shall be directed to the full development of the human personality and to the strengthening of respect for human rights and fundamental freedoms. It shall promote understanding, tolerance and friendship among all nations, racial or religious groups, and shall further the activities of the United Nations for the maintenance of peace.

(3) Parents have a prior right to choose the kind of education that shall be given to their children.

Article 27. (1) Everyone has the right freely to participate in the cultural life of the community, to enjoy the arts and to share in scientific advancement and its benefits.

(2) Everyone has the right to the protection of the moral and material interests resulting from any scientific, literary or artistic production of which he is the author.

Article 28. Everyone is entitled to a social and international order in which the rights and freedoms set forth in this Declaration can be fully realised.

Article 29. (1) Everyone has duties to the community in which alone the free and full development of his personality is possible.

(2) In the exercise of his rights and freedoms, everyone shall be subject only to such limitations as are determined by law solely for the purpose of securing due recognition and respect for the rights and freedoms of others and of meeting the just requirements of morality, public order and the general welfare in a democratic society.

(3) These rights and freedoms may in no case be exercised contrary to the purposes and principles of the United Nations.

Article 30. Nothing in this Declaration may be interpreted as implying for any State, group or person any right to engage in any activity or to perform any act aimed at the destruction of any of the rights and freedoms set forth herein.

93 Carolyn Forché, "The Colonel"

Carolyn Forché (1950–   ) is a prize-winning poet who has taught at several universities, including San Diego State University, the University of Virginia, and George Mason University, where she teaches writing. Two major collections of her poetry have been published under the titles *Gathering the Tribes* (1976) and *The Country Between Us* (1981). She is also the editor of *Against Forgetting: Twentieth-Century Poetry of Witness* (1993). As a human rights activist, she visited El Salvador in 1978, when many officers in the Salvadoran military bitterly resented President Carter's human rights policy. The following poem is a description of her visit to a colonel's home for dinner in El Salvador one evening in May 1978.

QUESTIONS TO CONSIDER

1. Initially Carolyn Forché insisted that this document was not a poem but, rather, a set of notes recording what she saw and heard at the colonel's house. Why would she resist calling her work poetry? Would you describe this as a poem?

2. Which of the lines or images in the poem captures best the mood of that evening?

3. What characteristics of El Salvadoran society does the writer reveal in her description of the colonel's home?

4. What is usually meant by the expression putting your "ear to the ground"? What do you think Forché means by using the expression?

What you have heard is true. I was in his house. His wife carried a tray of coffee and sugar. His daughter filed her nails, his son went out for the night. There were daily papers, pet dogs, a pistol on the cushion beside him. The moon swung bare on its black cord over the house. On the television was a cop show. It was in English. Broken bottles were embedded in the walls around the house to scoop the kneecaps from a man's legs or cut his hands to lace. On the windows there were gratings like those in liquor stores. We had dinner, rack of lamb, good wine, a gold bell was on the table for calling the maid. The maid brought green mangoes, salt, a type of bread. I was asked how I enjoyed the country. There was a brief commercial in Spanish. His wife took everything away. There was some talk then of how difficult it had become to govern. The parrot said hello on the terrace. The colonel told it to shut up, and pushed himself from the table. My friend said to me with his eyes: say nothing. The colonel returned with a sack used to bring groceries home. He spilled many human ears on the table. They were like dried peach halves. There is no other way to say this. He took one of them in his hands, shook it in our faces, dropped it into a water glass. It came alive there. I am tired of fooling around he said. As for the rights of anyone, tell your people they can go fuck themselves. He swept the ears to the floor with his arm and held the last of his wine in the air. Something for your poetry, no? he said. Some of the ears on the floor caught this scrap of his voice. Some of the ears on the floor were pressed to the ground.

May 1978

94 The Dalai Lama (Tenzin Gyatso), Nobel Peace Prize Lecture

The history of Tibet, the land often described as the "roof of the world," is marked by its struggles for survival as an independent Buddhist state against two powerful neighbors, the Mongol Empire to the north and Imperial China to the east. From the late fourteenth century until 1959, a line of rulers, both spiritual and secular, known as Dalai Lamas presided over this state. In October 1950, the Chinese People's Liberation Army invaded the land and reasserted China's control after a year-long suppression campaign. Since then, Tibet has been under the control of the People's Republic of China (PRC) as an autonomous region. In response to China's radical attempts to transform Tibet into a socialist system, the Tibetan people rose in an unsuccessful revolt in 1956, and their smoldering anger and frustration erupted again in a mass uprising in March 1959. The Tibetans were more brutally suppressed by China's People's Liberation Army than ever before. Lhasa, the capital of Tibet, was bombed; a great number of Tibetans were killed; and since then, Chinese settlers have continued to pour into Tibet with the encouragement of the Chinese government. This ever-increasing number of Chinese settlers threatens to outnumber the Tibetan population. The present Dalai Lama,[1] Tenzin Gyatso, fourteenth in line, fled with a group of 100,000 Tibetan followers and set up a government in exile in Dharamsala on the Indian side of the Himalayan Mountains. For more than four decades, the Dalai Lama, a firm believer in the Buddhist principle of nonviolence, has led his people to wage a historic struggle to free Tibet from Chinese oppression without resorting to violence. In 1989, in recognition of his nonviolent campaign to end Chinese domination of Tibet, he was awarded the Nobel Peace Prize. The following is his acceptance speech.

QUESTIONS TO CONSIDER

1.   Discuss the wisdom and effectiveness of a nonviolent approach to fight against injustice and oppression by citing two or three twentieth-century examples.
2.   How legitimate is the claim by the People's Republic of China that Tibet is such an integral part of the country that it cannot possibly be granted independence?
3.   How serious is the problem of the ever-increasing number of Chinese settlers in Tibet? Why? What is the prospect of Tibetan freedom from Chinese domination?
4.   Describe the proposed Zone of Ahimsa as peace sanctuary. Why would this be a good thing to establish in Asia?
5.   Compare Chinese population policies in Tibet with those suggested by Sir William Petty to the English for use in Ireland (see Reading 14).

Brothers and Sisters:

It is an honor and pleasure to be among you today. I am really happy to see so many old friends who have come from different corners of the world, and to make new friends, whom I hope to meet again in the future. When I meet people in different parts of the world, I am always reminded that we are all basically alike: we are all human beings. Maybe we have different clothes, our skin is of a different color, or we speak different languages. This is on the surface. But basically, we are the same human

---

[1]Dalai Lama is the office of the spiritual and secular leader of the Tibetan people. *Dalai* means "ocean of wisdom" and *Lama* "the monk."

From Sidney Piburn, *The Dalai Lama: A Policy of Kindness* (Ithaca, NY: Snow Lion Publications, 1993), pp. 15–25. Reprinted by permission.

beings. That is what binds us to each other. That is what makes it possible for us to understand each other and to develop friendship and closeness.

Thinking over what I might say today, I decided to share with you some of my thoughts concerning the common problems all of us face as members of the human family. Because we all share this small planet earth, we have to learn to live in harmony and peace with each other and with nature. That is not just a dream, but a necessity. We are dependent on each other in so many ways that we can no longer live in isolated communities and ignore what is happening outside those communities. We need to help each other when we have difficulties, and we must share the good fortune that we enjoy. I speak to you as just another human being, as a simple monk. If you find what I say useful, then I hope you will try to practice it.

I also wish to share with you today my feelings concerning the plight and aspirations of the people of Tibet. The Nobel Prize is a prize they well deserve for their courage and unfailing determination during the past forty years of foreign occupation. As a free spokesman for my captive countrymen and -women, I feel it is my duty to speak out on their behalf. I speak not with a feeling of anger or hatred towards those who are responsible for the immense suffering of our people and the destruction of our land, homes and culture. They too are human beings who struggle to find happiness and deserve our compassion. I speak to inform you of the sad situation in my country today and of the aspirations of my people, because in our struggle for freedom, truth is the only weapon we possess. . . .

The awarding of the Nobel Prize to me, a simple monk from far-away Tibet, here in Norway, also fills us Tibetans with hope. It means that, despite the fact that we have not drawn attention to our plight by means of violence, we have not been forgotten. It also means that the values we cherish, in particular our respect for all forms of life and the belief in the power of truth, are today recognized and encouraged. It is also a tribute to my mentor, Mahatma Gandhi, whose example is an inspiration to so many of us. This year's award is an indication that this sense of universal responsibility is developing. I am deeply touched by the sincere concern shown by so many people in this part of the world for the suffering of the people of Tibet. That is a source of hope not only for us Tibetans, but for all oppressed peoples.

As you know, Tibet has, for forty years, been under foreign occupation. Today, more than a quarter of a million Chinese troops are stationed in Tibet. Some sources estimate the occupation army to be twice this strength. During this time, Tibetans have been deprived of their most basic human rights, including the right to life, movement, speech, worship, only to mention a few. More than one sixth of Tibet's population of six million died as a direct result of the Chinese invasion and occupation. Even before the Cultural Revolution started, many of Tibet's monasteries, temples and historic buildings were destroyed. Almost everything that remained was destroyed during the Cultural Revolution. I do not wish to dwell on this point, which is well documented. What is important to realize, however, is that despite the limited freedom granted after 1979 to rebuild parts of some monasteries and other such tokens of liberalization, the fundamental human rights of the Tibetan people are still today being systematically violated. In recent months this bad situation has become even worse.

If it were not for our community in exile, so generously sheltered and supported by the government and people of India and helped by organizations and individuals from many parts of the world, our nation would today be little more than a shattered remnant of a people. Our culture, religion and national identity would have been effectively eliminated. As it is, we have built schools and monasteries in exile and have created democratic institutions to serve our people and preserve the seeds of our civilization. With this experience, we intend to implement full democracy in a future free Tibet. Thus, as we develop our community in exile on modern lines, we also cherish and preserve our own identity and culture and bring hope to millions of our countrymen and -women in Tibet.

The issue of most urgent concern at this time is the massive influx of Chinese settlers into Tibet. Although in the first decades of occupation a considerable number of Chinese were transferred into the eastern parts of Tibet . . . since 1983 an unprecedented number of Chinese have been encouraged by their government to migrate to all parts of Tibet, including central and western Tibet (which the PRC refers to as the so-called Tibet Autonomous Region). Tibetans are rapidly being reduced to an insignificant minority in their own country. This development, which threatens the very survival of the Tibetan nation, its culture and spiritual heritage, can still be stopped and reversed. But this must be done now, before it is too late.

The new cycle of protest and violent repression, which started in Tibet in September of 1987 and culminated in the imposition of martial law in the capital, Lhasa, in March of this year, was in large part a reaction to this tremendous Chinese influx. Information reaching us in exile indicates that the protest marches and other peaceful forms of protest are continuing in Lhasa and a number of other places in Tibet despite the severe punishment and inhumane treatment given to Tibetans detained for expressing their grievances. The number of Tibetans killed by security forces during the protest in March and of those who died in detention afterwards is not known but is believed to be more than two hundred. Thousands have been detained or arrested and imprisoned, and torture is commonplace.

It was against the background of this worsening situation and in order to prevent further bloodshed, that I proposed what is generally referred to as the Five Point Peace Plan for the restoration of peace and human rights in Tibet. I elaborated on the plan in a speech in Strasbourg last year. I believe the plan provides a reasonable and realistic framework for negotiations with the People's Republic of China. So far, however, China's leaders have been unwilling to respond constructively. The brutal suppression of the Chinese democracy movement in June of this year, however, reinforced my view that any settlement of the Tibetan question will only be meaningful if it is supported by adequate international guarantees.

The Five Point Peace Plan addresses the principal and interrelated issues, which I referred to in the first part of this lecture. It calls for (1) Transformation of the whole of Tibet, including the eastern provinces of Kham and Amdo, into a Zone of *Ahimsa* (non-violence); (2) Abandonment of China's population transfer policy; (3) Respect for the Tibetan people's fundamental human rights and democratic freedoms; (4) Restoration and protection of Tibet's natural environment; and (5) Commencement of earnest negotiations on the future status of Tibet and of relations between the Tibetan and Chinese peoples. In the Strasbourg address I proposed that Tibet become a fully self-governing democratic political entity.

I would like to take this opportunity to explain the Zone of Ahimsa or peace sanctuary concept, which is the central element of the Five Point Peace Plan. I am convinced that it is of great importance not only for Tibet, but for peace and stability in Asia.

It is my dream that the entire Tibetan plateau should become a free refuge where humanity and nature can live in peace and in harmonious balance. It would be a place where people from all over the world could come to seek the true meaning of peace within themselves, away from the tensions and pressures of much of the rest of the world. Tibet could indeed become a creative center for the promotion and development of peace.

The following are key elements of the proposed Zone of Ahimsa:

—the entire Tibetan plateau would be demilitarized;

—the manufacture, testing, and stockpiling of nuclear weapons and other armaments on the Tibetan plateau would be prohibited;

—the Tibetan plateau would be transformed into the world's largest natural park or biosphere. Strict laws would be enforced to protect wildlife and plant life; the exploitation of natural resources would be carefully regulated so as not to damage relevant ecosystems; and a policy of sustainable development would be adopted in populated areas;

—the manufacture and use of nuclear power and other technologies which produce hazardous waste would be prohibited;

—national resources and policy would be directed towards the active promotion of peace and environmental protection. Organizations dedicated to the furtherance of peace and to the protection of all forms of life would find a hospitable home in Tibet;

—the establishment of international and regional organizations for the promotion and protection of human rights would be encouraged in Tibet.

Tibet's height and size (the size of the European Community), as well as its unique history and profound spiritual heritage make it ideally suited to fulfill the role of a sanctuary of peace in the strategic heart of Asia. It would also be in keeping with Tibet's historical role as a peaceful Buddhist nation and buffer region separating the Asian continent's great and often rival powers.

In order to reduce existing tensions in Asia, the President of the Soviet Union, Mr. Gorbachev, proposed the demilitarization of Soviet-Chinese borders and their transformation into a "frontier of peace and good-neighborliness." The Nepal government had earlier proposed that the Himalayan country of Nepal, bordering on Tibet, should become a zone of peace, although that proposal did not include demilitarization of the country.

For the stability and peace of Asia, it is essential to create peace zones to separate the continent's biggest powers and potential adversaries. President Gorbachev's proposal, which also included a complete Soviet troop withdrawal from Mongolia, would help to reduce tension and the potential for confrontation between the Soviet Union and China. A true peace zone must, clearly, also be created to separate the world's two most populous states, China and India.

The establishment of the Zone of Ahimsa would require the withdrawal of troops and military installations from Tibet, which would enable India and Nepal also to withdraw troops and military installations from the Himalayan regions bordering Tibet. This would have to be achieved by international agreements. It would be in the best interest of all states in Asia, particularly China and India, as it would enhance their security, while reducing the economic burden of maintaining high troop concentrations in remote areas. . . .

In conclusion, let me share with you a short prayer which gives me great inspiration and determination:

> For as long as space endures,
> And for as long as living beings remain,
> Until then may I, too, abide
> To dispel the misery of the world.

Thank You.

Enduring Problems

T he disintegration of the Soviet Union, 1989–1991, and the end of the cold war at first inspired visions of a new world order with a reduction of international conflict, the triumph of liberal democracy, and a global free market. Soon, however, when crises erupted in Iraq, Somalia, Rwanda, Zaire, Bosnia, Liberia, Haiti, Sierra Leone, and Kosovo, to give only a sampling of affected locales, critics began predicting a very different version of the future. In some instances, their earlier pessimism had merely been suspended in the euphoria over the apparent end of world-threatening superpower conflict. Citing a variety of causes of current and projected disorder, including deadly epidemics of international scope, cultural and religious tensions, ongoing human displacement, the growing power of transnational corporations, and environmental concerns, along with population explosions, immigration issues, and north-south tensions, they foresaw a grim future for much of the world. Without dismissing the problems at hand, others analyzing the current state of world affairs have chosen to address the challenges humankind could very well meet.

While remnants of the cold war linger in China and the Koreas, an important part of the Chinese leadership's goals has been severely modified from its cold war stage: Chinese leaders, still officially following the dictates of their Communist Party, no longer view the market necessarily as a symbol of exploitation or even as a hostile force, but rather as a means for making *socialism* work. On the other side of the world, Pope John Paul II speaks for a need to modify capitalism with concerns for social justice. In Japan, a new generation struggles with the work-ethic orientation of parents and is modifying it in favor of more individualism and instant—or, at least, expedited—

gratification. Around the globe, as the twenty-first century unfolds, nationalism remains as strong as ever and international peace keeping has only modest successes to its credit, while globalization remains a two-edged sword of
threats and promises.

95 Deng Xiaoping, A Market Economy for Socialist Goals

China is entitled to a special place in discussions of problems and challenges at
the beginning of the twenty-first century. With well over a billion inhabitants and
consequently a fifth of the world's population, China is struggling with the challenge of continuing a commitment to Communist Party leadership in an age in
which Marxism in all its forms has suffered defeats. At the same time, the potential military and industrial strength of China, which has been notably lacking in
strength of any sort for the last two hundred years, presents a challenge to China's
neighbors and, in fact, the rest of the world.

After the death of Mao Tse-tung [Mao Zedong] in 1976, his successor, Deng
Xiaoping [Teng Hsiao-p'ing], steered the country sharply away from the Maoist
road to communism. Mao had tried to save China from poverty and "imperialism"
with his brand of socialism but failed after nearly thirty stormy years of revolutionary frenzy. Boldly dismantling Mao's institutions, one by one, including the collective farms, Deng Xiaoping forcefully put forth his vision for China, a modern industrial and prosperous socialist nation. He felt confident that socialism in China
could be saved by capitalistic means. The command economy, a principal feature
of any socialist system, has steadily been replaced by the principles of market-
oriented economy, and privatization of state-controlled enterprises has been
greatly expanded. Material and profit incentives, which were despised for reflecting a decadent bourgeois mentality during the Mao era, have been reinstated to
rekindle people's work enthusiasm. Deng also ended thirty years of isolation of
the country from the West: He opened the door to foreign capital and technologies, luring them to China by creating so-called "special economic zones," where
foreign investors enjoy tax breaks and low labor costs among other incentives.
In 1992, Beijing openly declared the building of a "socialist market economy"
as the central task of the government. The economic outcome of Deng's policies
has so far been phenomenal. China's overall industrial and agricultural productiv-
ities have soared sharply. China's annual rate of economic growth since 1980
has been close to double digits. The standard of living of the Chinese people has
risen sharply. In 1993, there were reportedly at least 40,000 millionaires in the
Canton region alone. The following excerpts show Deng Xiaoping's rationale for

introducing capitalistic principles to socialist China and his thoughts on the leadership succession.

Deng died in February 1997, but his bold vision for a prosperous China continues to live on in the policies of his successors.

QUESTIONS TO CONSIDER

1. What are Deng's justifications for injecting capitalistic principles into China's socialistic economic setting? Can socialism survive as a form of national ideology under the market-oriented economic reform?
2. What are the prospects for China's becoming a democratic nation? What problems do you see in a state where people experience an economic liberalization without political freedom?
3. Could the former Soviet Union have been saved had it adopted the reforms similar to those of Deng Xiaoping?
4. Deng talks about the leadership role of the Communist Party of China and about the need to combine socialism with a market economy. What do you think he means by "communist," as opposed to "socialist"? Or does he let these terms run together? Do *you* think there is a difference?

There is no fundamental contradiction between socialism and a market economy. The problem is how to develop the productive forces more effectively. We used to have a planned economy, but our experience over the years has proved that having a totally planned economy hampers the development of productive forces to a certain extent. If we combine a planned economy with a market economy, we shall be in a better position to liberate the productive forces and speed up economic growth.

Since the Third Plenary Session of our Party's Eleventh Central Committee,[1] we have consistently stressed the importance of upholding the Four Cardinal Principles,[2] especially the principle of keeping to the socialist system. If we are to keep to the socialist system, it is essential for us to develop the productive forces. For a long time we failed to handle this question satisfactorily. In the final analysis, the superiority of socialism should be demonstrated in a greater development of the productive forces. The experience we have gained over the years shows that with the former economic structure we cannot develop the productive forces. That is why we have been drawing on some useful capitalist methods.

It is clear now that the right approach is to open to the outside world, combine a planned economy with a market economy and introduce structural reforms. Does this run counter to the principles of socialism? No, because in the course of reform we

---

[1] It was held during September 18–22, 1978.

[2] The principles are to keep to the socialist road and to uphold the people's democratic dictatorship, leadership by the Communist Party, and Marxism-Leninism and Mao Zedong Thought.

From Deng Xiaoping, *Selected Works of Deng Xiaoping*, 3 (1982–1992) (Beijing: Foreign Language Press, 1994), pp. 151–52. 360–61, 368–70, *passim*. Reported by permission of China Books and Periodicals.

shall make sure of two things: one is that the public sector of the economy is always predominant; the other is that in developing the economy we seek common prosperity, always trying to avoid polarization. The policies of using foreign funds and allowing the private sector to expand will not weaken the predominant position of the public sector, which is a basic feature of the economy as a whole. On the contrary, those policies are intended, in the last analysis, to develop the productive forces more vigorously and to strengthen the public sector. So long as the public sector plays a predominant role in China's economy, polarization can be avoided. Of course, some regions and some people may prosper before others do, and then they can help other regions and people to gradually do the same. I am convinced that the negative phenomena that can now be found in society will gradually decrease and eventually disappear as the economy grows, as our scientific, cultural and educational levels rise and as democracy and the legal system are strengthened.

In short, the overriding task in China today is to throw ourselves heart and soul into the modernization drive. While giving play to the advantages inherent in socialism, we are also employing some capitalist methods—but only as methods of accelerating the growth of the productive forces. It is true that some negative things have appeared in the process, but what is more important is the gratifying progress we have been able to achieve by initiating these reforms and following this road. China has no alternative but to follow this road. It is the only road to prosperity.

The reason some people hesitate to carry out the reform and the open policy and dare not break new ground is, in essence, that they're afraid it would mean introducing too many elements of capitalism and, indeed, taking the capitalist road. The crux of the matter is whether the road is capitalist or socialist. The chief criterion for making that judgement should be whether it promotes the growth of the productive forces in a socialist society, increases the overall strength of the socialist state and raises living standards. As for building special economic zones, some people disagreed with the idea right from the start, wondering whether it would not mean introducing capitalism. The achievements in the construction of Shenzhen have given these people a definite answer: special economic zones are socialist, not capitalist. In the case of Shenzhen, the publicly owned sector is the mainstay of the economy, while the foreign-invested sector accounts for only a quarter. And even in that sector, we benefit from taxes and employment opportunities. We should have more of the three kinds of foreign-invested ventures [joint, cooperative and foreign-owned]. There is no reason to be afraid of them. So long as we keep level-headed, there is no cause for alarm. We have our advantages: we have the large and medium-sized state-owned enterprises and the rural enterprises. More important, political power is in our hands.

Some people argue that the more foreign investment flows in and the more ventures of the three kinds are established, the more elements of capitalism will be introduced and the more capitalism will expand in China. These people lack basic knowledge. At the current stage, foreign-funded enterprises in China are allowed to make some money in accordance with existing laws and policies. But the government levies taxes on those enterprises, workers get wages from them, and we learn technology and managerial skills. In addition, we can get information from them that will help us open more markets. Therefore, subject to the constraints of China's overall political and economic conditions, foreign-funded enterprises are useful supplements to the socialist economy, and in the final analysis they are good for socialism. . . .

The imperialists are pushing for peaceful evolution towards capitalism in China, placing their hopes on the generations that will come after us. Comrade Jiang Zemin and his peers can be regarded as the third generation, and there will be a fourth and a fifth. Hostile forces realize that so long as we of the older generation are still alive and carry weight, no change is possible. But after we are dead and gone, who will ensure that there is no peaceful evolution? So we must educate the army, persons working in the organs of dictatorship, the Communist Party members and the people, including the youth. If any problem arises in China, it will arise from inside the Communist Party. We must keep clear heads. We must pay attention to training people, selecting and promoting to positions of leadership persons who have both ability and political integrity, in accordance with the principle that they should be revolutionary, young, well educated and professionally competent. This is of vital importance to ensure that the Party's basic line is followed for a hundred years and to maintain long-term peace and stability. It is crucial for the future of China.

More young people should be promoted to positions of leadership. The present central leaders are rather advanced in years. Those who are a little over 60 are counted as young. They may be able to work for another 10 years, but 20 years from now they will be in their 80s, like me. They may be able to chat with people, as I'm doing today, but they won't have the energy to do much work. The current central leaders have been doing a good job. Of course, there are still quite a few problems in their work, but there are always problems in one's work. It is essential for old people like us to stand aside, give newcomers a free hand and watch them mature. Old people should voluntarily offer younger ones their places and give them help from the sidelines, but never stand in their way. Out of goodwill, they should help them when things are not being handled properly. They must pay attention to training successors of the next generation. The reason I insisted on retiring was that I didn't want to make mistakes in my old age. Old people have strengths but also great weaknesses—they tend to be stubborn, for example—and they should be aware of that. The older they are, the more modest they should be and the more careful not to make mistakes in their later years. We should go on selecting younger comrades for promotion and helping train them. Don't put your trust only in old age. I was already in a high position when I was in my 20s. I didn't know as much as you do now, but I managed. More young people must be chosen, helped, trained and allowed to grow. When they reach maturity, we shall rest easy. Right now we are still worried. In the final analysis, we must manage Party affairs in such a way as to prevent trouble. Then we can sleep soundly. Whether the line for China's development that was laid down at the Third Plenary Session of the Eleventh Central Committee will continue to be followed depends on the efforts of everyone, and especially on the education of future generations. . . .

We shall push ahead along the road to Chinese-style socialism. Capitalism has been developing for several hundred years. How long have we been building socialism? Besides, we wasted twenty years. If we can make China a moderately developed country within a hundred years from the founding of the People's Republic, that will be an extraordinary achievement. The period from now to the middle of the next century will be crucial. We must immerse ourselves in hard work: we have difficult tasks to accomplish and bear a heavy responsibility.

96 Pope John Paul II, *Centesimus Annus*

For two thousand years, popes have been writing "world letters" (encyclicals) to the faithful about the pressing theological, social, and moral problems of the day. On May 15, 1891, Leo XIII (Pope 1878–1903) published a revolutionary encyclical on the condition of labor and the need for social reform in the industrialized countries. Titled *Rerum Novarum* (*Of New Things*), the encyclical was a powerful defense of the rights of workers to organize and to form labor unions, to own private property, and to raise their families in dignity free from poverty and deprivation. *Rerum Novarum* attacked unregulated competition of free market capitalism and condemned the shallow materialism of Karl Marx's prescription of class revolution. To mark the centennial of *Rerum Novarum* and to reaffirm the Roman Catholic Church's commitment to speak out on matters of social justice, on May 1, 1991, John Paul II (Pope 1978–   ), issued a new encyclical titled *Centisimus Annus,* updating for the post–cold war world the Church's teaching on social justice.

QUESTIONS TO CONSIDER

1. Pope John Paul II, in speaking of the "idolatry" of market economy, argues that "there are collective and qualitative needs which cannot be satisfied by market mechanisms." Can this view be reconciled with free market capitalism?
2. What does the pope mean when he insists that Karl Marx's concept of "exploitation" has been overcome in Western society but the problems of alienation and consumerism remain inherent in Western-style capitalism?
3. How would you compare the pope's view of economics with that of Adam Smith (see Reading 16), Friedrich List (see Reading 37), and Karl Marx (see Reading 34)?
4. According to Pope John Paul, what is the proper role of the state in a capitalist society? Do you agree or disagree? Why?

It would appear that, on the level of individual nations and of international relations, *the free market* is the most efficient instrument for utilizing resources and effectively responding to needs.

But there are many human needs which find no place on the market. It is a strict duty of justice and truth not to allow fundamental human needs to remain unsatisfied, and not to allow those burdened by such needs to perish. It is also necessary to help these needy people to acquire expertise, to enter the circle of exchange, and to develop

From Pope John Paul II, *On the Hundredth Anniversary of Rerum Novarum: Centesimus Annus.* Encyclical Letter of May 1, 1991 (Washington, DC: Office for Publishing and Promotion Services, United States Catholic Conference, 1991), pp. 66–97, *passim.*

their skills in order to make the best use of their capacities and resources. Even prior to the logic of a fair exchange of goods and the forms of justice appropriate to it, there exists *something which is due to man because he is man*, by reason of his lofty dignity. Inseparable from that required "something" is the possibility to survive and, at the same time, to make an active contribution to the common good of humanity.

In Third World contexts, certain objectives stated by *Rerum Novarum* remain valid, and, in some cases, still constitute a goal yet to be reached, if man's work and his very being are not to be reduced to the level of a mere commodity. These objectives include a sufficient wage for the support of the family, social insurance for old age and unemployment, and adequate protection for the conditions of employment.

It would now be helpful to direct our attention to the specific problems and threats emerging within the more advanced economies and which are related to their particular characteristics. In earlier stages of development, man always lived under the weight of necessity. His needs were few and were determined, to a degree, by the objective structures of his physical make-up. Economic activity was directed towards satisfying these needs. It is clear that today the problem is not only one of supplying people with a sufficient quantity of goods, but also of responding to a *demand for quality:* the quality of the goods to be produced and consumed, the quality of the services to be enjoyed, the quality of the environment and of life in general.

To call for an existence which is qualitatively more satisfying is of itself legitimate, but one cannot fail to draw attention to the new responsibilities and dangers connected with this phase of history. The manner in which new needs arise and are defined is always marked by a more or less appropriate concept of man and of his true good. A given culture reveals its overall understanding of life through the choices it makes in production and consumption. It is here that *the phenomenon of consumerism* arises. In singling out new needs and new means to meet them, one must be guided by a comprehensive picture of man which respects all the dimensions of his being and which subordinates his material and instinctive dimensions to his interior and spiritual ones. If, on the contrary, a direct appeal is made to his instincts—while ignoring in various ways the reality of the person as intelligent and free—then *consumer attitudes* and *life-styles* can be created which are objectively improper and often damaging to his physical and spiritual health.

Widespread drug use is a sign of a serious malfunction in the social system; it also implies a materialistic and, in a certain sense, destructive "reading" of human needs. In this way the innovative capacity of a free economy is brought to a one-sided and inadequate conclusion. Drugs, as well as pornography and other forms of consumerism which exploit the frailty of the weak, tend to fill the resulting spiritual void.

It is not wrong to want to live better; what is wrong is a style of life which is presumed to be better when it is directed towards "having" rather than "being," and which wants to have more, not in order to be more but in order to spend life in enjoyment as an end in itself. It is therefore necessary to create life-styles in which the quest for truth, beauty, goodness and communion with others for the sake of common growth are the factors which determine consumer choices, savings and investments. Given the utter necessity of certain economic conditions and of political stability, the decision to invest, that is, to offer people an opportunity to make good use of their own labour, is also determined by an attitude of human sympathy and trust in Providence, which reveal the human quality of the person making such decisions.

It is the task of the State to provide for the defense and preservation of common goods such as the natural and human environments, which cannot be safeguarded simply by market forces. Just as in the time of primitive capitalism the State had the duty of defending the basic rights of workers, so now, with the new capitalism, the State and all of society have the duty of *defending those collective goods* which, among others, constitute the essential framework for the legitimate pursuit of personal goals on the part of each individual.

Here we find a new limit on the market: there are collective and qualitative needs which cannot be satisfied by market mechanisms.

Certainly the mechanisms of the market offer secure advantages: they help to utilize resources better; they promote the exchange of products; above all they give central place to the person's desires and preferences, which, in a contract, meet the desires and preferences of another person. Nevertheless, these mechanisms carry the risk of an "idolatry" of the market, an idolatry which ignores the existence of goods which by their nature are not and cannot be mere commodities.

Marxism criticized capitalist bourgeois societies, blaming them for the commercialization and alienation of human existence. This rebuke is of course based on a mistaken and inadequate idea of alienation, derived solely from the sphere of relationships of production and ownership, that is, giving them a materialistic foundation and moreover denying the legitimacy and positive value of market relationships even in their own sphere. Marxism thus ends up by affirming that only in a collective society can alienation be eliminated. However, the historical experience of socialist countries has sadly demonstrated that collectivism does not do away with alienation but rather increases it, adding to it a lack of basic necessities and economic inefficiency.

The historical experience of the West, for its part, shows that even if the Marxist analysis and its foundation of alienation are false, nevertheless alienation—and the loss of the authentic meaning of life—is a reality in Western societies too. This happens in consumerism, when people are ensnared in a web of false and superficial gratifications rather than being helped to experience their personhood in an authentic and concrete way. Alienation is found also in work, when it is organized so as to ensure maximum returns and profits with no concern whether the worker, through his own labour, grows or diminishes as a person, either through increased sharing in a genuinely supportive community or through increased isolation in a maze of relationships marked by destructive competitiveness and estrangement, in which he is considered only a means and not an end.

The concept of alienation needs to be led back to the Christian vision of reality, by recognizing in alienation a reversal of means and ends. When man does not recognize in himself and in others the value and grandeur of the human person, he effectively deprives himself of the possibility of benefiting from his humanity and of entering into that relationship of solidarity and communion with others for which God created him.

Man cannot give himself to a purely human plan for reality, to an abstract ideal or to a false utopia. As a person, he can give himself to another person or to other persons, and ultimately to God, who is the author of his being and who alone can fully accept his gift. A man is alienated if he refuses to transcend himself and to live the experience of self-giving and of the formation of an authentic human community oriented towards his final destiny, which is God. A society is alienated if its forms of social organization, production and consumption make it more difficult to offer this gift of self and to establish this solidarity between people.

Returning now to the initial question: can it perhaps be said that, after the failure of Communism, capitalism is the victorious social system, and that capitalism should be the goal of the countries now making efforts to rebuild their economy and society? Is this the model which ought to be proposed to the countries of the Third World which are searching for the path to true economic and civil progress?

The answer is obviously complex. If by "capitalism" is meant an economic system which recognizes the fundamental and positive role of business, the market, private property and the resulting responsibility for the means of production, as well as free human creativity in the economic sector, then the answer is certainly in the affirmative, even though it would perhaps be more appropriate to speak of a "business economy," "market economy" or simply "free economy." But if by "capitalism" is meant a system in which freedom in the economic sector is not circumscribed within a strong juridical framework which places it at the service of human freedom in its totality, and which sees it as a particular aspect of that freedom, the core of which is ethical and religious, then the reply is certainly negative.

The Marxist solution has failed, but the realities of marginalization and exploitation remain in the world, especially the Third World, as does the reality of human alienation, especially in the more advanced countries. Against these phenomena the Church strongly raises her voice. Vast multitudes are still living in conditions of great material and moral poverty. The collapse of the Communist system in so many countries certainly removes an obstacle to facing these problems in an appropriate and realistic way, but it is not enough to bring about their solution. Indeed, there is a risk that a radical capitalistic ideology could spread which refuses even to consider these problems, in the *a priori* belief that any attempt to solve them is doomed to failure, and which blindly entrusts their solution to the free development of market forces.

These general observations also apply to the *role of the State in the economic sector.* Economic activity, especially the activity of a market economy, cannot be conducted in an institutional, juridical or political vacuum. On the contrary, it presupposes sure guarantees of individual freedom and private property, as well as a stable currency and efficient public services. Hence the principal task of the State is to guarantee this security, so that those who work and produce can enjoy the fruits of their labours and thus feel encouraged to work efficiently and honestly. The absence of stability, together with the corruption of public officials and the spread of improper sources of growing rich and of easy profits deriving from illegal or purely speculative activities, constitutes one of the chief obstacles to development and to the economic order.

Another task of the State is that of overseeing and directing the exercise of human rights in the economic sector. However, primary responsibility in this area belongs not to the State but to individuals and to the various groups and associations which make up society. The State could not directly ensure the right to work for all its citizens unless it controlled every aspect of economic life and restricted the free initiative of individuals. This does not mean, however, that the State has no competence in this domain, as was claimed by those who argued against any rules in the economic sphere. Rather, the State has a duty to sustain business activities by creating conditions which will ensure job opportunities, by stimulating those activities where they are lacking or by supporting them in moments of crisis.

In recent years the range of such intervention has vastly expanded, to the point of creating a new type of State, the so-called "Welfare State." This has happened in some countries in order to respond better to many needs and demands, by remedying forms of poverty and deprivation unworthy of the human person. However, excesses and abuses, especially in recent years, have provoked very harsh criticisms of the Welfare State, dubbed the "Social Assistance State."

By intervening directly and depriving society of its responsibility, the Social Assistance State leads to a loss of human energies and an inordinate increase of public agencies, which are dominated more by bureaucratic ways of thinking than by concern for serving their clients, and which are accompanied by an enormous increase in spending. In fact, it would appear that needs are best understood and satisfied by people who are closest to them and who act as neighbours to those in need.

Faithful to the mission received from Christ her Founder, the Church has always been present and active among the needy, offering them material assistance in ways that neither humiliate nor reduce them to mere objects of assistance, but which help them to escape their precarious situation by promoting their dignity as persons. With heartfelt gratitude to God it must be pointed out that active charity has never ceased to be practised in the Church; indeed, today it is showing a manifold and gratifying increase. In this regard, special mention must be made of *volunteer work*, which the Church favours and promotes by urging everyone to cooperate in supporting and encouraging its undertakings.

In order to overcome today's widespread individualistic mentality, what is required is *a concrete commitment to solidarity and charity*, beginning in the family with the mutual support of husband and wife and the care which the different generations give to one another. In this sense the family too can be called a community of work and solidarity.

Apart from the family, other intermediate communities exercise primary functions and give life to specific networks of solidarity. These develop as real communities of persons and strengthen the social fabric, preventing society from becoming an anonymous and impersonal mass, as unfortunately often happens today. It is in interrelationships on many levels that a person lives, and that society becomes more "personalized." The individual today is often suffocated between two poles represented by the State and the marketplace. At times it seems as though he exists only as a producer and consumer of goods, or as an object of State administration. People lose sight of the fact that life in society has neither the market nor the State as its final purpose, since life itself has a unique value which the State and the market must serve. Man remains above all a being who seeks the truth and strives to live in that truth, deepening his understanding of it through a dialogue which involves past and future generations.

97 Japan: The Postwar Generation

The twentieth century was a remarkable time for Japan. The country went from triumph to tragedy, and then from utter ruin to prosperity. After having gained confidence in the Russo-Japanese War (1904–1905), Japan stepped up its imperialistic drive and waged one successful war of aggression after another until it was forced into unconditional surrender at the end of World War II in 1945. The Japanese Empire was reduced to its pre-Meiji borders, with its land laid in utter ruins, its people demoralized and exhausted; for the first time in its history, the country was placed under foreign military occupation for nearly seven years, from 1945 to 1952. Ironically, such a humiliation suffered by Japan was a blessing in disguise.

The foundations for Japan's postwar transformation into a democracy and an economic superpower were largely laid during this period of U.S. military occupation. Japan has not only rebounded so quickly and so successfully from the ashes of war but had also built the second largest economy in the world by 1982. By the mid-1950s, Japan had already regained its prewar economic level. During the 1960s, Japan forged ahead to become one of the great industrial and trading powers of the world. By 1970, Japan became the third largest world economy after the United States and the Soviet Union. Even though Japan has been struggling with economic recession since the early 1990s, it remains the second largest economy behind the United States. The new generation of Japanese, often referred to as the "new breed," were born and raised during this period of economic growth and affluence and have developed a world outlook and a work ethic quite different from those of their parents' generation, whose hard work, dedication, and boldness were behind Japan's postwar recovery and prosperity. Many of these older generation of Japanese are alarmed by the new trend. The following reading illustrates such changes on the part of the new generations of Japanese who will shape Japan well into the twenty-first century.

QUESTIONS TO CONSIDER

1.   Compare and contrast the ways of life and thinking of the younger generation of Japanese with those of their parents' generation. What are the social, political, and economic implications?
2.   How do you compare the lifestyle of the new generation of Japanese with that of their American counterparts?
3.   Discuss the views expressed by optimists and pessimists, respectively, about the changing attitudes and ways of thinking of the new generation of Japanese. With whom do you agree? Please explain.

As the new millennium approached, Japan's prospects remained unclear in many ways, but it took no crystal ball to see that the future ultimately rested in the hands of the generation born after economic growth began in the 1960s. Unlike their parents, who could remember the hard times of the wartime and early postwar years, this new cohort of Japanese seemed so different that the media referred to them as a "new breed" (*shinjinrui*). Shuffled onto the educational escalator at an early age, hustled to after-school cram schools and carefully protected during "examination hell," they had been carefully raised to enter the corporate society built by the older generation. While this generation was able to work "by the manual," many commentators feared that young people lacked the mettle and boldness to keep the economy going, let alone deal with the myriad other problems the country faced.

From Peter Duus, *Modern Japan*, pp. 365–68, First Edition. Copyright © 1998 by Houghton Mifflin Company. Used by permission.

The main complaint about the "new breed" was that they were less devoted to work than their parents. At the Seoul Olympics in 1988, for example, journalists lamented the "spineless, lackadaisical attitude" of young Japanese athletes who did not seem to care whether they won or lost but were satisfied merely to have participated. Certainly, Japanese athletes brought home fewer medals than their American, Chinese, or even Korean contemporaries, but obituaries for the Japanese work ethic were premature. By comparison with youth in the Western industrial countries, the "new breed" were much more likely to see work as their main interest in life, and most expected to be employed as long as they could. Neither were they much less inclined than their parents to work overtime or to spend time after hours with work mates. It was hard to shake habits of self-discipline drilled into them by the long hard climb up the educational escalator.

But in other ways, their attitudes toward life and society were significantly different from the older generation's. Unlike their parents, who grew up in families of four or five children, the "new breed" came from smaller, child-centered households. The average family in the 1960s and 1970s had less than two offspring, meaning that many children grew up with no brothers or sisters. The experience made them much more self-centered and self-contained than the older generation. Instead of spending after-school hours playing with neighborhood friends, they commuted to cram school, sat at their desks doing home work, or played video games on the family television set. Their sense of social and communal responsibility was much weaker than that of earlier generations. University students were as likely to amuse themselves with solitary computer games as join social and athletic clubs, or plunge into political organizations. The "new breed" was more atomized, if not more individualistic, than previous generations.

In the work place, this change brought a marked decline in loyalty toward the firm and an even greater decline in willingness to make personal sacrifices for it. The "new breed" was more inclined than their parents had been to take holidays, switch to new companies, or even embark on new careers after several years. The collectivist ethic remained strong, but it was no longer directed primarily toward the company. For most young people, work was not an end in itself but a means to some other end: leisure, consumption, or personal fulfillment. In contrast to parents who had scrimped and saved most of their lives, they had grown up accustomed to instant gratification. No longer did they feel that years of hard work and effort were necessary to reach a distant goal. Their weekly allowances had been generous, and their parents had bought the toys their children craved. As these children grew older it was only natural that they expected to buy or do whatever they wanted.

The "new breed" lived not by an ethic of scarcity but by one of acquisition. Bombarded from childhood with television commercials, they were eager connoisseurs of "name brands." Their avid consumerism provided a widening market for new weekly magazines stuffed with information about clothes, computers, electronic gear, rock shows, restaurants, and just about anything else that money could buy. Indeed, manufacturers talked about the shift from mass production to "micro-markets" or "micro-masses" as young consumers sought highly novel or specialized products, whether designer shoes or exotic beers. The huge weekend crowds of young people in the Harajuku section of Tokyo, a concentration of trendy boutiques and fast food shops, demonstrated their eagerness to bury themselves in the market place. While some pointed out that "individualism" was on the rise among young people, it seemed to be an individualism best symbolized by the personal credit card.

The "new breed" looked forward to marriage no less than their parents had. Surveys showed that young men supported the institution more enthusiastically than young women, but marriage rates remained high. Since more young people spent their early twenties enjoying their freedom, dating or even living with several possible partners, however, the marriage age rose. Arranged marriages, where family, friends, or neighbors brought young couples together, were also on the decline. Young people preferred to find partners on their own, and once married, they seemed to enjoy an easier and more intimate relationship with one another than older couples. While the younger generation was more tolerant of divorce than their parents, couples in their middle age were most likely to split, particularly when newly retired husbands began spending more time at home than they had while working.

Oddly enough, for all their materialism, many members of the "new breed" were attracted to the "spiritual" side of life. According to public surveys, young people were far less likely than the older generation to proclaim a personal religion, especially an established religion like Buddhism, Shinto, or Christianity, but were far likelier to believe in the existence of spirits, deities, and other supernatural forces. According to one hypothesis, the "new breed" had difficulty distinguishing fantasy from reality because they had grown up watching television. While the idea may seem farfetched, it does appear that many found the occult as plausible as the scientific. During the 1980s and 1990s, an upsurge in "new religion" sects attracted young people from mainstream middle-class families rather than from the socially marginalized or displaced. While affluence had increased opportunities for self-expression, the goals of "working hard" or "catching up" no longer had the meaning they did for older Japanese. Religious sects offered a sense of purpose that young people had not found in school, university, or workplace, and they satisfied a craving for solidarity, intimacy, and belonging that was no longer satisfied by the firm or company.

The dark side of the new religious cults was exposed dramatically in March 1995 when a deadly nerve gas was released on two major downtown subway lines in Tokyo, killing twelve passengers and sickening 5000 others. Within a few days, police raided the Tokyo offices and rural headquarters of Aum Shinrikyō, a "new religion" founded by Asahara Shoko, a sight-impaired guru who had once been arrested for selling fake medicines. The discovery of toxic ingredients used to manufacture the gas confirmed the sect's involvement. In May, Asahara and other sect leaders were arrested. What shocked the public, who were mesmerized daily by television reports about the sect, was not only the sect's involvement in murder, torture, extortion, and illegal drugs, but the fact that young people, lured by promise of perfecting themselves through meditation and other practices, made up the rank and file of its membership. The leaders surrounding Asahara, moreover, were highly educated, graduates of elite universities, many with advanced scientific or professional training, who avidly carried out criminal acts at his command. Not surprisingly, the incident shook the myth that Japan was the "world's safest country" and raised questions about how a society could have produced such an aberration.

In sum, in the mid-1990s, Japan seemed to be a country adrift, caught up in problems created by its spectacular economic success, but uncertain of what lay ahead. An air of public pessimism prevailed. Public opinion polls showed a steady rise in the number of people who thought Japan was moving in a "bad direction." In early 1997 more than 55 percent did. But pessimism has always galvanized the Japanese public rather than discouraged them. Although the mirage of "Japan as Number One" had faded, it seemed only a matter of time before the Japanese would define a new set of dreams—

whether as "life style superpower," "paradise for the elderly," "world leader in environment," or some other comforting identity. A society that had managed to escape colonization by Western imperialism, to rise to a position as a major power only to lose it in an ill conceived war, and then to recover from destruction and defeat to become an economic superpower was clearly facing a better future than it thought it did.

98 Henry A. Myers, "Now, in the Twenty-First Century"

As the twenty-first century dawns, most age-old questions and issues are still with us. History certainly does not repeat itself in any mechanical way—technological inventions by themselves assure that—but history does give us an idea of the options available to humankind in coping with challenges. What follows is an attempt to identify some of the main challenges and review of the range of possible reactions to them.

QUESTIONS TO CONSIDER

1. Assuming that present trends will continue can lead to bad predictions, such as one made in 1899—on the basis of the nineteenth-century trend in U.S.–Latin American relations—that by 1999 or 2000 what was then Buenos Aires would be called "McKinleyville." What present trends in global relations do you think will continue? Which are much less certain?
2. Are there problems with reasoning that (a) since the USSR freed itself from communism with relatively little violence, China can be expected to do the same thing, or (b) since East and West Germany were united quickly and peacefully after forty-five years of separation, the same should be possible soon for North and South Korea? Are these analogies valid?

CONFLICT AND CONFLICT RESOLUTION

As people centuries from now look back at the twentieth century, they may well give it the short name "Age of Social-Doctrine Conflict." Particularly in its core decades, roughly 1914–1990, no previous period in world history saw such continual struggle—coercive, psychological, and diplomatic—among protagonists of ideologies, with conflicts over nationalism, democracy, militarism, fascism, and communism, all in many variations, casting the longest shadows. Since the end of the cold war, the last four of these have faded somewhat as causes of conflict, whereas nationalism—in the sense of a force fueling struggles over ethnic claims—has assumed central importance.

As we have seen, nationalism is a powerful ideology, but it is more than a social doctrine: At the moment, it is a rationale for expansion and has had genocidal consequences; in fact, two of the most prolonged and wanton instances of mass killing since World War II, in the former Yugoslavia and in Rwanda, have taken place since the end of the cold war over "ethnic rivalries," which is a current media synonym for "nationalism." A third instance, in Cambodia (see Reading 87) had different, cold war–related roots. Although it is true that protagonists of "-isms" from Stalin and Hitler to Pol Pot hold an unchallenged world record for mass killings with tens of millions of victims in the twentieth century, it is also true that people seem able to recover more easily from even the rabid behavior induced by the worst of social doctrines than from ethnic hatreds. Identities based on "-isms" can be discarded. Most of the former believers in Italian Fascism or German Nazism abandoned their doctrinal persuasion with the defeat of their leaders—at least enough to blend in with the rest of their national populations. Former Communists in Russia are able to do the same thing; however, ethnic identities are nearly impossible to discard. There is no such thing as a *former* Bosnian Serb or *former* Hutu (see Readings 71 and 72). The likelihood is that intense ethnic conflict will continue to plague the twenty-first century.

INTERNATIONAL LAW ENFORCEMENT

If ethnic conflict is a fact of world life, the only responses are either to let the conflicts burn themselves out, until victors have subdued weaker enemies at high human cost, or to intervene. Intervention here means the use of outside, international forces to establish and keep peace among the warring parties. This role was seen as a main one for the League of Nations after World War I. The United Nations' stronger structure than its predecessor's and an American commitment to it raised high hopes in 1945 after World War II for its future as international peacekeeper.

Actually, for the half century after World War II, the United Nations did not work significantly better than the League of Nations in its peacekeeping role. It did establish the uneasy peace that followed the war establishing Israel (see Reading 83) with the partition of Palestine, and it kept peace most of the time on Cyprus—a very meager record of efficacy from a global-peacekeeping standpoint. Some of its members contributed to the Korean War, but the Korean War was waged by the United Nations only because the Soviet Union was boycotting the organization during crucial proceedings (see Readings 74 and 75) while Chinese seats in the United Nations were held by the Nationalist government of Chiang Kai-shek on Taiwan rather than by that of Mao Tse-tung on the Chinese mainland. The power to veto Security Council actions, which was given to the former main allies from World War II as its permanent members, meant that a veto could be expected any time a cold war conflict called for UN intervention, and nearly all significant international hostilities after 1946 were cold war conflicts or became so with Third World countries in surrogate roles. This state of affairs called the North Atlantic Treaty Organization (NATO) into being. Its members were not all North Atlantic countries, which the name implies; rather, they were united by a determination to prevent further Soviet expansion in Europe. In this original role, NATO worked well: After its formation, the USSR did not expand any farther into Europe, although its detractors could claim that it was not NATO but the U.S. Strategic Air Command that was the real deterrent to Soviet expansion. Others minimized Soviet expansionist tendencies, but NATO appeared justified to its supporters largely because the United Nations was incapable of doing its peacekeeping job.

With the cold war over, NATO should theoretically be unnecessary. In the absence of expected vetoes, the United Nations can return to its original role, that of international peacekeeper. It is true that China is still a Communist country, but there are so few other Communist countries and causes that they should not keep the Security Council from working most of the time. It appears, however, that NATO members have not the slightest intention of disbanding; in fact, NATO forces have done far more fighting *as* NATO forces since the end of the cold war than during it. The simple fact appears to be that leaders of the NATO countries, with at least the passive support of the people who elected them, prefer NATO as an organization of countries more like their own—more stable, more democratic, and more predictable—than any random sampling of UN countries.

People in other parts of the world seem to feel the same way, preferring to have conflicts in their areas countered with forces from countries resembling their own. In West Africa, that force was the Economic Organization of West African States (ECOWAS), which began as a free-trade association but developed military forces in the Economic Organization [of West African States] Monitoring Observer Group (ECOMOG). Under the leadership of Nigeria, ECOMOG successfully intervened in the Sierra Leonean civil war and established much more peaceful conditions than any other force did after the May 1997 coup (see Reading 89). Nigeria ran out of money to maintain its forces throughout the country, and so ECOMOG could not continue to enforce peace; but the point is that for more than a year this West African regional organization, rather than the United Nations, exercised peacekeeping functions in that country far better than the United Nations has been doing with its belated and less-than-focused effort there in 2000. The outlook, then, is for international but regional organizations to conduct peacekeeping operations, with the United Nations remaining mostly in the background.

GLOBALIZATION AND THE DIGITAL DIVIDE

With the rapid expansion of computer usage in the last two decades of the twentieth century, the gap in the standard of living between the developed North, with its increasingly digital economy and society, and the underdeveloped and distinctly less digital South has widened. The lines drawn are approximately those of the old First World (North) and Third World (South) of the cold war era, with the peoples of the Soviet bloc or Second World struggling with varying success to join the old First World in living standards. Almost no one opposes aid to alleviate poverty in the underdeveloped world; however, there is little current enthusiasm for how the World Bank or the International Monetary Fund has been tackling the problem with more loans, which often have not only failed to do much for progress in the underdeveloped countries but also left them with impossibly large sums to repay.

Immigration pressures on the developed world appear to be increasing. They keep the Mexican-American border porous in spite of U.S. efforts to control illegal entry and lead to tragedies such as that of the forty-seven Chinese who in June 2000 suffocated in a sealed truck at the port of Dover, in England. As the Digital Divide widens, people from the old Third World will desperately seek First-World jobs. This kind of pressure cannot be alleviated without making the old Third World considerably more like the First World economically. This means some—probably massive—displacement of local institutions and ways of life and, if past experience holds true, will lead to charges of imperialism, as if out of pure arrogance the new First Worlders wanted to refashion the poorer part of the globe into one that resembled their own. There will probably be increasing environmental concerns here as well. Cutting down rain forests may well continue to appeal to Brazilians as a means of gaining income and as a step toward developing Brazil's economy into one that provides well-paying jobs.

GLOBALIZATION AND NATIONAL INTERESTS

In the twentieth century, many countries, including the United States, saw internal political disagreement over how good an idea it was to strengthen international organizations and encourage global interaction, as opposed to focusing on domestic issues and aspirations. Protagonists of a more global outlook were the "internationalists" of the twentieth century, who were apt to term their opponents "isolationists." The 1990s saw a shift in enthusiasms and fears concerning globalization, and in the early twenty-first century the term centers most of all on international free trade or global capitalism. Large-scale business, which in the nineteenth century and first part of the twentieth century was inclined in most countries to favor tariffs and other restrictions on aspects of trade in which their countries could not compete well, adopted a much more international outlook. From the 1950s to the 1990s, politically conservative groups in the capitalistic countries increasingly favored free trade, whereas groups directed toward labor interests, human rights concerns, and environmental questions favored it less. There are exceptions, of course, but in general it is accurate to say that in the early twenty-first century, the right favors globalization with more fervor than the left.

Part of the reason for this is the growing association of globalization with the expanded role of multinational corporations. Democratic parties of the left had no problem with globalization in the twentieth century as long as it meant more cultural interchange and more authority for international organizations over national ones. However, if globalization today means increasing free trade with multinational corporations as the main players, this implies some restriction or stagnation of the public sphere at the expense of the private one.

Overall, the increasing public interest in economic developments—where private businesses, not governments, are the main players—is leaving government and politics in a less important role than before. Radio and television stations in the early twenty-first century report far more business and general economic news than they did a few decades earlier at the expense of governmental or political news. In doing so, they are appealing to what their publics consider to be important. Even public radio stations in the United States devote what thirty years ago would have seemed to be a disproportionate amount of time to reporting on "the marketplace." Globalization, the relatively good record of capitalism in the public mind in democratic countries, and the decreased interest in government and politics seem at least partly interrelated, with no change in that relationship in sight.

HUMAN RIGHTS

The failure of the United Nations to establish peace through its own interventions does not obscure the fact that the claims of human rights are taken more seriously in the early twenty-first century than before. NGOs (see Reading 89) and regional organizations are increasingly active and visible today. This raises the issue of national sovereignty and globalization from another perspective: How much sovereignty will nation-states have to give up to comply with the decisions of international bodies? After all, nation-states as we know them did not dominate the world map until the nineteenth century, and not completely until the twentieth century. Although more of them may emerge—a Palestinian one and one or more to establish more stable borders for peoples in the eastern Congo region and their neighbors—they appear to be subject to increasing influence by international, particularly regional, bodies.

As a sign of increased empowerment of women, the twentieth century saw four quite effective women prime ministers in different countries: Israel's Golda Meir, India's Indira Gandhi, Britain's Margaret Thatcher, and Pakistan's Benazir Bhutto, whereas Burma's Aung San Suu Kyi has been a leading and effective voice of the opposition to military dictatorship there for many years. There is enough consensus worldwide on the need to upgrade women's role in society to assure that the general trend toward treating women more as equals to men will continue, although the road in that direction is full of rough spots.

Internationally, the quest for women's rights runs into questions not only of national sovereignty but of different cultures' providing different standards of human rights. Are there really such things as "Asian rights" and "Muslim rights," for example, in which the group takes precedence over the individual, youth defers to age, and women defer to men, or do these attitudes and behaviors represent historical artifacts that might have claimed validity through the nineteenth and twentieth centuries but can no longer be defended in the twenty-first?

The evidence is overwhelming that the acceleration of economic, political, and social change in the twentieth century resulted in greater homogenization and less cultural diversity in the world. Against this background, China's special pleading for "Asian values" when accused of human rights abuses, such as harvesting kidneys and other human organs from prisoners, is a sham. Yet in Africa, the Middle East, East Asia, and other parts of the world, human rights activists are perceived as but another example of Western cultural imperialism. It seems possible that the seductive appeal of Western values, including human rights, will prove so strong that regional or cultural exceptionalism will not last to the twenty-second century. Nonetheless, the inherent tensions between the Western world's economic, political, and social values, including human rights, and the non-Western world's religious and cultural traditions will continue to collide and could well boil over into conflict. Thus, for example, a rich and powerful champion of non-Western values, such as Libya's Mu'ammar al-Gadhafi, could be tempted to order missiles to strike U.S. cities in retaliation for America's trampling of "Muslim values" in the name of human rights.

THE ASIAN CENTURY

While the United States dominated world events in the second half of the twentieth century and remains the sole superpower after the cold war ended, Asia was increasing in world importance as the century closed. Japan, South Korea, and Taiwan developed into stable and prosperous states with economies increasingly important for world trade. China was held back by drastic mismanagement under Mao Tse-tung (see Reading 79), but beginning with the leadership of Deng Xiaoping (see Reading 95) and his system of combining collectivist control with capitalist incentives, China has played an increasingly large role on the global political and economic stage. China has the look of becoming a superpower within a matter of decades. As much as we may say that the cold war is over, it lingers on in Asia with the issue of China and Taiwan, as well as in relations between North and South Korea.

The "One China" policy came to mean something very different from the 1950s through the 1990s. Originally espoused by Chiang Kai-shek and the Kuomintang and endorsed by the United States, it held that the government of the Republic of China (on Taiwan) was the legitimate government of China and anticipated the day when it would return to remove the Communist usurpers from the mainland. Thus Taiwan's Republic of China successfully laid claim to China's seats in the United Nations through the 1960s. Then with the increasing legitimization of mainland China's People's Republic in the Nixon and Carter administrations, ending with the U.S. recognition of Communist China as the real China and relegating Taiwan to a hazy lesser status, "One China" for the mainland Chinese leadership quickly became the policy of treating Taiwan as a rebellious province of China.

Although it is true that far enough back Taiwan was ruled by China, it is equally true that China controlled Taiwan for only four years in the twentieth century: The Japanese took Taiwan in 1895 and held it until the end of World War II. Then from 1945 to 1949, Taiwan was indeed under (Kuomintang-run) China; since 1949 it has functioned as an independent state. There are several scenarios for the China-Taiwan issue in this century, with the extremes ranging from a mainland Chinese military conquest of the island to a discrediting and removal of communism in China along the lines of the upheavals that transformed the Soviet Empire into more agreeable successor states in 1989 and 1990. Taiwan could easily become a model for mainland China, having achieved economic wealth and stability along with a democracy strong enough that it enabled the first change of government in which an opposing faction replaced the previously ruling group as a result of free elections in four thousand years of Chinese history. China is still a country that people escape *from;* Taiwan has been a country people escaped *to* in its half century of independence. This speaks loudly for Taiwan as a model; the problem here is that the leaders of China are not looking for a model that will make them unnecessary. To be sure, the same thing could have been said regarding the Soviet Union in the mid-1980s: Soviet leaders were not looking for a model that would relegate them to irrelevance, but events resulting from *perestroika* overtook them.

The Korean case is altogether different. For starters, in Korea—unlike in the China-Taiwan confrontation—the free and prosperous protagonist is at least equal in power to its poor and totalitarian adversary. Famine and general economic deprivation seem to have reached extremes in North Korea sufficient to prod its leadership into accepting aid from South Korea. The recent meeting of the two heads of state seems promising in terms of diffusing tensions; however, there appear to be limits on how unified the country can become as a result of negotiated settlements alone. North Korean Kim Jong Il must know full well that German unification meant the end of East German leaders as anything more than likely defendants in human rights cases, and he can scarcely welcome a Korean unification that bodes the same sort of outcome. Of course, no one asked head of state and Socialist Unity (Communist) Party General Secretary Erich Honecker if he wanted to step down as leader and be considered for trial as a human rights violator. Events simply overtook him, and they may well do the same in Korea. A more realistic scenario is probably one in which Kim Jong Il attempts to *use* capitalism either as aid for development or to provide incentives for economic progress along the lines of Deng Xiaoping's program (see Reading 95), although whether he could do so in the Korean context without drastically undermining his position and the system itself is doubtful.

Inter-Asian conflicts aside, Asia seems poised to take on a larger role on the world stage soon. The sheer size of Asia's population might not be much of a factor in determining Asian influence by itself; after all, India's very large population has done nothing for Indian influence on the global scene. Instead, it is the combination of large populations, economic development, and stable political systems in Japan, Taiwan,

South Korea, and the smaller Pacific Rim states that should indeed make an increasing difference in the global balance of trade, cultural influence, military relations, and diplomatic power.

RELIGION AND TECHNOLOGY

Present-day religion tends to be sparingly dealt with in world history textbooks, but it remains a strong thread in the fabric of civilization. America with its stridently secular culture and fervently free market economy is also one of the most religiously vibrant countries in the world. This seeming contradiction raises the obvious question: Why is this the case? In the world at large, what is the appeal of traditional religion in an age so geared to life's material considerations (see Reading 96)?

Part of the answer to both questions may lie in the ever-growing bureaucratic and technological control of twenty-first–century life. Religion may serve as an antidote to this phenomenon. So, too, the atomization and sense of isolation that is at the center of twenty-first–century materialism may account for the growth in religious affiliation, especially in those religious traditions that offer believers simple answers—simplistic, of course, for critics—to life's problems in an increasingly complex, technological world.

Since the major world religions include a stress on compassion in their sacred books, their influence on world affairs should be benign, as it is in the case of religiously affiliated NGOs (see Reading 89). There is a darker side to religious fervor, however, when it reinforces cultural rivalries, as in the case of the Ayatollah Khomeini's traditionalist Shiites in Iran against the West, or ethnic or national confrontations, as between Palestinians and Jews or between Hindus and Pakistanis. Protestant-Catholic tensions show only marginal signs of abating in Northern Ireland (see Reading 39), and the atrocities in the Balkans (see Reading 71) reflect both intra-Christian hostilities between Catholic Croats and Eastern Orthodox Serbs and the even deeper conflicts between Christian populations and Muslims in Bosnia and Kosovo.

Beyond the effects of the Digital Divide, one sure thing about the twenty-first century is that its technology will make it different. Here the twentieth-century–record is impressive, and the continually accelerating march of technological progress through the past three centuries shows no sign of slowing down. Examples in two fields, communications and medicine, may serve to make this—in contrast with other conjectures about historical trends—an uncontroversial point.

In 1900, hard-rubber, one-sided phonograph records that played for a few minutes sold in the United States for $3.00 to $5.00 each, the weekly salary range for average workers. Think of it: three minutes of low-quality audio for your week's wages! Progress in the industry relegated even the greatly improved, double-sided, long-playing, high-fidelity, inexpensive records of the 1950s and 1960s to the status of historical curiosities as audiotape cassettes replaced both phonograph records and reel-to-reel audiotapes in the 1970s, only to be challenged by longer-lasting CDs with much better sound quality in the 1980s; these in turn have had to compete with new audio products of the computer age. Consumer interest and promising returns for investment in research combine to ensure that new items will fuel the communications revolution well into—perhaps throughout and beyond—the twenty-first century.

The medical picture also seems promising with some surety in the industrial world and at least hope in the developing world. In 1900, diabetes was a terrifying, fatal disease, thought to come "from a fall" and treated with state-of-the-art prescribed mild, and sometimes not so mild, doses of arsenic. In 2000, it is "under control" for most of those who have it. Tuberculosis claimed lives in epidemic proportions in 1900. In 2000, it is rare: The national U.S. organization devoted to combatting it has had to begin fighting other respiratory ailments in order to stay in business, although multi-drug-resistant strains of tuberculosis still present a challenge, particularly in Russia and China, to its complete eradication. Heart disease had no effective treatments in 1900, nor was the relationship of diet to heart problems understood. The discovery of cholesterol and its clogging effect on arteries, along with surgical techniques for heart transplants and coronary-artery by-passes, has added decades to the lives of heart patients, as has research that has developed plastic and metal heart components.

These are only the most obvious improvements in medicine and health care of the past century. They apply foremost to the industrial world, but considerable progress has been made in the developing world as well. Leprosy is still a fact of life in parts of Asia and Africa, but it has been arrested for most victims in most areas. Health problems in underdeveloped areas are often not so much the result of ignorance in medical science as of problems in implementations of programs: The prevention and treatment of malaria has been understood for a long time, but malaria still kills tens of thousands of people annually because political and economic factors keep delivery systems for the medicines from being implemented or sustained. Diarrhea kills countless thousands of African children every year, not because medical science fails to understand cause and effect concerning it, but because the educational effort necessary for its control has been sporadic.

The medical challenge for the twenty-first century will be to see the technology of the Western world implemented by developing countries while pursuing cures in research centers for the still-rampant plagues, particularly AIDS, and other killers and debilitators, notably cancer and spinal-cord injuries. It is estimated that more than 20 million people will have died of AIDS between 1980 and 2005, a number that is beginning to approach world-war–level casualty statistics. In several African countries, HIV-infected people exceed 10 percent of the population. The twentieth century was the first to make any headway against cancer, but even with success stories from early detection and combinations of radiation, surgery, and chemotherapy, much remains to be done. At the moment there is some faint hope—no more than that—for developing remedial, perhaps regeneration-inducing treatments for spinal-cord injuries.

Some technological problems seem to be beyond the mind of humans to solve. In the days of Moses, ax heads would sometimes fly off their handles, occasionally killing someone. In 2000, ax heads are still flying off their handles, even those of molded fiberglass. Persistent technology does, of course, have a proud record of coping with problems of the physical world, and, who knows, the year 2080 or so may even see that nut cracked with an affordable, all-metal but lightweight, one-piece ax.

Such problems as are posed by the ax head and handle are, fortunately, rare. The outlook is for technology to rise to the occasion most of the time in improving humankind's material standard of living, but this is only a part of the unfolding scenario for life in the twenty-first century. Whether the "Age of Social-Doctrine Conflict" can give rise to an age in which ethnic toleration and human rights come into their own and in which "developing countries" really do develop the capacity for improving their peoples' standards of living is still a very open question.